RABBIS AND JEWISH COMMUNITIES IN RENAISSANCE ITALY

THE LITTMAN LIBRARY OF
JEWISH CIVILIZATION

Dedicated to the memory of

Louis Thomas Sidney Littman

who founded the Littman Library for the love of God
and as an act of charity in memory of his father

Joseph Aaron Littman

and to the memory of

Robert Joseph Littman

who continued what his father Louis had begun

יהא זכרם ברוך

'Get wisdom, get understanding:
Forsake her not and she shall preserve thee'

PROV. 4: 5

Rabbis and Jewish Communities in Renaissance Italy

◆

ROBERT BONFIL

Translated by

JONATHAN CHIPMAN

London
The Littman Library of Jewish Civilization
in association with Liverpool University Press

The Littman Library of Jewish Civilization
Registered office: 4th floor, 7–10 Chandos Street, London, W1G 9DQ

in association with Liverpool University Press
4 Cambridge Street, Liverpool L69 7ZU, UK
www.liverpooluniversitypress.co.uk/littman

Managing Editor: Connie Webber

Distributed in North America by
Oxford University Press Inc, 198 Madison Avenue,
New York, NY 10016, USA

First published 1990 by Oxford University Press
on behalf of the Littman Library of Jewish Civilization
First issued in paperback 1993
Reprinted 2004

Catalogue records for this book are available from the
British Library and the Library of Congress

ISBN 978-1-874774-17-4

Printed and bound by
CPI Group (UK) Ltd., Croydon, CR0 4YY

Preface and Acknowledgements

The work offered here to the reader examines the history of a specific institution among the Jews in Italy in a period to which many scholars have devoted their attention. In a sense, one might even say that this institution's history faithfully reflects the entire history of those Jews, touching as it does upon many aspects of Jewish society's relation to those individuals and institutions which, in its eyes, represented the normative framework of their unique collective life. I refer to the rabbis, and to the frameworks through which they participated in the life of society, constituting an integral part of it and serving at times as its leadership.

The period under discussion has often enjoyed a pre-eminent place in the interest of those studying the history of the Jewish people, whether due to the extensive documentation which has survived from it, the intellectual and emotional associations aroused by the paradigmatic impact of many aspects of Jewish life in those times, or simply due to the inherent interest in the situation and role of the Jews in developments of special significance for world history, as the Italian Renaissance was. This work therefore follows a long line of predecessors.

I must immediately add that the use of the term 'Renaissance' in the title of the book may be misleading. The manner in which the participation of the Jews in the Renaissance is traditionally presented may arouse expectations which will not be fully satisfied. At least one reason for this is that the history of the writing of the book itself had an inevitable influence on its contents. It may therefore be useful to explain in what sense this was the case. In fact, the main part of this book consists of a doctoral dissertation written for the Department of Jewish History of the Hebrew University in 1976. It was originally conceived as a complement to the general surveys of the history of the Jews in Italy, offering a more thorough understanding of one of its institutional aspects which was of paramount importance in the life of Jewish communities. But, as research progressed, I soon realized that the traditional picture was largely unacceptable to me. It seemed particularly necessary to reject the image of an Italian Judaism moving directly towards assimilation, in which assimilation itself was viewed in positive terms as the consequence of an ideal world of the Renaissance leading to acculturation. Nor did I feel that I could accept the image of Italian rabbis as opponents of secular culture, and thus as spearheading the fundamentalist, obscurantist, anti-rational and conservative trend in Jewish life. Indeed, I found no evidence in the sources of tension between rabbis and other components of the community on these grounds. The more I studied the sources, the more I recognized the need for reappraising the traditional picture as a whole. It was too great a task to approach all at once.

I therefore chose to write the history of the institution of the rabbinate as an initial step towards the more general enterprise, while following preliminary assumptions differing in part from those generally accepted and understanding that the onus of proof was obviously still on me. I thought, and I still think, that rather than postponing the entire project indefinitely, it was worth while to bring the results of my research to light in order to encourage others to join in the overall revision. A price was to be paid for that decision. Many aspects that would naturally be dealt with in a general study were here omitted or even taken for granted, to a degree sometimes beyond that generally accepted. For example, while I did not accept the idea that the acquisition of general (i.e. not specifically Jewish) learning was a symptom of trends towards acculturation, I did not take pains to prove this. As a consequence of the fact that the book was originally conceived as a work on an *internal* Jewish institution, the *history of the Jews* that emerged inevitably conveyed a sense of cultural isolation far greater than I would myself be prepared to maintain. I decided to accept that limitation.

Shortly after the dissertation was approved by the Senate of the Hebrew University, it was submitted for publication in Hebrew without substantial changes. That edition, entitled *ha-Rabbanut be-Iṭalyah be-tekufat ha-Renessans*, was published in 1979 by Magnes Press, Jerusalem; thus, the arguments here presented are nearly twelve years old. In considering the possibility of preparing an English edition, the weighty problem of updating obviously arose. To be sure, in the meantime many new books and articles dealing with the history of the Jews in Italy had been published. I myself offered several further contributions to the reappraisal of this chapter of Jewish history. As far as my ideas are concerned, the interested reader will find them expressed in my more recent articles listed in the Bibliography.

A new choice imposed itself: either relinquish the idea of having the book translated as it is while attempting to prepare a more comprehensive general picture, or take the risk of making it available to the English reader, notwithstanding its shortcomings. My decision is evident. I hope that the efforts expended on the translation and publication will be vindicated. In fact, as far as I can see, none of the publications which appeared subsequent to the Hebrew edition of the book has seriously challenged the conclusions reached here. On the contrary, most of the documentary evidence brought to light in these publications provides a clear-cut confirmation of my conclusions. In fact, most of these publications, important as they may be, are based upon archival documents (coming from State or Municipal Archives), so that they relate only marginally to the contents of this book. The interested reader will find most of these listed in the excellent bibliographical tool offered by Aldo Luzzatto and Moshe Moldavi, *Bibliotheca italo-ebraica: bibliografia per la storia degli ebrei in Italia, 1964–1973* (Rome and Tel-Aviv, 1982).

Needless to say, I did not feel it necessary to mention books or articles whose authors had had the opportunity to read the Hebrew edition of the book and nevertheless had chosen to ignore its conclusions. After all, everyone, myself included, is biased in his own way as to what he may consider convincing.

This book is thus essentially an unrevised version of Part One of the original Hebrew edition. Part Two of that edition, the appendices consisting of *pièces justificatives*, mostly in Hebrew, appeared impossible to translate in a manner that the English reader might find useful, while the reader familiar with Hebrew could obviously be referred to the original. Nevertheless, the work presented here is not merely a partial translation of the Hebrew edition. The translator has taken considerable pains to insert, at appropriate points within the text, substantial excerpts from the appendices, in order to make available to the reader all the evidence necessary to support the arguments presented. In a sense, then, although no new material has been added, he has created a revised edition of the original. Needless to say, I also have tried to eliminate the errors pointed out to me by those of my friends who were kind enough to do so. Apart from that, no updating has been carried out.

One notable exception to the general statement made above regarding post-1979 publications pertains to the very important editions of Rabbinic responsa and correspondence of Renaissance Italian Jewry by Jacob Boksenboim. Those relevant to the present work are duly listed in the Bibliography. On one occasion I have also introduced a change in the original wording of my text following a suggestion of Mr Boksenboim. Although, while working on the Hebrew edition of this book, I had consulted a good deal of the material gathered by him, its extensive publication thereafter made it possible conveniently to check omissions or errors resulting from my earlier consultation of the manuscript sources. The translator has taken special efforts to update the relevant footnotes in order to make reference to the sources easier. Such an updating was also carried out in certain other cases, in which the reader is referred to new or revised editions of various works, doctoral dissertations subsequently published in monograph form, etc., which are more convenient to consult than those which existed at the time of publication of the Hebrew book. Various works written in Hebrew are also generally referred to here in their English translations, where such exist.

In presenting the book to the English reader, I wish to reiterate my heartfelt thanks to those who helped and advised me during its writing. First and foremost to my mentors, Professor Hayyim Hillel Ben-Sasson, of blessed memory and—may he enjoy long life—Professor Giuseppe B. Sermoneta. Then to all my friends and colleagues with whom I discussed the book and whose comments assisted me.

I also wish to express my thanks to the various libraries and institutions which permitted me to make use of the documents and manuscripts in their collections. These are all duly mentioned in the Bibliography appended to the book. I am particularly indebted to my friends in the Manuscript Department and in the Institute for Microfilms of Hebrew Manuscripts of the Jewish National and University Library in Jerusalem for their co-operation in making many sources available to me.

I owe a special debt of gratitude to Magnes Press, which

released its copyright privileges, thereby making the present edition possible. A no lesser debt is owed to the Littman Library of Jewish Civilization for their warm assistance in all phases of preparation of this edition, and particularly to Mr Vivian Lipman, on whose initiative the project was launched and who was its main sponsor and advocate throughout.

I also wish to express my friendly thanks to Rabbi Jonathan Chipman, who took great pains in executing the translation and editing of the work. My good friends Elliot Horowitz and Miriam Bodian devoted much time to reading the English manuscript, suggesting both substantive and stylistic improvements. Enid Barker and Sylvia Jaffrey of the editorial staff of Oxford University Press deserve a special thanks for the painstaking and thorough manner in which they prepared the manuscript for publication.

Finally, I wish to reiterate here my thanks to all the members of my beloved family who patiently supported my solitary peregrinations in the remote reaches of the history of our people. I feel particulary indebted to my dear wife Eva, at whose initial suggestion and encouragement I turned towards academic life during the first difficult period in which we were finding our way to our Homeland. If this work contributes to the history of our people, then let it be said—her part is included in mine.

Robert Bonfil

Contents

List of Plates

Plates appear between pages 178 and 179

Introduction

The institution of the rabbinate is of importance both in its own right and in relation to the institutions in and alongside which it stands and acts: the yeshivah and the community. It is therefore appropriate that my discussion of this institution be preceded by a few words concerning these other two institutions, even if only in very general terms. Much of what I will say below concerning the Jewish community and the academies of Torah study in Italy applies to most Jewish communities in other places as well; nevertheless, even the points of similarity take on different nuances as a result of their inclusion in the unique Jewish milieu of the Apennine Peninsula during the fifteenth and sixteenth centuries.

Throughout the period under discussion, the Jewish community in Italy was a religious-national-social group organized in ways similar in many respects to those of the corporation. In this sense, it was one more link in the chain of manifestations of the national-social consciousness of the Jews in the Middle Ages.[1] Just as the various parts of any living organism are interdependent in order to fulfil the various tasks necessary for life, so were the various functions of the institutionalized organization of the medieval Jewish community in Italy, as elsewhere, created to fulfil functions connected with the very existence of the community, its integrity and uniqueness as a living body. These functions

[1] On this subject as a whole, it is sufficient to refer to Salo W. Baron, *The Jewish Community*, 3 vols. (Philadelphia, 1942), and the extensive literature cited therein. From the literature that appeared following the publication of that work, we may add: Y. Baer, 'The Origins and Foundations of Jewish Communal Organization in the Middle Ages' (Heb.), *Ẓion*, 15 (1950), 1–51; H. H. Ben-Sasson, 'The Place of the Community-City in Jewish History' (Heb.), in *Kovez̧ Harz̧a'ot she-hushme'u be-Kenes ha-Shneim 'Asar le-'Iyun be-Hisṭoriah*, and 'The Northern European Jewish Community', *JWH*, 11 (1968), 208–19. See the additional essays gathered in the volume, *ha-Kehilah ha-Yehudit be-yemei ha-Beinayim*, ed. H. H. Ben-Sasson (Jerusalem, 1976). On the Jewish community in Italy during the period under discussion, see: S. Simonsohn, 'The Jewish Community in Italy and the Christian Corporation' (Heb.), in *Dat ve-Ḥevrah be-Toldot Yisra'el uve-Toldot ha-'Amim*, i.e. lectures given at the 9th Conference of the Historical Society (Jerusalem, 1968), 81–102; idem, 'The Organization of Autonomous Jewish Rule in Mantua, 1511–1630' (Heb.), *Ẓion*, 21 (1956), 143–82; idem, *History of the Jews in the Duchy of Mantua* (Jerusalem, 1972), 318–24; and see the general surveys in M. A. Shulvass, *The Jews in the World of the Renaissance* (Leiden and Chicago, 1973), 44–113; A. Milano, *Storia degli ebrei in Italia* (Turin, 1963), 459–68.

were defined by the Jews of Verona in a straightforward way at the beginning of their communal ledger for the year 1539: 'to take care for and to deal with and to be involved in every trouble—may it not come—and other interest and involvement of the community—may the Rock guard and keep them—and if there occur any business problem or confusion to the individual . . .'[2] That is to say: its purpose was to be concerned with the existence of the Jewish community in the city generally, as well as of every individual therein, to stand guard against external dangers, as well as to show concern for the proper activity of the public in everything pertaining to the survival of the living Jewish body politic.

Organized communities had existed in southern Italy and in Sicily for years prior to the period under discussion, and during the fourteenth and fifteenth centuries communities were created in north central Italy by settlers from various places: from the region of Rome and south of it, from Spain, from France, and from Germany. The first half of the sixteenth century was clearly the period during which most of the Jewish communities in the cities of north central Italy took shape. This stage followed on one during which Jewish settlements in these cities were mostly built upon isolated families of bankers, who settled there after the authorities granted them the privileges known by the general name of condotta. We do not know at present which models were available to the members of the various settlements at the time of their organization. Almost all that we know about the organization of these communities in southern Italy and in Sicily comes from non-Jewish sources, which are obscure rather than clear.[3] We do not even know the role played by earlier traditions, originating in the communities of southern Italy,[4] upon the organization of

[2] See I. Sonne, 'Basic Premisses for the History of the Jews in Verona' (Heb.), *Kobeẓ 'al Yad*, 3/13 (Jerusalem, 1939–40), 151.

[3] See particularly the following: B. and G. Lagumina, *Codice diplomatico dei giudei di Sicilia* Part 1, 3 vols. (Palermo, 1884–95); G. di Giovanni, *L'ebraismo della Sicilia* (Palermo, 1748); N. Ferorelli, *Gli ebrei nell'Italia meriodionale dall'Età Romana al secolo XVIII* (Turin, 1915; repr. Bologna, 1966); M. Gaudioso, *La comunità ebraica di Catania nei secoli XIV e XV* (Catania, 1974); R. Straus, *Die Juden im Königreich Sizilien unter Normannen und Staufern* (Heidelberg, 1910); E. Munkácsi, *Der Jude von Neapel; Denkmäler des süditalienischen Judentums* (Zürich, 1939). See also S. Simonsohn, 'The Jews of Syracuse and their Cemetery' (Heb.), *Sefunot*, 8 (1964), 277–80.

[4] One must not forget that thousands of Jews left Sicily in the wake of the edicts of the kings of Spain, and a few of them were added to the populations of the Jewish centres of north central Italy. See A. Milano, 'La consistenza numerica degli ebrei di Sicilia al

the settlements in north central Italy, in comparison with the influence of models brought with them by the immigrants from France, Germany, and later on from Spain, nor how these traditions and influences were integrated into a conceptual structure which served as a basis for organizing society in the Christian world within which the Jews lived. But this much is known for certain: that wherever communities were set up, one can clearly distinguish the impression left by the various groups by whom they were founded. There are cases, for example, in which the community was defined as a sort of corporation, as in Padua[5] and Mantua,[6] while in others emphasis was placed upon the differences among the various groups; such was the case in Rome, which seems to have preserved at the time of its reorganization in 1525 the structural-social imprint of the communities of southern Italy.[7] Everywhere, each group struggled for the protection of its own interests, its defence, and its social stature within the community.[8] One need not add that, beyond the variations formed by these groups within Jewish society, there were other variations created by ethnic differences, so that in one community one might find a number of different congregations—an Italian congregation, an Ashkenazic one, Oriental (i.e. Levantine), and Occidental (Ponentine, i.e. Portuguese) ones, etc.[9] Thus, as R. Leone Modena once put it, 'the large community was composed of several "congregations" '.[10]

momento della loro cacciata', *RMI*, 20 (1954), 16–24 (also in *JSS*, 15 (1953), 25–32); Simonsohn, 'The Jews of Syracuse', 276 n. 8.

5 See D. Carpi (ed.), *Pinkas Padua* (Jerusalem, 1974) 14 ff.

6 See Simonsohn, 'The Jewish Community', 'Organization of Jewish Rule', and *Mantua*.

7 See A. Milano, 'I "Capitoli" di Daniel da Pisa e la comunità di Roma', *RMI*, 10 (1935–6), 324–38, 409–26. To my mind, the parallel (albeit not identity) between the three groups which chose the leadership of the community (namely: bankers, wealthy people, middle-class) and the method by which the twelve *proti* in Palermo were chosen during the early years—'quatuor . . . de statu maiori, quatuor de statu mediocri et alios quatuor de statu minori' (Lagumina, *Codice diplomatico*, 183–4)—is significant and deserving of study in its own right. One ought to compare this with *popolo potente*, *popolo grasso*, *popolo minuto*.

8 A struggle of this sort is portrayed in detail and with abundant documentation by Simonsohn, *Mantua*, 505 ff. Unfortunately, archival material such as that which was available to Simonsohn in Mantua has not been preserved for the other communities. This being the case, one must exercise caution in seeing the situation in Mantua as typical of that which prevailed elsewhere. See also M. A. Shulvass, 'On the History of the Community of Reggio' (Heb.), *Sinai*, 20 (1947), 198–205, and *Renaissance*, 49–51.

9 See ibid. 56–60.

10 Leone Modena, *Teshuvot Ziknei Yehudah*, ed. Simonsohn (Jerusalem, 1955), sect. 26, p. 43.

One thus found well-defined sub-groups within the communities, each with their own unique traditions, structures, and demands, for which they struggled with the other elements of the community. This situation would seem to justify the statement that the Jewish community in Italy was more like a city than a corporation. It constituted, so to speak, a kind of city within a city.[11] Obviously, one is not to understand by this that they enjoyed actual autonomy in terms of government and juridical arrangements, but that there was always present an aspiration for such autonomy, even though this was not always fully attained everywhere.[12] In fact, it is clear that the community was not a 'city within the city' except in a narrow sense, as the Jewish communities lacked at least two of the basic characteristics of a city-state: political independence and the means to carry out the decisions of its institutions by direct coercion.[13] Nevertheless, the Jewish public, always and everywhere, saw itself through its communities as subject to Jewish law alone for the determination of its parameters and identity. By this subjugation to *halakhah*, the communities developed forms of leadership which were expressed within the organizational structures in various places. A detailed description of these structures may be found in every survey of the history of the Jews in Italy as well as in the monographs devoted to specific communities; their common denominator was the establishment of quasi-municipal organizational frameworks,[14] which became more complex as the communities' populations grew.

As the public saw the determination of these frameworks as being subject to the norms of Jewish law, it sought the solutions to all questions, both public and private, within this normative

[11] Even the definitions given by R. Elijah Bachur for *kahal* and *kehilah* (terms here generally translated as, respectively, 'congregation' and 'community') contains an element of the parallel of *kehilah* to city, at least in its territorial aspect. According to him, there are some people who distinguish between *kahal* and *kehilah*, 'and call a gathering of Jews who live in one city a *kahal*, and the city, in which there is that *kahal*, they call *kehilah*, such as the *Kehilah* of Padua or of Venice', Elijah Bachur, *Sefer Tishby* (Isny, 1541), 201.

[12] This topic is discussed at length in Ch. 5.

[13] Cf. Milano, *Storia degli ebrei*, 460.

[14] It seems to me that this statement is true for the entire period, and that Shulvass's distinction (see e.g. *Renaissance*, 52, 56, 74) between the period prior to the ghettoization of the Jews and the period following the ghettos is artificial, and has no reliable foundation. Cf. also S. Simonsohn, 'The Ghetto in Italy and its Government' (Heb.), *Sefer Yovel le-Yiẓḥak Baer* (Jerusalem, 1961), 270–90.

system. The form of existence of these communities, as shaped by their aspiration to ensure the inner cohesion of Jewish society and as expressed in their activity and spiritual creation, as well as the relations and connections of this society with the surrounding world, were stamped with the mark of the *halakhah*. Great significance is therefore attached to understanding the ways in which the society related to the system of Jewish norms, and to the position and status within society of those people who represented this system—namely, the rabbis. The present study is dedicated to this issue, to which scholars have thus far not addressed themselves extensively.[15]

The above presentation of the purpose of this study implies a clearly defined meaning of the term 'rabbinate' from the semantic point of view, which may require some explanation. If any discussion involving semantic questions generally speaking requires great caution, particularly when the sources being used for the discussion are taken from halakhic literature,[16] such caution is doubly warranted in the subject under discussion.[17] In fact, it seems to me that the very growth of the institution of the rabbinate, many generations prior to the period under discussion, is still in need of basic semantic clarification. The

[15] Cf. Shulvass, *Renaissance*, 78.

[16] See B. D. Weinryb, 'Responsa as a Source for History (Methodological Problems)', in *Essays Presented to . . . Rabbi Israel Brodie* (London, 1967), 404–5, and an interesting example of a semantic problem relating to this question in S. D. Goitein, *Sidrei Ḥinukh* (Jerusalem, 1962), 152–3.

[17] For example, S. Assaf's definition of the rabbi as 'a scholar appointed over the public to judge, to issue halakhic rulings and to conduct its religious life'—'Towards a History of the Rabbinate' (Heb.), in *Be-ohalei Ya'akov; Perakim mi-ḥayyei ha-Tarbut shel ha-Yehudim be-yemei ha-Beinayim* (Jerusalem, 1973), 27—requires further elucidation, at least in so far as the nature of the appointment referred to in the definition is undefined. The very use of the Talmudic phrase, 'appointed over the public' (*memuneh 'al ha-ẓibbur*), rather than 'appointed *from* or *by* the community', leads to a certain ambiguity or confusion. From what Assaf states further on, it would appear that he is indeed referring to an appointment from the public or community. It follows from this that, were the title 'rabbi' awarded to an individual by the process of ordination, it would bear a different meaning from that which Assaf gives to it here. Assaf in fact seems to have understood ordination in this way: 'One who wished to stand for election to the post of rabbi needed to receive a kind of special "diploma"—the *semikhah*—and the title *Morenu*,' (ibid. 28). Throughout Assaf's discussion of ordination, we find that his use of the sources contains a covert assumption that ordination can only be given by a rabbi appointed over the community; we need not add that this assumption is totally groundless, even in those later sources which he invokes to support his opinion. Assaf generally makes substantial use there of late sources and, in the course of his synchronic approach to the subject, draws conclusions from the later period regarding the earlier one, leading to complete semantic confusion in his discussion of the period prior to the 17th century.

attempts to understand this institution as being defined within the framework of the communal organization,[18] and even to see the rabbi as fundamentally a holder of communal office, not only limit the overall picture of the phenomenon, but also involve a certain element of forced reading of the sources.[19] We are not concerned here with extending the discussion beyond the period in question, but I must emphasize that there is no justification for defining the rabbinate specifically within the framework of the communal organization. I prefer a concept of 'institution' in the sense used in sociology, i.e. referring to fixed and characteristic forms and conditions of behaviour with regard to the functioning of society in various contexts. The very definition of the rabbinate combined the idea of leadership and rulership[20] with that of study and scholarship. Thus, the 'rabbi' is placed in close relationship to the 'student', who is instructed by him and accepts his authority by virtue of the knowledge of the Torah he has imparted to him. I do not intend to elaborate here upon the question of what periods and in what contexts one or another of these concepts was predominant, but there is no doubt that throughout the Middle Ages the concept of the rabbinate was understood as drawing upon the reality of Torah study.[21] Thus,

[18] From the extensive literature touching upon this subject, directly or indirectly, see: Baron, *The Jewish Community*, ii. 66–70 and iii. 123 n. 15; Assaf, 'Towards a History of the Rabbinate'; M. Güdemann, 'Dei Neugestaltung des Rabbinerwesens und deren Einfluss auf die talmudische Wissenschaft im Mittelalter', *MGWJ*, 13 (1864), 68–70, 97–110, 384–95, 421–44; S. Schwarzfuchs, *Études sur l'origin et le developpement du Rabbinat au Moyen-Age* (Paris, 1957). See also M. Breuer, *Rabbanut Ashkenaz be-yemei ha-Beinayim* (Jerusalem, 1976); S. Heksher, 'Leader, Judge and Teacher' (Heb.), in *'Ish 'al ha-'Edah*, ed. Y. Eisner (Jerusalem, 1973), 161–93; S. Zeitlin, *Religious and Secular Leadership* (Philadelphia, 1943), 31–46; I. A. Agus, *Teshuvot Ba'alei ha-Tosafot* (New York, 1954), 18–29; idem, 'The Use of the Term Ḥakham by the Author of the Sefer Ḥassidim and its Historical Implications', *JQR*, 61 (1970), 54–62.

[19] See e.g., E. E. Urbach's review of Agus's *Teshuvot Ba'alei ha-Tosafot* in *KS*, 30 (1955), 204–5.

[20] The term *rav* in its literal sense of 'master' or 'great one' is even used in humble contexts, such as 'the *rav* (i.e. leader) of the donkey drivers', or even in a negative sense, as in 'the *rav* of the brigands'.

[21] It would perhaps not be superfluous to mention here that the hegemony or ascendancy of the institution of the Rabbinate was seen, from the viewpoint of the world of rabbinic learning and knowledge, as characterizing this historical period in contradistinction to the earlier period of the Gaonate. See R. Menaḥem ha-Meiri, *Bet ha-Beḥirah 'al Masekhet 'Avot*, ed. B. Z. ha-Levi Prag (Jerusalem, 1964), 52–4, as well as the introduction to his *Bet ha-Beḥirah 'al Masekhet Berakhot*, ed. S. Dikman (Jerusalem, 1965), 32.

leadership and halakhic authority were associated with the rabbinate by virtue of the fact that Jewish society turned to the rabbis for clarification of the details of the normative system which lay at the basis of their lives, to which appeal the rabbis responded.[22] The institution of the rabbinate is therefore defined simultaneously in two distinct areas: in that of scholarship and halakhic authority, and in that of communal leadership, in which the rabbis participated, both by virtue of the claims which they made based upon their own scholarship and authority, and by the dependence of the public upon their knowledge of the Torah and their halakhic rulings.

An exploration of this institution, like any other, will require that we pay attention to these fundamental characteristics of every social reality, and particularly to the distinction between 'status' and 'function'. In other words, we must take note of the nature of the status of the rabbis as halakhic authorities within the social system on the one hand, and their mode of realizing the rights, privileges, and duties involved in this status and constituting its dynamic aspect, on the other hand. To this end, we must inquire about the people who claim the status of rabbis in society: the nature of their implied claim to leadership,[23] and the relationship of society to that claim. We must also ask how these concepts became institutionalized in different ways in Jewish society, and how these forms were incorporated within the social structure, alongside its organizational aspects.

During the period under discussion, individuals in Italy claimed the right to religious leadership on the strength of the rabbinic ordination they had received, which gave them the right to rule on questions of Jewish law, and by virtue of which they were given the title of 'rabbi' (Heb. *rav*) by other 'rabbis'. We must therefore begin by examining the social and ideological background of those people who wished to be elevated to the status of 'rabbi', and the course of studies leading to it. A general survey in the first chapter of this book will be devoted to this question, relying primarily upon the extensive documentation recently gathered

[22] See J. Katz, *Tradition and Crisis* (New York, 1971), 169–70 and compare H. H. Ben-Sasson, 'Concepts and Realities in Jewish History at the End of the Middle Ages' (Heb.), *Tarbiz*, 29 (1960), 300.

[23] Cf. Baer, 'The Origins and Foundations of Jewish Communal Organization', 28 ff.; Ben-Sasson, 'The Place of the Community-City', 170; idem, 'The Northern European Jewish Community', 213 ff.

concerning Jewish education in Italy. One need not add that the aim of my examination of Jewish education in that country during that period is not to write its history, but rather to determine whether or not the rabbi in fact emerged organically out of his community, and was anchored in a world-view which belonged to the community as a whole. Those readers familiar with the literature pertaining to the culture of Italian Jewry during the Renaissance will realize that my mentioning this tendency in itself implies a certain stand on the question of the rabbis' involvement as the standard bearers of normative Jewish tradition in its ideal expressions, whereas Jewish historiography has stressed primarily the tendency towards greater distance from that tradition in the wake of involvement in the general culture. My stand on this question will find explicit and more extensive expression during the course of this work. In any event, my summary will be very succinct and I will not attempt to add to what is already known to us from the field of Jewish education in Italy during that period, but only to emphasize certain points, as an introduction to the general topics to be discussed in this work.

Let me add here that the question of the rising status of 'rabbi', within the general framework of the culture of the period, entails a certain attitude towards fixing the chronological boundaries of the work. That is, as the phenomenon known as the Renaissance is primarily cultural, reaching its maturation and greatest expression with the completion of the revolution in the realm of education in the Christian world in the middle of the fifteenth century, one may justifiably define this phenomenon in terms of the same time-frame within Jewish culture. In this work, I have defined the period of the Renaissance as beginning more or less in the middle of the fifteenth century and concluding at the end of the sixteenth century.[24]

As we have stated, during the Renaissance individuals in Italy acquired the status of 'rabbi' through ordination. No new arrangements for the granting of ordination different from those previously customary seem to have been introduced during this period. My initial question concerning the institution of the

24 There are several reasons for viewing the period of time referred to here as a distinct era in the history of Italian Jewry; I hope to deal with this issue extensively elsewhere. Meanwhile, see R. Bonfil, 'Expressions in Italy of the Uniqueness of the Jewish People during the Renaissance' (Heb.), *Sinai*, 76 (1975), 44–6, and cf. Ch. 6, Sect. 3 and the end of Sect. 4.

rabbinate will therefore concern the nature and constituent elements of the claim of the ordained, and the community's relation to this claim; Chapter 2 will be devoted to this problem. I will attempt therein to examine how the Jewish public evaluated the rabbis, and how this valuation was reflected in the relationships, on the one hand, between the public and the rabbis and, on the other, those of the rabbis among themselves. I will ask to what extent the identification of the concept of *talmid ḥakham* (i.e. 'scholar of sacred lore'), which had been accepted and honoured by a centuries-old tradition, with that of 'ordained rabbi' seemed justified in the eyes of Jewish society, and to what extent the results of this were problematic within society. In other words, I will attempt to evaluate the weight of the authority ascribed by the public to rabbis by virtue of their ordination, and the way in which the public attempted to participate in the promotion of specific individuals to the rank of rabbi. I will also attempt to determine the characteristics demanded of those ordained and the privileges they enjoyed by virtue of their ordination; I shall take note in this connection of the parallels between the granting of rabbinic ordination and the awarding of the title of doctor in the universities. As the rabbinic prerogative of excommunication was very significant in this connection, I shall dwell upon its meaning within the context of the rabbis' demand for ordination and a position of leadership.

In Chapter 3, I shall be concerned with defining the place of the rabbis within the established organizational framework of the communities and the extent of their participation in its leadership. The picture portrayed here is a varied and complex one, which at first glance might seem to dissuade one from reaching any general conclusions. Not only did conditions differ from one place to another, just as the central figures differed from one another, but the available documentation makes it impossible for us to derive a complete picture. I have of course attempted to examine the sources available from all those communities in which the office of 'community-appointed rabbi' existed, but these were not numerous. Moreover, particularly in the larger communities, no such rabbi was appointed throughout the sixteenth century. This fact, which on the face of it seems rather strange, will lead to a discussion of the means by which the office of the community-appointed rabbi took shape, while examining possible influences from both the Ashkenazic and Sephardic worlds. It seems to me here that all roads point towards one focal issue—namely, the rabbinic prerogative of issuing the ban (*ḥerem*), which was intended to strengthen the foundations of communal leadership. I will therefore attempt to determine to what extent this impression is correct. The participation of rabbis in communal leadership led in a natural way towards tensions between the rabbis and the lay communal leaders, on the one hand, and among the rabbis themselves, on the other. We must therefore clarify the nature of these tensions. I shall also concern myself in this chapter with the functions of the communally appointed rabbis, their status within the community and their salaries.

In the light of these findings, in Chapter 4 I shall attempt to re-evaluate the significance of the existence in one community of a person holding the office of community-appointed rabbi and of other individuals who, while ordained 'rabbis', stood outside the established framework of communal leadership. Isaiah Sonne built a comprehensive theory upon this fact, according to which during this period Italian rabbis were divided into 'official rabbis' and 'itinerant rabbis' in the service of wealthy individuals. In his opinion, the 'itinerant rabbis' undercut the authority of the 'official rabbinate'—a characteristic expression of the individualistic spirit of the Renaissance. Sonne attempted to explain entire chapters in the history of Italian Jewry during this period by means of this theory, from the implementation of Jewish law in the communities to the controversy concerning the publication of the *Zohar*. With regard to the latter question, I. Tishby[25] has demonstrated that there is little support for Sonne's theory. In my opinion, the very fact that there were no community-appointed rabbis in the major communities throughout the sixteenth century suffices to refute Sonne's theory completely, and not only in the matter of the printing of the *Zohar*. Nevertheless, we must attempt to understand the meaning of the difference between communally appointed rabbis and those who were not connected with any communal institutions. The latter supported themselves by various means, such as being in the service of wealthy individuals as a kind of 'private rabbi'. I will therefore wish to include certain aspects of the social meaning of that phenomenon to set against the background of the social framework of the Renaissance.

[25] See below, Ch. 4, n. 30.

Two other matters seem particularly important for a portrait of the institution of the rabbinate during this period. The first concerns the application of Jewish law, as understood by the scholars of those generations: that is, on the one hand, the role of the rabbis in the juridical realm and, on the other, their creativity as expressed in the composition of halakhic responsa. The question generally asked here is whether the situation in this area is to be seen as determined primarily under the influence of the spirit of the Renaissance, as is generally thought,[26] or whether an organic internal development took place, which was of course not entirely bypassed by the current conditions. For example, was the weakening of the institutions of Hebrew law in Italy at this time the result of a weakened relationship to those institutions in the wake of the widespread involvement in secular learning, or was this perhaps not at all the reflection of a weakening of commitment, but an organic development of the institutions of the Law themselves, due to various factors which had little or nothing to do with involvement in general erudition and culture? The very formulation of the question in this manner suggests a well-beaten path, albeit in so far as these matters are connected they of course correspond to the general tendency of this book, as I stated earlier when I presented its aim. In any event, the answer to this question will demand a detailed analysis of the situation of Jewish law in Italy during this period, and of the characteristic features of the responsa of the sages of Italy. Chapter 5 of this book will be devoted to this subject.

In the light of this tendency, and in a similar spirit, in the final chapter I will address the position of the rabbis and their role in shaping the cultural and spiritual life of those generations. In keeping with what has been said thus far, I will attempt to answer the question whether the rabbis were organically involved in the cultural activity of their contemporaries, or whether they were obscurantist opponents of an enlightenment towards which the members of that generation allegedly tended in the wake of their involvement in general culture. This question will require us briefly to discuss a multi-faceted development which took place in the cultural interests of the people at that time, until the

[26] See e.g., I. Sonne, 'On the History of the Community of Bologna in the Beginning of the 16th Century' (Heb.), *HUCA* 16 (1942), 35–100; M. A. Shulvass, 'The Study of Torah Among Italian Jews during the Renaissance' (Heb.), *Ḥoreb*, 10 (1948), 105–28.

emergence of the phase of spiritual involution at the end of the period, a phenomenon which in effect concluded the process of turning away from philosophy and the entry into the field of the mysticism of the Kabbalists, which ultimately signified the separation of Jewish thought from general philosophy in order to go in a different direction. We will need to discuss briefly two subjects which seem pertinent to this question: we shall attempt to understand the nature of the philosophical thought of the rabbis of those generations; and we will try to perceive the way in which the rabbis came into contact with the public among whom they lived by means of the sermon.

To summarize, I will attempt to examine the institution of the rabbinate generally in relation to an entire gamut of issues pertinent to understanding the history of the Jews in Italy during this period which has remained a focal point of interest for many scholars down to the present day. If the presentation of material is somewhat different from that found in standard works, this is a natural expression of my inclinations and historical consciousness, and is a reflection of the approach which I received at the Hebrew University of Jerusalem, where this work first came into existence, and from the people from whom I learned much pertaining to the history and thought of the Jewish people.

Some preliminary remarks about the footnotes are in order. In the references to bibliographical sources, I have provided the full details (sometimes with a short title) only on the first occasion per chapter on which a given work is mentioned; thereafter a shortened entry, with author and abbreviated title only, is provided. In addition, a selected Bibliography, containing full entries and, where applicable, short titles of each work listed, is given at the end of the book.

I have not provided bio-bibliographical information concerning the various rabbinic personalities mentioned in the body of the work, who play a dominant role in the aspect of history of the period discussed here. Exception has been made in only a few cases, generally speaking where it seemed necessary so as to provide background to a given figure's activity, and only then when there was no adequate entry concerning that figure in one of the standard encyclopaedias of Jewish studies, namely: *Encyclopaedia Judaica* (Berlin, 1928); *Jewish Encyclopaedia* (New

York, 1901–1905); *Encyclopaedia Judaica* (Jerusalem, 1971); *ha-Enẓeklopedyah ha-'Ivrit** (Jerusalem and Tel Aviv, 1951–81). In addition to these encyclopaedias, abundant material concerning the rabbis of Italy appears in the following works: M. Mortara, *Indice alfabetico dei rabbini e scrittori israeliti* (Padua, 1886); Neppi-Ghirondi, *Toldot Gedolei Yisrael u-Ge'onei Iṭalyah* (Trieste, 1853); S. Wiener, 'Mazkeret Rabbanei Iṭalyah 1520–1818', in his *Pesak ha-ḥerem shel ha-Rav Ya'akov Polak* . . . (St Petersburg, 1897); S. Simonsohn, Introduction to Leone Modena's *She'elot u-Teshuvot Ziknei Yehudah*, ed. Simonsohn (Jerusalem, 1955); idem, *History of the Jews in the Duchy of Mantua* (Jerusalem, 1972), 695–741.

I

The Socio-cultural Background to the Emergence of the Rabbis

The emergence of a rabbi within Italian-Jewish society in which, not unlike other contemporary Jewish communities, life revolved around the forms of a religious system, was organic. That is, an individual who aspired to the position of rabbi did not follow any particular course of study or 'professional' preparation which differentiated him from the rest of the community, in a manner analogous, for example, to that of the Christian priesthood. The course of study of those who ultimately entered the rabbinate was identical to that of all those who felt it their duty as Jews to undertake the traditional obligation of religious study. One can reasonably state that this programme of study was perceived by the community as designed to bring the best students up to the level of what we may perhaps define as 'religious leaders' (in Hebrew, *morei hora'ah*—a term implying rabbinic function and scholarship, but far more comprehensive). This may be sensed, for example, in a letter written by a teacher to the mother of a student, informing her of her son's progress in his studies: 'The fruit of your womb . . . does not depart . . . from the tent of study . . . He engages in study unceasingly. I am certain that the foundations of his family will yet be uplifted, making him a name among the great ones. Then you shall rejoice . . . and there will be fulfilled by him, "his name will be great in Israel, *he shall instruct*, and the islands shall hope at his teaching" [cf. Isa. 42: 4].'[1] In the eyes of this scholar, whose words may be assumed to reflect the dominant spirit of his age, one who received the title

[1] S. Assaf, *Mekorot le-Toldot ha-Ḥinukh be-Yisra'el* (Tel Aviv, 1928–43), iv. 20. Similarly, R. Raphael b. Joseph Helli recorded the birth of his eldest daughter in the list of his children at the end of his book, 'Ṭal Orot' (MS Los Angeles 1, 779 bx 5; IMHM 32361), 244a: Raphael said, 'In the year 5370 [i.e. 1610], on the 8th day of Shevat . . . God had grace on me and my wife bore . . . a daughter . . . May it be His will . . . that her birth be in a time of blessing . . . and that she merit to enter the marriage canopy and to see sons and grandsons involved in Torah and fulfilling the commandments and serving as "religious leaders" (*morei hora'ah*) in Israel . . .'

of rabbi was seen as having attained the pinnacle of achievement in his studies. Such a view was no doubt rooted in the nature of these studies, which Jewish society saw as stemming from a divine source and as an expression of holiness informing the whole of Jewish life. In fact, at least in theory, religious culture still represented what was considered as specifically Jewish culture. This being so, despite the deep involvement of Italian society of this period in humanism and Renaissance culture, to which we shall have opportunity to refer further, the revolution in general education during the period under discussion completely bypassed the Jewish community.[2]

Among the concrete and striking expressions of that revolution, the most important was the radical change in the texts which formed the curriculum of study. In the time-span of only one generation, all the old textbooks upon which generations of medieval youth had been educated completely disappeared. By the end of the fifteenth century, the well-known *auctores* ('authors'—i.e. authoritative educational texts), and particularly the *auctores octo*,[3] which the young had been required to learn mostly by heart and primarily by means of plain declamation, completely disappeared from Italy.[4] Not one of these eight texts was printed there, all twenty-nine *incunabula* of these works being printed in France.[5] The old educational system was subjected to the most severe and bitter criticism imaginable during those generations, alongside unqualified praise of the activities of the pioneers who destroyed it and established in its place a new system based upon the reading of classical sources. One senses a feeling of awakening following a deep sleep, of emergence into the light after an extended stay in the 'barbaric' darkness of the previous generations, and of self-confidence in daring to accept the challenge of confrontation with the *auctoritates*, on whose works they had been educated and against which they rebelled.[6]

[2] On this subject generally, see E. Garin, *L'educazione in Europa, 1400–1600* (Bari, 1966); idem, *La cultura del Rinascimento* (Bari, 1971).

[3] On the *auctores octo*, see G. Billanovich, 'Leon Battista Alberti, il Graecismus e la Chartula', *Lingua nostra*, 15 (1954), 70–1.

[4] See Garin, *La cultura del Rinascimento*, 71–6.

[5] See E. P. Goldschmidt, *Medieval Texts and their First Appearance in Print* (London, 1943), 29–30.

[6] See e.g. the letter written by Guarino Guarini to his son in the middle of the 15th cent.: G. Veronese, *Epistolario*, ed. Sabbadini (Venice, 1915–19), 581–4. For additional sources, see C. Vasoli, *Umanesimo e rinascimento* (Palermo, 1969), 311 ff.

By contrast, the Jewish educational system remained almost entirely unaltered. It was not completely bypassed by certain expressions of the new spirit, particularly that of greater openness to criticism or to polemic attitudes concerning the system of study, in which the status of talmudic disquisitions (*pilpul*) severely declined (see Chapter 5). But by and large the Jews in Italy continued to be educated on the sacred texts of their religious tradition. The many surviving documents relating to Jewish education in Italy during the period under discussion[7] present a clear picture of this subject, described in detail by nearly all the scholars who have dealt with it.[8] One may reasonably conclude that, at least in so far as visible expressions are concerned, no major changes took place in the general attitude of Jewish society to the religious tradition which this education was meant to instil. An illustration of this is that, throughout the entire period, they apparently found no fault in the system of rote learning of the Bible and vernacular translation[9] at an early age, the origins of which lay in early medieval tradition.[10]

To be sure, the scholars who have dealt with this subject have justifiably stressed certain characteristic features of the education of the Jews in Renaissance Italy: the cultivation of an elegant, even flowery manner of writing; the particular emphasis upon knowledge of the Hebrew language, based upon the tradition of the classical grammarians, whose importance remained undiminished throughout this period; the necessity of what were thought of

[7] Most of these documents appear in Assaf, *Mekorot*, vols. ii and iv.

[8] See esp. A. Marx, 'R. Joseph D'Arli as Teacher and Head of an Academy in Siena' (Heb.), in *Louis Ginzberg Jubilee Volume: Hebrew Section* [*Sefer ha-Yovel li-khevod Levi Ginzberg*] (New York, 1946), 271–304; M. A. Shulvass, 'The Religious Life of Italian Jewry during the Period of the Renaissance' (Heb.), *PAAJR* 17 (1947–8), 1–20; idem, 'The Study of Torah'; H. Z. Dimitrowsky, 'History of the Jews in Milano Before the Expulsion of 1597' (Heb.), *Talpiyot*, 6 (1955), 715–19; S. Simonsohn, 'The World of a Jewish Youth during the Renaissance' (Heb.), *Hagut 'Ivrit be-Europa* (Tel Aviv, 1969), 334–49.

[9] On the nature of the vernacular translations, through which traces of the ancient Judaeo-Italian dialect were preserved until a late date, see G. Sermoneta, *Un volgarizzamento giudeo-italiano del Cantico dei Cantici* (Florence, 1974), 21–31; idem, 'Considerazioni frammentarie sul giudeo-italiano', *Italia: Studi e ricerche sulla cultura e sulla letteratura degli ebrei d'Italia*, i/1 (1976), 1–29; i/2 (1978), 62–106.

[10] Even the need to substitute more up-to-date versions for the older vernacular translations was only felt at the beginning of the 17th cent. The fruitful life-work of Leone Modena was involved with this project. On the parallel phenomenon among Sephardic Jews in Italy during this period, see I. Sonne, 'Jacob Lombroso and the book *Ḥeshek Shlomo*' (Heb.), *KS*, 11 (1935–6), 499–506.

as 'secular' studies, such as Latin grammar and composition, mathematics, music, etc. None of these features required a break with the continuity of the scholastic tradition inherited from previous generations: on this point the Jews clearly differed from the Christians. Thus, the sense of continuity and legacy which the Italian Jew felt for his own cultural tradition is particularly striking when contrasted with the sense of discontinuity and alienation which the Christians felt.[11] In a word, we may conclude that throughout this period, the Jewish educational system still clearly expressed as an educational ideal the pursuit of the traditional goal of perfection in the above tradition, to the point of being able to pass it on to the generations to come; in other words, the goal of becoming a 'religious leader' (*moreh hora'ah*)—that is, a rabbi—if one were successful in one's studies.

1. The Yeshivah

The focus of intellectual activity within Jewish society was the Talmudic academy—the yeshivah. There is a certain confusion regarding the use of this term in the sources from the period. At times, one must refer to the context in which the term is used in order to understand what is being referred to: a group of students gathered around a master who regularly teaches at a given place; a group of students in some kind of framework within the social context of the time (e.g. a company of scholars;[12] a group who study together in the synagogue following prayers; any other framework of study, including one supported by a wealthy man in his own home and at his expense;[13]) or, finally, a meeting-place for established Talmudic scholars (*talmidei ḥakhamim*), who had

[11] I. Zinberg, *A History of Jewish Literature*, iv (Cincinnati and New York, 1974), 37–9, already stressed this aspect of Jewish culture in Italy in the linguistic-grammatical area. It seems to me that the picture may be expanded to include all manifestations of culture generally; this particular aspect constitutes one of the most striking features of the Jewish renaissance in Italy. See Bonfil, 'Uniqueness of the Jewish People'.

[12] See e.g. Leone Modena, *Ḥayyei Yehudah*, ed. D. Carpi (Tel Aviv, 1985), p. 57: 'Also some young men constituted a *yeshivah* and a society, and in order to earn some pocket-money I would read to them every day, and on the Sabbath I would read some words of Torah and a sermon . . .'

[13] *Ḥayyei Yehudah*, p. 49: 'In Iyyar 5354 [1594] the leader Kalonymus Belgrado established a *yeshivah* and a place of study in a garden, and I was at the head of the sermons . . .' Note the stress upon 'in a garden'—similar to the academies which were established in the pastoral atmosphere outside the city! See also ibid. 97.

already mastered the tradition and constitute a kind of *collegium* of scholars or jurists.

A number of sources from the period under discussion would suggest that the term yeshivah refers to the last of the above-mentioned meanings, being in a sense parallel to *academia* or *studium*, in the sense of a meeting place for the learned,[14] while the use of the term to refer to other study frameworks is apparently a freer, borrowed usage.[15] Thus, R. Elijah Capsali (*c*. 1483–1555), from the vantage-point of the Ashkenazic yeshivot in which he studied, saw the growth of the yeshivot in Italy occurring as the result of migration of Ashkenazic students. In his description, he writes: ' "Then they began to call upon the name of the Lord" [cf. Gen. 4: 26] in the land of Italy, and they fixed places of study and established yeshivot in every city and town . . . and in those days many swam in the sea of Talmud, and knowledge grew . . .'[16] R. Elijah (Baḥur) Levita (1468/9–1549) also defined the yeshivah as a place in which students study Talmud under the aegis of yeshivah heads (*rashei-yeshivah*), whom he calls *presides academie*.[17] The term yeshivah is also translated as academia in one of the glossaries composed in the sixteenth century.[18] It is uncertain whether the permission granted by the king in 1466 to the Jews of Sicily to open a *studium generale* implied permission to open a yeshivah, which was

14 See Assaf, Mekorot, ii. 127 ff.; iv. 55; cf. also Breuer, 'ha-Yeshivah ha-Ashkenazit be-Shilhei yemei ha-Beinayim' [The Ashkenazic Yeshivah at the Close of the Middle Ages], Doctoral Dissertation (Jerusalem: Hebrew University, 1967), 23, and n. 71, 72.

15 One must still examine the question as to whether the distinction between *yeshivat ḥaverim* ('collegial *yeshivah*') and *yeshivat baḥurim* ('*yeshivah* of young unmarried students') was a clear one during this period in Italy or not; cf. Breuer, ibid.

16 See N. Porges, 'Elie Capsali et sa chronique de Venise', *REJ* 79 (1925), 33.

17 Elijah (Baḥur) Levita, *Sefer Tishby* (Isny, 1541), s.v. *Ravaz*, 223–4: 'And those who spread Torah thus were called the masters of the yeshivah, *presides academie*, who have many students in the Talmud . . .' Cf. ibid. s.v. *Yeshivah*, 149–50: 'Ieschibah—locum ubi sunt qui faciunt ibi acubare seu quiescere legem ⟨per hoc intelligunt Rabbinos & doctores legis⟩ et in quo sunt discipuli, *yeshivah* appellant ⟨id est accademia, gymnasium, schola⟩ . . .' Thus, the term *yeshivah* is derived by him from the root *le-yashev* 'to resolve' [difficulties], and serves not only as a meeting-place for sages, but also as a House of Study. On an ancient tradition concerning this matter, see H. Merḥaviah, *ha-Talmud bi-re'i ha-Naẓrut* (Jerusalem, 1971), App. IV, no. 19, p. 456: 'Gessiva . . . est quod sessio et accipitur pro schola, pro illa precipue in qua talmut legitur et docetur.' See below, the description of the yeshivah by R. Judah Moscato. On the number of students as a sign of the importance of the yeshivah, see Breuer, 'The Ashkenazic Yeshivah', 44. See also ibid. 59 ff., on the centrality of the study of Talmud in the *yeshivot*.

18 See G. Sermoneta, *Un glossario filosofico ebraico-italiano del XIII secolo* (Rome, 1969), 458.

considered the equivalent of a university, or whether this referred to a university as such.[19] But there can be no doubt that the invitation of R. Jacob Reiner[20] to establish a yeshivah in Ferrara was understood in Christian documents from the year 1556 as a request to open a *studium*, justified by reasons similar to those conventionally offered for the establishment of a university in those days—namely, that the yeshivah, as the glory of the community, enhances the city, as does the *studium*, and that its presence brings profit and benefit to the community of the city as a whole.[21] We may thus easily understand that the community saw it as in its interest and as its responsibility, in so far as possible, to attract a group of prominent scholars and learned people, and to support the yeshivah.[22]

The life of the yeshivah centred around the activities of the yeshivah head (*rosh-yeshivah*, pl. *rashei-yeshivah*) and other local scholars, who met at fixed times every day, along with their students with whom they studied during the rest of the day. A detailed description of this activity has been preserved by R. Elijah Capsali:[23]

[19] See B. and G. Lagumina, *Codice diplomatico dei giudei di Sicilia*, ii. 28–9; and cf. what has been said above with C. Roth, *The Jews in the Renaissance* (Philadelphia, 1959), 41.

[20] See Simonsohn, *Mantua*, 730; H. H. Ben-Sasson, *Hagut ve-Hanhagah* (Jerusalem, 1960), 254. The source cited there may also yield evidence that R. Jacob Reiner was indeed the head of the yeshiva (*rosh-metivta*) in Ferrara over a certain period of time.

[21] Duke Ercole II indeed acceded to the Jews' request, while noting that 'ciò non può tornare se non ad honore et ornamento di essa nostra Cittade, per il profitto che ne potranno trarre molti Hebrei et christiani scolari si forestieri come sudditi nostri'—A. Balletti, *Gli ebrei e gli estensi* (Reggio-Emilia, 1930; rep. Bologna, 1969), 97. Cf. Breuer, 'The Ashkenazic Yeshivah', 10 and n. 9. It is clear that this statement is connected with the phenomenon of migration of the scholarly community, common both to the *yeshivot* and the universities during the Middle Ages; see Breuer, ibid., 18, 41–4. Cf. also Chap. 4, Sect. 2, near the end.

[22] See e.g. Sonne, 'Basic Premisses', 153. See the detailed survey of the support of the *yeshivot* in Ashkenaz from public funds within the framework of the communal organization in Breuer, 'The Ashkenazic Yeshivah', 13–16, 26–37. Most of what has been said about Ashkenaz is also correct with regard to Italy, certainly with respect to its Ashkenazic community. See also how, in the framework of a sharp controversy, the *rosh-yeshivah* was accused of misuse of the funds of the stipends, emphasizing that this deed entailed a deprivation of 'important young men and scholars', *Pesakim* (Venice, 1519), 29b.

[23] See Porges, 'Elie Capsali', 34–5; cf. Breuer, 'The Ashkenazic Yeshivah', 67–9; H. Z. Dimitrowsky, 'On the Method of *Pilpul*' (Heb.), *Salo Wittmayer Baron Jubilee Volume: Hebrew Section, iii* (*Sefer ha-Yovel li-khivod Shalom Baron*) (Jerusalem, 1975), 119–20. See also Breuer, 'The Ashkenazic Yeshivah', 52 ff., for a comprehensive discussion of the world of the Ashkenazi *yeshivot*. As we shall see directly below, there was no

After the [morning] prayers the rabbi went with his disciples, who lived with him in his home . . . to a small room, located in the courtyard of the Great Synagogue of Padua, called the yeshivah, which was filled with wooden seats and lecterns, where they sat on seats of judgement [after Ps. 122: 5], and after that the other rabbis and learned people would gather together with the students . . .[24]

In his own home, the *rosh-yeshivah* was expected to teach those students who were unable to pay:

And he gave each of them a room in his house, where he would live, and thus would he do to each person according to his level and value, and these students would be fed from their own funds, but they ate together at one table, and there they would discourse . . . and those students who lived in the rabbi's house would be instructed by him . . .[25]

Thus, the *rosh-yeshivah* served as a kind of private tutor to these students, his salary for this being included within the annual 'stipend' that he received from the community.[26] What the *rosh-yeshivah* did for 'those students who could not afford to pay' was performed by other rabbis for the 'children of the wealthy and the "nobility", who would hire a rabbi from among the other rabbis of the city, to teach them more intensively'.[27] Thus, all of the rabbis, including the *rashei-yeshivah*, acted in the capacity of *repetitores* outside the walls of the yeshivah, preparing their students for the discussions within that framework.[28] The situation depicted here by R. Elijah Capsali reminds one of the characteristic features of the *yeshivot* of ancient Babylonia and Palestine, in which the members of the yeshivah gathered with their pupils.[29]

The above comparison between the *yeshivot* of Italy and those of ancient times is not only suggested by isolated evidence. Testimony from another source adds to a picture in which we

substantive difference between R. Elijah Capsali's description of the activities in the yeshivah and that of an Italian yeshivah one hundred years later.

[24] Porges, 'Elie Capsali'.

[25] Ibid.

[26] This fact certainly helped to obscure somewhat the distinction between a '*yeshivah*' in the narrow sense of a meeting place for scholars, as we have noted above, and the overall framework focused around the activity of the *rosh-yeshivah*.

[27] See Porges, 'Elie Capsali'.

[28] Cf. *Pesakim* (Venice, 1519), 29*b*; A. Marx, 'Glimpses of the life of an Italian Rabbi of the First Half of the Sixteenth Century', *HUCA* 1 (1924), 617.

[29] See Goitein, *Sidrei Ḥinukh*, 146–8.

see a mixture of ancient Jewish traditions[30] with the lore of the universities of the period. In a description of the structure and activity of the yeshivah in a sermon given by R. Judah Moscato (*c.* 1530–*c.* 1593)[31] about a hundred years after the description of R. Elijah Capsali, we hear of the division of the yeshivah community into three 'customary levels—the yeshivah head; the "text-reciters" (*shonei halakhot*); and the "discussant-scholars" (*ba'aley ṭerisin*)'.[32] Moscato's description is based upon a sacral understanding of the yeshivah and of the task of the *rosh-yeshivah*,[33] the former envisaged as a kind of miniature Temple, performing a function similar to that of the Sanctuary in the wilderness and of the Temple in Jerusalem, according to the rabbinic tradition. The *rosh-yeshivah* is compared to Aaron, the High Priest; the 'text-reciters' to the beard of Aaron, 'which descends upon his cheeks' (cf. Ps. 133: 2); these (the cheeks) to the 'discussant-scholars' who surround him.[34] In this description which, in the spirit of the time, naturally reflects the influence of Neoplatonic ideas, intellectual activity within the yeshivah is depicted as 'the supreme influx which flows upon the head [i.e. the *yeshivah head*], descends upon the beard [*those who repeat halakhot*], the beard of Aaron . . . which descends upon his cheeks [*the discussant-scholars who surround him*]'.[35] Thus, the image of the *rosh-yeshivah* in relation to the community of scholars,[36] as well as the method of operation of the yeshivah as it emerges upon the rhetorical screen of R. Judah Moscato, does not substantially differ from that depicted by R. Elijah Capsali. Capsali also writes in his description:

> The other rabbis and scholars gathered together with their students, the rabbi began to ask questions, and each would answer according to

30 One might mention in this context, and with reference to what has been said above, the situation described in the Scroll of Ahimaaz, in which the community of scholars in the yeshivah is presented as composed of 'sages', 'colleagues', 'rabbis and sages and those who understand'; see *Megillat Aḥhima'aẓ*, ed. B. Klar (Jerusalem, 1944), 19, 36, 44.

31 Moscato, *Nefuẓot Yehudah*, Sermon 36.

32 Ibid. 76*a*.

33 We shall discuss the sacral understanding of the rabbi in Italy further in Ch. 2, Sect. 4.

34 Moscato, *Nefuẓot Yehudah*, 77*a*—all making use of homiletical parallelism to Psalm 133.

35 Ibid. One should mention that, in the allegorical approach of Philo, whose writings were greatly admired during R. Moscato's epoch, the high priest Aaron is compared to the *logos*.

36 Cf. Breuer, 'The Ashkenazic Yeshivah', 23–4.

> his own level. Afterwards, each one would ask and answer and bring to light hidden things, and this is what is called the discussion (*pilpul*) of the yeshivah. And each one would discuss with his partner, the great one with the great one, and the younger with the younger one, and the discussion was conducted from memory, that is, without opening a book, for the text[37] was well known to everyone, and there were no books there except for the rabbi's copy of the Talmud, in which he would show them the relevant text . . . and they would sit there in the yeshivah for about one hour . . . depending upon the discussion and the requirements of the particular text being studied, and at the end the yeshivah head . . . would open his book and show them to which point they were to study till the next gathering, not to add to or to subtract from it, and then they would stand up and go to their homes, and each of the masters would study for the next day with his students, and the *rosh-yeshivah* would do likewise with his own students—and thus would they do every day . . .[38]

Thus, the *rosh-yeshivah* opened with a discussion of a Talmudic unit learned outside of the walls of the yeshivah, the entire community of the yeshivah participated in the discussion, 'each one according to his level', and the *rosh-yeshivah* summarized the discussion and assigned the subject-matter for the next day's discussion.

R. Elijah Capsali's description makes no mention of the 'text-reciters' mentioned by R. Judah Moscato. Nevertheless, it makes no sense to assume that Moscato invented this category for the purposes of his sermon alone. In the absence of other detailed descriptions, I would suggest that the 'text-reciters' fulfilled a function similar to that of the *tannaim* ('repeaters' of the law—i.e., repositories of the Oral Tradition) in the ancient *yeshivot*[39]—particularly as at the time Moscato wrote these words the Talmud was not available to all the students, as it was in other, more settled periods. The consequences of the papal decree of September 1553, ordering the burning of all extant copies of

[37] i.e. the Talmudic text together with Rashi's commentary and the Tosaphistic glosses, upon which the discussion was based. Cf. E. E. Urbach, *Ba'alei ha-Tosafot* (Jerusalem, 1980), 31 n. 86; cf. Breuer, 'The Ashkenazic Yeshivah', 68.

[38] Porges, 'Elie Capsali', 34–5. Cf. M. Breuer, 'The Growth of *Pilpul* and *Ḥiluk* in the Ashkenazic Yeshivot' (Heb.), *Sefer Zikaron le-Morenu . . . Y. Y. Weinberg* (Jerusalem, 1970), 245.

[39] See Goitein, *Sidrei Ḥinukh*, 170–1.

the Talmud,[40] which was actually carried out by the rulers of most Italian states, were still vividly experienced everywhere. By the time R. Judah Moscato spoke to his audience, the censored Basle edition of the Talmud (1578–81) was available, but this edition was certainly not satisfactory. Thus, we might say that the 'text-reciters' preserved for the yeshivah community the complete, uncensored text of the topic being studied: during the years between the burning of the Talmud and the printing of the Basle edition, they presented from memory the texts which they had learned in secret,[41] while at the later period, when that edition was available, there was still need for someone to supply the correct reading in those cases in which there was a suspicion of substantive changes in the text of the censored edition.[42]

It has recently been noted, in a description of yeshivah activity from the beginning of the seventeenth century, that one finds the figure of a member of the yeshivah who read the text before the discussion. Hence, it has been suggested that the 'text-reciters' mentioned by R. Judah Moscato might be identified with these lecturers. It might then be possible that we have here a rather different model of yeshivah activity from that of Padua, one which is perhaps ultimately linked with some Spanish tradition.[43] While at the present state of our knowledge this possibility is a feasible one, it seems to me more likely that the figure found in the later description is a development of the model exposed above, one which more closely approached that of the university lecturer.

Be that as it may, from R. Judah Moscato's description we receive a picture of the *rosh-yeshivah* as the one who opened the discussion, and of the yeshivah community raising and answering questions in his presence. The *rosh-yeshivah*'s main function here is to eliminate the doubts raised by his interlocutors and to present a clear summary of the subject matter. He saw this as the

[40] See K. R. Stow, 'The Burning of the Talmud in 1553, in the light of Sixteenth-century Catholic Attitudes toward the Talmud', *Bibliothèque d'Humanisme et Renaissance*, 34 (1972), 435–59, and the bibliography listed there.

[41] Cf. the statement of R. Abraham Portaleone at the end of *Sefer Shilṭei ha-Gibborim* (Mantua, 1612).

[42] They certainly did not dare to bring copies of the Constantinople 1580–3 edition to Italy! On the presence of the Basle edition in Mantua during this period, see S. Simonsohn, 'Books and Libraries of the Jews of Mantua, 1595' (Heb.), *KS* 37 (1962), 121.

[43] J. Boksenboim, *Iggeroth Melammedim; Italia 5315–5351 (1555–1591)* (Tel Aviv, 1985), 6–7 and n. 19.

basis of his success, and it was for this that he prayed, elaborating upon the 23rd Psalm:

Even when I walk in the valley of darkness *of doubts* I will fear no evil, for Thou art with me *to show me the way towards solving them.* Your rod *of the questions of the scholars* and your staff *through the way of their solution* shall comfort me *for both of them are intended to bring the truth to light.* You set before me a table against my enemies *the discussant-scholars, in the sense of 'enemies in the gate'*[44] . . . You have anointed my head with oil *having appointed me a yeshivah head,* my cup runneth over. *May it be Thy will that you fill me with overflowing abundance, that I be able to give of it to my fellows, to the yeshivah students, as in the parable of the oil and the dew* . . .[45]

We may also add to these descriptions the evidence found in the description of the activity in the yeshivah of Verona at the end of the sixteenth century[46] and in the invitation directed to R. Isaac de Lattes (d. *c.* 1570) to serve as *rosh-yeshivah* in Pesaro in 1557.[47] In the light of all these, we may conclude that in its general outlines there is a uniform picture presented throughout the entire period under discussion, which in substance does not seem too different from that of the communities of students in the yeshivot in other places during the same period.[48]

We have already noted the semantic proximity in the consciousness of people of that generation between the concepts of yeshivah and *studium.* There were other significant points of similarity between the two, particularly in the pattern of their educational activities, both with regard to the technique of study and the structure of the lectures. The activity within the yeshivah, as described both by R. Elijah Capsali and by R. Judah Moscato,

[44] An allusion to Kiddushin 30*b*: ' "They will not be shamed when the enemies speak in the gate" [Ps. 127: 5]. What is meant by "enemies in the gate"? R. Hiyya b. Abba said: Even a father and son, or teacher and student, who are engaged in [studying] Torah in one place [lit. "gate"] become enemies to one another [because they challenge one another and one does not accept the other's words (i.e. *understanding of the text*)—Rashi] and do not move from there until they become reconciled to one another.'

[45] Moscato, *Nefuẓot Yehudah*, ibid. 77*b*. On the parable of the oil and the dew, see near note 35. Cf. n. 17.

[46] See Sonne, 'Basic Premisses', ii. 179, Document 23.

[47] See D. Frankel, 'Three Letters Concerning the Life of R. Isaac Joshua de Lattes' (Heb.), *'Alim le-Bibliographyah ve-Toldot Yisrael* iii/2 (1937–8), 24.

[48] I will not touch here upon the theoretical and scholarly aspects of this picture. Even the final chapter of this book will only deal tangentially with these questions, and only in so far as they touch upon the institution of the rabbinate.

clearly resembles the educational framework of a law class at one of the universities. There, too, the professor first lectured in a special manner (*doctoreo modo*), followed by various kinds of discussion—depending upon the tradition of the particular university—to remove difficulties which had arisen, particularly in the study of the *glossa*. This sequence of learning activities appears to be quite similar to the above-mentioned activity in the yeshivah.[49] In a like manner to that described by Capsali for the Padua yeshivah, a variety of different questions pertinent to the topic at hand were proposed in the universities as well and, at their conclusion, the professor summarized all that had been learned and discussed. Experienced scholars and doctors participated in such lessons, side by side with normal students.[50] Thus, it would not be inappropriate to conclude that the activity of the *rosh-yeshivah* in the Jewish academy closely paralleled that of the Professor-Doctor in the university. This activity is fairly well summarized by the tests by which candidates were examined prior to receiving the doctoral title, enabling them to teach in the university, in which it was determined whether they were able 'to lecture in the doctoral way, to summarize the arguments of the doctors, to respond to and solve them' (*doctoreo modo legendo*, *argumenta doctorum reassumendo*, *ipsis respondendo et ea solvendo*).[51]

But the yeshivah fulfilled more functions than did the university. The *rosh-yeshivah* also functioned as a kind of Chief Justice (*av bet din*) of a miniature Sanhedrin, composed of the community 'who sat on the seats of judgement'.[52] At times, he brought before the yeshivah community questions that had been addressed to

[49] On the methods of analysis used in the *yeshivah*—*pilpul* and *ḥiluk*—and their similarity to the discussions in the university, see Breuer, 'The Growth of *Pilpul*'; idem, 'The Ashkenazic Yeshivah', 91–3. See also Urbach, *Ba'alei ha-Tosafot*, 676 ff.; Breuer, 'The Ashkenazic Yeshivah', 92 n. 60; Dimitrowsky, 'On the Method of *Pilpul*', 116–19.

[50] On this, and on the structure of teaching in the Italian universities, see P. S. Leicht, *Storia del diritto italiano; le fonti* (Milan, 1956), 135.

[51] See e.g. the text of the doctoral diploma awarded to R. Obadiah Sforno, cited by Vittore Colorni, 'Spigolature su Obadia Sforno', *Volume . . . in Memoria di Federico Luzzatto*, *RMI* 28/3–4 (1962), 86. We shall see below that, just as the doctorate qualified an individual to fulfil these functions in any university, so did the rabbinic ordination authorize the rabbi 'to establish a *yeshivah* in any place'. Cf. Breuer, 'The Ashkenazic Yeshivah', 9.

[52] See the statement of R. Elijah Capsali quoted previously. This public was identical with the *benei yeshivah* referred to continually in the sources.

him, on which he ruled following discussion and clarification among the 'student-colleagues',[53] similar to the procedure followed by the *geonim* of the Babylonian academies during the High Middle Ages. For this reason, coming out of the consensus of a community of experienced scholars, illuminated by divine inspiration, and with the intermediacy of the *rosh-yeshivah* in the manner described by R. Judah Moscato, the rulings issued by the *rosh-yeshivah* in his capacity as Head of the miniature Sanhedrin held particular weight, and appeared almost as if they were emanating directly from God.[54] We may summarize by saying that the sacral understanding of the yeshivah and of the *rosh-yeshivah*, its hierarchical structure, and the function it performed in determining the *halakhah* in the sense of a minor Sanhedrin within the public domain—would all suggest deep roots, drawing upon ancient traditions.[55]

This ambience blended harmoniously with the university world, without any special efforts of adaptation, and certainly without producing any sense of tension at the adoption of outside customs within the sacred area of traditional intellectual activity. This point can hardly be overestimated, and must be kept in mind carefully in any reconstruction of the peculiar mentality of Renaissance Jews in Italy, particularly as it pertains to an area which would logically be thought of as the most resistant to outside influences, contrary to the mainstream of traditional Jewish trends.

It should be added at this point (in anticipation of discussion in Chapter 5) that the Jewish communities in Italy did not enjoy juridical autonomy throughout this period. For that reason, the possibility of developing the institution of the yeshivah into a kind of communal legislative body or law court was curtailed. On the other hand, there is clear evidence of a tendency to concentrate activity of this sort within the yeshivah. The yeshivah of R. Judah Minz (*c.* 1408–1506), which formed the model for R. Elijah Capsali's description from which we have already

[53] See e.g. the *Responsa* of R. Judah Minz (Venice, 1553), no. 5. Cf. Breuer, 'The Ashkenazic Yeshivah', 21–2.

[54] See the *Responsa* of R. Judah Minz, no. 12: 'they allowed him to be married like the owners of *yeshivot*'.

[55] Compare H. H. Ben-Sasson (ed.), *A History of the Jewish People* (Cambridge, Mass., 1976), 423 ff.

quoted, functioned as a genuine law-making body for the entire Jewish community. For example, in 1507, Minz, in the presence of a large community of scholars, published a collection of seven ordinances pertaining to a variety of areas of Jewish communal life—marriage law, public morality, ritual slaughter, and juridical procedure.

I have discussed these ordinances in considerable detail elsewhere[56] and will not do so again here, but shall confine myself to some general remarks. These ordinances seem clearly expressive of the manner in which the Ashkenazic community (which constituted the dominant group in Padua, and to which R. Judah Minz belonged), including its rabbinic leadership, adapted itself to the way of life of Renaissance Italy and how the rabbinic leadership understood its position and task within Jewish society. That understanding is clearly expressed here in particular by the fact that the ordinances are published without any reference to the lay leadership of the community, as if the yeshivah functioned as an independent, sovereign, legislative body.

The opposition of the Christian authorities to the granting of juridical autonomy, which curtailed this developing trend, combined over the course of time with a tendency towards allocation of authority to the communal leaders, creating a model of Jewish leadership in which decisions relating to matters were no longer made exclusively within the walls of the yeshivah. Instead, the rabbis participated in various ways, as we shall see when considering the appointed communal rabbi in Chapter 3.

Be that as it may, during the seventeenth century, once the communities had succeeded in gaining some sort of recognition for their right to juridical autonomy, there grew out of the framework of the yeshivah the institution of the 'general yeshivah'—the supreme authority for legal rulings by the sages of the community—in which the various congregations were represented in proportion to their strength within the overall community—but this goes beyond the limits we have set for the present work, and I shall not discuss it here.[57]

[56] See R. Bonfil, 'Aspects of the Social and Spiritual Life of the Jews in the Venetian Territories at the Beginning of the 16th Century' (Heb.), *Ẓion*, 41 (1976), 68–96.

[57] See Ch. 3, Sect. 11 n. 315.

2. The Emergence of the Rabbi

I have already said that the rabbi emerged in an organic way from the general community of scholars; the student's participation in its intellectual activity and debate was not intended to prepare him for the rabbinic title as such. However, the social importance attached to the rabbinic title, as shown in greater detail below, was a strong incentive in people's striving to have their name prefaced by the title 'Colleague [of the Rabbis]' (*Ḥaver*), and if possible by the title 'Our Master, Rabbi' (*Morenu ha-Rav*). We have already noted[58] certain expressions of the general mentality which considered that as an ideal.

Obviously, at least in theory, one was entitled to be ordained as rabbi after having displayed extensive knowledge in the pertinent subject-matter. However, the period of study was not defined nor, in a certain sense, were the contents of the studies. It was clear to everyone that the rabbi was expected to be expert in Talmud and in *halakhic* literature, but there is no evidence of a demand for expertise in specific Talmudic tractates. Even the works of *novellae* and legal rulings (*ḥiddushim* and *pesakim*) upon which the discussions were based were dependent upon the various traditions of learning followed by the community, a point to be briefly considered further.[59] It has been noted that Talmudic dialectical activity and creativity decreased noticeably in Italy during the period under discussion, but there seems no evidence that the study of the Codes replaced that of the Talmud in the *yeshivot*. There also seems to be no basis for assuming that the burning of the Talmud was the main cause of such a shift in the orientation of learning activity.[60] Even if there is considerable evidence for the lack of copies of the Talmud during the latter half of the sixteenth century, one can safely affirm that the study of Talmud and Tosaphists continued to occupy a central place in the *yeshivot*. It was rather the approach which changed; acuity in Talmudic discussion was no longer the crowning personal achievement of the scholars and, unlike the case in Ashkenaz, did

58 See at the beginning of this chapter.

59 See Ch. 5, Sect. 8.

60 See, on the other hand, Breuer, 'The Ashkenazic Yeshivah', 72–3, and the bibliography cited there.

not serve them in their struggle for communal leadership.[61] This change was the result of various factors, which we shall briefly discuss in Chapter 6.

When the scholars saw that a given individual had substantial scholarly accomplishments, they saw themselves as entitled to consider whether or not to bestow upon him the title of *Ḥaver*, and afterwards that of *Rav*—that is, to proceed to rabbinic ordination. Whether referred to as such or under another name,[62] there is no doubt that the formal act of ordination (*semikhah*),[63] through which an individual was elevated to the status of 'rabbi', is inextricably tied to the roots of the rabbinate. To the best of my knowledge, no systematic study has ever been conducted into the development of this institution from Gaonic times to the fourteenth century.[64] It would not be far amiss to state that this institution, similar to others in the Jewish people's history, moved west as part of the heritage of the European Jewish communities from the Babylonian Gaonate. The origins of the development of centres of Jewish learning in the West is involved with people who were ordained in Babylonia. For example, R. Sherira Gaon wrote to R. Jacob b. Nissim in Kairouan concerning R. Elḥanan b. Shemariah, who was one of the 'four captives' (that is, one of the four prominent Babylonian scholars who, according to a legendary tradition, were captured on the high seas by pirates, sold into slavery, and eventually became the leaders of several communities on the Western Mediterranean littoral, thereby transferring the centre of rabbinic authority to that region):[65] 'Also our only and very dear son, our colleague (*Ḥaver*), may

[61] On Ashkenaz and Poland, see ibid. 95–100; Ben-Sasson, *Hagut ve-Hanhagah*, Chs. 12–13.

[62] The term 'appointment' (*minui*), for example, is used as a synonym for 'ordination' (*semikhah*); see Pseudo-Rashi to Mo'ed Katan 22*b*, s.v. *ḥakham she-met bet midrasho baṭel*: '*Ḥakham*—the one appointed over the city, from whom they seek rulings . . .', *Perush Rashi le-Masekhet Mo'ed Katan*, ed. A. Kupfer (Jerusalem, 1961), 75, and see the editor's note there.

[63] Hebrew: *semikhah*. The Hebrew term comes from the root *smkh*, literally, 'to place hands upon', referring to the ancient gesture of bestowal of authority, blessing, or identity upon another person, animal or thing—in the case of ordination, the transfer of one's halakhic authority.

[64] Mordecai Breuer's study on the Ashkenazic institution of ordination, 'Ashkenazic Ordination' (Heb.), *Ẓion*, 33 (1968), 15–46, to be discussed, deals with the time-span beginning with this period until the end of the Middle Ages.

[65] Abraham ibn Daud, *The Book of Tradition* (*Sefer ha-Qabbalah*), a critical ed. with a translation and notes by G. D. Cohen (Philadelphia, 1967), 63 ff.

God protect him, whom I ordained in the yeshivah . . .'[66] It seems that the rabbis who taught in the Diaspora were originally ordained in Babylonia, and that gradually, during the course of its liberation from the centralized authority of the *geonim*, a new form of the institution took shape in the West. Evidence for the Oriental origins of the institution may be found in *Sefer ha-Shetarot*, a collection of formulas used in various legal situations, compiled by R. Judah b. Barzilay al-Bargeloni (late eleventh and early twelfth centuries). The following explanation is appended there to the document relating to rabbinical ordination:

> And thus it is, for example, that when one ordains one of the students, he is called . . . either 'learned man' (*Ḥakham*) or 'Rabbi' (*Rav*), and that one writes a document to this effect . . . If the elders of the city or those of the congregation and the study house agree to ordain one of the students, they . . . then write a document of ordination . . . And once that document of ordination is in his hands, from that day on everyone calls him 'Rabbi', and he is included in the judgements of the court and the gatherings of the *Ḥaverim*, and he is served and dresses like one of the sages and in their raiment, that of the ordained *Ḥaverim* and Rabbis (*Rabbanim*), and not like that of the disciples who have not yet been ordained . . .[67]

The source of R. Judah's formula has recently been uncovered in a formulary of R. Sa'adya Gaon, which was already composed by the year 926.[68] It does not seem possible to specify how, if at all, the shaping of the institution of ordination in the West was influenced also by practices which were still observed in the

[66] See the bibliographical notes by S. A. Poznanski, 'The People of Kairouan' (Heb.), in *Zikaron le-Avraham Eliyahu* [Harkavy Memorial Volume], (Petersburg, 1909), 187–8. Also the important remarks in that article concerning the titles used by the sages during that early period. Cf. the text of this letter cited by J. Mann, *The Jews in Egypt and Palestine under the Fatamid Caliphs*, (Oxford, 1922), ii. 171: 'We have already read your letter and seen that all of you love our great man, our master and teacher Abraham Berabi, the *ḥaver*, may he rest in Eden, and we ordained him in the *yeshivah* . . .' Cf. D. Rosenthal, '*Rabbanan de'Siyyum'a* and *Bene Siyyume*" (Heb.), *Tarbiz*, 49 (1979–80), 52–61; H. Y. Bernstein, 'The Law of Ordination and its History' (Heb.), *ha-Tekufah*, 4 (1913), 394–426.

[67] *Sefer ha-Shetarot le-R"i ha-Barzeloni*, ed. Halberstamm (Berlin, 1898; photo edn., Jerusalem, 1967), 132. See Breuer, 'Ashkenazic Ordination', p. 15 n. 2. See also the clear expression in *Ma'amar Seder ha-Dorot* by R. Saadiah b. Maimun ibn Danan, *Ḥemdah Genuzah* (Königsburg, 1856), 30*a*: 'Even though Rabbi Jacob son of R. Isaac [i.e. Alfasi] was a great sage and ordained to the rabbinate . . .'

[68] I owe this information to my friend and colleague, Menahem Ben-Sasson, whom I wish to thank here. Dr Ben-Sasson is currently working on an edition of Sa'adya's formulary.

Land of Israel.[69] Be that as it may, in twelfth-century sources we find numerous references to the ordination of individuals to the rabbinate, and it would appear that during this period the title *ha-Rav* came to be used following the name of the individual ordained, to distinguish it from the use of the terms *R.* or *Rav*, which preceded, as an honorific title, the names of those scholars who had not yet been ordained,[70] in a way which appears not dissimilar from a custom still in use in many contemporary traditional milieus.

Some have maintained that, from the twelfth century on, the title *rav* indicated one who held a specific office or function within the communal framework.[71] However, the question is a debatable one, and would seem to require more thorough research. Nor is it clear when the practice, still in use in the twelfth century, of placing the title *ha-Rav* after the person's name, fell into disuse. From the fact that it did fall into desuetude, we may reasonably infer that the number of ordained individuals steadily increased and that, consequently, ordained scholars might no longer pretend to exercise exclusive prerogatives within their community, simply because there were too many of them. This does not mean that the rabbis did not fulfil certain functions within the community, and it certainly does not mean that the rabbis did not wish to fulfil such a function. However, it would seem that the relationship between the rabbinic title of an ordained scholar and the functions associated with it within the communal framework needed to be restructured. One may naturally think of some additional conditions, which for the time being require further clarification, such as formal appointment by the community, or at least the agreement of the community that such-and-such a person would fulfil certain tasks within it. If this assumption is correct, it would constitute a tentative explanation of the strange fact that, during the course of time, the use of the term 'ordination' (*semikhah*) ceased to be used in Spain as the designation for the formal act by which one acquired the title of rabbi, even though the title itself continued to be used.[72] That is to say, it is possible

[69] See bibliographical notes in Breuer, 'Ashkenazic Ordination', n. 3.

[70] Cf. the references in *Sefer ha-Qabbalah*, ed. Cohen, 57, 58, 60, 61, with the refs. in the *Itinerary* of Benjamin of Tudela, ed. Adler (London, 1907), 3, 5, 9, 13, 15, etc.

[71] See the bibliography cited in our Introduction, n. 18.

[72] See e.g. the statements made by Nahmanides in his polemic with Pablo Christiani, *Kitvei ha-Ramban*, ed. H. D. Chavel (Jerusalem, 1963), 304–5.

that, while semantically *semikhah* may have continued to mean ordination, implying appointment, the process by which the appointment was separated from the ordination caused the term itself to fall into disuse. Be that as it may, unlike the situation in Spain, the term *semikhah* continued to be used in France and Germany, and possibly also in Italy, although we have no evidence as to the means of granting rabbinic titles in those areas prior to the fourteenth century.

Mordecai Breuer has devoted a detailed study to the institution of ordination in Germany and France from the fourteenth century onwards.[73] According to Breuer, from the generation of Rabbi Meir of Rothenberg (*c.* 1215–93), the use of the term 'Our Master' (*morenu*) for rabbis became more and more widespread. He further conjectures that what is generally known as the 'renewal' of Ashkenazic ordination at the time of R. Meir Ha-Levi of Vienna (d. 1404) and of R. Isaac b. Sheshet Perfet (1326–1408, known as *Ribash*), following the well-known controversy with the rabbis of France, was no more than a crystallization of the formal arrangements for ordination, such as the granting of the title 'Our Master' to the one ordained, as well as the transformation of ordination into an institution granting the authority and status of rabbi. Breuer discusses the historical circumstances which brought about this development in some detail: the dwindling of the community of scholars as a result of the persecutions and edicts which followed the Black Plague, and the various expressions of spiritual crisis which followed it; the creation of a vacuum of authority within the communities, and the tendency to fill this by communal lay leadership or by unqualified rabbis; the involvement of the city officials and the kings in the choice of communal rabbis; social tendencies, such as the pursuit of honour and titles among the scholars, prevalent at that time both within the Jewish community and in Christian society; the tendency of influential rabbis to impose their authority beyond the area of their own jurisdiction through the influence of students whom they had ordained; etc. All these brought about the crystallization of fixed arrangements for the elevation of an individual to the level of rabbi, and the bestowal of a formal document by means of which he could seek an appointment and status within the community. Breuer also noted the negative

[73] Breuer, 'Ashkenazic Ordination'.

phenomena which accompanied the institution of ordination in Franco-Germany, which ultimately hastened an involutory process causing the decline of the prestige of ordination.

There is no doubt that ordination, as described by Breuer, was also practised in Italy and that there is no substantive difference between the institution of ordination in Ashkenaz and the same institution in Italy during the period between the mid-fifteenth century and the end of the sixteenth century, even if one may still question Breuer's statement whether the spread of Ashkenazic *semikhah* occurred only where there were *yeshivot* following the Ashkenazic tradition,[74] or whether there was rather a parallel development of the institution, resulting from similar social problematics and ideals. We shall leave this unresolved here. It is the price we must pay for an attempt to study a relatively late period in the history of the development of the rabbinate. While the historian must always ask himself 'What happened previously?', the answer to such a question is not always within his reach.

I have already noted how the principal active preparation for ordination took place in the discussions of the yeshivah. However, we do not have clear information concerning the age of the young people who constituted the community of students at the yeshivah. From the testimony of R. David b. Messer Leon, who was ordained at the age of 18, and similar evidence which we shall discuss at greater length in Chapter 2,[75] we may conclude that whoever was able to study Talmud was allowed to accompany his teacher and to participate in the discussions within the yeshivah 'according to his level'. It is difficult to determine whether this took place at the age of 15, as it seemed to one of the scholars,[76] or possibly even earlier.[77] Apparently there were no clear norms set for this, and a boy of 10 or 11 was not barred from studying at the yeshivah if he was capable of doing so.[78]

[74] Ibid., 28.

[75] See below, Ch. 2, Sect. 3, re R. Azriel Diena's responsum on this subject.

[76] See Assaf, *Mekorot*, iv. 55 (apparently following the Mishnah in Avot 5: 21).

[77] See Breuer, 'The Ashkenazic Yeshivah', 44.

[78] It seems clear that boys began to study Talmud, Alfasi, and Codes from the age of 9 or 10 in the *yeshivot* of their teachers or at home with their private tutor. See Assaf, *Mekorot*, ii. 114; *Kitvei R. Yehudah Aryeh mi-Modena*, ed. J. Blau (Budapest, 1906), 56; the end of *Sefer Shilṭei ha-Gibborim* of R. Abraham Portaleone. As against this, 'young men' (*baḥurim*) who enjoyed public support were certainly considered 'young men who

Thus, in due course, the Italian rabbi emerged from this world of learning, in which he had taken his place according to his ability, to turn towards activity in other aspects of society. In the following chapters, I shall try to describe how the title 'Rabbi' was actually bestowed, to follow the rabbi within Jewish society, to investigate the prestige associated with his title, and the function he performed among his fellow Jews.[79] We shall discover a living, multiform picture of an environment filled with social and spiritual tensions, in the shaping of which the rabbis were central figures. A number of factors contributed to this unique picture: the involvement of Italian Jews in general culture; the impact of Catholic society in a region where the papal presence was felt; the direct and indirect pressure of the Church on communities; the diversity of the various congregations within the community; the deep changes which occurred in Jewish spiritual life in that period during which Kabbalistic mysticism became a central form of spiritual expression in Italy. All these factors left their impression on the institution of the rabbinate in that country, as well as on its activity and influence among the Jewish public. It is perhaps not an exaggeration to say that some of the subjects to be discussed further also have a bearing upon questions not altogether remote from the world of contemporary Jews.

study', that is to say, mature students. See Sonne, 'Basic Premisses', 153; in my opinion, the word *melamdim* is the correct reading.

79 See the bibliographical list appended at the end of this work. Some MS sources upon which I relied for this study are appended at the end of the Hebrew ed. of this book, *ha-Rabbanut be-Iṭalyah bi-tekufat ha-Renessans* (Jerusalem, 1979), Sect. II, 209–93. It did not seem necessary to quote these passages in full for the English reader; selected passages from some of these documents have been incorporated within the text. The interested reader is referred to the original Hebrew texts found in that edition; appropriate references will be found in the footnotes here.

2

The Social Meaning of Rabbinic Ordination

1. The Status of the Ordained Rabbi

As we have already mentioned, during our period the practice of ordination in Italy did not differ substantially from that in France and Germany. We cannot state with certainty whether this institution was brought to Italy from France and Germany by those who had migrated there during the preceding period, or whether traditions brought by the immigrants mingled on Italian soil with other, already existing traditions from earlier generations.[1] There were two different titles which were generally granted by ordination: *Morenu ha-Rav* (i.e. 'our Master, Rabbi'), granted in 'rabbinical ordination', and licensing its bearer to rule on questions of Jewish law; and *Ḥaver* ('Colleague', i.e. to some extent 'associate'), in what was known as 'collegial ordination'. The latter elevated its bearer to the level of a recognized scholar (*talmid ḥakham*), albeit not one authorized to rule on halakhic questions *per se*. Towards the end of the sixteenth century, a third title, *ḥakham* (sage), constituting a kind of intermediate stage, was added to these two titles.

The title *Ḥaver* harks back to the institutions of learning within the framework of the academies (*yeshivot*),[2] the heirs of the Great Sanhedrin of the Second Temple period, as they were known among Babylonian and Palestinian Jewry, whence it spread to other regions where Jews established centres of learning following the model of the ancient academies of Babylonia and Palestine.[3] The title was granted to scholars who fulfilled various

[1] See Ch. 1, Sect. 1.

[2] Even at the time of the Mishnah and the Talmud, the term *ḥaver* was used in the broad sense to refer to a scholar; see *Encyclopedia Talmudica*, xii (Jerusalem, 1967), s.v. *ḥaver*.

[3] See S. D. Goitein, *Sidrei Ḥinukh* (Jerusalem, 1962), 13-14.

tasks of communal and religious leadership,[4] participated in discussions within the academy, and were thus distinguished from ordinary Torah students.[5] It is not clear whether collegial ordination was practised in Europe continuously throughout the Middle Ages, or whether it was reinstituted after a period of desuetude.[6] What we have already said concerning the continuity of the practice, whether known by that or by some other name,[7] may well hold true regarding the granting of the title *Ḥaver* as well. This title appears in Jewish life from the beginnings of rabbinism,[8] and it would seem that, during the period in which the European communities became independent of the Babylonian centre and thereafter, it was commonly accepted as indicating a lower level than that of 'rabbi'.[9] Until the beginning of the period under discussion, the title *Ḥaver* was still reserved for yeshivah students 'who study all their days'[10]—i.e. student-colleagues of the *rosh-yeshivah*.[11] While the history of the institution of 'collegiality' (*ḥaverut*) has not yet been studied in its own right, there is no doubt that the title was perceived by contemporaries as clearly subordinate to the rabbinic title. One might cite, for example, Elia Levita, writing in the first half of the sixteenth century.[12] A *ḥaver* is 'a man who has been ordained as rabbi, but is not yet fit to rule on legal matters or to be called *Morenu ha-Rav*. They therefore call him *ḥaver ha-Rav*, that is, one who is "associated" with a fully qualified rabbi.'

Those holding this title were thereby entitled to the honours due .to one who devoted himself to Torah study. Such honours were expressed by visible changes in his social status, beginning

4 Ibid. 143. 5 Ibid. 175.

6 See M. Breuer, 'Ashkenazic Ordination' (Heb.), *Ẓion*, 33 (1968), 15–16 n. 5; idem, 'The Ashkenazic Yeshivah', Doctoral Dissertation, Jerusalem, 1967, pp. 54–55.

7 See Ch. 1, beginning of Sect. 2.

8 e.g. in a very early period R. Jacob, the father of R. Nissim Gaon, was known by the title *Ḥaver*. See S. Abramson, *Rav Nissim Gaon* (Jerusalem, 1965), 21; S. D. Goitein, 'New Information on the Negiddim of Kairouan and Rabbenu Nissim', *Ẓion*, 27 (1962), 21.

9 See Abraham ibn Daud, *The Book of Tradition* (*Sefer ha-Qabbalah*), ed. G. D. Cohen (Philadelphia, 1967) 61.

10 The expression is taken from Joseph b. Moses of Münster *Leket Yosher*, Y. Freimann (ed.) (Berlin, 1903), ii. 39. Cf. B. Klar (ed.), *Megillat Aḥima'aẓ*, (Jerusalem, 1944), 19, 36.

11 See e.g. J. Colon, *Teshuvot Mahari"k* (Venice, 1519) sects. 90, 93, 102, 132.

12 E. Levita, *Sefer ha-Tishbi* (Isny, 1541), s.v. *ḥaver*, 107–8. These remarks were quoted verbatim by David de Pomis (1524–93) at the end of the century in his *Ẓemaḥ David* (Hebrew, Latin, and Italian dictionary) (Venice, 1587), 57b–58a.

with the proclamation of his status as *Ḥaver* when he was called up to the Reading of the Torah and on every other occasion when he was addressed, analogous to the parallel designation of an individual as 'rabbi', which we shall discuss in greater detail below. In the yeshivah itself, this status was expressed by the inclusion of the ordained *Ḥaver* among the 'discussant scholars'.[13] In a certain sense, the title *Ḥaver* may be understood as a kind of undergraduate degree, constituting a significant milestone in an individual's progress towards the rabbinate. It was understood in this way by the Italian scholars of the period under discussion, against the background of a tradition known from ancient times both in the Ashkenazic world and in that of Italian Jewry.[14] There is no indication during this period of any further impact of the institution of collegiality on public and communal life in Italian Jewry. As an honorific title, it stressed the hierarchical division of Jewish society into categories of learning; the title as such also served to emphasize the importance of the ordained rabbis within that hierarchy. It was therefore only natural that the changes then occurring in the valuation of rabbinic ordination were paralleled by similar changes in the valuation of 'collegial ordination'.[15] Moreover, the appearance of the title *ḥakham* towards the end of the sixteenth century should evidently be interpreted as a restructuring of that very same hierarchy through the introduction of an additional rung, also reflecting the tendency to strengthen the importance of the ordained rabbis.[16]

From a formal, institutional point of view, rabbinical ordination was therefore a proclamation of the fact that, in the opinion of the ordaining individual or individuals, the person receiving ordination was a Rabbinic scholar (*talmid ḥakham*) at the top of the hierarchical scale of Jewish learning, and therefore capable of issuing halakhic decisions. This naturally implied that the one

[13] See Ch. 1, Sect. 1.

[14] See R. Jacob Israel Finzi's remarks, quoted in the Appendix to the Hebrew edition of this book, Document 3, p. 215, and R. Leone Modena's comments quoted below, n. 263. Compare with the text of the Rabbinic ordination granted to R. Isaac Levi by R. Israel Isserlein Freimann (ed.), *Leket Yosher*, ii. 88): 'As already several years ago he was ordained by my consent to be called by the title *ḥaver*, I now add to him strength and honour . . . and he shall be called . . . by the name "our Teacher, the Rabbi" '. Cf. also the passage from Klar (ed.), *Megillat Aḥima'aẓ*, previously cited in Ch. 1, Sect. 1.

[15] See R. Benjamin's second argument, Sect. 6 in this chapter.

[16] The context of these changes presumably indicated some sort of crisis. See Ch. 6, Sect. 3.

so ordained deserved those privileges which Jewish society granted to scholars who had attained this level. The respect which Italian Jewish society granted to its rabbinic scholars during this period did not differ in essence from that which any other medieval Jewish society gave to its religious scholars. The image of the *talmid ḥakham*, as seen by the society within which they lived, was one both of guide and spiritual leader, as well as an ideal towards which many aspired.[17]

A centuries-old tradition viewing intellectual perfection as the supreme human ideal naturally led to the elevation of the 'Masters of Torah' above the masses. Alongside this, there existed another view, which considered action the decisive value for the shaping of human perfection: the tension between these two points of view was always a central crux in the history of Jewish thought.[18] Here is not the place to discuss at length the ways in which this tension affected the image of the people's leader. However, we may say that speculation and action were combined, albeit in different proportions, in every such ideal image, so that the *talmid-ḥakham*, whose actions and wisdom would ideally complement one another, was raised to a position of leadership.

One may take as paradigmatic the following statement made by R. Samuel Judah Katzenellenbogen eulogizing R. Judah Moscato:

> There are four attributes which ought to be found in a complete scholar—two pertaining to perfection in himself, and two pertaining to perfection in the realm of his relations with others . . . The former are: perfection of intellect and perfection of deed . . . for the deed is the fruit of intellectual contemplation, as they said 'It is not study which is the main thing, but the deed' [Avot 1: 17] . . . and afterwards . . . two attributes which ought to be present in a scholar pertaining to the perfection in his relations with others, because it is the nature of those who are perfect to influence those around them by their wisdom, to expound [the Torah] in public and to inform the people of the laws of God and His statutes in accordance with the needs of the time.[19]

[17] See the beginning of Ch. 1.

[18] e.g. N. Lamm, *Torah li-shemah be-Mishnat R. Ḥayyim mi-Volozhin uve-Maḥshevet ha-Dor* (Jerusalem, 1972), 101–6.

[19] Samuel Judah Katzenellenbogen, *Derashot Maharshi"k* (Venice, 1594), Sermon 3, 18b–19a. The combination of perfection of thought and of deed which are present in the image of the scholar, as it appears in the eyes of R. Samuel Judah Katzenellenbogen, is so great that he regularly uses the term *talmid-ḥakham* as a synonym for *ẓaddik* (i.e. a saint). See, for example, ibid. Sermon 4, 22b, and compare also Sermon 5, 6, and 10; see also I. Rosenzweig, *Hogeh Yehudi mi-Keẓ ha-Renessans; Yehudah Aryeh Modena ve-sifro*

In these words, which in the full text make homiletical use of Psalm 1: 3, we find an echo of a similar statement by R. Obadiah Sforno (*c*. 1470–1550) in his commentary to that same Psalm, reflecting his own understanding of the spiritual leadership of the nation. R. Obadiah, who adhered to a strictly rationalistic world-view, albeit one deeply influenced by the profound changes affecting his generation,[20] saw the leadership of the people embodied in the scholars of each generation.[21] In his eyes, they embodied the ideal of the perfect man in thought and deed, particularly in those areas involving teaching others, preaching, and individual example. Hence, the central task which he assigned to them in assuring the nation's existence in exile and in paving the way for its redemption.[22] Working from a world-view in which the sacral constituted a vital element,[23] R. Obadiah Sforno compared the sages of each generation to the holy ark, towards whom the eyes of each generation were turned, because 'the purpose of all the actions [i.e. *their actions*] is to honour their Creator, to see marvellous things from His Torah, and to resemble Him'.[24] He incorporated the symbolism of the construction of the ark mentioned in the Torah in this intellectual construct: '"to make an ark of wood" symbolizing the body, which is easily destroyed; "covered with gold outside and in", to refer to one who is wise in His holy Torah, which enlightens his actions and the ways of His goodness to others, and indicating that he is identical within and without . . .'[25]

R. Obadiah's words here echo the rabbinic saying: ' "You shall cover it with gold within and without" [Exod. 25: 11]—Raba

Midbar Yehudah (Merhaviah and Tel Aviv, 1972), 85–7, for discussion of a similar approach in R. Leone Modena's thought.

20 See R. Bonfil, 'R. Obadiah Sforno' (Heb.), *Eshel Be'er Sheva'*, 1 (1976), 200–57.

21 e.g. his commentary on Exod. 3: 15.

22 Ibid. nn. 96, 97, and cf. *Derashot Maharshi"k*, Sermon 10, 53b: 'The righteous man, by virtue of his observance of the commandments and his devotion to the study of Torah . . . becomes another person, distinct from others'. These things are said with regard to R. Joseph Caro, following R. Samuel Judah Katzenellenbogen, according to whom the concept of 'righteous man' coincided with that of 'scholar'. Of all R. Caro's qualities, R. Samuel Judah saw fit to emphasize only one—namely, that which included 'all perfections, and that he taught much Torah and raised many disciples' (*Derashot Maharshi"k*, ibid., 56*a*).

23 See above, Ch. 1, Sects. 2 and 4.

24 Obadiah Sforno, *Kavvannot ha-Torah* (at the end of his *Bi'ur ha-Torah*) (Venice, 1567), 89a.

25 Ibid. 88a, etc.

said: we learn from this that any sage whose inside is not identical with his outside is not considered a sage' (Yoma 72*b*). Nevertheless, his analogy of the sage to the holy ark, carrying associations of leadership, dignity, and the protection of the nation by its leadership, is more than merely a repetition of ancient sayings. It derives from a specific, well-defined ideological outlook. The image itself reappears frequently in the words of other rabbis throughout this period, and was artistically articulated by preachers. It was nevertheless intended to strengthen public consciousness of this idea, upon which depended their respect for the rabbis, including the preachers. R. Judah Moscato, for example, made use of this imagery in eulogizing R. Moses Provenzali: 'upon the removal of the ark of God' [cf. 1 Sam. 4: 21] from the community.[26] The sages are described there as 'the central pillars upon which the house stands'. The whole image is based upon an outlook according to which:

> . . . just as those circumstances in which Israel enjoys an honourable position are not dependent upon the splendour of the government or of the mundane rulership, but only upon the perfection of Torah and of true wisdom, so must its decline and dishonour be understood, not in relation to its temporary lack of sovereignty, but in terms of its lack of knowledge and its catastrophic plummet into the depths of foolishness.

Thus, according to Moscato, the condition of the nation in exile, lacking political independence, calls for a stress upon the decisive importance of the Talmudic sage for the very attainment of its aims which, to him, belong exclusively to the realm of spirit.[27]

One further point will suffice to make this clearer. R. Mordecai Dato (1525–1591/1601)—while emphasizing the Messianic element in Jewish thought, as would be expected of a Kabbalist

[26] Judah Moscato, *Sefer Nefuzot Yehudah* (Venice, 1889), Sermon 33. Cf. Katzenellenbogen, *Derashot Maharshi"k*, Sermon 7, 39a.

[27] Cf. the remarks of the *Ga'on* R. Samuel b. Eli (in S. Assaf, *Tekufat ha-Ge'onim ve-Sifrutah* (Jerusalem, 1967), 58, which were certainly not known to R. Judah Moscato: 'and as for the king, they chose him because they needed someone to go before them in battle and war, and in the time of the exile they do not have [a king nor] wars, nor any of the things which require a king, and they have no need but for someone who will guide them and make them understand and teach them the commandments of their law and judge their judgements and rule for them in *halakhah*.' This appears to be an additional expression of the continuity of ideas from the world of the Babylonian academies through the world of the European sages, who demanded for themselves a position of leadership in accordance with what has been said in Ch. 1, Sect. 1.

who had studied in Safed—expressed the identical idea in his commentary to Ezekiel 34: 2:

'And the word of the Lord was with me, saying, prophesy to the shepherds of Israel' . . . The shepherds of Israel are two—the kings and the Sages. The task of the kings is to see to the needs of Israel in this world, while the Sages tend to their needs concerning the World to Come. The one is a temporal shepherd, the latter, a spiritual shepherd . . . likewise in Exile, the shepherds of the Exile [communities] are two: the wealthy and the learned . . .'[28]

The wealthy are mentioned because of their responsibility for the physical existence of the exiled nation, supplying its members with the funds necessary to insure their settlement rights and to meet the taxes imposed upon the community as a whole, as well as to support communal institutions, while the learned were seen as the nation's spiritual leadership.

As we shall see, the statements cited here were articulated by scholars representing the main streams of Jewish thought in Italy throughout the period under discussion. They would therefore seem sufficient proof that the image of the rabbinic scholar was seen in Italy as an ideal to be emulated by every Jew. That image implied the right to a position of leadership within a society which not only recognized this right, but saw it as strengthening its very foundations.

Within this framework, one ought also to mention the influence of the general environment, within whose social frameworks the non-noble intellectual approached the pedigreed nobility,[29] conforming to the medieval tradition which saw in learning a means of attaining human perfection and the happiness to which every person was deserving—*La felicità che si conviene al'huomo come huomo*.[30] Within Jewish society this atmosphere certainly contributed to the granting to rabbis, even of humble origin, an equivalent status to that of the wealthy families.

[28] Mordecai Dato, 'Derashot II', MS British Museum Add. 27007, 2*a*, Sermons of R. Mordecai Dato, IMHM 5686 and Margoliouth Cat. 381. In his comments reflecting the fashioning of the sacral understanding of the rabbi in Italy as a spiritual leader only, R. Mordecai Dato gives further expression to the impact of the Christian outlook and its terminology (*potere temporale* as against *potere spirituale*).

[29] See J. Burckhardt, *The Civilisation of the Renaissance in Italy* (New York, 1958), 360.

[30] A. Piccolomini, *Della istituzione dell'uomo nato nobile e in Città Libera* (Venice, 1542), 2; cf. P. F. Grendler, 'The Rejection of Learning in mid-Cinquecento Italy', *Studies in the Renaissance*, 13 (1966), 230 ff.

One may learn more about this from an unusual question asked at this time in Germany concerning whether or not one born out of wedlock might be appointed to the rabbinate. In a responsum containing more interesting details, R. Samuel Judah Katzenellenbogen also addressed himself to this question. R. Samuel Judah did not accept the view of the Ashkenazic rabbis, as transmitted by R. Moses Isserles (*c.* 1525/30–1572), that one ought not to ordain a bastard 'not [because it is forbidden] by the Law, but because it is a degradation to the Torah, because such a one is held in contempt by people'.[31] R. Samuel Judah answered R. Isserles:

> I have already written to Your honour that I am in agreement if you are of the opinion that he [i.e. *this specific person*] is not worthy of bearing that title, as that truly is the case. But if you wish to say that it is an insult to the Torah to ordain one who is blemished in this manner, in my opinion one born out of wedlock is no worse than a proselyte, and yet how many proselytes have we found among the *tannaim* and *amoraim* [i.e. *Mishnaic and Talmudic Sages*]! The sages already said (Horayot 3: 8): 'a bastard [i.e. *one born of an incestuous union*] who is a Sage takes priority over an ignorant High Priest'. I know that you may argue that a proselyte is considered like a new-born child, and is therefore preferable to an illegitimate child, and that even though a bastard who is a sage takes priority over an ignorant High Priest, he still may not be called up to the Reading of the Torah with the title 'rabbi', but the truth peeks through from every side . . . Be that as it may, it is my way, that of fools, to speak against kings without shame[32] . . . but heaven forfend that I should disagree with the conclusion of your righteous court. And already eight days ago I received an epistle . . . from the litigant himself, filled with dross and scum, and after I saw your statement I decided not to answer him.[33]

It was difficult in principle for R. Katzenellenbogen to accept the statement that one ought not to ordain one with a blemish of this sort on account of the Torah's honour, even though aware of the problems associated with the subject and a sense that, within the framework of an academic discussion, one might argue against his reservations. However, as on the basis of the information available to him the individual involved did not

[31] Moses Isserles, *Teshuvot ha-RaMA*, ed. A. Siev (Jerusalem, 1971), sect. 24, p. 147.

[32] Based on Pss. 49: 14; 119: 46. That is to say: by my nature I tend to enter into dispute with people greater than myself, but only in theory and not in practice.

[33] *Teshuvot ha-Rama*, sect. 69, p. 300, with references.

deserve the 'crown of Torah', R. Samuel Judah readily agreed with the decision of the Ashkenazic sages in practice. One strongly feels here the tension between, on the one hand, his own conscience and understanding as a scholar, loyal to the principle that the Torah uplifts those who study it and, on the other hand, the social reality in which a person of doubtful ancestry was 'taken lightly by others'. Certainly, people placed limits on their willingness to elevate learned men socially despite their humble origin; they accordingly disapproved of the ordination of a 'blemished one'. As we have already noted, the immediate practical expression of ordination was that one was called to the Torah by the title 'rabbi'—that is to say, the hierarchical order of Jewish society was restructured in favour of the advancement of the ordained. In the case of the 'bastard', this restructuring was perceived as quite simply turning things upside-down. The reluctance to accept such an extreme consequence of the general rule is therefore understandable. However, precisely because of the fact that this extreme case was perceived as a necessary exception to the rule, it is illuminating for our understanding of the rule itself.[34] That rule was that the declaration of an individual as a sage involved a certain ascent on the social ladder. One need not add that this was true even if a particular scholar were already wealthy or the scion of a prestigious family.

This being the case, it would seem that the first families of Italian Jewry practised a custom similar to that widespread in the Christian world, in which at least one of the sons of each prominent family attempted to enter the priesthood.[35] Our knowledge of the family background of many Italian Jewish scholars is still fragmentary, and does not allow for definitive conclusions on this subject. Nevertheless, a few individual cases will suffice to confirm the tendency: from the wealthy and prestigious Modena family, R. Solomon Modena was ordained to the Rabbinate;[36] from the banking family da Pisa, the well known R. Yeḥiel Nissim da Pisa; while, of the four sons of Isaac

[34] See n. 98 in this chapter.

[35] There is no doubt that this implied an attempt to gain a position within the frameworks of the Church, due to their importance within the complex of political and social tensions. A common expression in Italy even in our own day is *beata quella casa in cui c'è una chierica rasa*.

[36] See the Hebrew edition of this book, Document 6, p. 320.

Berechiah da Fano, R. Menaḥem Azariah da Fano was ordained. Further examples might easily be added.

2. The Demand for Status

Once it had been declared, through the act of ordination, that a given individual had attained the level of a learned scholar and the title of *ha-Rav*, it was only natural that this individual seek a place in society appropriate to his new status. Ordination itself served as the formal justification for the demand for privileges. Towards the end of the period under discussion, R. Samuel Judah Katzenellenbogen, citing the words of R. Solomon ben Adret of Barcelona (*c*. 1235–*c*. 1310), ruled that a scholar who demands the rights and privileges due to him as a rabbi asks no more than 'his portion of the inheritance and legacy, like a priest (*kohen*) asking for the priestly tithes who, in a place where he is unknown, may simply announce himself as such'.[37] Furthermore, what the scholar was asking as his due was no small matter for, according to R. Katzenellenbogen, 'the Scholar is the choicest of all creations, and all others are given to him as servants'.[38] In his view, all the sources support the conclusion that those who know a given person to be a scholar are 'without doubt required to publicize this fact . . . This is the reason for the ordination practised among us in all lands.'[39] In his comments, R. Katzenellenbogen relates concisely to the ways in which ordination had been understood in previous generations, from his own perspective at the end of the sixteenth century, when it had become a clearly defined institution.

What R. Isaac ben Sheshet (14th century) has written[40] concerning the reason for ordination, namely, that it was instituted because it is forbidden for a scholar to rule on legal matters during the lifetime of his master without his permission . . . and that ordination constitutes the act of granting permission to the disciples to instruct—this reason is inadequate, except in the case of a disciple who is ordained by his principal teacher, and even then only in the case of rabbinical ordination, in which he is granted permission to rule on legal matters, but not in

[37] *Derashot Maharshi"k*, Sermon 4, 23a.

[38] Ibid. Sermon 5, 25b. [39] Ibid. Sermon 4, 23a.

[40] Isaac b. Sheshet, *Teshuvot ha-Ribash* (Vilna, 1879), sect. 271.

the case of 'collegial' ordination (*ḥaverut*). Rather, one may argue that, according to the view of R. Isaac ben Sheshet, the main reason for ordination from the very outset was to grant permission from the master to his disciple, allowing him to pass judgement, and that it was afterwards extended even to those situations in which one did not need permission, as well as to the case of 'collegial' ordination (*ḥaverut*), in which no permission to teach is granted. But the reason which I have given as my opinion seems more correct, and is sufficient [explanation] for ordination in general.[41]

Katzenellenbogen expressed these opinions with a straightforwardness suitable to the solemn occasion of the ordination at which this sermon was delivered, ignoring the complex problematics implicit in his words. For that reason, this sage neither addressed himself to, nor answered, the question of the status of an individual who has been ordained and thereby proclaimed as a scholar, but to whom the community denies those privileges to which he should have been entitled by virtue of his ordination. In other words: does the act of ordination, in itself a formal, institutional act, carry a substantive value by which its holder automatically gains authority and status within the community in his own right, or are both the status and the ordination conditional upon other factors, such as communal opinion? A sharp debate raged around this point, beginning no later than the generation of R. Isaac ben Sheshet.[42] The application of the conclusions of this debate determined both the content and the practical implications of the rabbinic title.

Two clear pieces of evidence may be cited for the existence of this dispute in Italy at the beginning of our period: the comments of R. Benjamin of Montalcino[43] in the controversy concerning the edicts of R. Judah Messer Leon,[44] and the lengthy ruling by R. Judah son of R. David Messer Leon (*c.* 1470/2–1526), entitled *Kevod Ḥakhamim*, in the wake of a controversy in Valona.[45]

41 *Derashot Maharshi"k*, Sermon 4, 23a.

42 On the emergence of this problematic in terms of two conflicting tendencies which acted as a dynamic moment in the development of the institution of ordination, see Breuer, 'Ashkenazic Ordination', 17–18.

43 See U. Cassuto, *Gli ebrei a Firenze* (Florence, 1918), index, and esp. 191–4.

44 For a comprehensive bibliography of this controversy, see D. Carpi, 'R. Judah Messer Leon and his Activity as Physician' (Heb.), *Mikhael; Me'asef le-Toldot ha-Yehudim ba-Tefuẓot* (Tel Aviv, 1973), 279–81. See also R. Bonfil, 'Introduction to *Nofet Ẓufim* (Jerusalem, 1981), 7–53.

45 See D. Tamar, 'On R. David Messer Leon's *Kevod Ḥakhamim*' (Heb.), *KS* 26 (1950), 96–100.

R. Benjamin of Montalcino marshalled three arguments on behalf of the view that ordination does not possess substantive value making it a source of authority and rulership over the community. The first argument:

> Even though he [R. Judah Messer Leon] was properly ordained as a rabbi by virtue of his being learned in the Talmud . . . [he may not claim the authority which the Talmud . . . attributes to ordained rabbis because] it was interpreted that this [only] holds true[46] '[when] the House of Israel are dwelling upon their land'[47] . . . but as we have neither king nor prince in the Land of Israel, by whose power the elders are appointed, how can one accept appointments from one who lacks the authority to either appoint or to ordain? And if this power was retained by the exilarchs in Babylonia. . . how am I to know if they still exist, and if he [R. Judah Messer Leon] was appointed by their authority?[48]

That is to say: there is no central authority in this day analogous to the prince or king in *Eretz-Yisrael*, nor even anything similar to the Babylonian exilarchate. Therefore, there is no way in which ordination can serve as an independent source of authority.

R. Benjamin's second argument is that even during Talmudic times:

> There was no greatness or power conferred by dint of ordination, but only that [the one ordained] was able to judge by himself [i.e. *without a court of three*] and was exempt from paying [compensation in the event of judicial error] . . . But one may not promulgate edicts without the agreement of those upon whom they are imposed, even as a temporary measure, for such a power was only granted to the kings of Israel, and subsequently to the Great Court [i.e. *the Sanhedrin*] in Jerusalem . . . [Thus] if Maimonides wrote . . . that the punishments are delegated to them, indicating that the Court may give corporal and other punishments beyond the [letter of the] law as an emergency measure . . . he has also specified to which court or judge he was referring—namely, those ordained by the Great Court in the Land of Israel or the exilarchs in Babylonia . . . In any event, he wrote that even the permission of the exilarch cannot [convey judicial authority] to one who is not an expert . . . How much more so today, when there is no exilarch and none who may be considered 'expert', that we may not issue punishments or

46 Jerusalem Talmud, Bikkurim 3: 3.

47 Based on Ezekiel 36: 17. This verse is interpreted in the Jerusalem Talmud, ibid., as indicating that one may not ordain rabbis outside the Land of Israel.

48 *Divrei Rivot*, 4.

confiscate property save by [order of] those whom the members of the community have accepted over themselves, and with written [authorization] of one of the Gentile kings . . .[49]

That is to say, the lack of a central authority, as a result of which ordination no longer independently confers authority, creates the need to invest authority solely by the agreement of the community and of the non-Jewish rulers.

R. Benjamin's third argument was that the status of the ordained scholar is valid only in his own city. One who wishes that his decisions be accepted elsewhere can do no more than 'present them and fulfil them by becoming the master of many students from different places, so that, if they spread their master's decisions through their sermons or via their disciples, they may ultimately cause all Israel to obey—but that goal should certainly not be reached by cursing and banning those who do not study Torah from him or fail to submit to his authority'.[50]

R. Benjamin's statements are reinforced by the fact that we find the text of his own ordination by various prominent scholars at the end of this pamphlet.[51] Interestingly enough, all those who ordained R. Benjamin came from French circles.[52] One may conjecture that R. Benjamin simply gave expression here to the dominant opinion in French rabbinic circles. Support for this

[49] Ibid.

[50] Ibid. 4–5. Even if one claims that this alludes to the fact that disciples are subject to their teachers, it is clear that this refers to actual disciples, and not to the broader public. From the rabbinic statements cited by R. Benjamin, one may infer that he does not specifically refer to the restriction of the rabbi's authority to a specific place, but to the appropriate way of fulfilling this authority, in accordance with an earlier Jewish tradition.

[51] Ibid. 12–14.

[52] On R. Jacob ha-Levi, one of the French scholars who moved to Italy from Chambéry during the first half of the 15th century, see M. Mortara, *Indice alfabetico* (Padua, 1886), 33; H. Gross, *Gallia Judaica* (Paris, 1897; repr. Amsterdam, 1969), 597–8; H. Merhavyah, 'A Spanish-Latin Manuscript Concerning the Opposition to the Talmud in the Beginning of the 15th Century' (Heb.), *KS* 45 (1970), 593. On Meir Loans, see Gross, *Gallia Judaica*, 272. R. Solomon b. Gabriel Strossburg is evidently identical with R. Solomon Tarshburg (Strasbourg), who also migrated from Chambéry to Italy in the first half of the 15th century (see Merhavyah, 'A Spanish-Latin Manuscript'). Various French scholars with this family name lived in Italy in the second half of that century, and it would seem likely that they all belonged to one family. On R. Aaron Strossburg and his sons, R. Gabriel and R. Joseph Ḥayyim, see R. N. Rabinowitz, *Ma'amar 'al Hadpasat ha-Talmud; Toldot Hadpasat ha-Talmud*, ed. A. M. Habermann (Jerusalem, 1965), index. On R. Joseph Ḥayyim, see also Abraham Fuchs, 'Opposing Attitudes to the *Ḥerem ha-Yishuv* in the 15th Century' (Heb.), *Ẓion*, 37 (1972), 186 and n. 23.

view appears in the opinion of R. Joseph Colon (*c.* 1420–80),[53] the greatest French scholar in Italy during R. Benjamin's day. While his discussion revolves primarily around the question of the relationship between the ordainer and the ordained (to which we shall later return), even a superficial reading of his words demonstrates that ordination *per se* is of no substantive value in his eyes, but is a purely formal and public act. He clearly states that the permission to decide halakhic matters received by the ordainee is not analogous to that issued by the exilarch, and that only the latter conveys judicial authority autonomously (i.e. with the litigants' agreement).

Even in the early generations, and even at the time of the *tannáim* [*whose ordination carried the implication that its recipient was a 'public expert'*], ordination was not like receiving permission from the exilarch ... As Maimonides wrote ... 'If this was the case of a judge who had received permission from the exilarch, or who had not received such permission, but was accepted by [both] litigating parties' ... which clearly indicates that being considered as an 'expert' and 'receiving permission' are two separate things ... certainly ordination is not as efficacious as receiving permission ... and how much more so ordination as practised today, in our great sinfulness ...[54]

In R. Joseph Colon's remarks we find several of the elements present in the first two arguments presented by R. Benjamin of Montalcino. It therefore follows that it is hardly coincidental that Colon—who certainly cannot be characterized as one of the admirers of R. Benjamin of Montalcino,[55] as he opposes him both sharply and extensively in nearly every sentence of his halakhic discussion of the edicts of Messer Leon—was completely silent about R. Benjamin's statements pertaining to ordination and its significance.[56] We may, perhaps, speculate that the very wording

[53] Most of R. Joseph Colon's remarks on the subject of ordination appear in his responsa, *Teshuvot Mahari"k*, sect. 117, 169, and in Pines (ed.), *She'elot u-Teshuvot u-Piskei Mahari"k ha-Ḥadashim* (Jerusalem, 1970), sect. 40.

[54] *Teshuvot Mahari"k ha-Hadashim*, sect. 40, 178–9. The beginning of the responsum was printed by S. Assaf in *Minḥah le-David: Sefer ha-Yovel le-David Yellin* (Jerusalem, 1935), 222. On the inaccuracies in the edition according to which it is quoted here, see the criticism by J. Yudlov, *Sinai*, 67 (1970), 321–3, esp. 322.

[55] In another context, Colon wrote of him: 'Who has told him that he is my colleague, to the extent that I am not allowed to permit what he has forbidden? Even though I know my own shortcomings ... in any event in my opinion he is not my colleague, for behold he errs!' *Teshuvot Mahari"k*, sect. 171.

[56] *Teshuvot Mahari"k ha-Hadashim*, sec. 49, 229–252.

of the rabbinic title in R. Benjamin's own ordination—i.e. *Rav*, and not *Morenu ha-Rav*—is an expression of the difference in approach between the German and the French scholars.[57] Our knowledge of the French world of learning is still very poor, and it may be rather far-fetched to draw a general conclusion from a single observation, as opposed to the general historiographic trend of considering France and Germany as one and the same Ashkenazic world. Nevertheless, there may be a connection between this speculation and the opinion of the opponents of Ashkenazic ordination, as articulated in the words of their Sephardic champion, R. Isaac b. Sheshet. As we have stated above, and as may be seen by analysing his concept of ordination,[58] R. Isaac supported those French circles who did not attach substantive value to it. These circles therefore saw no reason to define the relationship between the ordained rabbi and the community as one of master and disciple, which would have given substance to the title *Morenu*—'our teacher'—and justified the community's subordination to the authority of the ordained scholar.

Indeed, there seems to have been a diametrically opposed outlook, which was evidently particularly predominant among Ashkenazic circles in Italy during the latter half of the fifteenth century. An expression of such a conception may be seen in R. David son of Messer Leon's lengthy discussion in *Kevod Ḥakhamim*. This œuvre is a detailed responsum, dealing with the controversy which arose at the beginning of the sixteenth century in Valona concerning the meaning and implications of subordinating a community to the authority of a rabbi who was no longer appointed by it. R. David devoted a considerable portion of this work to an examination of the concept of ordination in his day.[59] His words were expressed in the context of a polemic with some Sephardic rabbis who completely negated the value of ordination and mocked it.[60] R. David himself admits that, following the desuetude of ordination in the Land of Israel, the

[57] The procedures for ordination practised by the French rabbis have not been studied to date, and as far as I know no ordination documents from French sources have been published.

[58] See Breuer, 'Ashkenazic Ordination', 17–18.

[59] *Kevod Ḥakhamim*, 54 ff. R. David was ordained in the yeshivah of R. Judah Minz (ibid. 64).

[60] See Breuer, 'Ashkenazic Ordination', 29–30.

ordination practised in his day ought not to be seen as a 'true' or 'authentic' ordination. Nevertheless, relying upon an opinion which saw ordination as practised in Babylonia as an act of 'agency' of the 'early forefathers',[61] he maintains that 'even though there is no ordination today and no one [worthy of being] ordained . . . we rely upon the early ones, who in their day practised ordination . . . in the Land of Israel. Through their authority to ordain, they [as it were] . . . ordained whomever they saw as worthy of such, in every generation and every time, according to the procedure recorded in the Talmud . . .'[62] This being so, contemporary ordination is more than simply a 'vestige of [ancient] ordination', but is invested with substantive, independent value by virtue of these same forefathers, including 'a *real* ordination to be called "rabbi", as in Talmudic times'.[63] Stated more clearly: just as we rely upon the forefathers in calendrical matters, and upon their calculations for the sanctification of the New Moon—'so that we in our own place may be seen as if having been given permission in each generation to fix new months, as if we were acting in their stead'—so are we 'to do everything which is under the rubric of ordination exactly as if we were them . . . and [we] practise ordination as if they were the ones granting ordination here'.[64] This statement is a far-reaching one, as he himself immediately indicates: 'it would necessarily follow from this that, just as those ordaining practised all the types of judgement, and even [the penalties for] theft and fines, we may likewise do so'.[65] However, he does not dare to develop this idea to its logical conclusion. In any event, even though there is no 'authentic' ordination today, R. David sees it nevertheless as having substantive value and therefore deserving, in his view, 'to be called an "intermediate ordination", similar in some respects to the authentic ordination'.[66] This kind of ordination is comparable to the 'granting of permission' mentioned in the Talmud, barring one who is not thus ordained from issuing halakhic rulings.[67] The Talmudic discussion in the relevant passage concluded with the question of the validity of ordination 'from there to here and from here to there' (i.e. the degree of validity of an ordination granted in *Eretz-Yisrael* in Babylonia,

61 See Babylonian Talmud, Sanhedrin 5a, and *Tosafot* ad loc.

62 *Kevod Ḥakhamim*, 55.

63 Ibid. 50.

64 Ibid. 61.

65 Ibid.

66 Ibid. 63.

67 Ibid. 55, 63.

and vice versa),[68] concluding that the 'granting of "permission" (i.e. authorization to issue rulings) by the exilarch is valid in the Land of Israel, while "permission" granted by one's teacher in the Land of Israel is not valid in Babylonia'.[69] On the other hand, not only does R. David ignore the distinction between 'permission' received from one's master in the Land of Israel and that received from the exilarch or from the prince, but one receives the clear impression from the entire discussion that 'permission', i.e. ordination granted by one's master in the Land of Israel, is more important than 'permission' received from the exilarch. Thus, for R. David son of Messer Leon the value of ordination is in fact substantive; it is not merely a testimonial to one's expertise as a Talmudic sage, a public act of recognition as a scholar for the benefit of those who do not know him, but it confers actual authority, similar to that of those who received ordination in the Land of Israel. It follows that the status of an ordained scholar is infinitely greater than that of one who is not ordained, and 'one who is not ordained ought to be subordinate to one who is ordained'.[70]

At the time of the controversy in Valona, R. David ha-Kohen of Corfu expressed certain ideas parallel to those of R. David son of Messer Leon in his defence.[71] He further stated, regarding the central problem, that 'in our generation, because of our many sins there are people who have not served [the sages] at all', there is no way other than ordination to determine that a given sage is indeed worthy of ruling: 'and from this it is clearly known to all that whoever is not ordained, that is, has not permission to teach, may not do so and should not be relied upon [for legal decisions], unless it is known to all that he is a great man' (i.e. an important scholar). Immediately thereafter, he expressed his

68 Sanhedrin 5a.

69 See *Kevod Ḥakhamim*, 55 and the editor's note there (n. 4), and cf. the previously cited passage from R. Joseph Colon.

70 *Kevod Ḥakhamim*, 53–4. The main proof of this statement is that, in his view, 'the one ordained is subject to the one who ordained him'; see on this also below at the end of Sect. 6 of this chapter, and see H. H. Ben-Sasson, *A History of the Jewish People* (Cambridge, Mass., 1976), 598.

71 See R. David ha-Kohen, *Teshuvot Maharda"kh*, sect. 22. See also A. Marmorstein, 'R. David Kohen und das Rabbinerwesen in der ersten Haelfte des XVI Jahrhunderts', *Jeshurun*, 14 (1927), 182 ff. R. David ha-Kohen was ordained by R. Bendit Axelrad—see Pesakim (Venice, 1519), p. 24*a*. Like R. David son of Messer Leon, he was ordained in the yeshivah of R. Judah Minz.

doubts concerning the validity of writs of divorce and of levirate-separations (*ḥaliẓah*) performed by those who 'are not known by the sages as great scholars'.[72]

3. Jewish Society and the Rabbinate: Suspicions, Reservations, and Regulations

Thus far, we have heard the rabbis' opinions concerning only the legitimacy of the imposition of their authority upon Jewish society, and the related demand for recognition of rabbinic status on the basis of ordination alone. In the above-mentioned comments of R. Benjamin of Montalcino, however, the public already appears as a party to the discussion. The lack of fixed criteria for the evaluation of the personality and fitness of a given candidate for ordination led to a situation in which, in the final analysis, the granting of ordination was entirely dependent upon the judgement of the one granting it. In the natural course of events, therefore, doubts arose concerning the rabbi's motivations in taking the socially significant step of ordaining a given individual. Concomitantly, the large number of individuals holding ordination also aroused suspicions that there were among them unworthy individuals; these led to second thoughts, both within the public and among the rabbinate, as to the most suitable procedure for granting ordination.

In an incident that took place in Imola during the first half of the sixteenth century, an entire community refused to accept a young, newly-ordained rabbi who, in the course of seeking to establish his status, discovered himself displacing the scions of several prominent local families, including a certain R. David Yehiel, who had held the post of preacher.[73] The final outcome

[72] *Teshuvot Maharda''kh*, sect. 22: 'and my heart tells me [i.e. '*I have a feeling*'] that all divorces issued in our day by those who are not known to the scholars as great men, are suspect.'

[73] Two letters on this incident addressed to R. Abraham ha-Kohen by Isaac Morello, the leader of those who spoke in the name of the opponents, have been preserved. See 'Derashot R. Nathan b. Binyamin Finzi', MS London 932 (IMHM 5726), 99–104. The first letter is quoted in full in the Hebrew edition of this book, in Document No. 2, p. 212–14. I have found no further information about R. Jeḥiel from any other source. As to him being a preacher in Imola, see the second epistle, p. 101b: 'there is with us the great one Rabbi David Jeḥiel, who preaches in public . . .' Further on, the author states of himself that he never missed even one of his sermons. Perhaps he is to be identified with David b. Joseph ibn Yaḥya, author of 'Hilkhot Ṭerefot be-Kiẓur' (MS New York, Adler Collection 1500, 127a–128a).

was that the members of the community withdrew their opposition, giving in to the authority of R. Abraham ha-Kohen of Bologna, who had ordained the individual in question. The leading spokesman of the opponents was evidently frightened by the threatened ban of R. Abraham ha-Kohen,[74] and he sought forgiveness, promising never to insult the young rabbi again, and imposing silence upon himself. Thus, this incident indicates the authority exercised by R. Abraham ha-Kohen in the Romagna district,[75] as well as the influence which he exerted in places near Bologna through the network of young scholars whom he ordained and imposed upon the public in a way similar to that suggested by R. Benjamin of Montalcino in the previously cited passage. However, how could such a method not be open to the possibility that the ordaining scholar should exert undue influence by ordaining unworthy parties? Suspicions that the ordaining authority granted degrees merely as a means of gaining control over the public were inevitable.[76]

Clear evidence of such a possibility may be seen in the responsum sent by R. Jacob Israel Finzi to remove a rabbi 'who was ordained unjustifiably' by a certain scholar who is portrayed as travelling around the country on business, meanwhile ordaining rabbis as a means of achieving an influential, authoritative position against the will of the community.[77]

Rabbi so-and-so did not pay heed to the honour of the other rabbis, but only wished to create rabbis as if he were the prince and head of the entire exile. He did something which is not to be done, particularly in the present age, when there is no longer ordination [i.e. *in the classical Talmudic sense*] outside of the Land of Israel, but only appointment, and we are, so to speak, the spokesmen of the sages.[78] For we read in the Talmud . . .[79] 'R. Johanan said, "Who is a scholar that is to be appointed over the public? One of whom one may ask the halakhah in any place [i.e. *subject*] and he responds, even in *Tractate Kallah*" ' . . . Therefore, everything which that person did is null and void *ab initio* and is without substance, for we do not follow a person's name but his

[74] See at the end of the second letter: 'for [he] was angry with your servant over the curses which were invoked against your servant'. See also the Hebrew edition of this book, Document 2, p. 214 n. 32.

[75] The Romagna district, of which Bologna was the capital.

[76] Cf. Breuer, 'Ashkenazic Ordination', 24–6.

[77] R. Jacob Israel Finzi, 'Teshuvot', sect. 164; the full text of this responsum is published in the Hebrew edition of this book, Document 3, pp. 215–16.

[78] See Gittin 88b.

[79] Shabbat 114a.

flavour,[80] and particularly so if the people of that community did not wish to have him, and that person is unworthy of being appointed as a rabbi, for in so far as I know him, I have not heard anything from him but words of external wisdom and philosophy, of which[81] it is said, 'and awesome are all those whom it has killed'[82]—this refers to those students who have not gained as much knowledge of Torah as they should have, and glorify themselves before the ignorant and the people of their town . . .

While we are unable to identify this particular rabbi, R. Jacob Israel Finzi's account certainly seems to fit the general picture described here.[83]

Finzi's condemnation of this particular rabbi referred to his lack of professional and scholarly qualifications. However, far more serious were the accusations drawn up against the young rabbi in Imola who demanded that his authority be recognized. He was accused of lacking wisdom and understanding, while possessing a character blemished by arrogance and pride,[84] and

80 A word play upon Hullin 66a.

81 Maimonides' usage in Mishneh Torah, *Hilkhot Talmud Torah* 5: 4 follows from this.

82 Prov. 7: 26, and see how this verse is allegorically interpreted in Sotah 22a.

83 The absence from this responsum of the factor of monetary profit requires further study of the use of ordination as a means of gaining profit. See I. Sonne, 'On the History of the Community of Bologna', *HUCA*, 16 (1942), 47; Breuer, 'Ashkenazic Ordination', 33. R. Leone Modena mentioned without embarrassment, among his 'attempts . . . to earn' a living 'the title of Rabbi and Colleague'—*Hayyei Yehudah* (Tel Aviv, 1985), 104, while in Ashkenaz the head of the *bet-din* had the acknowledged right to receive sums of money in return for ordination (Breuer, 'Ashkenazic Ordination', ibid., 33–4). If R. Benjamin of Montalcino's comment that R. Judah Messer Leon was not among 'those who do not know how to make profit out of everything, and grant ordination for money' may be interpreted as alluding to the existence of unworthy individuals who received ordination in order to gain financial benefits, one must not exclude the possibility that his comments are simply borrowed from characteristic phrases appearing in the Talmud referring to judges who are appointed for money. The comments of R. Abraham Minz concerning R. David from Pizzighettone, of whom there was no basis 'for saying that he exploited the rabbinate . . . in that he refrained from taking bribery or ordaining one who was not worthy'—*Pesakim* fo. 20b—do not specifically indicate the impropriety of using ordination as a means of earning profit. I have not found a single clear case of an accusation, and certainly not an actual situation, of a rabbi using the granting of ordination as a means of earning money. See also *Teshuvot R. Azriel Diena*, sect. 180; the matter requires further study.

84 See Document 3 in the Hebrew edition of this book, p. 215–16. In the second letter, fo. 101a, he states: 'the man whom your honour seeks to place over us as our leader is all gall and bitterness [*!*] . . . he covers himself in a long prayer-shawl and mutters words to the Almighty. And then all the elders of the community rose, and banded against him . . . for what he had done . . . Shortly thereafter, he writes: 'that man did not care for piety or modesty, but only arrogance'.

with being motivated, not by the fear of God, but by the wish to exploit the rabbinate for personal aggrandizement.[85] So, how is one able to dismiss the possibility that even the great R. Abraham Ha-Kohen might have ordained him to serve his own purposes? In other words: here there fully emerges the problem of ensuring the complete identification of the concept of 'worthy rabbinic scholar' (*talmid-ḥakham*) with that of 'ordained rabbi'—that is, of ensuring that those who are unworthy are not ordained. As we shall see, the most prominent scholars in Italy weighed this problem with utmost seriousness. On the other hand, the very fact that the question was raised in this manner is itself an indirect indication that, in the absence of evidence to the contrary, this identification was generally considered self-evident. Evidence for this may be seen in another incident, in which the majority of the community supported a young rabbi, who enjoyed great esteem, against an aged and much respected layman's claim to seniority.[86] That community described the case in a question addressed to an authoritative rabbi:

Three of the elders of the generation who were . . . among the leading rabbis, saw fit to include a certain young scholar among the rabbis. They therefore ordained him, to rule in that which is permitted and forbidden and in [court] judgements, and to deal with matters of marital law like any veteran rabbi; and they ordered the reader of the congregation to call him to the reading of the Torah by the title, *Morenu ha-Rav*. They also publicized the fact that he deserved to be honoured in every holy matter, as is the law and custom of every ordained master of Torah. And, it being an ancient custom in Israel, when there is no *kohen* present [in the synagogue], that an ordained rabbi be called up to read instead of the *kohen*, even though there is a hoary elder present, the people of the congregation insisted that he go up first, although out of modesty he protested and refused several times.

And when he descended from the pulpit, two people—who were the sons of a certain elder, who was an ignoramus and whose habit it was

[85] See the second letter, 102a: 'A certain youth, one of his students, the son of R. Azriel of Corfu, used to study with him, and he was subjected by a writ of subjugation and swore an oath by the Torah to teach him for two consecutive years. And because that youth's strength weakened, and he lost his wealth, and the period of returning payment passed . . . he sent him away angrily and chased him out of the study house, for he was a cruel man. . .'

[86] 'Teshuvot R. Aharon b. Yisrael Finzi [of Reggio]', from a manuscript formerly in the possession of Isaiah Sonne, now MS Jerusalem—Makhon Ben-Zvi, No. 4040, Sect. 5. The responsum is published in full in the Hebrew edition of this book, Document 4", pp. 216-17.

to go up to the Torah in place of the *kohen*—rose up against him. And they attacked that ordained scholar, saying that it was fitting by law to give the priority to their elderly father. After that, on the Sabbath day, when the time came for reading the Torah Scroll, that scholar announced to the public that the elder should read in his place, for he waived his [rabbinic] prerogative, and did not wish to quarrel nor to go against the will of any person. And even though he said many things to appease the congregation, in order that they not press him to go up, they did not wish to listen to him and he was forced to go up, for they insisted to the point of embarrassment. Thus did it come about. And now, will your honour teach us the law—ought that elder to go up, since he is very elderly, or does the ordained scholar take precedence over the elder, as was the ancient practice? And will your honour also inform us what is meant in our sources by the term 'an outstanding elder' (*zaken muflag*) and 'an outstanding scholar' (*ḥakham muflag*)?

The rabbi answered this question in a very straightforward manner:

An outstanding scholar is one who was ordained to teach in the entire Torah, for Jephthah in his generation is like Samuel in his generation;[87] even if there is one greater than he in his generation, so long as there is no one greater in his city, he is still called an outstanding scholar. Therefore, [in this case] the sage takes precedence, and he ought to be called up first to the Torah.

But if the scholar wished to forgo his honour at any time, he may do so, as we have learned, 'The rabbi who waived his honour, his honour is waived,'[88] but his disciples must nevertheless show him respect. But he may not be called up following the elder, because of the saying of R. Johanan,[89] 'Every scholar who allows an ignoramus—even if he be the high priest—to bless before him is culpable of death, as is written,[90] "and those who hate Me loved death"—do not read "those who hate Me" but "those who make Me hated"—those who shame the Torah and make it hateful in the eyes of the people, allowing an ignoramus to be called up before him.' It is therefore fitting that that sage ought to minimize such forfeiture of honours, lest they come—Heaven forfend—to minimize the honour of Torah, [which] is very great.

As we have suggested, the rabbis, no less than the community, were interested in ensuring the legitimacy of the identification of *talmid-ḥakham* with 'ordained rabbi'. For them, an assurance that

[87] Rosh Hashanah 25b—i.e. that even the most insignificant person, if appointed to communal office, is entitled to the respect and authority of that office: 'for you have no other judges than those who live in your own time'.

[88] Kiddushin 32a. [89] Megillah 28a. [90] Should read 'all those who hate me'.

those called 'rabbi' would indeed be scholars and deserving of prestige was essentially a guarantee of the honour and status of the rabbinate itself. For this reason, the ordaining authorities practised a large measure of self-restraint, and by and large were extremely hesitant to grant ordination.[91] This is not to be interpreted as opposition to ordination *per se*, and certainly not as opposition to it in principle. On the contrary, all the statements in our sources expressing reservations about the granting of ordination are accompanied by statements indicating the paramount importance attached to that institution. For example, in the famous controversy concerning the quarrel between the Norzi and Finzi families,[92] R. Abraham b. Judah Minz, in a letter praising R. David of Pizzighettone to his antagonist R. Bendit Axelrad, mentions the fact that 'he never ordained one who was unworthy'.[93] R. Bendit, who saw these words as a sarcastic slur aimed at himself, replied: 'I too have never ordained any student who was not worthy', and proceeded to list all those he had ever ordained: their total number does not exceed five, two of whom had been previously ordained by others.[94] In the words of them both, one senses the splendour and honour of the ordaining rabbi which is somehow conferred upon the one ordained, and the great care that must be taken to avoid cheapening the value of ordination by awarding it to those who are undeserving.[95]

This term 'undeserving' is to be understood as applying, not only to wisdom, but also to personal character traits.[96] For example, in his previously cited sermon comparing the scholar to the Ark of the Covenant,[97] R. Samuel Judah Katzenellenbogen

[91] See Breuer, 'Ashkenazic Ordination', 29.

[92] See A. Marx, 'A Jewish *Cause Célèbre* in Sixteenth Century Italy', in his *Studies in Bibliography and Booklore* (New York, 1944), 107–54.

[93] *Pesakim*, 20a.

[94] Ibid. 24a; cf. Breuer, 'Ashkenazic Ordination', 29–32.

[95] See M. Benayahu and J. Laras, 'The Appointment of Health Officials in Cremona in 1575 and the Dispute Between R. Eliezer Ashkenazi and R. Abraham Menahem Porto ha-Kohen' (Heb.), *Mikhael*, 1 (Tel Aviv, 1973), 140–1, for an account of how a certain rabbi who was lying on his death-bed examined his conscience and attributed his sufferings to an error which he made when he 'covered up with the prayer-shawl [i.e., *ordained*] a colleague so-and-so [i.e. *who was unworthy*]'.

[96] See ibid.: 'that this man, in addition to being undeserving, lacking in knowledge and having not studied, moreover I heard that he behaves in the "13 ways in which the Torah is trampled and profaned"—and therefore the sage who had ordained him is asked to remove from him the collegial title. 'Trampled' is *nidreset*, a pun on *nidreshet*, meaning 'expounded'.

[97] See Ch. 2, Sect. 1.

mentioned the characteristics desired of a scholar who strives for ordination:

First, just as the ark was made out of pure gold . . . so ought the sage [to be], upon whose head the crown rests. In addition to that wisdom which he must first and foremost possess, he must also possess good traits and generous characteristics, and there should be no trace of any bad traits or low characteristics . . . Second—he must be the same within and without, just as was the ark, as our sages said, ' "You shall gild it within and without" [Ex. 25: 11]—this teaches that a scholar ought to be the same within and without'. Third, just as the outer part of the ark, which was a vessel for the inner ark, was also made of pure gold, so with this sage; it is not sufficient that he himself be as pure as gold in all his traits and characteristics, but the father of this scholar, who is to his son like the outer vessel surrounding the vessel in which the Torah rests, should also be as sage and pure as refined gold . . .[98]

This problem was raised explicitly by R. Azriel Diena (d. 1536) in his complaint against the rabbis granting ordination during the first third of the sixteenth century. He claimed that they only took note of the candidate's intellectual talents, but did not pay any heed to his character and ethical traits which, in his view, are essential. In a letter addressed to the rabbis, he writes:[99]

And on these my belly is like wine not yet opened [cf. Job 32: 19] . . . on seeing those who possess the Torah . . . when they deal with some talented young man who is sharp and clever . . . even if at times they did not see him, neither do they know him . . . but they unhesitatingly accept the laudatory testimony of others, calling him *Ḥaver* or . . . 'learned master'[100] . . . And even when they see or hear from nearby or far off of a man who is learned in books and is an elder, known among people . . . they place their hands upon him [i.e. *grant him ordination*], calling him *Morenu ha-Rav* (i.e. *bestowing upon him the title of the ordained*, '*Our teacher*, *Rabbi*') . . . and they are not acquainted with

[98] *Derashot Maharshi"k*, Sermon 7, 39a. 'The father of the sage' (*avi ha-talmid ḥakham*) evidently refers to the one ordaining. It may also be that this refers to a familial relationship in the literal sense: even though in terms of actual law, R. Samuel Judah thought that the question of lineage is of secondary importance in the valuation of a rabbinic scholar (see above, Sect. 1), he did not ignore lineage in citing the ideal qualities of one deserving of ordination.

[99] Cf. the complaint of the people of Imola, Ch. 2, Sect. 3.

[100] A play on words based upon Deut. 18: 10–11: 'there shall not be found among you one . . . or a charmer [*ḥover ḥaver*]) or a consulter with familiar spirits [*ov*] or a wizard [*yid'oni*]'—*ḥaver*—that is, the title of *Ḥaver*; *ov* = *av*, apparently based upon the exegesis of Gen. 41: 43 ('and they called before him Abrekh! [Make way!]'); *yid'oni*—'one who knows'.

him, nor do they know his ways . . . but only that he knows how to manage in Talmudic discussions and to confuse his opponents[101] . . . This is certainly a grievous sin, for those people who are ordained but whose heart has not been touched by God distort the Torah's paths and pervert its rounds, and it is to them like a trade and like a spade with which to dig silver and gold . . . May it be His will that this ordination not be a source of satisfaction for him, and that the one ordaining not see joy from his disciple . . . My eyes have seen that for years . . . how they ordain empty vessels, in whose hearts there was not the Law of God, and who feel their way in laws and legal rulings like blind people . . . Furthermore, I have seen scholars who were wise in knowledge of books and understood difficult things . . . but when they managed the double-edged sword of God in their hands,[102] they appeared as wishing to receive the reward of Phineas, while doing the deeds of Zimri[103] . . . Therefore, concerning these things my heart is very embittered, for how carefully must one examine the ways of the one ordained, whether his deeds are praiseworthy or not . . . and whether his ways conform to the ways of the eternal Law . . . Therefore, one who ordains and crowns and places his hands upon an elder or a young man must very carefully consider that ordainee, to measure the goodness of his deeds, whether his deeds conform to the eternal Law, if they are straightforward and open, and not spoiled and despicable. For even if he can show that he has learned Torah and Mishnah, the main thing is still lacking—whether he fears God, and whether his inward parts turn and tremble when he sits in judgement, lest he sin and be held responsible before God . . .

Following a colourful description of the crooked behaviour of an unworthily ordained rabbi, R. Azriel Diena goes on to blame the situation upon those who ordain unworthy candidates.[104] He then enumerates three conditions to ensure that those ordained will possess the requisite traits:

First, that they search and examine their ways and their deeds, if they are done with integrity and are faithful, and if they are steadfast, and if their fear of sin and their service of God indicate integrity and honesty. Next, they must examine their qualifications, if they have learned and studied thoroughly, and if they possess profound knowledge,

[101] In Hebrew: *le-falpel ule-valbel* ('to engage in *pilpul* [*Talmudic dialectics*] and to confuse'). On the use of this word-play to refer to inappropriate forms of legal argumentation, see the works cited in Ch. 1, n. 49.

[102] An allusion to the use of the *ḥerem*, to be discussed below at greater length.

[103] Sotah 22b, alluding to the incident described in Num. 25: 1–15.

[104] *Teshuvot R. 'Azriel Diena*, sect. 180, ed. Boksenboim (Tel Aviv, 1979), ii. 132 ff.; see also the next note.

and whether they are fit to instruct the children of Israel . . . Secondly, those who grant ordination may not place their hands upon anyone nearby or far off solely on the basis of hearsay, if they have not become acquainted with [the candidate] and know that he is worthy of the crown of Torah, and that the fear of the Master of Masters hovers over his head. Third, that a scholar who has been ordained may not be definitely considered as a rabbi until he has obtained the agreement and permission of three rabbis . . .

R. Azriel's third condition, at least, seems to have been accepted: Rabbi Meir Katzenellenbogen (1473–1565, known as the *Maharam* of Padua) introduced a regulation whereby ordination was only to be granted with the agreement of three rabbis,[105] an edict which the prominent rabbis of Italy followed for many years.[106] It was even required that at least one of those ordaining be 'one of the elder sages of the generation'.[107]

One hears echoes of this same tendency on the part of those receiving ordination, whose ultimate interest was also to protect the integrity of the concept of 'ordained scholar'. This may be seen in the attempt to restrict the act of ordaining others to a well-known yeshivah head. Thus, according to the statement of R. David son of Messer Leon, 'those who are deserving of ordination and those who are important . . . do not wish to be ordained except by a *rosh-yeshivah*, who has been well known for a number of years'.[108] Several years later, for example, in a letter addressed by R. Bendit Axelrad to R. Abraham b. Judah Minz in the course of the afore-mentioned bitter controversy,[109] he wrote:

105 See Sonne, 'On the History of the Community of Bologna', 47–8, 75; Breuer, 'Ashkenazic Ordination', 34–6.

106 Thus, e.g. the document of ordination granted to R. Aaron b. Israel Finzi was signed by three rabbis. The text of this document is in the Hebrew edition of this book, Document 9, 223–4. It is also evident from this document that, if R. Meir in fact intended that those ordaining should 'agree together to that ordination', and that the one granting ordination not simply append his signature after that of the others granting ordination without consultation among them all (according to Breuer, 'Ashkenazic Ordination', 35, a point which in my opinion requires further examination), then the ordinance itself did not go into effect, but only the condition that the ordination be signed by three. Some other documents of ordination are also published in the Hebrew edition of this book; see Documents 5–8, 217–22.

107 See Sonne, 'On the History of the Community of Bologna', 48; Breuer, 'Ashkenazic Ordination', 35. On the term *ga'on*, see below, Sect. 6.

108 *Kevod Ḥakhamim*, 64, and cf. Breuer, 'Ashkenazic Ordination'.

109 See above, Ch. 2, Sect. 3.

Now after you have blessed your neighbour with a great voice [i.e. *you have insinuated against me an accusation in that you praised my opponent, blessing him by saying that he never ordained one who was unworthy*] . . . you force me to answer you in a manner which is unpleasant for me. Thus I shall respond by saying that it may be that he never ordained one who was unworthy, lest people should not wish to receive ordination from him, because he was not a *rosh-yeshivah* anywhere before [he came] . . .[110]

In order to assure the good character of those seeking the rabbinic title, towards the end of the century a tendency emerged not to grant ordination to anyone below the age of 40. The determination of the age at which 'a [would-be] scholar is entitled to elevation to the status of a ruling scholar' involved a complex problematic, of which people were well aware.[111] Therefore, whenever younger people were ordained it was accompanied by explanations justifying the act. For example, R. David son of Messer Leon relates that, when he was ordained at the age of 18, 'many sermons were delivered on the day of my ordination, among them those containing proofs that, although I was but 18 years old, it was permitted to give ordination to such a one who was deserving of it'.[112] The youthful ordainee's age is apparently mentioned in order to note the exception to the usual practice, due to his distinguished character,[113] with a clear awareness that the case was an unusual one.[114] R. Jacob Finzi's request that, prior to the granting of rabbinical ordination, the candidate remain in the category of *Ḥaver* (Colleague) 'for many years' is clear evidence of the recognition that there ought to be a procedure, but also that this practice was not institutionalized. A concrete example of this appears in one of his responsa, in which he stipulates that a particular individual was not to be

110 *Pesakim*, 24a. The meaning of the last sentence is somewhat unclear; does he mean to say that at that time there was no one in the country who had been ordained by him because he was not a yeshivah head, or was R. David of Pizzighettonne the first rabbi in Italy to be ordained by R. Judah Minz?

111 See Babylonian Talmud, Sotah 22a–b, Rashi and *Tosafot* ad loc, and cf. R. Nissim on Avodah Zarah (Riva di Trento, 1558), iii. 267a.

112 *Kevod Ḥakhamim*, 65, and cf. 53, and Document 6 in the Hebrew edition of this book, pp. 220–1.

113 See, e.g. the statement by R. Elijah Capsali, in Porges, 'Elie Capsali', *REJ* 79 (1923), 36: 'Our Master R. David ha-Levi b. R. Eleazar [of Pizzighettone] was of Ashkenazic stock, and because of his sharpness for the honour of his ancestors, they ordained him when he was twenty-eight years old'.

114 Cf. Breuer, 'Ashkenazic Ordination', 40–1.

ordained as rabbi until he had been a *Ḥaver* for a number of years:[115]

Therefore, I say that this person is not to be called Rabbi until he first receives Collegial ordination from the rabbis, and uses it for many years, and increases in wisdom and ethics; then, if he seems deserving to the sages of that generation, they will ordain him. And to this my view inclines, if two or three other rabbis will agree with my opinion, and so shall the Torah be increased and honoured.

The rabbis made use of the limitation regarding age so long as they saw need, and even awarded ordination under the explicit condition that it only take effect after a period of time. This was true, for example, of the ordination granted to R. Asher Grassetto in Mantua on 17 January 1590, using the formula, 'We know . . . him to be God-fearing and deserving of being a rabbi in Israel, so we have agreed from this time on that, when he will be 40 years old, he will be crowned with the crown of ordination.'[116]

Retroactively, in order to deal with the possibility that an unworthy individual might be ordained, the rabbis attempted to introduce a procedure whereby the title could be removed through public declaration.[117] There are various testimonies of such

115 'Teshuvot R. Ya'akov Yisra'el Finzi', MS Jerusalem 8° 1992, sect. 164, fo. 1; quoted in full in the Hebrew edition of this book, Document 3, p. 215-6.

116 'Teshuvot Bat Rabbim', MS. Moscow-Ginzburg 129 (IMHM 6809), sect. 3, p. 89. See also, for a slightly later period, Yitzḥak min ha-Levi'im, *Medabber Tahapukhot* (1912), 176, 181, 185.

117 e.g. R. Joseph Colon's plea to remove the rabbinic title from R. Moses Capsali (Teshuvot Mahari"k, Sects. 83, 84): 'I hereby inform you and I decree upon you by power of the above-mentioned ban that you not ask any halakhic instruction or any judgement of this person, Moses Capsali, as I have seen with my own eyes that he does not even reach [the level of] a shepherd [i.e. *he is a perfect ignoramus*], and he does not know the form of halakhic traditions. What have we to do with this ordination of which he is not deserving? In fact, we do not follow the name of a thing, but its taste [i.e. *we can only base ourselves upon substantial evidence, and not simply upon the title he bears; a play on a concept appearing in BT Ḥullin 66a*], and he has neither the taste nor the fragrance of Torah . . . I furthermore hereby decree the ban against all those who see or know of this declaration, that they do not call that same Moses Capsali by the title of either rabbi or *ḥaver*, for he is not deserving of this whatsoever. Therefore, remove the crown from his head, that he be called neither rabbi nor *ḥakham* . . .' See also R. Meir of Padua's arguments for the removal of the title from R. Abraham of Rovigo: 'that it should be known to you that this man is not deserving of issuing halakhic rulings, but is only deserving to have the crown lifted from his head, not to be called rabbi or *ḥakham*, so that no man be ordained on the basis of his rulings. And I decree by power of the ban against every cantor . . . that he not call him [up to the reading] by the title of *rav* or of *ḥakham*, but only by his first name, Abraham. And you, the holy congregation, the sons of holy ones, do not ordain by virtue of his instructions, for he may not teach or

removal of the rabbinic title: R. Jacob Pollak removed the rabbinic title from R. Abraham Minz, and also placed him under a ban under the accusation of displaying contempt for scholars;[118] the rabbis of Venice stripped the rabbinic title from R. Benjamin Mattathias of Arta because of 'incorrect halakhic rulings' and because of the suspicion that he had forged signatures;[119] R. Joseph of Arles was twice stripped of the title of *Ḥaver*: the first time for some sort of forgery, and once because he had shown disrespect towards elder rabbis,[120] while some time later his rabbinic title was removed on the grounds of forging a signature and contempt for other scholars.[121] On one occasion, some people even attempted to unfrock one of the leading rabbis of that generation, R. Moses Provenzali.[122]

The most commonly given reason for removal of the rabbinic title appears to have been contempt shown for other scholars. This was at least one of the declared reasons, if not the major one, for the removal of ordination in most of the above cases.[123] As is well known, accusations of contempt for scholars were generally raised in connection with disputes among rabbis—that is, in those cases in which there was reason to assume that, alongside objective considerations, there was also an element of personal involvement, whose objectivity it is difficult to weigh. This may have been one reason why the removal of the rabbinic title could not serve as an effective tool of the rabbis for preserving

prohibit or permit or judge, either by prohibitions or by monetary matters, for this man is known to mislead people . . .' See E. Kupfer, 'R. Abraham b. Menahem of Rovigo and his Removal from the Rabbinate' (Heb.), *Sinai*, 63 (1967), 142–62, and compare the expressions appearing here with the parallel ones in rabbinic ordinations, to be discussed below.

118 See S. Wiener, ed., *Pesak ha-Ḥerem* (St. Petersburg, 1897).

119 See *Teshuvot Azriel Diena*, sect. 181; S. Assaf, 'The Responsa of R. Azriel Diena' (Heb.), *KS* 14 (1938–9), 551–2.

120 See *Teshuvot Azriel Diena*, sects. 182–7.

121 See E. Kupfer, 'The Disqualification and Reinstatement of Joseph of Arles as *Ḥaver* and Rabbi' (Heb.), *KS* 41 (1966), 117–32.

122 See E. Kupfer, 'The Removal of the Crown of Torah from R. Moses Provenzalo' (Heb.), *Sinai*, 63 (1968), 137–60.

123 On this matter see also A. Marx, 'The Removal of R. Joseph d'Arles from the Rabbinate and his Reinstatement' (Heb.), *Tarbiz*, 8 (1937), 171–84; Benayahu and Laras, 'The Health Officials in Cremona', 93–5, 140–2; Assaf, 'The Responsa of R. Azriel Diena', 113–19; J. Colon, *Teshuvot Mahari"k ha-Hadashim*, Introduction, 34–9; J. Minz, *Teshuvot Mahar"i Minz*, sects. 10, 13; and see also the Hebrew edition of this book, Document 4, pp. 216–17. On the parallel phenomenon in Ashkenaz, see Breuer, 'Ashkenazic Ordination', p. 38 and n. 149.

the honour of the institution—a point to which we shall later return.

When the communities attained a more fixed stage of organization, from the middle of the sixteenth century,[124] the possibility of criticism on the part of the community was added to the practice of self-criticism among the rabbis. This was expressed in the edicts issued by the communities to delegitimize ordination granted to outsiders, albeit following a discussion of each individual case, as well as by linking the reception of ordination to certain requirements which would guarantee the agreement of the community. Various regulations of this sort have already been noted,[125] their common denominator being the community's demand to participate in the decision. However, this demand appears in different forms. Generally, these regulations clearly indicate the high status enjoyed by the rabbis in public opinion in different places, and a corresponding clear tendency to limit the public's involvement in decisions, as the institutionalization of the rabbinate within the organizational framework of the community reached its culmination towards the end of the sixteenth century, and especially in the first half of the seventeenth century.[126]

A stringent edict observed in Rome, at least until the first half of the seventeenth century, stated that 'one cannot call any person rabbi without the permission of the Congrega'. Even when the question of ordination was raised on the public agenda, the Congrega continued to insist upon its own right to choose rabbis, even vehemently so, issuing a specific ruling on the subject.[127] On the other hand, it was agreed in Mantua in 1597 that nobody was to be ordained as rabbi except by the agreement of the majority of the rabbis in the city and of the members of the Council,[128] while in Verona a certificate of agreement, agreed to

124 See above, Introduction.

125 See S. Simonsohn, Introduction to *Teshuvot Ziknei Yehudah*, 24; idem, *Mantua* (Jerusalem, 1972), 576–7, and the sources quoted there; Breuer, 'Ashkenazic Ordination', 36–8; and cf. the words of the author from Imola, cited in the Hebrew edition of this book, Document 2, pp. 212–13 and the ordinances of the community of Rome, cited in Documents 33, 34, and 37, pp. 247–9.

126 This process will be discussed at greater length in the next chapter.

127 See Documents 33 and 34 in the Hebrew edition of this book, p. 247. The Congrega (in Hebrew: *Keriah*) was the Council of 60 chosen members of the congregation, according to an arrangement reached by Daniel da Pisa. See A. Milano, 'I "Capitoli" di Daniel da Pisa e la comunità di Roma', *RMI*, 10 (1935–6), 324–38, 409–26.

128 Simonsohn, *Mantua*, 576.

by the rabbis of the city, provided that no one would be recognized as ordained unless 'the majority of the rabbis of the city—those who are ordained and known as those who rule [on halakhic matters]—agree to ordain him and to call him "our teacher" (*Morenu*)'.[129] As we shall see in the next chapter, the difference in these expressions is but one aspect of the difference in the process of the institutionalization of the rabbinate in the communal framework in different places. Only in the seventeenth century, when this process reached its conclusion in the context of an all-encompassing communal organization, do we perceive clearly the tendency to transfer decision-making to the rabbinate. This phenomenon, however, is beyond the chronological confines of this work.[130]

4. Authority and Privileges

Those who held ordination enjoyed in its wake various prerogatives. These were detailed in the ordination document and included the authority to rule on matters pertaining to the ritually forbidden and permitted and to civil law; jurisdiction over issues of family law—i.e. marriages, divorces, and related matters; and, finally, the authority to excommunicate and impose bans.

129 I. Sonne, 'Basic Premisses', *Kovez 'al Yad*, 3 [13] (1939–40), 180–1.

130 See M. A. Shulvass, Introduction to R. Simone Luzzatto's *Ma'amar 'al Yehudei Venezia* [*Discorso sopra gli ebrei di Venezia*] (Jerusalem, 1951), 14; Simonsohn, Introduction to *Teshuvot Ziknei Yehudah*, 24; idem. *Mantua*, Introduction. See the text of the statute of the community of Mantua from 1637, mentioned by Simonsohn, p. 576 n. 242 from 'Pinkas Kehillat Mantova', Is Am, fo. 15b; the full text appears in the Hebrew edition of this book, Document 15, p. 234: 'For at that time there was presented before the Small Council an agreement made on 1 January 1597, wherein was written: the members of the Council may not ordain any person to be a rabbi, that is, to be called Rabbi, unless the majority of the rabbis of Mantua and a majority of the members of the Small Council agree. And before they agree to ordain the honourable Rabbi Cohen in question, the members of the Small Council shall examine the old agreement carefully. And they decreed that, according to their opinion, they may ordain the honourable Rabbi Cohen with the agreement of the *Ga'on* del Vecchio alone [*R. Abraham b. Shabbetai del Vecchio, who was the rabbi of the community of Mantua beginning in 1633*], and that they do not oppose that old ordination, because it is [well] known that the *Ga'on* del Vecchio is akin to a majority, for he is great and outstanding in wisdom and in seniority and is a yeshivah head, and is the teacher of that community, and he may be relied upon on in those cases where decision is required. Nevertheless, the truth is that [at that time] they also voted to temporarily nullify the old agreement mentioned above, and they likewise nullified everything which stood in the way of ordaining the honourable righteous teacher mentioned above, but they then stipulated that in the future they would not diminish any part of the old agreement, but allow it to remain in full force.'

We have already noted R. David son of Messer Leon's clear expression of the opinion that one who is not ordained ought not to be allowed to rule on halakhic matters.[131] By this remark, R. David seems to have been expressing more an emergent trend than an actual social reality. In fact, in so far as public opinion accepted the principle according to which a scholar (*talmid-ḥakham*) was necessarily one who was 'ordained', R. David's statement may be seen as reflecting the general consciousness. This consciousness was also fostered by the Talmudic discussions concerning scholars who, despite not having reached the stage of teaching, nevertheless rule on halakhic issues.[132] Thus, during the period under discussion, 'attaining the level of teaching' came to be more and more identified with the concept of 'ordination'. Put otherwise: while one might have some reservations about the general statement that an ordained person was in every case 'one who had attained the level of teaching', there is no indication to the contrary—namely, that one who was not ordained might be considered to have 'attained the level of teaching'.[133] True, we do find here and there people who disagreed with rabbinical rulings and saw themselves as possessing the necessary authority to rule on practical halakhic matters.[134] Nowhere, however, do we encounter the explicit view that halakhic decision-making is other than an exclusive rabbinic prerogative and that whoever wishes to issue rulings may do so. Even the expressions used by the rabbis when they wished to deprive their colleagues of the rabbinic title[135] seem to confirm the statement that the act of ruling on 'forbidden and permitted' (i.e. concerning prohibited foodstuffs and the like) was universally considered as an exclusive rabbinic prerogative.[136] This being the case with regard to ritual matters, it is not surprising that this should also be so with regard to marriage and divorce, considering the paramount gravity attached by Jewish Law to these issues. During this entire period, we do not find a single

131 See above, Ch. 2, Sect. 3.

132 e.g. Sotah 22a.

133 If there were still some renowned scholars who did not wish to accept ordination, the demand for the right to issue rulings alongside those ordained could not have come from them.

134 e.g. the opinion of the opponent of R. Abraham Menahem Porto's ruling concerning the wearing of *tefillin* during *Ḥol ha-Moed* (the intermediate days of Festivals). See *Teshuvot R. Abraham Menahem Porto ha-Kohen*, sect. 163.

135 See above, n. 117.

136 e.g. in *Teshuvot . . . Porto ha-Kohen*, sect. 163.

case in which a layman sought the right to perform marriages and divorces.

One might reasonably maintain that halakhic rulings in civil matters also fall under the rubric of what has been said here, whenever such rulings accord with Jewish Law. However, in Italy the situation in this matter was more complex. As we shall see later, the vast majority of rulings in civil matters were carried out by means of arbitration, the arbiters not necessarily being Talmudic scholars. In any event, we can definitively conclude that, throughout the period under discussion, there was no objection in principle to the rabbinic monopoly upon the three prerogatives mentioned above, which were included under the rubric of the Talmudic formula of ordination (Sanhedrin 5*a*) and appearing on the relevant document—*yoreh yoreh yadin yadin* ('he shall rule and he shall judge'). The same cannot be said regarding the issuing of bans and writs of excommunication, which subject was rife with disputes, appeals, and even disagreements between the rabbis and the public—a point deserving more extensive treatment.

We will not examine here the evolution of the institution of the ban before the period under discussion, either with respect to the role played by scholars as opposed to communal heads and *parnassim* (lay leaders), or the precise halakhic significance of a ban which was not imposed by a recognized scholar. These topics are worthy of study in their own right from both the halakhic and the historical perspective.[137] From the Talmudic period on, a certain ambivalence appears concerning the question of whose ban is efficacious. On the one hand, the sacral, magical aura which hovered over every curse uttered was of paramount importance in determining the seriousness with which people related to bans, even when those who imposed them were not rabbis.[138] On the other hand, from the tannaitic period on, the

[137] See, for the present, J. Katz, *Tradition and Crisis* (New York, 1971), 99–102; H. H. Ben-Sasson, *Hagut ve-Hanhagah* (Jerusalem, 1960), 212 ff.; *Encyclopedia Hebraica*, s.v. *ḥerem*; *Encyclopedia Judaica* (Berlin, 1930), s.v. *Cherem*. G. Leibson has recently begun to study this subject; see the first part of his work, 'Niddui va-Ḥerem be-tekufat ha-Mishnah veha-Talmud' (Jerusalem: Hebrew University Faculty of Law, 1973), Master's Dissertation, 183–8, for a bibliography of the numerous studies in which a variety of questions related to *ḥerem* have been studied. I do not distinguish here among the varying degrees of severity of the ban—*niddui*, *ḥerem*, and *shamta*—as in all documents from the period the terms are used without any relation to their precise significance, and certainly not to the halakhic differences dependent upon them.

[138] e.g. Babylonian Talmud, Moed Katan 16a.

ban was always, in practice, a prerogative of rulers and leaders, whether as a form of punishment and warning (as during the period of the Mishnah and Talmud)[139] or as a means of strengthening communal ordinances, which were essentially merely another form of warning (as in the later period).[140] Various factors joined to determine the role of the rabbis in using the ban, the most important of which were: the clear tradition that 'one under ban to the master is under the ban to the disciple, but one under ban to the disciple is not under ban to the master';[141] the analogy drawn between the concept of the ban (*ḥerem*) and the entire area of personal oaths (*shevu'ah* and *neder*;[142] the halakhic problematic requiring the agreement of an 'important person' for the enactment of communal regulations, particularly those pertaining to the ban;[143] and the custom, accepted as binding in most Jewish communities, not to treat one who has violated communal ordinances as being under the ban until declared as such, unless specifically stated otherwise in the edict itself.[144] All these factors were decisive in determining the role of the 'masters of the Law' in the practical implementation of the ban, in which the community heads and *parnassim* demanded their share. The tension between the lay leaders and the learned in relation to the question of ban has attracted the attention of scholars, who have primarily studied the late Middle Ages in Franco-Germany;[145] however, the roots of this tension, and its development throughout the medieval period, still require further study. In any event, what we have noted here certainly applies

139 See Leibson, 'Niddui va-Ḥerem', 80–104.

140 See L. Finkelstein, *Jewish Self-government in the Middle Ages* (New York, 1924; 2nd ed., 1964), 242.

141 Semaḥot 5: 15; Jerusalem Talmud, Moed Katan 3: 1; Babylonian Talmud, Moed Katan 15a; and compare Leibson, 'Niddui va-Ḥerem, pp. 80 ff.

142 These could only be nullified by a formal appeal to a sage or a court of experts [hatarat ḥakham], whose action provided the possibility of nullification by eliciting a formal expression of regret for having taken the oath; a similar procedure for the annulment of bans was proposed by way of analogy to this procedure. For the similarity of these terms even in the semantic realm, see S. Lieberman, *Greek in Jewish Palestine* (New York, 1942), 119. On the release of individuals from the ban, see Leibson, 'Niddui va-Ḥerem', 135–54.

143 This topic will be discussed at greater length in Ch. 3.

144 See *Ṭur Shulḥan 'Arukh: Yoreh De'ah* 228: 32; 334: 22. Cf. Ch. 5, Sect. 2 on edicts issued on the basis of the ban.

145 See Katz, *Tradition and Crisis*, 99–102; Ben-Sasson, *Hagut ve-Hanhagah*, 212 ff.; E. J. Schochet, *Rabbi Joel Sirkes* (Jerusalem, 1971), 143 ff.

to Italy in the period under discussion, and adequately establishes the point.

There is no doubt that, throughout this period, the ban was considered one of the 'rabbinical prerogatives'. Wherever the imposition of a formal ban occurred—that is, the public reading of one of the formulas entailing cursing of the banned one,[146] or the signing of such a document—it was imposed by the rabbis. True, there are exceptions to this general rule, some of which will be dealt with later; however, they all seem to be exceptions which prove the rule. In all of the many taxation regulations accompanying the explicit imposition of ban, the rabbis sign the ban.[147] The same is true for the ban formulas which accompany the approvals of published books (*haskamot*).[148] The role of the rabbis was likewise crucial in the ceremonies of oath-taking involved in assessment for tax purposes.[149] Even the government

[146] Such as the version cited in the *Kolbo*. On the use of formulas for oaths and bans from the *Kolbo* in Italy during this period, see below, Ch. 3 n. 352.

[147] Printed arrangements for valuation survive principally from the community of Mantua; see Simonsohn, *Mantua*, 377–84. On communal ordinances which were coupled with the *ḥerem*, see below, Ch. 3, Sect. 3.

[148] See the examples cited at the end of M. Benayahu, *Haskamah u-reshut be-defusei Veneẓia* (Jerusalem, 1971). Cf. also N. Rakover, *Ha-haskamot li-sefarim ki-yesod li-zekhut Yoẓrim* [Misrad ha-Mishpatim. Sidrat Meḥkarim u-sekirot ba-Mishpat ha 'Ivri. 9.] (Jerusalem, 1971), 1–94. Even the *ḥerem* which accompanied the approbation given to R. Jacob Soresina's *Seder ha-Nikkur* (Venice, 1595) was imposed by the *ge'onim* with the agreement of the lay leaders, there being no basis for Sonne's claim in his article, 'Documents concerning Rabbinic Messengers in Italy at the Beginning of the 17th Century' (Heb.), *Koveẓ 'al Yad* 5 [15] (1951), 208, that, from 1594 until the end of the 16th century 'the lay leaders overcame the rabbis in Venice, restricted their rights and removed from them the authority to proclaim a ban', something which was expressed, according to him, in the agreement referred to in the above book, in which 'the lay leaders are those who decry and ban and some of the rabbis answer Amen [i.e. *affirm*] after them'.

[149] See the 'arrangements for oath-taking and performing valuations agreed upon on Wednesday, 3 Iyyar, 5339 [1579] in the holy congregation . . . in the general council'. A copy of the only surviving example of this document, found in the archives of the community in Mantua, appears on p. 46 of the Hebrew edition of this book. It was likewise decided in the Community Council in Padua that all those taking the oath at the time of valuation should swear 'with a strict oath of the Torah, opening the Holy Ark in the presence of the judges of the Vaad and before R. Samuel Archivolti'; see Carpi, *Pinkas Padua*, for 1586, sect. 11a, p. 68a; for 1588, sect. 9, p. 74a; for 1591, sect. 9, p. 79a; and for 1593, p. 85a. See also below, Ch. 3, n. 352 and Documents 35, 36 in the Hebrew edition of this book. See also 'Teshuvot R. Azriel Trabot', sect. 44: 'This is the order of valuation . . . first-in order to give a good and suitable purpose to the involvements of the communities, concerning these new valuations, and an equitable rule for all, they decided unanimously, to bring here to Macerata two people who are wise and sound, crowned with Torah, to [administer] a solem oath of the Torah, with a strict and absolute ban, concerning all the ways and ordinances applying to every man and woman in the communities of La Marca.'

licences required in order to impose a ban[150] were only granted to the rabbis.[151] Outside requests to the Jewish community to ban specific individuals were likewise addressed to the rabbis.[152] R. Leone Modena (1571–1648), writing to Christians who were accustomed to the church prerogative of excommunication, mentioned as self-evident that the 'punishment of criminals by means of bans' was among the prerogatives of the ordained rabbis.[153] It seems to me that these words ought to be seen, not only as an additional indication of the coherence of Jewish mentality with that of the Catholic ambience in Italy upon the sacrality entailed in the concept of ban, but as evidence of a broader phenomenon—namely, the particular aura of sacrality which imbued the figure of the Italian rabbi during this period, a point to which we have already alluded and to which we shall return.[154] In any event, in Italy the ban was treated as a rabbinic matter; as a consequence, so long as it felt the need to use the ban, the public saw itself as dependent upon the rabbis.

Those isolated cases in which the lay leadership arrogated to itself the authority of imposing the ban[155] seem the exceptions which prove the rule. In 1585, the leaders of Padua took a vote in which they decided to give themselves the power to 'impose the edict of excommunication upon those to whom it seems appropriate', specifically regarding a certain matter in which they perceived the danger that 'heaven forfend there not come out of

150 See below, Ch. 5.

151 e.g. the formula granting rights to the Jews of Monferrato in 1592 (S. Foa, *The Jews in Monferrato* (Alessandria, 1914; repr. Bologna, 1965), 173): 'Che li Rabini Ebrei possano ordinare communiche . . .' (that the Jewish rabbis will be allowed to impose excommunication). Compare there other documents of this sort from subsequent years. Also in those places where the documents of rights did not include overall permission similar to that given to the Jews of Monferrato, this permission was also given ad hoc from time to time to rabbis. See, e.g. Simonsohn, Mantua, 352, n. 117. This permission is given there to 'Magistro Florio, Magistro Calimano doctoribus, et alijs doctoribus et magistris totius congregationis hebreorum' (to the doctors Florio, Master Calimano, and the other Doctors and Masters of all the congregation of the Jews).

152 See B. Pullan, *Rich and Poor in Renaissance Venice* (Cambridge, Mass., 1971), 562.

153 L. Modena, *Historia de gli riti hebraici* (Paris, 1637), 41–42: 'il *Cacam Rau*, o *Morenu*, decide i dubij circa le cose prohibite, e lecite, d'ogni materia, scriuono allegationi e sentenze . . . e castigano li disubidienti con scommuniche. . . ' (the *Ḥakham Rav*, [called] *Morenu*, resolves doubts in matters of prohibited and permitted things, writes summonses to judgement and rulings . . . and punishes with the ban those who violate them.)

154 See above, Ch. 1, Sect. 2; Ch. 2, Sect. 1 and 4.

155 On the situation in Ashkenaz and Poland, see the sources cited in n. 145.

this a certain destruction, and we lose a soul from Israel'.[156] The exact nature of the danger averted by these leaders is not clear. Shortly before this decision was adopted, the appointed rabbi resigned from his position as a member of the Communal Court; it therefore seems likely that this resignation took place against the background of some dispute over an issue related to that Court.[157] In any event, the language of the final decision on this matter states that the leaders felt themselves entitled to impose their ruling on this matter 'without the permission of any rabbi'. This would then seem to indicate their awareness that the accepted practice was for such things not to be done 'without the permission of the rabbis'. The decision of the *parnassim* of Padua began a period of great tension between them and the appointed rabbi, to which we shall turn in the next chapter. In any event, this decision was evidently the only one in which the lay leaders assumed the authority to impose the ban 'against whomever they saw fit' into their own hands. The community edicts, which were imposed by the leaders with the force of ban without the agreement of the rabbi, are no different from any other communal bans.[158] This being the case, the decision of the leaders of Padua does not contradict what we have said above. On the contrary, it confirms the idea that the imposition of the ban—by means of a declaration incorporating a curse against the one banned, or a signature on such a formula—was indeed a rabbinic prerogative, and that the community was supposed to turn towards the rabbis on such matters.[159] As we shall see in the next chapter, this

[156] See Carpi, *Pinkas Padua*, sects. 200, 205 (pp. 181, 183).

[157] I accept here the conclusions of Carpi, the editor of the *Pinkas*, ibid., 43–4. On this Court, see below, Ch. 3, Sect. 4b.

[158] See above, Ch. 2, Sect. 4.

[159] There is a good deal of speculation concerning the decision of the lay leaders of Venice 'to remove from the teachers of Torah all power and permission to ban and to excommunicate . . . and to take it' for themselves. See: J. Blau (ed.), *Kitvei R. Yehudah Aryeh Modena* (Budapest, 1906), sect. 183, p. 171; B. Klar, 'The Work *Sha'agat 'Aryeh 'al Kol Sakhal*' (Heb.), *Tarbiz*, 13 (1942), 145–7; Sonne, 'Documents Concerning Rabbinic Messengers', 207–9; Benayahu, *Haskamah u-reshut bi-defusei Venezia*, 35–9. Klar's statement, that the causes of the dispute and the unfolding of events are not fully clear, is still valid. Moreover, even what he considered clear seems to require further clarification; e.g. did the lay leaders really impose upon the rabbis a prohibition 'to wear the official garment which had been characteristic of them until now'? Or is the meaning of the communal officer's statement perhaps that one is not to recognize a rabbi except as one who has been ordained by their approval? And what does it mean that 'the members of the community did not pay attention to the rabbi's rulings in matters of unfit and fit things, prohibited and permitted' within the framework of the ordinances of the lay

understanding of the ban as a matter essentially pertaining to the rabbis alone was one factor aiding the process of appointment of a community rabbi, implying that the rabbi was required to impose the ban whenever he was asked to do so by the 'lay leaders'.[160]

If we are correct in stating that the broader community in fact saw the ban as a quasi-divine act, proscribed to all those who were not 'masters of the Law' except as an emergency measure, this very consciousness may have contributed to the status of clerical sacrality which the rabbis assumed. This same consciousness also encouraged the well-known tendency to make excessive use of the ban in disputes in which the rabbis were involved, particularly in order to ensure that those summoned to appear in court would not think lightly of the invitation, thereby imposing rabbinic authority precisely where their own weakness was felt.[161] Anyone perusing the sources pertaining to the history of the Jews in Italy during this period perceives how frequently the rabbis made use of the instrument of the ban in such circumstances. This situation, similar to that in Christian society,[162] clearly contributed to the fear that the ban would not be taken seriously, thereby dangerously reducing its effectiveness as an instrument of public discipline. It is superfluous to add

leaders? Only one thing is clear, namely, that the lay leaders of Venice forbade the imposition of the ban without their agreement. Against this, the rabbis of Venice decided 'to be in one band against anyone who would be appointed, Council or lay-leader, from whatever community it might be, or from all of them in this matter . . . to meet together all of us . . . and whatever would be agreed upon by the majority, all of us will be obliged to observe, whether it entail a positive act or passive acquiescence'. If this last phrase—i.e. to be 'obliged to do that which involves passive acquiescence'—is more than mere rhetoric, it must imply refusal to impose the ban at the request of the *parnassim* without the agreement of the other rabbis in the city, on the assumption that by this means the ban would not be imposed at all. If so, then even this case confirms what has been said above.

160 See below, Ch. 3, Sect. 4.

161 See Ch. 5, Sect. 6 on this subject. On the other hand, in so far as the practical result of this threat of the use of the ban upon the growth of the authority of the rabbinate is concerned, it is sufficient to mention here the effectiveness of that threat in connection with the dispute which took place surrounding the appearance in Imola of one ordained by R. Abraham ha-Kohen (see above, Ch. 2, Sect. 3). This is certainly adequate proof that, if the frequent use of the ban was also a sign of weakness, it was not exclusively so!

162 A striking example may be seen in the words of Montaigne, who was present in Rome at the time of the solemn proclamation of the ban against all those rulers who held Church property. He wrote in his journal: 'auquel article les Cardinaux de Medicis et Caraffe, qui etoint jouignant le Pape se rioint bien fort' (and here [i.e. *upon hearing the words of the ban*] Cardinals Medici and Caraffa, who were together with the Pope, laughed greatly), *Journal*, i. 260.

that this was hardly in the interest of the communities, as the ban was the most powerful principal instrument of coercion available to the Jewish communal leadership. Not surprisingly, a tendency developed to make the imposition of the ban contingent upon the permission of the community's lay leadership,[163] and to prohibit the publication within the community of bans brought from other places.[164] By these means, the communities applied their own primary mechanism of public control upon the rabbinic use of the prerogative of excommunication.

The rabbis saw these efforts to make the imposition of the ban contingent upon lay agreement as an affront to their own honour and authority. Thus, it is not surprising that they opposed this trend, even though certain expressions on this issue suggest that the rabbis did not entirely reject the argument that there was need for some sort of control over the use of bans (although they argued that this supervision ought not to be removed from the realm of the rabbinate). Thus, when the appointed rabbi of the community of Padua insisted that the lay leaders of his community present themselves before a Court of Venetian rabbis concerning their decision to use the prerogative of excommunication without consulting any rabbi, R. Samuel Judah Katzenellenbogen refrained from discussing the edict itself and contented himself with the brief comment: 'I shall not address myself to the *parte*[165] itself, for I hope that the intention was towards restricting regulations directed for the good of the whole; therefore, I shall not suspect you nor raise objections to it, and for my part let it stand as written.'[166] On the other hand, more extensive and emotional comments were conveyed by R. Abraham Menahem Porto ha-Kohen (1520–after 1594) to the lay leaders of Candia:[167]

[163] The ordinance regarding this matter was already in effect in Rome in 1525; see A. Milano, 'I "Capitoli" di Daniel da Pisa', *RMI* 10 (1935–6), 422. For Venice, at least in the year 1594, see S. Bernstein (ed.) *Diwwan le-Rabbi Yehudah Aryeh Modena* (Philadelphia, 1932), 113–15, and above, n. 159. For Padua, in 1585, see *Pinkas Padua*, sect. 212, pp. 185–6. On Verona, see Ch. 3, Sect. 4a.

[164] See Ch. 4, Sect. 4.

[165] i.e. decision.

[166] *Pinkas Padua*, sect. 214, p. 187.

[167] *Teshuvot R. Avraham Menahem Porto ha-Kohen*, sect. 18. The opening of this responsa is cited by M. Güdemann, *Ha-Torah veha-Ḥayyim* (Warsaw, 1897–9; Jerusalem, 1972), i. 279–80. The text of the ordinance of Candia, to which the responsum of Abraham Menahem Porto ha-Kohen refers, is cited by E. S. Hartom and U. Cassuto, *Takkanot Kandia ve-Zikhronoteha* (Jerusalem, 1943), 158–9. I have copied here those selections from the responsa of R. Abraham Menahem Porto ha-Kohen which seemed to be significant for my subject, from MS Jerusalem Heb. 3904 8°, fos. 143b–146b.

A voice of trouble comes from the holy community of Candia; there is dispute among the sages concerning edicts issued by the majority of the community . . . And anger has gone out . . . concerning one detail[168] of the edicts, paragraph number 14, in which it is said that 'under a fine of one hundred Venetian ducats and banishment for three years, the excellent rabbis cannot excommunicate any man, for whatever reason, unless they first approach the *connestabile*,[169] so that he will consult his advisors,[170] and only then the rabbis may rule upon that man and declare him to be banned and criminal, in accordance with the agreements of Our Excellent Government [i.e. *the Venetian ruler*].[171] And now we find that there are Rabbinic scholars who object to this section, arguing that each sage may excommunicate on his own, even without the consent of the community and without the knowledge of the *connestabile* and his advisers . . . I am disturbed because, even if they used to do so from ancient times, as it would appear from the language of the edict[172] . . . it is not to be considered an 'ancient custom' [*and therefore considered as valid as falling under customary law*], nor is it in accordance with the Torah and the Sages, for the laws of excommunication are capital matters, and more stringent even than the laws of corporal punishment . . . And what have the *connestabile* and his advisors to do with such laws of bans? . . . Is it possible that they should overrule the scholar, to withhold permission to the Masters of the Law to curse and to excommunicate and to promulgate various restrictions and edicts to prevent people from doing wrong? For this is to place a muzzle on the mouths of the sages and chains on their cheeks[173] and to uproot the soil of the Torah—not for them shall be the rule of redemption. Is it possible and can it be imagined by any intelligent person that the teachers and rulers of what is forbidden and prohibited not be allowed to move without the permission of those reed-cutters? . . . And if you fear that perhaps the Torah makes them [*the rabbis*] quick-tempered [i.e. *if you think the rabbis may act hastily out of anger*][174] . . . Then do not allow them to ban or to excommunicate unless all the ordained rabbis of the community gather together, and take a decision by the majority,

[168] i.e. decision.

[169] i.e. the head of the community.

[170] i.e. his advisers.

[171] In a non-Jewish ordinance, i.e. one from the government.

[172] The wording of the edict—'as registered in sect. 28 [or 58], and as established by His Excellency the Inquisitor in 1515 and by His Excellency the Governor in 1545'—indicates that it had been approved by the Inquisitor sixty years earlier, and by the authorities thirty years before. The reference to the inquisitor clearly reflects the closeness of the ties between the officials of the church and those of the government concerning the subject of the ban. The subject itself is deserving of fundamental definition, for which this is not the proper place. See also below, Ch. 5, n. 29.

[173] i.e. one places an obstacle before them. Based upon a phrase used in Ezek. 38: 4.

[174] The figure of speech is taken from Babylonian Talmud, Ta'anit 4a.

or by two-thirds of them. But there shall not be included among them men who are not ordained or properly trained. Thus, the law will emerge clearly out of the discussion among them.

Even R. Abraham Menaḥem Porto ha-Kohen did not entirely reject the possibility that 'the Torah makes them quick-tempered', at least in so far as those rabbis who had shown a tendency to make exaggerated use of the ban were concerned. In such cases, he would agree that some form of control be exercised over them; nevertheless, in his opinion, the agreement of two-thirds of all the rabbis in a given place was sufficient guarantee against all possible contingencies.[175]

An ordinance issued in Ferrara in 1554, which forbade any rabbi from imposing a ban without the agreement of the community rabbi, succeeded in reducing somewhat the tension between the rabbis and the communal leaders. As we shall see, this ordinance, which was only in effect in those communities where a communal rabbi had in fact been appointed, indicated the strengthening of the internal structure of community government more than it did that of the status of the rabbi. In those communities in which there was no communal rabbi, the Ferrara ordinance prevented only rabbis from other cities imposing their decisions elsewhere. In such cases, issues relating to excommunication were left to the dynamics of confrontation between the local rabbis and the lay leaders of their communities. In any event, the establishment of the community organization led to a clear and decisive involvement of the community in the use of the weapon of excommunication. As a result, the power of the ban became progressively weakened as a means of imposing personal authority, and increasingly became a means of enforcing the authority of communal institutions.

As opposed to the tendency to restrict rabbinic prerogatives in those areas in which such restrictions aided the orderly conduct of communal life, there are no indications of any attempt to curtail the rights of those who had acquired ordination in the publicly accepted manner. These rights elevated ordained individuals to an honourable status within Jewish society, well above that of the general populace.[176]

175 Cf. the objections of R. Moses Basola to the ordinances of Ferrara from 1554, below, Ch. 3, Sect. 5.

176 Even within the Christian camp, the status of the ordained rabbi was seen as one of *dignitas*. See e.g. how at the end of the 16th century a Christian inquisitor addresses

Generally speaking, the place of honour in the synagogue[177] and in other social or religious gatherings[178] was reserved for the ordained rabbis. Rabbis were considered especially trustworthy in community matters.[179] They also received presents—particularly during the three festivals[180]—but also on other occasions. Thus, for example, R. Mordecai Dato reports that, on the occasion of his visit to Ferrara, he gave a 'present to the excellent rabbi'.[181] Rabbis were freed from certain restrictions imposed upon the rest of the community, such as sumptuary laws. Thus, in the *pragmatica* of the community of Mantua from the year 1599, we read that 'the excellent ordained rabbis, by the agreement of the Committee, are allowed to dress as they please, as are the honourable physicians'.[182] The sumptuary laws of Venice from 1545 stated that the rabbis were not included within the restricted number of guests one was allowed to invite to a wedding, and that the rabbi who blessed the new mother on her first visit to the synagogue following childbirth was also entitled to a special gift of drink (or perhaps a 'tip').[183]

The wives of the rabbis also enjoyed a special status. Evidence

in all simplicity a Jewish Rabbi as 'an habet dignitatem Rabbini' (C. Boccato, 'Un processo contro ebrei di Verona alla fine del Cinquecento', *RMI* 40 (1974), 358). On the *dignitas* of the doctors, see below, Sect. 5. See also above, Ch. 1, Pt. 2.

177 Discussed at greater length in Ch. 3, Sect. 10.

178 See immediately below.

179 e.g. in the ordinances of the community of Ferrara assisting those communities expelled from the Papal states, there are added to those appointed over the collection of money 'the *parnas* who cares for that office and three Masters of Torah' (I. Sonne (ed.), *Mi-Pavlo ha-Revi'i 'ad Pius ha-Ḥamishi*, 224). Compare below, in Ch. 3, how this matter passed on to the rabbi who was appointed from the community.

180 See Sonne, 'Basic Premisses', 180.

181 See I. Elbogen, 'Una nota di spese sel secolo XVI', *RI* 3 (1906), 161. Similarly, it was decided in the Community Council in Padua to use a certain sum that had been collected by it—half of which was 'the gift to the *Ga'on* R. Samuel J. Katzenellenbogen in Venice, and the other half will be divided by the appointed ones, part of it to two virgins from our community known to them, and part for flour for Passover for the poor people of our community, and to repair the windows of the great Synagogue'. See 'Pinkas ha-Medinah be-Padua', fo. 71b.

182 The *pragmatica* was printed on a separate page, one copy of which (possibly the only one) has been preserved in the communal archive in Mantua; a microfilm exists in IMHM, no. HM 207. Note the comparison of the rabbi's status with 'the level of physicians'. See also below, Ch. 3 n. 72, and n. 358. I have not at present found that the ordained rabbis in Italy wore special garments unique to their status, as was the practice of other places; see Breuer, 'Ashkenazic Ordination', 42.

183 'Compozione'; see Sonne, 'Basic Premisses', 159; cf. Yiẓḥak min ha-Levi'im, *Medabber Tahapukhot* (1912), 179.

of this appears in a discussion by R. Judah Minz of a case in which the virginity of a bride was questioned.[184]

It transpired that my distinguished relative Rabbi Kaplan agreed to accept testimony from the honourable women, the wives of the colleagues ordained and licensed to rule, of whose wives it is said that 'the wife of a Colleague is considered like a Colleague'.[185] The custom here in the holy community of Padua is to take them alongside the other honourable women to show them the blood of virginity; and those women who testified to the blood of virginity of Mrs Yutlan . . . were, first, the Rabbanit[186] Mrs Olke, wife of Rabbi Zangwill, and second, the Rabbanit Mrs Mingeit, the widow of Rabbi Anshel Segal, of blessed memory.[187]

The example of the rabbi who blessed a woman after childbirth is but one of the ways in which sacral expression was given to the image of the rabbi in Italy. R. Leone Modena reports in his autobiography that his fiancée asked before her death 'that they call a rabbi for her to confess—and he came and she recited Confession',[188] and how, when he himself had a feeling of impending death, he recited confession 'before ten people, three of them being rabbis.'[189] He also told how he recounted a certain dream to R. Solomon Sforno, 'and he interpreted it, that in the future my wife would give birth to a daughter, and I would name her after my mother'.[190] At times, the rabbis' answers to their interlocutors contained magical elements, indicating the rabbis' sacral understanding of their own role within society. Thus, for example, a rabbi in Viadana[191] told a woman who had difficulty in childbirth 'that a Torah scroll should be brought and held to

184 J. Minz, *Teshuvot*, sect. 6. 185 Shavu'ot 30b; 'Avodah Zarah 39a.

186 This is further evidence of the fact that the term *rabannit* (wife of a rabbi) naturally went together with the title *Morenu ha-Rav*, at least in Ashkenazic circles in Italy. Compare, many years later, the statement of ownership at the beginning of MS Parma 653 (which includes the prayer book for the entire year): 'Tuesday, 4th day of the month of Av, [5311/1551], I purchased this prayer [book] from the Rabbanit the widow of Rabbi Elijah Ḥalfan . . .' Among the Ashkenazim, the title was in use for many generations prior to the period under discussion here.

187 See also Ch. 3, Sect. 10, on the special status enjoyed by the wife of the communally appointed rabbi.

188 L. Modena, *Ḥayyei Yehudah*, 45. 189 Ibid. 111.

190 Ibid. 53. He likewise asked R. Abraham of Rovigo whether his second marriage would be successful, and he was told that he would not be successful with her in business matters, and that if he married her she ought to change her name—and she therefore changed her name to Diana (ibid. 37).

191 A small town near Mantua.

her breast, and she would be saved from her travail'—a suggestion which aroused the fierce opposition of Rabbi Azriel Diena.[192] To this must be added the central role of the rabbis in issues related to bans and oaths, as already noted.[193]

This image was enhanced by the fact that some of these rabbis engaged in astrology, perhaps out of the desire for total knowledge in accordance with the best medieval tradition, the wish to fulfil the requests of their contemporaries,[194] or the wish to make use of this skill as an additional source of income. The most talented even offered their services to rulers as fortune-tellers. R. Bonet de Lattes worked in the service of the Pope at the end of the fifteenth century;[195] R. Kalonymos b. David Kalonymos was in the service of the Duke of Bari;[196] R. Abba Mari Ḥalfan, father of the well-known R. Elijah Ḥalfan,[197] similarly interested himself in these sciences, as may be seen from a list of his books which has been preserved.[198]

In the context of this sacral image of the rabbi, it is worth noting the constant demand of the rabbis to displace the members of the priestly tribe (*kohanim*), traditionally called up first to the public reading of the Law in the synagogue. In the middle of the sixteenth century, R. Jacob Israel b. Raphael Finzi wrote that 'by law a Talmudic sage ought to precede an ignorant *kohen*'.[199] Basing his decision upon a long list of important authorities from Maimonides down to R. Asher, he stated:

How much more so in our generation, when there are *kohanim* who cannot even read, these should not be called up before an ordained

[192] See S. Assaf, 'The Responsa of R. Azriel Diena' (Heb.), *KS* 14 (1937–8), 543.

[193] Above, Ch. 2, Sect. 4.

[194] For the interest of contemporaries in matters of astrology and magic see e.g. E. Garin, *Medioevo e Rinascimento* (Bari, 1966), 150–91.

[195] D. Goldschmidt, 'Boneto de Lattes e i suoi scritti latini e italiani', in *Scritti in memoria di Enzo Sereni* (Jerusalem, 1970), 88–94.

[196] See MS Parma 336, which is a collection of selections on astrological subjects, partially from R. David, the father of R. Kalonymos, and of his brother R. Ḥayyim. At the end of the manuscript, there is a prediction of the future for the 1490s, similar in form to that of the horoscopes of R. Bonet de Lattes, described by Goldschmidt in his article, 'Bonet de Lattes'. It ought to be noted that this R. Kalonymos understands astrology as 'among the other speculative and talmudic wisdoms' (MS Parma 336, 77a), that is, as part of a unity in which astrology is included in an organic way.

[197] The above MS, fos. 44–7, gives 'the reasons for the commandments from the tables of Alfonso, attributed by R. Kalonymos himself to 'R. Abba Mari, the father of my son-in-law R. Elijah Ḥalfan'.

[198] See below, Ch. 6, n. 25.

[199] 'Teshuvot R. Ya'akov Yisrael Finzi', sect. 5. The responsum is cited in full in the Hebrew edition of this book, Document 1, 209–12.

scholar . . . And to the objection that today there is no real ordination and no such thing as a real scholar (*talmid-ḥakham*),[200] I would reply that we are the agents of our forefathers,[201] and that Jephthah in his generation was as worthy as Samuel in his. And as in this generation there are wise people who know the Torah, they ought to be granted the honour of being called to the Torah prior to these ignorant *kohanim*, for the sages and priests of this generation are not inferior to the sages and priests in the time of the Talmud . . .

Although this responsum related to a specific case, the author gave it a programmatic tone by concealing any details which would enable us to identify the actual case which prompted his reply, publishing his ruling in his commentary on the Prayer Book among the laws pertaining to the public reading of the Torah.[202]

Implicit in R. Jacob Israel Finzi's responsum is a clear sense of the strivings of the rabbis of this period to alter ancient, well-established custom and to receive the prerogative of being called to the Torah even prior to the *kohanim*.[203] This wish led to great controversy within the community, clear evidence of which is reflected in an incident which occurred in Urbino in 1571, and was subsequently discussed among the rabbis of that generation.[204] In contrast to R. Jeḥiel Trabot, who addressed the members of his community with the request that they take care not to violate the respect due to the *kohen*, R. Isaac Finzi stated that 'it is permitted and desirable and required' to call up the rabbi before the *kohen*, who 'does not know how to read, so how can he recite the blessing over the Torah and read; to the contrary, it is forbidden to do so, for he is reciting a blessing for naught; moreover, by law a scholar who is not a *kohen* has priority over a *kohen* who is not a scholar'.

200 Note: 'there is neither ordination nor any Rabbinic sage'; i.e. put simply; ordained rabbi = talmid ḥakham.

201 Based upon Yoma 19a and Kiddushin 23b.

202 See J. I. Finzi, 'Makkabi: Perush ha-Tefillot ve-Ṭa'amei ha-Dinim', MS Cambridge Add. 512 (IMHM 16805), 240b–244a. There are certain changes and additions in the ruling found in the 'Perush ha-Tefillot', as compared with the ruling in his responsa.

203 Cf. the commentary of R. Obadiah of Bertinoro to Mishnah, Gittin 5: 3. See, on the other hand, Zedekiah b. Abraham Anav, *Shibbolei ha-Leket ha-Shalem*, sect. 32: S. Buber edn. (Vilna, 1886), 16, 1; S. Mirsky edn. (New York, 1966) 230. See also below, Ch. 3, n. 302.

204 J. Boksenboim (ed.), *Teshuvot Matanot Ba-adam* (Tel Aviv, 1983), sect. 1 (*Teshuvot R. Isaac Finzi*) and sect. 2 (*Teshuvot R. Yeḥiel Trabot*).

The analogy drawn between the dignity inherent in knowledge of the Law and that derived from membership in the 'priesthood' is clearly present in other rabbinic works of that generation. We may therefore conclude with reasonable certainty that there was a definite tendency to bring this notion to the attention of the community. For example, R. Obadiah Sforno saw in the symbolism associated with the Temple and its vessels a clear parallel between the tasks of the high priest in relation to those of the other priests and that of the scholars as compared to the people.[205] Similarly, R. Judah Moscato interpreted the verse, 'and you shall be for me a people of priests and a holy nation', (Exod. 19: 6) by stating ' "a kingdom of priests"—that is to say, a kingdom of sages, "for the mouth of the priest shall guard knowledge, and they shall seek teaching from his lips" (Mal. 2: 7)'.[206] It is possible that this particular understanding of the rabbi's function was influenced by commonly held views in the neighbouring Catholic world.[207] In any event, this sacral-clerical dimension added force to the widespread trend towards raising the rabbi above the rest of the community.

Despite their aggressive demand, the rabbis did not succeed in altering the ancient Rabbinic practice by having themselves called to the Torah before the *kohanim*. They were equally unsuccessful in preserving their special privilege of exemption from taxes. This privilege had a long and rich tradition in rabbinic literature,[208] in a sense similar to the parallel privileges of doctors within Christian society.[209] Already in 1460, the Jews of Sicily attempted to obtain an exemption from royal taxes for those rabbis defined as *magistri scolarium* on the argument that this was fitting according to Mosaic law as well as according to inveterate custom (*tam per legem mosaycam quam per continuam observanciam*).[210]

205 See principally *Kavvanot ha-Torah*, 89–90.

206 J. Moscato, *Nefuẓot Yehudah* (Venice, 1589), Sermon 33, 148a. Compare his comments concerning the *rosh-yeshivah* and the *yeshivah*, above, Ch. 1, Sect. 1.

207 See the comments of R. Mordecai Dato cited above, Sect. 1, n. 28, and see also above, Sect. 4.

208 See S. Shilo, *Dina de-Malkhuta Dina* (Jerusalem, 1975), 30–4, 252–7, the bibliography listed there, and the note appended.

209 On these privileges in Italy, see A. Pertile, *Storia del diritto italiano dalla caduta dell'Impero Romano alla Codificazione*, *II* (Bologna, 1968), Pt. 2, 357. We shall return to this point immediately.

210 i.e. both according to Mosaic Law and to the custom found in the tradition. See M. Gaudioso, *La comunità ebraica di Catania nei secoli XIV e XV* (Catania, 1974), 106, 118.

R. Obadiah Sforno still thought that a scholar should be exempted from paying taxes:

Even if he is very wealthy and successful in business, so long as a scholar devotes most of his time to Torah, his business occupation is temporary as compared with his involvement in study, which is considered his principal occupation, so that he belongs to the class of 'all his holy ones in your hands' [cf. *Deut. 33: 3*][211] . . . Who would dare to argue[212] against the Law of our God, to tax people who are His and holy, thus bringing guilt upon the people? Heaven forfend that there should be such a thing in Israel![213]

The sharp wording of this responsum is clear evidence that the right of scholars to this privilege was being questioned at the time of this author.[214] It seems likely that the considerable burden imposed upon Jews by the ruling authorities, together with the extensive involvement of ordained rabbis in highly profitable businesses, particularly banking, ultimately decided the issue in favour of abolition of the privilege claimed by the rabbis. A certain degree of tension between the rabbis' arguments and the needs of the community accompanied this process, and thus found expression in some of the forms of taxation, such as the temporary arrangement made in Mantua in 1572 to assist those who had been expelled from Pesaro.[215]

The strength of the rabbis' argument for tax exemption, even during the second half of the sixteenth century, may be inferred from the responsa of some scholars when the community of Bologna decided to demand taxes from four teachers, who had

[211] See Babylonian Talmud, Baba Batra 8a.

[212] i.e. one who wishes to strengthen his opinion—a word-play based upon Genesis 27: 33.

[213] The responsum was published in full by E. Finkel, *R. Obadja Sforno als Exeghet* (Breslau, 1896), pp. x–xi.

[214] That is to say, long before the end of the 16th cent. Cf. M. A. Shulvass, *The Jews in the World of the Renaissance* (Leiden and Chicago, 1973), 72, 96–7.

[215] The Holy Congregation (i.e. the merchants) are to pay a quarter, the bankers two-thirds, 'and the class of the rabbis, the remainder'. See Sonne, *Mi-Pavlo*, 213; S. Simonsohn, 'The Organization of Jewish Autonomous Rule in Mantua, 1511–1630' (Heb.), *Ẓion*, 21 (1956), 154. See also 'Pinkas Verona' ii, fo. 80a, for the decision concerning payment of 'the extraordinary taxes' in 1569: 'and R. Ephraim and Il, Yoez, will pay a third of the above, according to the sum imposed upon one couple'. See the ordinances of Forli from 1418: 'and no one shall be exempt . . . either the Colleagues or any man apart from those who receive charity'; that is to say, there was logical reason for thinking that the Colleagues were exempt, and against this reasoning their obligation to participate in payments is stressed.

previously been exempt.[216] As we have said, this argument was not sustained, and the communities required the rabbis to pay taxes like other members of the community. Not even a hint of a rabbinical exemption may be found in the communal registers, where one finds rabbis assessed like everyone else.[217]

On the other hand, there is a tendency to exempt them from paying taxes when they are appointed to communal office and their income comes from the communal coffers. This, however, does not seem a consequence of their being considered as scholars, but of their status as public, communal employees. This exemption was no more than a kind of hidden income, granted to other officials as well, and did not apply to the commercial profits of the rabbis.[218]

5. Ordination and the Doctorate

In a certain sense, the institution of rabbinic ordination developed in a manner parallel to that of the doctorate. We cannot survey here the long tradition relating to the institution of the doctorate from the beginning of the European universities.[219] It is sufficient for our purposes to recall certain essential features of the crystallization of the institution during the period under discussion. As is well known, the procedure by which one received the title of doctor was approximately as follows: after the academic doctoral committee, to whom the university had turned, had favourably recommended a particular candidate, the title was formally awarded in a special ceremony, proclaiming the recipient's

[216] See on this point the responsa given in full in the Hebrew edition of this book, Documents 13, 14, pp. 229–34.

[217] e.g. in an assessment from the Mantua community from 1571 (File No. 1, Document 32), R. Joshua Ḥay, R. Eleazar Ḥazan of Fano and R. Solomon Norzi are listed among those paying. In another list (File No. 1, Document 62) R. Kalonymos Noveira, R. Aharon and his son, R. Ephraim, and other sages are listed. In a list from 1581, there appear too R. Judah Moscato and R. Judah Provenzali.

[218] See the rabbinic contract of R. Abraham Menahem ha-Kohen Porto in Verona—Sonne, 'Basic Premisses', 170. It is thus also possible to explain why R. Samuel Romilli is not taxed in the later list, mentioned in the previous note, while on the other hand he does appear among those who pay in the list which preceded the last one.

[219] See Friedrich Karl von Savigny, *Geschichte des römischen Rechts in Mittelalter* (Heidelberg, 1826–31), Pt. 3, Ch. 7; Pertile, *Storia del diritto italiano*, 28. See also H. Rashdall, *The Universities of Europe in the Middle Ages* (London, 1936; repr. 1951), i. 224–33, and index, s.v. 'graduation'.

right to be called 'doctor' and to enjoy the privileges pertaining to his new status. This proclamation was issued by the chancellor of the university, or by some other functionary entitled to do so.[220] In some cases, a written document containing the text of the proclamation was then given to the new doctor.[221] The principal components of the diploma did not change substantially over the course of time[222] and, at least from the fourteenth century onwards, they included six main elements: (1) an introduction—including general phrases in praise of wisdom, as well as underlining the right of those who labour in the pursuit of wisdom to receive the title of doctor as a just reward for their labours; (2) the presentation of the candidate and the statement that he is indeed worthy of receiving the title. This section included a description of the candidate's scholastic attainments, his virtuous qualities, his noble lineage, etc., as well as a description of the formal procedures by which these attainments came to be ratified. Such procedures included consultation of the university with a collegium of prominent scholars who, after having investigated the candidate, examined him in public or private on a number of specific topics, in order to confirm his worthiness of joining the society of doctors; (3) the proclamation of the candidate as a doctor by the authorized representatives of the university; (4) the enumeration of the authority and privileges of the new doctor; (5) an attestation that those objects which served as symbols of his status (*insignia*)—i.e. the book, the cap, and the ring—had been conveyed upon the new doctor; (6) finally, the bestowal of the kiss of friendship and peace.

[220] *Cancellarius*, *vicarius*, etc.

[221] The earliest preserved ordination (doctoral) document seems to be one from 1276. See M. Roberti, *Storia del diritto italiano* (Milan, 1942), 244.

[222] See various versions in Savigny, *Geschichte der römischen Rechts*. Comparison of the doctorate awarded in Siena in 1409 with that granted to R. Obadiah Sforno in Ferrara in 1501 (see Document 11 in the Hebrew edition of this book, pp. 226–7), clearly proves that in practice they used formulas taken from a formularium, with minor changes. For a stereotyped formula of this sort, see *Formularium Instrumentorum . . . Petri Dominici de Mussis . . .* (Venice, 1530). fos. 55v–57. The formula used in the doctorate was not substantially altered even when it was granted to a Jew, except that in his case there were added words of encouragement for him to convert to Christianity, as well as certain restrictions upon the doctoral privileges; see V. Colorni, 'Sull'ammissibilità degli ebrei alla laurea anteriormente al secolo XIX', *Scritti in onore di Riccardo Bachi*, *RMI* 16 (1950), 202–16 and App. 2, n. 3. See also: H. Friedenwald, *The Jews and Medicine* (Baltimore, 1944; 2nd ptg. New York, 1967), 258–62, the version printed there by Friedenwald was reprinted in F. Secret, 'Juifs et Marranes au Miroir de Trois Médecins de la Renaissance', *REJ* 130 (1971), 190–1.

Our sources relating to the procedure for ordaining rabbis convey the clear impression that the procedure resembled the granting of the doctorate, save for the formal and ceremonial aspect; namely, the appeal to a committee of examiners and the examination by it, and the bestowal upon the scholar of special objects symbolizing his new status. While not many ordination diplomas have survived from our period,[223] the considerable similarity between these documents, as well as the resemblance between their structure and that of the doctoral diplomas,[224] leave no doubt that there was indeed a formal relationship between the rabbinical ordination and the doctoral diploma (examples of these two kinds of document are given in Appendix 1). The ordination documents likewise contain introductory formulas in praise of wisdom, which honours those who hold it; confirmation that the ordained rabbi is worthy of the title, thanks to his attainments in learning and his personal qualities;[225] a solemn proclamation of the rabbinic title; and details of the authority granted to him, and the privileges to which he is entitled in his new status. All these elements are present in the rabbinical diploma of ordination, often in an order which is not essentially different from that found in the doctoral diplomas. There are even certain similar expressions, which seem to serve as a substitute for the formal granting of *insignia* to the doctor:[226]

[223] See the text of the ordination granted by R. Israel Isserlin, *Leket Yosher*, ed. J. Freimann, Pt. 2, p. 38; the ordination of R. Benjamin of Montalcino, *Divrei Rivot*, pp. 13–14; that of R. Abtalyon b. Solomon, at the beginning of *Sefer Palgei Mayim* (Venice, 1605), 3a; the ordinations issued by R. Leone Modena (including one issued by R. Menahem Azariah da Fano) at the end of *Teshuvot Ziknei Yehudah*. See also A. Marx, 'R. Joseph d'Arles as Teacher and Head of an Academy in Siena' (Heb.), *Louis Ginzberg Jubilee Volume* (New York, 1946), p. 294, and Documents 5–10 in the Hebrew edition of this book, pp. 217–25. Goitein's remarks, *Sidrei Ḥinukh*, 191–2, concerning the rarity of this type of document during the period of the *genizah*, applies as well to the period under discussion here.

[224] For a comparison of the ordination granted by R. Isaac de Lattes with a typical doctoral degree, see Document 12 in the Hebrew edition of this book, pp. 227–8.

[225] Cf. above, Sect. 3. The idea of granting privileges as compensation for the effort invested by the ordained in order to ascend the scale of wisdom deserves to be compared with the similar idea, found already in the first *Privilegium Scholasticum*, published by Friedrich I in 1158. See P. Kibre, *Scholarly Privileges in the Middle Ages: The Rights, Privileges and Immunities of Scholars and Universities at Bologna, Padua, Paris and Oxford* (London, 1961), 10 ff.

[226] From the ordination granted by R. Isaac de Lattes to R. Samuel Kazani, 'Teshuvot R. Yiẓḥak mi-Lattes', MS Vienna—National Library 80 (IMHM 1303), fo. 128; published in the Hebrew edition of this book, Document 8, p. 222; cf. Documents 6 and 12, pp. 220, 227–8. These expressions were also based upon an internal Jewish tradition; see Ben-Sasson, *A History of the Jewish People* (Cambridge, Mass., 1976), 598.

and there shall be placed in your hands the garments of the rabbis:[227] a stick and a whip with which to beat those deserving of it by the needs of the hour; a *shofar* with which to excommunicate every man who rebels against your ordinances . . . a shoe with which to perform *ḥaliẓah*; and a quill with which to correct divorces and to issue judgement and to rule in marital issues, for you are expert in their nature.

It is clear that the two types of document differ in their details: the ordination diplomas by their nature contain expressions of the characteristic world-view of Judaism and its specific problematics. For example, one may sometimes detect a certain tension in the references to the newly ordained rabbi's attainments in the field of general secular learning, reflecting the differences of opinion among the sages concerning the value and role of 'external wisdom'.[228] Likewise, the fact that a given candidate's knowledge of Kabbalah is mentioned in an ordination diploma written by R. David son of Messer Leon[229] is a clear indication of that scholar's attitude to these studies. The detailing of the prerogatives granted to the ordained scholar is typical of the Jewish tradition—'he shall teach and he shall judge', etc. To these were added, with emphasis, the rabbi's right to excommunicate, a prerogative which, as we have noted already,[230] was of paramount importance in determining his role and authority in communal leadership.

Far greater emphasis than in the doctorate was placed upon the proclamation that the ordained scholar may bear the title, 'our illustrious teacher, the Master, Rabbi' (*Ma'alat Morenu ha-Rav Rabbi*), and the obligation incumbent upon the community to address him as such and to call him to the public reading of the Torah in the synagogue by this title. As we have already noted,[231] this was the primary expression in everyday life of the change in the social status of the ordained scholar; hence the importance of this emphasis. At times, the ordination diploma also contained details of the ceremonial expressions of honour to which the ordained scholar was entitled by virtue of his new

227 The phrase is borrowed from Babylonian Talmud, Sanhedrin 7b.

228 See Messer Leon, *Kevod Ḥakhamim*, p. 65; *Teshuvot Maharda"kh*, Ch. 20, Sect. 10; L. Modena, *Teshuvot Ziknei Yehudah*, 187, 188, 190, 191; and cf. also Documents 5 and n. 34, and Document 8 in the Hebrew edition of this book, p. 222; and also R. Jacob Israel Finzi's words cited in Document 3, pp. 215–16. See also below, Ch. 6, Sect. 1.

229 See Document 5, 217–19, in the Hebrew edition of this book.

230 See above, Sect. 4.

231 See above, Sect. 1.

title, such as to sit among the sages at every gathering and meeting,[232] 'to teach Torah in the *yeshivah*',[233] and to preach in public.[234] At times, the diploma even makes express mention of his right to ordain other rabbis.[235] This should be seen as parallel to the privilege granted to the doctor to license other doctors (*privilegium doctorandi*). It would follow from this that the statement by R. Isaac Abrabanel (1437–1508) that the practice of ordination is an indication of Christian influence on Judaism, 'who were jealous of the nations who make doctors, so they do the same',[236] was not entirely unwarranted.

We have already noted that the special status of the ordained scholar elevated him above the 'masses of the people'. One might then safely say that it was analogous to the social elevation of office holders in Christian society[237] or that accepted in the world of the universities, in which the doctorate conferred upon one 'nobility and dignity'.[238] How much more so was this the case until the period under discussion, when university study was primarily the privilege of a social élite. The status conveyed by university study was added to that of noble lineage, particularly in that it prepared one to fulfil various positions involving leadership and administration.[239] In fact, it is well known that

232 See Document 8 in the Hebrew edition of this book, and compare Document 4, pp. 222, 216–17.

233 See ibid. Document 6. The meaning of the phrase is evidently that one is to rise to the level of a 'text-repeater' in the yeshivah (see above, Ch. 1); cf. Israel Isserlein, *Terumat ha-Deshen* (Venice, 1519), sec. 342. There is no doubt that this is parallel to the privilege granted to the doctor to lecture (*legendi*) and to comment (*glosandi*), etc.

234 See the Hebrew edition of this book, Document 6, pp. 220–1. As we shall see below in Ch. 6, Sect. 4, those who were not ordained might also preach in public. Nevertheless, this is a further indication that the ordained rabbis were given preference as preachers (see ibid. and cf. Breuer's remarks in 'Ashkenazic Ordination', p. 43 and n. 199). See also below, Ch. 3, Sect. 8, for how, towards the end of the 16th cent., the communally appointed rabbis demanded preference over all others regarding this subject.

235 See the Hebrew edition of this book, Document 6, pp. 220–1.

236 Isaac Abrabanel, *Naḥalat Avot*, beginning of Ch. 6.

237 See A. Berger, *Dictionary of Roman Law* (Philadelphia, 1953), s.v. 'dignitas'.

238 In the language of the gloss, 'doctoratus tribuit nobilitatem' [the doctorate conveys nobility]; see A. Visconti, *La storia dell'Università di Ferrara*, (Bologna, 1950), i. 10; or, in the words of Bartolus, 'doctoratus . . . est dignitas'. This also explains the reason for the opposition of Christian jurists to elevating Jews to the status of doctors; see Colorni, 'Sull' ammissibilità degli ebrei', and also Carpi, 'R. Judah Messer Leon', 286–90.

239 See the analysis in J. Verger, 'Le Rôle social de l'Université d'Avignon au XVe Siècle', *BHR*, 33 (1971), 489–504, esp. 492–503. Cf. also Burckhardt, *Civilisation of the Renaissance*, 360, and what I have written above, Sect. 5.

the doctors were granted rights and privileges[240] which were expressed in specific benefits and ceremonial gestures.[241] The parallel to these things in the privileges granted to ordained rabbis conveys a clear feeling of the concrete dimension thereby added to the parallel between the rabbis and the doctors.

6. The Decline in the Prestige of Ordination

In the case of both the doctorate and rabbinic ordination, edicts and rules were introduced to prevent the granting of the title to those who were unworthy of it. In the university context, for example, we may recall that it was decreed in the theological faculties at Bologna and Padua in the fifteenth century that the degree of doctor would not be granted to anyone who had not yet reached the age of 30, having devoted at least eight years to the study of philosophy and an equal number to the study of

[240] See *Dictionnaire du Droit Canonique*, iv (Paris, 1949), cols. 1330–1, s.v. *docteur*; see also Kibre, *Scholarly Privileges*; Rashdall, *The Universities*, index, s.v. privileges.

[241] Particular importance was attached to the status of physicians and jurists, who throughout the 15th cent. were promoted to the status of noblemen, wore special clothes, and rode a horse given them by the commune, which also provided a special servant. For example, the doctors were granted special status on ceremonial occasions. Thus, the chronicler describes the reception of Emperor Fredrick III in Ferrara in 1452: 'andoli inanti... messer Borso marchexe da Este e tuti li altri signori, et andoli etiam inanti il vescovo Francesco di Ferara con tuta la chierexia e multi doctori ferrarexi' (i.e. there went out to greet him ... Messer Borso, the Marchese of Este and all the other *Signori*, and Bishop Francesco of Ferrara went out to greet him, together with all the priesthood and many doctors from Ferrara). Quoted from *Diario Ferrarese dall'anno 1490 sino al 1502, di autori incerti, a cura di Giuseppe Pardi* [*Rerum italicarum Scriptores. Raccolta delli storici italiani ... ordinata de L. A. Muratori*, vol. xxiv, Part 7 (Bologna, 1928), 34. See also I. Origo, *The Merchant of Prato* (London, 1957), 294. The fact of the physician's special status gives an added dimension to the tendency, throughout the period under discussion, for rabbis to gravitate particularly towards the medical profession; their qualification to judge and to rule gave them the status of physicians and judges at one and the same time. They attained the apex of social ascent when the profession of physician was given a status of knighthood, which Jews only rarely received. This is recorded very proudly in the memorial books of the members of their families. See V. Colorni, 'Note per la biografia di alcuni dotti ebrei vissuti a Mantova nel secolo XV', *Annuario di studi ebraici*, i (1934), 176–7; Carpi, op. cit. One must not forget that not everyone could aspire to medical studies, to the extent that, according to one testimony, only the sons of the wealthy or the sons of physicians could afford such a career—see Origo, *The Merchant of Prato*, 300. I do not know from where Falk derives the conclusion that 'this kind of study was available practically free'! Cf. J. Falk, 'R. Obadiah Sforno, The Humanistic Commentator' (Heb.), *Sefer Zikaron le-zekher David Niger* (Jerusalem, 1959), 280.

theology.[242] Only after the candidate had met these conditions was he permitted even to be examined towards the granting of the doctoral degree. During this period, a significant decline occurred in the prestige attached to the doctorate, far greater than that of ordination. Among the reasons for this decline were probably the fact that individuals were being elevated to the status of doctor by a non-academic authority, such as the Emperor or the Pope, for reasons of social prestige alone, without any prior consultation with any academic body.[243] In addition, the growth in the number of universities[244] combined with the new emphasis upon the national character of the doctorate under the influence of the Reformation, as against the universal character which it had held during the preceding period, tended to cheapen the value of the doctorate.[245] During the second half of the sixteenth century, there were increasingly frequent complaints in Italy that the title of doctor provided no guarantee of the erudition of the bearer of the title, that the ranks of doctors had become filled with unqualified people, that the physicians knew nothing of their own profession, etc.[246] There were complaints that doctors were abusing their status, that they had become bureaucrats rather than using their knowledge for the benefit of society, and that farmers and butchers sent their sons to the university in order to acquire a degree which would pave the way for them to acquire status and power.[247]

As we have seen, there were voices among Jews as well complaining about rabbis who were 'improperly' ordained, about the 'sin of the ordained and the ordainers', and the like.[248] It is difficult to know to what extent these complaints, which were articulated in a general way, reflected an actual decline in the level of those ordained. In any event, there is no doubt that the development of the institution of ordination brought about a

[242] See A. Sorbelli, *Storia dell'Università di Bologna*, i. *il medioevo sec. XI–XV* (Bologna, 1940), 139.

[243] Such as the title granted by the emperor to R. Judah Messer Leon; see Carpi, 'R. Judah Messer Leon', 286–9. See also *Diario Ferrarese*, 55, where it is stated that the emperor who granted the title to R. Messer Leon on 21 Feb. 1469, several days earlier visited in Ferrara and granted similar titles to numerous people.

[244] See Pertile, *Storia del diritto italiano*, 36.

[245] See *Dictionnaire du Droit Canonique*, ibid. s.v. docteur'.

[246] See Pertile, *Storia del diritto italiano*.

[247] See Grendler, *The Rejection of Learning*.

[248] See above, Sect. 3, and cf. Breuer, 'Ashkenazic Ordination', 30–1.

certain devaluation of the rabbinic title.[249] True, during this entire period nobody challenged the ordained scholar's right to make use of the title 'Our teacher, the Master' when called to the Torah or anything else pertaining to sacred matters;[250] however, one may detect elsewhere clear expressions of the above-mentioned tendencies. For example, in an ordination diploma granted to R. Benjamin of Montalcino, the only prerogative of authority explicitly mentioned is that allowing him to render decisions in the rather mundane matters of 'the prohibited and the permissible',[251] while other points were mentioned in a general phrase, which primarily stressed the educational image of the rabbi.[252] On the other hand, the ordination granted by R. David son of Messer Leon[253] is striking in its broad enumeration of prerogatives: 'he shall surely teach, and judge, hold accountable and exempt, find innocent or guilty, permit and prohibit, involve himself in matters of divorce and *ḥaliẓah* (i.e. *release from levirate marriage*), ban and excommunicate'. He praised the ordained scholar in great and specific detail, citing his extensive knowledge, his analytic and dialectical ability, his approach to the study of the Law, his influence upon his students, his knowledge of Kabbalah and his ethical qualities. Other details of the ordination diploma also give clear expression to his views: between the lines, one can plainly see that he wished to incorporate among the attributes of the ordained scholar, in addition to the crowns of Torah, those of Kingship and of Priesthood.

It is certainly no accident that even routine expressions

[249] A close examination of ordination diplomas will reveal additional expressions of the different viewpoints and transformations which took place in the valuation of ordination, even on the part of the ordaining rabbis themselves.

[250] Unlike the earlier period, during which there were sages who, despite being ordained, refused to be called to the Torah by the title *Kevod Morenu ha-Rav*; see *Pesakim*, 24a, and compare Breuer, 'Ashkenazic Ordination', 29.

[251] *Divrei Rivot*, 12–14.

[252] 'And grant him the honour of rulership, let him chastise wrongdoers . . . the stick and the whip in his hand, like all the earlier rabbis who ruled the people.' The 'stick and whip' are the 'garments of the rabbinate' already referred to. Cf. the responsum of R. Benjamin Montalcino to R. Judah Messer Leon (*Divrei Rivot*, 5): 'Therefore, if the loyal friend [*this was the expression with which R. Judah Messer Leon concluded his ordinance, and R. Benjamin added the equivalent of quotation marks to the word 'friend' to express his reservations about the term*] . . . wishes that his ordinances be kept, he ought to have introduced them and strengthened them by instructing many disciples from different places and they, if they are able [to do so] in their sermons or through their disciples, will be a reason for all Israel to listen to their voice . . .' See above, n. 51.

[253] See Document 5 in the Hebrew edition of this work, pp. 217–19.

referring to the granting of the crown of kingship and the rod of leadership to the ordained scholar,[254] such as those used by David ben Messer Leon, were still in use in the mid-sixteenth century among the older scholars, although at the end of the century they are no longer as prevalent.[255] Even the expressions of praise for the wisdom of the one ordained become weaker and almost meaningless. On the other hand, other factors, which one would normally expect to be of secondary importance in the granting of ordination—such as the age and honour of the ordained scholar,[256] his holding of a prominent social position,[257] and the like—are raised to central importance. One even begins to find Talmudic discussions in the body of the ordination document, brief because of their location, but significant in that they indicate a certain emptiness which they evidently come to fill.[258]

Towards the second half of the sixteenth century, the term *Ga'on* (Very Excellent) began to appear alongside the title *Morenu ha-Rav* (Our Master, Rabbi), in order to distinguish between an ordinary ordained scholar and an important rabbi. Here, too, one may cite a certain development of an earlier tradition. From the very beginning of the rabbinic period, the title *Ga'on* had signified greater scholarly acumen than did that of *Rav*. In a tradition attested by R. Menahem Meiri,[259] ordained scholars were considered *ge'onim* if they were expert in the entire Talmud, as against ordinary 'Rabbis' (*Rabbanim*), who were expert in only four of its six 'orders',[260] and 'learned men' (*ḥakhamim*), who were expert in only three.[261] We find in his tradition that '[the Hebrew term] *ga'on* alludes to the sixty tractates of the Talmud, corresponding to the numerical value of the word. Nevertheless,

[254] What could be more natural in this context than to make use of the Talmudic saying, 'Who are the kings?—The rabbis?'

[255] See Documents 6 and 9 in the Hebrew edition of this book, pp. 220–1, 223–4, and cf. all the ordinations which R. Judah Messer Leon granted, and that given by R. Menaḥem Azariah da Fano, at the end of *Teshuvot Ziknei Yehudah*.

[256] See Modena, *Teshuvot Ziknei Yehudah*, 179.

[257] See ibid., 190. Cf. also Yiẓḥak min ha-Levi'im, *Medabber Tahapukhot* (1912), 180–1.

[258] See e.g. the material cited in Documents 9 and 10 in the Hebrew edition of this book, pp. 223–25.

[259] B. Z. ha-Levi Prag (ed.), *Bet ha-Beḥirah 'al Masekhet 'Avot* (Jerusalem, 1964), 52–4.

[260] i.e. *Mo'ed*, *Nashim*, *Nezikin*, *Kodashim*.

[261] i.e. *Mo'ed*, *Nashim*, *Nezikin*.

according to Meiri, he did not receive the title unless he had been ordained by another *Ga'on*, with the agreement of the *yeshivah*, as the *yeshivah* heads in those days were called *ge'onim*.' Even those places in Europe which preserved a wide range of studies and expressed greater independence from the *ge'onim* of Babylonia preserved the title itself.[262] During a certain period, there even seems to have been a continuous tradition of special ordination for the title of *ga'on* preserved in Provence, France, Germany and Italy.[263] However, that tradition was interrupted at a time and under circumstances which are unclear. In Renaissance Italy, this title is no longer granted in any institutional way; however, those bearing it were considered clearly superior to other rabbis.[264] From now on, this title was used to express special respect for a rabbi who was called *Ga'on*,[265] and to present him as one 'noted for his teachings and behaviour'.[266] The restoration of the use of the title *Ga'on* would therefore appear to be an additional indication of the deterioration in the public status of ordination, and of the tension which accompanied the rabbis' demands for status concomitant with their rabbinic titles.[267] In the following chapter, we shall see how this semantic distinction between an ordinary rabbi and a *Ga'on* received concrete expression in the system of communal organization.[268]

The decline in the value of the title 'rabbi' was quite naturally accompanied by a decline in the status of the title 'Colleague' (*Ḥaver*) which, as we have seen, was by its very nature and definition dependent upon the former.[269] This title was no longer

[262] See B. Z. Benedict, 'Towards the History of the Torah Centre in Provence' (Heb.), *Tarbiẓ*, 22 (1951), 86 ff. On the use of the title *Ga'on* after the Gaonic period, see S. Poznanski, *Babylonische Geonim im nach gaonäischen Zeitalter* (Berlin, 1914), 104.

[263] See the tractate of R. Azriel Trabot Zarfati, published by David Kaufmann, 'Liste de rabbins dressée par Azriel Trabotto', *REJ* 4 (1882), 210–12.

[264] See David de Pomis, *Ẓemaḥ David*, fo. 27b: '*ga'on*—[means] rulership and ascendancy'; '. . . dominium et superbia, signoria. E superbia si pone anco per la significatione di eccellentissimo, particolarmente nella scienza della legge', and cf. Levita, *Sefer ha-Tishbi*, s.v. *ga'on*, 35: 'and I have heard that they were called this because they were expert in the entire Talmud, which consists of sixty tractates—the numerical value of the word *ga'on* being sixty' (and cf. also the words of Meiri, previously quoted). It is worthy of note that an additional development led to its being custom among Italian Jews to this very day to refer to the ordained rabbis as *eccellentissimo*—i.e. [the rabbi] *ga'on*.

[265] e.g. above, Sect. 4 and n. 181.

[266] See also the responsa of R. Eliezer Ashkenazi. ed. J. Boksenboim, *She'elot u-Teshuvot Mattanot ba-Adam* (Tel Aviv, 1983), 65–6.

[267] On this matter in 15th-century Ashkenaz, see Breuer, 'The Status of the Rabbinate'.

[268] See below, Ch. 3, Sects. 3 and 11.

[269] See above, Sect. 1.

reserved for scholars who 'study Torah all their days',[270] but was instead granted to young people as an incentive in their studies or even as an honorific on their wedding day.[271] Nevertheless, one should not forget that the scholars generally did not forgo their demand that candidates for 'rabbinic ordination' should have held the title *Ḥaver* for many years, until they reach the appropriate age for receiving the title 'our Master, Rabbi' (*Morenu ha-Rav*).[272]

During the latter half of the sixteenth century, a new title appeared, which served as a kind of intermediate level between *ḥaver* and *Morenu ha-Rav*—namely the title *Ḥakham* (learned man), granted to one who had not yet reached the age of 40. This title already seems to have been alluded to in a letter of R. Azriel Diena from the year 1533 or thereabouts concerning a 'rabbinical emissary' who, according to R. Azriel, came to him by means of a ruse, extracting his signature in order to authenticate his accrediting document.[273] In reference to this document, he wrote: 'However, he did not succeed in extorting from me that I place the crown of wisdom [i.e. *the title* '*Ḥakham*'] on his head, as he requested, and as some other Masters of the Law had already done.'[274]

A clear reference to the introduction of this title appears only at the end of the sixteenth century. In 1593, R. Samuel Archivolti of Padua was asked by the a group of rabbis from Venice to bestow the title of *Ḥakham* upon Isaac Treves, a prominent Venetian householder, upon the occasion of the marriage of his daughter. The exchange of letters concerning this invitation served as a forum for a general discussion of the validity of this

[270] See above, n. 10.

[271] R. Leone Modena and his 'grandson' Isaac were granted the title of *ḥaver* on their respective wedding days; see *Ḥayye Yehudah*, 46, 98. See also Breuer, 'Ashkenazic Ordination', p. 40 and n. 170. Cf. Modena, *Riti*, 41: 'questo e certo mezo titolo che si da a giovani o persone che non sono compitamente versati'. On the granting of the title as an encouragement to continue in one's studies, see the ordination granted by R. Leone Modena himself at the end of *Teshuvot Ziknei Yehudah*, pp. 183, 185.

[272] See e.g. how in 1605 R. Leone Modena was still referred to by R. Menahem Rava as *Kevod Morenu ha-Ḥaver* (when he was 34 years old) in the introduction to *Sefer Bet Mo'ed*. Cf. also above, end of Sect. 3.

[273] *Teshuvot R. Azriel Diena*, sect. 94.

[274] From what is said in this document concerning that same person 'who is on a mission on behalf of the Masters of Torah in Jerusalem', it would appear that he was an Oriental Jew (see below, Ch. 3, Sect. 6), so that it is doubtful whether anything definite concerning the general custom in Italy may be inferred from this incident.

new three-fold ranking of scholars, into *Ḥaver*, *Ḥakham*, and *Rav*. The rabbis of Venice—including R. Samuel Judah Katzenellenbogen, R. Jacob Cohen and R. Avigdor Cividal—wrote to R. Archivolti as follows:[275]

We know that this man is truly and justly deserving and fitting to receive additional honour. In fact, he is already felicitously wise,[276] so let him receive the honour deserved by sages. We have therefore decided and concluded among ourselves to honour him with greater honour and strength than he had previously enjoyed. . . Henceforth, this shall be the title by which he is to be called to the reading of the Law: '*ha-Ḥakham* R. Yizhak'.

Because of their love and respect for R. Archivolti, they wished him to be present at the synagogue on the Sabbath in question and to be the one publicly to confer this title upon R. Treves. In his reply, R. Archivolti expresses his surprise at the use of this term to denote a specific level of learning, between 'Colleague' (*Ḥaver*) and 'Rabbi' (*Rav*). Arguing from the relevant Talmudic sources, he states that the term 'Colleague' was used of one 'who had learned but not reasoned' (i.e. had not yet reached the level of independent deduction from the sources required for issuing halakhic rulings). On the other hand,

the crown of the rabbinate is suitable for those who have both 'learned and reasoned', so that he may teach and judge and release the first-born [animals] with justice and righteousness. Thus, we have the level of one who has 'learned and not reasoned', and of one who has both 'learned and reasoned'. Just as there is no [possible] third level between these two, so I would have thought that there is no crown [i.e. *honorific title*] between those two crowns. Moreover, in what respects is the *Ḥakham* to be considered superior to the *Ḥaver*, but inferior to the Rabbi?

Interestingly, despite these learned objections, he consented to the Venetian rabbi's request for his participation in this occasion, out of respect for their rabbinic stature, while concluding the letter with a 'personal' request that they explain and justify their halakhic reasoning on this point to him.

This is done in a third letter,[277] written by R. Avigdor Cividal, who replies that the principal source utilized by

[275] MS Budapest—Kaufmann 456, sect. vii–ix, fos. 11–14. Published in full in the Hebrew edition of this book as Document 16, pp. 235–7.

[276] *Ṭuveina de-ḥakhimei*; based upon Rashi to Ketubot 40a.

[277] MS Budapest—Kaufmann 456, sect. ix, pp. 13–14.

R. Archivolti for his definition of the distinction between *Ḥaver* and *Rav* (namely, Bava Batra 158*b*) in fact discusses the rather special case of *Talmid Ḥaver*, a 'Student-Colleague', which is in fact not a title at all, but refers to a particular kind of relationship of disciple to master. He then goes on to invoke a Gaonic tradition according to which three scholars are identified by three different titles—*Ḥakham*, *Rav*, or *Ga'on*—depending upon their knowledge and expertise in, respectively, three, four, or six 'Orders' of the Talmud.[278] The title *Ḥaver*, on the other hand, is no more than an honorific granted to young students 'whose souls are drawn to Torah and who know the nature of Talmudic dialectics' as a kind of incentive to further studies, as we have mentioned above.

The title *Ḥakham* thus seems to have acquired a meaning similar to that formerly attached to the title *Ḥaver*.[279] Thus, R. Leone Modena explained the granting of 'the title of *Ḥakham* and afterwards of Rabbi' to R. Benjamin Bavli as follows:

> I saw that he was good and deserving, to have the crown of gold, the crown of the wise, placed on his head, and from now onwards he should be called 'the *Ḥakham* Rabbi Benjamin Bavli', may he live long . . . for he is not yet of age to instruct the children of Israel (that is, to be called 'Our Master, Rabbi') . . . and I am certain that it will not be long before he will be a teacher in Israel (i.e. *receive this title*).[280]

From that time on, the title *Ḥakham* became quite widespread.

The decline in the prestige accorded to the title granted through ordination was accompanied by a toning down of the great debate which had agitated the rabbinic world at the beginning of our period, namely, that concerning the relationship between the rabbi granting ordination and the scholar receiving it. The granting of substantive value to ordination implied a certain concentration of authority in the hands of the one granting, who was the source of the authority granted. In fact, the growth in the number of those who were ordained was accompanied by a similar growth of the popular belief that the one ordained was somehow subject to the one granting ordination. This process may be illustrated by considering the way in which R. Joseph

278 See above, Ch. 7, Sect. 6.

279 From the statements of R. Avigdor Cividal, it would also seem that he now returned to the artificial use of the earlier distinction between *ḥakham* and *rav* mentioned in the tradition of Meiri (see above, Sect. 6). See how, in *Tapuḥei Zahav* (Rome, 1618), the author explained the initials *hḥ''r* as *ha-ḥakham rabbi*, 'sapiens rabbi, seu magister'.

280 Modena, *Teshuvot Ziknei Yehudah*, 187.

Colon's statements were transfigured some decades thereafter by R. David son of Messer Leon. Indeed, as R. Joseph Colon put it:[281] 'it is a common saying' or 'the custom of our forefathers' that the one ordained was thereby subject to the one giving ordination. Rabbi Colon articulates clearly the opinion of those who saw ordination as of substantive value. His conclusion, delivered in a long and complex discussion,[282] openly contradicts the opinions of his contemporaries, Rabbis I. Bruna and I. Isserlein, who claimed that there is a clear analogy between the rule demanding subjugation of the disciple to his teacher and the emerging relationship between the one granting ordination and the one receiving it.[283] Colon's conclusion is expressed in unequivocal and piquant terms: 'We have wearied of finding the source whereby the one ordained should be subject to the one ordaining';[284] 'The truth is that all my days I have been astonished, wondering what the world relied upon and from whence they learned to say that. Because he ordained him do we force him to be considered as his disciple?'[285] However, in an aside R. Joseph Colon remarks that 'it may be that we have here an argument in favour of the custom of our fathers that the ordained scholar is subject to the one ordaining'. Precisely these remarks, which were uttered casually and which do not express Colon's opinion, served as a source for R. David son of Messer Leon in his long ruling *Kevod Ḥakhamim*. He copied this section of the responsum almost verbatim, concluding that this is 'a clear indication that the one ordained is subject to the one ordaining'![286]

281 Responsa 117. Cf. Breuer, 'Ashkenazic Ordination', 27.

282 His argument revolved around the understanding of Maimonides' rulings in *Hilkhot Talmud Torah*, Ch. 5 and the comments thereon of the *Hagahot Maimoniot*.

283 There is no doubt that this is the authentic opinion of R. Israel Bruna here; cf. Breuer, 'Ashkenazic Ordination'. It seems to me that R. Bruna's understanding of this entire issue still requires clarification, but this subject is outside of my present argument; see *Teshuvot Mahar"i Bruna*, sects. 140, 141, 185–8, 269.

284 *Teshuvot Mahari"k*.

285 *Teshuvot u-Piskei Mahari"k ha-Ḥadashim*, sect. 7, p. 37.

286 *Kevod Ḥakhamim*, 76. David Tamar, who has noted the fact that many of R. Joseph Colon's responsa were copied by R. David son of Messer Leon in his rulings—D. Tamar, 'On *Kevod Ḥakhamim*' (Heb.), *KS* 26 (1950), 96–100—did not discuss the fact that the conclusions of the two sages are diametrically opposed to one another. This is evidently the reason why R. David did not mention Colon in his rulings, even in an allusion. R. David's tendency is particularly clear in the way in which he deals with the above statement of Maimonides and the *Hagahot Maimoniyot*; the main thrust of Colon's discussion is to refute the opinion of R. Israel Bruna, according to whom a disciple whose teacher has ordained him is not allowed to teach even beyond the limit of three *parsangs*

Moreover, the analogy between the student–teacher relationship and that between ordainee and ordainer enabled R. David to transfer the contents of the former relationship to the latter, and to derive from this his conclusion regarding the position to which ordination entitled the scholar within the community. He likewise concluded straightforwardly that 'one who is not ordained ought to be subject to one who is, and this by dint of the fact that the one ordained is subject to the one who ordained him'.[287] It therefore appears[288] that the question of the relationship between ordainer and ordainee is yet another expression of the conflict between the tendency which regarded ordination as being of essential value and that which did not.

With the decline in the value of ordination in the wake of the tendencies mentioned thus far, the importance of the debate concerning the subordination of the one ordained to his ordainer likewise declined. The general mood of the times seems to be well expressed in a lengthy responsum by R. Moses Provenzali,[289] which draws a kind of line of continuity between the period of the Tosaphists and that of the period under discussion. According to him:

> There is a great difference between study by memory, such as was done by the ancients in their day, and study from texts written in a book, as is our way, because in study by memory the students always needed their teachers . . . Even after they knew how to explain things well, having filled themselves with bread and meat [i.e. *having acquired extensive knowledge of the texts*] of received traditions . . . and it also follows from this that the opinions, teachings and rulings were almost all transferred to the students by their teachers, apart from the little which they had from their own reasoning; that new acquisition was doubtless, among the majority who received from them, like a new branch added to the tree. But even this little that was new was not acquired by the students through their own understanding, but from the words of their teachers, for they did not learn anything except that which was taught, nor understand anything but that which was understood by the former teacher [i.e. *everything depended exclusively*

from the former's residence unless he received explicit permission to do so from his teacher-ordainer. As against this, R. David, who copied the words of Colon almost verbatim, saw this entire discussion as a further indication of the subjection of the one ordained to the ordainer—see *Kevod Ḥakhamim*, 75 ff., esp. 102–11.

287 *Kevod Ḥakhamim*, 54.

288 Cf. Sect. 3 above.

289 *Teshuvot R. Moshe Provenzali*, sect. 6.

upon the transmission of learning from teacher to student], going back to the earliest ones, inspired by the wisdom which the Creator granted to mankind. Therefore, they owed so much honour to their masters from whose wells they drank, and particularly to those from whom they had learned most of their wisdom.

In contrast with this situation, things seemed radically different to him in his own day.

For the rabbi does not teach his students anything of his own, but explains to them the unclear words of the book, at the beginning of their study . . . In this form of study, the students never need the textual tradition of their rabbi, even at the beginning of their study, but his explanations. Therefore, once the students grow and reach the level of independent study, so that they may understand the words of the book by themselves, they no longer need any teacher other than the book, and those who wish to acquire wisdom and to be among the privileged who labour by themselves and study many books day and night . . . and rise to the level of teaching [i.e. *to be teachers themselves*], and these without doubt receive a good reward for their toil and acquire a good deal of wisdom by their great effort and not from their rabbi.

The conclusion is obvious:

As in our day the student needs his teacher less than in former days, so the power of the master over his student and the student's duty of respect for his master are also lessened.

These remarks by R. Moses Provenzali, together with the answers to the questions he was asked by his student,[290] may be seen as directly stemming from the teaching of the great Tosaphist, R. Moses of Evreux:

From the day we were exiled from our country and our Temple was destroyed and the nations were mixed up and the hearts were diminished, one can [no longer] say that the fear of one's own teacher ought to be as the fear of heaven [cf. Avot 4: 12]; similarly, those laws by which the student is obligated towards his master are likewise abolished, for the books and commentaries teach us, and everything depends upon the sharpness of their intellect and explanation.[291]

[290] Ibid., sect. 7.

[291] See Urbach, *Ba'alei ha-Tosafot*, p. 479, and n. 5. Cf. *Hagahot Maimoniyot* to *Talmud Torah* 5: 3; Y. Z. Kahane (ed.), *Teshuvot Pesakim u-Minhagim le-Maharam mi-Rotenburg* (Jerusalem, 1960), ii. 252 and n. 10, 11; *Shulḥan 'Arukh*, *Yoreh De'ah*, sect. 242: 9. I wish to express my thanks to Prof. Gerald Blidstein who called my attention to these sources. CF. also *Shulḥan 'Arukh* with the glosses of Gur Aryeh ha-Levi, *Yoreh De'ah* (Mantua, 1722), sect. 242, para. 6.

In R. Moses Provenzali's words, in which the dependence of the student on his master is negated, there is also great appreciation of the man who achieves the rabbinic level by his own powers. Thus, Provenzali indirectly implies that the question of who has really reached the level of rabbinate was no longer within the realm of judgement of his master, but depended upon the evaluation of the scholar himself and of the public to whom the question pertained. If this is true of the relationship between master and student, then it is *a fortiori* true of the relationship between ordainer and ordainee.[292] Provenzali's words clearly reflect the period in which he lived; we find there expressions characteristic of medieval scholars, as well as of a strong personality rebelling against many conventions on the basis of his confidence that his stand would elicit a positive reaction from the community in which he lives.[293] It is not surprising that the entire attempt to deprive him of the rabbinic title, in the light of his dispute with the Ashkenazic rabbis in Mantua,[294] left no impression upon his activity among his admirers and supporters. On the contrary, once a means had been found to put aside the vestiges of hatred and rivalry some seven years after the incident, shortly before his death at a hoary old age, those scholars who had agreed to excommunicate him were more anxious to accept him again on the level which he had enjoyed 'prior to the controversy' than he himself was troubled by the matter.[295]

Nevertheless, the afore-mentioned trend, removing the question of ordination from the exclusive domain of those authorized to grant it and shifting it to that of public opinion, together with the fact that ordination was not granted in the framework of an institution such as the university, but by the rabbis on an individual basis, seem indirectly to have reduced the importance

292 R. Moses Provenzali also clearly expressed this opinion in the only surviving ordination at his hand, in which he added to the reasons for granting the ordination that 'the distinguished ones of the land' where the person he ordained 'sit among them and are deserving to be the ones bestowing the crown . . . agree to this and desire it'. (See Document 9 in the Hebrew edition of this book, pp. 223–4.)

293 See how the members of the Community stood by him and signed a declaration of support during the course of the whole matter of the Tamari-Venturozzo divorce (*Eleh ha-Devarim* (Mantua, 1566), 13–14). Compare R. Bonfil, 'R. Moses Provenzali's Commentary to Maimonides' 25 Axioms' (Heb.), *KS* l (1975), 158.

294 See E. Kupfer, 'The Removal of the Crown of Torah from R. Moses Provenzali' (Heb.), *Sinai*, 63 (1968), 137–60.

295 See M. Benayahu and J. Laras, 'Health Officials' (Heb.), *Mikha'el*, 1 (Tel Aviv, 1973), 93–5, 141–2.

of the removal of rabbinic titles so long as it was seen as no more than an expression of controversy between irritable scholars. The impression gained is that rabbinic scholars used this tool rather excessively against their colleagues, in comparison with the norm in ecclesiastical or university circles, where titles seem to have been removed only under the most exceptional circumstances.[296] The removal of the title remained directly dependent upon the status which the *dramatis personae* enjoyed within the community—that is, the respective status of those removing the title and the one from whom the title was removed. The rabbi whom people wished to 'defrock' might at times have already established his position among his rabbinic colleagues and the public. If so, his prestige was no less and at times even greater than the one who attempted to remove the title from him. It is therefore not surprising that in such cases the act of removal left hardly a trace behind.[297] The opposite was the case if the one from whom the rabbinic title was removed was still at the beginning of his career, and the rabbi performing the act enjoyed greater public authority. A clear illustration of this point is seen in the difference in attitude of R. Joseph of Arles towards the removal of the title from him in the various instances in which he was involved.[298]

The rise of the public role in determining the importance of 'the one adorned with ordination' and his position among them in the light of the tendencies discussed above prepared the way for the creation of a new model—namely, the public function of the rabbi appointed by the community. In the next chapter, we shall discuss the emergence of that office.

296 Throughout the Middle Ages, it was customary for the bishop to unfrock any priest who had been subject to the death sentence; Doctors were subject to similar discipline. See Pertile, *Storia del diritto italiano*, v. 268 and n. 40. Compare Breuer, 'Ashkenazic Ordination', p. 38 and n. 149.

297 For this reason, I do not share E. Kupfer's astonishment—'R. Abraham of Rovigo and his Removal from the Rabbinate' (Heb.), *Sinai*, 61 (1967), 149–50—and so do not see the attempts to resolve the difficulties as serious.

298 See E. Kupfer, 'On the Denial of Rabbinic and Collegiate Status to R. Joseph from Arles and his Restoration' (Heb.), *KS* 41 (1966), 117–32. Kupfer also took note (p. 125) of the fact that '1548 was not like 1532–36, when R. Joseph was still a young scholar . . .' See also Ch. 2, Sect. 3.

3
The Community-Appointed Rabbi

1. When and How was the Office Created?

Even a superficial examination of the sources for the period clearly indicates, by the middle of the sixteenth century, the existence of some communities which had an appointed rabbi, alongside others in which no such appointment had yet been made. This state of affairs is implicit in the wording of the fourth ordinance approved by the representatives of the Italian communities in Ferrara in 1554:

In a place where one rabbi resides, another rabbi living outside the city cannot issue edicts accompanied by the threat of excommunication without the agreement of the rabbi of the city, or unless that rabbi declares himself unwilling to deal with the specific case in question . . . But in those places where there is a rabbi appointed by the community or by its leaders, even another rabbi of that same city may not promulgate any such edict, *either verbally or in writing*, except with the agreement of the community rabbi. Should he [nevertheless] issue such an edict it shall be null and void *ab initio*; however, if any person has dealings with the rabbi of the city, then other rabbis may rule upon him as they see fit.[1]

In other words, a distinction was drawn between 'a rabbi of the city', who is simply a rabbi living in a particular place, and a

[1] See L. Finkelstein, *Jewish Self-government in the Middle Ages* (New York, 1924; 2nd edn, 1964), 302. We shall return to the significance of this ordinance in sect. 5. As I understand it, the distinction between 'by the community' and 'by the leaders of the community' is based upon the different forms of organization arrived at by the various communities at the time the ordinances were made: in some communities, such as Verona, decisions were still accepted by the entire membership of the community, that is, by the taxpayers, while in others, such as Rome, the decision-making authority had been transferred to a body of chosen leaders. It may also be that the distinction is between those places in which the money-lenders were still dominant and were called 'the leaders of the community' (*rashei ha-kahal*) and those in which the public had attained full rule (see Introduction, n. 8). As far as we are concerned, this distinction is merely a technical one, for which reason from here on the appointed rabbi will simply be designated as the 'community-appointed rabbi' or 'the rabbi appointed by the community'.

'rabbi appointed by the community'.[2] In the absence of a community-appointed rabbi, this ordinance does not restrict the rights of the local rabbis to promulgate edicts,[3] but it does preclude the exercise of such a right by those rabbis living outside the city.

The earliest known written appointment was issued in Verona in 1539.[4] Abraham Yaari compiled a bibliographical list of rabbinic appointments which he discovered during his years of extensive research in Hebrew bibliography.[5] Of all the documents of this type discovered by Yaari in the numerous manuscripts and books which he examined, that of Verona is the earliest one known from any Jewish community in the world.[6] A similar document has been preserved from the latter half of the sixteenth century in Cremona. There were also community-appointed rabbis in Padua from 1579, and in Casale Montferrat from 1589.[7] It would also

[2] It follows from this that, even in the second ordinance, the 'rabbi of the city' was identical with the rabbi living in the city. For this reason, the wording of the ordinance was very precise: 'the one who first violated the agreement and brought his fellow Jew to the courts of the non-Jews without permission of *his community* or of *the rabbi of his city*, etc.'

[3] i.e. edicts implying the imposition of excommunication against transgressors.

[4] See Appendix 2 for a comprehensive list of the appointment documents known to us from Italian communities of this period. A number of those which have not been published to date appear in Part II of the Hebrew edition of this book. I should point out here that the term 'appointment document' (*ketav-minui*), as used here does not refer to an 'appointment' in the literal sense—i.e. a formal document issued by the leaders of the community to the appointed rabbi—but to the decision to appoint a rabbi as recorded in the communal register. I have not succeeded in discovering an appointment document in the literal sense, if any such existed.

[5] A. Yaari's widow has kindly allowed me to examine the collection of lists in her possession, now awaiting editing prior to publication. It is my pleasant duty to thank Mrs Yaari. I will specifically cite each item which I received from these lists.

[6] M. Benayahu has gathered together versions of appointments from Turkey and Greece, taken from various volumes of responsa; see M. Benayahu, *Marbiẓ Torah* (Jerusalem, 1953), 22–8. The first of these documents is from the year 1555. The earliest known appointment published to date from the Ashkenazic orbit is that of R. Isaiah Horowitz, issued in 1606; see M. Horovitz, *Rabbanei Frankfurt* (Jerusalem, 1972), 322–4. This has been briefly discussed and translated into English by E. Neuman, *Life and Teachings of Isaiah Horowitz* (London, 1972), 38–41, 200–1. J. Katz published three typical rabbinic appointments from Bohemia, Moravia, and Germany from the year 1640; see his study 'On the History of the Rabbinate at the Close of the Middle Ages' (Heb.), *Sefer Zikaron le-Binyamin de Preis* (Jerusalem, 1969), 281–94. Earlier appointments from the ledgers of the Frankfurt community (MS Jerusalem Heb. 4to 662), beginning with 1583, were copied by Yaari in the above lists. See also Y. Prener, 'Contrat d'engagement du rabbin d'Avignon en 1661', *REJ* 65 (1913), 315–18.

[7] See the list of appointments in the Hebrew edition of this book, pp. 298–9.

appear that there were such in Ferrara in 1556,[8] in Bologna in 1569,[9] in Modena during the 1570s,[10] and in Florence in 1608;[11] however, the record books (*pinkasim*) of these communities have not survived.

In any event, we may state that the office of community-appointed rabbi first emerged in north-central Italy towards the middle of the sixteenth century, although by the 1550s it had still not arrived in some communities.[12] By the middle of the century, most communities had reached the stage of more or less fixed forms of organization. The emergence of the office of the appointed rabbi should therefore be seen within that context. These facts point to the complexity of the general picture, making us aware of the need for exercising great caution in the use of accepted terminology and phrases, which can otherwise lead to an entirely distorted impression. Such expressions as 'Rabbi So-and-so *officiated* (*kihen*) or *served* (*shimmesh*) in the rabbinate in city so-and-so', or 'Rabbi X was *appointed* rabbi of place Y', or even 'Rabbi X was the rabbi of Y', are rather ambiguous unless accompanied by an explanation as to the nature of the office or appointment referred to in a given case. It is this question which the present chapter is intended to elucidate.

2. The Office of the Appointed Rabbi within the Structure of the Communal Organization

Those extant documents of appointment mention, as the primary reason for the community's decision to appoint a rabbi, the need

8 See E. Kupfer, 'R. Abraham b. Menaḥem of Rovigo and his Removal from the Rabbinate', *Sinai*, 61 (1967), 157.

9 An arbitration ruling issued by R. Moses Provenzali regarding a dispute which took place between the community of Bologna and R. Solomon of Modena (on R. Solomon see Section II of the Hebrew edition of this book, Document 6, p. 220 n. 2), who left Bologna shortly before the expulsion of the Jews from that city, is given in his 'Teshuvot', MS Jerusalem 8to 1999, sect. 198. The community demanded various payments of R. Solomon; among the other debts he had to pay, in R. Provenzali's ruling, was 'the rabbi's salary'.

10 See n. 54.

11 See U. Cassuto, 'I più antichi capitoli del ghetto di Firenze' *RI* 9 (1912), 208. It should be noted that Cassuto did not find in Florence, during the 1570s, 'a rabbi upon whom there was regularly imposed its supervision from a religious and spiritual viewpoint'. See Cassuto, *Firenze*, 214.

12 The phenomenon of Torah teachers of the type of R. David ibn Yaḥya, who appeared in the communities of south-central Italy from the beginning of the 15th cent., will be discussed later.

to ensure the continuity of local study of the Law.[13] This does not differ in principle from the reason usually offered for the decision to appoint a head of the academy (*rosh-yeshivah*). Even the teaching activity demanded of the communally appointed rabbi did not differ fundamentally from that expected of the *rosh-yeshivah*; indeed, there are a number of cases in which the rabbinic appointment explicitly included an appointment as *rosh-yeshivah*.[14] A particularly clear formulation of such a statement may be found, for example, in the invitation addressed to R. Isaac de Lattes to serve as *rosh-yeshivah* in Pesaro in 1557.[15] Like the rabbi appointed in Verona, the only thing required of R. Isaac was:

> to explain and to interpret a passage from a code, such as Alfasi's together with R. Nissim Gerondi's glosses, to the student-disciples once every day following the Morning Prayer, until time for the morning meal. And the rest of the day . . . he shall be free to spend according to his pleasure and benefit, and he will be free and master of himself.[16]

The community moreover assured R. de Lattes that if

> the income of one hundred gold *scudi* each year, and a free goodly house for him and his family to live in in keeping with his dignity would appear to him insufficient, then notwithstanding the fact that he himself was free to increase his income by some other activity . . . they will add to his salary . . .

As we shall see below, an income of one hundred gold *scudi* per year, plus a house 'in accordance with his dignity', were conditions far superior to those offered to community rabbis during the 1550s.

[13] See e.g. the first appointment issued in Verona: 'behold the land shakes . . . because of the abandonment of Torah; there is no one who learns or teaches . . . therefore we have agreed, in order to fulfil the obligation of heaven and our obligation, to spread Torah among us'. In the appointment from Cremona: 'it is incumbent upon us and our fathers to strengthen those who study Torah and to assist them. Therefore we have risen up . . . and besought the Excellent Rabbi (*Ga'on*) so-and-so, may he live . . . that he will consent to dwell among us.' A similar line of reasoning, at times even making use of similar language, also appears in appointments from outside Italy (see the sources cited at n. 6).

[14] See the first appointments of the community of Verona. On the educational activities of the yeshivah heads, see Ch. 1, Sect. 1.

[15] See D. Frankel, 'Three Letters Concerning the Biography of R. Isaac Joshua de Lattes' (Heb.), *'Alim le-Bibliographiya ve-Korot Yisrael*, 3/2 (1937–8), 24, and cf. the letters of appointment below.

[16] Frankel, ibid. The absence of any reference to the study of Talmud and *Tosafot* is clearly a result of the situation created after the burning of the Talmud.

Unlike the invitation addressed to R. Isaac de Lattes, the documents of appointment prepared by the communities incorporated other clauses, which established the framework for the joint participation of the community's lay leaders (*parnassim*) with the appointed rabbi in the realm of community leadership.[17] The essence of these conditions was that the rabbi was expected to reinforce communal ordinances by excommunicating transgressors whenever so requested by the lay leaders. This requirement, which appeared explicitly in most of the appointment documents,[18] was not shared by the *rosh-yeshivah*, who was not a communally appointed rabbi. This is not to say that the *rosh-yeshivah* did not participate in the communal leadership, but rather that his role remained independent of the organizational framework of the community. Thus, his authority rested upon the specific relationship between himself and those studying under his direction in the yeshivah. Naturally enough, these people saw themselves as committed to honour him and to follow his rulings, as a consequence of the relationship established between them, which was essentially no different from that of any teacher over his students. It is not difficult to perceive that, in a community where other scholars were present, the *rosh-yeshivah* could not automatically assume a status of seniority, unless this was recognized by some sort of general agreement. The best way to bring this about was by attracting all the scholars of the community to the yeshivah, and imposing upon them the authority of the *rosh-yeshivah* by virtue of his status within the hierarchical structure of the yeshivah.[19] Thus, we may say that the rabbi's

[17] One is struck, in the first appointment from Verona, by the separation between the two realms. Everything pertaining to the realm of study is concentrated in the first paragraph, while that which relates to the leadership of the community is contained in the second paragraph, which opens with the words 'and in matters concerning the congregation'. This separation well expresses the approach of those who appointed the rabbi, there being an addition here to what it was customary to stipulate with a *rosh-yeshivah*. In later appointments, this division is somewhat obscured, and the tasks and obligations of the rabbi are organized in sections according to the degree of importance attached to each section. For example, in the appointment of R. Abraham Menaḥem ha-Kohen Porto in Verona in 1584, sects. 9 and 11, which are also concerned with religious teaching, follow other sections concerning various matters of communal leadership.

[18] Where it does not appear, we will discuss further the reason for its absence.

[19] Such an experience seems to have been described by R. Elijah Capsali in his remarks concerning the scholars of Padua and the yeshivah of R. Judah Minz: 'our master R. Ḥayyim Carmi was one of the outstanding ones, and he was French and did not go to the *yeshivah*, for he had a different method of study; and my master and father, may he live long, asked his teacher, R. Judah Minz, to study together with him, and thus

authority in the community became a projection of his authority within the House of Study. A balanced combination of true scholarly skill and expertise with high sensitivity to the public's needs, when it subtly directed the involvement of the rabbi outside the limited area of academic activities, might give such a rabbi a position of uncontested leadership. On the other hand, insensitivity to the community, or even an error in judgement regarding the means by which to implement his personal authority, could undercut the basis of such authority. This model of rabbinic activity, in public teaching and in communal leadership, may be described in terms of charismatic personal leadership, independent of forms of communal organization. The limitations of this kind of leadership are rooted in the personality and talents of the rabbi, that is, in his personal stature, his confidence in his own intellectual capacities, his independence, and his sense of religious and moral responsibility.[20]

An outstanding example of this model of leadership is that of R. Judah Minz in Padua. One is struck by the sense of authority conveyed by the very language of the introduction to the ordinances which he instituted in 1507,[21] as head of a group of 'rabbis of the Venetian dominion':

> Since the [conditions of] the hour demand it, and these ordinances pertain to us Jews in accordance with our Law, and there being present in Padua many sages and rabbis of our Law who dwell in Italy under Venetian rule, therefore I, Judah Minz, with the rest of my colleagues and students, have seen fit to introduce the arrangements described below . . .[22]

they did, and they discoursed in the *yeshivah* in the Holy Tongue [*i.e. Hebrew*], so that he would also understand. And when he saw that they did not have ease from one another in matters of halakhah, he ceased to go to the *yeshivah*.' See N. Porges, 'Elie Capsali et sa Chronique de Venice', *REJ* 77 (1923), 35. In my opinion, it is significant that the initiative for this scholar's meeting with R. Judah Minz did not originate with R. Minz himself, but with one of those who went to the yeshivah. That is to say, the scholars of the yeshivah, who saw themselves as subject to the yeshiva-head, were interested, perhaps even more than he, in the general agreement to the authority of the rabbi!

[20] See J. Katz, *Masoret u-Mashber* (Jerusalem, 1958), 199 (from where I borrowed the phrase, 'intellectual certainty'); H. H. Ben-Sasson, *Hagut ve-Hanhagah* (Jerusalem, 1960), 163 ff.

[21] See R. Bonfil, 'Jews in the Venetian Territories' (Heb.), *Zion*, 41 (1976), 69–96.

[22] Compare the analogous feeling of leadership on the part of R. Judah Minz's cousin, Rabbi M. Minz, in his *Teshuvot*, sect. 60, and see also H. H. Ben-Sasson, *A History of the Jewish People* (Cambridge, Mass., 1976), 599.

Thus, the rabbis felt that the power to legislate was conferred upon them by the uncontested principle that 'ordinances pertain to us Jews in accordance with our Law', and that the rabbis were the 'Masters of the Law'. All those present on this occasion were the disciples of one individual; their feeling of subjugation to him had been formed within the walls of the yeshivah at Padua. The impact of these ordinances, signed by thirty rabbis who were his 'disciples', was felt for years thereafter, even though its details were forgotten;[23] the number itself is a concrete indication of R. Minz's power and influence.[24] The community heads are not mentioned as the promulgators of these ordinances; the legislating rabbis did not require their agreement in order to make these rules, nor did they indicate any doubt that these ordinances would be accepted by the public. Their expectation was, in fact, confirmed.

However, in creating the office of the appointed rabbi, Jewish society, which saw the basis of its existence as rooted in a sacred normative system, undoubtedly demonstrated its need to establish fixed and institutionalized organizational frameworks besides the informal authority of a *rosh-yeshivah*. What made the communities feel such a need? As we said, the appeal to a *rosh-yeshivah* depended solely upon the particular characteristics of a given rabbi, the admiration felt towards him by the community, and the sacral aura which surrounded the yeshivah. We may assume the fear arose that, in the absence of institutionalized norms in this area, such an appeal might itself not be possible, thereby hampering the proper functioning of the institutions of social organization. Such an undesirable development might occur as a result of several factors. For example, a particular rabbi to whom the society might need to turn for spiritual and legal support of the practical expressions of their institutional forms of organization, might suffer from certain personal limitations. Relevant also are the natural obstacles encountered by any community whenever confronted with the need to weigh the utility of an appeal to a scholar or to decide to which scholar to appeal, if

[23] See A. H. Freimann, *Seder Kiddushin ve-Nisu'in me-aḥarei Ḥatimat ha-Talmud ve-'ad yameinu* (Jerusalem, 1965), 131 ff.

[24] R. Benjamin of Montalcino alluded to the lack of such influence and power on the part of R. Judah Messer Leon, when he engaged him in polemic concerning his demand for the authority to introduce edicts for the community to which he did not see himself subject; see *Divrei Rivot*, 5, and Ch. 2, Sect. 27 n. 51, and Sect. 6 n. 244.

more than one existed in a given place. In other words: any community, the proper functioning of whose institutions depended upon a sacral normative system, would strive to ensure that its appeal to that system would avoid being dependent exclusively upon the personal involvement of a single individual, however great and respected he might be. Such a community would also attempt to ensure that its appeal to teachers of the Law was not undermined by the attempt of some sector of the public to avoid the very appeal itself, so long as the question as to which teacher to appeal might itself raise difficulties. Particularly in a case in which the community had no teachers who were accepted by the decisive majority of the public on the basis of their personality and charisma, such a situation was always a possibility.

This seems to have been the situation in Italy during the period following the death of R. Judah Minz. Throughout the sixteenth century, a series of rabbinic controversies raged within the Italian Jewish community. More or less satisfactory documentation is extant for some of them, such as the Finzi-Norzi controversy,[25] the Tamari-Venturozzo divorce,[26] and the dispute surrounding the ritual bath (*mikveh*) of Rovigo.[27] Each of these controversies involved many rabbis, no one of them possessing the authority to decide with finality. Indeed, the personal authority

[25] See A. Marx, 'A Jewish Cause Célèbre in Sixteenth Century Italy', in *Studies in Bibliography and Booklore* (New York, 1944), 107–54.

[26] See S. Simonsohn, *Mantua* (Jerusalem, 1972), 501 n. 8; E. Kupfer, 'Further Notes Concerning the Scandal of the Tamari-Venturozzo Divorce' (Heb.), *Tarbiz*, 38 (1969), 54–60. See also Bonfil, 'Jews in the Venetian Territories', 79–80 n. 64.

[27] See L. Modena, *Kitvei R. Yehudah Aryeh mi-Modena*, ed. J. Blau (Budapest, 1906), German Section, 127–37; A. Yaari, 'An Unknown Document concerning the Controversy in Reggio' (Heb.), in his *Meḥkerei Sefer* (Jerusalem, 1958), 420–9; K. Schlesinger, 'A Controversy Concerning the Matter of Gentile Wine in Italy in the year 1608' (Heb.), *Yuval Shay; Ma'amarim li-khevod Shmuel Yosef Agnon* (Ramat Gan, 1958), 211–20; G. Cohen, 'Towards the History of the Controversy Concerning the Matter of Gentile Wine in Italy and its Sources' (Heb.), *Sinai*, 77 (1975), 62–70. Only fragmentary accounts were published concerning other incidents, such as the engagement of Rosa in 1535—see Freimann, *Seder Kiddushin ve-Nisu'in*, 135–7; E. Kupfer, 'On the Denial of Rabbinic and Collegial Status to R. Joseph of Arles and his Restoration' (Heb.), *KS* 41 (1966), 121–5. Extensive material on yet more controversies is preserved in manuscript documents. For example, concerning the responsa of R. Meir of Padua (*Teshuvot Mahara"m mi-Padua*, sect. 13—and cf. I. Lattes, *Teshuvot R. Yiẓḥak mi-Lattes*, ed. M. Z. Friedländer (Vienna, 1860), 53 ff.), one finds responsa of other rabbis in at least three manuscripts: MS Jerusalem Heb. 8to 101; Heb. 8to 3904; and MS Montefiore 480. Likewise, in the latter two MSS one finds groups of responsa concerning the question of the wearing of *tefillin* during the intermediate days of the festival—and these are only two out of many; see also n. 167 in this chapter.

of the individuals involved was severely weakened by some harsh facts which came to light in the wake of these conflicts. To these factors must be added the social tension between the various 'ethnic groups',[28] which found particularly sharp expression in the area of rabbinical relationships[29] even if, within the context of rabbinic discussion, the ethnic differences were at times somewhat obscured under the influence of other factors, both personal and halakhic.[30] The ethnic factor is particularly striking within the narrow confines of the local communities, in which we can identify cohesive communities which stood behind the disputing rabbis. Even in the case of the Tamari-Venturozzo divorce, the Mantua community was divided into two camps: the scholars of the Ashkenazic *yeshivot* on the one hand, and R. Moses Provenzali and the Italian community on the other. In the controversy concerning the Rovigo ritual bath, R. Judah Saltaro da Fano of Venice expressed himself sharply against R. Ben-Zion Zarfatti:[31]

[28] On the contempt towards Ashkenazim during this period in Italy by the Italians and Sephardic communities, see Gerard E. Weil, *Elie Levita* (Leiden, 1963), 4, and the sources cited there. Cf. also the remarks of one of the members of the Rieti family, who wrote to his relative, a widower who intended to marry as his second wife a woman of Ashkenazic background: 'and how much more so when you set your mind to be assimilated amongst the hordes of the Ashkenazim, who are arrogant souls; you mean to compete with them, and from there you have chosen to build up a home for yourself! They were a source of trouble to all of the Jews in general, and to the Italians such as ourselves in particular. Their women go about with upstretched necks [cf. Isa. 3: 16] seeking adultery, with their legs they anger, the badge of arrogance and shame is on their foreheads, they always draw sin with the ropes of seductions and idle talk ... MS NY—JTS 73835, fo. 13. See S. Simonsohn, 'I banchieri da Rieti in Toscana', *RMI* 38 (1972), 414-15, in which the Italian translation of these remarks is published. See also M. A. Shulvass, *The Jews in the World of the Renaissance* (Leiden and Chicago, 1973), 57-60; S. Assaf, 'Responsa of R. Azriel Diena' (Heb.), *KS* 15 (1940), 125.

[29] See e.g. the response of R. Abraham ha-Kohen of Bologna to Rabbi Abraham Minz in the context of the Finzi-Norzi controversy, *Pesakim* (Venice, 1519), fo. 33a: 'Now you denigrate me with the term Sephardi, which is the very opposite of such ...' Cf. also fo. 35a, the words of another sage on the same matter, and see likewise the polemics of R. Isaac de Lattes against Ashkenazic rabbis, 'as their path is one of foolishness, to aid the Ashkenazim as a seal, whether the oppressor or the oppressed, and to hold guilty the Italians, without examining whether this is justified or not. Both the righteous and the wicked are killed by the speech of their mouths, unless salvation comes from another place [cf. Est. 4: 14].' (*Teshuvot R. Yiẓḥak mi-Lattes*, 144, and cf. also 144 ff.). See also the words of R. Abraham of Rovigo to R. Meir of Padua in Kupfer, 'R. Abraham of Rovigo', Addendum 5.

[30] See S. Simonsohn, 'The Scandal of the Tamari-Venturozzo Divorce' (Heb.), *Tarbiẓ*, 28 (1959), 387-8.

[31] See S. Simonsohn, Introduction to Modena, *Teshuvot Ziknei Yehudah* (Jerusalem, 1955), 57.

And if your honour believes that the leadership belongs to the Ashkenazim, and that God has withheld honour from the Italians and the Levantines and the Ponentines, heaven forfend . . . for one who says such things does not know the nature of the world . . . for these things do not depend upon climate and locale, but upon one's heart being filled with the spirit of wisdom, knowledge and intelligence, accompanied by good character and the fulfillment of the commandments, for by righteousness shall a king reign and a rabbi rule . . .[32]

Saltaro did not only allude to the fulfilment of the commandments—that is, to Orthodox practice—for the sake of rhetoric. During the course of the same controversy, it was announced 'on the Sabbath day by the servant of the holy congregation, in the courtyard of the ghetto, that there are Ashkenazic rabbis who permitted the use of Gentile wine, and published their decision on printed sheets'.[33] To these specific points of friction we must add the general atmosphere of competition, controversy, and scholarly jealousy, characteristic both of the world of study in the *yeshivot*[34] and of Renaissance Italy. Frequently, in the words of one or another of the sages involved in this controversy, 'it was clear that one skillfully . . . passed a camel through the eye of a needle'.[35] These events appear to have had a decisive effect upon the erosion of the personal authority of the rabbis in the community.

During this same period—that is, during the years following the generation of R. Judah Minz—communal organizations began to take shape in most of the communities of north-central Italy.[36] These two factors seem to have been decisive in bringing about and in shaping the institution of the community-appointed rabbi; the crystallization of the communal organization, together with

[32] J. Saltaro, *Mikveh Yisra'el* (Venice, 1607), 9a.

[33] These things appeared in a broadsheet published by R. Moses Kohen Porto on 13 Tammuz, 5368 (1608), a copy of which has been preserved in the Jewish National Library; see Yaari, 'The Controversy in Reggio', 420–9. The great authority relied upon by R. Abtalyon di Consilio (whom they mocked by saying that he was 'strict about water and lenient concerning wine') as 'permitting Gentile wine' was no less than R. Samuel Judah Katzenellenbogen, the son of R. Meir of Padua. See Yaari, 'An Unknown Document', 424.

[34] See Ben-Sasson, *Hagut ve-Hanhagah*, 173–8.

[35] R. Porto ha-Kohen's wording in his 'Teshuvot', MS Jerusalem Heb. 8to 3904, sect. 4, is based upon the phrase used in the Talmud, Berakhot 55b. It is certainly not an insignificant fact that this responsum deals with a controversy in which R. Eli'ezer Ashkenazi was involved!

[36] See Introduction.

the erosion of the rabbis' personal authority, brought about a definite tendency towards the creation of models of rabbinic leadership based upon office, personal charisma alone seeming insufficient.[37] To these we may perhaps also add the influence of the institution of the 'Torah Teacher' (*marbiẓ Torah*), brought by the Spanish exiles from their land of origin. As we shall see later, certain elements belonging to the office of community-appointed rabbi may have been borrowed from that institution.[38]

The process which brought about the creation of the office of community rabbi also led, by its very nature and character, to public involvement in the creation of this new model of leadership, as the source of the authority which created the office and appointed those who occupied it. A concrete expression of the change in this respect may be inferred from the phrases used during the period following R. Judah Minz's death in relation to the afore-mentioned ordinances issued by him and by his followers in Padua. R. Azriel Diena, who lived during the period of the transition was very precise in his wording in 1519. He wrote to R. Judah's son, R. Abraham Minz, that the ordinances were issued 'in Padua, by the great oak, your father of blessed memory, in the company of great men and men of deeds'.[39] When these same rules were reintroduced in the state of Montferrat in 1571, they were referred to as an ordinance 'made by the people of the holy congregation of Padua *and* by the members of the yeshivah there'.[40] In addition, the ordinance of Montferrat itself, although promulgated by the rabbis, was ratified by the elected leaders (*Va'ad ha-Medinah*) of the state:[41] there 'the perfect sages

[37] During the period of transition from one period to another, the rabbis frequently attempted to exploit the new situation in order to strengthen their personal authority through this office, on the basis of the argument that a community which appointed a rabbi placed itself in a situation of permanent subjugation to his rulings, even following the period of his contract, analogous to the relation of disciples to their teacher. The entire first section of Messer Leon's treatise *Kevod Ḥakhamim* is devoted to this argument, which is characteristic of those rabbis who grew up in the world of the Ashkenazic *yeshivot* during the period prior to the crystallization of the office of the community-appointed rabbi, who subsequently encountered this office in the world of Sephardic Jews, where it had for some time been fully shaped (as we shall see further), and attempted to enjoy the best of both worlds. In north-central Italy itself, when this office sprang up and took shape, in a manner which we shall see, arguments similar to those of R. David Messer Leon are not found. Cf. Ch. 2, end of Sect. 2.

[38] See Ch. 3, Sect. 6.

[39] See Freimann, *Seder Kiddushin ve-Nisu'in*, 132.

[40] See Finkelstein, *Self-government*, 307; Freimann, *Seder Kiddushin*, 141.

[41] On this council, see Shulvass, *Renaissance*, 112.

ordained these ordinances and the people of the province agreed'.[42] It therefore seems that those who made ordinances in Montferrat could no longer conceive of a situation in which the rabbis would introduce ordinances outside the framework of the communal organization. They assumed that, just as in their case 'the people of the region agreed' to their ordinance, the ordinances of Padua were likewise issued by 'the members of the community of Padua and the members of the yeshiva there'. We may thus conclude that the generation following R. Judah Minz was one which closed one epoch and opened another, not only in terms of communal organization, but in every aspect of the communal role of the rabbis and the nature of their authority over the public within that framework.

3. Communal Ordinances and the Promulgation of Bans

In fact, this new situation actually had its roots in ancient traditions of communal organization. The community's authority to enact ordinances, anchored in one specific Talmudic passage,[43] became accepted as a principle of internal organization.[44] In that passage, the actual validity of the ordinances is linked to the prior agreement of the 'senior person' (*'adam ḥashuv*) of the city.[45] Accordingly, the community's sovereign authority to enact ordination was related to the more general question pertaining to that subordination. The historical questions relevant to this issue,

[42] Thus the author of the responsum in sect. 3 of MS Kaufmann 150 (IMHM 32246). This manuscript is described by M. Mortara, 'Notizie di alcune collezioni di consulti MSS di rabbini italiani possedute e pubblicate da Marco Mortara', *Mosè*, 5 (1882), 265 ff.; in his view, its author is R. Raphael Joseph Treves.

[43] Tosefta, Bava Meẓi'a 11: 24-6; Babylonian Talmud, Bava Batra 8b-9a.

[44] See Y. Baer, 'The Origins and Foundations of Jewish Communal Organization' (Heb.), *Ẓion*, 15 (1950) 1-51; M. Elon, 'On the Nature of Communal Ordinances in Jewish Law' (Heb.), *Meḥkerei Mishpaṭ le-zekher Avraham Rosenthal* (Jerusalem, 1964), 1-54; S. Tal, 'The Halakhic-Legal Principles upon which are based Communal Ordinances' (Heb.), *Dinei Yisra'el*, 3 (Tel Aviv, 1972), 31-60; M. Elon, *ha-Mishpaṭ ha-'Ivri* (Jerusalem, 1973), ii. 558-630; S. Morell, 'The Constitutional Limits of Communal Government in Rabbinic Law', *Jewish Social Studies*, 33 (1971), 87-119; A. Grossman, 'The Relation of the Early Ashkenazic Sages to Communal Rule' (Heb.), *Shenaton ha-Mishpaṭ ha-'Ivri*, 2 (1975), 175-99.

[45] The basis for this condition has already been seen in Babylonian Talmud, Bava Batra 8b-9a.

as well as the related halakhic discussions, still require extensive study. Further research into this topic is likely to bring out the full significance of the tension between the lay leadership and the Rabbinic scholars within the communities, a tension noted already by Baer in his pioneering study of medieval Jewish communal organization.[46]

In the actual shaping of historical reality, there is a natural tendency for this tension to be somewhat blunted, and for a certain equilibrium to emerge between the opposing forces. Only the shifting of the centre of gravity one way or another reveals how tenuous this balance is, as well as its significance for the proper conduct of communal affairs. When R. Isaac Lampronti (1679–1756) wished to cite a precedent for what seemed to him a self-evident, undisputed matter—namely, that 'a decision to excommunicate without the approval of any of the city's rabbis is null and void, even if intended to prevent transgression'[47]—he cited R. Leone Modena's statement in support of his position from the period when the basis of this rule was challenged. Modena's words were uttered in opposition to a certain ordinance issued by the Communal Council of Venice 'under penalty of excommunication' without conferring with the leading rabbis of the community.[48] Modena's statement is one of the few clear sources for the customs and procedures which took shape in the Italian communities prior to the introduction of that specific ordinance in Venice:

And I remember that in my youth, during the lifetime of the three *Ge'onim*, R. Judah Katzenellenbogen, R. Jacob Cohen,[49] and R. Avigdor Cividal,[50] the 'Small Council' consisted of twenty princes of the community, including the *Ga'on* Y. Saraval[51] and other rabbis and *ḥaverim*. Nevertheless, when they or the community wished to issue any ordinance or pass any decision (*parte*) which would involve the imposition of a ban of excommunication, they would call the three above-named

[46] See Baer, 'Origins and Foundations of Jewish Communal Organizations', 38–9 and n. 34. Morell, 'Constitutional limits', 93 n. 56 explicitly refrained from dealing with this question. See, therefore, at present, Elon's remarks, 'On the Nature of Communal Ordinances', 32–9; idem, *ha-Mishpaṭ ha-'Ivri*, 607–14, and index, s.v. *'adam ḥashuv*.

[47] See Lampronti, *Paḥad Yiẓḥak*, s.v. *haskamah be-ḥerem*, and also sect. 2 above and n. 52.

[48] See Simonsohn, *Teshuvot Ziknei Yehudah*, sect. 78. On the term 'under penalty of excommunication' (*be-'onesh ḥerem*), see below, Ch. 5, n. 41.

[49] Ibid., Introduction, p. 43. [50] Ibid. 57. [51] Ibid. 51–2.

Ge'onim for their agreement. And whoever will search in the Communal Register of that Holy Community among the agreements made in those days will find that the decisions (*parti*) enforced by the threat of excommunication contain the agreement of those three giants, some of them signed in their own hand.[52]

R. Leone Modena's statement is confirmed by another source. R. Jeḥiel Trabot of Ascoli[53] stated that a community is not allowed to issue any ordinances without the agreement of the city's 'senior person', adding this evidence to his words:

I saw this in the Responsa of my grandfather, the *Ga'on* Rabbi Jeḥiel Trabot [of Macerata],[54] and I remember that when I was in Venice last year I saw the agreement of the Levantine community on the matter of the *grana*,[55] signed by all the members of that holy community, to which were also affixed the signatures of the *Ga'on* R. Meir Katzenellenbogen of Padua and his great son, R. Samuel Judah [Katzenellenbogen], and R. [Meshulam] Kaufmann [ben Shemaiah][56] and R. Eliezer Ashkenazi.

[52] Ibid. 110. In my opinion, R. Leone Modena's testimony is not only restricted to observing the fact that, as the *ḥerem* was a rabbinic prerogative, they were called upon to bring the ordinance into effect after the agreement of the Small Council, as one might understand from M. Benayahu's comments concerning the agreement of the sages of Venice and their leaders (see M. Benayahu, *Haskamah u-reshut be-Defusei Venezia* (Jerusalem, 1971), 34 and n. 3). It may be noted that the picture drawn here in the words of R. Modena differs from that perceived by R. Isaac Lampronti, who relies upon the former: Lampronti discusses agreement to the ordinance as if its wording were 'without the agreement of *any* of the sages in the city', while R. Leone Modena stresses the need for the agreement of *all* the important rabbis of the city. Lampronti wrote at a time when there were already rabbis in all the communities, while Modena based himself upon the situation in Venice, where there was no appointed rabbi at the time—a point which will be further clarified.

[53] See E. Zimmer, 'Biographical Details Concerning Italian Jewry from A. Graziano's Handwritten Notes' (Heb.), *KS* 49 (1974), 400–44. R. Yeḥiel was ordained rabbi on 16 Av 1569; see the remarks of A. Graziano, 'Teshuvot Ma'arvei Naḥal', fo. 2a, who was among the students at the yeshivah in Pesaro (see Lampronti's *Paḥad Yiẓḥak*, s.v. *ḥaliẓah*). In the 1570s he lived in Modena, where he was considered the 'master of the city' (*mara de-atra*); see J. Boksenboim (ed.), *Teshuvot Matanot ba-Adam*, sect. 22. On the meaning of the term during this period, see below, sect. 4d.

[54] See E. Zimmer, 'Biographical Details', 443 n. 18. He took part in the polemic concerning the excommunication issued by R. Jacob Polak against R. Abraham Minz; see S. Weiner (ed.), *Pesak ha-Ḥerem* (Petersburg, 1897), 5. His collection of responsa has been preserved in a manuscript in the Jewish National and University Library in Jerusalem, Heb. 8[vo] 194.

[55] I do not know to what this refers. It may be that this ordinance concerned the sale or transportation from outside the city limits of dry cheeses (*formaggi di grana*).

[56] See M. Mortara, *Indice alfabetico* (Padua, 1886), 9; on the rabbis of Venice at the time of the Tamari-Venturozzo divorce, see Simonsohn, 'The Scandal of the Divorce'. On the title page of the 1566 Venice edition of the *Ṭur Oraḥ Ḥayyim*, he is referred to as *resh metivta*—'the head of the Academy'.

All this is evidence that it is customary not to make any agreement without the consent of the sages of the city... And I also remember that when I was in Ascoli, where there was a great community, for every ordinance of the Council, issued by the people of that community, they would call my father, the *Ga'on* Azriel Trabot,[57] and they would act according to his word.[58]

The stipulation that all the prominent scholars of the city participate in the process of decision-making affecting the promulgation of ordinances was not only an excellent means of criticism for the community, but also clearly expressed the awareness of the need to link these ordinances to the sacrally perceived system of norms incumbent upon them as Jews.[59] However, the fact that the public turned to many rabbis at the time these ordinances were introduced testifies to the fact that none of them had acquired the stature of the 'senior person', possessing the uncontested authority to convey sacral validity upon the decisions of that community. Needless to say, this situation created difficulties in the very process of decision-making. On the other hand, even if a figure were found whom the public would be prepared to accept as a rabbinic authority, how could that community prevent the creation of a set of conditions in which the very functioning of its institutions would be totally dependent upon the decisions of that rabbi? How could the community be assured that the personal limitations of the rabbi would not hinder the proper functioning of its institutions?

The institution of the community-appointed rabbi arose out of this complex problematic, its basis being the consciousness of the sovereign authority of the community, which did not decline throughout the Middle Ages. This was well expressed by R. David son of Messer Leon, who quite simply stated that

We say that the majority of the people of the city are allowed to do whatever they wish, and no individual or individuals can prevent them. The basis of this ... is that the majority of the people of the city, are analogous [in authority] to the [ancient] Prince within all Israel, as R. Solomon ben Adret wrote in brief, without further evidence.[60]

[57] See Zimmer, 'Biographical Details'.

[58] *Teshuvot Matanot ba-Adam*, MS NY—JTS Rab. 1355, sect. 62.

[59] Cf. the remarks of R. Judah Minz quoted above, Sect. 2.

[60] Messer Leon, *Kevod Ḥakhamim*, 9, and at length. Cf. R. Jacob b. Asher, *Ṭur Shulḥan 'Arukh, Ḥoshen Mishpaṭ* 2: 1. See also the remarks of R. Benjamin of Montalcino, *Divrei Rivot*, 4, which indicate the acceptance of this principle in Italy during this period.

The simplest way of solving the problem of granting sacral force to the decisions of the public was to include a rabbi within the leadership, in the sense of a 'senior person'. In the light of the problematic outlined above, it seemed appropriate to stipulate in the appointment of the *rosh-yeshivah*, who was supposed to be the outstanding scholar of the city, an agreement on his part to respond to the public's demand to back its decisions by his power to excommunicate whenever asked to do so.[61]

As we have stated above, this obligation was unambiguously stated in most of the appointments of community rabbis. This situation, implying clear subordination of the rabbi's will to that of the communal leaders, would obviously have posed difficulties for the rabbis under all but very special circumstances. It was therefore necessary that the appointment be understood as leaving the *rosh-yeshivah* his status as a 'senior person', notwithstanding his explicit subjugation to the will of the community. This depended upon such factors as the specific personality of the rabbi concerned and his own self-esteem, the existence of a yeshivah which the community rabbi could influence by his appointment as a *rosh-yeshivah*, the presence in the city of other rabbis and their own self-image in relation to the appointed rabbi, the size of the community doing the appointing, and the degree of its homogeneity. These not only determined the status of the appointed rabbi within the community, but even made possible the very appointment itself. The 'ideal' conditions for the crystallization of a reality such as that outlined here would emerge in a place where there were no outstanding scholars apart from the community rabbi, in which the community was homogeneous, and in which the personality of the rabbi chosen allowed him to accept the obligation to impose the ban at the community's request without arousing in him a feeling of loss of independence and subjugation to the community.

[61] This obligation freed the public and the rabbi alike from the danger of paralysis, should the rabbi lack the self-confidence required in order to take a definitive stand on one of the questions under consideration. On the other hand, it is clear that if there was a conflict between the demands of the community and the rabbi's conscience, the rabbi had no option but to resign his position, as he saw himself as prevented from fulfilling the afore-mentioned obligation. Here we see, from another perspective, the need for a delicate balance between the wishes of the public and the rabbi's will, referred to above in connection with the situation outside the communal organization. Throughout the period under discussion, we do not know of even one case in which a community-appointed rabbi in fact resigned on grounds of conscience. See below, Sect. 4c, near the end.

4. Local Conditions

A. Verona

Conditions of the sort mentioned appeared during the first half of the sixteenth century in Verona, a small community[62] with a homogeneous Ashkenazic population.[63] Throughout the long period following the appointment of R. Joḥanan as community rabbi, there were no other rabbis in this community who exceeded or even equalled him in scholarly expertise.[64]

[62] The demography of Italian Jewry during the 15th and 16th centuries has not yet been properly studied; even general guidelines for dealing with this question have not yet been set. For example: the great mobility of merchants and bankers introduces an element of uncertainty into the general picture, even in those cases where we are able to establish more or less exact numbers on the basis of what is written in the communal registers. Considerable data concerning the demography of Italian Jewry has been gathered by A. C. Harris, 'La demografia del ghetto in Italia, 1516–1797 circa', *RMI* 33 (1967), Supplement. Regarding Verona, it is generally assumed that there were more than 400 people there at the end of the 16th century; see S. W. Baron, 'The Controversy of the Communities of Verona according to the Responsa of R. Mordecai Bassan' (Heb.), *Sefer ha-Yovel le-Shmuel Krauss* (Jerusalem, 1937), 217–54; Shulvass, *Renaissance*, 16; Harris, op. cit. This number however seems somewhat exaggerated. In the assessments from the years 1587, 1590, and 1592 (see 'Pinkas ha-Kehillah bi-Verona', ii, MS Jerusalem National Library, Heb. 4to 552, fos. 156a, 166, 171b–172a), the number of those registered did not exceed 55 'couples' (i.e. family units); one must further take into account that these 'couples' included widows and individuals who had not yet established a household (each widow was counted as half a couple, as was every self-supporting son living in his father's household). On the other hand, the list did not include those who did not pay taxes. Moreover, in the list of the seats of the men and women in the synagogue at the end of the century (ibid. 149a, 173b) the total number does not exceed 180, apart from those youths who sat together with their teachers, whose number is not noted. Among the documents found in the Venetian archives, there is an assessment for 1589 of 26 families (some 225 Jews), and for 1599 of 33 families (about 300 individuals); another assessment for the year 1600 increases the number to 60 families, totalling some 400 individuals. See B. Pullan, *Rich and Poor in Renaissance Venice* (Cambridge, Mass., 1971), 547. If we add these facts to what follows from the communal register, it would appear that the Jewish population of Verona fluctuated between 200 and 300 individuals during the 16th century, and was closer to the former than to the latter.

[63] See S. Simonsohn, 'The Communal Registers of Verona' (Heb.), *KS* 35 (1960), 128, 133.

[64] Apart from R. Joḥanan and his son-in-law, R. Yo'eẓ (who inherited his position), most of the lists of those assessed during this period make no mention of other ordained rabbis. See 'Pinkas Verona' i, MS Jerusalem National Library Heb. 4to 555: lists for 1545 (fos. 3b–4a), 1554 (27a–b), 1558 (46b–47a), 1560 (52b–53a). The list for 1547 (5b–6a) mentions R. Jacob (referred to as *he-Ḥaver* and not as *Morenu ha-Rav*!), evidently a young person who in the course of time became the son-in-law of R. Yo'eẓ (ibid. 150b). The list for 1549 (15a–b) refers to *he-Ḥaver* Seligmann: if he is identical with the one mentioned in earlier lists as Seligmann, then he must have just then been granted the title of *Ḥaver*. It may be that this individual was R. Seligman Ḥefeẓ, who afterwards moved to Cremona (see M. Benayahu and J. Laras, 'Health Officials' (Tel Aviv, 1973),

The requirement that the rabbi issue ordinances at the community's request was explicitly stated in his appointment. The language of the first appointment document—'that the rabbi will be required to enact or to excommunicate at the request of the *parnassim*'—still allows for the interpretation that the rabbi was also free to promulgate ordinances at his own initiative without the agreement of the lay leaders,[65] although this is not necessarily the case. In any event, over the course of time, perhaps in the wake of certain incidents whose details have not come down to us, this theoretical possibility of misunderstanding was removed. The appointment from 1557 states explicitly that: 'He has not the right to make edicts or to ban or to punish without the agreement of the *parnassim*.'[66] This does not imply a deterioration in the position of the rabbi in Verona. We must consider this statement in the light of the ordinance adopted at the 1554 Communal Synod in Ferrara, in which all rabbis were proscribed from imposing excommunication without the permission of the community rabbi.[67] We may thus conclude that, by the middle of the century, the authority to impose bans by means of the appointed rabbi was in practice recognized as belonging to the lay leadership. The afore-mentioned statement in the 1557 document from Verona must then be seen in terms of its strengthening the structure of the communal lay leadership in Verona, rather than as part of the decline in the status of the rabbi.[68]

81 n. 10). However, one may still argue that that there were other rabbis who were not included in the list of those assessed because they did not pay taxes. Such an argument seems to me improbable, because the exemption from taxes was evidently not even granted to the community-appointed rabbi until the term of R. Abraham Menahem Porto ha-Kohen in 1584. In any event, those taxes which were imposed on the basis of assessment by couples, were also paid by R. Yo'eẓ, the heir of R. Joḥanan, together with the other rabbi who joined the community in his day, R. Ephraim—if to a lesser degree than the other members of the community. See, for example, 'Pinkas Verona' ii. 80a: 'And Rabbi Ephraim and I myself, Yo'eẓ, will pay that third, as mentioned, according to the assessment imposed on every couple.' Once this R. Ephraim had joined the community, the members of the community included him, alongside R. Yo'eẓ, in special and sensitive functions: he was among those who participated in the tax assessments, together with R. Yo'eẓ (ibid. 62b and compare 63a, 70a), and there was imposed upon him, together with R. Yo'eẓ, the task of establishing whether a given individual was to remain in his position to deal with matters of orphans, even though he was not chosen to be a collector of charity funds (ibid. 80b).

[65] There is no such ordinance in the Verona Minute Books for that year.

[66] See I. Sonne, 'Basic Premisses', *Kobeẓ 'al Yad* 3 [13] (Jerusalem, 1939–40), 168.

[67] See Ch. 3, Sect. 1.

[68] See Sect. 5.

Despite the rabbi's subjugation to the lay leadership in the matter of bans, the activity of the rabbi in the small community of Verona clearly exerted influence upon the community leadership, thanks both to the special conditions which applied there and to the personality of R. Joḥanan. He participated in determining with the assessors the levy payments incumbent upon the various members of the community,[69] and judged appeals concerning these assessments in tandem with two appointed arbitrators. It was explicitly stated in that decision, that this was only because 'the *Ga'on* R. Joḥanan is acceptable to everyone'.[70] Understandably, he also participated with the lay leaders charged with the distribution of stipends to the yeshivah students.[71] He was raised above the community by the fact that certain ordinances did not apply to him, such as the peculiar ordinance concerning the special garment which those who officiated in the synagogue as cantor had to wear.[72] On one occasion, the Small Council (*Va'ad Katan*) of Venice appealed to him with the request that he select two representatives of the community for a meeting in the capital on an important and confidential matter.[73] More than anything else, it was stressed in the Communal Register that major ordinances required his agreement, particularly when it appeared that these ordinances pertained to various subjects of conflict and controversy within the community, such as the ordinance 'that one is not to open a store . . . until the end of *U-va le-Ẓion* [i.e. *the final prayer in the Daily Morning Service of the synagogue*]'.[74] He

[69] 'Pinkas Verona' i. 21a. [70] Ibid. i. 52b. See also ibid. ii. 26b. [71] Ibid. i. 48b.

[72] Ibid. ii. 41a. The wording of the ordinance is: '[On Sunday, the 7th day of Marheshvan 5317 (1557)], a *parte* was proposed by the three *parnassim* above mentioned and on the part of the Ga'on R. Joḥanan, the head of our Court (*av bet din*) that those leaders (*parnassim*) should have the authority to have a mantle made as they see fit, and that mantle will be worn by whomever goes before the Ark [i.e. *acts as cantor*] to pray, apart from that Excellent Rabbi (*Ga'on*), who is the permanent cantor, who may pray in his customary clothing. And the money which the leaders shall collect in order to make that mantle may be taken from whomever they wish, and whoever stands up to pray without that garment will pay a fine to charity, one *scudo* for each time that he went up [i.e. prayed without it]. The *parte* was unanimously approved.' On the special garment worn by the one officiating as cantor, see also Carpi (ed.), *Medabber Tahapukhot* (1912), 174. On the term, 'head of the court', see immediately below.

[73] 'Pinkas Verona', ii. 37a. This information was published by Sonne (ed.), *mi-Pavlo ha-Revi'i 'ad Pius ha-Ḥamishi*, 149–50, who also speculated on the possible nature of the confidential matter.

[74] 'Pinkas Verona', i. 47a. For a photo-reproduction of this page, see R. Bonfil, *Autonomous Leadership in the Jewish Communities of Italy in the 15th and 16th Centuries; A Sourcebook*' (Heb.), (Jerusalem, 1974), 78.

sometimes took the initiative to present the text of decisions to be voted on for adoption to the Assembly,[75] and towards the end of his life he headed a group of people who proposed the text of all community decisions.[76] This procedure, which at the time R. Joḥanan was no more than a customary practice shaped by the force of the rabbi's personality, became a fixed procedure in specific cases by the time of his heir, R. Yoʿeẓ,[77] a fact clearly indicative of the substantial change which had occurred in the standing of the rabbi. Not only was his agreement required in advance,[78] but he himself, at least formally, proposed ordinances.

We may conclude from this that the situation of the community of Verona is correctly reflected in the expressions which the community used in its documents of appointment, where it was stated, for example, that 'we accept and take upon ourselves as our head, as a prince and judge and teacher, the *Ga'on* R. Joḥanan';[79] or 'that he may be for us a master and prince and judge';[80] or 'to appoint upon us the *Ga'on* R. Menaḥem Katz . . . as a head and a leader';[81] 'to be a prince'[82] and the like. As we shall see, the absence of expressions of this sort in other appointment documents was particularly significant and fully understandable in the light of the variety of historical situations in the different communities.

In the case of Verona, it was even possible to project the authority implied in the title 'head of Court' or 'senior judge' (*av bet-din*), which usually was given *ex officio* to the *rosh-yeshivah*,

[75] e.g. arrangements pertaining to the cemetery; see 'Pinkas Verona', ii. 29a.

[76] Ibid. ii. 32a, 33a.

[77] Ibid. 98b. See the formula of the decision: 'As a controversy has arisen among the members of the community regarding who are entitled to propose *parti* [i.e. *proposals for voting*], even though the arrangement has always been that the lay leaders (*parnassim*) propose the *parti* to the congregation in all matters pertaining to the community, there are nevertheless those people in the community who say that a new situation has arisen in the congregation concerning matters of taxation and levies, that therefore people from within the community ought to be chosen who know how to deal with and arrange such matters, while others say that, as the *parnassim* have until now been those to propose all *parti* to the community, they should continue to do so. In order to uproot the seed of controversy, I, [Rabbi] Yoʿeẓ propose a *parte* to the holy congregation, that three men be chosen from the congregation to formulate the proposal, even though the arrangement until now has been that the leaders are the ones to propose the *parte*, as the new matter of the taxation has come up. And the thing shall be determined by the majority. The proposal was passed, 18 for, 8 against.' ('Pinkas Verona', ii. 98b. Printed as Document 31, p. 246, in the Hebrew edition of this book.)

[78] e.g. ibid. 64b, 65b.

[79] In the appointments of 1539 and 1542.

[80] In the appointment of 1549.

[81] In the appointment of 1586.

[82] In the appointment of 1592.

outside the context of the yeshivah. It seems more than mere coincidence that, once the community began to refer to the appointed rabbi as 'head of Court', beginning in the year 1555,[83] they ceased to include expressions indicative of judicial authority within the appointment, such as we have already noted. As we shall see further (in Chapter 5), a situation of considerable disorder reigned in the internal judicial system of the Italian communities towards the end of the sixteenth century. The dependence of judicial arrangements upon arbitration made it impossible for the rabbi's status to be strengthened by his position as 'head of a court', which might derive its authority from that of an institutionalized, fixed rabbinic court. Nevertheless, once the community of Verona had decided in 1545 that the rabbi and two lay leaders either judge or appoint judges to serve as arbitrators in those cases where the litigants did not reach agreement concerning the appointment of arbitrators within twenty-four hours,[84] we find that R. Joḥanan, who had not yet been designated as 'head of Court', became in effect the only permanent judge in the city. Both by dint of his scholarly expertise and his standing as *rosh-yeshivah*, R. Joḥanan was superior to the two lay leaders, so that he became *de facto* head of the court, even if he was not referred to by this term until close to the end of his life.[85] From then on, the title was inherited by those who succeeded him in this post. Notwithstanding, during the period under discussion, the title 'head of Court' carried no practical significance beyond the yeshivah context. On the contrary, the impression received is that the title is little more than an honorific affixed to that of the *rosh-yeshivah*, possibly under the influence of the Ashkenazic style in north-central Italy,[86] and certainly as a result of the scholarly atmosphere in the *yeshivot*.[87] It was, in short, an acknowledgement of the fact that the *rosh-yeshivah* was regarded as the highest religious authority within the community, even if this bore no practical consequences regarding the legal

[83] See Sonne, 'Basic Premisses', 167, and the appointments from 1557 on.

[84] Ibid. 158.

[85] It follows from this that Sonne was correct in arguing that this points to the strengthening of the status of the community rabbi (ibid. 167).

[86] On the significance of the title 'head of the court' in Poland during the 16th and 17th centuries, see Ben-Sasson, *Hagut ve-Hanhagah*, 163–4. See also M. Breuer, 'The Status of the Rabbinate in the Leadership of Ashkenazic Communities in the 15th Century' (Heb.), *Ẓion*, 41 (1976), 47–67.

[87] See Ch. 1, Sect. 8.

arrangements and internal organization of the communities. When R. Isaac de Lattes was invited to be a *rosh-yeshivah* in Pesaro in 1557,[88] he was also offered the title 'head of Court'; however, the wording of the document suggests that this title was no more than a synonym for *rosh-yeshivah*. This being so, in those places where there was no yeshivah or judicial court, the term 'head of Court' had no concrete meaning. Another proof of this may be seen in R. Abraham ha-Kohen of Bologna's letter to R. Abraham Minz, in response to the latter's use of the title 'head of Court' in reference to R. David of Pizzighettone: 'And you crown him with a crown which it is not yours to give to any man, namely, the title "head of Court", so that it is implied . . . that you consider yourself as the Prince.'[89] At the time of writing, there was no yeshivah in Ferrara. Thus, the community which held in its hands the authority of 'the prince'[90] had not appointed R. David of Pizzighettone as *rosh-yeshivah*. Therefore, according to R. Abraham ha-Kohen, this title was totally unsuitable to him!

We may thus conclude that there emerged in Verona, against the specific background of this community, a trend to create, from the combined roles of the *rosh-yeshivah* and 'head of Court', a model of a community rabbi required to implement measures of excommunication at the request of the community. This innovation had the appearance of an organic development, and did not detract from the status of the community-appointed rabbi. However, as we shall clearly see, such a development was prevented in other communities, in which prevailed conditions different from those in Verona.

B. Casale Montferrat

Similar, but not identical, conditions to those in Verona existed at the end of the sixteenth century in the town of Casale in the district of Montferrat. Although its Jewish population was then only about 200,[91] this included a number of ordained rabbis, in

[88] See Frankel, 'Three Letters' p. 14.

[89] See *Pesakim* (Venice, 1519), 30b.

[90] See above, Sect. 4.

[91] See S. Foa, *Gli ebrei nel Monferrato nei secoli XVI e XVII* (Alessandria, 1914; repr. Bologna, 1965), 68. This number indirectly confirms my conclusion regarding the size of the Jewish population in Verona (see above, Section 4), as in Casale there were also 40 families at the end of the 16th century (in the assessment for the year 1592 appearing on p. 14 of the 'Pinkas Kehillah Kedoshah be-Casale', MS in local community archives (below: 'Pinkas Casale'), there are 41 couples listed, while in the previous listing, from 1590, there are 32 couples—ibid. 9.

addition to the community rabbi.[92] The degree of homogeneity of this community is uncertain: it is difficult accurately to assess the tradition according to which the majority of its Jewish inhabitants were Spanish exiles;[93] indeed, a cursory glance at the list of its inhabitants from the end of the sixteenth century[94] clearly indicates the presence of some Ashkenazic elements. It is possible that from these sprang the opposition of six out of twenty-four electors to the appointment of R. Abraham Provenzali as rabbi.[95] In any event, even if the written appointment describes the task of the communal rabbi in a neutral way, reflecting a particular tradition,[96] the very contents of this document reflect a profound difference between the position of the rabbi in Casale and that in Verona. Especially noteworthy are the stress laid upon the rabbi's obligations and the restrictions imposed upon him,[97] as well as the fact that, apart from the honorific titles of *ha-Ga'on* and 'head of Court',[98] there was not even a rhetorical reference to any major position of leadership and authority due to him. His name is not even listed with those of the lay leaders (*parnassim*) who selected arbitrators in those cases where the

[92] In the year 1592, R. Moses Katz Rapa and R. Kalonymus Pavia are listed in the tax assessment. To these should be added the *ḥaverim* Jacob Segre, Menaḥem Chizighin, Shlomo Katz ('Pinkas Casale', 14); the same is true of the order of evaluation from the year 1596 (ibid. 18).

[93] See Foa, *Gli ebrei nel Monferrato*, 7.

[94] See the list of 24 heads of families who signed the appointment of R. Abraham Provenzali in Document 23 in the Hebrew edition of this book, p. 242. Most of these are bankers, for whom see Foa, *Gli ebrei nel Monferrato*, index, as well as R. Segre, *Gli ebrei Lombardi nell'età spagnola* (Turin, 1973).

[95] See the first appointment, cited here in Appendix 3.

[96] App. 3: '[They] will come to an agreement with Rabbi Abraham Provenzali son of R. David to be rabbi and teacher of the congregation, and upon him [is imposed] the office and the burden of this people, as has been until now the lay for any rabbi and sage in Israel . . . '

[97] See especially the appointment for the year 1599: 'And he will be required to arrange and to ordain . . . concerning everything that will be needed, even concerning the choice of the judges . . . on condition that he does not make arrangements in monetary matters, except with the agreement of two leaders (*parnassim*). . .' In the appointment from 1600: 'With an absolutely firm condition, that he does not make any arrangements for the members of the congregation concerning money matters except with the agreement of two leaders (*parnassim*).' Is this not a clear hint of the tension between the rabbi's desire to expand the scope of his authority in the choice of judges (see Chapter 5) and the community's desire to rein him in? It is unfortunate that we do not have at present any additional documentation concerning the nature of this tension.

[98] Even the titles *ha-Ga'on* (Excellent Rabbi) and *rav av bet-din* (Rabbi, Head of Court) do not accompany the name of the rabbi until after a certain period of time, some ten years after the first appointment.

litigants were unable to come to an agreement as to the appointment of specific individuals.[99] The rabbi is likewise not listed among the tax assessors,[100] nor included among those who formulate proposals for the community. Not only do we find no indication in the community *pinkas* (minute book) that his agreement is required for the introduction of ordinances, even those entailing the imposition of a ban, but it would appear that the rabbi had no impact whatsoever in this area. A typical example of this occurred with the introduction in 1540 of sumptuary laws (*pragmatica*), when the community was divided as to whether or not to impose the ban upon those who violated them. A decision was reached by a slender majority of 13 to 11, the rabbi's opinion on this issue not having been mentioned, even obliquely, despite the fact that he sat, together with two lay leaders, on the court which judged criminals and imposed fines upon them.[101] In any event, his obligation to 'enact' seemed self-evident from the very definition of his task. The 1599 appointment leaves no doubt in this matter: 'he shall be required to arrange and to decree, with the necessary permission, as the rabbi of the holy congregation, as in olden days'.[102]

This does not mean to imply that the rabbi was not accepted by the community. He was charged with various sensitive tasks (such as the resolution of a dispute concerning burial plots in the 'old cemetery'),[103] reflecting a positive attitude and feelings

[99] The procedure to be followed in such cases is described in the Casale Communal Record Book; cf. Document 53, pp. 275–6, in the Hebrew edition of this book.

[100] See 'Pinkas Casale', 12—decision concerning the appointment of assessors from the 2nd Intermediate Day of *Sukkot*, 5353 [1593], and p. 16—decision from 29 Shevat 5356 [1596]. The fact that, alongside the first decision, it is stated that the members of the community did not succeed in appointing a deputy assessor, is deserving of special note: 'On that night they voted on different people in order to appoint the deputy assessor, and none was elected.' This indicates the intensity of social tension within this small community. Nevertheless, the rabbi of the community is not described as 'acceptable to every man' (cf. Sect. 4a).

[101] See 'Pinkas Casale', 4–5. For the Hebrew version of the decision and of the pragmatica, see Bonfil, 'Self-government', 70–4. The Italian translation of R. Abraham Provenzali, together with the approval by the duke, was published by Foa among the appendices at the end of *Gli ebrei*, 183–9.

[102] i.e. with the permission of the ruling authorities. See the discussion at the beginning of Ch. 5, Sect. 2.

[103] In this dispute, those with established claims (*ḥazakah*) to certain burial plots demanded reimbursement from the heirs of those without such claims who had already been buried there. See 'Pinkas Casale', 9. To this should be added what has already been said concerning his task pertaining to judging those who violated the *pragmatica*.

of respect. However, generally speaking, one may say that the communal rabbi's status in Casale was quite different from that in Verona. The fundamental reason for this was the absence there of a yeshivah. In the absence of a yeshivah in Casale, the rabbi was not automatically considered a *rosh-yeshivah*—a point which clearly had a deleterious effect upon his status in relation to the other rabbis of the town. This hindered the natural development of a communally appointed rabbi who was also *rosh-yeshivah*, whereby the title 'head of Court' might signify real judicial power within the four walls of the yeshivah, whence his leadership might spread even in the absence of a permanent court. Thus, without the presence of a rabbinic Court, the title of 'head of Court' was equally meaningless.

C. Padua

It seems appropriate to discuss the situation in Padua at some length,[104] as a good example both of the particular situation which prevented the creation of autonomous communal courts in the Italian communities during the sixteenth century,[105] and of the tendency mentioned previously, of making the authority to impose excommunication[106] contingent upon the contents of the office and the status of the community-appointed rabbi.

The communal register does not stipulate the role to be played by the community rabbi. The lay leaders of Padua initially wished the adjudication of bans to be entrusted to the local rabbinic court, whose establishment was announced on the 26th day of Heshvan, 1579 (5340). On that same occasion, the Community Council selected two individuals to

> sit in council with the *Ga'on* R. Samuel Archivolti (1515–1611), over the course of one year, the three of whom together shall be known as the Court of the Holy Community of Padua, which may issue sanctions against whomever refuses to fulfil any of the laws of our holy Torah . . .[107]

Those who formulated this decision expressed their intention quite clearly. It echoes a variety of ideological concepts indicative

[104] On the degree of homogeneity of the community, which was primarily Ashkenazic, as well as the size of the Jewish population in that city, see Carpi's remarks in *Pinkas Va'ad Kehillah Kedoshah Padua, 5338–5363*, ed. D. Carpi (Jerusalem, 1974).

[105] Ch. 5 deals at length with this point.

[106] See Ch. 2, Sect. 4 and Ch. 3, Sect. 3.

[107] *Pinkas Padua*, sect. 47, pp. 90–1.

of the wish to create a kind of miniature Sanhedrin whose edicts would be considered 'as if performed by the Great Court of Israel', symbolizing the autonomous rule of the community. Even the formulation of the authority of this institution was decisive and clear, 'as if the judges and rulers were appointed by the Princes of Israel and by the authorities of Venice'.[108] The reference here to the non-Jewish government is intended both to guide the public in its perception of the institution, as well as to define the only limitation on its authority—i.e. 'it is a condition of our words that they not be opposed to our rulers' will . . .'[109] The purpose of the institution was to improve the world in the kingdom of God—'to impose edicts upon those who refuse to fulfill that which is written in the law of our holy Torah . . . to hear the cry of the oppressed . . .' Further evidence of the community's intention to set up an institution which would express the authority of the rabbi and the institutionalized participation of the communal leadership in this authority is indicated in the choice of judges: alongside R. Samuel Archivolti were R. Abraham Heilpron, the *parnas* (lay leader) of the community at that time, who held the title of *Ḥaver*, and R. Simeon Kohen, the scribe and apparently also cantor of the community (although this latter point is not clear). In order to explain this matter, we must first examine what happened to the Court following its establishment.

Beginning in 1583, it is recorded in the register of the community of Padua that 'three judges from that holy community' were elected periodically 'to judge all incidents that may occur or already have occurred in that community'.[110] One might thus legitimately argue that these three judges in fact comprised the communal court, and that this court acted continuously from 1579. However, this clearly was not the case.[111]

On 25 Tishri 1577, the Padua community decided that the two lay leaders 'would serve as judges in cases involving up to twenty lire between all litigants, following the formula reported on in

108 Cf. with what has been said above, at the end of Sect. 3.

109 Cf. above, n. 124.

110 *Pinkas Padua*, sect. 107, p. 140.

111 My understanding of the situation in the Padua community differs on many details in this respect from the understanding of Carpi in his introduction to *Pinkas Padua* (pp. 41–5), a point which will be evident to the reader who compares my presentation with his.

the old Register . . . all this was done in December 1556'.[112] We learn from this that it had been customary to constitute a court of two lay leaders, whose task was to judge disputes involving minor sums—possibly similar to the 'householders' courts' known to us from the Ashkenazic world.[113] On that same day it was decided, in a separate ruling, that 'the lay leaders will be the judges of the holy community in all things pertaining to the needs of the community and the like'.[114] The function of these 'community judges' is quite distinct from that of 'judges up to the sum of twenty lire' referred to in the preceding decision—even if *de facto*, as a result of the latter decision, both functions were in the hands of the same people, i.e. the *parnassim*.[115] In what follows, I will attempt to define more closely the difference between the two functions.

In the 1579 decision establishing a court, the community was asked to grant it the functions of 'judges of the community', as referred to in the earlier decision (i.e. from 25 Tishri 1577).[116] Instead, the community reiterated its original decision concerning the 'judges of the community', at least from 25 Nissan 1582,[117] from which point two judges were chosen each year from among those exempt from payment of taxes[118] for the limited function

[112] *Pinkas Padua*, sect. 2, p. 68.

[113] See Ben-Sasson, *Hagut ve-Hanhagah*, 186; J. Katz, *Tradition and Crisis* (New York, 1971), 95–7. The difference between Padua, with this court of lay leaders, and Verona, which was under the leadership of a Rabbinic Court, ought to be stressed here even though in Verona also the court only dealt with small sums. These points will be further explained.

[114] *Pinkas Padua*, sect. 3, p. 68.

[115] Very soon after, there was felt a need to separate such tasks, and it was decided 'to make two judges of the community . . . in order that there be no cause for any man to say that the communal judges are [also] the assessors', *Pinkas Padua*, sect. 14, pp. 76–7.

[116] From the language of this decision, it seems clear that those who formulated it wished to remove any suspicion, lest it be thought that the task of 'judges of the community' was not to be transferred to the newly established court. If this were not the case, what would be the meaning of 'and they shall *also* be judges in the community' after it had been stated that 'the three of them together will be called the court of the Holy Congregation of Padua'? It seems to me that the continuation of the text of the decision ('and they . . . will attempt to hear the cry of the poor at least once a week') indicates that the task of judging cases involving small sums was also meant to be transferred to this court. Nevertheless, the matter requires further study, and Carpi's reconstruction in the introduction to *Pinkas Padua*, p. 42, according to which this task was not transferred by this decision to the court headed by the rabbi, is also possible.

[117] Ibid., sect. 83, p. 129 and cf. also sect. 107, p. 140.

[118] Even though one of those elected was the rabbi appointed from the community, they did not necessarily choose only scholars whose main occupation was religious study; the second judge chosen was a student in the university (see ibid. p. 130, n. 10).

of judging 'all those cases concerning the taxation of the community'. We may infer from this that the task of the 'community judges' was to handle appeals concerning matters of taxation, assessments, and other disputes between the community and individuals or groups within it. This is also explicitly formulated in a 1588 decision, in which it was decided 'to appoint three judges to whom every difficult thing will be brought—in matters of the community, between an individual and the community, and between the public, as is customary . . .'[119] As this was the sole task of the 'community judges', they were appointed for 'the entire period of the valuation, as is customary',[120] and the decision relating to their appointment was again recorded, close to the time specified for the decisions concerning the tax assessment and the choice of assessors. This election took place once every two years, with the exceptions of 1580, when it was decided that the members of the court headed by the rabbi would also serve as community judges, of 1581, for which there are no decisions recorded in the register save some isolated decisions from the end of the year,[121] and of 1594, during which the election of community judges is not mentioned at all.[122]

119 Ibid. sect. 312, p. 231. This specifically states 'between an individual and the community and between the public [*bein rabbim la-rabbim*] as is customary', and not between individuals.

120 Ibid. sect. 458, p. 297.

121 Ibid. pp. 42–3 and n. 14.

122 Cf. ibid. sect. 14, p. 76 (14 Adar 5338 [1578]—the decision in sect. 13 concerning assessments was accepted on 26 Shevat of that year, pp. 74–6); sect. 83, p. 129 (25 Nissan 5342 [1582]—decision in sect. 79 concerning the assessors was adopted on 15 Shevat of that year, p. 127); sect. 139, p. 155 (9 Shevat 5344—the decision in sect. 131 concerning the assessors: 17 Tevet 5344, p. 152); sect. 244, p. 197 (6 Adar 5346—the decision in sect. 243, is the ruling of assessment: the eve of 6 Adar 5346, pp. 196–7); sect. 312, p. 231 (4 Shevat 5348—decision in sect. 308, is the ruling of assessment: 10 Tevet 5348, pp. 227–9); sect. 376, p. 266 (26 Tevet 5350—decision in sect. 375, is the ruling of assessment on the same day, pp. 263–6); sect. 458, p. 297 (21 Iyyar 5352—decision in sect. 455, is the ruling of assessment: 7 Iyyar 5352, p. 296); for 5354 there is no mention made of election of the judges of the community; sect. 584, p. 340 (1st Intermediate Day of Passover—decision in sect. 586, is the ruling of assessment: same day, p. 340). Regarding this same question, I wish to indicate that I diverge from the opinion of the editor of the *Pinkas* that already in 1590 the ruling that community judges were not to be assessors was no longer observed (p. 42). The decision in sect. 394 cited by the editor (ibid. n. 11) relates to those who assessed the assessors (who in that particular year turned out to be the judges of the community, for which reason this decision was accepted ad hoc) and not to the assessors. A similar case occurred in 1584 (cf. sect. 145, p. 158), but on that occasion the Council's decision was different from that of 1590. In the state council as well, 'judges' were appointed to a similar task, as can easily be seen by perusal of the 'Pinkas ha-Medinah' (Minute Book of the Regional Council) of Padua, conserved in the Archives of the Jewish Community of that city. See n. 244 below.

As the 'judges of the community' and the court established by the edict of 1579 were two different bodies, at least from 1582 onwards, they no longer selected two people to join the rabbi of the community, but all judges were elected, the rabbi standing for election to a position in this court, at times being elected and at times not.[123] Why did the people of Padua reverse their 1579 decision to draw a distinction between the task of the communal judges and that of the court which they set up in that year? It seems to me that this may have been as a result of the abolition of the court of three headed by the community rabbi. Moreover, I would conjecture that this took place in response to opposition on the part of the government who (as we shall see in Chapter 5) had also opposed the establishment of autonomous Jewish judicial authorities in other Italian cities.[124] Not only is there no trace following 1579 of a court of three headed by the rabbi,[125] but even the decision referring to the creation of a court headed by the rabbi was not included among other decisions ratified or promulgated in an updating of their decision by the community to 3 Shevat 1580.[126] Thus, the adjudication of minor disputes returned to the lay leadership,[127] while major disputes were adjudicated, by the old method in which each side selected one judge, and these two together selected a third.[128] Thus, the

[123] Carpi (*Pinkas Padua*, 42) sees the question in terms of the tension between the lay leaders and the rabbi 'in everything pertaining to the division of tasks between them in matters of judgement'. However, the fact is that already in 1583, two years prior to the dispute with the *parnassim*, the rabbi was not chosen to be one of the judges of the community (p. 43 n. 16). We have already discussed this dispute in the discussion of the role of the *ḥerem* in Ch. 2, Sect. 4.

[124] This problem will be discussed at length in Ch. 5. It was not for nothing that those who formulated the decision on 26 Heshvan 1579, in total opposition to other decisions, emphasized the condition that the words of the decision not be 'against our rulers in Venice and the governors of this city'!

[125] The only ruling signed by R. Samuel Archivolti and two other judges is that from 27 Tammuz 1582 (*Pinkas Padua*, sect. 830, p. 457). R. Israel Luria and R. Abraham Heilpron, who were not 'judges of the community' at that time (sect. 83, pp. 129–30), signed there together with Archivolti. When the latter two were selected as 'judges of the community' on 28 Shevat 1583 (sect. 107, p. 140), R. Samuel Archivolti was not appointed with them.

[126] I disagree on this point with Carpi, who sees a connection between the decision of 26 Heshvan 1579 and that in sect. 57: xi–xii (see his comment there, p. 44, n. 31); cf. immediately below.

[127] *Pinkas Padua*, sect. 57: xl, p. 112.

[128] Ibid., sect. 57: xi–xii, p. 101. Cf. Carpi's comments, p. 41.

abolition of the central court of three headed by the rabbi could have taken place no later than 3 Shevat 1580.[129]

If we are correct, the abolition of this court led to the reinstatement of the original procedure for imposing bans. The dispute which broke out in 1585 between R. Samuel and the lay leaders[130] indicates that, prior to that same dispute, the *parnassim* saw themselves as subordinate to the rabbi in all matters involving bans. However, even if no specific decision was taken on this matter, the contents of various decisions confirm the role of the community rabbi in this area. He participated with the lay leaders in their discussions concerning those who were suspected of violating community ordinances.[131] Thus, violators of community ordinances came to him 'to request forgiveness' and to be released from the ban to which they had been subject.[132] After 1585, in the aftermath of his dispute with the lay leaders, R. Samuel ceased to be involved in excommunications, and the efforts of the lay leaders to ensure a functioning system of leadership in his absence grew. Nevertheless, not only did the Council fail to execute its decision to impose the ban against a certain individual, apropos of the same matter which had aroused the ire of R. Samuel Archivolti, but even the power of communal bans became markedly weakened. We read of people 'who did not bend their ear to hear the voice of the *parnassim*, and said "who is master over us?" [cf. Ps. 12: 5] following their crooked hearts and opening their mouths without restraint to say that the *parnassim* have no right to command any one.'[133]

On the other hand, a year after these matters were recorded in the Register, R. Samuel Archivolti informed them of his intention to leave the city.[134] This evidently served as a stimulus for renewed negotiation with him. It was decided to appoint a committee of three people who were given the authority 'to make a compromise[135] with that notable . . . and they may engage him to do as seems right in their eyes'.[136] This decision was issued

[129] There may perhaps be a connection between the problem of the court and the emphasis placed one year later by the Cattaveri, the Venetian magistrates responsible for the Jews and for problems relating to them, upon the prohibition against establishing Jewish courts. See V. Colorni, *Legge ebraica e leggi locali* (Milan, 1945), 337, 371–2, and cf. also in Ch. 5, Sect. 2.

[130] See above, in Ch. 2, Sect. 4.

[131] *Pinkas Padua*, sect. 98, pp. 134–6.

[132] Ibid. sect. 57: xxiv, xxxix, pp. 105–6, 112.

[133] Ibid. sect. 278, p. 212.

[134] Ibid. sect. 328, pp. 241–2.

[135] i.e. to set terms of payment with him.

[136] Ibid.

on 19 Iyyar 1588. The first member of the committee was appointed a month later, on 23 Sivan,[137] and two more another week after that, on 2 Tammuz.[138] The negotiations were not completed until the end of that year, or perhaps at the beginning of the Hebrew year 5349 (i.e. Autumn 1588).[139] Meanwhile, the lay leaders made their first concession towards R. Samuel: in a lengthy decision concerning the updating of the juridical procedures in the community, he was granted certain supervisory tasks over the activities of the leaders in this area.[140] Unlike the earlier decisions, the declaration of the ban against those who had refused to pay taxes, or their readmission into the community, was formulated here with great caution: 'He who refuses will be considered as a sinner . . . and one who does so deliberately shall be called before the *parnassim* because of his rebellion, and must make apologies, and do whatever is imposed upon him . . . and if they [i.e. the *parnassim*] wish to fulfil the will of both God and man, they should call R. Samuel, and everything shall be decided by them.' We may conclude from this that Archivolti's position of authority had begun to be reinstated even prior to the negotiations concerning his retention of the office of community rabbi. Indeed, from 1589 on, R. Samuel gradually began to return to his previous position; for example, we again find communal decisions stating that those who violate communal edicts will be excommunicated until they pay the fine imposed upon them 'and take it upon themselves to do whatever the community leaders and R. Samuel Archivolti impose upon them'.[141] He again participated with the lay leaders in discussions concerning individuals suspected of having violated communal ordinances[142] and, immediately following the above decision, his right to excommunicate without consulting the *parnassim* was restored in cases involving violation of ritual law.[143] This final decision, early in 1601, symbolizes practically the end of the process of reconciliation with the rabbi; it was subsequently decided to erase

[137] Ibid. sect. 333, p. 243.

[138] Ibid. sect. 335, p. 244.

[139] Ibid. sect. 345, p. 251. This decision is not dated, but the editor has quite justifiably placed it between 14 Av 5348 [1588] and Tishri 5349.

[140] Ibid. sect. 337, pp. 245–8: 'and if Heaven forbid the *parnassim* should neglect this . . . then the plaintiff may go before the *Gaon* Samuel [Archivolti] . . . and then, as seems fit in his eyes, they shall send the warden to the lay leaders with a fine of up to two ducats, that they shall make order [i.e. *see to the matter*]', p. 247.

[141] Ibid. sect. 367, p. 260; sect. 707, pp. 395–7; sect. 805, pp. 445–6; sect. 806, p. 446.

[142] Ibid. sect. 690, p. 387.

[143] Ibid. sect. 691, p. 388.

from the record various decisions in which R. Samuel was mentioned unfavourably.[144] Even earlier, in 1590, it was decided that, in those cases where the edict of ban could be sent personally, as in the case of those assessors who were elected *in absentia* by the session of the Council, so that the oath sworn by the assessors on that occasion did not apply to them, 'R. Samuel will send them an order of ban via the clerk of the court, that they not speak a word to any man concerning the matter of those assessed'.[145] It was likewise stated there that the act of excommunication, 'with all the sanctions and curses entailed', was to be publicized by the rabbi.[146] Thus, at the end of the period of dispute between R. Samuel and the lay leaders, the rabbi emerged with his position strengthened. It seems clear that R. Archivolti's public prestige was a decisive factor in this struggle,which was clearly expressed in the decisions of the Council, both before and after the dispute: he was chosen to supervise the procedure and the secrecy of the assessment,[147] as well as the distribution of houses in the ghetto.[148] He turned to the community to assist various needy people known to him, and supervised matters relating to orphans;[149] he was also given various sensitive tasks relating to the collection and distribution of charitable funds,[150] as well as the collection of moneys for funding special activities of the community.[151] It is superfluous to add that the people also turned to him in all matters concerning divine worship[152] and education.[153] However, the main indication of his improved position following the dispute was his inclusion

[144] Ibid. sect. 692, p. 388.

[145] Ibid. sect. 375, pp. 263–6. It seems that the commands of the warden mentioned in sect. 660, pp. 372–5, and sect. 734, p. 409–12 should also be understood in this manner.

[146] Ibid. sect. 707, pp. 395–8.

[147] Ibid. sect. 625, pp. 359–60; sect. 631, p. 362; sect. 707, p. 398, and cf. sect. 77, pp. 125–6; sect. 314, pp. 232–5; sect. 375, pp. 263–6; sect. 623, pp. 355–8; sect. 660, pp. 372–5; sect. 734, pp. 409–12.

[148] Ibid., sect. 790, pp. 448–9 and sect. 791, p. 440.

[149] Ibid. sect. 82, p. 129; sect. 134, p. 153; sect. 295, p. 221; sect. 366, p. 260; sect. 517, p. 316; sect. 801, p. 444.

[150] Ibid. sect. 297, p. 222; sect. 299, p. 223; sect. 378, p. 267; sect. 453, p. 295; sect. 746, p. 416; and cf. also sect. 464, p. 299, and sect. 872, pp. 458–9. Similar tasks were assigned to him in the State Council. See 'Pinkas ha-Medinah be-Padua', fos. 8a, 85a.

[151] *Pinkas Padua*, sect. 78, p. 127.

[152] See ibid. sect. 67, pp. 119–20; sect. 69, p. 120; sect. 350, p. 254; sect. 402, pp. 275–6; sect. 422, p. 285; sect. 481, p. 303.

[153] Ibid. sect. 423, p. 285.

with those lay leaders who decided whether those who had not come to the Council meetings had in fact been unable to do so;[154] he was also given certain supervisory functions over the judicial activities of the lay leaders themselves, as well as hearing the claims of those who had established rights in the area where the ghetto was erected.[155] Even in the matter of the ghetto, he was considered above the community, and was allocated a house without participation in the lottery.[156] He was likewise sent to represent the community in Venice, together with the lay leaders.[157]

After the failure of the attempt to establish a court, whose 'acts were to be considered as if performed by the Great Court in Israel', the community rabbi's leadership is manifested against the background of the tendency to subject the community to his authority by the imposition of the ban, and in the light of the tension between the rabbi's own view of his position within the community and the members' view of him. It seems clear that the main factor hindering Rabbi Samuel Archivolti from consolidating his position was the abolition of the institution of the court,[158] along with the absence of a yeshivah in Padua, making it impossible for him to be either a head of Court or a *rosh-yeshivah*. This latter factor is connected with the decline of Padua as a centre of Jewish learning, parallel to the rise of Venice. R. Meir Katzenellenbogen of Padua was the last *rosh-yeshivah* to occupy the office held by R. Judah Minz and his son R. Abraham. By the time of R. Samuel Archivolti, the rabbi of Padua was no longer a *rosh-yeshivah*,[159] so that from then on the inhabitants of Padua were subject to the influence and rule of the rabbis of

[154] Ibid. sect. 507, p. 313.

[155] Ibid. sect. 337, pp. 245–8; sect. 761, pp. 424–5; sect. 799, p. 443; sect. 814, pp. 449–50.

[156] Ibid. sect. 786, p. 435.

[157] Ibid. Appendix 24.

[158] R. Samuel Archivolti was not even referred to as Head of Court in his own community, although in the light of what has been said above one should not ascribe too much importance to this fact.

[159] A remnant of this change in the situation has been preserved in R. Isaac Ḥayyim ha-Kohen's description, *Paḥad Yiẓḥak* (Amsterdam, 1685), fo. 10a): 'Our teacher Judah Minz of blessed memory . . . was the head of the academy . . . and after him his son, R. Abraham, o.b.m., sat on his seat, and after him his son-in-law, the great light, R. Meir Katzenellenbogen, known as the *Maharam* of Padua, and the seat of his glory was in the synagogue of the Ashkenazim . . . and no one has sat there until this day . . . and his son, the *Ga'on* R. Samuel David Katzenellenbogen became *rosh-yeshivah* and Master of the Place (*resh mata*) in Venice—and in Padua the head was R. Samuel Archivolti . . .'

Venice. Even natives of Padua saw themselves as subject to the ordinances of 'the Masters of Venice', both prior to Archivolti's appointment and during his term of office.[160] Thus, the dispute between the rabbi and the lay leadership was ultimately resolved by accepting the decision issued by the rabbis of Venice.[161]

In R. Samuel Archivolti's first certificate of appointment,[162] there is evidence that the lay leadership did not, at least initially, see the activity of the rabbi as much more than that stated in the definition of his office: 'to teach the holy community'[163]—i.e. the lay leaders of Padua felt no need to define the rabbi's position as that of an office-holder in the community, nor to include in his appointment terms which would be likely to be interpreted as implying that his status was that of a 'senior person'. Thus, whatever R. Samuel accomplished as the result of personal struggle, he never achieved the same status as the rabbi of Verona—namely, that the ordinances of the community would be made by his agreement, and that he would bring the ordinances to the vote before the community.[164]

D. Cremona

To what has already been said, we may add what is known about the situation in Cremona, where a number of rabbis were of greater stature than the official community rabbi. As in Padua, the proximity of major rabbinic figures had a negative effect upon the status of the communally appointed rabbi within his own community. One formula of rabbinic appointment from this community has survived, which may be viewed as typical for this

[160] e.g. *Pinkas Padua*, sect. 1, p. 67; sect. 57: xliv, p. 114.

[161] Ibid. sect. 690, p. 387.

[162] Although the old *pinkas* of the community of Padua has been lost, so it is difficult to determine whether the appointment from the year 1579 was the earliest one, I agree with Carpi's conclusion that the one extant is indeed the first (ibid. p. 49).

[163] Rabbi Joseph Basevi's words, in the précis he prepared of the decisions incorporated in the *pinkas*, rightly seemed to Carpi inexact and useless (ibid. p. 56, n. 4). However, it seems to me worthwhile quoting here the statement concerning the rabbinic appointment of 1579 from that précis: 'Si dà incarico a Moise Eilpron di condurre per due anni come maestro pubblico di Religione il Rabbino Samuele Archivolti verso il corrispettivo di Ducati cinque al semestre.' It is clear that Archivolti was not appointed as a school teacher, which the community of Padua evidently had already (see *Pinkas Padua*, sect. 165, p. 167, and in Sect. 9 here). Nevertheless, it seems important to point out that Basevi did not feel that the office (which he knew well, having himself been the rabbi of a community) included much more than 'maestro pubblico di Religione' (i.e. public teacher of religion)!

[164] See above, Sect. 4a.

office.[165] Throughout the sixteenth century, until the expulsion of the Jews from the duchy of Milan at the end of the century, Cremona was among the major centres of Jewish learning in Italy.[166] While the majority of the community was of Ashkenazic origin, in the second half of the century it was joined by Italian families, thereby upsetting the homogeneity of the population.[167]

Several sources[168] suggest that R. Abraham Menaḥem ha-Kohen Porto (Rappaport, 1520–after 1594) was appointed rabbi of the Cremona community during the second half of the sixteenth century. This was done by a document identical, or at least similar in its major details, to the one mentioned above. As *rosh-yeshivah*, he was honoured with a place at the head of the yeshivah and had the prerogative of expressing a final opinion in the discussions of 'their honours of the Torah, the Masters and students, members of the yeshivah'—but he is called neither 'head of Court' nor 'head and leader'. Moreover, Porto's signature comes after those

[165] See the list of sources for the appointment of rabbis from the community. The comments of Jacob Katz ('History of the Rabbinate', pp. 281–5) concerning this kind of document are also applicable regarding rabbinic appointments from Cremona.

[166] On this community, see the bibliography listed by S. Simonsohn, 'Cremona', *Mikha'el*, 1 (Tel Aviv, 1973); Benayahu and Laras, 'Health Officials'. It is certain that the size of the Jewish population in this community near the date of the expulsion did not exceed that of the Jews of Casale: archival documents confirm that there were 37 families in Cremona in 1597. See Segre, *Gli ebrei Lombardi nell'età Spagnola*, 112. While it is true that many more families lived in the town in the 1560s and 1570s, and that many Jews abandoned the duchy of Milan during the years preceding the expulsion in 1597, having foreseen what the future held, one may nevertheless not equate the numerical size of the community of Cremona with that of such communities as Mantua or Ferrara.

[167] See the responsum of R. Abraham Menaḥem Porto ha-Kohen, sect. 26 (MS Jerusalem Heb. 8to 3904, 163–4; MS Montefiore 4870, fo. 461): 'The inhabitants of the city from earlier days were entirely Ashkenazic, and they followed their custom of donning [i.e. *tefillin* (phylacteries) on *Ḥol ha-Mo'ed*] without a blessing, and recently newcomers came who were from other countries, following their own custom in all innocence, not to wear them at all, and they have [authorities] upon which to rely ... and as it is inappropriate that there be different groups, I expounded to them ... that they should all wear *tefillin* without a blessing, according to the practice of Ashkenaz. And those whose conscience prevents them from altering their [ancestral] custom will be blessed, but should stay at home or in a place in the synagogue where they will not be seen ... and they all—both new and old, Ashkenazim and Italians—said Amen, and they wore *tefillin* throughout *Ḥol ha-Mo'ed*, with the exception of this one man, who for two years has been adorned with the crown of [*the title*] *Ḥaver*, R. Moses Porto, an Ashkenazi, all of whose [ancestors] are from Ashkenazic stock, who was arrogant and said no ...' This controversy concerning the wearing of *tefillin* during *Ḥol ha-Mo'ed*, is one of many which arose in Italy at this time against the background of the spread of Kabbalah.

[168] See the sources mentioned by Benayahu and Laras, 'Health Officials', and in Sect. 4b.

of R. Aaron David Norlingen[169] and R. Isaac Seligman Ḥefetz[170] on the communal ordinances which they signed.[171] It would therefore seem that the appointment as *rosh-yeshivah* in Cremona did not necessarily convey upon its holder the status of an 'important person', and even the integrity of his status within the yeshivah may have depended upon his ability to bring to a conclusion halakhic discussions without antagonizing other local scholars. While the appointment of the rabbi in Cremona does contain several phrases referring to his supervision of religious study in the city, reminiscent of similar documents from Ashkenazic communities,[172] and subsequently carried over by R. Porto ha-Kohen to Verona,[173] those phrases suggestive of authority found in parallel documents from Ashkenazic communities are completely lacking.[174] This is a far cry from the status of the rabbi in the latter communities, whom all the people of the city, including the other rabbis, were explicitly forbidden to contradict. Not only is no protection provided against the other rabbis living in the city in case they should violate his rabbinic prerogatives, but there is not even any indication that the community at large is subject to his discipline. Needless to say, there is no mention of sanctions or punishments brought against those who violate his rulings.[175]

Unlike the situation in Verona and Casale, the terms of appointment of the rabbi in Cremona did not require him to issue ordinances at the community's request. At first glance, this would appear to express the community rabbi's independence in this matter, but such was not the case. If one carefully reads the section describing the rabbi's prerogatives to issue ordinances and set restrictions, one immediately senses the weak and rather vague tone, which is far from unambiguous. While it does stress the public's looking for initiative on the part of the rabbi, it does not state how that initiative is meant to operate. One clearly senses that other factors are taken into consideration here—i.e.

[169] See Simonsohn, *Mantua*, 722.

[170] See Simonsohn, introduction to Modena, *Teshuvot Ziknei Yehudah*, 41. Cf. n. 64.

[171] See Benayahu and Laras, 'Health Officials', p. 100; Simonsohn, 'Cremona', 263.

[172] We have already seen that in Padua similar prerogatives were also granted to the appointed rabbi.

[173] See the ordination appointment from Verona of 1584.

[174] Compare Katz, 'History of the Rabbinate', 291–2, sects. 4, 7, 8.

[175] Cf. ibid. 286, 289, 294, sect. 33.

the other *ge'onim* in the city, whose agreement is required for making decisions.[176] Thus, as the status of the community-appointed rabbi as the 'senior person' of the city was not unchallenged, he could not be required to issue ordinances with the ban. Instead, he was charged with searching for the means of issuing ordinances, on the assumption that the delicacy of the rabbi's position would require him to behave with the requisite caution in order to avoid dispute. Hence, although R. Abraham Menaḥem Porto ha-Kohen seems to have been the official rabbi of Cremona, he explicitly states that he was unable to issue a ban against those who read *Me'or 'Einayim*[177] by R. Azariah de Rossi (*c.* 1511–78) without the agreement of Rabbi Eli'ezer Ashkenazi, who was not present in the city at the time that the problem arose, 'because in the place of great men, it is not my place to step over the heads of the holy people'.[178] If, on one occasion, he had seen fit to overstep this limitation—thanks to the confidence he gained from the special appointment he received at the time of the plague emergency to issue ordinances of the 'health officials', and from the support of R. Isaac Seligman Ḥefetz, who was appointed together with him at that time—in the final analysis, and in the light of the opposition of R. Eli'ezer Ashkenazi, the ban imposed by the health officials was abolished. Much to

[176] See the wording of the appointment: 'and he shall seek to silence the contentious and to make peace between the members of our people, and to decree and make limitations in accordance with the needs of the times, for this is the office which the honourable rabbi carries on his shoulders'. Cf. sect. 7 of the appointment granted to R. Abraham Menaḥem Porto in Verona (Sonne, 'Basic Premisses', 170–1): 'he may not excommunicate . . . any person of those who dwell in our holy congregation, save with the agreement of the lay leaders or the majority of them'. That is to say, in Cremona the rabbi is the one who takes the initiative, requiring only the agreement of the majority of the lay leaders in order to act.

[177] This work, first published in Mantua in 1573, was one of the first Hebrew books to deal with traditional sacred texts in a critical manner. It questioned especially the validity of many Talmudic and Midrashic legends and of the traditional chronology of biblical history, and was at the centre of a bitter controversy throughout Italy and in many other parts of the Jewish world.

[178] See his remarks regarding the question of the prohibition against reading *Me'or 'Enayim* in D. Kaufmann, *Gesammelte Schriften* iii (Frankfurt-on-Main, 1915), 92–4; Judah Aryeh Leib Wadislowski, *Sefer Toldot Rabbenu Menaḥem 'Azaryah mi-Fano* (Piotrkow, 1902), 18. Cf. the remarks by R. Abraham Menaḥem Porto ha-Kohen in his responsa, sect. 5, regarding another controversy involving R. Eli'ezer Ashkenazi: 'and although I loved the Excellent Rabbi Eli'ezer Ashkenazi, whose net is spread over all the people of the Exile, and it is known . . . that he is a great prince in Israel, and that the radiance of his light particularly enlightens the members of the congregation here, in the Holy Congregation of Cremona, and it is exceedingly hard for me to oppose his intention . . .'

his distress, Porto was forced to sign the compromises agreed upon by R. Eli'ezer Ashkenazi and R. Isaac Seligman Ḥefetz.[179]

In any event, the facts recorded by R. Abraham Menaḥem Porto ha-Kohen about the appeal addressed to him by the community heads concerning de Rossi's book, coupled with the fact that he was prevented from imposing the ban, indicates that both sides saw this as a matter pertaining to the definition of his office. This would support the assumption that he was indeed the official communal rabbi at that time. Thus, we find that his status depended upon his skill in manœuvering among the scholars, whom he himself acknowledged as his superiors in learning. It is therefore not surprising that he preferred the office of assistant rabbi in Verona, leaving his appointment in Cremona in the hope (which was in fact realized) that he would eventually be appointed communal rabbi in the former city.[180] This decision is particularly significant in the light of his ongoing opposition to any restriction on the rabbi's freedom to impose excommunication, expressed in the afore-mentioned letter which he sent from Cremona (where the rabbi's authority to issue bans had not yet been formally restricted)[181] to Candia in 1574[182] or shortly thereafter.[183] The clause in his appointment in Verona, explicitly enjoining him from imposing excommunication without the agreement of the lay leadership, should also be read in the light of that opposition.[184]

It follows from all this that, even if R. Abraham Menaḥem

179 See Benayahu and Laras, 'Health Officials'.

180 See Sonne, 'Basic Premisses', 170–1. Benayahu and Laras, 'Health Officials', 82, sensed the strange nature of this decision by R. Abraham Menaḥem Porto ha-Kohen, which they explained by suggesting its attribution 'to the increased troubles in the community, or to the increasing number of ordinances against the Jews'. As a further clarification, it should be stressed that Porto did not adopt this decision until after a referendum among all the members of the community of Verona 'to examine. . . whether they are satisfied and pleased with his honour'! This referendum presented a considerable problem for the leaders of the congregation, who agreed to this innovation only on condition that it should not become a precedent which would detract from 'the power of the *parti* and our ordinances and customs, whether [applying to] the future or the past' (see the full text of the decisions in the Hebrew edition of this book, Document 29, p. 245.

181 Nothing is said in the appointment of the communal rabbi concerning this matter.

182 See the discussion of communal ordinances pertaining to the *ḥerem* in Ch. 2, Sect. 4.

183 The ordinance, to which R. Abraham Menaḥem Porto ha-Kohen objected, is from the year 1574, and in this year he was certainly already in Cremona (see Benayahu and Laras, 'Health Officials', 81; Simonsohn, 'Cremona', 263).

184 See the rabbinic appointment, Simonsohn, 'Cremona', sect. 7.

ha-Kohen Porto served as the community rabbi in Cremona, he was clearly not the 'master of the city'.[185] This latter term, *mara de-atra*, was applied to R. Aaron David Norlingen who, as we have seen, lived in Cremona at the same time as Porto. In 1608, R. Judah Saltaro da Fano wrote of Norlingen in his book *Palgei Mayim* as follows: 'he was the head of the yeshiva (*resh metivta*) and the Master (*mara de-atra*) of the holy community of Cremona, and is now the elder of the sages of Mantua'.[186] One might of course argue that R. Aaron David Norlingen, and not R. Abraham Menaḥem ha-Kohen Porto, was the official rabbi in Cremona. This would invalidate what has been said concerning the status of the appointed rabbi in Cremona on the basis of the latter's situation. But this argument appears very problematic: as we have seen above, Porto issued halakhic rulings to all of the inhabitants of Cremona, and they turned to him to rule upon the proposal to excommunicate all those who read de Rossi's book. He was likewise the one to take upon himself the struggle against R. Eli'ezer Ashkenazi on the matter of the 'health ordinances', even though he added to his responsa the argument that 'if your honour will defeat me, my colleagues will say that you have defeated a layman'.[187] In the absence of additional evidence, I tend to accept the view that R. Abraham Menaḥem ha-Kohen Porto was Cremona's official rabbi, as well as the *de facto* head of the yeshiva, even though he did not enjoy the full status of *rosh-yeshivah* in his community due to the influence of the other sages of the city.

A similar situation, albeit of a totally different order in terms of the stature of the figures involved, emerged in Verona at the end of the sixteenth century. There, the position of community-appointed rabbi overlapped with that of *rosh-yeshivah* and of the 'great one of the city'. For this reason, he maintained the prerogatives of *rosh-yeshivah* even when he was unable to 'come daily to sit in the yeshivah' due to the burden of communal responsibilities, and was forced to appoint another rabbi to fill his place and to sign on his behalf.[188] On the other hand,

[185] He is designated thus by Benayahu and Laras, 'Health Officials', 100. This is also how Sonne designates all the rabbis appointed by the communities (see Sonne, 'History of the Community of Bologna', *HUCA* 16 (1942), 40).

[186] R. Judah Saltaro, *Sefer Palgei Mayim* (Venice, 1608), fo. 15a.

[187] See Benayahu and Laras, 'Health Officials', 102.

[188] See Sonne, 'Basic Premisses', 179, Document 23.

R. Abraham Menaḥem ha-Kohen Porto served in practice as *rosh-yeshivah* in Cremona by virtue of his appointment as communally appointed rabbi, even though he did not bear the title of 'yeshivah head and teacher of the community'.[189] The one to enjoy this status in Cremona was R. Aaron David Norlingen!

In the source referring to R. Norlingen as '*rosh-yeshivah* and Master in the Holy Community of Cremona', only one other rabbi is honoured with the title *mara de-atra*—namely, R. Samuel Archivolti.[190] But one cannot argue that this constitutes prima-facie evidence that the communally appointed rabbi is always designated by the title of *mara de-atra*: in fact, R. Mordecai Bassan, who was certainly the official rabbi in Verona, is mentioned in this same document without that title. We may therefore conclude that the title *mara de-atra* did not serve during our period in any way other than in its original sense in classical rabbinic literature—i.e. to emphasize that a particular rabbi was considered the most important rabbi in his town. Further evidence of this is the fact that in the book *Mikveh Yisra'el*, in which many rabbis are mentioned by name, the only rabbi designated as *mara de-atra* is R. Abtalyon di Consilio,[191] who was at the time the only ordained rabbi in his community.

To summarize: the office and status of the community-appointed rabbi depended upon the conditions in those particular localities where the office first took shape from its earliest development out of the model of the *rosh-yeshivah*, and in the light of the need to grant sacral power to the community ordinances by means of 'a senior person'. The concepts of yeshivah-head and of head of Court, which naturally accompanied it, were an integral part of the concept of 'communally appointed rabbi', although during the process of the actual shaping of this office they were not identical in the various communities, and at times these concepts became exclusively ideals. Wherever the homogeneity of the population and its numerical size encouraged the tendency to

[189] There is perhaps a certain similarity here to the tension which arose in the Ashkenazic communities between the Head of Court and the *rosh-yeshivah* (see Ben-Sasson, *Hagut ve-Hanhagah*, 168–70).

[190] See *Sefer Palgei Mayim*, fo. 15a, and, at the end of the book, the list of those sages who prohibited the ritual bath in Rovigo.

[191] R. Judah Saltaro, *Mikveh Yisrael* (Venice, 1607), fo. 6b. R. Abtalyon's ordination is cited at the beginning of *Sefer Palgei Mayim*.

appoint a community rabbi, the rabbi's personality and the presence or absence of other important rabbinic scholars in or near the community had a decisive effect on the shaping of the office. In those communities where the concept of 'the great one of the city' was organically associated with that of *rosh-yeshivah*, the title 'head of Court' gained distinct definition and the rabbi was able to strengthen his position and to impose his influence upon the community leadership. It is therefore not surprising that in Verona, where such conditions were created, things reached the point that, towards the end of the period under discussion, the power of the rabbi was like that of 'one of the leaders [*parnassim*] of the community and his voice . . . is considered as one of them'.[192] In no other community have we found a community-appointed rabbi enjoying a similar status. In so far as various different factors, the most important of which we have mentioned, hampered the possibility of identifying the appointed rabbi with the 'great one of the town', the concepts of *rosh-yeshivah* and head of Court were emptied of their contents, and at times the rabbi was not even referred to by these titles at all. In such cases, the rabbi's status was also harmed and the value of accepting such office became doubtful, as the example of Cremona clearly illustrates.

5. R. Moses Basola's Critique

Once created, it was only natural that the communities should attempt to strengthen and consolidate the office of community rabbi. By reinforcing the rabbi's position, that of the internal communal leadership was also strengthened. This attitude is especially evident in the ordinance issued by the Synod of Ferrara in 1554, prohibiting other rabbis from imposing the ban in any community without the permission of the community-appointed rabbi.[193] We have already seen that in most communities the official rabbi was himself proscribed from imposing the ban

[192] See Sonne, 'Basic Premisses', 182, Document 27.

[193] See Sect. 1 above. There were cases in which the communities participated in the granting of this permission. Thus, in Verona, many years after 1554, it was stressed that every promulgation of a ban was conditional upon 'the permission and agreement of . . . the [communal] rabbi with the majority of the lay leaders' (Sonne, 'Basic Premisses', 179, Document 22).

without the permission of the *parnassim*.[194] Thus, the obligation imposed upon the community rabbi to issue ordinances in accordance with the will of the *parnassim*—which was at times expressed in blunt terms, such as 'he cannot refuse'—suggests that the very point which is intended to symbolize the authority of the community-appointed rabbi also reflects the severe restriction of his freedom. In fact, the above ordinance was a means of strengthening the leadership of the *parnassim*, even if from a formal point of view it enhanced the respect and authority of the official community rabbinate.[195]

It is therefore not surprising that, throughout the period under discussion, not a single leading rabbinic figure was appointed to this office by any of the local communities. R. Moses Basola (1480–1560) makes this point very clearly in his objections to the ordinance of Ferrara:

> This arrangement cannot be a lasting one, for how can it be that the rabbi be considered as the lord or the duke of the city, absolutely sovereign to do whatever he decides? . . . Furthermore, they did even worse in saying that no other rabbi in that town may issue ordinances wherever there is a rabbi appointed by the community or by the communal leaders. Thus, they have elevated themselves in order to do as they wish with the rabbi they have set up for themselves, a man who eats that which is not his and is afraid[196] to look at them. In fact, it is proper to chasten those rabbis who unjustly issue edicts which do not conform to *halakhah*.[197]

In other words: while one may legitimately issue regulations against those rabbis who rule their communities arbitrarily and impose excommunication alongside the rulings themselves[198] this ought not be done by adding to the prerogatives of the community rabbi, as this simply strengthens the lay leaders of the community.[199]

[194] See Sect. 4a, and the appointment of the rabbi in Casale.

[195] Cf. Shulvass, *Renaissance*, 55.

[196] Following a different reading, the source would be: 'one who eats at his fellow's [table] is afraid to look at him [thereafter].' (Cf. Jerusalem Talmud Orlah 1: 1, fo. 61b.)

[197] See S. Z. H. Halberstamm, 'The Ordinances of 1554' (Heb.), *'Ivri Anokhi*, 31 (1879), 267.

[198] This is a sign that even R. Moses Basola was aware of this, as there was exaggerated use of bans and excommunication in his day. See on this Ch. 2, Sect. 4, for Porto ha-Kohen's comments on this matter.

[199] It is not clear whether Basola's objections that 'he eats that which is not his and is afraid to look at them' alludes to the rabbi's economic dependence upon the community.

These comments of R. Moses Basola, who was among the greatest rabbis of his day in Italy, and whose name was well known even in non-Jewish circles,[200] clearly expresses that subjugation to the lay leadership which was part and parcel of rabbinic appointment. This situation certainly made some distinguished rabbis reluctant to succumb to the temptation embodied in the image of rulership associated with the office of the communally appointed rabbi. An additional factor making for such reluctance was certainly the local presence of other prominent rabbinic scholars who were not subject to the *parnassim*. We can therefore state in conclusion that the status of the community-appointed rabbi was inversely proportionate to that of the other scholars in the community.

R. Moses Basola's contempt for the community-appointed rabbis, hinting that they made cynical use of their titles, was certainly exaggerated. In fact, although the office was not particularly attractive to individuals of R. Moses Basola's stature, one cannot say that those who served in it were unqualified. Many of those who were seen by their communities as worthy of the office and who, in fact, accepted it, such as R. Abraham Menaḥem ha-Kohen Porto, R. Abraham Provenzali, and R. Samuel Archivolti, while not the greatest scholars of their day, were far from being mediocre. Nevertheless, Basola was correct in his comparison of the stature of those community-appointed rabbis whom he knew in his day to that of the great rabbis of the period. One must again emphasize that criticism of the type issued by R. Moses Basola can only be properly understood in the context of a situation in which the office was considered an innovation, and therefore subject to discussion and negotiation. That is to say, while both the critic and the public to whom his criticisms were directed knew that not every community had an

If this is the case, his zeal for the rabbis' independence was exaggerated: it is difficult to imagine that the modest salaries received by the appointed rabbis would be sufficient cause for them to become so subjugated to the lay leaders as to be transformed into 'puppet rabbis', whose concern for their daily bread took precedence over their fear of God. It may be that Basola wished to formulate his objections in blunt terms, and that what he really meant was that the appointed rabbi had ('eats') an authority which was not really his, but was granted to him by the leaders of the community, to whom he became subjected by his very appointment, so that 'he is frightened to look at them'. This matter will be discussed at greater length.

200 See I. Tishby, 'The Controversy Concerning *Sefer ha-Zohar* in 16th Century Italy' (Heb.), in his *Ḥikrei Kabbalah u-Sheluḥoteha*, i (Jerusalem, 1982), 96–9.

appointed rabbi as yet, one could still hope that negative criticism of the institution might prove constructive.[201]

6. The Sephardic Model of 'Torah Teacher'

Another possible source of the institution is revealed by examining the definition of the office of community-appointed rabbi in those appointments extant in the record books (*pinkasim*) of the communities of northern Italy: namely, the tradition of the Sephardic communities adopted by the communities of southern Italy during the late fifteenth and early sixteenth centuries. Discussion concerning the situation in southern Italy must necessarily be focused exclusively on the kingdom of Naples, and particularly on the city itself, where the Jewish community continued to exist after the Expulsion of 1492—i.e. after settlement in the rest of the southern portion of the kingdom had been abolished. Nevertheless, several comments on the situation in southern Italy prior to the expulsion, i.e. including Sicily, are in order.

There are hardly any extant sources clarifying the position and function of the rabbis within the framework of the internal leadership and spiritual life of the communities of southern Italy prior to the arrival of the exiles from Spain and Portugal. Most of our knowledge of those communities is based upon studies undertaken by Christian scholars, who examined the archival material in their own way, giving us only a rather fragmentary picture of the subject.[202] Moreover, there are no extant Hebrew sources explaining how, prior to the emergence of the institution of ordination as described in Chapter 2, a given individual became recognized as a 'rabbi' in these communities. As far as matters can be reconstructed from the published documents, the framework of the religious-spiritual leadership of the communities of southern Italy had, prior to the arrival of the exiles from Spain and Portugal, been rooted in older forms known from various medieval

[201] However, as is well known, Sonne and others saw the opposition of R. Moses Basola to the ordinances of Ferrara as an aspect of the tension between 'itinerant rabbis' and 'official rabbis'. We shall return to this point at greater length in Ch. 4.

[202] A comprehensive survey of the communities of Southern Italy and the pertinent literature may be found in S. W. Baron, *A Social and Religious History of the Jews*, 16 vols. (Philadelphia, 1952–76), x. 220–46, 398–406; idem, *The Jewish Community*, 3 vols. (Philadelphia, 1942), i. 230–2; ii. 58–9, 75–6; iii. 54–5, 121, 125.

sources. We know that cantors were of particular significance within the framework of the communal organization,[203] together with the scribes and synagogue beadles. The definition of the task of the cantor, who was designated in a 1392 document as the 'elder of the Jews' (presbyter), was 'to sing the prayers in the synagogue and to prepare and write Hebrew documents according to their [*the Jews'*] custom'.[204] A 1455 document refers to the cantor, along with the scribe and the beadle, as performing functions essential to the proper functioning of the Jewish community.[205] In some cases the functions of scribe and cantor were concentrated in one individual, while in others there were scribes appointed whose only job was to produce Hebrew documents.

From the evidence of published non-Jewish documentation, it would seem that, during the second half of the fifteenth century, excommunication procedures were entrusted to the rabbis 'who sat at the head of the synagogue, delivered sermons and expounded the holy Writ, and ruled on matters of law and banned offenders'—even in southern Italy.[206] The overall impression gained is that, as in the well-known picture one gains from the Scroll of Ahimaʿaẓ, the rabbi's activity was focused within the yeshivah, from whence radiated his influence over the public.[207] He also evidently

203 On the medieval cantor, see S. Lieberman, 'Yanai's *Ḥazzanut*' (Heb.), *Sinai*, 4 (1939), 222–3; E. E. Urbach's review of A. I. Agus's edition of *Teshuvot Baʿalei ha-Tosafot*, *KS* 30 (1955) 204–5; S. Schwarzfuchs, *Études sur l'origine et le developpement du Rabbinat au Moyen-Age* (Paris, 1957), 20; Mortara, *Indice alfabetico*, p. 27 n. 1. Cf. also L. Landman, 'The Office of the Medieval Hazzan', *JQR* 62 (1971–2), 156–87, 246–76.

204 According to the list of rights granted by King Martin to the bishop of Mazzara, as quoted in F. Lionti, 'I ministri della religione presso gli ebrei di Sicilia', *Archivio storico Siciliano* n.s. 10 (1885), 131: 'ad cuius officium pertinet canere officia in Synagogis, et conficere contractus et scribere instrumenta hebraica et secundum ritum eorum'.

205 See B. and G. Lagumina, *Codice diplomatico dei guidei di Sicilia* (Palermo, 1884–95), i. 559; Lionti, 'I ministri della religione presso', 133–4 (letter of Alphonso to the heads of the community in Trapani): 'Alfonsus . . . prothis Iudaice terre Drepani . . . visis et recognitis literis vestris quibus exponitis quod, volentibus vobis creare et ordinare quosdam officiales necessarios et utiles eidem Iudaice et presertim notarios, chasenos et sacristanos . . . volentes nos huic rei salubriter providere, vobis dicimus et mandamus quatenus . . . officiales ipsos creatos, faciatis et ordinetis necessarios et utiles eidem Iudaice et presertim chasenos, notaros et sacristanos . . .' Cf. Lionti, ibid. 134.

206 Ibid. 132; N. Ferorelli, *Gli ebrei nell'Italia meridionale* (Turin, 1915; repr. Bologna, 1966), 104–5. Cf. *Megillat Aḥimaʿaẓ*, ed. Klar (Jerusalem, 1944), 37, and L. Modena's remarks quoted above, Ch. 2, Sect. 4 and n. 146.

207 It is worth remarking that the rabbis required the permission of the heads of the congregation and of the lay leaders (*ṭuvei ha-ʿir*) in order to preach in the synagogue or to impose bans. See Lionti, 'I ministri della religione presso', 134.

received payment for adjudicating disputes upon request.[208]

Into these forms were merged the distinctive institutions brought by the Spanish and Portuguese exiles from their lands of origin. This process should not be thought of simply as a result of the migration of Spanish and Portuguese exiles into Italy. Southern Italy had been subject to Spanish influence for centuries; even in Jewish institutions one can see certain similarities, such as the institution of the general judge, which resembled that of the *rab de la corte* (the rabbi appointed by the king to rule over Jewish affairs).[209] However, to date no Hebrew sources have emerged likely to shed light upon the nature of the similarity between the forms of communal organization *vis-à-vis* the rabbinate in southern Italy and in Spain and Portugal. I must therefore confine myself to noting the massive migration of the Jews of Spain and Portugal to southern Italy at the end of the fifteenth century. Even without relying upon various speculative assumptions,[210] there is no doubt that many of the exiles from Spain and Portugal found refuge in the towns of the kingdom of Naples, where they became for a while an extremely important factor within the Jewish population; their traditional forms of leadership emerged clearly wherever they settled.

From the early fifteenth century on, every Jewish community of Spain was required to appoint a Torah teacher (*marbiẓ Torah*). The first section of the 1432 ordinances of Valladolid states that:

> wherever there are forty householders or more, they are required to do everything within their power to maintain among themselves a Torah teacher to teach Talmud, *halakhah*, and *aggadah*. The community is obliged to support him in a fitting manner, with items of the best quality, from the income of the taxes on meat and wine, and from the charity fund . . . or of the free-offerings for the Torah study, so that he need not beg for his needs, or need to appeal to the wealthy individuals of the community. He is to serve as a preacher, chastener and guide in all things related to the service of the Creator . . . And if

208 See Ferorelli, *Gli ebrei nell'Italia meridionale*, esp. p. 105 n. 1.

209 See I. Loeb, 'Réglement des Juifs de Castille en 1432 comparé avec les réglements des Juifs de Sicile et d'autres pays', *REJ* 13 (1896), 206–16.

210 Such as Ferorelli's calculations, *Gli ebrei nell'Italia meridionale*, 78–98. His main assumptions (pp. 96–8) are that the taxes paid by the Jews to the government were identical to those paid by the Christians, and that the average family contained five members. Compare S. Simonsohn, 'The Jews of Syracuse and their Cemetery' (Heb.), *Sefunot*, 8 (1964), 276.

the community does not reach an agreement with the Torah teacher with regard to the sum he is to be paid, they are to pay him the amount of the tax of Torah study in that place, or to add to it if it is insufficient—all in accordance with the judgement of the *rab de la corte*.[211]

The same ordinance states that it is preferable that all Torah teachers have a 'fixed place to study with whomever wishes to hear the Law from him'.

This ordinance prescribed three clear tasks of the Torah teacher: to preach in public, to rule in matters of Jewish law when asked to do so by members of the community, and to teach. This was summarized in the following way by R. Isaac Abrabanel: 'the preacher of Torah . . . is the teacher, is the one who rules on matters of law, and is the admonisher.'[212] The nature of this teaching is not explicitly stated in the regulation, but from the prevailing situation in the communities of the Spanish exiles, we may infer that this refers to lecturing in Talmud with the *Tosafot* or the Code of Alfasi, as well as lectures on the halakhic codes (e.g. Maimonides' *Mishneh Torah*, R. Moses of Coucy's *Sefer Miẓvot ha-Gadol* [*Semag*] or, in a later age, the *Arba'ah Ṭurim* of R. Jacob ben Asher) which the rabbi delivered in the synagogue at fixed times every day. The comment concerning the desirability of the Torah teacher having 'a fixed place to study with whomever wishes to hear the Law from him' suggests that the establishment of the yeshivah might have been seen as a positive development in the office of the rabbi, because it would raise the level of religious knowledge within the community, and possibly because it would tend as well to strengthen the status of the 'Torah teacher'. As defined in this ordinance, the office need not be directly connected with the administration of justice and the government of the community.[213] The 'Torah teacher' was not necessarily synonymous with the 'Torah scholar' (*talmid ḥakham*), who determined whom the judges of the community were supposed

[211] See F. Baer, *Die Juden in christlichen Spanien, ii* (Berlin, 1936), 283. The text here cited is based upon Assaf, *Ḥinukh*, ii. 83. See also Finkelstein, *Self-government*, 354; F. Baer, *History of the Jews in Christian Spain* ii. 263; M. Benayahu, *Marbiẓ Torah* (Jerusalem, 1953), 13.

[212] R. Isaac Abrabanel, *Naḥalath Avot*, on Avot 4: 5.

[213] Compare Finkelstein's remarks, *Self-government*, as noted at the beginning of this chapter.

to fine and punish as transgressors,[214] although it was natural that they would turn first of all to him, in those places were there were no greater scholars. However, in the third section of the ordinances of Valladolid, it is stated explicitly that permission to sue one who did not obey a ruling or summons from the Jewish courts in non-Jewish courts was subject to the agreement of the judges and the scholar of the community. The Torah scholar to whom the judges of the community turned for advice in their battle against the informers and slanderers was not necessarily identical with the Torah teacher; it is explicitly stated that the judges ought to follow 'the decision of the greatest Torah sages they can find'.[215]

The Spanish exiles reconstituted the office of 'Torah teacher' in their new places of exile. The new office of community rabbi (*ḥakham*), as well as his position within the legal and political arrangements of the community, was based upon it,[216] in conformity with the new situation which took shape in the various communities. I do not intend to investigate here this development within the communities of the Spanish exiles. However, there seems little doubt that, in the tradition which the Spanish exiles brought with them, the office of Torah teacher was clearly defined by its contents, and that a salary went with it, in order to enable the rabbi to 'make the Torah his fixed occupation and all labour despised and abandoned',[217] even though the discussion concerning the legitimacy of accepting such a salary never completely ceased.[218]

Don David ibn Yaḥya (1465–1543) was appointed to such a

[214] See Baer, *History of the Jews*, 263–4.

[215] Ibid. 265.

[216] See the appointments from Magnesia (from 1555) and from Patras (from before 1592) cited by Benayahu, *Marbiẓ Torah*, 22–6. Compare D. Benvenisti, *Yehudei Saloniki be-dorot ha-Aḥaronim* (Jerusalem, 1973), 180–3.

[217] Based upon the wording of the rabbi in Rhodes from 1612; see Benayahu, *Marbiẓ Torah*, 26.

[218] See Baer, *History of the Jews*, 221–3; Abrabanel, *Naḥalat Avot*, on Avot 4: 5; R. Simeon b. Ẓemaḥ Duran, *Teshuvot* (*Tashbeẓ*) (Amsterdam, 1738–41), Pt. I, sect. 142; R. Yosef Ya'veẓ, *Ma'amar Ḥasdei ha-Shem*, commentary on Avot 4: 5 (in the 1533 Constantinople edn., fos. 95–8), and cf. the introduction by his son, R. Isaac; R. Obadiah Sforno's commentary to the same *mishnah*; R. Moses Yakar Ashkenazi, at the end of *Sefer Petaḥ 'Einayim* (Cracow edn., 12–13); R. David b. Messer Leon, based upon the *Tashbeẓ*, in S. Schechter, 'Notes sur Messer David Leon Tirées de Manuscrits', *REJ* 24 (1892), 127–8. See also Ben-Sasson, *Hagut ve-Hanhagah*, 160; Katz, *Tradition and Crisis*, 95–6.

position in Naples at the beginning of the sixteenth century.[219] In a letter to other scholars,[220] he justified his request for salary from the community by citing the fact that a similar practice existed in Otranto and Sulmona.[221] He reported that the community had assigned him the task 'both of preaching on the Sabbath day[222] . . . and of ruling upon those legal questions which occur daily, both here and in nearby communities,[223] as well as to hear litigants and arbitrate disputes.[224] And I also began to teach and to learn Talmud and commentaries and other things, until the number of students grew.'[225] His teaching activities are portrayed by R. David in a manner which suggests that he did far more than was required of a Torah teacher under the formal rubric of the office given above:

And apart from all that, I was the *repetitor* for the younger students, and I studied with them until mealtime, and in the afternoon I studied a different subject with them until the Afternoon Prayers, and on winter evenings until six o'clock. In addition, I studied with them[226] a daily chapter of Talmud, and other subjects such as grammar and poetics and logic and [*al-Ghazali's*] *Intentions of the Philosophers* and [*Jedaiah Bedersi's*] *Book of the Examination of the World*. And on the Sabbaths [I would] sometimes teach [*Judah ha-Levi's*] *Kuzari* and at times [*Maimonides'*] *Guide for the Perplexed*. And all this, even though I was only required to teach one Talmudic lesson every morning, in order that they should know what is required, and to rule on what they ask me each day. But in order to fulfil what is required of me by heaven

[219] See A. Marx, 'Life of an Italian Rabbi', *HUCA* 1 (1924). It is superfluous to stress that it is beyond all doubt, from the figures mentioned by R. David ibn Yaḥya in his letter, that the entire communal framework within which he worked was of a clearly Spanish character.

[220] Sonne has speculated that the letter was sent to a conference of rabbis or of representatives of communities. See I. Sonne, 'The General Synod in Italy, Father of the *Va'ad Arba 'Araẓot* in Poland' (Heb.), *ha-Tekufah*, 32–3 (1948), 665–7.

[221] See Marx, 'Life of an Italian Rabbi', 621.

[222] I have deleted here four words, translated 'and also to write their letters and epistles'—which I shall discuss further.

[223] This certainly refers to those communities which were within the orbit of the central community in Naples.

[224] It is clear that he is not alluding here to an appointment as a community judge; rather, disputants came to him voluntarily to seek halakhic rulings. If in other passages, such as in R. Gedalyah ibn Yaḥya's *Shalshelet ha-Kabbalah*, he is referred to as a 'judge', this does not match his description here, and one is not to take it as meant literally. See *Sefer Shalshelet ha-Kabbalah* (Amsterdam, 1697), fo. 52b.

[225] Marx, 'The Life of an Italian Rabbi', 616.

[226] This certainly means, 'among the members of the congregation'.

and by the people, I went beyond my [required] quota, with great effort and painful labour.[227]

In other words: the formal definition of the office required of him no more than 'to teach one Talmudic subject every morning . . . and to rule on what they ask me each day'.

The other task which constituted R. David's position, 'acting as scribe of the community, to write their letters and epistles',[228] was undertaken voluntarily, out of a sense of moral responsibility as a Torah scholar to assist in the needs of the community.[229] At the end of his proposed request he again emphasized that:

I have troubled myself *much more than was required of me* . . . for I was only required to teach the Talmudic subjects, but I served as *repetitor* . . . I was only required to teach in the morning, but I taught morning and mid day, and in the evening until six o'clock. I was only required to teach Talmud with commentaries, and I taught grammar and poetics and music and *Intentions of the Philosophers* and *The Book of the Examination of the World*. And I was not required to be their scribe . . . nor was I required to judge and to issue rulings, but only to rule 'yes' or 'no' [i.e. *to decide one way or another on halakhic issues*]. And I exhausted myself in inviting litigants to my home, to charm them and to force them to accept a compromise and to make peace among them, and it never occurred that a matter came to me which I judged according to the letter of the law, but only by way of compromise with the agreement of the two parties involved, taking great trouble with them. Nor was I required to compose the documents regarding transactions of individuals between one another—and in this matter also I humbled myself, to save them the cost of taking a Christian scribe, for there was no Jewish scribe in the whole community upon whom they could rely.[230]

It follows from this that R. David saw his appointment as demanding of him only that he preach, rule on halakhic matters, and teach Talmud and its commentaries every morning. Everything else he did of his own free will and, because he counted upon a

227 Marx, ibid. 617.

228 Ibid. 616, and see Documents 4 and 8 in the Hebrew edition of this book, 216–17, 222.

229 'And I also made myself the scribe of the communities, for all of their many communications . . . and I even served as the scribe for individuals for documents of *compromesso* to arbitration and receipts and rulings and business matters and betrothals and all other matters between man and his fellow, without [taking] salary or fixed payment.'—Marx, ibid. 617. My emphasis.

230 Ibid. 621. My emphasis.

salary from the community, he was prepared to forgo any subsidiary income. He testified that:

I never received as much as a penny from private individuals, and even in those matters which Torah scholars are accustomed to receive: not for performing marriages or divorces or levirate marriages, or for arbitrating [disputes], or for writing letters, or for composing halakhic decisions sent outside [i.e. *of the community*]. And if on occasion some individual would send me a gift out of politeness, I returned it, until people became acquainted with my character and ceased doing so.[231]

Only when his salary was overdue did he permit himself to accept gifts. In fact, he defended such actions in words which were intended to refute the accusations of those who thought that these gifts weakened his claim to a salary.[232] Thus, despite the narrow formal definition of the office, based upon the previously mentioned tradition of the Spanish communities, the rabbi considered that office as a fairly good basis upon which to build, and to widen its scope in accordance with his understanding and his talents. Once these hopes were disappointed, he asked for his salary retroactively, on the basis of that same limited understanding of the office.

7. Different Approaches among Ashkenazim and Sephardim

In his responsum relating to R. David ibn Yaḥya's request,[233] R. Meir of Padua stated in summary that 'the principal payment which a rabbi requests is for his teaching, and it would appear that his task is to teach the Talmudic subjects, to preach, and to issue rulings on matters of divorce and marriage and forbidden

[231] Ibid.

[232] Ibid. 623.

[233] *Teshuvot ha-Maharam mi-Padua*, sect. 40. At present, I see no way of answering the question as to why R. Meir cited Otranto rather than Naples as the place of residence of his correspondent, other than Marx's hypothesis ('The Life of an Italian Rabbi', 615, n. 30) that there was indeed a confusion in his responsum. Schwarzfuchs, who has devoted a full-length study to the analysis of R. Meir's responsa as a historical source, does not touch upon this question, nor mention Marx's article. See S. Schwarzfuchs, 'I responsi di Rabbi Meir da Padova come fonte storica', in *Scritti in memoria di Leone Carpi* (Milan and Jerusalem, 1967), 121–2.

and permitted things'.[234] R. Meir found the request itself, as stated in R. David's letter, astonishing:

Wherefore did your honour see fit to demand payment for these, and even to ask [payment] for that which you have done in the past, notwithstanding the fact that no payment had been set, according to the conclusion of the Talmud in the [4th chapter of Tractate *Nedarim*].[235] We are not entitled to receive payment save for the teaching of Scripture—either as payment for guarding [the children], according to Rav's view, or for teaching them the cantillation of the text, according to Rabbi Joḥanan—but that one is not allowed to do for teaching Midrash and *halakhot* and *'aggadot*, as is written, ' "As I have commanded you" [236]—just as I [instructed you] for nothing, so should you do so for nothing.'

He nevertheless acknowledged the legitimacy of one of the arguments that could have been propounded by R. David—namely, that his teaching required special effort on his part, as 'the students did not understand the Talmudic text after it was stated only once, and on this ground he could demand a salary from them'.[237] However, as R. Meir also recognized that the community could reasonably 'argue in their defence, as R. Isaac of Corbeil's *Sefer Mizvot Katan* states, that it is nevertheless a meritorious act [*mizvah*] to repeat [the lesson] several times, one could reasonably argue that his [R. David's] intention was [to teach] only for the sake of this meritorious act; perhaps they actually thought that such was the rabbi's intention[238] and they did not set aside salary for him'. On what grounds then could R. David base his claim? 'He could find no justification for taking salary retroactively for being their authority in matters of ritual and divorce and marriage!' Rabbi Meir added: 'And if your honour will state that in these times a rabbi takes payment from the community, it is only on the basis of the argument given by R. Isaac in the *Tosafot* [in the 13th chapter of Tractate

[234] It should be stressed in this context that R. Meir nowhere in his writings mentioned R. David's teaching activity, nor his ruling in controversies, so that Marx's criticism ('The Life of an Italian Rabbi', 613 n. 24) of M. Güdemann's remarks ('Die Neugestaltung des Rabbinerwesens', *MGWJ* 13 (1864), 423) seems to me quite superfluous.

[235] Nedarim 37a.

[236] Deut. 4: 5.

[237] On this point R. David argued that he did not wish for anything, but that he became a *repetitor* of his own will!

[238] Indeed, 'such was the rabbi's intention', by his own testimony!

Ketubot],[239] in which he explains that the judges [who issued] ordinances sat in judgement at all times, and were not engaged in any labour, having no other source of income, so that it was incumbent upon the community to support them.'

According to his statement, R. Meir was well acquainted with the 'reward' which scholars received from communities, but he saw this as a payment 'based upon the answer of R. Isaac'—that is, what the Talmudic sources define as 'trouble and loss of time' alone and not based upon the actual parameters of the task of the Torah teacher as defined by R. David ibn Yaḥya in his letter. If R. David in fact based his demand upon these parameters, 'he could not find any basis for doing so' for [God said] 'just as I [taught] for nothing, so shall you [teach] free of charge'! This response is nevertheless surprising. Did not R. Meir know of many rabbis who received large salaries from their communities outside the framework of 'R. Isaac's answer'—that is, even without any obligation on their part to be available for the needs of the public at all times and to refrain from engaging in any other occupation?[240] We may conclude from this that a clear distinction was drawn between a definite grant allocated by the community to a rabbi who might also perform other tasks, and one which the community had not promised to the rabbi in advance and for which, in R. Meir's view, there was no justification in terms of the services rendered by the rabbi to the community. Thus, his assumption was that such a grant is unrelated to the actual content of the office, for which reason the rabbi's services cannot be assessed retroactively. This was true even in such cases as that of R. David, in which the community had promised him a given amount from a certain date onwards. R. Meir did not explain the grounds for the community supporting a *rosh-yeshivah* such as himself,[241] a point to which I shall return. In any event, the difference between the approaches of R. Meir and of

[239] Ketubot 105a, s.v. *gozrei gezerot*.

[240] To concretize this matter, see the formulation of the appointment of R. Isaac de Lattes in Sect. 2 of this chapter. Even the stipend received by R. Judah Minz 'from the communities' was only for his position as *rosh-yeshivah* and for teaching in his own home, as a *repetitor*, those students who were unable to pay (see Porges, 'Elie Capsali', 34–5).

[241] As we have noted, R. Meir occupied the office of *rosh-yeshivah* in Padua. It is likely that the custom of granting the *rosh-yeshivah* a generous stipend was not altered in that place, as had been the practice at the time of R. Judah Minz, who received one hundred florins a year.

R. David on this question may be summarized as follows: R. David saw the specific definition of the office as essential, the other components being eventually added depending upon local conditions, while R. Meir considered such an office as invalid *per se*, but saw its contents as providing a possibility for the natural expansion of the role of the *rosh-yeshivah* in public life.

We find here a striking example of the difference in approach between the Ashkenazic and the Sephardic worlds within Italy, in the wake of the reconstitution there of the Sephardic model of the 'Torah teacher'. It may reasonably be claimed that the Spanish exiles brought with them the model of the Torah teacher wherever they settled in sufficient numbers to allow them to organize an independent community, or at least to have a tangible influence upon the life of the community at large. We have mentioned already the existence of this office in various places in southern Italy. Evidence from the beginning of the sixteenth century may also be brought from central Italy, as demonstrated by the testimony of R. Eli'ezer ibn-Ẓur, a Sephardic *marbiẓ Torah* in Recanati.[242] Another document from the same region concerns the presence in the area of the Marches of a scholar who received an annual salary from the Regional Community Council; the document relates how that scholar sent a letter to the community heads requesting that they continue to pay his annual salary.[243] The author of the document, R. Jeḥiel Trabot, does not state the exact reason for which the salary requested was paid 'as they have been accustomed until now' and 'as is written in the Register of the Community'. He stressed only that 'he always has a heavy burden from those who come to him every day, requesting rulings in disputes which occur among them or to write for them, and nobody thinks of giving me so much as a penny'. It is difficult to determine from this whether his implied complaint refers only to his work writing documents on behalf of individuals, or whether it also refers to the loss of time involved in issuing halakhic rulings on questions of everyday disputes. The juxtaposition of the two subjects would suggest that the rabbi did not see himself as formally obliged to perform either task. In any event, there is a striking similarity between the wording used here and that used by R. David ibn Yaḥya: they both imply that the salary received

[242] See Sonne, 'The General Synod in Italy', 651–5.

[243] Ibid. 655–8.

from the community created a framework of moral obligation on their part towards the community, of which both sides are aware. Because of this, they took upon themselves certain tasks, despite the fact that from a formal point of view they were not obliged to fulfil these tasks. On the other hand, there is a striking difference between the formulation of the elderly R. Jeḥiel Trabot, who was of French origin, and that of the Spaniard R. David. The latter laid claim to additional payment on the basis of a well-defined office, while the former requested a continuation of payment by pointing out the benefit to the public from the presence of a scholar, free to involve himself with their needs upon request.

Why did the communities decide to pay R. Jeḥiel Trabot, as evidenced by the community records? It has been suggested that this is evidence of the existence of a model of a 'rabbi of the Regional Community Council', whose main function was to serve as scribe of the Council when its leaders met, and perhaps to rule on inter-communal disputes.[244] However, it is difficult to imagine that R. Jeḥiel Trabot was granted the relatively high salary of 48 florins a year in order to fulfil these two functions alone. It seems rather to have been an expansion of the position of the (community-supported) *rosh-yeshivah*, such as R. Judah Minz in Padua, a model of Ashkenazic origin created after the establishment of the rabbinate within the framework of the community organization, following the influences from the Sephardic world. In substance, it would seem that R. Jeḥiel Trabot's ideological axioms and his understanding of his own role in the community closely matched that of R. Meir of Padua.

We may thus conclude that the institution of 'Torah teacher', brought by the Spanish exiles, coalesced with other factors mentioned above in shaping the office of community-appointed rabbi within the specific situation in northern and central Italy, where the German and French Jews played a major role in the shaping of the intellectual atmosphere. R. Meir of Padua's responsum was in fact recorded one year before the first rabbinic

[244] Ibid.; Shulvass, *Renaissance*, 100. The Regional Community Council (*Va'ad ha-Medinah*) was the council of the representatives of the communities, who were united from a territorial point of view into one organizational framework, primarily for the purpose of relations with the non-Jewish government.

appointment from Verona.[245] We have already seen how the status of the communal rabbi in northern Italy depended largely upon the specific way in which the office took shape in a given community, in accordance with local conditions and population. Both the exchange between R. Meir of Padua and R. David ibn Yaḥya and the statement of R. Jeḥiel Trabot suggest that this interdependence had its roots in a theoretical dialectic. Thus, the model of the community-appointed rabbi emerged from the ideological tension generated by the meeting on Italian soil between the form of the rabbinic office defined in the Sephardic tradition and the institution of *rosh-yeshivah* accepted in the Ashkenazic world. Chronologically, the period of growth of this institution in the communities of northern and central Italy overlapped with the final years of the Jewish community in southern Italy.[246] Thus, during the period under discussion, the office of community-appointed rabbi existed in practice in a framework other than that of the Sephardic model of 'Torah teacher' only in northern Italy, and in the light of the above-mentioned trends.

8. Special Tasks

All the functions of the Torah teacher reappear in the office of the community-appointed rabbi. This was similar to what took place in the encounter with the Ashkenazic model of the *rosh-yeshivah*. In the first rabbinic appointments from Verona, the task of teaching the members of the community is defined in the same way as it is defined in the office of Torah teacher.[247] In rabbinic appointments from other communities, at least thirty years later than that of Verona, a considerable emphasis is placed upon the teaching functions of the community rabbi, even though

[245] As R. David ibn Yaḥya's letter is dated 1538, it is reasonable to assume that R. Meir answered him the same year. As we mentioned above, the first rabbinical appointment, from Verona, was in 1539. A discussion similar to that of R. Meir in his responsum may be found in M. Isserles, *Teshuvot ha-RaM"A* (ed. A. Siev), sect. 50. See also Ben-Sasson's discussion, *Hagut ve-Hanhagah*, 170.

[246] As is well known, the Jewish settlement in southern Italy terminated in 1541.

[247] See the appointments from Verona for the years 1539 and 1542, and cf. the appointments of 1569, 1583, 1584, 1586, 1589, 1592, and 1593. Notice that the first appointment document even defined the office in general terms by the words 'to spread Torah' (*le-harbiẓ Torah*).

the exact programme of study is not always stated in detail—perhaps because these matters were considered as self-evident by virtue of well-established tradition.[248] The same is true for the obligation to deliver sermons on Sabbaths and holidays. While this obligation is explicitly stated in the appointments issued in Verona beginning in 1588, in Padua in 1596, and in Casale in 1598 and 1599, even in those documents in which it was not, this would seem to be simply because it was so self-evident.[249] Possibly, as well, the emphasis in the later appointments upon the rabbi's obligation to preach may be one of the indications of the crystallization of the office towards the end of the sixteenth century. At this point, rabbis already tended to see their position integrated in an organic way within the leadership structure of the community, and not only in terms of specific services in return for which they received a fixed salary. For this reason, they might be tempted to excuse themselves from the burden of delivering a sermon every Sabbath. A clear indication of such a possibility appears in the appointment of R. Mordecai Bassan in Verona in 1599: the community exempted him from preaching every Sabbath, employing another fixed preacher instead, but they did require him to preach at least on those three sabbaths every year 'on which it was a fixed practice to pledge donations for the Holy Land, for its scholars and its poor—namely: on *Shabbat Naḥamu* [*the Sabbath following the fast day of Tisha be-'Av*], *Shabbat Teshuvah* [*the Sabbath between New Year's Day and the Day of Atonement*], and *Shabbat Shekalim* [*the first of the four "special sabbaths", on which the Torah portion regarding monetary gifts to the Temple was read*]'.[250] In any event, the rabbi retained the right to preach whenever he wished to do so, without anyone having the right to protest.[251] The 1593 appointment from Padua also explicitly mentions his obligation to rule on ritual questions, as does that of Cremona. It seems quite clear from the latter

248 Cf. the appointment from Padua for the years 1585 and 1596 and that from Casale for 1598 and 1599.

249 Cf. the phrasing of the appointment from Padua for the year 1596: 'and he will be required to preach in public on Sabbaths and holidays, as well as to teach every morning in the great synagogue, as was customary in olden times.' Likewise, the wording of the appointment in Casale from 1598: 'and he is required to study and to preach in public as in early days.' This confirms Shulvass's comment in 'The Study of Torah', 122 n. 66.

250 Here also, the influence of the Ashkenazic patterns is doubtless reflected. Cf. Katz, *Tradition and Crisis*, 172–3.

251 See on this point Ch. 6, Sect. 4.

document[252] that those unqualified expressions referring to the rulings of the rabbis applied to ritual matters; this seems to have been the case from the very first appointments to the rabbinate.[253]

In Verona in 1588, those who sought a rabbi to succeed the elderly R. Yoʿeẓ were told 'to seek a master who is a preacher and teacher and shall lead the people in the right path'.[254] There is no doubt that this sentence, in which all three of the previously mentioned functions of the Torah teacher appear in the explicit definition of the office, indicates the shape it had taken until that year. To these tasks there was gradually added, in the communities of northern Italy, another function reminiscent of that found among the Ashkenazim—namely, the supervision of study arrangements within the community.[255] However, what essentially determined the status of the appointed rabbi in the communities of northern Italy, and even made such an appointment possible, was the potential for the position's organic growth through its combination with the function of *rosh-yeshivah*, as well as the involvement of the appointed rabbi in the community leadership, particularly in the area of legislating ordinances. These two aspects, which arose against the background of the ideological problem inherent in the conflict between the theories of R. Meir of Padua and of R. David ibn Yaḥya, brought about a situation in which the borrowing from the 'Spanish' office of Torah teacher not only involved additional tasks, but also substantive change in the understanding of the task of this office.

9. The Salaries of Community-Appointed Rabbis

An examination of rabbis' salaries in the sixteenth century will confirm the conclusions reached thus far. Obviously, in order to

252 The following is the wording of the text: 'If the members of the congregation or any individual should need to know the true law concerning forbidden and permitted matters, they shall turn to the above-mentioned Excellent Rabbi (*Ga'on*), and his honour shall show them the path by which they shall go, according to God's goodness upon them.'

253 Cf. e.g. the appointments from Verona ('we accept upon ourselves as head, prince, judge *and teacher* the *Ga'on* R. Joḥanan'), from Padua from the years 1579 and 1585 ('to teach'), and from Casale from 1596 ('to be a rabbi and teacher of the congregation') and 1606 ('that he should be again as at the beginning a rabbi and righteous teacher').

254 'Pinkas Verona', ii, fo. 141a; Sonne, 'Basic Premisses', 169, Document 15.

255 See Sect. 4d.

understand correctly the value of a certain sum of money in any given period, one must first know its purchasing power; that is, one requires information concerning the cost of goods and the average consumption of these goods at various levels of society. As such an undertaking would be too complex within the context of the present work, I will limit myself to a few scattered considerations which, while admittedly less useful for constructing an overall picture, will require far less digression from the subject. As a basic parameter, I shall try to compare the salaries of rabbis with the daily wage of builders. While one might argue that such a parameter is unsuitable to our purposes, both because of the difference in social level between the rabbis and the builders and because of the seasonal nature of building, its use will be justified on the basis of the fact that the initial comparisons may be complemented by comparative study of the daily wages of builders and the price of basic commodities, a task already performed by economic historians of the Middle Ages.[256] In this manner, we can also examine in a concrete way the extent to which the concept of 'payment for loss of time',[257] by which the rabbi's salary was designated, was a mere *modus loquendi* and to what extent it had real meaning.[258] Table 1, indicating the size of the daily salary of master builders (*maestri*) and apprentices (*lavoranti*) in Venice during the second half of the sixteenth century, is taken from the study by Brian Pullan, whose work on the economic history of Italy during this period is well known.[259]

We may reasonably assume that the salary of builders did not greatly vary from region to region,[260] and certainly not within the borders of the same region, such as between Padua and Verona. Let us now compare the salaries of the community rabbis

[256] e.g. E. H. Phelps Brown and S. V. Hopkins, 'Seven Centuries of the Prices of Consumables Compared with Builders' "Wage Rates" ', *Economica*, NS 23 (1956), 296–314.

[257] e.g. the first appointment of the rabbi of Verona and the appointment of R. Samuel Archivolti in Padua from 1593.

[258] As is known, in *halakhah* 'payment for idleness' (paid to rabbis, cantors, teachers, and the like) is calculated on the basis of the wages of a day-labourer.

[259] See B. Pullan, 'Wage-earners and the Venetian Economy, 1550–1630', *The Economic History Review*, 16 (1964), 407–26; idem, *Rich and Poor in Renaissance Venice*, 180.

[260] Cf. e.g. G. Parenti, 'Prezzi e salari a Firenze dal 1520 al 1620', in *I prezzi in Europa dal XIII secolo a oggi; saggi di storia dei prezzi raccolti e presentati da Ruggiero Romano* (Turin, 1967), 205–58. The author of this article cites, as the daily wages of a construction worker in Florence: in 1520, 15.8 *soldi*; in 1556, 24 *soldi*; in 1573, 35 *soldi*; in 1581, 35 *soldi*; in 1602, 40 *soldi*.

Table 1. Daily wages of builders in Venice, in *soldi di piccoli* (1 Corinthian ducat = 124 *soldi*)

Year	Master builder	Apprentice
1545		18.00
1546	24.75	
1551–5	29.41	20.18
1556–60	28.71	19.30
1561–5	30.20	22.98
1566–70	32.04	19.82
1571–4	34.91	24.14
July 1577	33.71	22.18
1580	38.33	22.84
1581–5	44.37	26.82
1586–90	42.87	27.08
1591–5	46.95	33.30
1596–1600	50.24	36.70

Table 2. Rabbinic income compared with that of builders in Venice

Year	Annual rabbinic salary as stated in appointment	Annual rabbinic salary in Venetian *soldi*	Days worked for equivalent income	
			Master builder	Apprentice
Padua				
1579	25 + 10 ducats	4,960	147.13	223.62
1581	25 + 10 ducats	4,960	111.78	184.93
1584	25 + 10 ducats	4,960	111.78	184.93
1588	25 + 17 ducats	5,208	121.48	192.31
1593	25 + 15 ducats	4,960	105.64	148.94
1596	10 + 10 *scudi*	2,720	54.14	74.11

Table 2 (*cont.*)

Year	Annual rabbinic salary as stated in appointment	Annual rabbinic salary in Venetian *soldi*	Days worked for equivalent income: Master builder	Days worked for equivalent income: Apprentice
Verona				
1543–5	15 ducats	1,880		104.40
1549	8 ducats[a]	992	40.08	
1557	6 ducats[b]	744	25.91	38.54
1559	6 ducats + 8 *scudi* for teaching	936	32.60	48.49
1565	6 ducats + 8 *scudi*, as above	936	30.99	40.73
1567–9	6 ducats + 8 ducats[c]	1,736	54.18	87.58
1579	14 ducats (total, exclusive of scribal fees)	1,736	45.29	76.00
1580	16 ducats (as above)	1,984	51.76	86.86
1584	75 *scudi muzingo*	1,800[d]	40.56	67.11
1593	30 ducats + free rental equiv. 22 ducats	6,448[e]	137.33	193.63
1596	ditto	6,448	128.34	175.69
1599	18 ducats + free rent as above (45 ducats total)[f]	5,560	110.66	151.49

[a] The reason for the deterioration in the terms of salary is explained in the appointment.

[b] The younger R. Yo'eẓ was appointed in this year, and it was natural that his salary be determined accordingly, particularly as the previous rabbi was still alive.

[c] The salary conditions in 1567 were identical with those in 1569. The text of the 1569 appointment is cited in the Hebrew version of this book, Document 21, p. 240.

[d] This was the salary given to R. Abraham Menaḥem Porto ha-Kohen at his appointment as assistant to R. Yo'eẓ.

[e] This was the salary given to R. Mordecai Bassan, but he accepted it only with great reluctance.

[f] See the appointment.

in Padua and Verona, as stated in their letters of appointment, with that of the builders (see Table 2).[261] In calculating the salary of the appointed rabbi in Padua, the extra sums which the rabbi received from the various confraternities for study and for charitable works throughout the period of his appointment have been taken into account.[262] However, in calculating the salary of the rabbi in Verona, the sums received for his services as scribe have not been considered, as in most of the documents this sum appears separately from the stipend granted to the rabbi for his 'loss of time' in performing the task of *av bet din* and in teaching the community.[263]

In order to clarify the picture further, the salary of the community-appointed rabbis should be compared with those of cantors and teachers. In Verona in 1572, the cantor received an annual salary of 16 ducats, plus an exemption from ordinary taxation;[264] in 1573, 12 ducats;[265] in 1575, 18 ducats.[266] In Padua, the cantor received 12 ducats in both 1586 and 1587;[267] in 1588, 15 ducats, plus rent-free use of the apartment in which he lived;[268] the same was true in 1590;[269] in 1591, 20 ducats;[270]

261 See Appendix 2 for a list of these appointments.

262 See *Pinkas Padua*, 49, and the editor's notes there. The community saw itself as responsible for the payment of that addition, in those cases where the Confraternities for Torah study and Free Loans were unable to meet the promised payments. In other words, it saw itself as responsible in every event for paying the additions over and above the fixed salary. See especially on this matter the appointment for the year 1596.

263 See also at the end of Sect. 6 of this chapter. It is stated in the appointments of 1542, 1549, and 1569 that the ducat referred to is based upon a value of 4 lire and 13 *soldi* (which is the equivalent of the Venetian ducat). From the time of the conquest of Verona by Venice, the Veronese currency continued to be used, based upon the ratio that these coins bore to the Venetian currency at the time of the conquest, i.e., 3:4. Venice minted coinage for the conquered areas of different values from its own, so that the Venetian coins were known to have different values when they were quoted in local terms. Likewise, the ducat of Venice, valued at 6 lire and 4 *soldi*, was converted to Veronese money according to the ratio of 3:4, that is to say, 3/4 of 124 = 93 *soldi* of Verona, which was exactly 4 lire and 13 *soldi*, as mentioned in the appointment. On all this, see Q. Perini, *Le monete di Verona* (Rovereto, 1902), 40–3. Another coin mentioned in the appointments is the *scudo mocenigo*, whose value was set as the equivalent of 24 *soldi* of Venice from 1525. See on this N. Papadopoli, *Le monete di Venezia* (Venice, 1907), ii. 140. I do not refer here to the value of the gold *scudo* of Verona, mentioned in these appointments only in connection with the salary received by the appointed rabbi in Verona for his services and by the scribe of the community.

264 'Pinkas Verona', ii. fo. 88a. 265 Ibid. fo. 90b. 266 Ibid. fo. 99b.

267 *Pinkas Padua*, sect. 234, p. 193; sect. 254, p. 201; sect. 289, p. 216.

268 Ibid. sect. 321, p. 239. 269 Ibid. sect. 377, p. 267.

270 Ibid. sect. 418, p. 283.

in 1593, 24 ducats;[271] in 1594, 26 ducats;[272] in 1597, 24 ducats;[273] and in 1601, 28 ducats.[274] In Casale, a schoolteacher was hired 'to be the slaughterer and to assist with other needs of the community, such as to assist in leading prayers and other matters'. In 1591, his salary was '50 *scudi* or 9 florins';[275] in 1596, 40 *scudi*, exemption from communal taxes, and a free seat in the synagogue for himself and his wife.[276] In 1582, in exchange for teaching the children of one wealthy man, a teacher in an unidentified place received 60 ducats;[277] in 1593, a tutor in Pesaro received 4 florins a month for teaching one girl and, in 1596, 3 florins a month.[278] These examples might easily be multiplied. By comparing the monthly wages for teaching one child with the annual salary paid to teachers by their communities, it would appear that the latter was based upon the addition of children of limited means to the roster of these same teachers' private students.

From all that has been said, one arrives at one simple, clear conclusion: that the salary of the community-appointed rabbis[279] did not represent an adequate living wage.[280] Particularly striking is the contrast between the 'reward' offered to R. Isaac b. Emmanuel de Lattes when he sought the position of *rosh-yeshivah* in Pesaro in 1557[281]—100 gold *scudi*, as well as a suitable apartment—with that of the community rabbi in Verona during that same year—6 ducats all told! If we remember that the value of a gold *scudo* (which was slightly less than that of a gold ducat) was, at the time, nearly eight lire, and if one assumes the value of rent-free accommodation as approximately 20 ducats a year,[282]

271 Ibid. sect. 500, p. 310.

272 Ibid. sect. 536, p. 321.

273 Ibid. sect. 619, p. 354.

274 Ibid. sect. 685, p. 385.

275 'Pinkas Casale', fo. 10. These florins are actual silver coins (*fiorino di Monferrato*).

276 Ibid. fo. 17.

277 See R. Y. Heilprin, *Teshuvot Naḥalat Ya'akov* (Padua, 1623), sect. 14.

278 See S. Assaf, *Mekorot*, ii. 121.

279 These statements are made here by way of generalization, although one might obviously argue that note should be taken of further distinctions between one community and another, and even between one rabbi and another in two different periods in the samecommunity.

280 To define this point further, let me add that these rabbis earned in one year what a construction foreman received in one month, or even less. Thus, a construction foreman in Venice, who also kept the books on the basis of which Pullan prepared the table cited above, received as his monthly salary before 1578 the sum of 24 ducats; from Feb. 1578, 30 ducats; from Mar. 1582, 36 ducats; from Feb. 1587, 46 ducats; from Feb. 1596, 72 ducats. See Pullan, 'Wage-earners and the Venetian Economy', 425 n. 2.

281 See Frankel, 'Three Letters', p. 24 and cf. the various rabbinic appointments.

282 See in Table 2 the salary of the rabbi of Verona from 1593 onwards.

we find that the 'reward' offered to R. Isaac de Lattes was some twenty-five times greater than the salary of the appointed rabbi in Verona at the same time! Also we must not forget that the community-appointed rabbi in Verona was, from the very beginning of his term of office, the *rosh-yeshivah* of the community as well. We may therefore conclude that the essential parameter for determining the minimum salary of the appointed rabbi was actually the concept of 'payment for loss of time', the assumption being that the rabbi would devote no more than a small portion of his time to the community, and that his primary income would be derived from some other source.[283] On the other hand, one

[283] It is sufficient to verify this with regard to the rabbis of Verona, Padua, and Casale, whose salaries are discussed above in detail. Thus, R. Joḥanan, the rabbi of Verona, was a school teacher, so that the community saw fit to state explicitly in his first appointment in 1539 that 'he shall not be allowed to teach more than seven hours daily, at most'; this is elaborated in his second appointment, in 1543: 'he may not teach more than seven hours daily, and the rest of the time which is left over he shall deal with matters pertaining to the welfare of the congregation . . .' His son-in-law R. Yo'eẓ, who succeeded him in this post, was apparently a money-lender; his name twice appears in the list of people who received back the money which they loaned 'to the city to buy in exchange grain to provide sustenance for the poor people of the city' (see 'Pinkas Verona', i. fo. 16b, 29b). It is not clear what R. Abraham Menaḥem Porto ha-Kohen's occupation was. It is possible that he also worked as a teacher, a hint of which may appear in the phrase, 'and his Torah is his occupation', which appears on his appointment in 1588. This expression is not to be understood as an obligation to engage exclusively in teaching members of the community and dealing with their needs, as the community did not provide him with an adequate livelihood. However, the community did exempt him from 'every tax and burden' upon those incomes deriving from 'his Torah which was his profession', as against that income deriving from 'some business . . . in trade', in which case it was stated that he should also 'stand . . . before the assessors of the Holy Congregation like one of the members of the congregation'. In addition, he engaged also in proof-reading books and possibly also in medicine (see Benayahu and Laras, 'Health Officials', 80–1)—two professions neither of which is considered as trade, and are therefore exempt from taxes and levies. R. Mordecai Bassan also taught schoolchildren and was a bookkeeper. In 1590, he declared of himself before the Inquisition, before he was appointed as community rabbi: 'et ho 43 anni incirca; la mia professione era ch'io attendeva ai studii, et son Rabbi, et tenevo scolari ai quali insegnava, ma da tre anni in qua incirca ho cambiato professione, perchè con questo modo non potevo acquistar a me il vivero et alla mia famiglia, andai . . . in una bottega a tener conto de libri . . .' (quoted by C. Boccato, 'Un processo contro ebrei di Verona alla fine del Cinquecento', *RMI* 40 (1974), 360). Despite the phrasing which he used here in his testimony before the Christian judges, it seems to me that he was not so poor, as prior to his appointment he even served as *parnas* of the community. R. Samuel Archivolti, the appointed rabbi in Padua, was known not to be particularly wealthy. Before he came to Padua, he was a proof-reader—for example, of *Sefer ha-'Arukh* (Venice, 1553), and *Bi'ur Sefer Kohelet* of R. Elisha Gallico (Venice, 1578)—and, as was the custom, also published various short books which were dedicated to wealthy patrons (see Ch. 4, Sect. 2). In 1602, when he was rabbi in Padua, he published under his own imprint *Sefer 'Arugat ha-Bosem* (see the phrase in the imprimatur [licence] of this book by the Rabbis of Venice: '. . . and he did not spare his bundle of money to publish

should not dismiss completely the value of the sums which were disbursed: even if they were inadequate to enable the rabbi to support himself, their value was not entirely symbolic; they were certainly significant for people who did not earn their own livelihood easily during the great 'price revolution'. Moreover, during a period of increased fiscal pressure on the Jews, in which their continued residence in certain locations often depended upon their ability to provide generous bribes and 'gifts' to the Christian officials, even the wealthiest individuals tended to become stingier, and the possibility of fund-raising for purposes other than sheer physical survival became limited, and in some cases was not related to the actual economic situation in a direct manner. For this reason, we must suppress the temptation to smile when we encounter such decisions as that of the community of Verona to reduce the salary of their rabbi from 15 to 8 ducats a year 'for the members of the community cannot afford any more, as we have until now'.[284] The rabbi agreed to this 'of his own free will'. Indeed, slightly more than half a ducat a month was hardly worth squabbling over; nevertheless, he had to find these pennies elsewhere; if he was a teacher, this meant the addition of another pupil from the ranks of the poor. The emphasis on the problem of salary in the community decisions pertaining to the hiring of rabbis, together with the anxiety lest there not be enough money in the treasury from which it was meant to come, clearly indicate the importance attached to these sums, and the fact that they were not perceived as symbolic only. But for that very reason, it is doubly important to see things in their proper perspective. Indeed, throughout the entire period during which the office of community rabbi was taking shape, the salaries paid to the rabbis were little more than 'payment for idleness', in the most literal sense.

If so, on what basis did the community grant the yeshivah heads a stipend so much higher than the 'payment for idleness' of the community rabbis? We must have recourse here to a set

it . . .'). Nevertheless, one should not assume that all these were adequate to support him, and we can only conjecture that his primary income also came from schoolteaching the other sources, such as being the scribe of the Regional Council. For this office he received 8–12 ducat p.a.; see 'Pinkas ha-Medinah be-Padua', fos. 7b, 69b, 76a, 78b, 83b, 91b. R. Abraham Provenzali, the community-appointed rabbi in Casale, was a physician (see the conclusion to *Sefer Shilṭei ha-Gibborim* by R. Abraham Portaleone).

284 See the appointments of 1549.

of concepts based, not upon the functions or tasks performed by the rabbi, but on the prestige which the community felt that it gained from his presence among them. This naturally related to the prominence of the rabbi himself and the importance of the yeshivah at whose head he stood. One finds a similar situation among university lecturers:[285] during this period, university instructors did not receive a salary in the accepted sense of the word, but a sum fixed by special contract, which might vary greatly.[286] Already between the years 1485 and 1488, the teachers in the major universities of Florence received between 200 and 300 florins per annum, while the lower salaries were in the region of 60 florins per annum.[287] At the same time, there were lecturers in Padua and elsewhere who received 1000 ducats annually.[288] In the light of such a situation, it is not surprising that R. Isaac de Lattes, who was among the leading rabbis of his generation, would be offered a sum of 100 gold *scudi* and a free apartment to be *rosh-yeshivah*, while the *rosh-yeshivah* in Verona, who was also the community-appointed rabbi, only received a total of 6 ducats all told in that same year!

This conclusion corresponds to the ideological framework proposed by R. Meir of Padua in his response to R. David ibn Yaḥya, and our own conclusion as to the change which took place when the model of Torah teacher was transferred to the communities of northern Italy. Despite the above situation, and in contrast with it, the Torah teachers received living salaries, albeit rather modest ones: R. David requested 100 *scudi* per year, while reporting that R. Ariel, who received only 80 *scudi* a year in Sulmona, and R. Isaac Corcos, who received 70 *scudi* per year

[285] One may perhaps also point out another similarity between university teachers and community-appointed rabbis in the length of their term of appointment, which was for 2–3 years, and in certain rare cases 5 years. See A. Visconti, *La storia dell'Università di Ferrara* (Bologna, 1950), i. 23. Perhaps this fact, which also points to the way in which the office was understood by contemporaries, ought to be added to the fact that there is no indication of a struggle in Italy, throughout the period under discussion, to convert the community-appointed rabbinate into a fixed office, as it was in Germany and Poland. See Ben-Sasson, *Hagut ve-Hanhagah*, 178–80. Nevertheless, we do not know of a single community-appointed rabbi who left his congregation against his will.

[286] See Visconti, *La storia dell'Università di Ferrara*, 27–8.

[287] See C. Trinkaus, 'A Humanist's Image of Humanism: the Inaugural Orations of Bartolomeo della Fonte', *Studies in the Renaissance*, 7 (1960), 91.

[288] See G. de Sandre, 'Il Collegio dei Filosofi e le prime vicende del Monte di Pietà in Padova', *Quaderni per la storia dell'Università di Padova* (Padua, 1968), 86; E. Ashtor, 'I salari nel medio oriente durante l'epoca medievale', *RSI* 78 (1966), 321–49.

in Otranto, 'were poor'.[289] Similarly, at the beginning of the century R. David ben Messer Leon received 70 florins a year in Valona.[290] These salaries may reasonably be compared with that received, for example, by the private physician of Pope Leo X—8 ducats a month.[291] In other words: in a situation in which the office of Torah teacher was defined, as we have seen, in terms of its specific contents, its occupant was treated as the equivalent of an expert in the natural sciences, providing fixed services in the area of his expertise. All this must likewise be understood in terms of the revolution in thought taking place during that period with regard to the determination of salaries: namely, the concept of salary as offered in exchange for specific services rendered, and not only as a means of providing a livelihood.[292] R. David ibn Yaḥya understood the concept of salary in this way with regard to the community-appointed rabbi. As we have seen, this concept was not accepted by the communities of northern Italy, and throughout the sixteenth century the salary of the community-appointed rabbi continued to be viewed as 'payment for idleness' in the most literal sense, even though the contents of the office of Torah teacher had been incorporated within it. A clear distinction was drawn in Verona between the 'payment for loss of time' given to the rabbi for the lessons he gave to the community, and the salary he was paid as 'Head Judge of the Court',[293] and certainly for such tasks as scribe of the community.

289 See Marx, 'The Life of an Italian Rabbi', 621.

290 Messer Leon, *Kevod Ḥakhamim*, 5.

291 See the data gathered by L. Geiger at the end of his edition of J. Burckhardt, *Die Kultur der Renaissance in Italien*, (Leipzig, 1919), 314–16. Compare Shulvass, *Renaissance*, 78–9. Marx ('Life of an Italian Rabbi', n. 28) has proposed drawing a comparison between these statistics and the salary of R. David ibn Yaḥya, but he himself has never actually done so.

292 See R. Romano, 'Storia dei salari e storia economica', *RSI* 78 (1966), 311–20. Particularly interesting is the argument put forward by a judge at the end of the 17th century for his request to free the determination of the salary of clerks of his type from the parameter of the cost of living: in his view, one must take into account that the judges must save money from their salaries against old age or for the benefit of their heirs ('iudices et Magistratus. . . quotannis summam, aliquam in arca reponant, qua vel suae senectuti vel posteritati consulant').

293 See the appointment documents from 1559 on. The renewal of the appointment as Head of Court was not necessarily considered as a renewal of the appointment to teach, unless this was stated explicitly. See especially Document 27, p. 244 in the Hebrew edition of this book. Other tasks, which one would naturally think of as implied in the rabbinic office, in fact were not, and special payment was given for them. See Appendix 3, and cf. the statements of R. David ibn Yaḥya quoted above.

It therefore seems clear that, despite the fact that the combination of the task of scribe with that of the community rabbi was quite common,[294] the former was not seen in any substantial way as connected with that of the community rabbi. The task of the scribe, which incorporated the distinguished tradition of the medieval *notarii*, was given to the Talmudic scholar because of his professional expertise even if he was not a community-appointed rabbi.[295]

Far more than the protestations of poverty on the part of the leaders of the community of Verona, the above distinction between the payment given for teaching members of the community and that for 'serving as Head of the Court' is indicative of the understanding of the office in its formative years. Throughout these years, the duties of the office holder continued to be seen in terms of well-defined tasks performed within the community, and not as a single, organic whole integrated within the framework of communal leadership. The disappearance of this distinction towards the end of the sixteenth century would therefore indicate the final integration of the office within that framework. This fact provides a more significant indication of the change in the valuation of the office than does the fact that the money for payment of the rabbi's salary, originally taken from special contributions, now came from the communal treasury.[296] One must not forget that the communal treasury was established primarily to provide stipends for scholars and charity for the poor, and that even in those places where the office was well established the rabbi's salary was taken from various types of charitable funds.[297] In any event, this means of funding the rabbi's salary is certainly no indication of his being an 'inconsequential community official',[298] whose status depended exclusively on the treasury from which his salary was drawn. One should rather stress the fact that the salaries were simultaneously made more consistent (in the proportional sense we have noted above!), and that there began to appear stipulations that, if the rabbi was absent from his community, another one should temporarily fulfil

[294] Cf. Shulvass, *Renaissance*, 77, and the sources cited there.

[295] But see Sect. 12.

[296] See the first rabbinic appointment from Verona as well as that of Casale.

[297] See in Sect. 6.

[298] Thus Shulvass, *Renaissance*, 78. In general, from everything which has been said until now and from what will be added below, such a definition is difficult to accept.

his functions at the former's expense,[299] or that this was to be deducted from his salary.[300]

10. Etiquette and Prerogatives

The emergence of the office of community-appointed rabbi was therefore dependent upon the specific conditions in the community involved. The office itself was in practice subjugated to the communal leaders; the salary which came with it was clearly inadequate to assure a sufficient income to the one holding it, while the rabbi's status in the community was less a function of his position than of his own personality. As a result, it tended to attract comparatively mediocre figures, who saw in it an opportunity for involvement in communal leadership. In the final analysis, and with all the reservations required in any generalization, we may describe these rabbis (to invert the tannaitic metaphors of Avot 4: 15) as preferring to be the 'head of foxes' rather than the 'tail to lions'.[301] But if R. Moses Basola and his like thought of these rabbis as second rate, within their own communities they were the leading figures; the various privileges and gestures of deference shown to them certainly contributed to their feeling of prominence. We have already mentioned some of the signs of deference which the members of the communities exhibited to their rabbis. Some of these, which have been maintained to this very day by the communities of Italy—such as the calling of the rabbi of the community to the reading of the Ten Commandments and the Chapter of Rebuke (Deut. 28) from the Torah Scroll, that the entire congregation rises when he is called to the Torah, etc.—clearly originated during the formative period of this office, although I have not found any allusion to them in the sources available to me.[302] However, one

299 See the appointments for Casale of 1599.

300 See the appointment for Verona of 1599. If it is mere coincidence, it is striking that the two conditions should appear in the same year in two different places. Such conditions also appear in the appointments of the Ashkenazic rabbis. Cf. e.g. the first clause in the appointment of the community rabbi of Amsterdam in 1665 (*De ambtsdata van de oudster opper-rabbijnen bij de hoogduitsche joodsche gemeente te Amsterdam . . . doore D. M. Skluys* (Amsterdam, 1917), 25-7). I owe this reference to the lists compiled by A. Yaari.

301 Cf. on the other hand, Shulvass, *Renaissance*, 77.

302 See, for a slightly later period than that under discussion, Yiẓḥak min ha-Levi'im, *Medabber Tahapukhot* (1912), 175, and cf. Ch. 2, n. 196.

special and unique privilege does emerge clearly from the sources from our period: namely, that of a special seat in the synagogue. As an individual's place in the synagogue may be taken as one of the indications of his status within the community,[303] an examination of the seating arrangements in the synagogue will reveal the importance given to rabbis in general, and to official community-appointed rabbis in particular. As in all communities throughout the Jewish world, those places adjoining the eastern wall were reserved for the most distinguished people, the most important of these being the seat to the right of the Holy Ark. During this period, seats in the Italian synagogue were arranged along the walls of the hall, with the Holy Ark (*aron ha-kodesh*) in the middle of the eastern wall, and the reader's desk situated in the centre of the hall. The community rabbi sat on the seat to the right of the Ark and next to him, on either side of the Ark, sat the other rabbis resident in the community, and other notables.

The description of the seating arrangement for the synagogue in Verona, found in the record book for 1563, relates that R. Yo'eẓ sat adjacent to the Ark, with R. Ephraim next to him.[304] The same is true in the seating plan for 1572.[305] In 1582 the number of rabbis and *ḥaverim* within the community grew: R. Yo'eẓ sat in his usual place to the right of the Ark, his son-in-law sat next to him, while the other rabbis and *ḥaverim* took their places to the left of the Ark and at the head of the two rows along the northern and southern walls of the synagogue.[306] In 1592 the rabbi of the community, R. Mordecai Bassan, sat to the right of the Ark, next to him sat his assistant and substitute in the yeshivah, R. Baruch Bassan, while the other rabbis and *haverim* occupied the other places on the two sides of the Ark. A similar arrangement is recorded for 1597.[307]

In the seating plan for the synagogue in Casale, the spot to the right of the Ark is marked simply 'rabbi of the community', while the occupants of the other places are listed by name: next to the rabbi of the community sat R. Moses Rapa, one of the

[303] See Maimonides, *Mishneh Torah*, *Hilkhot Tefillah* 11: 4.

[304] 'Pinkas Verona', ii. fo. 270a. A third person, known as R. Jacob, was also given an important seat, but not among the rabbis. See n. 64.

[305] Ibid. fo. 268b. [306] Ibid. fo. 269a.

[307] Ibid. fos. 173b, 188b. And see Y. min ha-Levi'im, *Medabber Tahapukhot*, 50, where it is stated that there was a 'bench for colleagues' in the synagogue in Venice. See also below, n. 310.

major figures and *parnas* of the community during this period.[308] The rabbi's wife likewise occupied a place of honour at the eastern end of the women's gallery, while the wife of R. Rapa sat next to her.[309] Similar arrangements took effect in other communities: the most important place was reserved for the rabbi of the community, while the places closest to him were seen as next in importance, so that they remained empty and one was proscribed from sitting there unless one had rabbinic ordination or was an elder. Thus, it was decreed in Florence in 1608 that 'on the bench of the synagogue where the rabbi sits, in the absence of rabbis or other distinguished people, shall sit R. Mahalallel de Blanis, and the other places to the corner shall be reserved for the others, or the elders shall sit there'.[310]

Another universally enjoyed privilege involving financial benefit was the exemption of community-appointed rabbis from the payment of taxes and tariffs.[311] This was true even though there were other religious functionaries who were also exempt from taxes; the exemption of the community rabbis from taxation was in effect an indirect addition to their salary, but it was primarily conceived as an indication of their privileged status. This matter appears to have been discussed in terms of the general question of the right of scholars to exemption from taxes.[312] One frequently senses that the rabbis insisted upon their exemption from taxes, not so much because of the actual financial benefit involved, but because it implied recognition that the category of *talmidei ḥakhamim* applied to them as individuals.[313]

As the office began to take shape towards the end of the sixteenth century, the custom of giving gifts to the rabbi on the occasion of a wedding became another sign of their special status. This may be seen in the rabbinic appointment from Verona from the year 1580, in which it is stated that the rabbi was to receive

[308] 'Pinkas Casale', 89.

[309] Ibid. 90. The practice of reserving an important place in the women's gallery for the rabbi's wife has been preserved by the Italian communities until our own day.

[310] 'Che nella banca della scuola dove siede il dottore non ci essendo altri dottori o huomini d'authorità e qualità, sia lecito sedersi a Laudadio de Blanis, e il resto sino al canto sia serbato per altri, o vero possino sederci uomini vecchi.' Quoted in U. Cassuto, 'I più antichi capitoli del ghetto di Firenze', *RI* 10 (1913), 74. Cf. also above, n. 307.

[311] In Padua this is also stated in the first appointment; in Verona in that of 1584.

[312] See above, Ch. 2, the end of Sect. 4.

[313] An example of this is R. Mordecai Bassan of Verona, who was among the leaders of the community before he was appointed as communal rabbi (see above, n. 283), and did not relinquish this exemption (see his rabbinic appointment).

'from every bridegroom who gets married . . . one golden *scudo* in the manner and order customary in previous years, but R. Yo'eẓ shall be required to recite the nuptial blessings'. Such a statement of the rabbi's obligation to officiate can only be understood against the background of the tendency to view this payment as a privilege to which the rabbi was entitled by virtue of his office. In my opinion, this also indicates the manner in which this privilege became established in the specific conditions of a small community, which had for a long time known no rabbi of distinction other than the communally appointed rabbi. On the other hand, the very remark appended to the above statement, that 'in the manner and order of years past' indicates that it was an accepted tradition. As this tradition had not been specified in the rabbi's appointment, we must assume that it was seen as self-evident. It is therefore possible that this testimony is indicative of the situation in other communities as well, in which conditions similar to those in Verona developed, although at present no conclusive evidence is available.

11. The Absence in Large Communities of the Office of Appointed Rabbi

Unlike the smaller, homogeneous communities, in the larger, more heterogeneous ones, particularly those in which there were several distinct sub-communities, it was more difficult to arrive at a situation in which a single rabbi would be appointed over the entire community, despite the fact that the most prominent rabbis of the period lived there. The history of several important Italian communities remains to be written; further research may perhaps add new details to the picture known to us thus far. In any event, no record has been found to date of a community-appointed rabbi in three of the major communities of sixteenth-century Italy: Mantua,[314] Venice,[315] and Ancona.[316]

[314] See Simonsohn, *Mantua*, 579–80.

[315] Most of the communal ledgers of Venice prior to the 17th century were evidently not preserved (see M. Benayahu, *Haskamah u-reshut be-Defusei Veneẓiah* (Jerusalem, 1971), 10, and n. 1). The collector M. Lehman has made it known that he has in his possession ledgers of the Venetian community (see the introduction to *Lev Shlomo*, by R. Shlomo Helma (Jerusalem, 1972)). However, as Mr Lehman has pointed out to me in a personal communication, these *pinkasim* (now lost!) only begin in 1623. In any event, Cecil Roth, in his survey of the history of the Jews of Venice, did not find the office of

community-appointed rabbi present there until a late date—C. Roth, *Venice* (Jewish Community Series; Philadelphia, 1930), 144–5. M. Benayahu, who has studied the *haskamot* of the rabbis of Venice in detail, concluded, like Roth, that in the 16th century 'there was no general rabbinate nor a chief rabbi' in Venice (ibid., 34). However, he added a point of his own in that he saw the phrase, 'the Excellent Rabbis of Venice', as an allusion to a council of rabbis composed of the rabbis of congregations, although their number was not fixed until 'in the 17th century the members of the general yeshivah (*yeshivah ha-kelalit*) constituted the institutionalized rabbinate'. As this institution took shape only in the 17th century, it cannot be dealt with in the framework of this book. However, it should be emphasized that the term, *ma'alat ha-Ge'onim* ('The Excellent Rabbis'), is too general to define it as a 'Rabbinic Council', and in my opinion the reality did not differ from that described in Sect. 3. In any event, let it suffice to state here the agreement of scholars that, throughout the 16th century, there is no mention in Venice of the institution of the community-appointed rabbi.

316 The list of rabbis, on behalf of whose souls prayers were recited in Ancona, and which begins with those of the 17th-century rabbis (see C. Roth, 'The Rabbis of Ancona' (Heb.), *Sinai*, 21 (1947), 323–6), is not a list of community-appointed rabbis; see also M. Wilensky, 'On the Rabbis of Ancona' (Heb.), *Sinai*, 25 (1949), 64. I do not know on what grounds Rosenberg states that R. Isaac Leon b. Eli'ezer ibn Ẓur the Spaniard 'was evidently the official rabbi of the community' in the first half of the 16th century (see H. Rosenberg, 'Alcuni cenni biografici di rabbini e letterati della communità israelitica di Ancona', Introduction to *Kitvei R. David Avraham Ḥai ve-Rabbi Yiẓḥak Refa'el Ashkenazi* (Ancona, 1932), p. xlviii, and compare Sect. 7. There were two congregations in Ancona—the Italian and the Levantine. The ordinances issued jointly by the two congregations in 1594 concerning various prohibitions applying to the sale of cheeses and meat, similar to earlier ordinances from 1588, by the assembly of 'sages, elders, lay leaders, appointed persons, and delegates by the two holy congregations, Levantine and Italian', it is concluded that 'in all of the above-mentioned matters . . . the granting of permission and the receiving of permission, to prohibit and permit, there were appointed four individuals, two from each congregation, and these are, from the Holy Congregation of the Levantines, the *ḥakham* R. [Jacob] Ibn Habib and the Honourable R. Samuel Ḥamiẓ, and from the Holy Congregation of the Italians, the distinguished elder, R. Shlomo Maẓliaḥ di Cagli and the *ḥakham* R. Joab da Rieti. As these four individuals shall enact, so shall it be'—see 'Takkanot Ancona', MS Los Angeles 44 (IMHM 28088). In confirmation of the edicts, there are affixed the signatures of the sages of the communities and its leaders, headed by R. Michael Codoto, who was among the important rabbis of the period. Had there been an appointed rabbi over the (general) community, there is considerable doubt whether a committee of four, only some of whom were rabbis, would have been appointed to examine certifications of *kashrut* and the granting of permission to sell products, instead of placing this task in the hands of the appointed rabbis, in a way similar to that done in the community of Padua (see above, at the end of Sect. 4c) and other communities, such as that of Amsterdam in the year 1665 (see the afore-mentioned appointment, in n. 300). It is worth pointing out that, at a later date, this task was imposed upon 'the distinguished rabbis'—evidently the rabbis of the yeshivah whose names appear at the end of the ordinances ('Takkanot Ancona', date 1675). The first rabbinic appointment in Ancona published to date is from 1692 (see Dario Disegni, 'Due contratti di Rabbini Medici di Ancona del 1692 e 1752', *Annuario di studi ebraici 1969–1972*, 97–104). Analysis of the transformations which took place in this city towards the middle of the 17th century, and the relationship between the appointed rabbi and the scholars of the yeshivah, is beyond the scope of this study. It is enough to conclude here that, so long as new documents are not uncovered, one ought to accept as fact the absence of any mention of a community-appointed rabbi in Ancona throughout the 16th century.

How is this fact to be accounted for? Several factors seem to have been operative here, each of which would perhaps by itself be insufficient to prevent the emergence of this office in the large communities. The first of these was the sense of competition with other rabbis who lived within the boundaries of the community, within the context of the tense atmosphere alluded to above. The responsa literature of the Sephardic sages, particularly from the area of the Ottoman empire, where situations of this type were frequent, is replete with controversies relating to attempts on the part of other rabbis to undercut the authority and status of the community rabbi.[317] While it is certainly not in the nature of people to whom even the Talmud permitted a modicum of pride to be frightened by such things, the weight of this factor should nevertheless not be entirely dismissed, especially when combined with other factors.

Another element may have been the situation in which the rabbis were subjugated to the public in matters of excommunication, although if taken by itself this condition would not be one to discourage rabbis from accepting the office. At least the negative side of this regulation—that is, the prohibition against the rabbi imposing the ban without the permission of the lay leaders—was a matter of hoary antiquity, the interdependence of the community lay leaders and the rabbis in this area accompanying the history of the Jewish community throughout the Middle Ages.[318] Indeed, in the smaller communities of Italy this same situation did not prevent rabbis from accepting the office. Even in the communities of Franco-Germany and Spain, where the communal rabbinate became highly developed towards the end of our period—under such names as *ḥakham ha-kahal* (sage of the community), *ha-rav de-mata* (rabbi of the place), *mara de-atra* (master of the place) and, in some Sephardic communities, *ḥakham ha-kolel* (the sage of the community)—this condition was also required of the rabbi. However, the restriction on rabbinic autonomy implied by it in those countries may have

[317] Significantly, confrontations did not take place in the major Italian communities, where by the nature of things one would expect to find them. If one would still maintain that even so we are not allowed to argue ex silentio, one ought to take note that, throughout the entire lengthy discourse on *ḥakham ha-kahal* (scholar of the community) appearing in *Paḥad Yizḥak*, R. Isaac Lampronti did not even once cite the responsa of the rabbis of Italy, which he knew so well!

[318] e.g. Finkelstein, *Self-government*, 228, 242, n. 4.

been seen as inconsiderable in comparison with the high status which the rabbi enjoyed by virtue of his appointment. The appointment of the Ashkenazic 'local rabbi' granted him a 'ruler's rod' in the full sense of the word, even if the public held on to the other end.[319] Likewise, in the Sephardic communities, even if at times the leaders decided that 'the sage will not be allowed to excommunicate without the agreement of a majority of the court' (similar in a sense to the decisions of the lay leaders in Italy), some reservation might also be appended to such decision. They might, for example, wonder 'if there is actually support for this ordinance, since it was not stated with the agreement of the rabbi mentioned, while there is another ordinance written and sealed in the record book of the community that ordinances cannot be made without his consent . . .'[320] The community's ordinances were made only in the presence of the rabbi who was to countersign them, and they insisted that such ordinances could not be abolished without the rabbi's consent, particularly if they involved the use of the ban.[321] On the other hand, if the agreement involved did not entail the use of the ban, then the very right of the majority to coerce the minority was held in question.[322]

In any case, the factors mentioned above, combined with the inter-ethnic tension[323] which was particularly sharp in the larger communities, and especially the lack of judicial autonomy (to be discussed at length in Chapter 5), seem to have prevented these communities from offering the position to any of the resident rabbis throughout the sixteenth century. At times, these communities solved the problem of the need for rabbinic authority by appealing to all the major rabbis of the city—that is, those referred to by the public as *ge'onim*—whenever it was necessary to institute important ordinances, particularly those entailing the imposition of the ban. We have already seen that this practice

[319] See the rabbinic appointment of R. Isaiah Horowitz in Frankfurt (cited in Ch. 2 n. 6), in which the community reaffirms the main prerogatives granted its rabbi in his ordination—'he shall teach, and judge, (*yoreh yoreh yadin yadin*), permit, and in his hand shall be the ruler's rod . . .' The difference is that those points which are stated in the ordination as recognizing the abilities of the one ordained and granting him permission to make use of certain prerogatives appear in the rabbinic appointment in terms of obligations on the part of the congregation and declaration of their subjugation to the rabbi. Compare Ben-Sasson, *Hagut ve-Hanhagah*, 180 ff.

[320] R. Meir Melamed, *Teshuvot Mishpaṭ Ẓedek* (Salonica, 1799), ii, sect. 4.

[321] Ibid. sect. 66.

[322] *Teshuvot Mishpeṭei Shmu'el* (Venice, 1599–1600), sect. 95.

[323] See Sect. 2.

took shape in Venice and Ascoli,[324] and was also customary in Mantua.[325] A typical example is described in the following document:[326]

On Thursday, 21 June, 1590, here in Mantua, it was agreed by an act of the members of the Council to attempt to fulfill the clause in the edict issued by his honour the Duke to the holy congregation concerning the outsiders who had come to live here in Mantua. This was to be done by those people who had been selected to be responsible for the fulfilment of that clause, and the members of the community are warned not to do anything against the efforts of those selected, either by action or by speech, to prevent them from attaining their aim, or to delay them from completing their aim in bringing about the fulfillment of that clause. *This agreement is made in the presence of and with the agreement of the Geonim.*

In this way, the principle of reliance upon the scholars to give sacral force to the edicts of the community was preserved in practice, while simultaneously avoiding the complex of problems which would have arisen with the appointment of an official rabbi. There were some cases, as we have mentioned above,[327] in which the scholarly world and public opinion themselves fixed a definite hierarchy among a number of different rabbinic scholars. In such cases, all these scholars met within the walls of one yeshivah, where this hierarchy found clear expression in their status in relation to the *rosh-yeshivah* and in the order of their signatures on documents. Thus, in the book *Mikveh Yisra'el*, the four most important scholars in Venice are referred to as 'the chief *Ge'onim* of the Holy Community of Venice',[328] each of them being allotted a definite status in relation to the *rosh-yeshivah*: R. Samuel Judah Katzenellenbogen, head of the Academy, was the 'first in rank', R. Jacob Abraham Baruch Katz was second to him, R. Avigdor Cividal third, and R. Ben-Zion Zarfatti fourth in rank 'to the *Ga'on* our teacher, R. Samuel Judah Katzenellenbogen'.[329] The yeshivah head thus enjoyed the status of the

[324] See Sect. 3.

[325] See Document 30, p. 246, in the Hebrew edition of this book, for the text of the decision taken by the Communal Council in 1590.

[326] 'Pinkas ha-Kehillah be-Mantova', Document 24, IMHM Microfilm HM 204, published in the Hebrew edition of this book, Document 30, p. 246.

[327] See Sect. 2 above.

[328] R. Judah Saltaro, *Sefer Mikveh Yisra'el* (Amsterdam, 1607), fo. 8a.

[329] Ibid. fos. 6b–7a, and see also Document 16, pp. 235–7 in the Hebrew edition of this book for discussion of the titles *Ḥaver*, *Ḥakham*, *Rav*.

leading scholar of the city without the subjugation to the community entailed in the office of community-appointed rabbi, and without eliminating the possibility for the community to criticize him via the other rabbis of the yeshivah. On the other hand, in those places where there was more than one assembly place for scholars, this hierarchical ranking could not be clearly expressed, and the situation was left undefined. This was the case in Mantua, for example, where, until the founding of the 'general yeshivah' in the seventeenth century, the Ashkenazic and Italian scholars each gathered in their own Study House. In any event, the different congregations constituting the overall community, as well the confraternities for charity and for Torah study, each appointed their own rabbis to fulfil the tasks of Torah teachers (*marbiẓei Torah*), without bearing any clear consequences within the overall communal framework. The homogeneity of the public within each particular congregation, and especially in each confraternity, helped remove the sting from the appointment of a Torah teacher or rabbinic authority. Moreover, the limited nature of the activity of any one congregation, and particularly that of the confraternities for the study of Torah, in economic and political matters in comparison to the scope of activity of the general community, served in a natural way to blunt the tension involving the leadership, as well as easing the process of rabbinic appointment. It is reasonable to assume that each rabbi served as a kind of Torah preacher within the limited framework of the social body over which he was appointed as head, and that at times he was even viewed as the most prominent one in the public, all decisions being made with his agreement.[330] The confraternities likewise lifted their rabbi above the flock, and did not impose the same conditions upon him as were placed upon the other members of the group.[331]

We may thus conclude: even though each organized group, whether one of the constituent congregations of the overall

330 Thus, e.g. in the *Pinkas* of the Italian congregation of Padua, R. Joḥanan Treves was mentioned as rabbi of the congregation, whose ordinances were accepted with his approval. See also D. Kaufmann, 'The Ordinances of *Ḥevrat Yeshivat Shalom* of 1589' (Heb.), *ha-Assif*, 3 (1886), 215. On confraternities for study and charity see A. Farine, 'Charity and Study Societies in Europe of the Sixteenth-Eighteenth Centuries', *JQR* NS 64 (1973-4), 16-47, 164-75.

331 See, e.g. R. Pacifici, 'I regolamenti della scuola italiana a Venezia nel secolo XVII', *RMI* 5 (1930), 395.

community or a confraternity for the study of Torah, usually appointed its own rabbi and Torah teacher, these appointments had no effect upon the broader framework of overall communal leadership—nor, for that matter, did they have one in the more restricted framework of those social bodies themselves, where in the final analysis what counted was not the appointment, but the charisma of the individual rabbi.

12. The Community of Rome

The situation of the Jewish community of Rome deserves a separate discussion. Despite its centrality and its importance in the history of Italian Jewry owing to its proximity to the Papal See, this community had no prominent rabbinic scholars throughout the period under discussion. None the less, the concept of 'rabbi of the community' was already in use there at the end of the fifteenth century, and possibly earlier. The way in which this concept is referred to in those few documents extant suggests that the incorporation of the rabbinate within the framework of the community organization took place in Rome in a rather different manner from that in the other Italian communities, perhaps the main difference being that, during certain periods, the term 'rabbi of the community' was applied to several rabbis simultaneously. It seems worthwhile to dwell a little upon the evidence found in several responsa concerning incidents which occurred in Rome at the end of the fifteenth and beginning of the sixteenth centuries.[332] While these documents have been known for some time to scholars of the history of the Roman Jewish community, there remain several details of which sufficient note has not been taken.

In the late fifteenth or early sixteenth century, a certain couple in Rome became engaged to be married, and the young man sent the customary gifts to his intended bride 'and also gave her fruits to eat in the presence of witnesses'. Later on, the two sides wished to break the engagement, and the question was raised—'in the presence of the rabbis of the Holy Congregation of Rome, who were R. Solomon Treves Ẓarfatti,[333] may he rest in Eden,

[332] See 'Teshuvot mi-Rabbanei Italyah', MS Kaufmann 150, fo. 45 ff.

[333] See H. Vogelstein and P. Rieger, *Geschichte der Juden in Rom* (Berlin, 1896), ii. 82, 93. I do not know if he is the same as that mentioned by N. Brüll, 'Das Geschlecht der Treves', *Jahrbücher für jüdische Geschichte und Literatur*, i (1874), 109.

and R. Emmanuel Provenzal,[334] may God protect him'-- whether these gifts were to be treated as formal betrothal gifts (*sevlonot*), therefore requiring the young woman to receive a proper divorce before being allowed to marry another person.[335] In the description of the case, recorded in 1519 in the wake of a similar incident,[336] there is a lengthy description as to how the case

> came before the above-mentioned rabbis and the other sages of the community . . . The rabbis mentioned and the other sages called upon the community officials and the heads and elders of the community, and in their presence and before them, through the local scribe, named R. Delli Piattelli, questioned and examined [the parties] with a solemn oath in the Central Synagogue (*Kenesseth ha-Kahal*), as to whether they knew that the community's practice was to give bridal gifts before the formal betrothal (*kiddushin*) [*in which case the girl would not be considered as formally married*] or after that [*in which case she would be considered as legally married*] . . . And then the rabbis and the other sages declared in the presence of these officials and heads of the community that the bridegroom needed to give her a divorce out of doubt, should he not wish to marry her; but this notwithstanding, if he actually wished to marry her, he ought to perform the formal marriage ceremony a second time, according to the law of Moses and Israel.

The would-be bridegroom gave the writ of divorce and everyone was satisfied. In the aftermath of this incident, an edict was instituted 'written and signed by all the heads of the community' that, from then on, it would be normal practice first to send the bridal gifts and afterwards to perform the formal betrothal, against the opinion of those who thought that the proper practice was first to betroth and afterwards to send the gifts. Two years later another such incident took place, and again 'they came before the heads of the community of Rome to decide whether one is to presume binding betrothal where bridal gifts have been sent, and likewise whether, in the case where fruit has been given her in the presence of witnesses,[337] one requires a divorce'.[338] Even

[334] See Vogelstein and Rieger, *Geschichte der Juden in Rom*.

[335] 'Teshuvot mi-Rabbanei Italyah', fo. 45.

[336] For detail, see A. Freimann, *Seder Kiddushin ve-Nisu'in*, 129–31; A. David, 'On the Identity of R. Israel Ashkenazi of Jerusalem' (Heb.), *Ẓion*, 38 (1973), 172–3.

[337] It is hard to tell whether this incident was similar to the first in all its details. If so, it attests to a custom unique to the Jews of Rome; or possibly the first account was borrowed from the latter in editing these documents. Cf. the testimony brought before R. Avigdor Kohen-Zedek (Freimann, *Seder Kiddushin ve-Nisu'in*, 47).

[338] 'Teshuvot mi-Rabbanei Italyah', fos. 45–6.

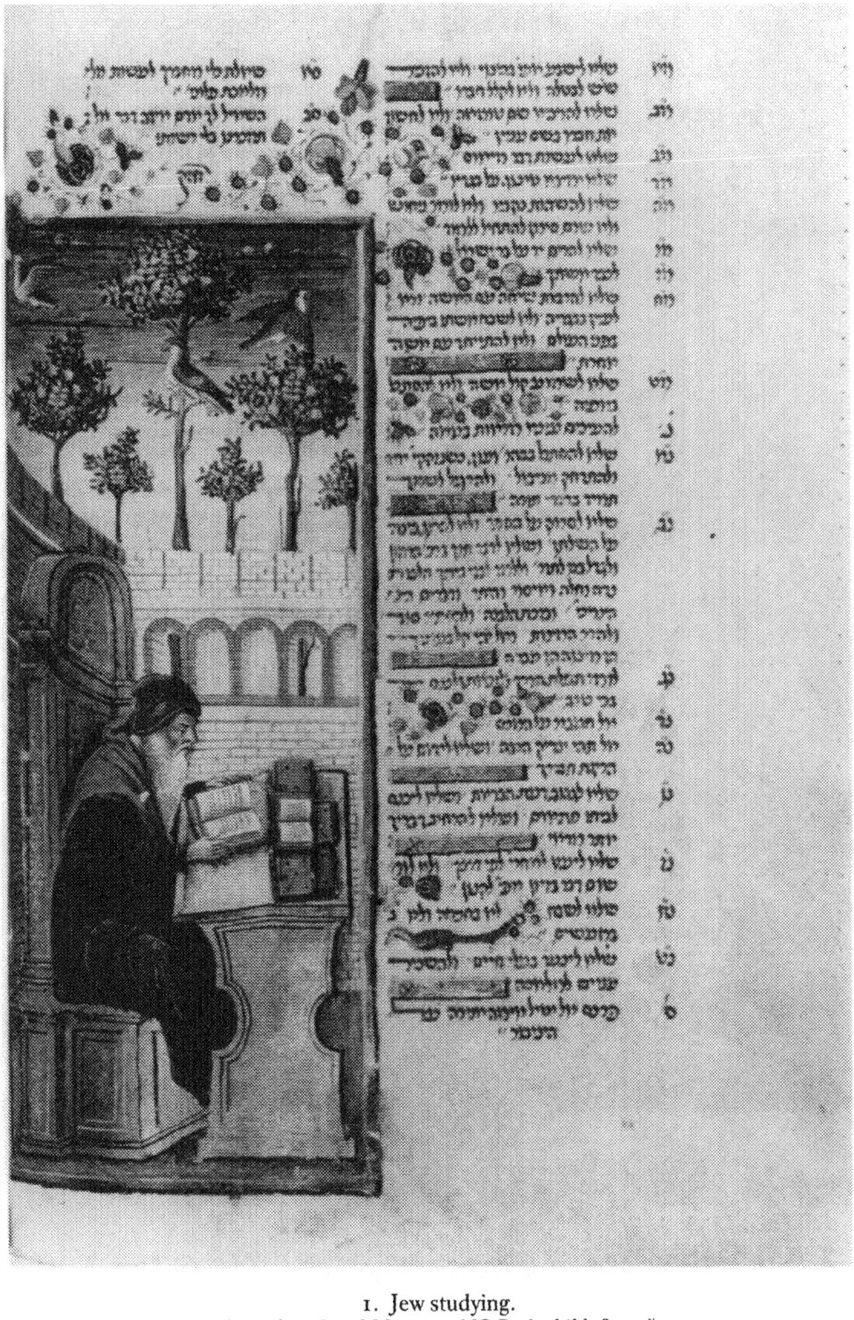

1. Jew studying.
Jerusalem, Israel Museum, MS Rothschild, fo. 44v.

2. Magisterial lecturer.
Vatican, Biblioteca Apostolica, MS Rossian 498, fo. 2[v] (detail).

3. 'O how love I thy law! It is my meditation all the day' (Ps. 119: 97).
Jerusalem, Jewish National and University Library, MS 4° 1193.

4. Jewish marriage. *Vatican, Biblioteca Apostolica, MS Rossian 555, fo. 220ᵛ.*

צורת הרב שונה לתלמידיו את כל הלכות
הספר וסידוריו

5. Rabbi teaching.
From Jacob ben Asher, Arbaʿa Turim, *Brescia, 1500*

6. A Jewish tribunal. *Vatican, Biblioteca Apostolica. MS Rossian 555, fo. 292–3.*

7. Marriage contract (*ketubbah*), Padua, 1561.
Jerusalem, Jewish National and University Library.

8. (*above*) The world of study.
Jerusalem, Israel Museum, MS Rothschild 24, fo. 330ᵛ.
9. (*below*) A Jewish author.
Jerusalem, Israel Museum, MS Rothschild.

though the young man agreed to give a divorce, one rabbi, R. Usigli the Spaniard, declared that the young woman needed no divorce, concluding 'and may the sin fall upon my head'. On the other hand:

The rabbi of the community, whose name was Messer Bonet Provenzali,[339] answered, saying the following in front of all the community and in front of all wise of heart. . . 'Let us present the case to the great authorities, the rabbis and sages of the yeshivah of Padua, or to other expert rabbis and sages who are closer to us, and let a third [i.e. *outside*] party come and decide among us, and let us not so hastily "put our head between the great mountains" [i.e. *presume certainty in such serious halakhic issues*] to release a woman who is possibly married . . . And even though I am an ordained rabbi, accepted by the community, and I also have the authority given by the court of our ruler the Pope, may his glory be augmented, to enact ordinances and to command those who will listen to my voice for the honour of our holy Torah, I do not wish to enact and to command until a third party come and decide among us. But as for the lenient [i.e. *Usigli*] and those who listen to him, may the sin fall on their head, and we will be clean before God and Israel.'[340]

The bride's relatives were angered and told the rabbi that they would not obey him, 'and will not consider you rabbi of the community in this matter. . .' The manuscript goes on to quote the rulings of the Spanish sage and of R. Bonet de Lattes, the letter sent by R. Bonet to R. Judah Minz, and the reply of R. Judah Minz as it was preserved in Bologna, confirmed by the signature of R. Abraham ha-Kohen and his court. In his response,[341] R. Judah Minz did not defer to R. Bonet's status at all, but affirmed the earlier ruling, concluding: 'We learn from this, that when one issues bans in the synagogue, if the majority of the community are there, then the others are required to submit themselves; but if not, they need not, unless there is a senior authority there to whose edicts every one is required to submit.'[342]

339 He was R. Bonet de Lattes—see D. Goldschmidt, 'Boneto de Latis e i suoi scritti latini e italiani', *Scritti in memoria di Enzo Sereni* (Jerusalem, 1970).

340 'Teshuvot mi-Rabbanei Italyah', fo. 47. These have already been mentioned by M. Mortara, 'Notizie di alcune collezioni di consulti MSS di rabbini italiani', *Mose*, 5 (1882), 266, and all subsequent scholars based themselves upon his conclusions, designating R. Bonet de Lattes as the chief rabbi of Rome. See e.g. Vogelstein and Rieger, *Geschichte* ii. 81, and cf. Shulvass, *Renaissance*, 94.

341 Sect. 15 in the above MS, fos. 57–60.

342 Ibid. fo. 60. These expressions are definitely in line with R. Judah Minz's approach to the leadership role of a great scholar, as mentioned in Sect. 2.

Thus, beginning with the period prior to R. Bonet, there were 'two rabbis of the holy congregation', as well as other 'sages of the community', all of whom together 'enacted . . . before the community officials and the heads of the community'.[343] The distinction drawn here between 'rabbis of the community' and 'the other sages of the community' indicates a clear difference in status, even though its exact nature is not defined. In any event, the impression received is that this refers to all the sages of Rome who gathered together at the yeshivah (or in some other kind of meeting house), whose status, like any group of yeshivah students, depended upon their scholarly knowledge. This group of rabbis debated the various halakhic questions which arose in the community, as was done wherever there was a yeshivah, and together constituted the 'rabbis of the community'. It is not clear in what way the manner in which they were addressed by the community at large reflected this valuation, nor how it was incorporated within the communal organization.

R. Bonet de Lattes was alone called 'the rabbi of the community'; hence, the Spanish sage was said to have 'jumped to the head' when he ruled on a practical halakhic issue in opposition to his opinion. R. Bonet himself defined his authority in the community on the basis of the fact that he was 'an ordained rabbi and accepted by the community', but here too it is not clear, either from his own words or from any other source, how he obtained the community's agreement to accept his rulings as authoritative. As an additional source of authority, R. Bonet cited the permission given him by the Pope 'to enact edicts and to command'. In the light of what is known concerning the practice of excommunication in Italy[344] during this period, it seems clear that R. Bonet exploited his position as the papal physician to receive blanket permission to impose the ban, without requiring special permission each time. As he was 'accepted by the community', this did not contradict their wishes, but actually served the public. It is therefore not surprising if we find no mention made here of opposition on the part of the public, of the kind familiar to us from those places where rabbis were appointed by the secular powers against the will of the public.[345] But, despite the

343 On the other hand, the 'local scribe' (*sofer mata*) was not known by the title 'rabbi of the congregation' (*rav ha-kahal*); cf. further.

344 See above, Ch. 2, Sect. 4 and Ch. 5, Sect. 2.

345 Cf. above, Ch. 2, Sect. 2.

permission of the authorities to impose the ban without the community's agreement, and despite the existence of a 'signed and sealed document from the heads of the community', who certainly would have backed him in this case had he wished to impose the *ḥerem*, R. Bonet nevertheless preferred to address an inquiry to 'the great authorities'—that is, the renowned scholars of the time. It is difficult to know whether this was merely an expression of modesty and of reluctance to rule on such a serious issue,[346] or whether he feared a challenge to his rabbinic status—a conclusion he might easily have drawn from the declaration of those who disagreed with him that 'we shall not consider you rabbi of the community in this matter'—and that he thus made a wise decision in seeking the support of the great Torah authorities. In short, the overall impression gained is one of competition, in the context of which the rabbi needed to protect his status by strengthening his personal influence rather than by relying upon the authority of the framework of communal organization. It follows from this that there may not have even been an actual appointment of a communal rabbi, although for the moment there is no substantive evidence in support of this assumption.

In any event, during the period following R. Bonet, we again encounter a kind of collegial definition of the communal rabbinate in Rome. This model, which emerges from documents preserved from the latter half of the sixteenth century and the beginning of the seventeenth century, has been summarized by historians of the community of Rome.[347] In fact, it has been quite properly emphasized that there was one office which definitely existed in sixteenth-century Rome—namely, 'the scribe of the place'.[348] It has also been noted that at least three different rabbinic figures

[346] One must remember that the extreme gravity of adultery in Jewish law rendered all questions pertaining to marriage and divorce, even those which revolved around seemingly minute, technical points of procedure, of the utmost seriousness.

[347] This refers primarily to the works of A. Berliner, *Geschichte der Juden in Rom von den ältesten Zeiten bis zum Gegenwart*, 2 vols. (Frankfurt-on-Main, 1893) and Vogelstein and Rieger, *Geschichte*. Generally speaking, I shall refer to the latter work, which contains detailed references to Berliner's works.

[348] An ordained rabbi of known stature within the congregation was appointed to this task. See Vogelstein and Rieger, *Geschichte*, 118, 130. During the period of R. Judah b. Shabbetai's service as scribe, he was a delegate of the community of Rome to the 1554 Convention of Delegates of the various communities which took place at Ferrara in 1554; see Finkelstein, *Self-government*, 303.

were designated in some documents by the title 'servant of the Holy Congregation of Rome',[349] from which it may be inferred that a kind of collegial rabbinate of three must have taken shape in Rome.[350] This conclusion also fits what we have seen of the situation at the end of the fifteenth century, although there seem then to have been two community rabbis. In the light of what has been said thus far, we may conclude that at no time throughout this period was there only one community rabbi in Rome; that at times there were several 'community rabbis' there, although not necessarily three in number; and that all of them were considered as 'community servants'. What is the significance of this, and how did the community address those rabbis for purposes of internal government? Examination of the available documents leads us to the conclusion that the community scribe enjoyed a special status, which at times makes it seem that he alone was designated by the title 'rabbi of the community', although the decision about whom to consult in matters pertaining to the rabbinate was left to the lay leaders of the community, who turned to all of the rabbis together on important decisions.

Thus, at the end of the sixteenth century, the Council (that is, the committee of the sixty chosen members of the community) did not rely upon one communally appointed rabbi in the ritual supervision of the meat sold in the butcher shops, but rather upon all the rabbis of the community.[351] The same is true of the invocation of oaths and the imposing of the ban in matters relating

[349] See Vogelstein and Rieger, *Geschichte*, ii. 99, 101, 107, 155. A letter 'concerning the matter of the books', dated 27 Adar 5323 (1563), IMHM microfilm HM 204, signed by several Roman rabbis—'Abraham b. R. Joshua Carmi, servant of the Holy Congregation of Rome; Shelomi b. R. Shlomo Corcos of blessed memory, servant of the Holy Congregation of Rome; Judah b. R. Benjamin Ẓaddik, servant of the Holy Congregation of Rome'—is preserved in the communal archive in Mantua.

[350] See Vogelstein and Rieger, *Geschichte*, ii. 127–8.

[351] The document containing the decisions of the Council in this matter appears in the collection of documents preserved in the archives of the Jewish community in Rome (IMHM microfilm HM 4803), fo. 14b. The document has no date; the preceding one is from 1588, and the following one from 1604. The following is the text of those sections relevant to our subject: 'In prima si ordina, et commanda, che si debba mondare, e nettare la carne . . . conforme al rito della legge Mosaica, secondo é stato dechiarato, et ordinato alli Macellari Hebrei dalli *Rabbanim* in presenza delli Magnifici fattori della Università di Roma, per ordine datoli dalla Congrega delli sessanta . . . Item, tutti quelli Hebrei che venderanno carne mondata . . . conoscendo non esser mondata secondo li sopradetti Capitoli, siano obligati publicarlo, et manifestarlo alli Rabbini, et Fattori conforme alla scommunica sopracio buttata.' This is signed by R. Joseph Ascarelli, scribe of the community.

to communal taxation, as may be seen from the final section of the sumptuary law of 1610.[352] At the end of that document, the ban is invoked against those who will violate it, at the order of R. Azriel Ascarelli, referred to there as 'the communal scribe'.[353] In 1617, his successor in this office, R. Ḥananel b. Israel Sforno,[354] appears as the 'rabbi of the Holy Congregation' at the head of the members of the Italian community in the list of 'the names of distinguished people of the Council who are still alive'.[355] The 'communal rabbi' is likewise mentioned in a decision of the Council from 1615.[356] In the assessment and oath dated between 1610 and 1617,[357] the Council specifically decided that Ascarelli was to be the one to swear in those individuals assessed. The 'scribe of the community' was thus identical with the 'rabbi of the community', at least at the time of rabbis Ascarelli and Sforno. Although the Council continued to appeal equally to all the rabbis of the community in everything which they saw as important, these two rabbis enjoyed a special status[358] in

[352] Ibid. fo. 35b. This is the text of the clause: 'Che li rabbini, no altri hebrej in materia de giuramento che [occorrendo dare] non debbano dare altro giuramento, che l'ordinario sopra li teffelim e no sopra lo cherem, o seffer del colbo, e cosi anco in materia de schomuniche non habbiano fare e dare ogni sorte de giuramento ne publicare altre schomuniche che l'ordinarij e anco pero che in materia delle [?] o datij della Communità, nel qual caso si ponno fare et dare ogni sorte di giuramento e scommunica et no in altro caso.'

[353] '[By order of] R. Joseph Ascarelli, scribe of the Holy Congregation of Rome, under penalty of excommunication . . .' This is the same 'Joshua Ascarelli' mentioned in Vogelstein and Rieger, *Geschichte*, ii. 193, following E. Natali, *Il ghetto di Roma* (Rome, 1887).

[354] Many responsa of this scholar, who was evidently a descendant of R. Obadiah Sforno, have been preserved, scattered among various manuscripts (among others, 'Teshuvot u-Pesakim mi-Rabbanei Italyah', MS Copenhagen Royal Library 115; MS Strasbourg 154, 155; MS Mantua 88).

[355] In a collection of documents preserved in the Jewish Communal Archives in Rome (IMHM microfilm HM 4804), fo. 1; cf. Berliner, *Geschichte*, 54; Vogelstein and Rieger, *Geschichte*, ii. 266. The decision to appoint R. Ḥananel Sforno as scribe of the congregation bears, in the same collection, the date 22 Sivan 5377 (1617).

[356] In the collection of documents mentioned in the previous note, for the date 9 Aug. 5375 (1615); and see below, n. 358.

[357] The above-mentioned collection, in IMHM microfilm HM 4803, fo. 38b. Evidently, R. Joseph Ascarelli was no longer alive at the time, as R. Ḥananel Sforno was named in his stead to serve as communal scribe.

[358] Thus, for example, on 9 Aug. 1615 (see above, n. 356), it was 'unanimously decided not to distribute gloves, that is, *guanto*, at the carnival, except to the Honourable appointees and the rabbi of the congregation and the treasurers and the [?], but no more'. I do not know what the significance of the glove is here. It was likewise decided, on 24 Tevet 5378 (1618), that whoever would have in his possession 'bills and letters and brevi which were made in our day and in the days of our fathers, pertaining to the Holy

comparison with the others. The following two documents from 1616 and 1618, respectively—that is, from the period during which R. Ḥananel Sforno served as 'rabbi of the congregation' (or 'scribe of the community') --clearly indicate that the Council was not content with addressing itself only to the 'rabbi of the community', but often reserved the final word to itself, or else delegated authority to the rabbi on an *ad hoc* basis in specific individual cases:[359]

On that same day [17 Menahem Av 5376 (1616)] Shelomo, known as Grizzo, came before the Council[360] and appealed to them to forgive him for what he had spoken and done [i.e. *he had boasted of eating non-kosher food*]. And the Council declared that the three rabbis who had removed his presumption of reliability [i.e. *as a God-fearing Jew*] would see whether by law they might restore him to his former status, and would do so, and they [i.e. *the Council*] would be satisfied with that procedure. And so I, Sforno,[361] went to all the distinguished members of the Council [to ask] whether they would agree to restore him, and every one of them answered that they would be satisfied that the rabbis do what seems right to them, and if they see fit to restore him, they may restore him.

On that day [27 Nissan 5378 (1618)][362] the members of the Council[363] and the distinguished appointed ones[364] debated whether they ought to call R. Abraham of Cammeo, the physician, by the title 'Rabbi', as there had been general agreement that no one was to be called 'Rabbi' without the agreement of the Council. And they voted by ballots,[365] whether it was fitting that they allow the distinguished rabbis and the appointed ones to do in this matter as seemed fit to them. And the proposal which stated that the rabbis and appointed ones should decide

Community and its interest, should be deposited with R. Ḥananel Sforno, under penalty of ban'. This special status of the 'rabbi of the congregation', who was the 'scribe of the congregation', also found expression in documents in which R. Joseph Ascarelli is designated as Rabbino principale. See Natali, *Il ghetto di Roma*, 242. In the light of the above, it is difficult in this case to accept Rieger's translation as 'Hauptrabbiner der Stadt' (see Vogelstein and Rieger, *Geschichte*, ii. 193; cf. also A. Milano, *Il ghetto di Roma* (Rome, 1964), 304).

359 From the Archives of the Community of Rome (IMHM microfilm HM 4804); published in the Hebrew edition of this book as Document 32, p. 247.

360 The Council of 60 members, selected by the procedure established by Daniel of Pisa. See A. Milano, 'I "Capitoli" di Daniel da Pisa', *RMI* 10 (1935–6).

361 i.e. R. Ḥananel Sforno, scribe and rabbi of the Holy Congregation.

362 From the same collection, IMHM HM 4804; published in the Hebrew edition of this book, Document 33, p. 247.

363 As just noted in n. 360.

364 i.e. the leaders (*parnassim*) who were serving at that time.

365 i.e. with balls.

whether or not he was fit to be called such won, and they determined that the agreement decided in this matter would be carried out.

Finally, once the Council decided not to recognize anyone in Rome as 'Rabbi' except those upon whom the Council itself would agree,[366] and to allocate equal tasks in the structure of the community organization to each of the available rabbis, there were no ordained rabbis left who were not also servants of the community and its scribes, as illustrated by the following decision:[367]

On that day [16 August 1620] the members of the Council voted and decided, together with the distinguished appointed ones, that all the needs of the community to write ordinances and other things would be served by the four rabbis, R. Hezekiah Manoah Corcos, R. Ahavah Kohen Manoscrivi, R. David della Rocca and R. Samuel of Castelnovo, each one of them for three months, with the condition that none of them would have the right to vote within the council. Likewise, each one in his turn would preside over the ceremony of oath-taking pertaining to taxation, and the wages would be divided among them, one quarter to each one.

This situation did not change at least until the second half of the seventeenth century.[368] Thus, the possibility of the appointment of a rabbi of the Roman community, at least in the sense in which this institution existed in the smaller communities discussed above, was prevented. On the other hand, the absence of prominent scholars in this community prevented a development similar to that mentioned above with regard to the other large communities, in which the *Ge'onim* remained outside the communal structure. A process took place in which, alongside the 'rabbi of the community', other rabbis also served as 'servants of the community'; the specific decision as to whether and under what situations to turn towards them was left in the hands of the Council, until

366 See Berliner, *Geschichte*, ii. 54. The text of the document which formed the basis for Berliner's statement appears in the Hebrew edition of this book, Document 32, and cf. also Document 33, p. 247.

367 Archive of the Roman Community; IMHM HM 4804; published in the Hebrew edition of this book, Document 35, p. 248. Cf. the decision from 1626 given in full in Document 36 in the Hebrew edition of this book, p. 248.

368 See the decision of 15 Ellul 5410 (1649), mentioned by Berliner, *Geschichte*, and given in full in the Hebrew edition of this book, Document 37, pp. 248–9. Cf. the similar document from 1661 published by A. Berliner, *Sarid me-'ir* [*Kovez 'al Yad*. 5 (Cracow, 1893)], 17.

in the final analysis there were no ordained rabbis left in Rome who were not 'communal servants', all of them being incorporated in the framework of the organization of the community on the college model.

13. Conclusion

To conclude: since it is impossible to identify certain general trends common to the majority of communities, in terms of the underlying operational models and motivations, it is doubtful whether the situation in Italy during the period we are dealing with can be described in an overall manner. The history and traditions of particular local communities, the personalities of certain central individuals and their intellectual, psychological, and social background, were of decisive importance. No less important is the fragmentary nature of the majority of the documents available to us. All these factors hinder the scholar's attempt to arrive at an overall picture of the multi-faceted reality. We must therefore be satisfied to close this chapter under the sign of this pluralism.[369] The fragmented picture presented here allows us to say only one thing with certainty: that, contrary to the views of those who held that in this area things were fixed and 'standardized',[370] the actual situation was a complex and intricate one, and in each place unique.

369 A striking confirmation of this reality is the fact that, in *Sefer Yefeh Nof*, published in Venice at the end of the 16th or beginning of the 17th century, there is not even one model of a rabbinic appointment, although the book contains various documents, including one for 'the document of delegation that the congregation makes for a private individual from among them to deal with the matters of the community in its name'.

370 Needless to say, one could refer here critically to other works adopting such a perspective. I again emphasize the caution that must be exercised with regard to the use of generalizations, which are not absent even in the works of the greatest scholars in this field.

4
Outside Sources of Rabbinic Income

1. 'With his Soul he Earns his Bread'

In the last chapter, we observed that, throughout the period under discussion, most of the rabbis in Italy were unable to earn a livelihood within the framework of their communal activities. With the exception of the Sephardic Torah teachers, who during the first half of the sixteenth century still received an adequate salary, and of certain yeshiva heads, who received grants from their community, in accordance with their personal prestige and greatness, the overwhelming majority of ordained rabbis received an adequate living salary neither within the context of the organized community nor from public money. This was even true of the appointed rabbis, in those communities in northern Italy which had them. How, then, did they earn their living?

The rabbis naturally served as teachers and tutors[1] but, as a main source of income, this occupation was certainly not one to guarantee either status or economic security. Nor did the fact that a given individual was a teacher of small children or a *repetitor* add to his prestige, and one could even insult a rabbi by calling him such. Thus, R. Bendit Axelrad reacted to a rebuke from R. Abraham b. Judah Minz in these sharp words:

> You thought to insult me by writing that I am a teacher of small children. It is indeed true that most of my life, for some forty years, I have taught pupils the Talmud, with [*Rashi's*] commentary and the *Tosafot*, and I have in exchange received payment for guarding them and for teaching the cantillation of the text,[2] as was done by some of the most prominent *ge'onim* of the entire world. The *Ga'on* R. Joseph Colon was formerly hired to teach, as was Rabbi Vitza Katz; the *Ga'on*, our teacher, your father of blessed memory [i.e. *R. Judah Minz*] was also hired by R. Asher Meshullem Segal, at the beginning of his studies at the *yeshivah*, to teach him the Codes, the Talmud and its Commentary.

[1] See M. A. Shulvass, *The Jews in the World of the Renaissance* (Leiden and Chicago, 1973), 154–5.

[2] Cf. Ch. 3, Sect. 7.

Similarly, the pious one and *Ga'on* of his generation, R. Jacob Margalit, and R. Jacob ha-Kohen the Pious, and other great ones [did likewise]. I also followed in their path and studied with the pupils . . . And I have thus earned my livelihood engaged in the labour of heaven, and not like yourself, who have all your days made your living through theft and injustice, even when you ate at your father's table . . . And when our teacher, the *Ga'on* [i.e. *R. Judah Minz, R. Abraham's father*], became old . . . you took the one hundred ducats which the communities gave him each year as a means by which to pay stipends to all the young men and students who came to study at the *yeshivah* . . . for yourself and chased away those distinguished young men and students without giving them any of that stipend . . . And after your father's death you took all of your father's money for yourself, both that which came from that stipend and the rest of your father's money, and you pushed aside the other heirs of your father and gave them 'Purim money' [i.e. *a small symbolic sum*]. Thus, your whole life you made a livelihood by theft and injustice, and you now dare to taunt me because I have made a livelihood from [teaching] my students.[3]

R. Bendit presents himself here as a poor but honest man, in contrast with those who have gained their wealth dishonestly, mentioning in passing other scholars who did so. One senses that he did not make a comfortable livelihood, for he only received 'payment for guarding [the children] and for teaching the cantillation of the text'; he was obviously aware of the halakhic problem involved in receiving payment for teaching as such, and would have evidently preferred to avoid it altogether had he been able to do so without having to resort to 'theft and injustice'.

The status of the teachers and *repetitors* did not improve during our period.[4] For this reason, the vast majority of ordained rabbis did not occupy themselves exclusively with the 'sacred page', but attempted to earn a living in one way or another, each one within the context of his particular talents, personality, and circumstances. They also hoped thereby to achieve economic independence, enabling them to hold their own beside those rabbis who had inherited wealth, such as R. Jeḥiel Nissim da Pisa. There are many reports of the varied and at times unusual ways in which rabbis earned their livelihood, independently and by personal

3 *Pesakim* (Venice, 1519), fo. 29b.

4 See the remarks of R. Aaron Berechiah of Modena in *Sefer Ma'avar Yabbok* (Mantua, 1626), 'Minḥat 'Aharon', sect. 4, Ch. 14—cited also by S. Assaf, *Mekorot* (Tel Aviv, 1928–43), iv. 54.

initiative. One could write an entire monograph about the detailed classification of these occupations—a task which I will not attempt within the framework of the present work, as it would require extensive biographical clarifications. Scholars have already dealt with the salient points, and I could hardly offer information which would substantially add to the picture already known.[5] I will therefore limit myself to a brief summary of those facts which seem most worthy of emphasis in the context of the present discussion.

Many of these rabbis were physicians, continuing a centuries-old tradition[6] whereby the healing profession accompanied 'the art of Torah'. This profession was an ideal one, freeing the rabbi from anxieties about his livelihood without requiring him to take payment for religious teaching.[7] Moreover, the position of the physician in those days was an extremely honourable one, and it seemed particularly appropriate that it be combined with that of the ordained rabbi.[8] This fact was even taken into consideration by R. David Provenzali in his plan for establishing a Hebrew University in Mantua.[9] One finds many prominent rabbinic names among the Jewish physicians of this period, including R. Judah Messer Leon and his son David, R. Elijah del Medigo, R. Bonet de Lattes, R. Obadiah Sforno, R. Abraham de Balmes, R. Isaac b.

[5] See, e.g. Shulvass, *Renaissance*, 148–55.

[6] See J. Walk, 'R. Obadiah Sforno, Exegete and Humanist' (Heb.), *Sefer Zikaron le-Zekher David Neiger* (Jerusalem, 1959), 280, and the literature cited there; C. Roth, *The Jews in the Renaissance* (Philadelphia, 1959), 213–29; H. Friedenwald, *The Jews and Medicine; Essays*, 2 vols. (Baltimore, 1944; 2nd printing, New York, 1967), esp. 221–40, 257–62, 551–612; S. W. Baron, *A Social and Religious History of the Jews* (Philadelphiia, 1952–76), xii. 80–90; C. Roth, 'The Qualification of Jewish Physicians in the Middle Ages', *Speculum*, 28 (1953), 834–43; M. Steinschneider, 'Jüdische Aerzte', *ZfHB*, 17 (1914), 63–96, 121–67; ibid. 18 (1915), 25–57; and N. Koren, *Jewish Physicians; a Biographical Index* (Jerusalem, 1973).

[7] R. Simeon b. Ẓemaḥ Duran attributed Maimonides' adamant opposition to receiving payment for teaching Torah to the fact that Maimonides was a physician: 'and if he, of blessed memory, was blessed by fortune to be close to the king and honoured in his generation because he was a physician, so that he did not need to receive any remuneration from the communities, what shall those rabbis and sages do who are not as talented as he was? Shall they die of starvation or be shamed of their honour to throw the yoke of Torah off their necks?' (*Tashbeẓ*, beginning of sect. 14). Compare I. Barzilay, *Yosef Shlomo Delmedigo* (Leiden, 1974), 125.

[8] See Ch. 2, Sect. 6.

[9] See the text of the programme, sect. 10 (Assaf, *Mekorot*, ii. 118): 'those who are expert in the Latin tongue shall study the books of wisdom—logic and philosophy and medicine—in such a way that whoever wishes to become a physician will not need to spend all his days and years in a *studio* among the Gentiles . . .'

Emmanuel de Lattes, R. Elijah b. Abba Mari Ḥalfan,[10] R. Eli'ezer Ashkenazi,[11] R. Abraham Portaleone and his son R. David, R. Abraham Provenzali, the appointed rabbi in Casale,[12] and many others.[13]

The income earned by these individuals from the practice of medicine stood them in good stead, some of them even becoming successfully involved in business activities as a result. Among these latter activities, one should particularly mention their involvement in financing the publication of Hebrew books. Thus, R. Elijah Ḥalfan 'was moved by his spirit to publish . . . the *She'iltot*' (an important Rabbinic work from the Gaonic period)[14]; R. Jacob Marcaria was a central figure in the Hebrew press in Riva di Trento[15]; R. Isaac b. Emmanuel de Lattes and two partners published the responsa of R. Nissim Girondi.[16] Examples might easily be multiplied. Also deserving of mention here are those whose main occupation was the study of Torah, such as R. Joseph Ottolengo[17] and R. Meir of Padua,[18], for whom the new world of printing opened possibilities of employment.[19] From this time on, many rabbis were employed in the printing trade in the task of 'proof-reading' which, as is well known, in those days primarily involved the editing or preparation of manuscripts for setting in print, and not the simple correction of printed galleys.[20]

[10] It is worth noting that a list of his books, including many medical works, has been preserved (see Appendix 1 to the Hebrew edition of this book, item no. 36).

[11] See M. Mortara, *Indice alfabetico* (Padua, 1886), 4.

[12] See the conclusion of Portaleone, *Sefer Shilṭei ha-Gibborim*, which conveys a clear echo of the importance of the physician's status in the eyes of his contemporaries.

[13] A comparison of Mortara's list (*Indice alfabetico*) with that of Steinschneider, *Jüdische Aerzte*, will yield the names of dozens of rabbi-physicians.

[14] Printed in Venice, 1546.

[15] See M. Benayahu, *ha-Defus ha-'Ivri be-Cremona* (Jerusalem, 1971), 107 ff.

[16] Printed in Rome, 1545-6. To this edition R. Isaac de Lattes added his own glosses and references to laws, which spread over 33 pages. See also S. Simonsohn, *Mantua* (Jerusalem, 1972), 717, and Friedenwald, *The Jews and Medicine*, 611.

[17] See Benayahu, *ha-Defus ha-'Ivri be-Cremona*, index, and esp. 53-8, 111-18.

[18] It is perhaps worth mentioning his involvement in the publication of the *Mishneh Torah* (Venice, 1550-1), as well as the book sent to him by R. Joseph Caro for printing which was lost in a shipwreck (see Ch. 6, Sect. 4) and also *Orḥot Ḥayyim* by R. Aaron ha-Kohen of Lunel, which was sent him 'from the city of Candia, to attempt to print it'—Solomon Luria, *Teshuvot Maharshal* (Lublin, 1574), sect. 37.

[19] See E. L. Eisenstein, 'The Impact of Printing on Western Society and Thought', *JMH* 40 (1968), 1-56.

[20] It is enough to mention the activity of R. David Pizzighettone and R. Mordecai Basola (father of the noted R. Moses Basola) in printing the Talmud at the end of the 15th century and the beginning of the 16th century—see R. N. Rabinowitz, *Ma'amar 'al*

R. Leone Modena wrote that his grandson was engaged in 'a clean and easy occupation in printing, which is in the final analysis also a religious occupation',[21] thereby indicating the tendency to see printing as a natural area of employment for a scholar, whose main occupation was religious scholarship, but whose livelihood had to come from other sources.

Even some of the greatest rabbis engaged in bookselling. Thus, R. Meir of Padua wrote to R. Moses Isserles:

There is a Jew among us who purchased the entire edition of the *Rif* [*R. Isaac Alfasi's glosses on the Talmud*] printed in Sabbioneta, and they are very beautiful, and he will give them to me here for four and a half of our *scudi* per copy. Will your honour kindly advise me whether I ought to buy them and send them to you, and for how much they may be sold there if I send fifty copies. Your advice will guide me.[22]

At times, rabbis printed small books at their own expense and sold them. R. Leone Modena invested 250 ducats in the publication of his *Bet Yehudah*,[23] and he also recorded that the sale of his books, *Galut Yehudah* and *Lev Aryeh*, brought him a profit of more than 250 ducats.[24]

On more than one occasion rabbis dedicated small works to wealthy patrons.[25] Thus, R. Samuel Archivolti dedicated his *Ma'ayan Ganim* to Abraham b. Asher Segal of the famous Meshulam family,[26] although it is clear that it was published at his own expense, as was his other book, *'Arugat ha-Bosem*.[27] These rabbis spoke quite openly about their hopes of profits from the dedication of their books. R. Leone Modena received 25 *scudi* from Bishop Ermolao Barbaro for dedicating one of his books to

Hadpasat ha-Talmud (Jerusalem, 1965), index—as well as that of R. Meshulam Kaufmann, proof-reader of *Sefer Rav Alfasi* (Venice, 1552) and of R. Joḥanan Treves, R. Samuel Archivolti, and many others.

21 L. Modena, *Ḥayyei Yehudah* (Tel Aviv, 1985), 96. See the title-page of the 1546 Venice edition of the *Sifrei*, containing a note that 'it was proof-read by R. Joḥanan of Treves, whose main occupation is Torah'.

22 *Teshuvot ha-RaMA*, sect. 69 (in Siev, ed., p. 301). Note that this entailed a commercial investment of some 400 ducats—which should be compared with the annual salary of the appointed rabbi in Padua a few years later!

23 1636 Venice edn. (see *Ḥayyei Yehudah*, 89).

24 Ibid. 33.

25 See Shulvass, *Renaissance*, 149.

26 1553 Venice edn. See the dedication at the beginning of the book, and the praises which R. Samuel heaped upon Abraham Segal in the poem with which the book concludes.

27 1602 Venice edn. and see the approbation given by the rabbis of Venice at the end of the book.

him: a modest sum, because the bishop 'while a great saint, is very careful with his money'.[28] Leone Modena later recorded that he printed the book *Tefillat Yesharim* [*the Prayer of the Upright*], 'with various additions, which I gave as a gift to the holy congregation of Rome, and I received 25 ducats from them as a gift. But as I mentioned the names of the donors in detail, there was confusion [regarding] their relative priority, and now I have reprinted the dedication a third time, and I stayed far away from them'.[29] Admittedly, the business of dedications did not always go smoothly!

I do not know whether R. Leone Modena, who recorded in his autobiography no less than twenty-six different occupations in which he engaged during his lifetime, was exceptional in this respect. It is quite possible that, were we to examine in depth the biographies of various rabbis in Italy during this period, we should find that other rabbis also engaged in not a few of these different occupations.[30] We may therefore conclude by saying that rabbis engaged in different, and at times unusual, occupations out of a desire for independence and personal initiative. Their income from outside occupations was sometimes supplemented by that from public funds, as with the community-appointed rabbis, only a small proportion of whose needs came from their communities.

2. What were Itinerant Rabbis?

Deserving of special mention among the various occupations in which the rabbis engaged is the tutoring of private pupils in the homes of the wealthy. There do not seem to have been very many

[28] *Ḥayyei Yehudah*, 33. The dedication of Hebrew books to outstanding Gentile figures was not uncommon. Thus, for example, R. Obadiah Sforno dedicated his commentary on Ecclesiastes and his Hebrew translation of Euclid's *Elements* to the King of France; see Walk, 'R. Obadiah Sforno', 281.

[29] *Ḥayyei Yehudah*, 62.

[30] e.g. the last occupation which he recorded was 'marriages' (*ḥittunim*). If this refers to income from performing wedding ceremonies, this has already been found to be received by other rabbis (see Ch. 3, Sect. 10). However, if it refers to money accepted for matchmaking, we already know that R. Samuel Archivolti sent to R. Jacob Marcaria (the physician and printer from Riva di Trento) six ducats for the match which he successfully made; see S. Bernstein, 'New Poems by R. Samuel Archivolti' (Heb.), *Tarbiz*, 8 (1937), 56, 65. In my opinion, this refers to both.

rabbis who engaged in this occupation, in which they became a kind of 'private rabbi' to their employer, who in turn took upon himself the rabbi's entire livelihood. The number of wealthy families who could allow themselves this luxury was very small. Nevertheless, the phenomenon represents an interesting example of patronage, typical of the Renaissance, and because of its nature it has received attention on the part of scholars, especially following Isaiah Sonne's theory of the itinerant rabbi, to which he assigned a central place in his picture of the Italian Rabbinate.[31] According to his thesis, these itinerant rabbis undercut the authority of the established rabbis, a phenomenon which Sonne saw in terms of the general Renaissance trend to 'destroy the structure of the general, abstract concepts of the Middle Ages and base the world on the individual'.[32] By this process, the Renaissance also undermined 'the existence of the community as a general entity, and scattered it into its individuals'. Against this background, there emerged according to Sonne, 'ordained rabbis who were not connected to any community, but to wealthy patrons alone . . . these rabbis wandered from place to place, accompanying their master or changing him periodically, similar to the humanists attached to the courts of the rulers. Such rabbis served their masters for a fee in every place and at all times', in their disputes with the communities, thereby creating antagonism between the itinerant rabbis and the rabbis of the establishment.[33]

One of the corner-stones of Sonne's theory is an ordinance introduced in Bologna in 1512, imposing the ban against 'whomever brings any letter or edict containing a curse or excommunication from any court outside of Bologna . . . even if it be a verbal edict'.[34] Yet there is not even the slightest hint in this ordinance that the community rabbi in that particular place had the authority to impose the ban, while this prerogative was denied other rabbis who lived in the same city—and one certainly cannot argue that all the rabbis of Bologna, which was in those days a centre of Torah learning, were community-appointed

[31] See I. Tishby's summary, 'The Controversy Concerning *Sefer ha-Zohar*' (Heb.), *Meḥkerei Kabbalah u-Sheluḥoteha*, i (Jerusalem, 1982), 96–7, and cf. e.g. Shulvass, *Renaissance*, 52–3.

[32] Cf. M. A. Shulvass, 'On the History of the Community of Rovigo' (Heb.), *Sinai*, 20 (1947), 198 ff.

[33] See I. Sonne, 'On the History of the Community of Bologna' (Heb.), *HUCA* 16 (1942), 38–43.

rabbis! The rabbis and *parnassim* are mentioned under one rubric in the ordinance itself: the cantor announced the ban which accompanied the edict in the synagogue, in the name of 'the rabbis and the *parnassim*'. The publication of edicts of excommunication from outside Bologna are made contingent upon 'the agreement of the rabbis and leaders'; when it occurred that an edict was brought from outside Bologna, the 'righteous judges, the rabbis and *parnassim*' discussed the matter, declaring the one who had brought the ordinance as himself under the ban. In the aftermath of this incident, there was renewed debate concerning the authority of the community to enact such an ordinance, an interpretation being proposed which would limit its application:

> There were those among the founders of this ordinance who did not feel comfortable with it, but supported a decision to nullify any ban brought from outside the city of Bologna against those who live there, in order to constrain Bologna's residents from presenting themselves in a court outside Bologna. As for those sinners who have performed sins and are deserving of excommunication, even the righteous and holy from outside the city of Bologna may constrain them, and rule bitterly over them.[35]

Thus, in the view of those who objected to the ordinance, not only did it not affect the right of any rabbi living within Bologna from imposing bans, but even those living outside the city should not be barred from doing so. The sole exception was in those specific cases in which the ban was used to force an individual from Bologna to appear at a hearing of a rabbinic court outside Bologna. R. Abraham ha-Kohen composed a lengthy ruling against this approach, in which he affirmed the community's authority to issue ordinances. He emphasized that 'the force of this ordinance is applicable to all kinds of edicts' and not only a ban 'not to take an individual outside the city'.[36] In any event, nobody even suggested that this ordinance was intended to prevent rabbis living in Bologna from imposing the ban on Bolognese Jews.

After some time, things changed in Bologna and, in 1537 (or perhaps earlier), an additional ordinance was introduced in order to prevent mishaps in matters relating to justice and bans. This ordinance also bears upon our subject, and is deserving of

[34] The text of the ordinance was published by Sonne, ibid. 56 ff.

[35] Ibid. 58. [36] Ibid. 71.

attention. The situation of the Jewish courts in Bologna is described by the lay leaders in 1537 as one in which:

each one builds a high place for himself against the law and the *halakhah*, secretly to make a court of three laymen and youths, and capriciousness reigns. They do not know or understand, and there is none among them who has studied [Torah] . . . And after they convene a court and have received testimony, they send their testimony far afield with the seal of the court, and they strike that man with blindness according to their will, with the approval of prominent scholars . . . for the *ge'onim*, the masters of Torah, who do not know what deeds they are doing in darkness, think that what they did conforms to the law of Torah . . .[37]

In other words, certain individuals within the community established lay courts in Bologna which accepted testimony improperly. This testimony was then presented to the 'great ones of the world' outside Bologna as if ratified by a proper court; these rabbis in turn relied upon it, issued rulings on its basis, and even imposed bans upon those who would not accept their ruling. In properly run communities, in such a situation, the community would naturally issue an ordinance prohibiting anyone but the official communal court from collecting testimony, but the people of Bologna were unable to do so because of the peculiar situation of the Italian communities. Thus, the people issued an ordinance in 1537:

that no member of our community . . . may make any court to accept testimony . . . in secret and on the sly upon any man in Bologna, or that any man may come from outside Bologna and establish a court to collect testimony in Bologna, except in the presence of the litigant. And that all the members of that court be learned and over twenty-five years of age . . . and in this manner we may save the oppressed from those who oppress them, and their oppressors will not have the strength to trap them in this net which they have set, as has been done until now.[38]

This being the case, it is quite clear that the question was not one between the 'rabbis of the establishment' and of the 'Master of the Place'. What the community hoped to accomplish by this edict was merely to ensure that the members of the court who collected evidence in Bologna would be 'learned . . . and over twenty-five years of age': 'private rabbis' were therefore clearly included within the rubric of this formula! The ordinance of

[37] Ibid. 73, and see *Pesakim*, fo. 4a. [38] Ibid. 74.

Bologna from 1512 and the additional one from 1537 were thus intended to prevent the involvement of figures from outside the city in matters concerning the people of the city,[39] as well as to prevent any further breaches in the legal system, such as had been made by people who were not learned or even mature individuals. The ordinances of Bologna therefore have nothing whatsoever to do with the phenomenon of private rabbis,[40] neither can we infer from them anything concerning the correct interpretation of it.

In order to understand properly the phenomenon of private rabbis, we must restate some of the conclusions which we have reached thus far. During the period under discussion, a class conflict between the itinerant rabbis, who allegedly undermined the foundations of the communal organization under orders from their wealthy patrons, and the official, appointed rabbis would have been impossible[41] for one simple reason. As we have shown at length in the previous chapter, there was during this entire period no existing model of an official rabbi who enjoyed the authority of master of the place (*mara de-atra*) within the framework of the communal organization. Indeed, in several large communities, wherein resided those wealthy individuals who were able to afford the luxury of a private rabbi, there was no appointed rabbi whatsoever. In those communities which did appoint a rabbi, the tension between the appointed rabbis and those not integrated within the community organization concerned the interplay between the forms of activity and influence of the appointed rabbis and those of the other rabbis within that same system. In other words, whatever tension existed involved com-

[39] Such regulations were instituted wherever the communities wished to protect themselves against outsiders, even where the phenomenon of itinerant rabbis did not exist. Cf. e.g. J. Halperin (ed.), *Pinkas Va'ad Arba' 'Arazot* (Jerusalem, 1945, 7, 16.

[40] We have already discussed the significance of the ordinance of Ferrara regarding this matter in Ch. 3, Sects. 4a, 5.

[41] Tishby questioned Sonne's theory of the itinerant rabbis in his discussion of the latter's interpretation of the controversy concerning the publication of Kabbalistic texts (see Tishby, 'The Controversy'). There is no doubt that Tishby is correct in his cautious conclusion that 'in any event, the general outlook that the identification of a given Italian rabbi of the 16th century to the class of "itinerants" or "official rabbis" was decisive in determining their stand on one or another side in public controversies, has been upset, albeit one must not deny the possibility that this factor did influence them at times, depending upon its bearing upon each specific controversy', p. 117. I shall attempt further to demonstrate how, in my opinion, rabbis were influenced by their being the servants of the wealthy classes.

petition between the rabbis for their place within the community. We have already seen how this tension affected both the contents of the office of the community-appointed rabbi and the very possibility of achieving such an appointment. Moreover, even in those communities where a community rabbi was appointed, the establishment of courts of law with broad juridical authority was prevented. This automatically prevented the granting to the official community rabbi of broad, exclusive authority to rule on halakhic questions, so that there was no possible reason for the creation of a class of rabbis who would protect the interests of the wealthy from the rulings of the community-appointed rabbis.[42] On the contrary, we have seen how in Padua, where there was a community-appointed rabbi, the subject of tariffs between the individuals and the community was adjudicated by 'the communal judges', who generally did not include the rabbi.[43] In cases of great importance, the communities and their opponents turned to the arbitration of rabbis from outside the community.[44] In this matter, the situation during the period when there was a communal organization was no different from that prior to it.[45]

In their appeals to arbitrators, everyone, including both the community officials and their adversaries, made use of the services of rabbis who served as advisers and, on occasion, as barristers to argue their case before the arbitration court.[46] If, from 1549 on, the people of Padua adhered to the ordinance by which 'no

[42] Cf. Shulvass, *Renaissance*, 77. [43] See Ch. 3, Sect. 4c.

[44] In this respect, the situation in Italy was no different from that elsewhere—cf. Jacob b. Asher, *Ṭur Shulḥan 'Arukh, Ḥoshen Mishpaṭ* 7: 12, and *Bet Yosef*, ad loc.

[45] e.g. just as the society of bankers, who claimed a monopoly in Mantua, and those who opposed their claim both turned for arbitration to R. Joseph Colon in the 1460s (see *Teshuvot Mahari"k*, sect. 192), so did the community of Bologna on the one hand, and R. Shelomo of Modena on the other, turn to R. Moses Provenzali for arbitration at the end of the 1560s (see 'Teshuvot R. Moshe Provenzali', sect. 198). See also the many arbitration rulings issued by R. Azriel Diena between litigants in cities where he did not live, such as sect. 282 (Mantua, between creditors and the congregation), sect. 285 (ibid. among various creditors), sect. 100 (Reggio, between the congregation and heirs), and others.

[46] Just as the opponent to the claim for a monopoly of the bankers of Mantua (in the case mentioned in the previous note), used R. Jacob Sforno as their representative, so did the community of Bologna, in the other case mentioned, make use of four delegates. On the other hand, R. Shelomo Modena, who was an ordained rabbi, did not have need of a representative. See likewise MS Vienna 80, fo. 43b, where R. Raphael Joseph b. Joḥanan Treves is referred to as 'delegate of the Holy Community of Viadana'. On the subject of delegates, see the ruling pertaining to them in the arbitration agreements (e.g. Document 50 in the Appendix to the Hebrew edition of this book, pp. 263 ff.).

rabbi, whether local or outsider, may serve as a barrister unless the rabbi himself is the plaintiff or defendant, [in which case] he may take a rabbi as barrister for himself',[47] we are entitled to assume that there was a definite trend to turn towards rabbis as barristers. Naturally, a barrister defends the interests of the one who has appointed him and who pays for his services; there is no real difference whether the barrister in question is the private rabbi of his client or whether he has been hired *ad hoc*. So long as the activity of the private rabbis was limited to protecting the interests of the wealthy in whose service they were engaged, this did not deviate from the general cultural framework, in which law and patronage went hand in hand.

There is considerable similarity between these private rabbis and the humanists who were part of the ruling courts during the period of the Renaissance.[48] This similarity, however, suggests a rather positive evaluation of the private rabbi in the eyes of his contemporaries, akin to the image of the court humanist.[49] A proper view of this phenomenon demands that we free ourselves of any tendency to see this in a negative light.[50] A contemporary expert in the social and intellectual history of Renaissance Italy has rightly warned against the tendency to write about courts and *cortigiani* during the Renaissance without explaining the significance of the terms being used:

The Renaissance courtier . . . is similar in every respect to Locke's gentleman. He is the significant person in society, the active element in society. A trader such as Manetti in Florence, a knight, a statesman, not necessarily wealthy and at times even poor, who by virtue of his culture becomes a teacher, involves himself in the liberal arts, and ascends to the level of knight and adviser to the highest authorities . . .

[47] *Pinkas Padua*, sect. 57: xi, p. 101.

[48] Shulvass has justifiably noted the parallel between the private rabbis and the humanists in the ruling courts—see Shulvass, *Renaissance*, 148–55; compare Sonne, 'On the History of the Community of Bologna', 40.

[49] On the concept of the courtier as the model for the perfect man of society during this period, see J. Burckhardt, *The Civilisation of the Renaissance in Italy* (New York, 1958), 382 ff.

[50] This attitude seems to have greatly influenced, perhaps unconsciously, the image of the rabbis in Italy during this period, both of Sonne and of those who followed him. This attitude incorporated the historiographic tendency of the Jewish Enlightenment (*Haskalah*) of the 19th-century and its epigones, which saw in Italian-Jewish culture of this period a kind of Enlightenment *ante litteram* (see further in Ch. 6). One thus finds a specific, and predominantly negative, image of the rabbis of this period, which to my mind is definitely unjustified; see Shulvass, *Renaissance*, 192–4.

a man who carries the responsibility for the society in which he lives, one upon whom depends the collective lot, a man whose *humanitas* alone allows for the existence of a more humane collective life.[51]

These words are very impassioned, and perhaps need to be toned down somewhat, but there is no doubt that they contain a large measure of truth. A superficial reading of Baldasar Castiglione's *Courtier* should suffice to indicate the keen admiration which the courtiers enjoyed in the eyes of their contemporaries, who considered them as perfect in every respect.

The absolute economic dependence of the private rabbis upon those who provided them with their daily bread did not affect the respect and honour which both they and their patrons saw themselves as deserving. These rabbis added to the prestige of their patrons, just as the talented courtiers added to the glory of the Christian rulers.[52] Some of the most prominent rabbis in Italy during the period under discussion here were private rabbis in the homes of wealthy men;[53] one may assume that the wealthier a given individual, the greater the stature of the rabbi he was able to hire. This practice even brought about the transformation of the homes of some wealthy men into actual *yeshivot*[54] headed by these private rabbis, a development which obviously augmented their prestige. Thus, Ishmael da Rieti's home in Siena became a yeshivah, and R. Joseph of Arles, who had previously been a teacher in that household, became a yeshivah head.[55] The Rieti family was proud of R. Joseph of Arles, referring to him as 'our *Ga'on*, the righteous teacher'[56] and boasting of his ability to hold his own in a disputation with the apostate Ḥananel da Foligno.

[51] E. Garin, *La cultura filosofica del Rinascimento; motivi della cultura filosofica Ferrarese nel Rinascimento* (Florence, 1961), 408–9 and 140–1.

[52] See A. Marx, 'R. Joseph d'Arles and R. Joḥanan Treves' (Heb.), *Kovez̧ Mada'i le-zekher Moshe Shur* (New York, 1945), 271, for a brief and attractive description of the phenomenon of rabbis teaching in the homes of the wealthy. My own description adheres closely to that of Marx, and my stress is primarily intended to refute Sonne's view of the itinerant rabbis.

[53] See Shulvass, *Renaissance*, 150. It is surprising to me how Shulvass could argue elsewhere (ibid. 77) that 'while there were men of stature among these private rabbis . . . the official rabbinate far surpassed them in both communal prestige and authority'.

[54] The maintenance of *yeshivot* by wealthy people within their own homes was known in Italy from the beginning of the period under discussion. See, for example, MS Montefiore 367, fo. 116a, for the verses written by R. Joseph Zark, sent with a gift to R. Mordecai Finzi, 'to the *studio* which he made in his home, Kislev 5193 [1433]'. On the parallel between *studium* and *yeshivah*, see Ch. 1, Sect. 1.

[55] See Marx, 'R. Joseph d'Arles'.

[56] See S. Simonsohn, 'I banchieri da Rieti in Toscana', *RMI* 38 (1972), 29.

Those who turned to the office of 'private rabbi' were not necessarily dependent for their entire sustenance upon the kindness of their patron and their ability to fulfil his or her will in every situation. R. Isaac de Lattes, a physician of independent means enabling him to make extensive investments in the area of publishing,[57] was apparently not dependent upon the mercy of any patron. If he took upon himself the office of 'private rabbi', it was presumably because this in no way detracted from his rabbinic dignity. Moreover, the salaries enjoyed by the private rabbis were far higher than those of community-appointed rabbis. R. Joseph of Arles wrote of his terms in the home of Menaḥem of Monte dell'Olmo: 'my salary with him is one hundred *scudi*,[58] two loads[59] of wheat and two loads of wine, and living accommodation for my wife, may she be blessed among women, in accordance with her honour; and I eat at the table of the patron, as does my beloved son as well'.[60]

As I stressed above with regard to the use of the services of barristers, it was only natural that wealthy individuals should turn to their private rabbis wherever a solution to halakhic questions was needed, particularly prior to taking decisions in business matters. This practice was an integral part of social life in those days, and there was no suspicion of conflict of interest regarding the sincerity of the various parties acting in this matter. A good example of this involves Ishmael da Rieti, who sent R. Joseph of Arles to various places to gather the opinions of the sages of Italy on the question of whether he could accept the offer of the Duke of Tuscany to open a bank in Pisa, despite the opposition of other Jewish bankers who had previously been expelled from there when a prohibition against lending on interest was imposed, while now, this edict having been repealed, they sought precedence in the right to lend there.[61] According to his own account, given in a fierce polemical letter to R. Joḥanan Treves, R. Joseph of Arles went to Padua 'visiting all of the

[57] See the end of Sect. 1 in this chapter. [58] i.e. in cash.

[59] A measure of volume of solids and liquids. It seems likely that this refers to the unit known as *soma*, which in Florence measured approximately 91 litres.

[60] See I. Sonne, 'The General Synod in Italy' (Heb.), *ha-Tekufah*, 32–3 (1948), 677; Shulvass, *Renaissance*, 137. Cf. the salary of the community-appointed rabbis, discussed in Ch. 3, Sect. 9.

[61] See on this matter Marx, 'R. Joseph d'Arles', 189–219. On the privilege of lending money in Pisa, see Simonsohn, 'I banchieri da Rieti', 4, n. 5.

rabbis there in order to clarify whether any man was permitted by the law of our holy Torah to attempt to receive conditions of loan on interest from the Duke of Florence'.[62] Word of this mission became known to R. Joḥanan Treves, communal rabbi of the Italian congregation in Padua[63] and, according to R. Joseph, R. Joḥanan replied with exaggerated enthusiasm:

> Then you answered, 'Do you conceal from me such a thing? I will ascend the palm tree of evidences and will rise to assist a prince in Israel, who was formerly my patron, the prince of Rieti, and I shall keep evil lips away from me.' And with the eyes of a scribe you composed a great poem . . . And you have revealed explicitly what I only alluded to, for I did not inquire about the right to Pisa, but only posed the question in general terms, speaking of the entire duchy. And you thought in your heart to receive a reward for the interpretation; by my life [i.e. *I swear*], I could not tell whether what you wrote was a halakhic ruling or a dirge. And it is still doubtful to me, for you have shown anger, and have written of those who oppose as if they were evil-doers, and you made many remarks of slander and condemnation, by which I was much pained. And also the nobleman, my patron, of Rieti, was very much pained, for he cares not to offend anyone, and judges every man favourably.[64]

Even if one may cast some suspicion on R. Joseph's words regarding his intention to conceal the precise details of the case under discussion, so that he might objectively clarify the absolute truth by the law of Torah, it is clear that R. Joḥanan Treves, who had, after being a 'private rabbi', become a 'communal rabbi', saw it as perfectly proper to come to the enthusiastic defence of the banker, who was his former patron. This enthusiasm, according to R. Joseph of Arles, added a bad taste to the entire business. Obviously, the relation of individuals to such questions depended more upon their personality than upon their status.

One small detail concerning that case from a different source should be added here. There is an extant responsum, dated Rosh Hodesh Adar II, 1547, by Shabbetai Elḥanan, son of Ishmael da Rieti, concerning the same question involving the renewal of money-lending in Pisa, written as an exercise in halakhic ruling

62 Marx, 'R. Joseph d'Arles', 204.

63 See R. Pacifici, 'I Regolamenti della scuola italiana', *RMI* 5 (1930).

64 See Marx, 'R. Joseph d'Arles'.

under the guidance of R. Joseph of Arles.[65] In the beginning of his responsum, the son declares that his father had asked him to discuss the question, 'and I ask you to tell me, according to the Torah which has been told us by our rabbis, the masters of law who sit in the seats of judgement, whether the Jews resident in Pisa, who earlier held the presumption of this prerogative, can prevent you'.[66] This would indicate that the question of the opening of the bank in Pisa and the halakhic controversy which raged round it sincerely interested the Rieti family, and they discussed the substantive issues involved within the context of religious study, albeit from the perspective of an interested party.

The private rabbis, who lived in close proximity to their patrons, were themselves influenced by this situation—each one according to his particular personality and reactions. An interesting illustration of this problem emerges from a case involving a dispute between an orphaned girl who had reached maturity, and a woman who was the guardian of her father's property. R. Moses Provenzali's responsum concerning this matter, from the second half of the sixteenth century, has been preserved.[67] The case was as follows: at the orphan's request, a court of arbitrators ruled that the guardian was to submit a detailed account of the property which had been under her custody. In a second ruling, which was not immediately published, the judges ruled that, if the account did not satisfy the orphan, both sides were to choose expert accountants who would examine the books and draw their conclusions. The judges likewise ruled that 'they reserve for themselves the authority to clarify any question which may arise regarding this ruling, throughout the duration of the

[65] This responsum has been preserved, bound within a copy of the book Eleh ha-Devarim, Mantua 1566 edn., in the Mediceo-Laurenziana Library in Florence. It includes 15 small pages, containing 20 lines on each page, apart from the last, which includes only 3 lines. It seems to me that this responsum can add a number of details to complete the picture, such as the reference to the pressure exerted by the Pisan public against the Church authorities to restore lending at interest to its former place, and the role of the university students in this incident. This last detail combines with other information known to us, in which the opening of banks for lending money at interest is justified in terms of the needs of university students; see also Ch. 1, Sect. 1.

[66] It is clear that his teachers 'who are Masters of teaching on the seats of judgement' are none other than R. Joseph d'Arles, the head of the yeshivah established by Ishmael da Rieti in his home, so that his son could be educated there.

[67] 'Teshuvot R. Moshe Provenzali', sect. 159. The question and the responsa are cited in full in the Hebrew version of this book, Document 38, pp. 249–55.

compromesso'.[68] The guardian delivered her accounts to the orphan, to which the latter raised objections. The arbitrators then published the second ruling, mentioned above; in accordance with this latter ruling, the orphan requested that the books be examined by two accountants. The guardian ignored this request so that, in accordance with the second ruling, the arbitrators demanded the right of final ruling. The guardian refused to submit to their judgement, on the basis of various arguments which she put forward at the suggestion of a rabbi 'who had received generous payment from her for many years'. The orphan argued in return that this rabbi's arguments were invalid because he was 'dependent' on the guardian, 'being supported together with all the members of his household' by the guardian. We find here a case of a wealthy aristocrat who generously supported a rabbi along with his entire household; it is argued that, because the rabbi is dependent upon this woman, his various arguments are intended to assist her in escaping from justice. This incident was a typical one in Italy during the period under discussion. The orphan was unable to appeal to a communal court because such courts did not exist—a point which has already been made several times, and which will be explained in detail in the next chapter. On the other hand, the existence of 'private rabbis' supported by patrons enabled these same wealthy individuals to define their family and entourage, who worshipped in their own private synagogue, as an autonomous 'congregation'.[69] This made it possible for the recalcitrant guardian to answer in all seriousness that she wished to be tried before 'the judges of her community'. R. Moses Provenzali related to this claim with all seriousness, recognizing that the guardian's synagogue in principle constituted a distinct, separate community. For this reason, one could reasonably argue that the respondent could force the claimant to take the case to her community, on the grounds that 'the litigants are to be judged before the judges of the community of the respondent'. Provenzali stated in his responsum that such a claim could only be invoked where one was dealing with expert judges who were not appointed by the litigants *ad hoc*, 'but in this generation, where there are no experts, but each [litigant] selects one arbitrator, how can one think that the respondent should

[68] The exact significance of the terms appearing here will be discussed at length in Ch. 5.

[69] See Shulvass, *Renaissance*, 192.

come and say, "Come and choose with me judges from such and such a community"? Is there not a well-known mishnah [which states] "This one selects one judge, and that one selects one judge"? '

The situation alluded to by this rabbi was obviously not one in which there were permanent courts which might judge without the prior consent of the two sides, but one in which the parties each chose arbitrators; this situation disqualified the guardian's argument in principle, irrespective of the specific status of her private rabbi. R. Moses Provenzali addressed several comments towards the lady's rabbi, who was presumably ordained, and whom he did not consider an utter ignoramus, concerning the proper behaviour for a rabbi in such a situation, in terms of both decency and the honour of the Torah. In his view, such a private rabbi 'ought not to be a judge [in such a situation]' and may even be formally disqualified 'by law, even if he is chosen by the arbitrator of the orphan'. It follows that such a private rabbi may at best serve as the legal adviser to the guardian. As one who understood the mentality of such rabbis, supported by wealthy people and subjected to the peculiar psychological pressures entailed in this status, Provenzali added that: 'My heart tells me that if things are as my inquirer states, it would be better for that sage to be disqualified by others; but so long as others do not disqualify him, he has not the power to avoid participating in this case, because the hand of the guardian is stronger than his own . . .'

We may conclude from this that there were certainly some rabbis during this period who accepted payment from the wealthy and shared their tables. At times, this situation was selfishly abused, but this is no more than the negative side of the general phenomenon of patronage, to which each patron and rabbi reacted in his own individual way. In the sentence, 'my heart tells me . . . that it were better for that sage were others to disqualify him', R. Moses Provenzali succinctly summarized the delicate situation in which the private rabbis found themselves. It involved continual tension between the desire for intellectual independence and the sense of psychological pressure owing to their peculiar situation of economic dependence. This tension left its mark on all areas, and not only on that of the specific economic interests of the patrons. In the final analysis, what determined the behaviour of the individuals involved, among the infinite possibilities presented by reality, were the degree of intellectual honesty and piety of both the rabbi and his patron, and the nature of the specific question on which the rabbi's opinion was asked.

Interesting light is shed on this matter by a small incident in which Provenzali himself found a way of compromising on an issue—albeit one of considerably less weight than the one discussed above—in which he himself was not ashamed to propose a certain *modus vivendi*. Many Italian Jews were accustomed to combine the second and third Sabbath meals during the short winter Sabbath days, separating them from one another by reciting the Grace After Meals and immediately thereafter ritually beginning a 'new' meal by washing their hands and reciting the blessing over bread. Provenzali, asked whether this custom was a proper one, replied as follows:[70]

> I will now answer you concerning your [practice of] eating with those who advance the third meal prior to its proper time, eating it before noon. Know that in the home of my patron they also follow this practice, and they incorporate it into the morning meal, dividing that meal into two. Although I have heard nothing on the matter [i.e. *I have no specific tradition concerning a ruling from earlier rabbis*], the custom does not seem right to me. In any event, I eat with them, in order not to deviate from their custom, but I do not recite Grace after the first meal, but rather they recite Grace and I am silent, for it is my intention to eat another meal [later in the day], so that what is two for them is one for me. When they wash their hands a second time, I wash my hands [for the sake of form], but I do not recite the blessing, because it is superfluous for me, nor do I recite the blessing over bread, but I answer 'Amen' to their blessing.

This constitutes clear evidence that R. Moses Provenzali earned his living in the home of a patron. He referred to that wealthy householder by the same term used by R. Joseph of Arles to refer to his patron, R. Ishmael da Rieti:[71] 'my wealthy master' (*geviri*). Provenzali compromised here with his conscience 'for the sake of peace', thereby avoiding a confrontation over a matter which did

[70] This responsum does not appear in the collection of his responsa published by his grandson; see R. Bonfil, 'R. Moses Provenzali's Commentary to Maimonides' 25 Axioms', *KS* 50 (1975), 164. It is included in the collection of his miscellaneous responsa in MS Los Angeles 12 (IMHM 28085), fo. 28b.

[71] See the above quotation in this section.

not seem to him one of principle; there are certain matters in which a rabbi must know how to use his common sense!

We may thus conclude that the institution of the private rabbinate in Italy during the period under discussion constituted the Jewish equivalent of patronage, so characteristic of the Renaissance, in both its positive and negative aspects. This phenomenon took shape against the background of a general situation in which the decisive majority of the rabbis were not part of the community organization. As we have frequently mentioned above, one of the primary causes of this situation was the failure of the communities to establish autonomous judicial institutions in which the rabbis could have found a broad framework for activity within the communal organization. We shall now turn to examining more fully the situation in the judicial realm, which will aid us in forming an overall picture of the period.

5
The Judicial Function of the Rabbis

1. Christian Opposition to the Establishment of an Autonomous Jewish Juridical System

With the efflorescence of Roman law from the eleventh century onwards, Christian jurists turned their attention to the question of the interpretation of the basic Roman laws pertaining to Jews. As is well known, according to the literal reading of these laws, Jewish autonomy is not recognized, except within the realm of civil law, and even there only concerning arbitration, when the agreement of both litigating parties is required.[1] It seems fairly well established that, throughout the period under discussion, the Jews in Italy never lost their theoretical status as *cives*, in so far as Roman law was concerned.[2] This apparently implied that Jewish law was not recognized as the personal law of the Jews. It should be added that the binding character of Mosaic law was denied by Christian theology, a fact which influenced the opinion of the jurists, who were generally under the influence of that theology.[3] This opinion was not universally accepted, however, and room was left for the argument that, in a manner parallel to the acceptance of local legal codes alongside Roman law, Jewish law ought to be considered valid as the personal law of the Jews, as a sort of species within the genus.[4] But even this line of

[1] See e.g. *Codex Justinianus* i. 9, 7: 'Nemo Judaeorum morem suum in coniunctionibus retinebit nec juxta legem suam nuptias sortiatur nec in diversa sub uno tempore coniugia conveniat.' Cf. on the other hand, *Codex Theodosianus* ii. 1, 10 and, with a slight but significant change, *Codex Justinianus* i. 9, 8: 'Judaei, romano et communi jure viventes, in his causis quae non tam ad superstitionem eorum quam ad forum et leges ac jura pertinent, adeant solemni more judicia omnesque romanis legibus inferant et excipiant actiones: postremo sub legibus nostris sint. Sane, si qui per compromissum ac similitudinem arbitrorum apud judaeos vel patriarchas ex consensu partium in civili dumtaxat negotio putaverint litigandum sortiri eorum judicium jure publico non vetentur; eorum sententias provinciarum judices exequantur, tamquam ex sententia cognitoris arbitri fuerint adtributi.' See also J. Juster, *Les Juifs dans l'Empire Romain* (Paris, 1914), ii. 101–6, and cf. his discussion there concerning the legal framework for specifically religious matters.

[2] See V. Colorni, *Legge ebraica e leggi locali* (Milan, 1945), 33–94. [3] Ibid. 166–70.

[4] Such is the opinion of the canonic jurist Calderini (d. 1365), ibid. 161.

reasoning did not imply actual recognition of an autonomous Jewish judicial system. It implied only that the regular judges should be obliged to judge Jews according to their own personal law.[5]

In any event, the only model which could possibly serve as a basis for the establishment of an internal Jewish juridical system was that of arbitration. In other words, since Roman law allowed Jews to turn to arbitration according to general consensus, and arbitration was acknowledged and incorporated in the judicial system, the arbitrator's decisions being binding upon the local governments, the Jews could try to build a system of internal jurisdiction over their co-religionists by in some way transforming arbitration into a compulsory procedure.[6] Two primary means were open to the Jews for attaining this goal: the introduction of *ad hoc* legislation on the part of the ruling Christian authorities and the promulgation of internal ordinances within the communities. The Church establishment was adamantly opposed to both of these.

Ad hoc legislation on the part of the authorities might be accomplished by introducing clauses relating to this matter into the text of the privileges granted to the Jews. It is known that in these clauses one may at times find some of the most striking examples of the ambivalence characteristic of the policy towards the Jews. This was but one aspect of the more general tension in the Jews' existence, caught as they were between central and local authorities, i.e. between the emperor and the Church, on the one hand, and, especially in Italy, between ecclesiastical authorities and local governments.[7] As we have seen, Christian jurists might be tempted to deny the validity of Jewish law as a consequence of the abolition of the Old Testament by the New.

[5] See ibid. 159 ff. and esp. 177–81. I shall return to this point later.

[6] Ibid. 306.

[7] See H. H. Ben-Sasson, 'The Northern European Jewish Community', *JWH* 11 (1968), 208–19. This is likewise the source of the papal statements, such as that of Pope Martin V to the Jews of Germany, Savoy and Bresse in 1418, declaring that there is no judicial authority over the Jews other than the local authorities; see M. Stern, *Urkundliche Beiträge über die Stellung der Päpste zu den Juden*, 2 vols. (Kiel, 1891–3), i. 21–5, Documents 9 and 10. It is perhaps worth mentioning here the view of some scholars who see the differences between the formulations of the two documents mentioned as reflecting differences in the papal tendencies with regard to the Jews in Italy, as against those beyond its borders; see S. Grayzel, 'The Papal Bull *Sicut Judaeis*', *Studies and Essays in Honor of Abraham A. Neuman* (Leiden, 1962), 271–5.

Such an approach found practical expression in the official position within the Papal States. Moreover, one of the main conclusions drawn by the Christians from their own theological teachings in the public realm was the absolute refusal to permit Jews to serve in positions of rulership and power,[8] including positions which might be perceived as involving any kind of *dignitas*.[9] The ecclesiastical authorities thereby forcefully prevented any recognition of compulsory jurisdiction of Jews over other Jews, even if only in the realm of arbitration.[10] One may therefore schematically say that opposition to granting rights to the Jews in this area was directly related to the ecclesiastical authorities' influence over local governments.[11]

In those places where the Jews were subject directly to the Church, the local government had exclusive legal authority even over internal Jewish disputes.[12] One therefore searches in vain

[8] e.g. B. Z. Dinur, *Yisra'el ba-Golah*, (Tel Aviv, 1965), I, i. 150, sect. 10; ibid. II, i. 235, sect. 48 [English: *Israel and the Diaspora* (Philadelphia, 1969)]; S. Grayzel, *The Church and the Jews in the XIIIth Century* (Philadelphia, 1933), 27, 198–200.

[9] See V. Colorni, 'Sull'ammissibilità degli ebrei', *Scritti in onore di Riccardo Bachi*, *RMI* 16 (1950), 203–8.

[10] However, the Church did not attempt to interfere in matters such as dietary laws, Sabbath observance, and the like, despite their importance from the theological point of view. One may see a justification for that in the distinction between *cerimonialia* and *judicialia* as stated in Thomas's *Summa Theologica*, Secunda Secundae, x. 11 (cf. also Prima Secundae, civ. 1): The Jews observed the *cerimonialia* alone, and even though these had the character of 'non solum mortua, sed etiam mortifera observantibus', they were the exclusive concern of the Jews. On the other hand, 'judicia exercentur officio aliquorum Principum, qui habent proprietatem judicandi'. It follows that a *princeps* who recognizes a system of Jewish law within the region under his authority sins towards the Church, as by this fact he acknowledges that, for a portion of the population under his rule (i.e. the Jews), those *judicialia* constituted laws which 'habent vim obligandi ex veteris legis'.

[11] This is particularly striking if one compares two documents issued by Pope Martin V (as already noted). The one pertaining to the Jews of Italy states explicitly that the Pope wishes that disputes among Jews be brought before the local authorities alone: 'decernentes ulterius, quod causas, lites seu controversias pro tempore orituras inter ipsos Hebraeos *domini locorum*, ubi huiusmodi lites motae fuerint, videre, decidere ac terminare ac videri, decidi et terminari facere ab eorum officialibus et ministris deputatis de jure, summarie, simpliciter de plano et sine figura iudicii . . .' (Stern, *Urkundliche Beiträge*, 42).

[12] See the 1429 version of Pope Martin's edict, cited in the previous note, and cf. the expression given to the same outlook in *Reformatio Tribunalium Almae Urbis et eius officialium* in 1611 (H. Vogelstein and P. Rieger, *Geschichte der Juden in Rom* (Berlin, 1895–6), ii. 196). One must emphasize that this was not an innovation, but was and remained the policy of the Church towards the Jews throughout the period, both before 1611 and for many years following; see Colorni, *Legge ebraica e leggi locali*, 319–20, and his perceptive comment on Vogelstein and Rieger's remarks. One might apparently derive a somewhat different conclusion from article 22 of the ordinances of Daniel of Pisa; see A. Milano, 'I "Capitoli" de Daniel da Pisa', *RMI* 10 (1935–6), 324–38, 409–26. The text of that article reads: 'Elessero et determinorono . . . che se occorresse qualche lite o

among the privileges granted in these places for any clause referring to arbitration among Jews.[13] One likewise finds no such clause in the privileges granted to the Jews in those regions in which the influence of the Church was particularly great, such as Naples[14] or Umbria.[15] In most cases, it is difficult to state definitively whether the absence of such a clause was a function of pressure from the Church, or whether this is related to the fact that the *condotta* was granted only to individual banking families.[16] But the very fact that *condotte* exist which delegate

differenza . . . in qualsivoglia negotio fra oltramontani, siano tenuti a chiamare arbitri della congrega italiana col terzo . . . e cosi se la lite fosse fra itagliani gli arbitri siano oltramontani per cosa dell'universale o vero che occorresse differenza tra gl'uomini della Congrega che non potesse vincersi per partito che le palle fossero mezze nere e mezze biandre in questo case definiranno e termineranno loro lite e differenze secondo la giustizia comportara l'Ill. mo . . . Vicario del nostro Pontefice o suoi ministri.' However, it is clear that this clause only applies to controversies concerning public matters (*per cosa dell'universale*); one must therefore interpret it by the addition of a full stop following the word 'universale'. It is difficult to imagine that one would find, combined together in one article, matters referring to jurisdiction in the private realm combined with those pertaining to decisions of the Council. The Italian syntax (che se occorresse . . . o vero che occorresse . . . in questo caso . . .) would apparently support our interpretation. Moreover, if this refers to disputes among Jews, one would have expected to find here a clause referring to those cases in which one side was from the Italian community and the other from the *oltramontani*.

13 The reference is obviously to the privileges (*condotte*) granted to the Jews as a group or community, and not to those granted to individual Jews. A systematic analysis of the contents of the many extant privileges (published or still in manuscript in archives) is still an outstanding *desideratum*. On the specific point dealt with here, see M. Radin, 'A Charter of Privileges of the Jews in Ancona of the Year 1535', *JQR* NS 4 (1913–14), 225–48. It appears that conditions were not appreciably different in the other cities of the Marche region. According to H. Rosenberg, 'Alcuni documenti riguardanti Marrani portoghesi in Ancona', *RMI* 10 (1935), 311 n. 1, the privileges published by Radin were not granted to the Jews of the Ashkenazic community of the city of Ancona, but only to bankers from other cities of the region; however, the matter requires further examination. If one may conclude from the sentence in the privilege granted to the Jews of Ascoli in 1470 ('super capitulis ebreorun qui hactenus steterunt in hac nostra civitate . . . confirmentur et prorogentur') that this was a confirmation of the conditions granted to the Jews from the year 1297, then in this city as well there was nowhere mention made of the clause pertaining to the law of arbitration between Jews, neither in the privileges, nor in the other documents published in the antisemitic book by G. Fabiani, *Gli ebrei e il Monte di Pietà in Ascoli* (Ascoli Piceno, 1942).

14 See D. Kaufmann, 'Contributions a l'Histoire des Juifs en Italie', *REJ* 20 (1890), 56–66.

15 See the documents published by A. Fabretti, *Sulla condizione degli ebrei in Perugia dal XIII secolo; Documenti* (Turin, 1891); see also A. Toaff, *Gli ebrei a Perugia* (Perugia, 1975); idem, 'Gli ebrei a città di Castello dal XIV al XVI secolo', *Bollettino della deputazione di storia patria per l'Umbria*, 72 (1975), fasc. 2.

16 See e.g. A. Ivo, 'Juives et Monts de Piété en Istrie', *REJ* 2 (1881), 188–95; L. Zdekauer, 'I capitula hebraeorum di Siena, 1477–1526', in *Archivio giuridico 'Filippo Sefaffini'*, 5 (repr. 1900), 4–9.

exclusive judicial authority over the Jews to the local authority[17] may be assumed to indicate a clear tendency, which may or may not have derived from the Church's influence in those places, as it did in the Papal States themselves.

This assumption is further confirmed by a draft of a memorandum, addressed to the ruler by the attorney of a Jewish widow, apparently in Reggio, in the latter half of the sixteenth century or the early seventeenth century.[18] This attorney discusses three questions: Are Jews allowed to benefit from the legislation recognizing courts of arbitration in those civil cases and controversies which pertain only to them? If so, must the arbitrators rule according to local law or according to Jewish religious law? Finally, are Jews allowed, or perhaps even obliged, to choose Jewish arbitrators or judges?[19] After answering the first question in the affirmative, the author built his case upon a series of references in juristic literature, according to which the parties may agree in advance that the arbitrators are to rule in accordance with Jewish law, provided that the following six conditions are

[17] In Florence, we find that jurisdiction over the Jews was already turned over to the special authority of the *otto di Guardia e Balia* in the conditions from 1437, which were reconfirmed under the later conditions. See M. Ciardini, *I banchieri ebrei in Firenze* (Borgo S. Lorenzo, 1907), App. I, p. viii (for 1437), App. VI, p. xxxi (for 1448), App. XXI, pp. lxxiii–lxxiv (for 1481); cf. also U. Cassuto, *Firenze* (Florence, 1918), 151, 344; Colorni, *Legge ebraica e leggi locali*, 320. This being the case, the Jews were not required to appeal to Jewish arbitrators (see Ciardini, *I banchieri ebrei*, 7–8), while if they did so of their own free will, they had the right to appeal against the arbitrator's ruling before the 'eight' in all cases. This situation was changed in the Duchy of Tuscany only after the granting of the privilege to the Jews of Livorno and Pisa in 1593, where it was expressly stated that the Duke was aware of the fact that in granting judicial rights to the Jewish lay leaders he agreed 'che la giurisdizione e l'autorità del . . . nostro giudice sia deminunita' (see Colorni, *Leggi ebraica e leggi locali*). This was a marked innovation, which took place within the specific context of Ferdinando di Medici's plans for developing the Duchy, in the framework of which he granted an unusually liberal privilege, opening a new period going beyond the chronological boundaries of this work. On Mantua, see S. Simonsohn, *Mantua* (Jerusalem, 1972), 765 ff.; ibid. 775–8 (for 1587); and cf. Colorni, *Legge ebraica e leggi locali*, 338–41. See also the privilege of the Jews of Asolo from 1508 and 1521, in M. Lattes, 'Documents et notices sur l'histoire politique et litteraire des Juifs en Italie', *REJ* 5 (1882), 230.

[18] This memorandum is preserved among the documents in the Modena Archive, available on microfilm in IMHM, pp. 6–13 (in Italian) and 14–20 (in Latin translation).

[19] '. . . se gli hebrei nelle loro cause, er questioni possano goder del priuilegio dello statuto sotto alla Rubrica de compromissis. Se questi Arbitri nel sentenziare debbano seguitare lo stile, e gli statuti della legge comune o pur della mosaica. E per ultimo se delle medesime cause pur anche possano, o pur si debbano essere hebrei Arbitri, e Giudici.' It follows from this that the term 'giudici' is a synonym for 'arbitri'. I shall return to this semantic point in Sect. 6.

fulfilled, that: the discussion revolve around a question of civil law; the dispute itself be one among Jews; nothing in the arbitrator's decision contradict civil law; nothing in such a decision touch upon the Christian religion; the procedure involve only the issuing of the decision itself (without those preliminary stages characteristic of the activities of a recognized judicial system, such as the acceptance of testimony before a notary, the requirement that witnesses appear before the judges, etc.); and the discussion be conducted entirely in accordance with Jewish law.[20] In his opinion, the response to the second question implies that the arbitrators ought to be Jews, as they are more expert than Christians in matters of Jewish law.[21] Thus, according to this lawyer, who presents the arguments of the Jewish side, there is no obligation on the part of the Jews to seek the arbitration of Jewish arbitrators, either by force of the *condotta* or by force of local legislation. The argument for the right to appeal to Jewish arbitrators is rather presented as a logical demand, which in no way follows from the principle established in the response to the second question—i.e. that Jewish law is the personal law of the Jews.

2. Means of Establishing a Jewish Judicial System on the Basis of Arbitration

In those states where the Jews obtained the inclusion of a special clause in the *condotta* by which individual Jews were compelled to turn to Jewish arbitration, the situation was different. This was true, for example, in the duchy of Milan, after Duke Francesco Sforza II decided in 1533 that:

[20] '. . . deuono le liti ciuili fra gli hebrei essere decise, et terminate conforme alla legge di Mosé, quando habbiano queste sei circostanti che seguono: Che siano ciuili. Che siano fra hebrei, et hebrei. Che non siano contro la legge ciuile. Che non tornino in pregiuditio, et in isprezzo della religion Christiana. Che concernano la decisoria, e non l'ordinatoria de giuditij. e che finalmente siano tali che nominatamente et in particolare uengano decise, e terminate dalla legge Mosaica.'

[21] 'Finalmente[te] quanto all'ultimo conchiudo si debbano elegger più sotto Arbitri hebrei in casi ciuili fra hebrei et hebrei che Arbitri Christiani: la ragione è questa: Gli Arbitri che sono per giudicare fra hebreo et hebreo debbono giudicar conforme alla legge di Mosé, come s'è prouato nel 2° quesito. Ma gli Arbitri hebrei in cotal leggi sono più pratichi di gran lunga che non sono li Christiani. Adunque ne' casi ciuili fra hebrei, et hebrei debbono essere Arbitri hebrei, e non arbitri Christiani.'

whenever there shall be a dispute or controversy in the civil realm, for every dispute and argument among the Jews, they shall select two Jewish doctors[22] or two Jewish arbitrators who will see and judge in accordance with their laws and statutes. And if a Jew will violate these ordinances, he shall receive a penalty of twenty imperial lire . . .[23]

This liberal privilege evidently served as a model for the privileges granted in later years in the adjacent states of Montferrat[24] and Savoy,[25] and we may reasonably assume that, for this very reason, a copy was preserved in the communal archives in Mantua.[26] It

[22] e.g. two rabbis.

[23] This privilege was published by S. Simonsohn, 'Un privilegio di Francesco il Sforza agli ebrei del ducato di Milano', in *Scritti in Memoria di Sally Mayer* (Jerusalem, 1956), 308–24. The privilege was ratified by Charles V in a letter from Barcelona dated 20 Mar. 1538. As the cease-fire between the King of France and the Emperor went into effect, Charles V published, on 27 Aug. 1541, a collection of laws pertaining to the Duchy of Milan, including several applying to the Jews. Despite the hostile nature of these regulations, as well as of the laws enacted by the same Emperor on 3 Apr. 1564, the clause pertaining to the internal legal system of the Jews did not change. In any event, on 12 June 1544 the ruler of the Duchy, with the agreement of the Emperor, published a new privilege which was in effect for eight years, in which he reaffirmed the validity of that issued by Francesco Sforza II: 'imo siano mantenuti e preservati nelli privilegi immunita et comodita franchixie, come sono stati mantenuti et preservati nel tempo del predetto Signore Ducha Francesco II et dopo sino al presente per vigore delle concessione et confirmatione prefate . . .' This indicates to us the power of local custom, despite the dramatic change in rulership, other examples of which will be cited. This privilege was again reaffirmed in 1556 for a period of twelve years. After four years (1569–73), during which the Jews lived in this Duchy without renewing their privilege, its contents were yet again renewed several times between 1573 and their final expulsion in 1597. On this matter, see C. Invernizzi, 'Gli ebrei a Pavia', *Bollettino della Società Pavese di storia patria* (Pavia, 1905) [offprint at the Jewish National Library in Jerusalem], 55–67, and cf. R. Segre, *Gli ebrei Lombardi* (Turin, 1973), 6–14. See also Colorni, *Legge ebraica e leggi locali*, 329. Prior to the privilege of Francesco Sforza, not only was there no obligation on the part of the Jews to turn to Jewish arbitration—as we learn from a dispute between two Jews in Pavia, who turned to two Christian arbitrators on 26 Sept. 1525 (Invernizzi, *Bullettino della Società Pavese*, 41 n. 1)—but even if they did turn to Jewish arbitrators, and these were unable to agree upon the choice of a third arbitrator, they were obliged to appeal to the local judicial system of the Duchy (ibid. 23 n. 2).

[24] See S. Foa, *Gli ebrei nel Monferrato* (Alessandria, 1914; repr. Bologna, 1965), 159, 162, 165, 167, 169, 170; cf. Simonsohn, 'Un Privilegio', 310 n. 5; see also Colorni, *Legge ebraica*, 326–8.

[25] See M. Lattes, 'Documents et Notices', 235. Cf. G. Borelli, *Editti antichi e nuovi dei Principi di Savoia* (Turin, 1861), 1230, 1243; Colorni, *Legge ebraica*, 325; and cf. H. Beinart, 'Jewish Settlement in the Duchy of Savoy in the Wake of the *Privilegio* of 1572' (Heb.), *Sefer Zikaron le-Aryeh Leone Carpi* (Milan and Jerusalem, 1967), Hebrew sect., 72–118.

[26] See Simonsohn, 'Un Privilegio', 308 n. 1. It seems, however, that the text of this privilege was based upon an earlier source, namely, of a privilege granted in the regions under the rule of Francesco Sforza from the middle of the 15th century; see S. Simonsohn, 'Alcune note sugli ebrei a Parma nel '400', in *Studi sull'ebraismo italiano in memoria di Cecil Roth* (Rome, 1974), 227–60.

is also worth noting here that, although following the marriage of Federico Gonzaga with Margherita Paleologo (who together initially granted the privilege in 1539) the state of Montferrat was ruled by the Mantuan dukes of Gonzaga, there was still a considerable difference between the judicial rights of the Jews in Montferrat and in Mantua itself.[27] Obviously, the power of tradition and of local conditions was sometimes stronger than the demand for uniformity and consistency in governmental policy, even within the same state.

Where the Jewish communities were unsuccessful in obtaining the permission of the government to require its members to turn to Jewish arbitration, they nevertheless attempted to create an autonomous judicial system through the introduction of internal communal ordinances prohibiting recourse to Gentile courts[28] and requiring recourse to Jewish arbitrators. However, the promulgation of such ordinances was no easy matter, as the ruling authorities generally reacted immediately and decisively once such ordinances became known to them. One must also keep in mind that the effectiveness of such ordinances was limited so long as they were not reinforced by the imposition of the ban, which required special permission by the local authorities, including the ecclesiastical ones.[29] The latter of course reacted severely to any

[27] See Colorni, *Legge ebraica*, 327–8.

[28] Such ordinances were also introduced in communities whose rulers acknowledged the necessity of turning to Jewish arbitrators, such as Cremona; see S. Simonsohn, 'Cremona', *Mikha'el*, 1 (Tel Aviv, 1973), 259. These ordinances, which carried with them the penalty of the ban, were introduced there in order to prevent people from turning to non-Jewish courts, despite the fact that this involved the payment of a penalty under the conditions of the privilege. Explicit permission was likewise granted in the privilege of the Duke of Savoy to impose the ban upon those who refused to turn to Jewish arbitrators; see Lattes, 'Documents et Notices'. On the negative attitude of the Jewish rabbis to appeals to non-Jewish courts, and on the means of pressure utilized to force them to turn to Jewish courts, see S. Assaf, *Batei Din ve-Sidrehem Aḥarei Ḥatimat ha-Talmud* (Jerusalem, 1924), 11–33.

[29] The question of the relation of the local authorities to the Church authorities in this matter has not yet been studied in depth. But see, in general, Simonsohn, *Mantua*, 256–8; Benayahu, *Haskamah u-reshut be-defusei Venezia*, 33; J. Shatzmiller, *Recherches sur la Communauté Juive de Manosque au Moyen-Age* (Paris and The Hague, 1973), 40–9; and see also Ch. 2, n. 172. In any event, one must take care not necessarily to link the question of the permission to impose the ban with that of the overall framework of Jewish law, despite the close connection between them. The opposition of the Church to recognizing the Jewish system of law was absolute, while with regard to the ban it demanded no more than the right to decide in which cases to allow the Jews to impose it.

attempt on the part of the Jews to evade governmental policy[30] so that, under the best of circumstances, the matter ended with the nullification of the ban.[31] It nevertheless seems that there was no place in which communal ordinances were not introduced on this subject, as we learn clearly from the numerous reactions on the part of the authorities.

At times, such ordinances were promulgated within the statutes of the various confraternities. Thus, for example, an ordinance of the Confraternity for Mutual Assistance (*Ḥevrat Gemillut Ḥesed*) of Ferrara in 1553 states that:[32]

whoever among the members of our confraternity shall have a dispute with another member of the confraternity may not go to the courts of the Gentiles, nor to any person[33] other than to the officials then serving in office. And the latter shall rule by law or close to law, or by compromise, as they see fit.[34] And if one of these officials is a relative of one of the litigants, or is suspect in his eyes, then the two will be required to choose two arbitrators from the confraternity, and these shall rule for them by law or close to law or by compromise; thus shall it be, and this shall be required of them from the appointed ones. And

[30] See e.g. the repeated declarations in Ferrara in 1556, 1559, and 1564, the full text of which is in Part II of the Hebrew edition of this book, Documents 39–41, pp. 255–6.

[31] See Colorni, *Legge ebraica e leggi locali*, 335–37, esp. n. 7, as well as the documents in App. 4, pp. 371–2. From all these documents, it is clear that the republic of Venice opposed both the establishment of Jewish courts and the imposition upon all Jews of the obligation to turn to Jewish arbitrators, as correctly surmised by Colorni. It is not impossible, for various reasons which we cannot expand upon here, that the republic behaved differently in its colonies and provinces, such as Candia and the Venetian colony in Constantinople. However, this question still requires further research. See D. Jacoby, 'Les Quartiers Juifs de Constantinople a l'Époque Byzantine', *Byzantion*, 37 (1967), 221–7; idem, 'Les Juifs de Constantinople et leur communauté du XIIIe au milieu du XVe siècle', *REJ* 131 (1972), 406–9.

[32] See the ordinances of the *Gemilut Ḥasadim* Confraternity of Ferrara from 1553, sect. 22–23.

[33] In other words, the members of the confraternity are not allowed to appeal to arbitrators who are not members thereof, even if they are their fellow Jews. However, it seems clear that special emphasis is placed here on the prohibition against turning to Gentile courts because in that locale such a prohibition did not apply to all the Jews with the force of a communal ordinance. The combination of the prohibition against turning to Gentile courts with the requirement that they turn only to arbitrators from the confraternity is clearly intended to remove the sting of that prohibition in Gentile eyes, by making the entire subject one of an internal ordinance of the confraternity, taken upon themselves by its members of their own free will. We shall see that in the later ordinances of the society, due to changes that had taken place in this matter within the Jewish community, those clauses which applied to the obligation of members of the society to appeal to Jewish arbitrators disappeared; see also n. 48 and Sect. 5 in this chapter.

[34] The precise meaning of these terms will be explained further.

the arbitrators, should they themselves be officials, or other ones, shall be given a period of ten days during which to complete the case, so that they may take counsel with the outstanding rabbis[35] as to what to do in this case according to law.

Whoever calls his fellow to judgement before the officials by the beadle of the confraternity and does not come will be required to pay five *bolognini* to the treasury for each occasion on which he refuses, but his fellow must have summoned him three consecutive times before he complains before the officials. And if his opponent does not come, then the officials may issue a ruling between them as they see fit, and treat the one who refuses to come as one who disobeys the ordinance itself, and he will be required to accept their ruling.

In the case of the internal rules of the confraternities, these ordinances were protected, not only by the sense of internal discipline binding the members of the group, but by the secrecy surrounding the group's arrangements. This was particularly true in those states which were subject to Church rule. Thus, for example, the abstract of the regulations of *Ḥevrat Nizharim* [*The Confraternity of the Meticulous*] in Bologna stated:[36] ' "The honour of God is the hidden thing" [cf. *Prov. 25: 2*]. It is forbidden to reveal to any person, in speech, in writing, or by hint, the counsel of the confraternity, save with the permission from the officials, "and the secret of God is with those who fear Him" [*Ps. 25: 14*].'[37] Shortly before that, it states:[38] 'Not to make [of] our enemies our judges [cf. *Deut. 32: 31*] by going to the courts of the Gentiles . . . Heaven forfend, concerning any Jew, even if he is not [a member] of the Confraternity of the Meticulous'. The ordinances presumably date from 1546, or even earlier, since the version here preserved was promulgated in that year, and that same year the society's meeting-place was established. The section dealing with the prohibition against appeal to non-Jewish courts in its full version is:

So that none of the members of *Ḥevrat Nizharim* even think of 'making our enemies our judges', Heaven forfend, we have stated and enacted and prohibited that none of us shall be permitted to go to the courts

35 This is evidence of the role played by the rabbis in issuing halakhic rulings within the framework of arbitration, a point to which we shall return.

36 See Ḥevrat 'Nizharim', Bologna, 'Takkanot', MS New York Public Library, Jewish Items 34 (IMHM 31161), sect. 16.

37 'to no man' (*le-shum adam*) means: even to Jews. See n. 33.

38 Ibid., 'Takkanot', sect. 12.

of the Gentiles when there comes before him any complaint or dispute or appeal against any Hebrew man or woman, whether a member of our confraternity or not... He shall be called before the officials and the trustees who shall serve in those days and at that time, and by them shall be [judged] every dispute and separation and compromise [cf. *Deut.* *17: 9ff.*], and they shall not pass out of the congregation, nor shall their memory depart from their seed [cf. *Est. 9: 28*], under penalty of half a gold *scudi* ... And if the one who violates this says that he is engaged in a complaint with one who is not one of our brothers [i.e. *a member of Ḥevrat Nizharim*] ... nevertheless, in that case too it is not appropriate, and he should not separate himself from the community without the permission of the officials [i.e. *he should not go to a Gentile court without their permission*], for theirs is the right and not his, and he is required to act in accordance with the teaching by which the above-mentioned officials shall instruct and guide him, and it is incumbent upon them to finish the work ... And the litigant shall not deviate in any way from their counsel concerning this penalty, and shall take to heart that there is a God in Israel.[39]

It is clear that the long tradition of earlier rulings upon which they could draw stood the Jews of Italy in good stead in this matter. We are not interested here in analysing the various approaches, for almost each of which precedent may be found in medieval rabbinic legal literature. We are concerned here only with noting the principal means by which things were carried out in practice, within a specific historical context.

On occasion, the communities introduced ordinances without even mentioning the word 'ban' (*ḥerem*),[40] or with the phrase 'with the force of a ban'[41] or like phrases in which, even though

[39] Cf. the ordinances of *Ḥevrat Yeshivat Shalom* in Ancona, sect. 1 (the prohibition against turning to Gentile courts) and sect. 12 (obligation of secrecy).

[40] e.g. the earliest ordinances instituted in Verona during the first half of the 16th century. Thus, in an ordinance dated 19 Av 1539, it was ruled—under penalty of monetary fine, but without the ban—that anyone selected by the litigants, or by the lay leaders together with the rabbi, to serve as an arbitrator may not refuse. An additional ordinance with the same contents was introduced there on 28 Aug. 1539 (see the full text of the ordinance in the Hebrew version of this book, Documents 42–43, p. 257).

[41] All this is only a part of the complex problematic pertaining to the ban; see Ch. 2, Sect. 4, and esp. n. 144 there. For distinctively Italian formulations from the period under discussion, see David b. Messer Leon, *Kevod Ḥakhamim* (Berlin, 1899; photo edn. Jerusalem, 1970), 30: 'but if the arrangements agreed upon are not formulated in this manner [i.e. *that they state "he shall be under the ban" or "we ban one who violates"*], but they state that "we received the agreements under force of ban", as is customary among us today when undertaking any agreement, this is not included under [the rubric of] public bans ... The explanation of this is that, when we examine this phrase, that is, "by force of the ban", [we find that] it is not found in the Talmud or in other sources

the ban was not explicitly mentioned, it was alluded to.[42] At times these ordinances were more cautiously formulated, reflecting fear of the Christian authorities in this sensitive area.[43] At other times the ordinances were strengthened by imposing the ban upon those who refused to be arbitrators after they had been chosen—a point which the Christian authorities did not regard as a violation of local jurisdiction, for reasons already mentioned.[44]

[in the writings of] the halakhic authorities, who never wrote "by force of" [*be-koaḥ*]. Rather, this phrase was invented by the lay leaders of the communities, who borrowed it from the vernacular, where we are used to saying, "do thus and such by force of this penalty" or "by force of this ban", and this was evidently taken from the vernacular, where one says "*sotto pena* so-and-so", meaning that if one violates this thing I will penalize you or excommunicate you.' See also J. Boksenboim (ed.), *She'elot u-Teshuvot Matanot ba-Adam* (Tel Aviv, 1983), sect. 60, p. 268, for the responsum of R. Yeḥiel Trabot II, known as 'from Pesaro' or 'from Ascoli' [for Trabot, see Zimmer, 'Biographical Details Concerning Italian Jewry from Abraham Graziano's Handwritten Notes' (Heb.), *KS* 49 (1974), 400–44, which states that those who violate the agreements of the community which had been declared under penalty of ban 'are not excommunicated until they are formally declared as such, and this was also written by the Excellent Rabbi R. Yeḥiel Trabot [*the first, from Macerata, known as 'the Elder'; see Zimmer, ibid.*], of blessed memory, in his responsa, that one must excommunicate [a person] before the ban is efficacious' (the text of this question appears near the end of Sect. 5 of this chapter). In other words, the clause in the original communal ordinance that those who violate such and such a rule shall be under the ban or excommunicated does not automatically place under a state of ban those individuals who violate the ordinance at some later date. In order to reinforce his view, Trabot cites there other opinions, concluding with *Ṭur Yoreh De'ah* 229–end.

42 Thus, the ordinances of Verona from 4 Tishri 1541 instruct the appointed rabbi 'to force and to oppress' those who go to Gentile courts or who refuse to be judged by Jewish law (see the full text of the ordinance in the Hebrew text of this book, Document 44, p. 258). In the ordinance issued on 21 Av 1584, we find a prohibition against selecting arbitrators who are not residents of the city 'and no one may say "I have gone to another court" . . . and this clause shall have the same validity as if drawn up with all the necessary procedures . . .' (for the full text of this ordinance, see Part II of the Hebrew version of this book, Document 45, p. 258).

43 See the 1580 ordinance of the Italian Congregation in Ancona in the Hebrew version of this book, Document 46, p. 259. This ordinance relies upon the authority of the non-Jewish government, which is mentioned in the Hebrew document and appears again immediately after a document in Italian, which I have not succeeded in deciphering because of the poor condition of the manuscript. In any event, it would seem that the formulation of the permission was no different from that of 1604, also cited in the same document. Note there the clear significance of the imposition of ordinances under force of ban, without imposing the ban *per se* prior to receiving explicit permission to do so from the authorities.

44 See the ordinance from Verona dated Rosh Ḥodesh Ṭevet, 5343 [1583], obliging all members of the community to appeal to Jewish arbitrators, albeit without the imposition of the ban: 'and whoever refuses to serve as a judge or arbitrator, if chosen by one of the parties, shall be separated from every holy thing in Israel, and shall also pay a fine . . . and if it seems to the leaders that one must be stricter with the one refusing, they may use whatever means they see fit . . . and they may impose excommunication until

It should to be emphasized that, despite the weak legal basis for the afore-mentioned ordinances, the feeling of internal discipline within the Jewish community helped to bring about a situation not much different, *de facto*, from that in those communities in which the authorities recognized the community's right to impose arbitration. This sense of discipline was of course greater in smaller, more homogeneous communities, and even more so within the various confraternities and special congregations. Thus, in the light of the situation here described, it is clear that there is no justification for describing those cases in which Jews did turn to Gentile courts in Italy during this period as reflecting a weakened Jewish consciousness or a lack of inner cohesiveness among the Jews.[45] Even in the admonitions given by the rabbis at the end of the sixteenth century, which were aimed at strengthening the awareness of the prohibition against turning to Gentile courts, it is clear that the main difficulty was not the decline in this awareness within Jewish society, but the proscription by the authorities against establishing Jewish courts. R. Samuel David Katzenellenbogen, for example, preached to his community that

> for many years now our Holy Torah has been lying in an abandoned corner . . . the Law of Torah has already been abolished among us, and one does not even think to force litigants to submit to Jewish law . . . and there is none who says 'return', for our hands are tied, being unable to chastise those who violate [the law] because of the oppressor and the fear of [his] punishment and the penalties placed upon us . . .[46]

Katzenellenbogen hoped to encourage the leaders of his community to 'restore and to put the Law of Torah in its proper place', with a feeling of confidence that the work would not be too difficult, 'for our princes are merciful leaders, and they will easily be

their decree is carried out' (see the full text of this ordinance in the Hebrew edition of this book, Document 47, p. 260). These things reappear more forcefully, and with the explicit use of excommunication, in an edict from 17 Jan. 1594 (see the text in the Hebrew edition, Document 48, pp. 260–1).

45 See M. A. Shulvass, 'The Religious Life of Italian Jewry During the Period of the Renaissance' (Heb.), *PAAJR* 17 (1947–8), 3–5; cf. L. Landman, *Jewish Law in the Diaspora: Confrontation and Accommodation* (Philadelphia, 1968), 97–8. Their summary is indirectly supported by the regnant Jewish historiography of the period, according to which the tendencies towards close contact with Christians increased in Italy during the 16th century, as a result of which the centrifugal forces likewise grew. We shall return to this question at greater length in the following chapter.

46 J. Katzenellenbogen, *Derashot Maharshi"k*, Sermon 1, p. 7a–b.

appeased and wish that we live by the law of our Torah'.[47] Both the admonition and the confident hope that 'the princes . . . are merciful leaders' and that the Jews would not meet too many difficulties in establishing an autonomous judicial system clearly entailed an element of rhetorical exaggeration, combined with political persuasion, directed from the pulpit of the synagogue towards the rulers of the city. But the rulers were not such 'merciful leaders' and were not so easily persuaded—while the Jews for their part were continually trying to persuade them! These Jews were certainly not always entirely *bona fide*. But it is clear from this that the emphasis is on the communities' success in preserving some sort of internal Jewish juridical system, despite the situation of weakness forced upon them by the authorities, more than it serves as evidence of a weakening of internal Jewish social cohesion in the wake of the centrifugal forces acting upon it, particularly the pull of the general culture.[48]

3. Strengthening the System of Arbitration

Alongside the tendency during this period to require recourse to Jewish arbitrators, there was a distinct effort made to strengthen the system of judicial arbitration by exploiting all available formal means for this purpose, whether within the realm of Jewish law or within that of the general judicial system. In fact, a unique situation evolved during this period in Italy in which, even in the Christian milieu, arbitration was raised to a status of *judicium* proper. Slowly, by a long and gradual process which began generations earlier, the Christians came to accept an arbitrator's decision as being equivalent to a judicial sentence (*tantum compromissum quantum iudicatum*).

[47] Ibid.

[48] Consequently, one should not see the prohibitions issued by the Talmud Torah confraternities against turning to non-Jewish courts as a 'public reaction', within the framework of the growth of the pietistic phenomena at the end of the period; cf. Shulvass, *Renaissance*, 55, 194. On the contrary, as we have already hinted earlier in this section (n. 33), and as we shall further see, with the easing of the pressure of the authorities concerning this subject towards the end of the 16th century, and with the commensurate strengthening of the autonomous judicial system of the communities, those clauses pertaining to the prohibition against turning to Gentile courts disappeared from the ordinances of the confraternities!

Unlike Roman law, in which the term *arbiter* was used indiscriminately, in the legal thought of the Middle Ages a distinction was drawn between *arbiter* and *arbitrator*: the *arbiter* ruled according to law and followed a formal procedure similar to that used in proper court cases, while the *arbitrator* ruled according to a compromise, *bono et aequo*, without appeal to formal procedures or to any system of law. Over time, this distinction became refined in many of its details. It was argued that, at least in theory, the ruling of an *arbiter* might be appealed, but not that of an *arbitrator*; that the *arbitrator* might issue rulings on holidays, but not the *arbiter*; etc. Thus, there was a degree of innovation in this area, involving a modification of Roman law; in Roman law arbitration was used only when there was preliminary agreement between the litigating parties, and the arbitrator's ruling was regarded as no more than a suggestion which either side could choose to reject, on condition that he pay a fine fixed in the *compromessum*. This option was closed to the litigating parties only after they had actually signed the ruling (*laudum homologatum*).[49] In contrast, during our period, despite the doubts raised by jurists in many details, arbitration was accepted both in theory and in practice without any distinction drawn between *arbiter* and *arbitrator*. The arbitrator's decision had the binding force of a ruling of any regular court of law, while the *compromessum* took the place of the *judicium*. To quote one of the greatest scholars of Italian law, 'Arbitration entered boldly into the structure of public law, even though it was in fact nothing but an expression of private will. This was [admittedly] an act without jurisdiction—but both doctrine and custom recognized

[49] See F. Bonifacio, 'Arbitro e arbitratore (diritto romano)', *Novissimo digesto italiano*, i (Turin, 1958), 925–8; L. Garetto, 'Arbitro e arbitratore (diritto intermedio)', ibid. 928–30; G. Crifo, 'Arbitro (diritto romano)', *Enciclopedia del diritto*, ii (Milan, 1958), 893–5; V. P. Mortari, 'Arbitrato (diritto intermedio)', ibid. 895–9; G. Salvioli, 'Storia della procedura civile e criminale', in *Storia del diritto italiano di P. del Giudice*, iii, part II (Milan, 1927), 181. Apart from the encyclopedia articles, the work by Salvioli is the most recent one to deal with this subject; we shall therefore refer to it in particular in the following notes. See also J. Juster, *Les Juifs dans l'Empire Romain*, ii. 102: with regard to the Jews, the decision of the arbitrators, even in Roman law of the Theodosian Code, had the force of a *res judicata*, as though it had been the decision of a Roman judge. Regarding the transformation in Roman law on this subject during the period of Theodosius, see A. M. Rabello, 'Sui rapporti fra Diocleziano e gli ebrei', *Atti dell-Accademia Romanistica Costantiniana—2° Convegno Internazionale 1975* (Perugia, 1976), 193–5. See also Juster, *Les Juifs dans l'Empire Romain*, 103–4, on the changes which came about in the Justinian Code.

the arbitration ruling as the equivalent of a court ruling.'[50] While earlier jurists dealt primarily with consensual arbitration between the two sides, sixteenth-century jurists saw it as imposed by force of law.[51] Generally speaking, local authorities preferred imposed arbitration, and arbitration was imposed upon relatives almost everywhere. Moreover, in those cases where relatives were unable to arrive at an agreement concerning the choice of arbitrators, it was the government's responsibility to appoint them.[52] Arbitration was also required in disputes between artisans and their fellow workers, among partners, between communes, between groups and individuals, among indigents, between indigents and wealthy individuals, and in many other cases.[53] It is interesting that this obligation derived in principle from canon law, according to which the Pope had the right to force resort to arbitration in every instance.[54] A doctrine emerged in Italy according to which the judge could require both sides to turn to arbitration whenever he anticipated complications or whenever the law itself was ambiguous.[55] Local ordinances likewise fixed rules for the selection of arbitrators, which at times included the selection of two names by lottery from the council of the 'good ones of the town' (*boni viri de tabula*).[56] If the two arbitrators could not agree among themselves regarding the appointment of a third, the government-appointed judge would make the appointment; there were even those who argued that in such a case the ruler had the right to excommunicate the arbitrators. Almost all local legislation fixed a certain period of time during which the arbitration ruling was to be issued, although the arbitrator had the right to correct or to extend his ruling even after it was issued. The arbitrators were also required to issue the ruling in the presence of all parties, and during daylight hours.[57] The elevation of arbitration to the level of proper jurisdiction obviously brought in its wake complex dialectical arguments. Many jurists asked various theoretical questions and at times, in the course of attempts to appeal against

[50] See Salvioli, 'Procedura civile e criminale', 182. [51] Ibid.

[52] Ibid. 183. It is worth noting in particular the edict of the Duke of Savoy, issued at the beginning of the 15th century (1409): 'inter parentes vel affines vicinos aut magnates ad simplicem requisitionem cuiuslibet amici vel vicini teneatur potestas seu iudices . . . per arrestationem personarum compellere ad compromittendum in . . . arbitratores et communes amicos'. See Pertile, *Storia del diritto italiano*, vol. vi, part I, 175–7.

[53] Salvioli, 'Procedura civile e criminale', 184. Compare also my previous comments concerning the situation within the Jewish confraternities.

[54] Ibid. [55] Ibid. [56] Ibid. 186. [57] Ibid.

the arbitrator's rulings, even practical ones. For example: Was the arbitrator required to rule in accordance with his conscience, or perhaps only according to the letter of the law? Must he rule in accordance with local ordinances or not?[58] What we have mentioned here was more clearly expressed in the many fine points of distinction introduced into the documents of arbitration, which were intended to prevent any appeal against the arbitrator's ruling and to render his ruling equivalent to a *laudum homologatum*. A lengthy interpretation by R. Abraham del Vecchio of the standard Hebrew text of the *compromessum* has also been preserved, examination of which amply illustrates this point.[59]

The entire set of problems discussed above may be clearly discerned in Jewish arbitration agreements. So, too, we find among the Jews the tendency to grant to the arbitrators' decision judicial status, against which no subsequent appeal was possible. This was a natural expression of the institution of arbitration in Jewish law, as it had evolved under the particular conditions of Italian Jewry during the period under discussion. Outside influences were absorbed and incorporated into the existing halakhic tradition. In fact, the Italian sages emphasized the continuity of their rulings with those of their predecessors. Del Vecchio's afore-mentioned interpretation clearly demonstrates this.[60]

Indeed, nearly all of the problems confronted by the Italian rabbis were dealt with in one form or another by the halakhic authorities of earlier generations. Given the spirit of the time and the nature of the problem, they certainly did not strive to introduce novelties in this area. We are not concerned here with the possible novelty inherent in their legal solutions, but with the very fact of the widespread interest in the subject of arbitration, and the way in which Jewish law was implemented in practice. This phenomenon may provide a very good example

[58] Ibid. 189.

[59] See Document 49 in the Hebrew edition of this book, pp. 261–3. Cf. *Formularium instrumentorum . . . Petri Dominici de Mussis . . .* (Venice, 1530), fos. 34r–35v, where one finds a long list of rules which the notary must follow in formulating *compromessi*, in order to provide the arbitrators with the broadest possible authority to rule 'tantum iuris ordine seruato & non seruato'. For del Vecchio's commentary, see Document 50 in the Hebrew version of this book, pp. 264–74.

[60] See App. 4 for a translation of a typical Hebrew *compromissum*, compared with its Latin equivalent.

of the flexibility of halakhic institutions within a given historical reality.

As is well known, the document stating the litigants' readiness to solve their dispute by way of arbitration, known in Latin as *compromissum* (plural, *compromissa*; Italian: *compromesso*; plural, *compromessi*), was drawn up in the presence of witnesses, like any other document.[61] Various versions of these documents were printed, some of them in collections of formulas.[62] In a comparative study of these documents, the most striking indication of the process by which arbitration was transformed into a proper form of jurisdiction is the initial obfuscation, and later the total absence, of any indication of the litigating parties' voluntary consent to the authority granted to the arbitrators in the document itself.[63] Such sentences as 'how by our free will, without any compulsion whatsoever'[64] or 'how of our own free will, without any compulsion or pressure whatsoever, but with full heart and consenting soul and clear and settled mind',[65] became transformed towards the end of the sixteenth century to the more neutral 'decided and agreed . . . and chose and took between them as judges, etc.'.[66] Such phrases seem to have disappeared completely at the beginning of the seventeenth century.[67] There can be little doubt that this fact is significant, and marks the end of the period mentioned.[68]

[61] See A. Gulak, *Yesodei ha-Mishpaṭ ha-'Ivri* (Jerusalem and Berlin, 1923), iv. 24–32; idem. *Oẓar ha-Sheṭarot ha-nehugot be-Yisra'el* (Jerusalem, 1926), 282–7; B. Cohen, *Roman and Jewish Law* (New York, 1966), 651–709; *Encyclopedia Talmudica* (Heb.), s.v. *zeh borer lo eḥad*, xi. 684 ff.; M. Elon, *ha-Mishpaṭ ha-'Ivri* (Jerusalem, 1973), i. 17–18. It is clear that the use of the legal term *compromesso* is not to be seen as a sign of assimilation to Christian society and distancing from Jewish tradition on the part of Italian Jewry of this period, as has been suggested by some scholars. See on this Bonfil, 'Jews in the Venetian Territories', 93 n. 134.

[62] e.g. Gulak, *Oẓar ha-Sheṭarot*, Documents 303–5, 307—the latter taken from Eli'ezer Melli, *Sefer le-kol Ḥefeẓ* (Venice, 1552); *Sefer Yefeh Nof* (Venice, 1552), fo. 30b; Sonne, *Mi-Pavlos*, 212–14; and cf. Document 50 in the Hebrew edition of this book.

[63] This specifically refers to the details of the document, and not to the obligation to turn to arbitration, as the locality under discussion here had no permanent Court, and one may argue that in such a case even Talmudic law allows one to force the litigants to turn to arbitration (see the sources cited in the *Encyclopedia Talmudica*, op. cit., xi. 684–85, nn. 1–13).

[64] See Gulak, *Oẓar ha-Sheṭarot*, Documents 303, 304.

[65] Ibid. Document 307 (i.e. *Sefer le-kol Ḥefeẓ*) and, with minor variations, Sonne, *Mi-Pavlos*, 213.

[66] *Sefer Yefeh Nof*, fo. 30b.

[67] See Document 50 in the Hebrew edition of this book.

[68] See Ch. 5, Sect. 2 and cf. Sect. 4. This process began in the communal ordinances which were made in this spirit, in those localities where such ordinances were possible.

An additional step, which combined with the one above, was that even here, similar to the accepted practice in Gentile courts, the arbitrators were given the option to explain or to interpret their ruling even after the time fixed by the arbitration-document.[69] There were those who introduced a sentence into this document entitling the arbitrators to do so even if their interpretation seemed broader than or contradicted the earlier ruling.[70] The principle by which the litigating parties were denied the option of withdrawing after the ruling was issued or requesting a new hearing was likewise accepted.[71] This latter principle involved a double expression: on the one hand, a phrase identical to that appearing in the *compromissa* to be introduced in non-Jewish courts. That is, the phrase 'without *appellazione* (the right of appeal) and without *revisione*' (the right to demand revision)—was introduced, in order to make the ruling immediately applicable by action of the authorities.[72] On the other hand, the document included an explicit agreement on the part of both sides by which they relinquished their right to demand to 'show us on what grounds you have judged us' (i.e. a detailed statement of the reasoning behind the arbitrator's decision),[73] required by the opinion of those rabbinic authorities who held that, even where the two sides selected their own arbitrators, they still had the

[69] See 'Teshuvot R. Moshe Provenzali', MS Jerusalem Heb. 8[to] 1999, sect. 159 (cited in full in the Hebrew edition of this book, Document 38, pp. 249–55). Provenzali stated there clearly and simply the right of the arbitrators, in his opinion, 'to clarify their words within the time and following it, so long as they do not add or subtract from their original words'.

[70] See Document 50 in the Hebrew edition of this book.

[71] Admittedly, Jewish law states that the two sides may not renege once the arbitrators' decision has been issued. However, as compromise was generally included among those forms of judgement which the two sides took upon themselves in a *compromesso*, as we shall see below, in the case of compromise there is an accepted rule that 'even though the litigants were satisfied with the compromise, they may renege in court so long as they did not perform an act of *kinyan* [*ceremonial agreement to whatever decision would be issued*]' (*Shulḥan 'Arukh, Ḥoshen Mishpaṭ* 12: 7). Thus, allowance is made for the litigants to cancel the ruling even after it is issued, provided there was no act of *kinyan* made at the time the ruling was drawn up. This reason combined with others to bring about a situation in which, at the end of our period, no *compromesso* was performed without a formal act of *kinyan* (see Document 50 in the Hebrew edition of this book).

[72] See e.g. the remarks by Samuel da Perugia, the central figure in the famous Tamari–Venturozzo divorce: 'after the time agreed upon . . . I pressured him concerning the execution of the ruling in their [i.e. *Gentile*] courts, and I came out guilty under their law, by virtue of the *compromesso* in which it was written, "without any *appellazione*" ' (*Eleh ha-Devarim* (Mantua, 1566), p. 3a).

[73] Cf. Horayot 6b, Ḥullin 48b.

right to demand this. It must be remembered that this was a right which automatically entailed, in the event of error, the convening of a new hearing.[74]

Of particular concern to us here is the establishment of the legislative framework binding the arbitrator. This refers, first and foremost, to the formula 'by law or close to law' (*be-din o karov la-din*), which appears in nearly all the *compromissa* from this period, in place of the earlier phrase, 'in accordance with what they shall be shown from heaven'[75] or 'as shall seem right in their good judgement'.[76] Moreover, we must try to overcome a certain ambiguity concerning the use of the formula, used immediately after the former words, 'as their eyes see fit'. Is this formula to be understood as extending the former, or as explaining it? That is, is it meant to grant the arbitrators authority to draw up a compromise as well, or must we understand it to mean, 'to rule by law or in accordance with that which seems to them close to the law'? There were those who opposed the very inclusion of the sentence 'as their eyes see fit' within the *compromissum*, as argued by R. Abraham Menaḥem Porto ha-Kohen in a brief but carefully reasoned responsum.[77] A certain member of the Levantine congregation of Venice had appealed to him:

> Will his Honour guide me in the paths of justice so as to determine whether the representatives of the Holy Congregation of Venice may force me to write in a *compromesso* . . . that the judge and the merchant[78] may judge my case as they see fit . . .

In his responsum, Porto wrote to the leaders of the congregation as follows:

> Let not this stumbling-block emerge from you, for such a person is not to be treated as a rebel [i.e. *one who refuses to listen to the Court or*

[74] See Document 50 in the Hebrew edition of this book.

[75] See *Sefer ha-Sheṭarot* of R. Judah al-Bargeloni, Document 8, cited by Gulak, *Oẓar ha-Sheṭarot*, Document 302. See also the version taken from *Sefer Naḥalat Shiv'ah* in *Encyclopedia Talmudica*, xi. 697 and n. 133.

[76] See Gulak, *Oẓar ha-Sheṭarot*, Document 303.

[77] 'Teshuvot R. Abraham Menaḥem Porto ha-Kohen', sect. 9, cited in full in Document 51, p. 274, in the Hebrew edition of this book.

[78] It is not clear whether this is meant to refer to two different judges, one of whom was a scholar ('the judge') and the other a layman ('the merchant'), thereby constituting a quasi-court (similar to that which existed in Verona, where the rabbi sat with the lay leaders of the community), or whether this refers to a court of lay arbitrators, in which the 'merchant' was transformed into a 'judge'. From what follows, it seems more likely that the second interpretation is the correct one.

revolts against communal discipline], as he wishes to be obedient to the law, for even if they are accustomed . . . to write this phrase, that is, when both of them agree to do so . . . or if the judges are sages and ordained rabbis . . . who know the law, one could force him to write 'as their eyes see', that is, according to what seems to them close to the law . . . But according to the custom of this generation, in which each one chooses arbitrators who are not ordained . . . Heaven forbid that one compel a person to submit to a ruling on the decision of one who is not an expert judge . . . you [i.e. *the Court*] cannot force him to write 'as they see fit', for that wording implies whatever is the arbitrator's own judgement . . . even if what seems to him to be correct is in fact close to the law . . .[79]

As a result of these disputes, a substantive change in the language of the documents came about: there were cases in which the formula 'as their eyes see' was added to the phrase 'by law or close to law', to which was also added the formula, 'and not by compromise',[80] while there were other cases in which the phrase 'as their eyes see' was entirely missing.[81]

The use of the formula 'by law or close to law' and/or 'as their eyes see' involved an additional problem, namely, who might serve as an arbitrator. As we have seen in the responsum of R. Abraham Menaḥem Porto ha-Kohen, the elimination of the formula 'as they see fit' came in the wake of the claim that such a clause was unwarranted unless the arbitrators were scholars and ordained rabbis. It follows from this that, if the ruling of the arbitrators was to be other than a compromise, not necessarily based upon the law, then the arbitrators must be expert scholars, that is, ordained rabbis, so that they might rule 'by law or close to law'. R. Isaac de Lattes went even further. He ruled that, in those places where the phrase 'by law or close to law' was written in

[79] Cf. the remarks of Samuel of Perugia (*Eleh ha-Devarim*, fo. 3a): 'And they made from this a *compromesso*, that is, a document of arbitration, but it did not work out, because I definitely insisted upon a [proper] judicial ruling by law or close to it, while the document was written in another manner, and I therefore nullified it.' In 'Teshuvot Matanot ba-Adam', sect. 109, there is likewise a discussion of a case in which 'R. Jacob wished them to write in the *compromesso* "as they see fit", and his brother did not wish this'. The author of the responsum adds that 'we have not seen any authority who says that today we do not arrange compromises'; further on in the same responsum, it becomes clear that the said R. Jacob wished that they write 'by law or close to law', and explicitly opposed a compromise.

[80] See Gulak, *Oẓar ha-Sheṭarot*, Document 307.

[81] Ibid., Document 304, and see Appendix 4 below, and at greater length in Document 50 in the Hebrew edition of this book.

the *compromesso*, the case was to be reopened in the event that an error was made in the interpretation of the law by the arbitrators—even if the respective sides had waived their right to ask 'on what ground you have judged us' or to appeal. In this rabbi's formulation, if the sides agreed between themselves

not to appeal . . . it is as if one said, 'Your father is acceptable to me, an unfit witness is acceptable to me' [i.e. *that he was prepared to waive the legal procedures rendering certain witnesses unfit*], or if they agreed that they would not ask the judges to write the reason for their decision, but simply stipulated that they judge by law or close to law . . . it nevertheless does not follow from this that they can issue an [extra-halakhic] compromise. So much more so that according to this, one who complains . . . that they erred in knowledge of the law or in a matter of *halakhah* based upon the Gaonic rulings, that in such a case the case is reopened.[82]

It follows that, according to the view of this rabbi, the arbitrators must also be scholars, or at least turn to ordained rabbis for assistance in clarifying the *halakhah*. R. Meir of Padua even noted that these matters were explicitly implied in the rule that when one of the two sides in a dispute

sought to go before arbitrators who were rabbis, knowledgeable in law and judgment, and the other party wished [to go to] idlers, there is no justification for this [latter] claim, as each one may force his neighbour

[82] See e.g. the following text of an ordinance requiring an individual to go to court together with his litigant, in the case of a claim where the chosen arbitrators had erred in knowledge of the law, and the case is therefore to be reopened: '*A* came before me on his own behalf and on that of *B* and his brother *C*, and he told me in truth that he had a claim against you, Rabbi *X* . . . and that they had agreed to call as arbitrators two brothers, *Y* and *Z*. Their opponents agreed to this procedure . . . They furthermore agreed that they were not to ask the judges to write the grounds on which they decided the issue, but stipulated that they should judge 'by law or close to law'. [Nevertheless,] they ruled on the basis of compromise, implying that they [understood the phrase] 'near to law' as implying compromise . . . but this wording does not imply that they can arrange a compromise, and certainly not in this case, where it was claimed that they erred in knowledge of the Law . . . And I, the undersigned, have been asked to require them to go to court before two other arbitrators, more righteous and expert in law than the previous ones . . . I therefore order you, with the power of my blessing [a euphemism for 'the power to ban'], that you go to judgement [again] before a proper court which is close to you, within three days of your being informed of this ordinance, or that each of you choose one arbitrator, etc.'—from 'Teshuvot R. Yiẓḥak mi-Lattes', MS Vienna-National Library 80, fo. 20; the text of the responsum is brought in full in Document 52, p. 275, in the Hebrew edition of this book. Cf. analogous practices regarding arbitration in the Christian milieu, as referred to in the discussion of Garetto, 'Arbitro e arbitratore', 144 n. 50.

to come to judgement before expert judges and not before laymen ... Likewise all of the recent Rabbinic authorities rule that ignorant people who have been appointed are inferior, and he may disqualify them.[83]

R. Meir summarized by saying 'it is self-evident that each one may force his fellow to be judged before those who know Torah'.[84] Now, once the system of arbitration had become strengthened, with the sense of authority and power of the rabbinic authorities reduced as a result of developments discussed in Chapter 1, the time had come to strengthen the status of the rabbinic authorities within that same system.[85] This further contributed to the evolution of arbitration as a complete legal system, suitable to the new situation, in which rabbis were central figures. From this point on, the personal prestige of the rabbis brought about a situation in which the circle of people to whom requests for arbitration were addressed became drastically reduced, and a kind of *de facto* court system emerged whose rulings were signed by the most distinguished and well-known scholars.[86] In cases where the arbitrators were not ordained rabbis, the latter generally turned to the rabbis for detailed legal instructions upon which to ground their ruling,[87] in order to avoid the danger of a demand

[83] *Teshuvot Mahara"m mi-Padua*, sect. 53, p. 91. Cf. Ch. 4, Sect. 2.

[84] Ibid.; see also sect. 43. R. Meir did in fact draw the distinction that the essential thing is that they be 'knowledgeable in Torah' and not necessarily 'rabbis', but this nevertheless indicates that in the popular mind those who 'knew the Torah' were not seen other than in the image of 'rabbis', as we have seen above in the responsum of R. Abraham Menaḥem Porto ha-Kohen and R. Isaac de Lattes.

[85] On the other hand, at the beginning of the 16th century, the rabbis were more concerned about establishing the institution of arbitration than about establishing their own rabbinic position. I discuss this point at length in R. Bonfil, 'Jews in the Venetian Territories', *Ẓion*, 41 (1976), 93–5.

[86] e.g. in Bologna R. Abraham ha-Kohen appears at the head of those signing the arbitration ruling, and he is joined by other rabbis, some of whose names are repeated several times. In Venice, in the second half of the 16th century, R. Samuel Judah Katzenellenbogen generally appeared at the head of the signatories, followed by the other Venetian scholars, in order of importance, whose names are repeated in numerous contexts—R. Leib Saraval, R. Avigdor Cividal, and others (cf. at the end of Ch. 3, Sect. 11). In Mantua, R. Moses Provenzali's name generally appears in the company of the community scribe, R. Phineas Elia of Melli, often joined by that of R. Samuel Ḥezekiah Romilli. It would seem superfluous to add other names, as anyone who peruses books concerning the history of Italian Jewry will come across them at every step.

[87] See e.g. the responsa of R. Menaḥem Azariah da Fano, *Teshuvot RM"A mi-Fano*, (Jerusalem, 1963), sect. 42: 'We have seen ... that the documents presented by Reuben and Simeon are clear ... and we have heard what each of them has to argue ... and now may the inquirer ... who is one of the arbitrators, receive his answer.'

for an appeal, as required by the afore-mentioned opinion of R. Isaac de Lattes.[88]

As against these practices, by which arbitration was transformed into a fully-fledged judicial system in every respect, reducing the freedom of action of both litigants and arbitrators, the various conditions whose intention was to preserve the original character of arbitration—that is, to preserve the theoretical distinction between arbitration and the formal procedural limitations binding upon regular courts which operated according to *halakhah*—were stated explicitly in the *compromissum*.[89] The general procedure, which was also found among non-Jews, as already mentioned, further strengthened this tendency. For example, the arbitration agreements included conditions allowing the judges to hear the testimony of the different sides separately, to hold hearings at night, to accept the testimony of (formally) unqualified witnesses, etc.[90] In this respect, the practice among Jews seems to have been influenced by the arbitration procedures of non-Jewish courts, as may be clearly demonstrated by a comparison of the later versions.[91]

On this point, they also clearly seem to have been influenced by the fact that the arbitration ruling was executed by non-Jewish authorities; the Jewish arbitration agreement therefore needed to be formulated in such a way as not to arouse any doubts as to its validity in the Gentile courts.

4. Communal Ordinances

Another means of transforming arbitration into a proper juridical instrument was the introduction of ordinances (*takkanot*) establishing rules for the imposition of the law of arbitration. In this respect, the communities operated in a manner analogous to a commune. For example, ordinances were introduced stating that the two sides were to appear before the lay leaders of the

[88] Judging on the basis of the privileges granted in 1626 to appeal arbitration decisions before the rabbis of the general yeshivah in Mantua (see Colorni, *Legge ebraica e leggi locali*, 342–3), the opinion of R. Isaac de Lattes was not an isolated one.

[89] See *Encyclopedia Talmudica*, xi. 692–4.

[90] See Document 50 in the Hebrew edition of this book.

[91] Cf. Document 50 in the Hebrew edition of this book with Document 49, pp. 261–3, and the notes to that document.

community whenever they were unable to find arbitrators. Together with the community-appointed rabbi who served as the third member of the 'court', these leaders had the authority to appoint arbitrators in accordance with certain rules. In the ordinances introduced by the communal leaders of Casale, we read as follows:[92]

One frequently finds that one is unable to find a person willing to act as judge in cases of law, [as he wishes] to avoid cause for hostility and theft and needless hate [i.e. *directed against him*] . . . Therefore, in order to remove a stumbling block from the path of our people and to enhance peace between man and his fellow and to uproot the sources of controversy, the distinguished *parnassim* have decided to issue this *parte* . . . that in every incident of complaint and suit and dispute that shall come about between man and his fellow, whether these be inhabitants of this city or from outside it . . . they are to come here, so long as either one or both of them are unable to find a judge by the usual procedure by which each selects an arbitrator. [In such a case] the one who cannot find a suitable arbitrator shall go to the distinguished *parnassim* . . . and they shall select by lot, drawing from the lottery box where they have placed a total of——[93] names of people appointed to serve as judges in every disagreement of this sort. And the one whose name is drawn first shall be a judge on behalf of him who does not have a judge; thus, also, if both of them [need to select a judge]. This is on condition that the chosen ones are not relatives or enemies, as defined by law, in which case another is to be named in his stead . . .

The ordinances also fixed, in broad outlines, the text of the arbitration agreements to be used by members of the community.[94] Thus, in an edict of the leaders of Verona,[95] we read:

[92] 'Pinkas Casale', 20; see the full text in Document 53, pp. 275–6 in the Hebrew edition of this book. In a similar fashion, the community in Mantua received permission from the authorities (albeit only in 1620) to prepare a list of rabbis, from among whom arbitrators would be appointed by lot; see Colorni, *Legge ebraica e leggi locali*, 341–3, and cf. also the parallel practice in non-Jewish courts mentioned above, Sect. 3.

[93] Here the scribe left a small blank space.

[94] See the edict from Casale just mentioned. A reminder of the fact that the Levantine community in Venice established their own form of *compromesso* appears in the responsa of R. Abraham Menaḥem Porto ha-Kohen (Document 51 in the Hebrew edition of this book, p. 274); cf. the words of Samuel da Perugia cited above, n. 72. It was also ruled in Verona on 17 Jan. 1594 that one was to write in the *compromesso*, 'from now on the litigants may not sue or force or [demand to] know from the arbitrators the reason by which they judged' (see Document 48 in the Hebrew edition of this book).

[95] 'Pinkas Verona' ii. fo. 179a–b; published as Document 48, pp. 260–1, in the Hebrew edition of this book.

[Monday, 17 January 1594] Judgement, which is the foundation of the heavens, and peace, that vessel which contains everything, being shaken; and the small sanctuary, the house of prayer, being without one to pay heed, but every day the number of those who interrupt the prayers for every complaint or claim increases, even if [the claim] is not for more than two pennies . . . We have therefore decided that whoever is selected as a judge, from this day on, may not refuse to serve, under penalty of fine and punishment and excommunication . . . and not to delay justice, but that all one's deeds be for the sake of heaven, so that as soon as the beadle finds him and informs him that he has been chosen to be a judge, he is to go to the synagogue with his fellow, the second arbitrator. And the two arbitrators will decide between themselves the time to be appointed for the litigants to come before them, at a time convenient to them . . . And whoever does not come at the appointed time shall be considered as though he had admitted all of the claims of his fellow-litigant. And the judges are to rule in accordance with the claims presented by the parties, and shall hear the opposite side as well, and all these shall be considered like testimony of a litigant, and as if sworn by oath from Mount Sinai . . . Nor may one select either me[96] or my children as judges, as I have been selected by the holy congregation to compel the litigating parties to accept the decision. Nor shall one select any official receiving salary from a householder,[97] as the authority of others is over him, nor a teacher who eats at the table of a head of a house, unless the latter agrees to it, in which case he is allowed, or even compelled, to be a judge . . .

From now on, no one may interrupt the prayers in the synagogue [*see Section 6*] unless his hearing is delayed by the *parnassim* [not being present in the synagogue] on the days appointed for hearing cases, namely, Monday and Thursday morning after the prayers, and on their [*the Gentiles'*] holidays, after Evening Prayers. And if for this reason he does interrupt the prayers, he shall first give ten *soldi* on deposit to the beadle . . .

Another development granted these same lay leaders—who were required to be available for such purposes in the synagogue at certain fixed times, along with the rabbi[98]—the right to judge certain cases by themselves, when it did not seem necessary to designate arbitrators. In those places where the imposition of arbitration under penalty of ban was prohibited by the govern-

[96] The community-appointed rabbi, who was the scribe of the community, and recorded the decisions in the Ledger.

[97] A director of a bank or other business which served others.

[98] See n. 40 above and the next note here.

ment, such ordinances were promulgated by the means mentioned above.[99] This was, in effect, the most fully developed form of the communal court in Italy until the end of the sixteenth century. No particular objection to this limited development seems to have been raised so that, even where the right of the Jews to judicial authority was not officially recognized, it was accepted, so long as the issues of principle involved in this matter were politely ignored by the tacit agreement of the government and the Jews,[100] this being in the interests of both sides. Thus, for example, in a decision of the community of Verona from 1594, certain sanctions were imposed against those who had recourse to Gentile courts. The decision issued on 21 December of that year[101] begins by stating that, because of the celebration of a circumcision, the communal institutions were unable to meet in the usual way, so the outgoing *parnassim* were authorized to name three new

[99] Ibid. See also the ordinance adopted in Verona on 2 Shevat 1543, when three lay leaders were chosen, and various tasks were imposed upon them, including that 'they will also be required to sit every Sunday for one hour following the Afternoon Prayer, to hear and to judge between each person and his neighbour, all those who have any quarrel or claim, so that the fixed [synagogue worship] shall no longer be interrupted here in Verona' ('Pinkas Verona' i. fo. 50a). The same principle is stated more clearly in an ordinance from 18 Tammuz 1545, in which the rabbi appointed by the community is required, along with the two leaders, to sit every Sunday in the synagogue, 'and before them shall come every dispute and judgement, and from them the ruling shall go out clearly, or they shall be given as judges people from the holy congregation'. This document was published by I. Sonne, 'Basic Premisses' (Heb.), *Kovez 'al Yad*, 3 [13] (Jerusalem, 1939–40), 158. Some time later, this same clause was incorporated within the contract of the community-appointed rabbi (see ibid. 170, sect. 6).

[100] In this case, the element of compulsion was carried out in a somewhat unclear manner, so that in order to strengthen it a 'kind of ban' was imposed, under the explicit condition that it would not be 'against the will of the exalted king or against the advice of the ruler'. At the beginning of the ordinances, it was always stated that they were instituted 'by the power given by the rulers' or by 'the permission given by their honours the rulers'. See the edicts of Verona from 21 Dec. 1595 and 25 Dec. 1596 (the full text is given in Documents 54 and 55 of the Hebrew edition of this book, pp. 276–77). These ordinances constitute a substantial change in the situation in Verona, as only then was the authority of that same communal Court just described established without question. It may be that further research in the archives of Verona will reveal the document which the Jews received from the authorities allowing them to make such regulations. In any event, it is worth mentioning that, until the end of 1593, there did not yet exist in Verona 'a straightforward arrangement . . . concerning the summoning to judgement [in disputes] between one person and his fellow, nor how and when one who refuses [to appear] is prosecuted for this refusal, or whether he may take him to a non-Jewish court, so as not to pervert justice [i.e. *by allowing the dispute to lapse entirely*]'. For the text of the regulations introduced on 12 Aug. 1593, see Document 56, p. 277, in the Hebrew edition of this book.

[101] Decision of the Council of Verona from 21 Dec. 1594, in 'Pinkas Verona' ii. fo. 181a, published in Document 54, p. 276, in the Hebrew edition of this book.

parnassim and two substitutes who would begin their terms immediately:

on condition that the new *parnassim* shall take upon themselves by oath, in the presence of R. Mordecai Bassan. . . to restore the laws of Israel to their proper place and to battle with all their strength against those who resort to Gentile courts—and this in accordance with the power granted to them by the . . . governor of the city—without favouring either the old, the wealthy, or poor. And the rabbi, together with the incoming *parnassim*, will arrange the procedure for sending the beadle, who is the messenger of the Court, to each man and his fellow . . . And in order to arrange this most important matter, the rabbi and the *parnassim* and the incoming ones will take counsel and find an appropriate way, and publicize it in the community, that no man may counter their word . . .

A second ordinance on this same subject was issued the following year.[102] The Jewish community might regard such an ordering of affairs as an achievement in the task of self-government; individual Jews had a interest in it because they were thus spared the exhausting and long drawn-out procedure involved when they turned to a recognized judicial system, as well as the expenses entailed in such an appeal (one must remember that at times even an agreement to turn to arbitration entailed the payment of expenses to the arbitrators). The non-Jewish government, for its part, viewed favourably the easing of the burden upon the local magistracy brought about by this arrangement.[103] Apart from this limited gain which, for reasons mentioned above, remained the accomplishment of small communities with homogeneous populations, and only in those localities where the ecclesiastical influence was not predominant, throughout the sixteenth century,

[102] 'Pinkas Verona', ii. 184a, published in Document 55, p. 277, in the Hebrew version of this book; cf. the regulation from 12 Aug. 1593, 'Pinkas Verona' ii. 177b, published in Document 56, p. 277, in the Hebrew edition of this book.

[103] This reason is explicitly mentioned in the appeals of the Jews to the authorities. See e.g. the fourth clause of the formula of request by the community of Reggio for a privilege, apparently from the second half of the 16th century (this document is preserved in the Governmental Archives of Modena, and is available on microfilm, IMHM, film HM 5416c, p. 31): 'che nascendo differenze ciuilli tra gl'hebrej habiano da stare al ritto hebraico come altra uolta li fu conceso, intendendo però solamente sino alla soma de Lire sessanta, e questo per ouiare li continui tedij, che giornalmente simili minutij aportano a ministri di S.A.S.' It should be mentioned at this point that, generally speaking, the Jews attempted to break through the government's opposition to granting them autonomy during periods of unusual pressure upon the local courts; see e.g. the appeal of the community of Mantua in 1577 in the wake of the plague (Simonsohn, *Mantua*, 355).

Jewish law in Italy did not go much beyond the limits and restrictions defined by arbitration.[104]

5. The Establishment of the Rabbinic Court in Ferrara

What is known about the single case in this period in which a Rabbinic court was established, in Ferrara, confirms and exemplifies the above conclusion. Scholars have been misled both in the dating of this event and in their interpretation of its significance.[105] In fact, even in the case of this court, the Jewish judicial system in Italy did not go beyond the limits of arbitration.

In 1574, members of the Italian and Ashkenazic communities in Ferrara asked permission from government officials to be allowed to appoint

[104] To the best of my understanding, even in the privileges given by the Duchy of Savoy from 1582 on, there was no extension of the principle of imposed arbitration. There, the Jews were required to turn to 'their rabbis, whether those who dwell in our province or those who dwell outside it, in order to receive an appropriate decision (*provisione*), as is customary among them and in accordance with their ancient law, and these rabbis may make use of their authority to impose [sanctions] upon whoever refuses to observe their commands, even by means of bans, and these bans shall be publicized, but no man may go outside the jurisdiction of our state' (see Colorni, *Legge ebraica e leggi locali*, 325–7). In the expanded version from 1616 (in full ibid. 326, n. 4), it is explicitly stated that the rabbis in question are selected (*Rabini eligendi*). However, from the language of the edict of 1667 (ibid. 327 n. 6) it seems that the Jews in Piedmont attempted to combine matters from the strictly religious realm with judicial ones, and in the wake of this to impose the authority of the rabbinic courts. In reaction to this, there follows the qualification: 'l'autorità dei Rabini si limita alla decisione delle differenze cerimoniali, dalle sentenze dei quali come dal laudo degli arbitri si farà l'appelatione al Conservatore', etc. In any event, this development goes beyond the chronological limits of this work (see further for a similar attempt in Ferrara during our period).

[105] This error is based upon the erroneous reading by Andrea Balletti (*Gli ebrei e gli estensi*, 94–5) of 1524 for 1574, and 1525 for 1575, in the documents from the State Archives of Modena, cited in full in Documents 57–60, pp. 278–81, of the Hebrew edition of this book. This error led him incorrectly to see a connection between these documents and those mentioned in note 30. Balletti likewise concluded that the authority of the rabbinic court in Ferrara was recognized during 1524–25, an error adopted by Colorni as well (*Legge ebraica e leggi locali*, 329–30). As one can now conclude from the names mentioned in the documents, there is no doubt that the entire theory was unwarranted: the notary Cesare del Sagrato, who signed the afore-mentioned documents, was active only between the years 1532–86, as we know from a list of notaries found in the state archives at Ferrara. I wish to express my thanks to Prof. Colorni, who examined this point for me, thereby confirming that what he wrote in his book on this subject was based purely upon Balletti's error.

three prudent individuals, who will take care of the necessary arrangements concerning the Jewish way of life in issues touching upon permitted and prohibited food and ceremonies of marriage and divorce, and operate in such a manner that people will not come every day to cry out in the synagogues[106] with complaints of one Jew against another, and force each one of them to select arbitrators.[107]

Three rabbis were proposed for this task: R. Ishmael Ḥaninna (Laudadio) of Valmontone,[108] R. Samuel del Vecchio,[109] and R. Ḥezekiah (Cesare) Finzi.[110] This fact is in itself a clear indication that the community in Ferrara saw this request as an initial step towards the establishment of communal courts with broad judicial authority.[111] The request was approved, in the very ambiguous wording in which the Jews had framed it: it was stated that the three rabbis were 'to take counsel in the Great Synagogue, and the burden shall be upon them, and they have

106 This clearly refers to the practice of *biṭṭul ha-tamid*—i.e. the interruption of the synagogue service in order to set right a wrong that had been done to someone.

107 'Nel di soprascritto proponendo gli deputati di detti hebrei alli huomeni della lor congregatione che fosse opera ben fatta il prouedere che questa università hauese continuamente una ressidenza di tre persone inteligenti che hauesserro cura di fare osseruare gli termini necessarij al uivere hebraico circa alli cibi liciti et inliciti et ordinationi di congiunger matrimonij e disgiungere e far che no' si uenghi tutto il giorno a far rumori nelle Sinagoghe per interesse che habbia qualsivoglia hebreo l'uno con l'altro per conto di dare e hauere a stringerli ciascun di essi a chiamar arbitri insieme, hano fatto ellettione delli tre infrascritti cioè M. Laudadio de valmontone M. Samuel del vecchio et M. Cesare Finzi i quali essi e non altri habbino autorità et podestà in tutte le cose suddette per mesi 19 seguenti cominciando dal di sopraddetto et che sieno tenuti tutti tre, o una parte di essi ritrouarsi nella sinagoga maggiore sera e mattina nel hora della oratione et il lunedi et il giovedi mattino far quiui residenza per spatio di mezz'hora doppo che si è orato senza dar grauezza a detta uniuersità di premiare detti huomeni, intendendo che questa resolutione sia di buona gratia dell'Ill.mo et Ecc.mo Sig.r Dica et non altrimente . . .' (Summary of a decision in Ferrara regarding the establishment of a communal court; from the Government Archives in Modena, Ebrei, Busta 15, fasc. 8; published in full in Document 57, p. 278, Hebrew edition of this book).

108 See D. Carpi, 'The Expulsion of the Jews from the Papal States During the Reign of Pope Pius V and the Inquisition Against the Jews of Bologna, 1566–1569' (Heb.), *Sefer Zikaron le-Ḥayyim Anzo Sereni* (Jerusalem, 1971), 148 n. 16; M. Benayahu, 'Eulogies of Italian Rabbis for R. Joseph Caro' (Heb.), *Kovez Rabbi Yosef Karo* (Jerusalem, 1969), 320–1.

109 See M. Mortara, *Indice alfabetico* (Padua, 1886), 68. Sections 120 and 146 of the responsa collection, *Matanot ba-Adam*, are by him.

110 The teacher of R. Leone Modena; see *Ḥayyei Yehudah*, 17, and Mortara, *Indice alfabetico*, 22.

111 Cf. this formula of request with the reasons given by the Jews of Piedmont mentioned in Ch. 3, Sect. 6.

the authority to attend to the disorders which may come about among the Jews'.[112]

But precisely the opposite occurred: the Jews opposed this new communal measure, objecting to the limitation of the authority of the local courts which would result from it; their appeal obviously could not but be accepted favourably by the ruler. But even the acceptance of this appeal, evidence of which has been preserved in the documents, did not abnegate the right of the community to demand that its members appear before Jewish arbitrators. The absence in the regulations of the Mutual Aid Confraternity of Ferrara, from 1588 on, of a specific clause requiring appeal to Jewish arbitrators is, if not absolute proof, at least partial evidence of this point.[113] A unique situation came about, in which the community possessed authority, but means existed to evade it through appeal to non-Jewish courts. The community was thus confronted with the delicate problem of how to adopt a clear-cut and firm posture *vis-à-vis* evaders.

One may add here the evidence found in a responsum of R. Jeḥiel Trabot, in which it is mentioned that the members of the Portuguese community in Ferrara had earlier received permission similar to that requested by the Italian and Ashkenazic communities in 1574. The question addressed to Trabot reads as follows:[114]

I saw the form of the agreement . . . made by the people of the holy community of the Portuguese, against those who break the fence [around]

[112] 'Ill.mo et Ecc.mo S.r Duca: Trouandosi gli hebrei habitatori in Ferrara Italiani, e Thedeschi fedelissimi di V. E. Ill.ma non hauere nelle lor sinagoghe Dottori hebrei che tenghino particolar cura di prouedere alli disordeni che gionalmente posseno occorrere come già altre uolte hano hauuto fecero ellettione a giorni passati di tre loro Rabbi quali assistentemente habbino a ridursi alla principal sinagogha dando loro carico et autorità di prouedere alli disordeni che potessero nascere tra essi hebrei, il somario della quale loro terminatione si esibisce qui annessa per informatione di V. E. et per che detta ellettione e fatta con condetione che ui sia il consenso di V. E. Ill.ma et non altrimente ricorsero a piedi di quella supplicandola si degni conceder loro il detto consenso et accio che non si possi credere chel dar tal facultà a detti Rabbi fusse un scemare della podestà del Ill.re Sig.r Giudice de sauij sopra le cose della natione hebrea desidreno et supplicheno V. E. che dia facultà al detto S.r giudice di accrescere et sminuire l'autorità di detti Rabbi secondo che a lui parerà di bisognoso in tutte le cose pertinenti al offizio suo che tutto riconosceranno da lei per gratia singolare alla quale pregano dal Sig.r Iddio felicità et esaltatione. Judex XII sapientum circa narrato prouideat et faciat quod ei conueniens videbitur Jo. Battista Pegna ultimo ottebris 1574. (Appeal of the community in Ferrara to the Duke concerning the establishment of a court, and the Duke's approval. Document 58, p. 279, in the Hebrew edition of this book.)

[113] See nn. 33 and 48 in this chapter.

[114] *Teshuvot Matanot ba-Adam*, sect. 60, fos. 68a–69a.

the Torah . . . and who wish to follow the statutes and customs and laws of the Gentiles . . . Therefore the members of that congregation arose and imposed a limit and restriction on this, and all of the congregation enacted and agreed as one, to impose a fine upon any one of the community who would violate their agreement and against anyone who would rise and attempt to make crooked the straight, to nullify their agreements and arrangements and the privileges which they received from our Lord, the Magnificent Duke of Ferrara; that [such a person] would be subject to the ban and not be called up to read the Torah for a set period, and other penalties, as enumerated in the said agreement, so long as he does not bring down the haughtiness of his heart to repent full-heartedly and humbly submit to the authority of the Holy Community. And as there were people from the Holy Community who rose and violated the laws and altered the ordinance, and even though law-abiding people spoke to them privately to persuade them to act justly, they did not wish to hear . . . Their hand is powerful, and they may act according to their will, because they are violent and strong and do not feel fear. And should the people of that Holy Congregation wish to chastise and criticize them and return them their just deserts, certainly the flame of disagreement and dispute would flare up in that holy congregation, and none could extinguish it. Therefore, the members of that congregation decided this time to bury their faces and eyes in the earth, and to forgive their shame in order to uproot the roots of controversy and to increase peace in the earthly family, and that there may not arise opportunities of damage, and that peace may rule among them. And I, the young one, was asked. . . whether the members of that Holy Congregation are required to do thus, and to violate their regulations and to forgive those who violated the agreement even though they have not repented . . . and whether or not there is any sin in their not chastising them on this . . .

The rabbi allowed them to nullify the agreement if the members of the community wished to do so 'so that the sinners will no longer have contempt of it'. We may infer from this that he did not see this agreement as an effective means of strengthening the status of Jewish Law. In his opinion, it would have been better not to 'offer an opportunity to the opponent to disagree', thereby upsetting the delicate balance between the government's willingness to tolerate the imposition of internal Jewish arbitration and the option offered to individual Jews to avoid this by appeal to non-Jewish courts.

As we mentioned above, the appeal to the rulers of Ferrara by the Italian and Ashkenazic congregations for permission to establish courts came only a few years after the permission granted to the Portuguese community to excommunicate all those who refused to turn to Jewish arbitrators. This right, granted to Portuguese ex-*conversos* who returned to Judaism in Ferrara, was among the special privileges granted to them in order to attract them to Ferrara, as had been done in Savoy in 1572.[115] One therefore receives the impression that the tendency to appeal to the government on judicial matters, specifically in the 1570s, was strengthened by two factors: on the one hand, the increased pressure upon non-Jewish courts due to the large number of suits involving questions of inheritance following the Great Plague[116] and, on the other hand, the granting of special privileges to the Portuguese *conversos*. These privileges stimulated other Jews to renew their own attempts, and also made it more difficult for the government to reject such attempts. For if the *conversos* were given this privilege, did it not stand to reason that it should also be granted to the previously established Jews, who had neither been Christians nor 'betrayed' Christianity?!

6. Arbitration as the Basis for Jewish Law in Italy

All in all, we may now conclude that Jewish law in Italy did not go beyond the limits of arbitration throughout the period under discussion. As stated at the beginning of the chapter, this conclusion does not differ in principle from that reached by Colorni,[117] although the detailed description given above would seem to demand an additional conclusion, namely, that throughout this period, and in fact at least until the end of the seventeenth century, one may not make use of the term Rabbinical Court (*bet-din*) without a qualifying explanation. One must certainly reject any blanket statement that the Rabbinical Court was one of the institutions of the Jewish community in Italy during this period, unless the term is taken in the more restricted sense as explained above.[118] Such terms as 'court' (*bet-din*), 'judge', 'to

[115] See Beinart, 'The Jewish Settlement in the Duchy of Savoy'.

[116] See Ch. 3, Sect. 6.

[117] Colorni, *Legge ebraica e leggi locali*. Cf. also Pertile, *Storia del diritto italiano*, iii. 215–16.

[118] See e.g. how Cassuto, who did not find any mention of a rabbinic court in Florence, reached the conclusion, based on the later period, that 'in civil disputes it was also

go before the court closest to him', 'a proper court', or even 'the Head of the Court' (*av bet-din*)[119] cannot be used in all other cases. One must be particularly aware of the danger of any literal understanding of such terms, which halakhic scholars used either out of habit[120] or because they were quoting sources.[121]

permissible to judge in accordance with Jewish law before a rabbinic court, when the two litigants agreed to do so; but in this case the Jews of Florence were forced to turn to another Jewish community, because no rabbinic court existed in Florence during the period under discussion' (U. Cassuto, *Firenze*, 156, and cf. his remarks on p. 164). In point of fact, what was lacking in Florence did not exist in any other community during that period either.

119 On the term 'court head' (*av bet-din*), see Ch. 3, near the end of Sect. 4d.

120 See *Ṭur Shulḥan 'Arukh*, *Ḥoshen Mishpaṭ*, sect. 14, and the different opinions summarized there by R. Gur Aryeh ha-Levi in his gloss to sect. 5: 'Today the [*equivalent of the*] Great Court is the greatest sage of the generation, there being no one higher than him.' Cf. *Tashbeẓ*, sect. 516. Similarly, in the *Responsa* of R. Joseph Colon the term 'court' (*bet-din*) is synonymous with scholar who is authorized to sit in judgement, and whose very presence in a given place determines the claimant's obligation to follow the respondent to that place, if he wishes a hearing based on Jewish law. See e.g. J. Colon, *Teshuvot Mahari"k*, Responsum 58: 'therefore I impose upon you excommunication . . . that you come here to Pavia, where she [*the respondent*] is, to go to judgement with her; but if the Court in Pavia is not acceptable to you, choose one judge yourself and she will choose one for herself, and the two of them will select a third, but in all events they must sit in judgement here in Pavia'. Our interpretation of these words is confirmed by comparison with a statement written by Colon in Responsum 21, addressed to a rabbinical gathering in Frankfurt which had authorized R. Simon ha-Kohen to sit at the head of the court and to force the members of the community to come before him for judgement (see M. Horowitz, *Rabbanei Frankfurt* (Jerusalem, 1972), 18). Colon wrote there as follows: 'Moreover, have I not been written to by Rabbi . . . R. Shimon Katz, who is foremost of the great rabbis of Germany, that they strengthen and support his court in Frankfurt by the strength of their ordinance, not to force any man to remove anyone from his court. Even if one of the litigating parties should open his mouth and say that the Nobleman R. Shimon Katz is unacceptable to him, by reason of marriage or consanguinity, in all events the said R. Shimon shall convene the court in his city and it shall be sustained by his word . . . therefore I, the young one, also join with them, and I declare with the power of the ban that no man can take R. Hirtz outside of the Court of Frankfurt . . .' See also Responsum 90.

121 See e.g. *Teshuvot Mahar"ik*, Responsum 154. The term *bet-din* is used there in connection with earlier sources: 'Third, that he ought not to have brought him to the courts of Gentiles until after he had received permission from the Court . . . for even if you say that receiving permission from the members of the congregation is efficacious . . . as implied in the words of our teacher R. Meir, in any event he ought to have empowered those members of the congregation who were fit to judge his son Asher, to the exclusion of those who beat him in the synagogue, who were not fit to judge him on several counts; and he should have done it [on the basis of] a majority of the others . . .' The permission of the Court referred to here is mentioned in the words of Maimonides and of R. Moses of Coucy, quoted in extremely abbreviated form by Mordecai ben Hillel (*Sefer Mordekhai* to Baba Kamma, sect. 74, quoted in *Bet Yosef*, *Ḥoshen Mishpaṭ* sect. 26): 'But I found [in the responsum] of R. Meir that one is not allowed to force him [to be judged] at the hands of the Gentiles, unless the Court or the heads of the community allow him . . .' It is therefore clear that one may not conclude from this responsum of R. Joseph Colon

Moreover, by virtue of their ordination, rabbis perceived themselves as 'seated upon the throne of justice' and naturally tended to see the place where they lived as 'a place where there is a Court'. It was therefore natural for them to summon people to come before them to be judged according to Jewish law, while those who refused such summonses were treated as violating communal discipline—a point which at times created controversy. Many of these controversies strengthen the thesis that, within the existing communal framework, Italian communities at this time were unable to establish permanent courts at which Jewish individuals could be required to be judged on the basis of communal ordinances. For this reason, one might reasonably argue that readiness to undergo arbitration was in fact tantamount to readiness to be judged according to Jewish law and to refuse to obey any further injunction. R. Abraham Menaḥem Porto ha-Kohen summarized this in his discussion of the hypothetical case of the 'Court of Sepphoris', which attempted to require Reuben, 'who lived in the region of the court of Tiberias', to submit to its jurisdiction (i.e. to undergo arbitration in 'Sepphoris'). He added:

> I have also seen what was written by R. Meir of Padua concerning the dispute between Eliakim and Eli'ezer from Guastalla. The situation was such that the former wished to force the latter to choose a judge, and I remember very clearly that in that case Rabbi da Rosa [i.e. *R. Moses Provenzali*] and those who followed his opinion argued that, according to R. Joseph Colon, this is the accepted [lit. '*simple*'] custom among the Ashkenazim, and that it is only their custom to do so.[122]

that there was a fixed court in Verona in his day. On the contrary, a reading of the entire responsum will reveal that Colon did not know of any other way to conduct a hearing in practice except before specially picked judges or arbitrators. There is therefore no ground for the claim that Colon's words here and in similar passages constitute a defence of the prestige and authority of the institution of the communal court, as argued by Harry Rabinowitz, 'Rabbi Joseph Colon and the Jewish Ban', *HJ* 22 (1960), 64–5. There is similarly no basis for the assumption, at least in the case of Italy, that at Colon's time 'each community had its own court (*bet-din*) whose judges administered rabbinical law'. Cf. in terms of the actual wording used by Colon, the phrasing of the second ordinance made in a gathering in Ferrara in 1554: 'whoever violated the covenant first and brought his Israelite brother to the courts of the Gentiles without the permission *of his congregation or of the rabbi of his city* . . .'

122 'Teshuvot R. Abraham Menaḥem Porto ha-Kohen', sect. 25, fo. 163a.

Porto is referring in these last comments to R. Joseph Colon's responsum.[123] Provenzali was inclined to reduce the entire question to one of Ashkenazic custom: if the obligation to appear for judgement before the rabbis of the place, who are known as the Court, is merely a matter of Ashkenazic custom, then this custom does not oblige those who are not Ashkenazim, so that one possesses full liberty in choosing one's arbitrators. Had there been a communal court in Mantua, the distinction between Ashkenazim and those who were not Ashkenazim would have seemed ridiculous!

One must emphasize that this situation applied to the body of civil law, including the realm of family law.[124] One need only mention here the extended dispute concerning the Tamari–Venturozzo divorce. As is known, in this case a court of arbitrators ruled that Samuel of Perugia was to divorce his betrothed within five days, and thereafter to receive from his father-in-law those objects which had been kept in his house, together with a certain

[123] 'Concerning the rabbi who wished to force them to be judged in his city, it is the accepted custom among the Ashkenazim that, when a given person finds his litigant in a place where there is a court, he may force him to be judged there.' *Teshuvot Mahari"k*, sect. 14.

[124] Even in the kingdom of Naples, where many traditions and practices from earlier periods were certainly preserved, in which one may detect the granting of juridical authority to the Jewish judges by the authorities, there seems to me to be no proof that, during the period under discussion here and until the expulsion of the Jews from that kingdom in 1541, the exclusive authority of Jewish judges in matters of family law was in fact recognized, and that the appeal to them was obligatory. See N. Ferorelli, *Gli ebrei nell'Italia meridionale* (Turin, 1915; repr. Bologna, 1966), 110–15; cf. Colorni, *Legge ebraica e leggi locali*, 319. Certainly, the listing of wedding contracts by the notary in Latin translation does not support this conclusion, as such registration was customary throughout Italy during this period, and these contracts were no more than 'documents which are presented in the [Gentile] courts', which facilitated the execution of the decisions of the arbitrators. Cf. also the document published by I. Joel, 'Italian *Ketubot* in the Library's Treasury' (Heb.), *KS* 22 (1945–6), 270–2. On the contrary, this practice led to not inconsiderable complications concerning the halakhic possibility that one had to relate to these documents within the framework of the rule, 'the law of the land is the law', leading to the conclusion that, because they were recorded in Gentile courts, they were applicable even against the usually accepted *halakhah*—for example, with regard to the right of the wife to collect the money stipulated in her wedding contract even during her husband's lifetime (see further below). The notary's registration of the marriage contract likewise confirms the fact that, in matters of family law, the *halakhah* was generally accepted in Gentile courts as the personal law of the Jews, within the framework of the legal system; see Colorni, *Legge ebraica e leggi locali*, 181–97. It follows from this that even halakhic rulings which were issued by rabbis were included in what is referred to above, when confirmed by the courts.

sum of money. On the basis of this ruling, Samuel obtained a divorce from another court than the one which issued the above ruling. Subsequently, certain doubts arose concerning the validity of the writ of divorce (*get*), so that R. Moses Provenzali of Mantua, together with his colleague R. Elia Melli, delivered a letter to Samuel, to be presented to the girl's father, Joseph Tamari, in which he was asked to agree to the arbitration of the matter before a board of arbitrators in a neutral place. Provenzali was attacked for this step, on formal grounds, that is, for failing to appeal directly to the rabbis of Venice. He replied to this charge as follows:

My colleagues have asked me why I did not direct my steps towards the great scholars of Venice, who sit there on the throne of judgement, so that my modesty would be greatly recognized [through this] . . . To whom of the holy ones ought I to turn, for were I to pour out my words to the judges [i.e. *to the arbitrators who ruled that Samuel was to give the divorce*] or to the arrangers [i.e. *to the 'Court' who presided over the divorce ceremony*], I would not be dealing even-handedly with the disputants, for they are suspect in the eyes of the young man, nor will I deny that truthfully in my eyes they also seem somewhat of an interested party . . . And if I would chance to turn towards the Oriental [i.e. *Levantine*] scholars who dwell there with them, I do not even know how to approach them or who they are. And I also feared lest [the anger] of the Ashkenazic sages burn at me for this reason, and they would say that I did not respect their honour . . . apart from the fact that it would seem as if I were taking too much authority upon myself were I to arrange that the judgement be decided by those who initiated it. Both sides would ignore the judgement and would not take heed of it . . .[125]

The essential point is that a number of different rabbinic bodies existed in Venice which could legitimately claim to possess the authority of a Court so that, were he to turn to any one of these bodies, his choice would necessarily be an arbitrary one, and it was not his prerogative to determine which of them was to be granted the authority of a court in this or another instance. One may infer from this that, within its institutionalized organizational framework, the community did not grant final authority to any one particular court. Thus, according to R. Moses Provenzali,

125 *Eleh ha-Devarim* (Mantua, 1566), 28.

all matters requiring the intervention of a court automatically remained a matter for arbitration.

It follows from Provenzali's words that, even in matters of family law, one must go before a court of arbitration in a situation such as the one described above. Provenzali was likewise attacked for this statement, on the basis of the ruling of R. Solomon ben Adret of Barcelona that arbitrators may not deal with prohibitions relating to marriage and divorce.[126] Provenzali wrote an entire treatise to refute this argument.[127] The halakhic intricacies of this question are irrelevant to the present discussion, as even Provenzali's opponents did not ask to raise the matter before the court of permanent judges in Venice,[128] but argued that the matter was to be decided by the majority of those contemporary scholars who were competent in matters of family law. Against them, R. Moses Provenzali argued that 'this can only be in one court, or in one in which they have agreed after negotiation'.[129] In any event, no communal court, by whose authority the incident of this divorce could have been dealt with, existed in Venice. This was the source of the confusion in this matter, which agitated Italian Jewry for years.

We may also add here, as another indirect confirmation of the non-existence of recognized, binding, legal, rabbinic authority, the repeated cases of the interruption of public worship by persons with a complaint, either against another individual (e.g. a respondent who refused to come to Court) or against the community in general. This practice, within the context of the medieval Jewish community, provided the individual with direct access to public opinion, and was thus a 'bulwark of strength for the weak and oppressed against the powerful'.[130] The practice, known as *biṭṭul ha-tamid* (the abrogation of public prayer), is already mentioned in the ordinances of R. Gershom Me'or ha-Golah (*c*. 960–1028), and there is evidence that it was used throughout most of the sixteenth century.[131]

[126] Sect. 1209.

[127] This commentary was published first.

[128] As, on the face of it, one might easily conclude from the above ruling of R. Solomon ben Adret.

[129] This commentary was published first, fo. [10]a.

[130] L. Finkelstein, *Jewish Self-government* (New York, 1924; 2nd edn. 1964), 18; cf. 15–18, 33.

[131] Cf. R. Emmanuel b. Jekutiel of Benevento, *Sefer Livyat Ḥen* (Mantua, 1557), 6a: 'I am deeply disturbed . . . when I hear that in the synagogues, when the public is

Once the arbitrators' ruling had been issued, it was approved by a notary and made enforceable by the decision and declaration of the appointed official (*praetor*).[132] As mentioned above, after such a decision became the equivalent of the decision of a court of law, its execution was turned over to the same non-Jewish authorities responsible for the execution of regular court decisions. These governmental officials were not associated with the judiciary, but with the administrative system,[133] and their action in carrying out the rulings of the arbitrators was in no way different from their activities in executing decisions of the courts, even if the ruling was one issued by Jewish arbitrators.[134] Many arbitration rulings of Jewish arbitrators appear in the archives of notaries in Italian cities,[135] most often in Italian or Latin translation, and at times even together with the Hebrew text of the ruling.[136] These documents are of great importance for understanding the transfer of concepts and terminology from Hebrew into Italian or Latin. In fact, a study devoted to such transfers might be of great value in understanding how Hebrew was translated into other languages, as well as in clarifying certain points concerning the remnants of the Judaeo-Italian dialect at the close of the Renaissance. However,

praying and during the reading of the Law, there is a sound of tumult from the city and a noise from the sanctuary, that they go into their assembly and interrupt during the reading of *Shema'* or before the Silent Prayer. My heart is pained when I am told by those who sit in the gate about the evil that has beset my people in some places; that in the Small Sanctuary [i.e. *the synagogue*] at the time of communal prayer people come forward and, because of some dispute or quarrel, interrupt the fixed offering [i.e. *the regular service of prayer*] and trouble the congregation to hear words of discord and a voice cursing and blaspheming, striking with a wicked fist. Is this called the House of God and the gate to heaven?! . . . Would it not be better for him to go to the study house of the sages or to the house of the person who shall be judge in those days, that the judge may tell him words of judgement; but in the synagogue he shall not speak out, and they will rejoice that he is silent, and does not trouble the worshippers nor disturb the people from their acts.' Cf. Documents 46, 50, and 57, pp. 259, 263–74, and 278 in the Hebrew edition of this book, and in Sect. 5 above.

132 See C. Lesona, *Manuale di procedura civile* (Milan, 1932), 44.

133 Ibid. 364.

134 See n. 1 above for the formulation of the basic Roman law, which concludes with the statement: 'Eorum sententias provinciarum Judices exequantur.'

135 See e.g. V. Tedeschi, 'Il diritto giudiziario israeliano', *Annali della Facoltà di Giurisprudenza dell'Università di Genova*, 10 (1971), fasc. 2, 16–17; R. Segre, *Gli ebrei Lombardi nell'età Spagnola* (Turin, 1973), 124–5. A long list of documents of this sort in Padua is given by D. Carpi, 'ha-Yehudim be-Padua be-tekufat ha-Renessans', Doctoral Dissertation, Jerusalem, 1967, p. 212 n. 9.

136 e.g. an interesting arbitration agreement is preserved in the 'Archivio Notarile' in Cremona (fondo notarile, Notario G. B. Raimondi, filza 120).

it seems to me that documents of this sort have no special characteristics which would make them particularly important to the historical issue at stake here, for which reason I see no need to dwell on them.

7. 'The Law of the Land is Law'

The situation described above, in which the pressure of the Christian world became a factor of central importance in the way in which Jewish law was applied, was quite naturally reflected in the contents of Rabbinic rulings. It seems to me that this phenomenon may best be understood by examination of the ways in which Jewish scholars in Italy during this period interpreted the famous Talmudic rule of the Babylonian scholar Samuel, 'the law of the land is the law' (*dina de-malkhuta dina*). A full discussion of this subject, even within the limited orbit of our study, would go far beyond the scope of the present work. This is one of the few halakhic subjects in which elements of socio-political philosophy, on the one hand, and historical reality, on the other, are intertwined in such a complex and manifold way that it is impossible to discuss it briefly in a satisfactory manner.[137] We must therefore content ourselves with a brief allusion to the turbulence caused by the legal situation in the realm of halakhic rulings in this area, while noting that a proper explanation of the political and social approaches of the various sages, as well as the practical expression of those questions which pertained to the rule, 'the law of the land is the law', certainly merit a separate study.

As to the basic question of whether or not this rule applies to civil cases, it would seem that, in Italy, during the period under discussion, there was no objection to the tendency, which began to emerge as early as the fourteenth century, to restrict the applicability of this rule to those matters which were regarded as 'the direct concern and interest of the King', while interpreting as narrowly as possible those sources which would apply this rule to civil law as well.[138] To a certain extent, this tendency was

[137] For a general survey of the subject, see L. Landman, *Jewish Law in the Diaspora*. For a more profound discussion, see S. Shilo, *Dina de-Malkhuta Dina* (Jerusalem, 1975).

[138] For sources, see *Encyclopedia Talmudica*, s.v. *dina demalkhuta dina*, vii. 299–301; cf. Shilo's discussion in *Dina de-Malkhuta Dina*, 131–45.

strengthened by the parallel tendency to prevent individuals from having recourse to non-Jewish courts. Evidence of this appears in the discussion by R. Joseph Colon which is intended to demonstrate that

> even according to those opinions quoted by Mordecai ben Hillel (1240?–98) in his [Talmudic] commentary, that even in other civil matters we say that [*the rule of*] 'the law of the land is the law' is applicable, this seems to apply only to tariffs and levies of the King's law . . . but it seems obvious that in cases between two [Jewish] parties, this is not so, for otherwise all the laws of the Torah would be made null and void, Heaven forbid.[139]

It has been rightly noted that Colon's conclusion here relies upon a particular line of interpretation of the statements of R. Asher b. Jeḥiel (1250–1327) and his son R. Jacob b. Asher, author of the *Arba'ah Ṭurim* (1270–1340) in their discussions of court litigation, and that from a purely theoretical halakhic perspective, the inclusion of civil cases under the rubric of 'the law of the land is the law' may coexist with the prohibition of resort to a Gentile court.[140] It would therefore seem that an additional element was introduced in this halakhic discussion, which reinforced the opinion that the application of this rule to civil matters might also encourage the resort to Gentile courts. There was thus an opposing halakhic tendency to restrict this rule to exclude civil cases, thereby averting this danger in those places where the Jews did not enjoy legal autonomy.[141]

In any event, following Samuel's rule, the principle was accepted that one might recognize the validity of documents which were validated by Gentile courts, including deeds of gift, without recognizing the Christian laws pertaining to such documents—'documents which were validated in Gentile courts were not allowed, except for their being considered valid *per se*, that is, that we do not consider them as invalid documents; but not that we are to depart from the law of Torah, even by a hair's breadth'.[142] Nobody directly challenged the authority of R. Joseph Colon and the tradition of the French sages, from

139 *Teshuvot Mahari"k*, Responsum 188.

140 See Shilo, *Dina de-Malkhuta Dina*, 138–42.

141 Cf. Shilo's comments, ibid. 143–5. Evidence for the presence of this consideration in Colon's thought may also be seen in his handling of the rule, 'the law of the land is the law', in *Teshuvot Mahari"k*, Responsum 192.

142 *Teshuvot Mahari"k*, Responsum 192; cf. Shilo, *Dina de-Malkhuta Dina*, 362.

which he drew proof for his position.[143] Nevertheless, it became customary[144] to draw up documents only in Gentile courts, since a situation had developed in which the Christian authorities were required to execute the decisions of Jewish arbitrators provided that these were based upon documents that had been validated (i.e. in Gentile courts). This situation created a multitude of questions, and effectively reopened the entire discussion from a number of different angles.

It is in the nature of such documents to contain conditions pertaining to economic matters, and it is a well-known principle of Jewish law that in such matters any conditions made between the parties are valid, even if they contradict the laws of the Torah, provided that they are drawn up in accordance with certain procedures.[145] It follows from this that even within the framework of these rules, if one were to say that Samuel's rule, 'the law of the land is the law', applies only to matters defined as pertaining to 'the interest of the King', and that one has to follow the rules of the Torah strictly in granting validity to documents validated in non-Jewish courts, there is nevertheless still room for disagreement concerning any specific document. Was it drawn up in accordance with Jewish law or not? In a case

143 *Teshuvot Mahari"k*, Responsum 65: 'It is likewise written in *Sefer ha-Terumah* xlvi, 8, 5, as follows: "I received from my teachers, who received a tradition from the French [scholars], that one does not assume that 'the law of the land is the law', except in those matters which are the concern of the king . . . but in those matters which are between man and his fellow, the Sages did not assume that 'the law of the land is the law' ".'

144 The Italian scholars refer to this custom as the one usually practised, and generally without the slightest hint of criticism. See e.g. *Teshuvot Matanot ba-Adam*, sect. 156, p. 220: 'as it is the custom in all the regions of Italy to register documents by non-Jewish expert scribes.' Cf. the remarks made by R. Meir of Padua, Responsa 47: 'but in our matter, if we believe the scribe that the borrower admitted truthfully that it (the note of indebtedness) was paid off, what have we to do with testimony that is unfit according to our law [i.e. *that of Gentiles*], for are not witnesses required only in order to determine the truth in such matters? But as the authorities take care to trust the scribe as much as one hundred witnesses of ours, therefore in our matter as well we will trust the scribe. And what have we to do with unfit witnesses, because of consanguinity or some other defect? . . . When it is written by a notary who is appointed by the King or by the Gentile courts, we validate the document, as in their law it is valid, for we rely upon the trustworthiness of the scribe, that he would not deliberately lie, or upon [the rule that] the law of the land is law.' See also ibid., sects. 54 and 60, and R. Joshua Boaz, *Shilṭei ha-Gibborim*, on R. Isaac Alfasi's code, to Bava Batra 71a. (I wish to thank Prof. S. Shilo for bringing this source to my attention.)

145 For Italy during the period under consideration, see the discussion of R. Abraham del Vecchio in Document 50 in the Hebrew edition of this book.

in which a formal halakhic defect in the drawing up of the document is found, what are the possibilities of validating it on halakhic grounds, given that it is valid according to Gentile law? Behind such discussions there always lurked, in practice, the shadow of the Gentile magistrates: in the final analysis, all those who wished to validate halakhically deficient documents proposed, by means of a halakhic argument, essentially to accept the non-Jewish law regarding them, while those who wished to disqualify them did so on the grounds of the presumption that one may not apply Samuel's rule, 'the law of the land is the law', in such cases. In all of these cases, one can sense the confrontation of Jewish law with non-Jewish law in a society which wished to live in accordance with *halakhah*, but was subject to Christian judicial bodies. Jewish law, Christian authority, social pressures, the socio-political views of the scholars, and of course individual interests—all contributed to the overall picture. The problem of documents which were invalid under Jewish law but valid under Christian law was but one aspect of a wider set of problems, in which Jewish law openly contradicted the laws accepted in Christian courts. Thus, there was a serious argument concerning a certain dowry document drawn up in Gentile courts which did not contain the phrase required in order to make non-Jewish practice valid according to Jewish law, i.e. 'to collect it according to the local custom'. It was asked whether the woman could still collect her dowry on the basis of this document during her husband's lifetime, 'as was the custom'.[146] The leading figure among those answering in the affirmative was R. Baruch Chazachetto of Ferrara, who argued in defence of this custom,[147] citing a statement in the Responsa of R. Isaac ben Sheshet Perfet (*Ribash*, 1326–1408), sect. 102, concerning the collection of the *ẓadak* during the husband's lifetime.[148] The leading opponent

[146] See 'Teshuvot R. Moshe Provenzali', sects. 85, 96, 97; *Teshuvot Matanot ba-Adam*, sect. 123. In addition to R. Moses Provenzali and R. Baruch Chazachetto, there also participated in this controversy R. Eli'ezer Ashkenazi, R. Aaron Norlingen, R. Phineas of Melli, R. Seligman Ḥefetz, and R. Azriel Trabot.

[147] 'For this was the custom of the generations from the beginning, also to be saved there from the kingdom and the other duties of the Gentiles.' Attention must also be given to the secondary consideration, which reflects a definite political and social outlook which clearly influenced the rabbi-decisor in the course of arriving at his decision.

[148] On ben Sheshet's approach generally, and the question of the *ẓadak* in this context in particular, see Shilo's discussion, *Dina de-Malkhuta Dina*, 346–8.

was R. Moses Provenzali, supported by R. Eli'ezer Ashkenazi,[149] who adhered to the principle that one must rule only according to Jewish law. Without discussing the halakhic argument *per se*, it seems clear that we find here indirectly a renewal of the discussion concerning the general rule of 'the law of the land is law'. Provenzali states this explicitly at the end of his responsum: 'Also because of the principle that "the law of the land is law", we are not to abandon the presumption that this rule applies only in cases pertaining to the 'interest of the King', but not in matters between man and his fellow [i.e. *between two Jewish litigants*].'[150] Even a superficial glance at the collections of responsa of Italian rabbis will reveal to the reader a wide range of similar cases.[151]

One of the immediate results of this situation was the emergence of a practice whereby documents were drawn up in the presence of the local Jewish scribe in order to prevent formal halakhic violations.[152] When a dispute on this point nevertheless arose, the sages did not hesitate to reinterpret the statements of earlier authorities in a manner which conformed to their own approach, using the general formula (which leaves wide latitude for interpretation): 'In our day the rule, "the law of the land is law", does not apply to matters regarding documents presented before non-Jewish courts.'[153] Thus, we discover here at least one

[149] It is perhaps not superfluous to add that R. Eli'ezer Ashkenazi mentioned in every case the fact that he was among the descendants of R. Joseph Colon, 'his grandfather'.

[150] 'Teshuvot R. Moshe Provenzali', fo. 94b.

[151] e.g. in *Teshuvot Matanot ba-Adam*, sect. 297, a question is asked concerning a will drawn up in Gentile courts by a Christian scribe, the validity of which was questioned by several of the beneficiaries, 'saying that it was not performed in accordance with *halakhah* and the ordinances of the rabbis'.

[152] Thus, R. Azriel Trabot tells us of an individual in Mantua who, 'because of his anxiety concerning death, by means of the scribe of the city [i.e. *the Christian notary*] and by the "scribe of the place" [i.e., *the Jewish communal scribe*], and in the presence of nine witnesses, all of them [gathered] in the Gentiles' court', ordered a certain sum to be given to each of his sons and left his wife as 'generally the heir of all of his remaining property; and if this wording shall be invalid if formulated in language of inheritance, he annotated this command by saying that he would give everything to his wife, using the wording of gift' (*Teshuvot R. Azriel Trabot*, sect. 26, p. 57b). See also n. 151.

[153] See the afore-mentioned passage from the Responsa of R. Azriel Trabot, in *Teshuvot Matanot ba-Adam*, sect. 309: 'the Gentile courts are considered as a judge appointed by the king; therefore, we do not draw up our documents in the Gentile courts at all, for such are entirely invalid. How much more so [is this true, considering] what R. Asher and many other authorities wrote, that today [the rule] "the law of the land is law" does not apply in matters of documents of non-Jews.' Prof. S. Shilo pointed out to me that in fact R. Asher nowhere said that the rule, 'the law of the land is law', does not apply to documents. It follows from this that, if the sense of R. Azriel's interpretation of R.

interesting development: it seems that, when the accepted custom was to present documents in Gentile courts, there developed the practice, in order to safeguard Jewish law, of including a Jewish scribe in the drafting of the document in the Gentile court, to reduce the conflict between Jewish and Gentile law as far as possible. There is no doubt that the legal and halakhic aspects of these developments merit serious study.

8. Some Reflections on the Responsa of Italian Rabbis during the Renaissance

Rabbinic rulings being among the very foundations of Jewish law, even within the limited orbit described here, a few remarks concerning the characteristic tendencies of the responsa of Italian sages during this period seem in place here.[154] I will attempt to describe certain very general, overall tendencies appearing in these responsa, particularly in terms of methodology and formal structure, which may indicate a certain specific development. This issue has not drawn much attention from scholars, with the notable exception of Isaiah Sonne.

In dealing with the system used by Italian sages of the Renaissance in writing their halakhic rulings, Isaiah Sonne attempted to distinguish 'three characteristics of the responsa of the Italian sages during the Renaissance', corresponding to three characteristics 'in relation to Aristotelianism'.[155] Upon reading what Sonne wrote on this subject, one cannot avoid the impression

Asher's words is that there is a general disqualification of such documents, and not only that contemporary Gentile courts are not proper 'Gentile courts' according to Jewish law, then his ruling requires further examination. However, in this case we are speaking specifically of a grant document; that being the case, it does not seem to be the intention to invalidate *all* documents which are drawn up in Gentile courts. Anyhow, this general formulation requires further study.

[154] It is of course not my intention in the present context to analyse various halakhic works and to clarify different halakhic approaches, nor to explain the effect of historical circumstances upon the different kinds of halakhic responses of the various sages to the problems presented here—each one according to his own outlook and as the result of his own thought. A comprehensive monograph devoted to the major personalities and works which marked the halakhic creativity in Italy throughout this period remains to be written, nor has there yet been a systematic publication of the collections of responsa from the period.

[155] See I. Sonne, 'On the History of the Community of Bologna at the Beginning of the 16th Century' (Heb.), *HUCA* 6 (1942), 53–5.

that he was heavily conditioned by his characteristic tendency to establish didactic schemes, on the one hand, and by his attraction to that creative spirit which he saw as the authentic and deep-rooted spirit of the Italian Jews, on the other.[156] In any event, Sonne apparently did not examine this question in depth, so that his statements on this subject, based as they are primarily upon his own personal impressions, were largely subjective. Elsewhere, Sonne has discussed the nature of halakhic studies in Italy during this period on the basis of bibliographical information.[157] There, too, he established elaborate schematic structures, founded primarily upon the ethnic differences within the Jewish population. The danger entailed in presenting things in such a schematic manner is obvious.[158] Sonne discusses all these matters at considerable length, including numerous bibliographical questions in the development of his theory and its related offshoots, requiring fundamental clarification which we cannot undertake here. He was nevertheless correct in noting the need for an explanation for the change that occurred in the writing of responsa and in pointing to the significance of this change. However, the very definition of the change itself is not clear, as the entire question, both of the means of issuing halakhic rulings and the means of writing responsa, still requires study and explanation—and not only with regard to those of the Italian scholars.[159] Moreover, at times the stress upon change and transformation may be dictated by the need of historians to seek

156 Thus e.g. Sonne combined together 'the remnants of the medieval school, with all the barbarity of their presentation', with the world of the majority of Ashkenazic scholars of Italy, whom he saw as distinguished for 'the lack of imagination and breadth in their thought' and the 'slackness of their presentation', ibid. 55.

157 I. Sonne, 'Excursions into History and Bibliography' (Heb.), *Alexander Marx Jubilee Volume* (New York, 1950), Hebrew Section, 209 ff.

158 e.g. after stating that the *Sefer Miẓvot ha-Gadol* was the favoured work of the French scholars (ibid. p. 211), he explained its disappearance by means of a second statement: 'the influence of the French circles gradually diminished, so that their influence is barely noticeable' (p. 217). However, he fails to explain such facts as that the importance of R. Moses Basola was as great as that of R. Meir of Padua during the 1560s, being perceived by Christian eyes as 'the Pope of the Jews' (see I. Tishby, 'The Controversy Concerning *Sefer ha-Zohar*', in *Yesodei Kabbalah u-Sheluḥoteha*, i (Jerusalem, 1982), 96–99), or that the rabbis from the Trabot family of France were among the foremost scholars throughout the century, and many other facts. We will dicuss the role of the *Sema"g* further.

159 On the form of Ashkenazic responsa during the 15th century, practised also in Italy, see, to date, Y. A. Dinari, *Ḥakhmei Ashkenaz be-Shilhei yemei ha-Benayim* (Jerusalem, 1984), 229–50.

changes in order to tell their story, even where in fact stability and continuity are clearly dominant features. In any case, there is no doubt that further research on this subject is sorely needed. I will try to make here a small contribution to that research, focusing, on the one hand, on the methodological-structural area and, on the other hand, on the realm of form and content.

Was Sonne correct in seeking parallels to a certain type of responsa and ruling of the Italian scholars of the Renaissance in the intellectual world of scholasticism? At first glance, there would seem to be some basis to his argument, at least as a working hypothesis. Apart from such rulings as those of R. Abraham ha-Kohen, published by Sonne himself,[160] where the scholastic structure is striking, one may doubtless point to other similar rulings, such as R. David b. Messer Leon's *Kevod Ḥakhamim* and R. Vitale da Pisa's *Ma'amar Ḥayyei 'Olam*.

The essential feature of the system is that the halakhic ruling is structured like a scholastic lecture,[161] i.e. opening with a presentation of the definitions necessary for a discussion of the subject; followed by 'introductions' or 'preambles' to the discussion itself, presenting the axioms;[162] then the division of the subject *ab initio* into well-defined sections; and finally the derivation of the conclusions in each section by means of analogy through the use of the axiomatic 'introductions'.[163] To make this point more clearly, I shall briefly quote here some remarks of R. Vitale (Jeḥiel Nissim) da Pisa (d. 1490), made in the course of discussing questions related to lending money on interest, concerning the method of *pesak*:

It is imperative for the complete understanding of any matter to examine the factors and origins, just as one examines the foundations of a building in order to acquire true knowledge. Consequently, we must study the fundamental factors of our problem and search back to its origins. This is all clear from the science of logical inquiry. Therefore, in this inquiry, it is my intention, in examining the prohibition against

160 See Sonne, 'The Community of Bologna'.

161 In the words of R. David b. Messer Leon, *Kevod Ḥakhamim*, 28: 'according to the order of speculative and comprehensive learning.'

162 Such as the 25 propositions found in the Introduction to Book Two of Maimoides' *Guide for the Perplexed*.

163 i.e. if the sentence contained in the introduction is true, it is sufficient to establish that the subject under discussion is identical or similar to that described in the introduction; thereby, the sentence contained in the introduction is also applicable to the subject under discussion.

interest, to cite the principles and sources of the matter which are indispensible for our exposition of the problem. Only the stubborn or foolish person can refute these arguments, and it is futile to debate with such people. For whosoever does not know the origin of a matter will surely not understand its consequences, but whoever knows the true origins, will come to the proper conclusions. Therefore, we shall, by way of introduction, offer two introductory statements . . .[164]

His two introductory remarks are:

first, that whosoever goes by the name of an Israelite and enters the religion of Moses, of blessed memory, is consequently obliged to observe the positive and the negative commandments of the Torah.[165] . . . Second, that the matter of lending on interest between one Jew and another is prohibited by the Torah. It is impossible to refute this and it has been explained explicitly in the section of *Mishpaṭim*, and in *Be-Har Sinai* and in *Ki Teẓe* [i.e. *Exod. 22: 24*, *Lev. 25: 35–8*, *and Deut. 23: 20 -1*].[166]

Following these two prefatory remarks, he continues:

it follows that every Jew is obliged to refrain from taking interest from his fellow Jew . . . We know that, in general, whoever enters the fold of the Torah of Moses must beware of taking interest from a fellow Jew, since it is one of the negative commandments. It is customary, after ascertaining the general rule, to deal with the particulars, for that is true knowledge. We must explain in detail the various kinds of interest, how many there are, which are Biblically prohibited, and which were prohibited by the sages by way of precaution . . .[167]

The subject is then divided into several sections: (1) interest according to Torah law; (2) 'dust' of interest; (3) circumvention of the prohibition against interest.

The true knowledge of anything depends upon the understanding of the definition of the subject, due to the fact that it is the definition that differentiates and distinguishes one thing from another. By that means, we can arrive at true knowledge of anything, and since true definitions depend upon the general qualities and the individual qualities that distinguish one thing from another, it is important for us to define carefully Biblical intent . . .[168]

[164] J. Nissim da Pisa, *Ma'amar Ḥaye 'Olam 'al 'Inyan Ribit* (New York, 1962), 12; English trans. 43.
[165] Ibid. [166] Ibid. 15, Eng. trans. 47–8. [167] Ibid. Eng. trans. 48.
[168] Ibid. 16, Engl. trans: 48–9).

He continues by enumerating and defining all of the different kinds of interest, discussing each one separately. I have quoted R. Vitale da Pisa's remarks at some length because they are a striking illustration of this systematic tendency, adhered to fanatically both when necessary and not. Otherwise, it would be difficult to understand the need this scholar felt for prefacing his halakhic discussion with the statement that every Jew is required to observe the commandments of the Torah!

On the other hand, the halakhic rulings of R. Abraham ha-Kohen show no sign whatsoever of this scholastic structure.[169] His rulings are similar in every respect to those of the Ashkenazic and French scholars in Italy, such as R. Azriel Diena and others. Is there a dichotomy here, rooted in the difference in subjects? Or does this difference reflect the influence of Ashkenazic learning, which superseded other traditions? Or were the rulings written in a scholastic structure perhaps the final remnants of a more widespread mode of thought, which became progressively weaker (as we shall discuss in detail in the following chapter)? In any event, it seems to me that one may conclusively state that towards the end of the sixteenth century the 'scholastic' form of halakhic writing no longer appears. For this reason, I tend to accept the third of the above possibilities as that closest to the truth.

Even among the scholars of the Ashkenazic and French schools, who had a decisive influence on the halakhic world of northern Italy, one finds a certain change in the character of their responsa towards the end of the period of the Renaissance. The long and tiresome dialectical argumentation (*pilpul*), which in previous generations had characterized the responsa of these scholars, became rarer and rarer during this period, and gradually began to disappear entirely. Was this an indication of a diminished skill? Or was it but one aspect of a more general change in the intellectual life of the times, in which interest was transferred from one sphere to another? It seems to me that the latter is the case, a point to which we will return both in this chapter and the next.

In terms of both form and contents, Maimonides' *Mishneh Torah* lost the pre-eminence which it had enjoyed until the middle of the fifteenth century, together with the rapid spread of the

[169] Such as those found in *Pesakim* (Venice, 1519).

influence of R. Jacob b. Asher's *Arba'ah Ṭurim*, which was heavily relied upon for practical halakhic rulings. The latter fact hardly needs to be proven. Sonne has already noted that, beginning in the fifteenth century, numerous manuscripts of the *Ṭurim* appear in Italy 'written in all sorts of scripts: Ashkenazic, Italian, Sephardic, and Provencal'.[170] This statement is confirmed by the list, published in Freimann's pioneering work,[171] of scribes who worked in Italy during the fifteenth century, particularly during the latter half of the century; many additional examples may be gleaned by perusal of the catalogues of various libraries throughout the world.[172] Yet precisely the appearance of manuscripts 'written in all sorts of scripts' leads one to question Sonne's statement drawing a direct causal connection between the 'migration of the first Ashkenazic printers from the circle of R. Judah Minz at the end of the fifteenth century' and the introduction and dissemination of the *Ṭurim* in Italy.[173] Not only did the appearance of the *Ṭurim* precede the coming of these printers by a significant period of time, but the attitude towards the *Ṭurim* of the Ashkenazic scholars of the generation of R. Judah Minz and those who preceded him has not yet been fully explained or clarified. On the one hand, Minz's testimony may be accepted at face value—namely, that precisely in his circle 'there are rabbis who do not even wish to read the *Ṭur Oraḥ Ḥayyim* [i.e. *the section of the Ṭurim dealing with daily prayer observances, Sabbath, and festivals*], claiming that the householders [i.e. *the non-learned people*] study it'.[174] On the other hand, R. Joseph Colon's responsa are filled with references to the *Ṭurim*; he hardly wrote a single responsum in which this code is not cited. One need hardly add that there is something over-simplistic in Sonne's tendency to present his discussion in terms of 'a kind of competition between the writers [following] and the printers of

170 Sonne, 'Excursions', 210.

171 See A. Freimann, 'Jewish Scribes in Medieval Italy', in *Alexander Marx Jubilee Volume* (New York, 1950), English Section, 294, no. 305 (written in 1440); 29, no. 322a (1472); 259, no. 112a–c (1474–9); 323, no. 488 (1476–83); 284, no. 246f (1478); 309, no. 402 (1478–9).

172 e.g. MS Vatican Ebr. 555 IX 245 (written in Mantua in 1335); MS Parma 64 (written in Ferrara, 1459); MS Vatican Ebr. 442 (written before 1467); MS Bodleian 708 (written in Piacenza, 1479); MS London 546 (written in Carpi, 1492); MS Bodleian 697 (Ancona, 1494), and others.

173 Sonne, 'Excursions', 210.

174 R. Judah Minz, *Pesakim u-She'elot u-Teshuvot* (Venice, 1553), 30b.

Maimonides, on the one hand, and the writers [following] and the printers of the *Ṭurim*, on the other,'[175] until Soncino came and 'mixed the boundary lines . . . publishing Maimonides, the *Semag* [*R. Moses of Coucy's Sefer Miẓvot ha-Gadol*] and the *Ṭurim* together, and weaving them into a triple-threaded band',[176] the situation thereafter continuing under the sign of that same 'confusion'. True, nobody would seriously doubt that any discussion of the history of culture from the time of Gutenberg must closely relate to the influence of printing. But even if we grant that the influence of the printers was very prominent and at times decisive in conditioning public opinion on the level of popular literature, it seems to me that their influence was far less in the realm of 'professional' literature, aimed at circles of scholars and those close to them. In this area, perhaps far more than in the field of popular literature, the 'consumer' was the one who had the decisive voice in determining whether a book was worth printing, especially in the light of the considerable financial investment entailed. The printing of a small book such as *The King and the Nazirite* cannot be compared to the printing of works of broad scope, such as the *Mishneh Torah*, the *Ṭurim*, or even *Sefer Miẓvot ha-Gadol*. We must therefore attempt, first of all, to understand the more complex picture of the world of scholarship and only afterwards turn to the history of the printing of books.

Throughout nearly the entire period under discussion here, the situation was dominated by a far-reaching and multi-faceted phenomenon: namely, the question of the role of the *Mishneh Torah* in halakhic ruling. Maimonides' critical spirit, drawing upon the world of philosophy, certainly left its impression in this area also. But if the weak points in his philosophical writings were easily picked up by his critics,[177] in the realm of *halakhah* the picture was far more complex. Many and diverse forces—whose weight and influence have not yet been fully determined, despite the many studies which have been devoted to this subject—played a role here.[178] Beginning with the very pointed

[175] Sonne, 'Excursions', 219. [176] Ibid. 212. [177] On this point see Ch. 6.

[178] See Y. Z. Kahane, 'The Controversy Concerning the Deciding of Halakhah in Accordance with Maimonides' (Heb.), *Sinai*, 36–8 (1955–6), *passim* (reprinted in the collection, *Hara"m Bamza"l, Kovez Torani Mada'i*, ed. Y. L. Maimon (Jerusalem, 1955), 215–45); I. J. Dienstag, 'The Attitude of the Tosafists to Maimonides' (Heb.), *Sefer Yovel le-khivod Shmuel Kalman Mirsky* (New York, 1958), 350–79.

criticisms in the glosses of R. Abraham b. David of Posquières (*Rabad*; *c.* 1125–98); continuing with the formal criticism summarized by the thirteenth-century authority, R. Moses of Coucy, in his introduction to the *Sefer Mizvot ha-Gadol* as to the absence of source references in the *Mishneh Torah*—to the extent that everyone 'may rule from his books and seek from him written proof . . . that will be for him like a dream without solution'; concluding with the rejection by R. Asher of Maimonides' rulings wherever he disagrees with R. Isaac b. Samuel of Dampierre (*ha-R"I ha-Zaken*; thirteenth century) and R. Jacob Tam (*c.* 1100–71), the two pillars of the Franco-German Tosaphistic school, as expressed in R. Asher's comment cited by R. Solomon Luria (*Maharshal*, 1510?–74)[179] that 'it is a tradition accepted by R. Asher that R. Tam and R. Isaac of France were greater in wisdom and in number [i.e. *possessed greater authority* than Maimonides'—one constantly encounters attempts to clarify the question of the place of the *Mishneh Torah* in halakhic rulings. Perhaps no other issue better exemplifies the tension introduced into the spiritual world of that generation by the conflict between the great respect for Maimonides' writings, on the one hand, and the vitality of the traditions and interpretations which were opposed to it, on the other hand. From the viewpoint of R. Joseph Colon, it would seem that:

> Among all the halakhic authorities, there is none clearer than R. Moses; and even if his proofs were not stated, many have interpreted his words . . . And if in some places one may challenge his conclusions on the basis of the approach of the Talmud, [this is because] we in our poverty are unable to find the solution, but if our Rabbi [i.e. *Maimonides*] were before us, he would open for us an entrance even wider than the gate of a palace.[180]

Clear evidence of the powerful clash of traditions and customs in Italy along these lines appears in two edicts issued by Messer Leon in 1455,[181] pertaining to certain details of the laws of

[179] In the introduction to Bava Kamma and Ḥullin; see also the remarks by Kahane, 'Deciding of Halakhah', 228 n. 99.

[180] Colon, *Teshuvot Mahar"ik*, Responsum 121.

[181] See Ch. 2, Sect. 2. In an essay that appeared after this book was completed, I attempted to demonstrate that this date should probably be corrected to 1475. See R. Bonfil, 'Introduction to *Nofet Zufim*' (Jerusalem, 1981).

menstruation and purification.[182] These ordinances, which were intended to alter the previous custom practised by Italian Jews in the direction of greater strictness, bringing it into line with Franco-German practice, touched upon one of the most intimate areas in the life of every Jewish family, and was reinforced by the imposition of the ban upon those who violated it. In other words, these ordinances were intended to bring about a minor revolution in the life of the Italian Jewish family, based upon the rulings of Ashkenazic and French authorities, beginning with the *Sefer ha-Terumah* by R. Baruch b. Isaac of Worms (late twelfth to early thirteenth centuries), and ending with the *Ṭur*, from which he copied an entire sentence in the second edict. It was not merely a matter of chance that Maimonides' opinion was not adduced in either of these two ordinances. When R. Joseph Colon was asked to express his opinion of these ordinances,[183] he stated his theoretical agreement with their halakhic foundations, which were based upon the opinion of the French and Ashkenazic sages mentioned there, and even noted that, in view of the rulings of R. Asher and his son, the author of the *Ṭurim*, these things had spread 'also into Ashkenaz and France . . . and so was the custom in all the French Diaspora'.[184] He nevertheless disagreed with Messer Leon's step in practice, for:

> It is in any event obvious that we may not prevent those places and regions which are accustomed to be lenient in this matter, following the words of . . . our teachers the *ge'onim* and of Maimonides. For even though it is doubtless fitting that anyone who is a God-fearing person ought to be strict about this matter . . . it is clear that one should not heap abuse upon those who are lenient, because they have followed this custom in those regions since ancient times . . . and particularly in this matter in which there are many opinions . . . for in all of Italy, they are accustomed to follow the practice of Maimonides . . . and certainly we are unable to stop them.[185]

[182] In *Divrei Rivot*, 1, he ruled that the 'seven clean days' were not to begin until five days following the last incident of marital intercourse; the effect of this ruling was to increase the period of menstrual separation between husband and wife to a minimum of twelve days. He likewise ruled that women were allowed to clean their hair during the daytime, but were to wait until evening to perform the ritual immersion in the *mikveh*—again, a stricter ruling following Ashkenazic practice.

[183] Colon, *Teshuvot Mahari"k ha-Ḥadashim*, 49.

[184] Ibid. 231. [185] Ibid. 249.

Thus, R. Joseph Colon indirectly agreed with Messer Leon's opponent, R. Benjamin of Montalcino[186] (despite his severe criticism of the latter for his polemical style and form of expression). R. Benjamin saw these edicts as a deviation 'from the approach of our master R. Moses ben Maimon, for from what we hear the Italians always turn only to him'.[187] The reference to the *Ṭurim* in the context of this controversy is very significant, and Messer Leon's error in copying from it served as a convenient object for R. Benjamin's attack: 'and if it pleased our loyal friend to follow the words of the *Ṭurim*, why did he add to them and say that it was a general agreement? And if he wished to copy his words verbatim, why did he not copy them as they are, for rather than "so that they not become confused" (*yitbalbelu*) he wrote "that they not become soiled" (*yitlakhelekhu*).'[188]

Echoes of this controversy concerning ritual immersion could still be heard at the end of the sixteenth century, as we learn from R. Leone Modena's responsa.[189] From this, we may infer that the change in the halakhic atmosphere began with the confrontation between the leaders of Ashkenazic and French Jewry and those of the local Italian community, even though the latter did not necessarily follow Maimonides in all of their practices. Another rabbi involved in this controversy, R. Joseph Treves,[190] explicitly emphasized, while mentioning those customs which were contrary to Maimonides:

All the people . . . follow the custom of their ancestors as Torah, based upon those authorities who are accepted among them . . . Will any Jew come to mockery and to shame because of several lenient rulings which we follow against the opinion of some other authorities, such as cooking the meat of the brain, which Maimonides prohibited, or using the fat which is on the abdomen underneath the skin, which according to

[186] See his remarks in *Divrei Rivot*, 1.

[187] *Teshuvot Mahari"k ha-Ḥadashim*, 240.

[188] *Divrei Rivot*, 6.

[189] 'During the rabbinate in the community of Venice of the Gaon R. Zilmelen, of blessed memory, he instructed the women to go to the bathhouse during the daytime, and would rebuke and send home whomever went at night; but after he passed away, when the Gaon R. [Samuel] Judah [Katzenellenbogen] served in his stead, he did not prevent them from going at night.' *Teshuvot Ziknei Yehudah*, ed. Simonsohn, sect. 4, p. 11; also printed in *Kitvei R. Yehudah Aryeh mi-Modenah*, ed. Y. Blau (Budapest, 1906), sect. 10, p. 12.

[190] See N. Brüll, 'Das Geschlecht der Treves', *Jahrbücher für jüdische Geschichte und Literatur*, 1 (1874), 100.

R. Yakir [*one of the Tosafists*] falls under the rubric of prohibited animal fats?[191]

However, as the majority of the Italian customs conformed with Maimonides, as we have already stated, we find that the confrontation between customs indirectly affected the status of Maimonides' rulings as well.

The process itself was a long and protracted one, affected by a variety of factors; it is doubtful whether we can enumerate them all. Among the major factors was that of the personalities of the scholars involved and their approach to problems. As we have seen, the approach of R. Joseph Colon differed from that of Messer Leon, even though the two agreed in practice. An additional factor was that of personal prestige and self-image among the sages who took part in the debates, as well as in their influence upon the public—and it need not be said that the decisive majority of rabbinic scholars in Italy during this period were French and Ashkenazic.[192] One should also add to this the strength or weakness of the particular custom under discussion; the presence or absence of a tradition of halakhic rulings of a specific ethnic-local character, as well as the sensitivity of the scholars to the question of customs;[193] the sensitivity of the public to the questions under discussion, and the changes which it sought to introduce into the community's way of life in light

[191] *Divrei Rivot*, 10.

[192] Cf. Shulvass, 'The Study of Torah', 106–8.

[193] R. Azriel Diena was 'greatly astonished'; 'I cannot understand it, for his Honour [i.e. *the author of the responsum on which he is commenting*] is a French scholar, and the mourner [*who was the subject of the question at hand*] is also a Frenchman. How then could you have abandoned the opinion of our French scholars, and particularly ought not we, who are their descendants, to pay them honour and not to refute their teachings?' (Sonne, 'The Community of Bologna', 50). Cf. *Teshuvot Mahari"k*, Responsa 144: 'It was the custom of the Italians that a woman not immerse herself in the ritual bath during the first forty days following the birth of a male, or the first eighty following the birth of a female, even if she did not discharge blood [i.e. *throughout that period of time*].' The question is specifically asked there because the local custom, based upon the *Sefer ha-Tanya*, 'by whom the Italians do everything', was opposed to the ruling of Maimonides, and some authorities wished to reject it because 'we build our foundations upon our master Moses'. R. Joseph Colon's view was that 'one is not to protest against the Italians, for they behaved thus as a stringency and a fence [i.e. *around the Law*], and it is based upon some precedent—that is, that authority whom the Italians are in the habit of following'. See also Document 61, p. 281, in the Hebrew edition of this book. It may be added that, to this very day, in many places in Italy women are accustomed to refrain from going to the synagogue following childbirth for a period of 40 days for a boy and 80 days for a girl.

of the outcome of their discussions;[194] the skill of the scholars in their attempts to 'harmonize views' by means of *pilpul*;[195] the extent to which the particular sages respected Maimonides, and the consequences of this for the nature of the discussions of 'comparing his opinions' with that of those opposed to him—a subject which clearly left its mark upon the philosophical 'background' of the rabbis. In any event, *Mishneh Torah* continued to be studied in Italy.[196] Clear evidence of this is to be seen in the many beautiful and elaborate editions of the *Yad* which were published during this period.[197]

What we have said concerning the confrontation between the *Mishneh Torah* and other authorities, primarily those in the Ashkenazic world, applies to some extent also to the *Hilkhot ha-Rif*, the halakhic compendium of the eleventh-century North

[194] It is perhaps interesting to add that R. Gur Aryeh ha-Levi, many generations after the controversy of Messer Leon, still cited, in his glosses to *Shulḥan 'Arukh* (Mantua, 1721–3), *Yoreh De'ah* 196: 11, the views of those who opposed R. Joseph Caro and supported that of the *Ṭurim* on the question of the timing of post-menstrual purification. He himself made no decisive ruling on the matter.

[195] According to the testimony of R. David b. Messer Leon, intellectual effort in the Ashkenazic *yeshivot* in Italy was focused upon dialectical novellae, based upon the commentaries *Hagahot Maimoniot* and *Mordekhai* (see *Kevod Ḥakhamim*, 79–80, 101–2) as well as on the *Tosafot* and *Sefer Mizvot ha-Gadol* (*Kevod Ḥakhamim*, 129–30; and see further). As most of the discussions of *Hagahot Maimoniot* quoted in his book are copied nearly verbatim from *Teshuvot Mahari"k* (see above, Ch. 2, Sect. 6), then the conclusion that R. David applied to himself in the various matters was also true of the yeshivah of R. Joseph Colon and his circle. On Ashkenazic *pilpul* in Italy, see Shulvass, 'The Study of Torah', 107; on *pilpul* in Ashkenazic *yeshivot* generally, see M. Breuer, 'The Growth of *Pilpul* and *Ḥilluk*' (Heb.), *Sefer Zikaron le-Morenu . . . Y. Y. Weinberg* (Jerusalem, 1970); H. Z. Dimitrovsky, 'On the Method of Pilpul' (Heb.), *Salo Wittmayer Baron Jubilee Volume*, Heb. Sect., iii (Jerusalem, 1975). It is unnecessary to add that, in the process of 'harmonization of views', the Italian rabbis saw themselves as obliged to take into consideration the opinions of indigenous Italian scholars as well, such as R. Isaiah of Trani (see *Kevod Ḥakhamim*, 43–6), and especially those books which were primarily devoted to customs, such as R. Zedekiah min ha-'Anavim, *Shibbolei ha-Leket*, 'which is a book written to strengthen our custom, the custom of the Italians, for this sage was from Rome, and was an outstanding authority' (ibid. 39). On the importance of the study of *Shibbolei ha-Leket* and *Sefer ha-Tanya* among Italian Jews, see Shulvass, 'The Study of Torah', 106–7, 117; idem, 'Religious Life', *PAAJR* 17 (1947), 14–15. To the Ashkenazic *pilpul*, one should add the method of discussion of the Sephardic sages, found in *Ḥiddushei ha-Ramban* (cf. *Kevod Ḥakhamim*, 129), although no Spanish sages of the first rank settled in Italy, so that the impact of their method of study was not felt.

[196] See the sources cited by Shulvass, 'The Study of Torah', 120. I can personally attest that, in my own childhood in Italy, my earliest exposure to the study of *halakhah* was through an edition, worn with use, of the first three sections of Maimonides' code (*Mada'—Ahavah—Zemanim*).

[197] See now J. Dienstag, 'Maimonides' *Mishneh Torah*—A Bibliography' (Heb.), *Sefer Yovel li-khevod Yizḥak Kiov* (New York, 1972), 21–41.

African authority, R. Isaac Alfasi (1013–1103)[198] which, after the arrival of the Ashkenazim, was generally bound together with the *Sefer Mordekhai*. Even if Maimonides' statement as to the small number of rulings of R. Alfasi with which he disagreed—'and they certainly do not exceed ten in number in any event'[199]—is not literally true, his differences with *Rif* are probably limited to about thirty *in toto*.[200] Nevertheless, Alfasi was less exposed to criticism because of the character of his work, which was a kind of abbreviated version of the Talmud, containing only those laws applicable in our day, and largely eliminating those legal discussions and debates which are extraneous to the actual legal ruling. In Italy, this work was generally studied together with R. Joshua Boaz's commentary *Shilṭei ha-Gibborim* (Shield of the Mighty), along with the rulings of other authorities commenting upon Alfasi, particularly the novellae of R. Isaiah of Trani.[201]

We thus discover a complex, open, and far-reaching confrontation, revealed sharply in the realm of custom, but not only there. This process deserves study in its own right, a study which certainly cannot be undertaken here. In any event, the challenge to the pre-eminence enjoyed by the *Mishneh Torah* in previous generations symbolizes, more than a diminishing of its importance, an intense process of ferment and an expansion of halakhic horizons. The dissemination of the *Ṭurim* and the reliance upon it for practical rulings must also be seen within this framework, although there were also additional factors which brought about a situation in which, by the end of the period under discussion, the *Ṭurim* had acquired a position of prominence, which it later

[198] Cf. the remarks of R. Joseph Colon at the beginning of Responsum 52: 'I found it written that, wherever there is a dispute between great men, one follows [R. Isaac] Alfasi when the *Tosafot* does not disagree with him. Regarding this, you wrote that the *Tosafot* is indeed the final authority, and we have nothing but their words . . . However, I would not infer from what you wrote concerning this point that one may in fact follow them to take a lenient position [even] in Torah law . . . On the contrary, one might say that, although when they disagree with Rav Alfasi we must take account of this, in that we are then uncertain whom the *halakhah* follows [e.g. *we would reject a lenient ruling of Alfasi if there were a stringent one of Tosafot*], we do not necessarily say that we must follow them for the [actual] halakhic ruling in the way we rely upon Rav Alfasi . . .' See also 'Teshuvot Mahara"m mi-Padua', sect. 71, fo. 106b: 'And the words of R. Alfasi are established precedents for fixing the *halakhah*, as R. Meir has written . . . for it is our practice to follow him whenever the *Tosafot* are not in disagreement.'

[199] See the *Mishnah* with Maimonides' commentary, ed. J. Kapah (Jerusalem, 1963), *Seder Zera'im*, 47.

[200] See S. Shefer, *Ha-Rif u-Mishnato* (Jerusalem, 1967), 106 n. 29.

[201] Ibid. 99.

shared with R. Joseph Caro's (1488–1575) commentary *Bet Yosef*, following the widespread printing of the *Ṭurim* together with the *Bet Yosef*. The particular character of this book, which does not deal with any laws except those applicable at the time,[202] and which was rooted in the practices of both Ashkenazic and French Jewry[203] as well as those of the the Sephardim,[204] made it popular among Jews who studied in the synagogue and elsewhere,[205] together with the *Semag* which, even though used in the *yeshivot* as well, was primarily studied in synagogues.[206] An additional factor contributing to the popularity of the *Ṭurim* was the time factor—that is to say, the status of the *Ṭurim* as the more recent authority increased the authority of its rulings.[207]

To these immanent factors mentioned above may be added one more point: the gradual decline of the tendency to engage in dialectic analyses, paralleled by the growing inclination to study the earlier authorities (*rishonim*) and to rule according to the more recent authority. This phenomenon was reinforced by analogous tendencies in the civil law in Europe, as well as by the spread of Kabbalah. In fact, it has been established that there was a clear inclination in the development of Church law, and of civil law in its wake, to turn directly to the original sources in Roman law, in contrast to the earlier tendency which stressed the

[202] See the remarks of Sonne, 'Excursions', 219–20.

[203] An examination of the influence of the literature concerning customs upon Ashkenazic rulings in those generations is likely also to clarify the process of the spread of the *Ṭurim* among the Ashkenazic sages. This is not the place for such a clarification, but see Dinari, *Ḥakhmei Ashkenaz*, 165–9.

[204] See A. Freimann, 'Die Ascheriden', *JJLG* 13 (1920), 191–204.

[205] See the remarks of R. Judah Minz cited in this section, and those of R. David b. Messer Leon cited in the following note.

[206] See *Kevod Ḥakhamim*, 78: 'How much more so those who study every day in the synagogue the rulings of R. Jacob, the author of the *Ṭurim*, by thorough memorization and pilpul, that is, in a way similar to the Talmud; even according to them, who say that they have not heard anything like it in all Spain . . . and even though the ruling unique for *pilpul* in Italy and in Ashkenaz and France is *Sefer ha-Miẓvot ha-Gadol*.' Perhaps there is testimony here that the beginning of the pushing aside of the *Semag* took place under the influence of Spanish immigration; see Sonne, 'Excursions', 211. See also *Kevod Ḥakhamim*, 79: 'Because we have become used to these books in the great *yeshivot* from our youth, as people were used to the Semag, which we delve into by means of *pilpul*, as we study the *Tosafot* deeply . . .' Certainly, the wide spread of the *Semag* within the general public took place as a result of its characteristic simplicity of presentation, *halakhah* and *aggadah* being mixed there together (see Urbach, *Ba'alei ha-Tosafot* (Jerusalem, 1980), 475–6.

[207] See the remarks of R. Judah Minz cited above, and cf. the remarks of R. Joseph Caro in the introduction to *Bet Yosef*.

importance of commentaries, whether in academic discussions or in practical rulings.[208]

The influence of the Kabbalah on this subject may perhaps be found in the words of the Kabbalist R. Abraham da Sant' Angelo:

I will express myself briefly, why it is vanity to bring a cartload of [quotations] from the words of the authorities (*poskim*), as many as they may be, both old and new, who composed books and many words, which are weariness to the flesh [cf. *Eccles. 12: 12*]; for even if a man lived a thousand years twice over, it would be nearly impossible to exhaust their fulness, as was stressed sternly by the great Excellent Rabbi Elia da Genazzano, who wrote in his *'Iggeret Ḥamudot* as follows: 'Behold, two evils were done to us in this exile. One, that they abandoned the source of living waters, the words of the Kabbalah, which are prophecy, and dug for themselves broken wells or wells of clay, to seek after the philosophers, and they drowned in the deep mire [cf. *Ps. 69: 2*] from which they cannot rise. And secondly, the many doubts which came about after the completion of the Talmud, which are a great reason to waste much time, for what difference does it make if I fulfill the *mitzvot* according to Maimonides, who codified them in clear and concise language, or if one fulfills them according to the *Mordekhai* or the *Semag* or the other authorities, study of which is more difficult and deeper than study of the Talmud? And apart from this, there arose between them controversies, this one says thus, and that one says thus, and if it seemed in the eyes of the later ones (*aḥaronim*) that Maimonides was too brief on a certain subject, they ought to have written a commentary on his work, it being a general work, and that would have been sufficient. And not everyone who wishes to take upon himself the name [i.e. *of being a scholar*] may do so, and in this I praise those who dwell on the south-eastern extremity of the Ocean, of whom R. Obadiah of Bertinoro wrote that some of them [i.e. *the Yemenites*] came to Jerusalem, and they say that they have only one [halakhic] authority, and all of them are expert in it.'[209]

In a similar but more extreme vein, R. Asher Lemlein described one of his visions:

Evil to me is the deed that I hear of multitudes who mislead the people of God, saying that the study of Kabbalah is secondary to the study of

[208] See C. Lefebvre, 'Juges et savants en Europe, 13ᵉ–16ᵉ s.', *Ephemerides Iuris Canonici*, 22 (1966), 84.

[209] Boksenboim (ed.), *Teshuvot Matanot ba-Adam*, sect. 39. Sonne (*Mi-Pavlo*, 132–6) wished to read this as referring to the confrontation between itinerant rabbis and official rabbis. See there the list of other Kabbalists, such as R. Moses Basola, upon whom R. Abraham of Sant'Angelo relied.

Talmud, and that there is no need to learn it as a book, [but] that the Talmud alone gives goodly words. And you, my son, know the true Kabbalah, and place your fear in the land of life [cf. *Ps. 27: 13*]; and you complained that you are not a Talmudist, and why did not God give you a tongue to learn, in order to discourse upon the Mishnah and the *aggadot*, to solve many riddles. Know, my son, that your thoughts ought not to confound you, but let your wellsprings be poured into your studies, and do not bother to learn in the way of the Talmudists, for they should be to you like servants and like craftsmen, while you are like those who sit first in the kingdom . . . Know that the laws of what is prohibited and permitted are not hidden from the work of butchers; the laws of damages and of deliberate [misdeeds] are fitting to the work of jurists and magistrates; the laws of mixed fibres to tailors and seamstresses; the laws of seeds to farmers and villagers; the laws of tithes and priestly gifts and coins to the work of treasurers and bookkeepers; the laws of prohibited sexual unions to eunuchs[!]; the hours and months to the work of astronomers . . . [etc.] . . . but the law of knowing that He created all, is the labour of the righteous Kabbalists, in clear truth . . .[210]

Thus, in Lemlein's view, it is not worthwhile to engage in *pilpul* and to waste one's time in Talmudic study, which is in the final analysis a professional matter, but it is far preferable to devote oneself to Kabbalah.

It is clear that such a presentation of the matter was not typical of the great Torah scholars who lived at the end of the period we are dealing with, not even of the enthusiastic Kabbalists among them, such as R. Menaḥem Azariah da Fano.[211] Nevertheless, these comments deserve mention, indicating as they do how the tension between 'Talmudic' dialectics and the study of Kabbalah was understood by ordinary people.[212] When tension exists, great minds may manage to transcend it, but lesser individuals are affected by it, and a dynamic momentum is created which can no longer be ignored. In this case, that momentum was an additional factor contributing to the inclination to rely on a recent authority who could definitively determine how one ought to behave, freeing one from study and *pilpul* in halakhic subjects, leaving

[210] See the visions of R. Asher b. Meir, known as Lemlein Roitlingen, published by E. Kupfer, *Kovez̧ 'al Yad*, 8 [18] (1976), 403–4.

[211] See also Ch. 6, Sect. 3.

[212] See on this matter R. J. Z. Werblowsky, *Joseph Karo, Lawyer and Mystic* (Oxford, 1962), 158 ff.

people time to engage in Kabbalistic studies. These 'latter authorities' were identified in a natural way with the *Ṭurim*, later with the *Ṭurim* together with the *Bet Yosef*, and finally with the *Shulḥan 'Arukh* alone.

However, there would seem to be no contradiction between this tendency to rely upon later authorities and the other tendency to refer to the sources. On the contrary, the reliance upon 'the very latest' authority reduced the degree of daring needed in order to ignore the study of glosses and Tosaphot. To a certain extent, one finds here a phenomenon parallel to that of humanism within the Christian camp. The Italian rabbis avoided the endless discussions based upon scholastic distinctions and drew directly upon the earlier scholars (*rishonim*) without even taking the trouble to discuss whether they possessed the right to decide in controversies involving the outstanding authorities of the past. This had been done for them by the 'later ones'—R. Jacob ben Asher, author of the *Ṭurim* or, in the case of French Jewry, by Rabbi Moses of Coucy, author of the *Semag*. However, one should also not ignore in this context the general tendency, never absent in the world of rabbinic scholars, to view in a negative light most contemporary attempts to establish in practice an independent position on the great controversies of the past. One may recall, for example, in the period under discussion, the complaint of R. Elijah Ḥalfan in his approbation of the *Ṭur Yoreh De'ah* with *Bet Yosef* (Venice, 1551):

> Those who study and those who teach [Torah] have almost disappeared . . . for the vain ones are many, and the scholars are rare, and there is no one to teach knowledge or to understand tradition, save one in a city or two in a family . . . then each one, who was unique in his generation, strove to leave behind [him] a blessing . . . in their compositions . . . They tirelessly tried to establish the halakhic ruling . . . setting forth markers so that the reader might find in their books a prepared table, with little difficulty. However, because of their [excessively] great wisdom they drowned in the deep waters, so that those who came after them nearly brought up broken vessels [i.e. *were not successful in following their predecessor's steps*] because of the large number of authorities and numerous different books which have been published in the world since the dissemination of the works of the press [*invention of printing*]. Each one takes the crown to himself, to compose books and to glean after the sheaves, in saying that our forefathers left us enough room to show our skill . . .

To all that has been said until this point one must add the impact of the burning of the Talmud, which interfered with the discussion of sources found in Talmud and Tosaphot, and also contributed to the appreciation of the *Bet Yosef*, even though discussions in the *yeshivot* never ceased to be focused upon study of the Talmud and Tosaphot.[213]

It seems to me, that the most extreme example of a halakhic ruling in which the impact of the new spirit can be clearly distinguished may be found in a responsum by R. Azriel Trabot of Ascoli, in which he copied nearly verbatim from the responsa of R. Joseph Colon, while deleting entirely the dialectical discussion, quoting only the passages cited from the *rishonim* and, at the end, summarizing each topic by means of a quotation from the *Ṭurim*—and even this at times copied from the writing of Colon. The character of such a responsum can be fully appreciated by comparing how this scholar copied from Colon's responsa and how R. David Messer b. Leon did so![214] R. Aaron b. Israel Finzi summarized matters as follows at the end of the sixteenth century: 'It is our custom here in Ferrara to follow in all matters the ruling of the *Ṭur*, as these are interpreted [there] by R. Joseph Caro . . .'[215]

[213] See Ch. 1, Sect. 2, and cf. Sonne, 'Excursions', 217; Benayahu, *Haskamah u-reshut be-Defusei Venezia*, 28–9. On the lack of copies of the Talmud in Italy during these years, see Shulvass, 'Torah Study', 125–7; A. Yaari, *Serefat ha-Talmud be-Iṭalyah* (Tel Aviv, 1954). It is interesting to note that there was a kind of parallel to the process which led to the spread of the *Sefer Mizvot ha-Gadol* following the burning of the Talmud in France (see Urbach, *Ba'alei ha-Tosafot*, 476), although this time at the expense of the *Semag*. After the Bomberg edition of 1547, the *Semag* was not reprinted until the beginning of the 19th century (Livorno, 1808).

[214] This responsum is given in full in Document 62 of the Hebrew edition of this book, pp. 282–8. However, this is a responsum of a unique sort, which was written during a difficult period in the life of R. Azriel, when most of his books were not with him. But for this very reason, one may learn some details which are important for our subject: Maimonides' words were copied by R. Azriel from the *Piskei Mahari"k* alone, as may clearly be seen from comparison of the responsa, while we see that he did have a *Ṭur* with him for study. This is an indication that, when sending his other books to another province, where they encountered destruction, he specifically chose the *Ṭurim* and the *Piskei Mahari"k* to keep with him for everyday perusal, and for assistance in making halakhic rulings. The manner in which he copied from Colon's responsa also indicates that he presumed that the one receiving it should see it as the result of his own analysis, and not only as something based upon Colon's words (cf. in particular the final section of the responsum).

[215] 'Teshuvot R. Aharon b. Yisrael Finzi', sect. 41. See also Document 61, p. 281 in the Hebrew edition of this book for the full text of the responsum, which gives us indirect confirmation of part of the issues summarized above.

There is no doubt that a more profound examination of those works of the Italian scholars of this period which are still in manuscript will add many details to the picture presented in this chapter. Nevertheless, what we have said should suffice to demonstrate the uniqueness of the Italian Renaissance even in the realm of halakhic study and rulings, and to hint at the manner in which influences, pressures, and echoes from the Christian world were reflected in a uniquely Jewish spiritual world—particularly by its spiritual leaders, the rabbis. In the coming chapter, I will attempt to show further how the rabbis belonged organically to the cultural milieu in which they lived.

6
The Cultural World of the Rabbis

1. Torah and 'Wisdom'

The inclusion within the rubric of a study devoted to the history of the rabbinate of a chapter dealing with the history of culture and thought—which are properly speaking the concern of Italian Jewry as a whole—calls for some introductory remarks. Certainly, conventional wisdom would have it that the majority of those who participated in the cultural creativity of the milieu in question were rabbis. But it is not only for this reason that this chapter has been included here.

We have already seen how, throughout the period under discussion, the image of the Italian rabbi was that of guide and spiritual leader, the ideal of human perfection towards which people were educated, being regarded as 'the central pillar upon which the house rests'.[1] Thus the nature of a given rabbi's erudition determined his character, not only as a man, but also as a leader. Moreover, the idea of a given man being 'crowned with the crown of the rabbinate' elicited primarily the images of learning, erudition, and ability to make halakhic rulings. This being the case, the image of the rabbi as a figure of human perfection, as a sage, learned man, and teacher, has a bearing not only upon the attitude of the public to the rabbi, but upon the broader issue of the attitude of the public to the body of learning which constituted the cultural world of the rabbi and which the latter was supposed to convey to his students. In turn, the public's attitude, whether of assent or dissent, influenced the formation of the rabbinic cultural world. This being so, we cannot refrain from asking some elementary questions regarding the cultural image of Italian Jewry and the function of the rabbi in its shaping, even if in a very limited, general way.

When R. David b. Messer Leon attempted to describe the image of the scholar who was worthy of being called a rabbi, he

[1] See Ch. 2, Sect. 1.

stated quite simply that 'the sage who is learned in all the wisdoms, in addition to the Talmud, is more deserving of ordination than one who is simply a Talmudist'.[2] In writing these words, he overcame certain doubts which he had felt in his youth when he had asked R. Jacob Provenzali concerning the secular wisdoms: 'Are they beloved or rejected by our honourable rabbis, of blessed memory, who were Masters of religious behaviour? For from their words it would seem that they hated philosophy.'[3] By that time, R. David had decided clearly in favour of 'Aristotelian logic . . . which is the essence of the discourse of the wise men of our generation'.[4] In fact, in asking this question, he had in mind the figure of his own father, R. Judah Messer Leon. It will be remembered that the latter's leadership of the Jewish community was based upon a series of strict ordinances in the spirit of Ashkenazic halakhic rulings.[5] Nevertheless, his entire intellectual world was based upon Aristotle and Averroës, Cicero and Quintilian.[6] R. Jacob Provenzali replied to R. Judah's son that he ought not to involve himself with Aristotle, but rather follow the approach of the students 'in the faraway *yeshivot* at the end of the east, who . . . desire Torah and love the Talmud'. That is to say, he ought to choose a different way from that of 'the rabbis of this region' who, because of their excessive involvement in philosophy, seemed in Provenzali's opinion 'not to value those things [i.e. *Torah and Talmud*] at all'.[7] In other words, the implied message was that he ought to reject the path of his father in favour of that of the students 'in the faraway *yeshivot* at the end of the east'!

[2] David b. Judah Messer Leon, *Kevod Ḥakhamim* (Berlin, 1899; photo edn. Jerusalem, 1970), 65; cf. Document 5 in the Hebrew edition of this book for the use of the term 'communal sage' (*ḥakham kollel*) in the ordination given by R. David.

[3] S. Assaf, *Mekorot* (Tel Aviv, 1928–43), ii. 99.

[4] This sentence is taken from the responsum of R. Jacob Provenzali to a question asked by R. David—Assaf, ibid. 100.

[5] See Ch. 5, Sect. 8, on Messer Leon's *takkanot*.

[6] To date, the literary and philosophical work of R. Judah Messer Leon has not been sufficiently studied. See, thus far, I. Zinberg, *A History of Jewish Literature* (Cincinnati, 1974), iv. 39–42; I. Husik, *Judah Messer Leon's Commentary on the Vetus Logica* (Leiden, 1906); and the summaries in J. Guttman, *Philosophies of Judaism* (Philadelphia, 1964), 257–8; and I. Husik, *A History of Medieval Jewish Philosophy* (Philadelphia, 1948), 431. See also the doctoral dissertation of S. Rosenberg, 'Logika ve-Ontologyah be-Philosophia ha-Yehudit be-me'ah ha-arba' 'esreh', Jerusalem, 1973, 46–9, 107–10, and my remarks in the Introduction to the photo-edition of the first edition of *Sefer Nofet Ẓufim*. There can be no doubt that this figure is deserving of a comprehensive monograph.

[7] Assaf, *Mekorot*, 101–2.

Both question and answer epitomize the continuing vitality in Jewish thought of this inherent problematic, one which counterposes the view of those who affirm the value of the study of 'wisdoms' against those who reject such study. This problematic was a constant in the history of medieval Jewish thought, and was approached in a variety of ways.[8] During the period under discussion, a radical change took place in Italy, culminating in the removal of Aristotle and 'wisdom' from the pedestal upon which they were still ensconced during R. David b. Messer Leon's times, and their replacement by the study of Kabbalah. What were the reasons for this change? How were these factors related to the problem referred to above? What was the role of the rabbis, 'the masters of Torah', in shaping this change? Did the cultural creativity of the rabbis belong organically to the general phenomenon, or did it perhaps remain aloof from it and bring about change from without, with an attempt to channel the cultural interests of the Jews in directions which the rabbis might consider of primary importance within their own *Weltanschauung*? In the following discussion, I shall attempt to provide tentative answers to at least some of these questions.

2. The Libraries of the Jews

Cultural changes do not occur in a sharp and sudden manner. Furthermore, the use of literary works as historical evidence, that is, as a criterion for testing a given cultural ambience, requires great caution. For the purposes of our study, we may assume that a cultural ambience can be usefully tested by examining those channels through which the culture reaches out to the broader public—that is, first and foremost through the literary works which the public reads and by which it forms its own cultural world.[9] An examination of the dissemination of certain works in

[8] Jewish medieval literature is full of references to this problem, which has been studied only fragmentarily, and mostly in relation to the controversy concerning the writings of Maimonides and the ban placed upon them by R. Solomon ben Adret. See H. H. Ben-Sasson, *Trial and Achievement: Currents in Jewish History from 313* (Jerusalem, 1974), 230–42; and n. 66 here. On the vacillations concerning this subject in Italy during the Renaissance, see M. A. Shulvass, 'The Study of Torah', *Ḥoreb*, 10 (1948), 106–98; idem, 'Religious Life', *PAAJR* 17 (1947–8), 18.

[9] One must of course add to this that cultural activity which took place verbally, to be discussed further.

comparison with others is therefore likely to yield considerable information concerning the cultural interests of the public. Thus, if a given work was not frequently recopied in manuscript or was not printed often or at all, one may assume that it did not leave much of an impression upon, and certainly did not influence, the cultural life of the period, even if its contents may be of great interest to the historian of ideas. In our quest for the characteristics of the culture of our period, we must draw a clear distinction between those books which the public read and enjoyed and those which interested the minority, albeit the élite.[10] Inventories of books from the period are therefore of great importance. In these lists, which were generally preserved on blank pages of books, one may find clear testimony to the cultural interest of the books' owners.[11]

These remarks apply primarily to the period prior to the invention of printing in Europe, as well as that of the incunabula and the early post-incunabula. However, even during the later period a great deal can be learned from books, especially if the book-lists of an entire community have survived, as was the case concerning Mantua at the end of the sixteenth century, where the censors required inventories of the books owned by Jews. It is certainly ironic that what was without doubt felt at the time as an oppressive decree is now of benefit to the contemporary historian of the culture of Italian Jewry.[12] However, as far as this later period is concerned, one may entertain some reasonable doubt as to the degree to which book lists may serve as reliable cultural indicators. Even though towards the end of the sixteenth century people did not yet buy books casually, and the type and number of books in an individual's library may still be taken as indicators of his social and cultural status and interests,[13] the

[10] See E. Garin, *L'educazione in Europa, 1400–1600* (Bari, 1966), 15 ff.

[11] See P. Kibre, 'The Intellectual Interests Reflected in Libraries of the Fourteenth and Fifteenth Centuries', *JHI* 7 (1946), 257–97; G. Tamani, 'Codici ebraici Pico Grimani nella Biblioteca Arcivescovile di Udine', *Annali di Ca' Foscari*, 10 (1971), *Serie Orientale* 2, 1–25; V. F. Stern, 'The Bibliotheca of Gabriel Harvey', *RQ* 25 (1972), 1–62; S. Connell, 'Books and their Owners in Venice, 1345–1480', *Journal of the Warburg and Courtald Institutes*, 35 (1972), 163–86, and see also R. Bonfil, 'A List of Hebrew Books from Imola from the End of the 14th Century' (Heb.), *Sefer Zikaron li-Shelomo Umberto Naḥon* (Jerusalem, 1979), 47–62.

[12] See S. Simonsohn, 'Books and Libraries of the Jews of Mantua, 1595' (Heb.), *KS* 37 (1962).

[13] See e.g. A. Labarre, *La Livre dans la vie amienoise du seizième siècle* (Paris, 1971). According to this study, during the years 1503–6 one does not find any library containing

great revolution in the distribution of books during those generations caused by printing certainly brought into the home books which did not necessarily indicate clearly defined cultural interests, even though they do reflect the impact of printing upon the shaping of the culture of the times.[14] Furthermore, books which were passed down from father to son remained in inherited libraries even though the latter may have had no special interest in them. The profit they were likely to realize from the sale of these books or their exchange for other books was insufficient to counterbalance their sentimental value or to bring about their removal from the libraries. It therefore follows that, the further we advance into the era of printing, the more uncertain becomes the historical value of book-lists, and their proper evaluation requires a combination of many additional elements. On the other hand, during the period prior to the invention of printing and that of the incunabula and early post-incunabula, the high cost of books and their scarcity greatly reduced the tendency of a person to acquire books in which he had no particular interest. Inherited books whose contents or emotional value were not meaningful would then be more likely to be exchanged for others more desirable. Extant lists of books from this period therefore tend to be be more indicative of the actual cultural interests of their owners. Thus, if we can establish the composition of an average library of people who lived at that time from an examination of a sufficiently large number of different lists in one area, we may assume, at least as a working hypothesis, that this will reflect the degree to which certain books were circulated, as against others. This will serve as an important indicator of the cultural interests of the average person of those times, and not merely that of an intellectual élite.[15]

more than 100 books, except for those belonging to priests, jurists, or physicians, while after 1550 there is a marked rise in the number of books found, in the 887 lists that were examined.

[14] See A. M. Habermann, *Toldot ha-Sefer ha-'Ivri* (Jerusalem, 1945), 28 ff.; E. L. Eisenstein, 'The Impact of Printing on Western Society and Thought', *JMH* 40 (1968), 1–56, and esp. 2–6. See also the preceding note.

[15] On the other hand, comparison of these inventories of books with the lists of books recommended by scholars as being useful for the formation of the ideal human type, is likely to indicate the character of those proposing these lists as well as the cultural interests towards which they sought to direct their contemporaries. An ideal list of this type is that which R. Johanan Alemanno thought the ideal man ought to learn; see M. Idel, 'The Study Programme of R. Johanan Alemanno' (Heb.), *Tarbiz*, 48 (1979), 303–30.

To date, no studies of this type have been attempted and, apart from the pioneering surveys of M. A. Shulvass[16] and I. Sonne,[17] this entire area may still be considered as virgin territory. I will touch here only on a few isolated points pertaining to our subject. When the corpus of book-lists is published, it will be possible to expand the picture and to encompass the cultural phenomenon in general. This study has been confined to the lists of books preserved by Jews from northern and central Italy up to 1540. A total of more than forty lists, both published and in manuscript, has been examined.[18]

These lists indicate a clear decline of interest in philosophy within the Jewish public. Philosophical treatises are increasingly

[16] See M. A. Shulvass, 'Books and Libraries Among Italian Jews during the Renaissance' (Heb.), *Talpiyot*, 4 (1910), 591–605; and also idem, 'The Study of Torah', 122; idem, *Renaissance*, 257–67.

[17] See I. Sonne, 'Book Lists through Three Centuries; A. First Half of the Fifteenth Century, Italy', *Studies in Bibliography and Booklore*, 2 (1955), 3–19.

[18] A full catalogue of the lists which I examined appears in Appendix II to the Hebrew edition of this book, p. 295. Apart from these, additional lists have been preserved, but these have not been included in my catalogue for various reasons: there were cases in which the microfilms in the IMHM were illegible; there were others in which the ascription of the lists to Jews living in Italy seemed uncertain, and whose verification would require extensive research, which seemed unnecessary for the purposes of the present study; there were other cases in which the microfilms themselves were not availabe to me for various technical reasons. Prof. Nehemiah Aloni had spent more than ten years collecting material for the publication of a corpus of book lists—see S. Goitein, *Sidrei Ḥinukh* (Jerusalem, 1962), 150—which he had hoped to publish, a hope frustrated by his untimely death. In any event, I saw no justification in investing further energy in gathering material from manuscripts and in copying additional lists; for the purposes of the present work, the lists which I have examined seem definitely adequate to confirm my conclusions. I likewise did not take account, in the list in Appendix II, of the publications by C. Trasselli, 'Sulla diffusione degli ebrei e sull'importanza della cultura e della lingua ebraica in Sicilia e particolarmente in Trapani e in Palermo nel secolo XV', *Bollettino del Centro di Studi Filologici e Linguistici Siciliani*, 2 (1954), 7–8, and H. Bresc, *Livre et société en Sicile (1299–1499)* (Palermo, 1971), even though those works were available to me. The major focus in my discussion of the Italian rabbinate during this period is in the area north of Rome, due to the almost complete lack of internal Jewish documents pertaining to the Rabbinate in Sicily and in the Kingdom of Naples (see the Introduction and Ch. 3, Sect. 6). Now, even though these two works do confirm my general conclusions with regard to southern Italy as well, as I shall discuss further in the notes, it seems to me that the material cited there requires additional study, both in order to remove doubts pertaining to the identification of the books and to ascertain the extent of indicativeness of the lists with regard to the overall cultural life of the Jews of Sicily (see Bresc, *Livre et société*, 68). In addition, I think that the clear evidence to be gleaned from the material mentioned ought to be combined with other evidence, so as not to make book-lists in themselves the corner-stone of our argument. I have therefore preferred to leave this material pending further scrutiny until further internal Jewish evidence be discovered which, together with the book-lists, will make possible the construction of a picture of the cultural world of Sicilian Jewry.

scarce on the lists: the works of Aristotle and those attributed to him, which were widespread during the first half of the fifteenth century, become rarer in the second half of that century, and are no longer found at all in the first half of the sixteenth century except in special cases, which may well be the exceptions that prove the rule. Of six extant lists from the first half of the fifteenth century,[19] one is from a synagogue library, where one would not expect to find philosophical works, but which otherwise also reflects a definite interest in philosophy.[20] Three of the remaining five lists include philosophical works.[21] During the period from the middle of that century until the beginning of the sixteenth century, books of philosophy are found in only two[22] out of seventeen lists of books,[23] while in the first half of the sixteenth century, by which time the historical value of these lists had diminished for the reasons described above, we find works of philosophy in four lists out of seventeen.[24] Two of these belonged to unusual personalities, well known for their broad intellectual interests,[25] while one was a list of inherited books which may be more indicative of the interests of the deceased, who belonged to the previous generation, than those of the beneficiary—who nevertheless did not discard what he

[19] Lists 2–7 in Appendix II in the Hebrew edition of this book.

[20] Ibid. List 6. The presence in this list of the work *Malmad ha-Talmidim* is clear evidence of the philosophical interests of the public who studied in this synagogue.

[21] In List 4: Aristotle's *de Sensu et Sensatu* and *de Generatione et Corruptione* and the pseudo-Aristotelian *de Pomo*. On List 5: ibn Kaspi's *Sefer ha-Higayon*, R. Jedaiah ha-Penini's *Sefer ha-Hitnazlut* and *Ma'amarei ha-Philosophim*. In List 7: Aristotle's *Introduction*, *Categories*, *Rhetoric*, and *Analytica Priora* and *Posteriora*. Most of the lists mentioned here containing philosophical works have already been published (see Appendix II in the Hebrew edition of this book). It did not seem necessary to speak extensively here about the books included in those lists, nor to attempt to guide the reader towards an evaluation of the importance of philosophy in the libraries of those who owned books. Such an evaluation seems to me to require basic statistical examination.

[22] In List 14: *Introduction*, *Categories*, *Rhetoric*, *Logic*. List 18: *Sefer ha-Shema'*, *Philosophical Ethics* and *Sod ha-Sodot* attributed to Aristotle.

[23] Lists 8–24. [24] Lists 30, 33, 35, 36.

[25] List 33 is a list of the books belonging to Leon Sinai (or Segni), evidently the father of Joseph Sinai, the teacher of R. Abraham Portaleone, author of *Sefer Shiltei ha-Gibborim*, who valued the study of philosophy particularly highly (it should be noted that List 27 is a list of the books belonging to the nephew of that same Leon Sinai, which seems to constitute clear evidence that the family was one of scholars and book-lovers). The list of books belonging to Leon Sinai includes 112 items, among them many Kabbalistic works (including *Sefer ha-Zohar*) which do not appear in any other list—a further indication of the uniqueness of this list. List 36 is of the books belonging to the noted physician, Elijah Ḥalfan, an individual whose cultural interests were certainly not typical of the general public.

inherited.[26] In the last list of the four mentioned,[27] we find two copies of the *Analytica Priora* and another work of Aristotle, whose title I was unable to decipher. The presence of two copies of the same book in one list may indicate that here too we are dealing with a case of inheritance. In brief, of five lists from the first half of the fifteenth century, three contain philosophical texts and one indicates definite philosophical interests, while of the thirty-four lists from the latter half of the fifteenth and the first half of the sixteenth centuries, only six—at least two of which are exceptional in one way or another—include works of philosophy.[28] All of this constitutes clear evidence of a decline in the Jewish public's interest in philosophy between the middle of the fifteenth and the middle of the sixteenth century.[29]

To all that has been said thus far, one ought to add the fact that the books of Aristotle and those attributed to him, as well as those of Averroës, were hardly printed at all during the period under discussion,[30] and were nevertheless not extensively copied. Of the hundreds of Aristotelian and other philosophical manuscripts of which microfilms are available at the Institute for Microfilms of Hebrew Manuscripts in Jerusalem, and whose date of copying has been established with some degree of accuracy, the smallest number comes from the sixteenth century. Moreover, several of these were copied by or on behalf of individuals whose philosophical interests are well known to us from other sources.[31]

[26] i.e. List 35. [27] List 30.

[28] It should be noted that, in the inventories published by Trasselli and Bresc, no mention is made of philosophical works, a fact which led Bresc to doubt the indicativeness of these inventories in general for the overall picture of the cultural life of Sicilian Jewry (Bresc, *Livre et société*, 68).

[29] One should also note here that the activity of such Jewish scholars as R. Jacob Mantino, R. Abraham di Balmes, and their like, who participated in the translation from Hebrew to Latin of the works of Aristotle with the commentary of Averroës (which were included in the classical edition of Aristotle's works in Venice) is indicative of the interests of only a small circle of scholars, who were primarily oriented towards the world of the universities rather than to the Jewish world.

[30] The only works published were: (1) Aristotle's *Organon*, condensed by Averroës (Riva di Trento, 1560); (2) Averroës' abbreviated version of Aristotle's *Physics* (Riva di Trento, 1560); (3) Aristotle's *Ethical Letter* (Riva di Trento, 1560); (4) *De Pomo*—in *Likkutei ha-Pardes* (Venice, 1519), and in *Goren Nakhon* (Riva di Trento, 1562).

[31] MS Vienna 155, which includes the middle commentary of Averroës to *Physica*, copied by R. Vitale da Pisa in 1524; and MS Modena-Estense 75, which includes Averroës' commentary to *Metaphysica*, copied by R. Abraham Provenzali for himself. For other manuscripts, see MS Milano-Ambrosiana 75; Firenze-Laurenziana Pt. ii. 25; Paris 924, 1341; München 31, 32. There is no doubt that, were a systematic and comprehensive

It would appear that book publishers examined the possibility of printing philosophical works other than those which had already been published, and finally decided not to risk the investment. This, at least, would seem to be the conclusion to be drawn from the fact that R. Ezra da Fano copied a book containing Averroës' Commentary on *The Book of Heaven and the World* and other works for Cornelio Adelkind.[32]

Of the philosophical texts widespread during the Middle Ages, it would seem that only Maimonides' *Guide for the Perplexed* and the related literature, namely, its commentaries, continued to retain the interest of the public. These works are found consistently in lists,[33] a fact which must be explained in view of the disappearance of other philosophical works.

In the realm of Kabbalistic literature, we generally find in these lists only collections, usually designated by the generic name—'a book of *Kabbalah*', 'knowledge of *Kabbalah*', or 'collections of *Kabbalah*'[34]—and the commentaries on the Pentateuch by R. Moses Nahmanides (1194–1270)[35] and R. Menaḥem Recanati (late 13th–14th century).[36] Apart from these, we find only a few of those early Kabbalistic works which R. Joseph Ashkenazi, the '*tanna* from Safed', considered as containing authentic Kabbalah, 'and in which all the words of the Torah are explained', as opposed to the works of 'the modern Kabbalists'.[37] Thus, we occasionally find in those lists *Sefer ha-Bahir*,[38] *Baraita shel Ma'aseh Bereshit*,[39] and *Sefer Yeẓirah*.[40] Other Kabbalistic works which appear slightly more frequently include

study of this matter to be conducted and the dates of the copying of these manuscripts in Italian writing, which are listed in the catalogue in a general way as having been copied 'during the 15th or 16th century', were to be determined with greater accuracy, it would be possible to point to additional manuscripts to those mentioned here. However, this would not alter this general observation.

[32] See MS München 31 (pp. 15–17 in Steinschneider's catalogue).

[33] In lists dated from the second half of the 15th century onwards: see nos. 14, 18, 19 (*Guide for the Perplexed*), 20 (*Perishah mi-Moreh ve-Ruaḥ Ḥen*), 21 (*Guide*, *Eight Chapters*, and *Ruaḥ Ḥen*), 24 (*Guide*), 25 (*Guide* and *Ruaḥ Ḥen*), 30 (*Mesharet Moshe*), 33 (ibn Kaspi's *Commentary* to the *Guide* and *Millot ha-Higayon*), 34 (*Guide* and *Ruaḥ Ḥen*), 40, and 41 (*Guide*).

[34] In Lists 4, 7, 15, 16, 19, 33, 35.

[35] In Lists 3, 4, 6, 10, 19, 41.

[36] In Lists 5, 13, 14, 30, 40.

[37] See G. Scholem, 'New Information Concerning R. Joseph Ashkenazi, the "Tanna" from Safed' (Heb.), *Tarbiẓ*, 28 (1959), 84–5.

[38] In Lists 2, 19, 24, 33.

[39] In List 14.

[40] In Lists 24, 30, 33.

Sefer Ma'arekhet ha-'Elohut[41] and R. Abraham Abulafia's *'Or ha-Sekhel*.[42] The entire Zoharic corpus—the *Zohar*, *Tikkunei ha-Zohar*, *Midrash ha-Ne'elam*, *Midrash Ruth*, etc.—is found in only one isolated case,[43] a fact which confirms the comment made by the *Zohar*'s first publishers concerning the rarity of the *Zohar* in Italy prior to their edition.[44] These details seem to me to be sufficient both to indicate the existence of a special tradition of Kabbalistic study among Italian Jews prior to the printing of the *Zohar*, and the beginnings of close contact with the Kabbalists of Spain and afterwards those of Safed. That is, there was a tradition of study directed primarily towards the field of biblical exegesis to which there was added, in esoteric circles, a tradition of study of the works of early Jewish mysticism. Thus, one may consider the process of transformation which began to occur during the first half of the sixteenth century, and which reached its apex with the publication of the *Zohar* in the late 1550s, as a direct result of the contribution to the study of Kabbalah in Italy by rabbis who came from the sphere of influence of Spanish and Provençal Jewry—that is, Jews from Provence, Spanish exiles, and possibly also Jews from Candia, and the remnants of certain circles within Sicilian Jewry. This conjecture may be partially confirmed by the fact that, among the manuscripts from the fifteenth and early sixteenth century found in the Vatican collection,[45] including the *Zohar*, *Tikkunei ha-Zohar*, *Midrash ha-Ne'elam*, *Midrash Ruth*, or selections therefrom, ten originated in Candia,[46] two from the collection of a Christian humanist in Sicily,[47] and one from Germany.[48] All of these found their way into the Vatican collection by means of a gift from Maximilian I, Duke of Bavaria, to Pope Gregory XV in 1622. Of the remaining

41 In Lists 2, 19, 24, 35. 42 In Lists 2, 32, 33.

43 In List 33 which, as mentioned already, was unique.

44 See I. Tishby, 'The Controversy Concerning *Sefer ha-Zohar* in 16th Century Italy' (Heb.), *Ḥikrei Kabbalah u-Sheluḥoteha*, i (Jerusalem, 1982), 91–2. Even in the lists published by Trasselli and Bresc, no mention is made of Kabbalistic works; see n. 18.

45 The summary here is primarily based upon U. Cassuto, *I manoscritti Palatini della Biblioteca Apostolica Vaticana e la loro storia* (Vatican City, 1935), and upon the list of manuscripts in the Vatican Library, published by the Institute for Microfilms of Hebrew Manuscripts at the Jewish National and University Library.

46 Lists 105, 199, 200, 202, 206–8, 213, 226, 428.

47 Lists 68, 290. The source of both is evidently in Syracuse, which was a centre of Messianic speculation; see A. Z. Ashkoly, *ha-Tenu'ot ha-Meshiḥi'ot be-Yisra'el* (Jerusalem, 1956), 240–7. 48 List 212.

manuscripts in the Vatican collection containing Zoharic literature, the decisive majority are from the 1530s onwards.[49] It is doubtful whether any of the remaining manuscripts[50] were written in Italy, and even if there are exceptions, these would only serve to prove the rule.

3. Philosophy and Kabbalah

It is therefore clear that the flourishing of the study of Kabbalistic literature related to the *Zohar* was preceded by a prolonged period of decline in the prestige of scholastic philosophy. The intellectual vacuum gradually created was filled by the study of Zoharic literature. What were the reasons for this decline? In conventional terms, one might say that there was a strengthening of the anti-rationalistic trends at the cost of rationalistic scholastic ones. But one must immediately add that, as the decline of scholastic philosophy preceded the Counter-Reformation by a considerable period of time, and as the growth of interest in the *Zohar* increased gradually, at least from the 1530s onwards—that is, approximately one generation prior to the burning of the Talmud and the printing of the Zoharic literature—there is no justification for the explanation commonly found in Jewish historiography that this was simply a response to such external circumstances as the confinement of the Jews to ghettos and the increase in Church pressure during the Counter-Reformation. According to this approach, these external circumstances unconsciously aroused certain dark, anti-rationalistic elements inherent in Judaism. Thus the Jews, isolated from the external cultural world, became turned in upon themselves and were forced against their own interests to develop the conservative elements within their tradition. This explanation seems to be a product of the excessive emphasis placed by current historiography upon the alleged involvement of the Renaissance Jews in the cultural and social life of their milieu. Many phenomena which were in fact characteristic of Jewish life in Renaissance Italy were understood by Enlightenment German Jewish historiography and its offshoots

[49] Neophiti 22, 24, 25, were written in 1531; 204 was written in Rome in 1551; 210 was written in Ferrara in 1550; Neophiti 23 also seems to belong to the 16th century.

[50] If I have not erred in my searching of the catalogue, they are 487, 530, and 699.

as an expression of Enlightenment trends *ante litteram*, in contrast to Jewish tradition's essentially anti-rationalistic bent. The picture of Jewish life in Renaissance Italy was contrasted with that of Ashkenazic Jewry, which during that same period seemed closed and impervious to the influences of non-Jewish culture.[51] The Italian Renaissance appeared to be a period of victory for enlightened rationalism, while those cultural trends which seemed to characterize Italian Jewry at the end of the sixteenth century were interpreted as reflections of an involutionary process, that is, a return to the dark, fundamentalist anti-rationalism of the Middle Ages. Jewish anti-rationalism won the day by some kind of hidden alliance with Catholic reaction.[52] In this vein, the dynamics of the inner Jewish problematic involved in the historical process, together with the organic continuity of the cultural phenomenon, were considerably obscured by being consistently described exclusively in terms of challenge and response, adjustment or reaction to the world of general culture, acculturation or refusal to acculturate. Concomitantly, the nature of the relationship between general culture and specifically Jewish cultural expressions was obscured to no small degree.[53] This approach was doubtless fostered by the negative attitude to

[51] But cf. H. H. Ben-Sasson, 'Conceptions and Reality in Jewish History of the Late Middle Ages' (Heb.), *Tarbiz*, 29 (1960), 297–312; see also the remarks by J. Katz concerning this article in *Tarbiz*, 30 (1961), 62–8, and Ben-Sasson's rejoinder, 68–72; idem (ed.), *A History of the Jewish People* (Cambridge, Mass., 1976), 623–4; E. Kupfer, 'Towards the Cultural Image of German Jewry and its Sages in the 14th and 15th Centuries' (Heb.), *Tarbiz*, 42 (1973), 113–47; R. Bonfil, 'Jews of the Venetian Territories' (Heb.), *Zion*, 41 (1976).

[52] See e.g. M. A. Shulvass, 'The Jews of Italy in the Framework of the Culture of the Renaissance' (Heb.), *Sinai*, 22 (1948), 44–8; idem, 'Religious Life'; I. E. Barzilay, 'The Italian and Berlin Haskalah: Parallels and Differences', *PAAJR* 31 (1960–1), 17–54; idem, *Between Reason and Faith; Anti-Rationalism in Italian Jewish Thought, 1250–1650* (The Hague, 1967). There is no need to add that the approach outlined above departs from the common idealization of the Renaissance. On the subject generally, see: W. K. Ferguson, *The Renaissance in Historical Thought: Five Centuries of Interpretation* (Cambridge, 1948); P. O. Kristeller, 'Changing Views of the Intellectual History of the Renaissance since Jacob Burckhardt', in *The Renaissance: A Reconsideration of the Theories and Interpretations of the Age*, ed. T. Helton (Madison, 1961), 27–52. Likewise, the above approach would not insist upon emphasizing the contrast between the pagan, heretical Renaissance and the Middle Ages, imbued with uncritical religious faith. On this question, see the survey by H. Weisinger, 'The Attack on the Renaissance in Theology Today', *Studies in the Renaissance*, 2 (1955), 176–89, with regard to the Jews.

[53] Only recently have critical voices been heard concerning this historiographical tendency; see G. Sermoneta's review of Barzilay's *Between Reason and Faith* in *KS* 45 (1970), 539–46; R. Bonfil, 'The Historian's Perception of the Jews in the Italian Renaissance: Towards a Reappraisal', *REJ* 143 (1984), 59–82.

Kabbalah displayed by students of Jewish philosophy during the nineteenth and early twentieth centuries. To this should be added, perhaps, the impact of Burckhardt's understanding of Renaissance culture, which de-emphasized the importance of Renaissance philosophy *vis-à-vis* other areas of spiritual creativity.[54] In any event, scholars were not particularly drawn towards the study of the philosophical creation of Italian Jewry during this period, which they saw primarily as a 'reworking of the medieval tradition',[55] while their negative view of the Kabbalah led to an interpretation of the mass interest in it during the second half of the sixteenth century as an intellectual development even worse than a 'reworking of the medieval tradition', totally undeserving of serious study.[56]

Within this conceptual framework, the rabbis, 'the masters of Torah', were viewed as the natural representatives of the cultural-religious-traditional complex. This being so, the alleged 'submission' of the Jews to external cultural influences and their participation in the cultural movements of the Middle Ages and of the beginning of the Renaissance were very favourably evaluated, while these very same phenomena were regarded as signs of the weakness of the rabbis and of the institutions to which they belonged. That is, the rabbis were, so to speak, unsuccessful in halting the penetration of 'secular' culture into the Jewish milieu. On the other hand, the increase of Kabbalistic tendencies towards the second half of the sixteenth century, and the accompanying pietistic spirit, were seen as a kind of triumph, given to those rabbis totally unexpectedly from the Christian Church in the period of the Counter-Reformation.[57]

However, even a superficial glance at the chronology of the period should lead one to reconsider such a presentation. The simultaneous publication of the *Zohar* in two neighbouring places, in open competition and in an atmosphere of intense polemical turbulence, is striking evidence of the enthusiasm of the publishers and their feeling of confidence that they had in fact found a

[54] On this last factor, see the first section of R. Bonfil, 'R. Obadiah Sforno' (Heb.), *'Eshel Be'er Sheva'*, 1 (1976), 200–57.

[55] See J. Guttmann, *Philosophies of Judaism* (Philadelphia, 1964), 257.

[56] Ibid. and cf. Zinberg, *History of Jewish Literature*, iv. 3–4.

[57] See e.g. Shulvass, 'Religious Life', 2–8. Shulvass also found 'religious scepticism' in Italy in this period, which he also ascribed to 'the failure of the rabbis to serve as leaders in religious life'.

market thirsting for their work. Thus, the publication of the *Zohar* at the end of the 1550s should be understood as reflecting the final stage of a process of cultural transformation,[58] and not its beginning, as is generally assumed by those who advance this historiographical argument, seeing in it a direct consequence of the war of the Church against the Talmud and halakhic literature.

Isaiah Tishby has recently called attention to the internal Jewish problematic which underlay the polemic surrounding the printing of the Zoharic literature.[59] In the course of his discussion, Tishby showed that the historiographic approach discussed above confused tangential factors with primary ones, while either distorting or missing entirely the actual roots of the spiritual awakening, which were expressed in an explicit spiritual-ideological programme.[60] Various signs of the ideological dilemma connected with the polemic surrounding the printing of the *Zohar* had generally been interpreted in terms of other problems, such as the alleged class antagonism between 'itinerant rabbis' and 'appointed rabbis'. We have already seen that it is doubtful whether such an antagonism had any place at all in the historical process under consideration here. There is no reason to see this controversy as contradicting that conclusion.[61]

Tishby is no doubt correct in stressing the sense of missionary zeal with which the publishers of the *Zohar* were imbued—a mission intended to save that generation from the dangers of religious and ethical corruption which they saw as threatening those who were not involved in the study of Kabbalah. Such a sense of mission did not emerge suddenly from frustration following the burning of Talmudic literature. This consciousness in fact expressed the mood of people who saw themselves confidently clearing a new path, and not a hesitant attempt to find a possible alternative to the study of Talmud. Tishby further demonstrated how the claims of those who supported the publication of the *Zohar* and its dissemination contain clear signs of the battle against philosophy.[62] However, he did not develop this idea nor explain how the same spiritualistic trends which involved a rejection of philosophy and a turn towards Kabbalah

[58] As we noted above, this process continued for at least one generation.

[59] Tishby, 'The Controversy Concerning *Sefer ha-Zohar*', esp. 121–30.

[60] Ibid. esp. 124–130. [61] See Ch. 4, Sect. 2.

[62] Tishby, 'The Controversy Concerning *Sefer ha-Zohar*', 128–9.

developed. Nor does he explain the difference between the battle of the Kabbalists against philosophy and the danger of religious and ethical corruption which they believed was threatening the 'ordinary masters of *halakhah*'.[63]

There was indeed a great difference between these two complementary phenomena: even though there were abundant expressions of opposition on the part of Kabbalists to the exclusive preoccupation with *halakhah*, and even though involvement in such study was not perceived as sufficient protection against the dangers of distance from the source of pure faith,[64] in the final analysis, Kabbalists were not opposed to the study of *halakhah per se*, that is, to the *contents* of such study. The profound involvement in halakhic studies by those who were among the outstanding personalities within the Kabbalistic camp, such as R. Moses Basola and R. Menaḥem Azariah da Fano (1548–1620), was in no way considered a fault. By contrast, the battle with philosophy was deep-rooted and intense.

Umberto Cassuto has identified the polemic between R. Vitale (Jeḥiel Nissim) da Pisa and the poet Moses b. Joab da Rieti, following the publication of the 'apology of R. Jedaiah ha-Penini' from Beziers in the 1539 Bologna edition of the *Responsa* of R. Solomon ben Adret,[65] as an expression of the controversy between the advocates of rationalistic philosophy and their opponents, the advocates of the mystical tradition of the Kabbalah. On the face of it, this is no more than a late echo of the controversy which exercised the generation of Adret himself. However, even though many details of the earlier controversy still require study,[66] the intention of Adret and those who sided

[63] Ibid. 129.

[64] Ibid. n. 178, and see also the end of Ch. 5. In any event, these phrases indicate that the study of Talmud continued even after its burning, motivated both by persistence and devotion, which involved an element of risk; cf. Ch. 1, Sect. 2 and Ch. 5 n. 213.

[65] Moses ben Joab da Rieti's poem in defence of philosophy, 'ha-Ẓo'eket be-kol ram neged . . . ha-Rashb"a' ('The Loud Cry Against . . . R. Solomon ben Adret'), was first published by Hirschfeld, *JQR* 14 (1901–2), 778, and again, with corrections, by Cassuto, 'Ein hebräischer Dichter des 15. Jahrhunderts', *MGWJ* 77 (1933), 381–2. Cassuto also noticed Moshe ben Joab's polemical barbs against R. Vitale da Pisa's book, *Minḥat Kena'ot* (see U. Cassuto, *Firenze* (Florence, 1918), 267), and the textual parallel between R. Moshe's remarks and those of R. Jedaiah ha-Bedersi (*MGWJ* 77 (1933), 381–2).

[66] See the material noted by J. Shatzmiller, 'Between Abba Mari and ben Adret: the Bargaining which Preceded the Ban of Barcelona' (Heb.), in *Meḥkarim be-Toldot 'Am Yisra'el ve-'Ereẓ Yisra'el*, 3 (Haifa, 1975), 121–2 n. 2. See also the sound remarks of Y. H. Shor, 'R. Nissim son of Moshe of Marsilia' (Heb.), *he-Ḥaluẓ*, 7 (1895), 89 ff.

with him was rather different from that of those who opposed philosophical rationalism during the period under discussion here. Adret and his circle opposed the study of philosophy 'until the student and the teacher are twenty-five years of age and have filled their bellies with "dainties of Torah" ', since otherwise one who studies philosophy 'will deny it [*the Torah*] mastership'. On the other hand, 'he who has from his youth cherished her shall not depart from her even when he becomes old'. In other words, the Jew ought to be placed in a situation in which he will not be influenced by philosophical studies to the detriment of his Torah studies or his adherence to the principles of faith. This is neither the place to discuss the question as to whether or not opposition to philosophical rationalism existed within Adret's circle, apart from this one explicit declaration, nor to discuss in general the nature and source of the opposition to philosophical study. In any event, it seems clear that the battle against philosophical studies in Adret's generation was essentially a defensive war against the danger of apostasy which, according to its opponents, was inherent in the nature of the studies themselves or at any rate the possible negative influence of such studies.

Conversely, the emphasis in R. Vitale da Pisa's work is placed, not upon the danger posed to those who study philosophy, but on the lack of religious certainty expressed by those who turned to philosophy with the aim of finding therein the answer to their existential problems as men and as Jews. The emphasis now is placed upon the bankruptcy of philosophy and the need to fill the vacuum with new contents—namely, Kabbalah.

There was much that was paradoxical in Rabbi Vitale da Pisa's position. As far as I have been able to ascertain, throughout the period under discussion, there is no philosophical work written in Italy that equals da Pisa's *Minḥat Kena'ot* in clarity, breadth of knowledge, and systematic analysis. This work is an up-to-date abstract of the state of philosophical studies in his day. The presentation of ideas in the book, the structure of the discussion, and the precision with which he cites the Aristotelian sources[67] indicate that R. Vitale da Pisa did not refrain,[68] nor did he wish to prevent others, from studying philosophical works.[69] On the

[67] See e.g. the definition of the soul given on p. 52, and cf. the editor's note there.

[68] On the books which belonged to or which were copied by him, cf. Cassuto, *Firenze*, esp. 275–8.

[69] See *Minḥat Kena'ot*, 71–2.

other hand, it is clear from his work *Ma'amar Ḥayyei 'Olam*, concerning the halakhic ramifications of lending money at interest, that da Pisa did not flee from halakhic studies to engage in contemplative mysticism.[70] In short, we find here the image of a scholar, highly expert in Talmudic literature, but also deeply involved in the world of philosophy, who yet deliberately turned away from that world out of a deep feeling of dissatisfaction,[71] even if not necessarily opposed in principle to the study of 'wisdoms'.

At the very beginning of his book, da Pisa stresses that his complaint is directed against 'the hastening towards and pursuit of wisdom' and 'not upon the searching out of its hidden depths . . . because wisdom, in terms of its being wisdom and that from it may be known the causes of things . . . is deserving of being sought and pursued'.[72] What is meant by 'hastening towards and pursuit of wisdom' as distinct from 'searching out its hidden depths'? R. Vitale da Pisa's quarrel is with those who 'place their principal [efforts] in philosophy' because they are convinced that 'it is a handle and vessel to the Torah . . . without which it [*the Torah*] would not lift up its hand or foot'. By contrast, he is convinced that 'the faith of the Egyptians is not like that of the Hebrews, for they are lively [cf. *Exod. 1: 19*] . . . it is not divided as happens in human wisdom . . . [in which] this one says that . . . and this one says that . . . because they did not receive the truth from the truth in itself'.[73] In other words, he is not opposed in principle to the study of 'wisdom', a concept which for him—

[70] See his remarks in *Minḥat Kena'ot*, 88, concerning the importance of the study of *halakhah*.

[71] Cf. the summaries given by R. Vitale da Pisa in a Kabbalistic spirit with his philosophical summaries: they provide clear confirmation that his knowledge of Kabbalah was greatly inferior to his philosophical knowledge, and perhaps even to his halakhic knowledge. It also seems that his teaching is not at all free from the influence of naturalistic outlooks which were common in his generation. See e.g. *Minḥat Kena'ot*, 76–7; in general, R. Vitale seems to resemble R. Mordecai Dato who, like him, was an eclectic Kabbalist—see at the end of this section. This is not the proper place for a detailed analysis of da Pisa's Kabbalistic doctrine. Such an analysis properly belongs within the framework of a comprehensive study of this thinker, against the background of the specific Italian tradition of Kabbalistic study (cf. the beginning of Sect. 3), and thorough examination of his sources (see Ch. 3, Sect. 2). Sonne has noted the influence of Spanish circles in Bologna upon R. Vitale, an influence which even left its impression upon the style of his handwriting; see Sonne, 'The Community of Bologna', 87 and n. 13. A full monograph devoted to this figure and his thought is a desideratum.

[72] *Minḥat Kena'ot*, 9.

[73] Ibid. 9–10.

as well as for his contemporaries—includes 'all the rules of the wisdoms—physics, mathematics, and metaphysics'.[74] But in his opinion, to use a formula very close to the conclusion of R. Jehiel Nissim da Pisa, although not accepted in his time, 'wisdom' is good for everything which lies within the limits of 'natural science' (i.e. physics),[75] while knowledge which is 'beyond nature' (i.e. metaphysics) is subject to doubt—and from this stems its harmfulness. Anyone who wishes to be convinced of this need only open the philosophical works themselves:

Whoever wishes to know all these opinions and conjectures and what [was thought] by our predecessors and the later ones, and the sages of the Christians and their proofs and arguments, should study the works of the commentators [i.e. *of Aristotle*] and in particular the works of the greatest of the later philosophers of our generation, Agostino Nifo da Sessa.[76]

His words thus include a distinct appeal to the works of the philosophers for proof of the conclusion stated above.[77] It was thus a process of thorough examination and study, and not uncritical flight, that brought R. Vitale da Pisa to his refutation of that rationalistic approach which saw philosophy as the means of confirming most of the metaphysical beliefs of the Torah, and which regarded as impossible any contradiction between the philosophical outlook and the religious tradition—an approach according to which the Jewish scholar ought to rely upon his faith only in those few subjects concerning which philosophy had not reached conclusions or to which it did not address itself at all, such as prophecy.[78] According to da Pisa, this was incorrect; philosophy is incapable of reaching a definite conclusion on any major metaphysical question concerning mankind as a whole or the Jewish people. 'This one says this, and another says that': that is, there are profound differences of opinion, so that it is impossible to eliminate doubt.

[74] Ibid. 12. [75] Principally geometry and medicine, ibid. 110.

[76] Ibid. 71–2. [77] Cf. his remarks on p. 33.

[78] See e.g. for the period we are concerned with, Elijah del Medigo's Averroistic work, *Beḥinat ha-Dat*. On this scholar and his thought, see Cassuto, *Firenze*, 221–33; Guttmann, *Philosophies of Judaism*, 258–9; B. Kieszkowski, 'Les Rapports entre Elie del Medigo et Pice la Mirandole', *Rinascimento*, series 2/4 (1964), 41–91, which contains a listing of earlier literature; and D. Geffen, 'Insights into the Life and Thought of Elijah del Medigo Based on his Published and Unpublished Works', *PAAJR* 41–2 (1973–4), 69–86.

Thus, R. Vitale da Pisa's entire work is a kind of reasoned confession of a man who has turned his back upon philosophy. In the bulk of this work, one finds the clear awareness that philosophy is powerless to free man, and *a fortiori* the Jew, from doubts concerning the burning questions of existence, as these presented themselves in the author's milieu.[79] The main focuses of the discussion in *Minḥat Kena'ot* are those questions which pertain to the understanding of Godhead and the aspiration for a positive apprehension of God;[80] the problem of the separate intelligences and their nature, including the problem of God's action in the world and the stress upon the voluntaristic-teleological aspect of this activity; the refutation of that approach which identifies the divine messengers, that is, the angels, with the separate intelligences, with the aim of granting the angels a concrete personal existence and thereby enriching the personalist understanding of God and His ways of acting;[81] the wish to shift the centre of gravity in the understanding of prophecy from the intellectual to the practical-ethical domain, unique to the Jewish people;[82] and, particularly, the problem entailed in the nature, aim, and eternity of the human soul, and specifically of the Jewish soul. These latter issues constitute the main elements of the book,

[79] See e.g. *Minḥat Kena'ot*, 11: 'We therefore see explicitly that the human intellect cannot ascend on high to [the realm of] subtle opinions and argumentations, were it not for the light of Torah that rose upon His servant the true one of His house [i.e. *Moses*], by whom it was given to the congregation of Israel, whose righteousness is like the mighty mountains.' Cf. ibid. 14, 73–4, 113, 117. Even theological disputes within the Christian camp, such as the question of works and of predestination, were expressed within this context; cf. p. 11.

[80] *Minḥat Kena'ot*, 18–28. It should be noted that the very same problem echoes from the first chapter of R. Moses Cordovero's *Pardes Rimonnim*; cf. the comments of R. Leone Modena in *Ari Nohem* (ed. Leibovitz, 16–21).

[81] *Minḥat Kena'ot*, 28–36. Cf. the comments of R. Leone Modena directed against the Kabbalists, who claim to know the fundamentals of concentration in prayer, in his *Ari Nohem*, Ch. 9 (ed. Leibovitz, 24–9).

[82] *Minḥat Kena'ot*, 36–44. This latter subject should be seen in light of the value of deeds as against intellectual understanding, as expressed in the critique of the Maimonidean approach, particularly that of R. Ḥasdai Crescas. This valuation is given an added dimension within the complex of Renaissance thought, in which even those thinkers who follow the established path of scholastic rationalism would not allow themelves to avoid its problematic. See Bonfil, 'R. Obadiah Sforno'. These trends were now joined by the mystical understanding of human acts as influencing the cosmic system; cf. *Minḥat Kena'ot*, 75, 88. Cf. also R. Leone Modena's remarks, in *Ari Nohem*, Ch. 8 (ed. Leibovitz, 22–4), against the Kabbalists, who argue that they know the reasons for the commandments. Concerning the matter of prophecy, particular to the Jewish people, the approach of simple faith, perhaps in a certain Christian vein, stands out against the rationalistic approach; cf. *Minḥat Kena'ot*, 26.

both in terms of quantity[83] and emphasis. R. Vitale da Pisa's discussion is a striking expression of the failure of scholastic rationalism to give to man the consciousness of his individual spiritual uniqueness, and to the Jew the sense of uniqueness involved in his commitment, acquired by blood and tears, to a system of observance of the precepts of the Torah among the hostile nations in Exile.

At the same time, that is, in 1538, R. Barkhiel ben Kaufmann, at the age of fifty-three, set down in writing his great work, *Lev Adam*. At the beginning, he states that from the age of fifteen years onwards 'I had always longed to understand the depths of the reasons of the [*commandments of the*] Torah and its secrets'. He goes on to describe how his spiritual world grew out of the realization that Aristotelian philosophy is not useful except in the realm of 'natural sciences':

> Therefore, one is prevented from receiving true benefit from his [Aristotle's] books concerning the essence of truth, for the true axioms were concealed from him, and his words were nothing but intellectual speculation. Thus, he departed from the paths of truth, for he completely denied creation *ex nihilo*, that is, he denied that something may come into existence from nothing. From this there followed many other things which caused great destruction of faith, such as the theory of eternity of the world, and many other things from which followed, heaven forbid, the negation of the Torah. In fact, his intellect proved useful in understanding the nature of the world alone . . .[84]

Certainly, opinions such as these involve a certain return to ideas, motifs, and uncertainties which were previously articulated, in one form or another, in Jewish circles. We shall not examine here the differences between the various systems. In a certain sense, R. Barkhiel, who evidently found it difficult to free himself totally from scholastic philosophy, and attempted to incorporate Kabbalah into philosophy,[85] returned to the criticism directed by R. Judah ha-Levi against Aristotle: 'for he troubled his mind and thoughts because he did not have a tradition from one whose message he could believe.'[86]

Indeed, it is no accident that a renewed flowering of interest

[83] *Minḥat Kena'ot*, 51–95: i.e. more than a third of the book.
[84] See D. Ginzburg, *Me'asef; Pirkei Divrei ha-Yamim ve-Divrei Mada'* ii (St Petersburg, 1902), 10.
[85] See E. Gottleib, *Meḥkarim be-Sifrut ha-Kabbalah* (Tel Aviv, 1976), 423.
[86] See *Kuzari* 1: 65.

in R. Judah ha-Levi's historical-philosophic œuvre took place in Italy during those years.[87] Even R. Judah Moscato, the author of one of the most important and comprehensive commentaries upon the *Kuzari* written towards the end of the sixteenth century, who knew R. Barkhiel b. Kaufmann's writings and derived from them inspiration,[88] saw certain points of contact between the thought of R. Judah ha-Levi and that of the anti-rationalistic Kabbalists concerning the evaluation of the practical religious precepts:

Know now that the root of all the controversy over this depends upon the difference in opinion pertaining to the practical precepts: whether they are directed towards themselves, or if they are a means to reach the apprehension of the intelligences, as stated in [Maimonides'] *Guide*. And the *Ḥaver* [i.e. *the Jew in the Kuzari*] took it that all is done properly in its time, that [precepts] are absolutely essential and primordial, and the true Kabbalists agree with the *Ḥaver* on that point . . .[89]

Another matter is also involved here. There is no doubt that the mystical direction of the Kabbalists, which R. Vitale da Pisa proposed to his co-religionists as an alternative to philosophy, was a definite expression of the feeling of uniqueness of the Jewish people—a feeling which, as I have tried to show elsewhere, was common among the Jews in Italy during the period under discussion.[90] There thus follows from da Pisa's presentation a tendency to emphasize the uniqueness of the Jewish individual *vis-à-vis* other human beings, and the uniqueness of the Jewish people *vis-à-vis* other peoples;[91] to stress how this uniqueness was obscured, if not completely negated, by scholastic thought:[92] to stress strongly the substantive difference between

[87] See the end of Sect. 4 and nn. 191, 192.

[88] See H. Michael, *Or ha-Ḥayyim: Ḥakhmei Yisra'el ve-sifreihem* (Jerusalem, 1965), 644.

[89] See the commentary *Kol Yehudah* on Ch. 1, sect. 79, end.

[90] See Bonfil, 'The Uniqueness of the Jewish People'.

[91] See e.g. *Minḥat Kena'ot*, 13: 'If, therefore, God has revealed His Holy right arm upon Israel and upon His Holy ones, to give them a crown of glory, that they are as the mistress of all kingdoms, and to place a precious stone at their head, their king going before them and God at their head, how can we be so guilty as to descend to Egypt, and to the other descendants of Keturah, for help? . . .' Cf. ibid. 41.

[92] See e.g. *Minḥat Kena'ot*, 14: 'For if it were thus [i.e. *that philosophy is no more than a commentary and elaboration of obscure Rabbinic sayings, such as the curious aggadot*], why then are they hidden and why do they speak in riddles and parables, if these are things which man can bring to his knowledge by means of logic and rational proofs. And if this

the Jew and other human beings[93] (a point of clear divergence between the rationalistic understanding of man and that of the Kabbalists); and to stress the feeling of a Jew who, even though it was not within his power to influence the political world in which he lived, might nevertheless believe himself, by virtue of the simple performance of Jewish ritual, to be influencing the entire cosmos[94] and to be participating in the process of the redemption of his people and all mankind.

The traumatic experience of the Expulsion from Spain and the consequent heightening of expressions of longing for immanent redemption served as an overall framework for all of these ideas. Within this context, the works of philosophy were understood to be works of the *sitra aḥra*—the demonic 'Other Side' of Kabbalistic metaphysics. As is known, many would identify the turn towards philosophy as one of the decisive factors contributing to the tragedy of the Expulsion; thus, the abandonment of these books and the return to Jewish practice via repentance, prayer, and good deeds, coupled with the mystical intentions attached to all of these, might be seen as paving the way for the realization of redemption. Such ideas were promulgated in Italy particularly by such preachers as R. Joseph Javez (d. 1507). Even though the immediate impact of his sermons does not seem great, and we have not to date found any significant echoes in the response of the public in Italy to these and their like,[95] there nevertheless

were so, they would all be united in this—Jew and Christian and Persian and Hagarite [i.e. *Muslim*]—and there would not be among the secrets of Torah those which were only given to Moses our master at Sinai, and which the prophets received generation after generation . . .'

[93] See e.g. *Minḥat Kena'ot*, 81: 'This is the matter of the souls of the Israelite nation, but as for other nations whose souls do not originate and descend from a holy place . . . the power of the pure soul does not devolve upon them, except after they accept the yoke of the Kingdom of Heaven [i.e. *become converted to Judaism*] and circumcise themselves. [Nevertheless] they do not merit to cling to the supernal light as do Israelites, and our rabbis said of this that one is not to teach Torah to a Gentile until after he has been circumcised . . .' Cf. 73–5, 79. The same things which R. Vitale da Pisa here addresses to the scholars who read his book were in the following generation said from the pulpit of the synagogue; see R. Bonfil, 'The Uniqueness of the Jewish People', 42–4, and cf. Samuel Judah Katzenellenbogen, *Derashot Maharshi"k*, Sermon 11, p. 58a. Katzenellenbogen's position within the context of the thought of his time will be discussed below. See also R. Bonfil, 'One of the Italian Sermons of R. Mordecai Dato' (Heb.), *Iṭalyah*, 1 (1976), 1–32.

[94] See *Minḥat Kena'ot*, and also above, n. 82, and cf. *Derashot Maharshi"k*, Sermon 8, p. 41b.

[95] See Gottlieb, *Meḥkarim be-Sifrut ha-Kabbalah*, 355.

was a place for them within that cultural environment, even if a marginal one. Thus, we find that the cultural atmosphere in Italy was one in which the Kabbalah might be seen, not as an aristocratic, esoteric doctrine, but rather as the corner-stone of a popular movement which would grow towards the end of the century. At that time, the Kabbalah broke through into the sermons of the enthusiastic preachers in Italy, who combined a call for repentance and good deeds with the mystical doctrine of the Kabbalists and, at times, apocalyptic interpretations of history,[96] to which we shall return at greater length. But let us go back to our subject.

Who were these people who put all their energy into 'the hastening towards and the pursuit of wisdom', and whom Moses b. Joab da Rieti wished to serve as spokesman and defender?[97] Was the confrontation one between an anti-rationalistic rabbi and an intellectual élite of seekers after rationalistic wisdom who were not understood by the 'Masters of Torah'? In order to answer the latter question unequivocally in the negative, it is enough to note the restrained response of R. Joḥanan Treves to R. Vitale da Pisa:

> You, the mighty cedar of Lebanon, have sent the hyssop in the wall to enter into the thick of the struggle of the living God, Saviour, and Great Redeemer, in their internal speculations, and to separate the great ones, the Revered Rabbis and wise sages, as it is understood from your proposal to join the controversy. And I fear lest my skull be smashed or lest I be burned up by the breath of their mouths, if I place a small finger between them . . .[98]

It is clear from this answer that the struggle was not one between a camp of 'Masters of Torah' and one of devotees of philosophy! In 1539, a figure of the stature of R. Joḥanan Treves felt that to take a stand on the issues treated by R. Vitale in his work would require taking sides in a lively and tumultuous controversy involving the major rabbinic figures of the age.

A striking figure among these rabbis was R. Obadiah Sforno. I have discussed elsewhere at length the way in which this sage sought to find his way into Averroistic mysticism, as this developed

[96] On the phenomena in general, see G. Scholem, *Major Trends in Jewish Mysticism* (New York, 1961), 244–51.

[97] See above, in Sect. 3.

[98] *Minḥat Kena'ot*, 4.

among the university circles, which in his day were still strongly devoted to scholasticism.[99] R. Obadiah imagined that he would be a kind of spokesman of the *Hebraica Veritas* in his battle, but his hope was not realized. It seems to me that the proofs which he wished to establish in his book *Or 'Ammim* (*Lumen Gentium*) and in his other works, while making use of scholastic analogies, did not leave much of an impression. We nevertheless have here a clear example of an original, living scholastic creation, written by a rabbi known throughout Italy.

Sforno's attempt, undertaken in the same Bologna in which R. Vitale da Pisa wrote his work,[100] seems to have been the last significant attempt to defend the structure of Jewish scholasticism by means of dialectical discussion. The very path which he chose provides clear evidence of his awareness that the criticism directed against scholasticism upset the very foundations of scholastic thought in both the Jewish and Christian camps.[101] This criticism was supported, in not insignificant ways, in Jewish works, such as that of R. Hasdai Crescas, which was in turn echoed among Christians, such as Pico della Mirandola;[102] but neither this criticism nor the growing mystical trend of the Kabbalists

[99] See Bonfil, 'R. Obadiah Sforno', which also contains a discussion of this phenomenon in general within the Christian milieu.

[100] R. Obadiah Sforno's book, *'Or 'Amim*, was published two years before R. Vitale da Pisa wrote his *Minḥat Kena'ot*. Most of the subjects discussed in the former are likewise treated in the latter, which suggests that these were the main questions which interested people during that period. R. Vitale certainly read *'Or 'Amim*, and included clear allusions to his criticism of it in his own book (see Bonfil, 'R. Obadiah Sforno', 214 n. 57), albeit there was no head-on confrontation here. It may be that da Pisa hesitated to attack Sforno because of the latter's age and position. However, it seems more likely that he saw no grounds for a substantive discussion, as such a discussion would, by its very nature, need to focus upon the scholastic distinctions through which Sforno attempted to strengthen his own logical arguments. These very assumptions were rejected by da Pisa. He himself indeed objected to Plato and Aristotle, Alexander and Themistius, Averroës and Avicenna—in short, to all those *auctoritates* upon whom R. Obadiah Sforno's own position was based. He therefore had neither common ground nor reason to argue over the details of *Sefer 'Or 'Amim*.

[101] An extreme expression of such criticism, albeit one which in the final analysis was of only marginal weight in the overall picture, is to be found in the writings of Nicolo Franco, an Italian scholar who was a contemporary of R. Vitale da Pisa and R. Obadiah Sforno, published in the very same year that R. Vitale wrote his opus: 'Veggo prima i philosophi, e con essi la gran confusione de i lor scritti, i lor ciarlamenti, tutti sono impecciati di Principii, e di fini; di corporeo e d'incorporeo; di generabile, e di sensibile e d'incorruttibile; di mortate e d'immortale; di finito e d'infinito e di materie prime, d'atomi e d'Idee'—N. Franco, *Le Pistole Vulgari* (Venice, 1539), fo. 85. Cf. P. F. Grendler, 'The Rejection of Learning', *Studies in the Renaissance*, 13 (1966).

[102] See H. A. Wolfson, *Crescas' Critique of Aristotle* (Cambridge, Mass., 1929), 34 ff.

succeeded in totally obliterating the traces of Jewish scholasticism. Many rabbis whose mental constitution was explicitly rationalistic continued to adhere to it, albeit cautiously and with the definite aim of developing the theological foundations of the scholastic structure, and not its philosophical elements. This was accomplished by following Maimonides' approach, while attempting to limit, or even to ignore, the criticism directed against it.[103] The aura of sanctity which surrounded the Maimonidean corpus—including the *Guide for the Perplexed*, which never entirely left the Jewish bookshelf in Italy—served to buttress those who adhered to the scholastic structure. Study of the *Guide* therefore continued, in a somewhat peculiar and dogmatic way, accompanied by elementary commentaries,[104] although alongside it the scholars also began to learn R. Judah ha-Levi's *Kuzari*.[105]

We may infer from this that the dispute between the opponents of philosophy and those who continued the scholastic tradition in their own way, was a central element of the cultural expression of Italian Jewry, being related to the wider debate among Christians. Prominent rabbis took part in this debate, taking positions on one side or the other, while one can find a wide gamut of schools of thought between the two extremes, combining philosophical and Kabbalistic elements in varying degrees, from the claim for complete equivalence of Kabbalah and philosophy to the total rejection of philosophy in favour of Kabbalah. Even the not uncommon approach which sought to make use of philosophy in order to strengthen Kabbalah, an approach which was becoming increasingly popular, brings into relief three developments: first, the quite powerful status still enjoyed by philosophy; second, the severity of the criticism directed against it, which upset the status of exclusive primacy which philosophy had enjoyed within the overall cultural context; third, the widespread desire for a synthesis between Kabbalah and philosophy.

For example, R. Leone Modena testified that he had heard 'from R. Israel Sarug . . . who said that there was no difference between *Kabbalah* and philosophy, and that whatever he learned

[103] I presented a typical example of this in some detail in Bonfil, 'R. Moses Provenzali's Commentary on Maimonides' 25 Premises' (Heb.), *KS* 50 (1975), 157–64.

[104] See the end of Sect. 2.

[105] See Bonfil, 'R. Obadiah Sforno', 157 n. 2, and see also Sect. 3 above.

in *Kabbalah* he interpreted in a philosophic manner'.[106] Interestingly, Sarug (*fl.* 1590–1610) presented himself as a disciple of R. Isaac Luria.[107] It seems unlikely that Sarug learned his doctrine in the Land of Israel; it seems more likely that he adjusted himself to the general atmosphere in order to recruit disciples for his own teaching. In this context, one must remember that the inspiration coming from Safed would tend to take issue with those who sought to buttress Kabbalah by means of philosophic arguments, preferring to view philosophical knowledge as belonging with other branches of human knowledge, as part of human experience and natural sciences and on a par with them. An interesting testimony to this effect has been preserved in the correspondence of R. Mordecai Dato with R. Ezra da Fano, the teacher of R. Menaḥem Azariah da Fano.[108]

R. Ezra da Fano, who still debated this subject within himself during the 1570s, received a letter from R. Mordecai Dato following the latter's return from Safed in which it is maintained that one should not study Kabbalah except through the words of the Kabbalists themselves, and that the Kabbalistic tradition is sufficient in itself to assure the truth of the things studied, requiring no assistance from philosophy:

Let me inform you of two things: first . . . that whatever is said by one of the sages of Safed . . . in the introduction to the works of Truth and Justice [i.e. *Kabbalah*], is based upon the words of the *Zohar*; their words are its words; they emerged from its radiance, and without them no man might raise his hands or feet . . . in learning or in criticism, to speak about this wisdom, for they fear the great fire which consumes that man who makes things up from his heart, who has not heard [them] from his teacher as required in the *Zohar* . . . They ought not to rely upon their understanding or their dialectics (*pilpul*), [though] they are very great, save in the interpretation of some few sayings of the *Zohar* which seem to contradict one another . . . and even this only under certain conditions [stated in] the *Zohar* itself. Secondly, that the words of the *Zohar* are based upon tradition, and that one may not question them . . .[109]

106 Modena, *Ari Nohem*, ed. Leibovitz, 52–3.

107 See G. Scholem, 'Israel Saruk—Was He a Disciple of Luria?' (Heb.), *Ẓion*, 5 (1940), 214–43.

108 R. Mordecai Dato's letters to R. Ezra da Fano are found in MS Parma 130, fo. 23–34.

109 Ibid. fo. 23a.

When Dato was again asked whether one was to understand that 'one is not to question those views found in the *Zohar*, but [only] to reconcile them, and if they are tradition one is to accept them', he gave a long, elaborate answer, in which he explained that he did not intend to prevent those who wished to understand the words of the *Zohar* by way of analogy or reconciliation with what is known from reason, from experience, or even from philosophy, from doing so. Such a stand seemed to him rather hasty and simplistic: 'It is rash to enter into their circle, the circles of righteousness, in which every breach [i.e. *contradiction*] is strengthened without seeking reason and understanding of its words, *Kabbalah* being above reason.' In his opinion, 'everything which is probable ought to be accepted graciously—and that which is without reason ought to be confirmed by reason'. That is: if it is possible to explain things by means of reason—good; if not—their contents are themselves acceptable to reason. 'And I know that the two of them—*Kabbalah* and reason—travel together in my answers . . . and it is an eternal argument, that nature and feeling and philosophy all acknowledge, and I did not suffice with my saying . . . for the words of the *Zohar* are [authentic] tradition.' What does R. Mordecai Dato intend to teach us? In his words:

One is not obliged to find a [rational] explanation of the kind which I have mentioned for all the words of the *Zohar*, for many have fallen [in the attempt]. Go and see how one of the sages of the nations, Johannes Reuchlin,[110] . . . made himself wise in one work which he made, which I saw many years ago, bringing selection after selection, at random . . . to find words of favour and natural philosophic reason in the words of the *Zohar*. And in his many clever words, albeit he avoided corporealization, he compared the Creator to [His] form, and the servant to his master . . . heaven forbid.[111]

One is therefore allowed to combine with Kabbalah 'an eternal reason, which is acknowledged by nature and intuition and philosophy', that is, an argument in which philosophical knowledge is combined with the natural knowledge so beloved by the members of his generation, as well as with the personal experience

110 Johannes Reuchlin, in his *De verbo mirifico*.
111 MS Parma, fos. 24a–25a.

of the thinker.[112] However, one ought not to follow Johannes Reuchlin's path in seeking 'natural philosophical proofs for the views of the *Zohar*'; that is to say, one is not permitted to attempt a kind of synthesis of natural philosophy[113] and Kabbalah.[114]

We can discern here a third type of eclectic thought, also represented primarily by rabbis. This path appears to be similar in nature to those syncretistic cultural positions which are so characteristic of any transitional period between the decline of one period of thought and the emergence of a new one. Here, too, there is no substantive difference between what took place in the Jewish world and that which occurred in the Christian world. Just as—apart from certain isolated cases, which are essentially the exceptions which prove the rule—in the final analysis the new Platonic enthusiasm fused with Aristotelianism, along with the writings of the Alexandrian school, in which such a synthesis was formulated for the first time, so did the concepts of the Kabbalah and its aggadic context fuse with the philosophical, cultural background. In the final analysis, this experiment, which suited well the taste and style of the times, did not exclude the construction of an encyclopaedic-eclectic structure which would include under one rubric various streams of philosophic thought—Greek, Arabic, and Jewish—along with

[112] Examples of such association appear in the sermons of R. Mordecai Dato, such as the sermon on *Lekh Lekha*, in which he nicely combined the natural reasons for the commandment of circumcision, which he found in R. Isaac Arama's '*Akedat Yiẓḥak*, and the mystical ones of the Kabbalah. See R. Bonfil, 'One of the Italian Sermons of R. Mordecai Dato'.

[113] *Philosophia naturalis.*

[114] This seems to have been the most extreme position within the spectrum of the eclectics, whose thought came to be dominated by the Kabbalah, out of all proportion to the philosophical-naturalistic element. The transition to this position can only have come about among people who turned to Kabbalah through a total rejection of philosophy, a rejection which was not based upon an immanent critique of philosophy, but upon a programmatic opposition to the very idea of philosophical studies. One such person was R. Joseph Ashkenazi, the '*tanna* from Safed', who stayed in Italy *en route* from Germany to Safed and there composed a work in which he criticized those who turned to philosophical studies, which they then used in order to give allegorical interpretations of difficult Rabbinic legends; see G. Scholem, 'New Information Concerning R. Joseph Ashkenazi'. This work by R. Shalom Ashkenazi was copied in Asti in 1582 by R. Abraham b. Meshullam (Scholem, ibid. 66), an individual whose statements against the study of *halakhah* and in favour of total devotion to Kabbalistic studies has already been noted. There is thus clear evidence that R. Joseph Ashkenazi's words found a receptive ear specifically in those circles which embraced the Kabbalah dogmatically, and not via a dialectical encounter with the philosophical problematics in whose wake it emerged.

the Kabbalah.[115] This path was followed by a number of talented sages during the second half of the sixteenth century, whom the public loved and admired precisely because they fused these different elements: R. Abraham Provenzali, the rabbi of the community in Casale Montferrat,[116] R. Judah Moscato, R. Samuel David Katzenellenbogen, and R. Samuel Archivolti.

4. Sermon and Midrash

That the afore-mentioned sages were well-known preachers, who operated specifically during the latter half of the sixteenth century, complements the picture drawn thus far. The realm in which one feels most clearly the transformation which took place in the Jewish cultural atmosphere during the period under discussion would seem to be that of the sermon. Due to its public nature,[117] the sermon brought the rabbis, as the Masters of the Torah, to encounter the public in a shared cultural atmosphere. That is to say, if the preacher did not belong to the type of the moralistic sermonizer, who is not typical of the cultural-social atmosphere in which he lives and acts, his sermon would generally blend into the cultural atmosphere within which it was given, the preacher attempting to exploit this atmosphere to the maximum in order to achieve his goals. The need fulfilled by the sermon in Italy was no different in principle from that which it fulfilled in any other Jewish community: namely, the need to reinforce adherence to the system of values to which the society was committed in principle, a *genre* which gave a certain pleasure to its audience, strengthening social bonds around these same values, as well as conveying a contemporary dimension to the cultural heritage of

[115] See Cassuto, *Firenze*, 245–6. See also E. Panofsky, 'Artist, Scientist, Genius—Notes on the "Renaissance-Dämmerung" ', in *The Renaissance; Six Essays*, by W. K. Ferguson *et al.* (New York, 1962), 129–31, and the literature cited there. See also H. Wirszubski, *Sheloshah Perakim be-Toldot ha-Kabbalah ha-Nozrit* (Jerusalem, 1973), 11–12.

[116] Although his writings have not been preserved, we may rely upon the testimony of his disciples, who depicted him as 'possessing both extensive knowledge and sharp analytic acuity . . . the Kabbalist, the physician and the divine philosopher' (see the conclusion of *Sefer Shilṭei ha-Gibborim* by R. Abraham Portaleone).

[117] See J. Dan, 'Hebrew Homiletical Literature (*Derush*) and its Literary Values' (Heb.), *ha-Sifrut*, 3 (1971–2), 559–60.

the group.[118] In other words, in Italy as elsewhere, the sermon first and foremost served a didactic-educational function.

One must remember that, within the framework of the Aristotelian-Ciceronian tradition of thought, rhetoric was always viewed as a means of persuasion,[119] and therefore as an instrument of education. As summarized, for example, by R. Joseph ben Shem-Tov in his book, *'Ein ha-Kore*,[120] which deals with the technique of the sermon, the 'purpose of this labour in itself, and in terms of those who listen and of the one that speaks and expounds', is solely 'to remove the spiritual illnesses from the souls of men and to preserve their health'.[121] It follows that, within this ideational framework, public preaching would be understood as a means of healing the spiritual ills of its listeners. Thus, 'the essence of preaching' turns out to be 'remembering the sins and transgressions and wrong-doings in which they sin . . .'[122] The preacher's individual character and ethical qualities are obviously of some importance: according to R. Joseph ben Shem-Tov, he ought to be a person of good deeds, 'upright in the city', wise, a master of clear speech, wealthy, mature in years, respected, modest, and one who makes an effort to correct even small faults.[123] Such an approach was commonly accepted in Italy throughout the period under discussion.[124] At the beginning of the period, R. Judah Messer Leon taught his fellows, in the wake of Cicero and Quintilian, that 'the perfect preacher must have three things: he must be wise, perfect in his ethical virtues, and able to speak appropriately according to the nature of his

118 See J. Katz, *Tradition and Crisis* (New York, 1971), 173–5; J. Dan, *Sifrut ha-Mussar veha-Deruch* (Jerusalem, 1975); H. H. Ben-Sasson, *Hagut ve-Hanhagah* (Jerusalem, 1960), 39–42; I. Bettan, *Studies in Jewish Preaching* (Cincinnati, 1939), 9.

119 Cf. Aristotle, *Rhetoric*, Sect. I, Ch. 1. In a debate at the beginning of our period concerning the subject of rhetoric, an important role was played by R. Judah Messer Leon's book *Nofet Ẓufim*; cf. my 'Introduction to *Nofet Ẓufim*'. On the function of the sermon in raising the cultural-social level of the public in the Renaissance milieu, see Burckhardt, *Renaissance*, 236 ff., 371.

120 The book is still in manuscript form. A. Jellinek published the Introduction only in *Kuntres ha-Mafteaḥ* (Vienna, 1881), 30–2. Here, I used MS Paris 325.

121 Ibid. fo. 92a, and see also fos. 102b ff., the second section on 'The Nature of Health and the Nature of Sickness and its General and Secondary Causes'.

122 Ibid. fo. 99b.

123 Ibid. fo. 102b, and cf. Bettan, *Studies in Jewish Preaching*, 60–1, 65–6.

124 Cf. Ben-Sasson's remarks in *Hagut ve-Hanhagah*, 41 ff., regarding Germany and Poland.

subject'.[125] At the end of this period, R. Moses b. Samuel ibn Bassa of Blanes, a preacher in Florence and Siena, elaborated upon this matter in the same spirit in his work *Tena'ei ha-Darshan*.[126] At the beginning of the book, he states that 'the perfect man who is worthy of serving his Creator . . . is none other than the perfect preacher, who fulfills all the conditions incumbent upon him'.[127] He then goes on to enumerate those negative qualities which a preacher ought to avoid,[128] and the virtues which he should cultivate. Regarding the latter, he states, first and foremost, that the preacher must be 'wise, understanding and learned and, as the [task of] the sage-preacher is to chastise others, he must also possess another wisdom, which is very delicate, such that his wisdom does not cause harm to others—namely, that he [knows how to] chastise in such a way that the good [people] will accept it from him, but the evil ones will not receive it . . .'.[129] Among other virtues, he expects the perfect preacher to possess eloquence,[130] 'to be precise and sharp' and 'that he be a master of proper behaviour',[131] 'that he say things clearly . . . words of substance . . . sweet and pleasant words . . . words of kindness and mercy . . . elevated words in profound matters, [but] in such a way that his words will be understood by those who hear them'.[132] All this is based upon rabbinical dicta and biblical verses, the clear assumption being that there were no outstanding figures among the Jews, from the time of the patriarchs onwards, whose greatness was not also expressed in the area of homiletics.[133]

We have seen that one of the tasks of the rabbi appointed by the community was to preach in the synagogue, primarily on Sabbaths and festivals, or at least on certain specific occasions during the course of the year. Even in those places which did not have a community-appointed rabbi, or where there were many

[125] Messer Leon, *Sefer Nofet Ẓufim*, Pt. I, end of Ch. 1. Cf. Bettan, *Studies in Jewish Preaching*, 235. For the extent of R. Judah Messer Leon's impact on subsequent generations in the realm of rhetoric, see the remarks by R. Baruch Uziel Chazachetto in his suggestions concerning the divorce, *Haẓa'ah 'al 'Odot ha-Geṭ* (Venice, 1566), 27b: 'Two letters have arrived signed by two of your rabbis . . . who are as people expert in the art of rhetoric, who know how to present their words in such a manner as to win the hearts of their hearers, as is the custom of orators, and like the learned things written in *Sefer Nofet Ẓufim* . . .'

[126] I quote from MS Columbia X 893 T 15 Q. The places where R. Moses ben Bassa was active are noted in the MS on fos. 13b and 15a.

[127] Ibid. fo. 14b.

[128] Ibid. fos. 16a–18b.

[129] Ibid. fos. 19b–20a.

[130] Ibid. fos. 20a, 23a.

[131] Ibid. fo. 23a.

[132] Ibid. fo. 24a.

[133] Ibid. fos. 20a, 41a ff.

synagogues, means were found to ensure the delivery of a sermon in the synagogues on Sabbaths and holidays,[134] usually by ordained rabbis who could serve as examples for the public who listened to them, although not exclusively by them.[135] In practice, as have seen,[136] the community-appointed rabbis sought the right of priority in the delivery of sermons, so long as they saw this necessary, including also their demand to lead the education of the public. This is confirmed in the comments of R. Jacob b. Kalonymos ha-Levi, in the introduction to his book *Kol Ya'akov*, in which he included topics for sermons listed in alphabetical order:[137]

And when the wheel of time turned around, and the holy diadem, my master and teacher, the pious Kabbalist R. Ezra da Fano passed away, I delivered the eulogy [over him] in the great congregation. And his merit assisted me so that from heaven my words found favour in the ears of those who heard me, and among them were the very erudite and profound scholars, the Excellent Master of the generation, my master and teacher R. Ben-Zion Zarfatti of blessed memory, who commanded me sternly to pursue this holy task; and because I was skilled at it . . . I did not refuse. And he insisted that I make it a fixed custom to speak every year on the festival of Sukkot, and [in this connnection] I several times eulogized and preached about those who had departed from the earth . . . I did not forbear to be the 'tail of lions' and to stand in the place of great men, the distinguished Masters of preaching before the congregation, both when they were outside [i.e. *away*] and when something prevented them, Heaven forbid, [from preaching] . . .

It is the nature of a sermon to be addressed to everyone. Thus, with the possible exception of those sermons which were delivered within certain closed circles of learned people or guest sermons by visiting rabbis who did not know the language of the country, it seems certain that throughout this period Jewish sermons were delivered in Italian,[138] as was the practice in the Christian

[134] See e.g. Documents 13–14, pp. 229–34, in the Hebrew edition of this book.

[135] See the comments of R. Leone Modena, who describes the form of the synagogue sermon extensively in his *Historia di gli riti hebraica* (Paris, 1637), 36–7. Modena states there that anyone who wished to do so was allowed to ascend to the pulpit and preach: 'che facilmente ad ogn'uno é concesso'.

[136] See Ch. 3, Sect. 8.

[137] The book remains at present in manuscript form. In the only copy preserved in Columbia University, the introduction is bound at the end of the book.

[138] See L. Della Torre, 'In qual lingua si predicò in Italia nei tempi passati', *CI* 1 (1862–3), 94–8, and the sources cited there. In addition, we have the explicit testimony

milieu.[139] The contents of the sermon were recorded in abbreviated form, sometimes by the preacher himself and sometimes by one of his listeners; this served as a kind of outline, more or less detailed, for the preacher himself or for other preachers. During the later period, preachers sometimes prepared their sermons for publication.[140] Those sermons preserved in Hebrew from the entire medieval period, at least until the second half of the sixteenth century, bear clear signs that they were not originally delivered in the form in which they appear in writing. Their dry and schematic form, almost completely lacking reference to current events and to the surroundings; the extreme brevity of many of the sermons (so that, if they were in fact delivered as published, they could not have taken more than five minutes to deliver); and, in other cases, the digressions into complex matters, difficult both in terms of content and in terms of the terminology and the philosophical or Talmudic dialectic contained within them: all these attest to the fact that the text of the majority of sermons as they have been preserved in writing was quite different from the form in which they were originally delivered in public. There are cases in which clear evidence has been preserved of the

of Montaigne, *Journal du voyage . . . en Italie . . . 1580–1581*, Ch. 7: 'L'après-disnée tour à tour leurs docteurs font leçon sur le passage de la bible de ce jours-làs, le faisant en Italien. Après la leçon quelque autre docteur assistant choisit quelcun des auditeurs et parfois deus ou trois de suite, pour argumenter contre celui qui vient de lire, sur ce qu'il a dict. Celui qui nous ouïmes . . . sembla avoir beaucoup d'eloquence et beaucoup d'esprit en son argumentation.' See also Bonfil, 'One of the Italian Sermons of R. Mordecai Dato'.

139 It seems a well established fact that, at least from the 10th century, Christians preached in the vernacular and not in Latin, except within certain closed clerical frameworks. Nevertheless, the majority of Christian sermons from earlier times until the 14th century have been preserved in their Latin form, in which they were recorded by their authors due to the impossibility of expressing the full clarity and scope of their ideas, which were rooted in scholastic thought, in the vernacular. These ideas were presented in the vernacular in simplified form and only by allusions, which were unsuitable to the presentation of systematic philosophical ideas; see A. Galletti, *L'eloquenza dalle origini al XVI secolo* (Milan, 1938), 53–70. In the Christian milieu, the use of the vernacular even in written form spread mainly from the 14th century (ibid. 162). In the Jewish milieu, by contrast, the change to writing sermons in Italian took place significantly later; I will attempt to explain the reasons for this below.

140 Ibid. 94 ff., 150 ff.; J. Dan, 'Hebrew Homiletical Literature', 561–2; Ben-Sasson, *Hagut ve-Hanhagah*, 39–40. This is certainly the reason for the small number of sermons preserved, in comparison with the other areas of literary endeavour; as most were delivered on days when writing was forbidden, if the preacher himself did not record his words either before or after delivering the sermon, generally for purposes beyond the sermon itself (cf. Dan, 'Hebrew Homiletical Literature', 566), the probability that one of his listeners would do so from memory after the end of the Sabbath or festival was very slight.

editing of sermons following their delivery. Thus, for example, in the text of the sermon delivered on *Shabbat ha-Gadol* (i.e. the Sabbath preceding Passover, on which it was customary to deliver a lengthy excursus on the laws of the Passover festival and on the text of the Haggadah), R. Samuel Judah Katzenellenbogen recorded:

Here I made a brief interruption in my exposition [of the laws] and I began to exhort the people concerning the baking of the *matzot*—particularly that they should be made with great speed, and that everyone should make them himself. And I expounded the verse, 'that a man does and lives by them' [Lev. 18: 5]—i.e., that they should perform the commandments with vitality and energy, not drowsily and lazily, and I explained to them some of the laws of *matzot*, and then I returned to my exposition and said . . .[141]

Similarly, in the midst of the text of the eulogy for R. Joseph Caro, he wrote:

I then began to relate the praises of the deceased scholar . . . that we can truthfully say without any exaggeration that since Maimonides and Nahmanides there has not been his like in Israel, to raise up and adorn the Torah; for apart from his printed books, he also publicized and improved many books, some of which he sent to me on the ship Contarina, with R. Baruch, who is with us here, except that the pirates stole them together with the spoils of the ship. And in a document which he directed to me, he told me of many novellae which he wrote upon the entire *Bet Yosef* [*Caro's classical halakhic commentary on R. Jacob ben Asher's halakhic codex*, *Arba'ah Ṭurim*] and of a large number of responsa which he would send to me, and concerning this I said, 'seek to be near to him' [Deut. 12: 5] . . . And then I expounded the rabbinic saying, 'The death of the righteous is as difficult as . . .' . . . and I again recited the verse 'seek to dwell near him and go there' . . .[142]

Thereafter, the note is integrated within the sermon in an organic way.

From a structural point of view, the Jewish sermon in Italy was not much different from what was customary in the Christian world. There were generally three main parts: 'the theme'—that is, the verse or short group of verses, generally accompanied by

[141] Katzenellenbogen, *Derashot Mahari"k*, Sermon 8, 44b.
[142] Ibid. Sermon 10, 56a.

a Rabbinic saying; the body of the sermon, in which the preacher developed the theme, expounded each of its elements at length, and incorporated elements of an ethical nature, which enabled him to relate to contemporary problems; and the conclusion, containing words of exhortation to repentance and good deeds, and a prayer for redemption.[143] To these there were occasionally added, following the presentation of the theme, an introduction (*exordium*), which included expressions of humility and apology, along with remarks pertaining to the art of sermonizing itself.[144]

In contrast to the conservatism reflected in the structure and style of delivery of the sermon during our period, one is struck by the transformation in its contents. Sermons based primarily upon philosophical ideas, such as those given by Moses ben Joab in Florence during the second half of the fifteenth century,[145] seem to have disappeared completely towards the second half of the sixteenth century. This transformation no doubt has its roots in the challenge to the status of scholastic thought already discussed. This challenge which was clearly expressed in dialectical confrontation within the realm of speculative creativity, made the philosophical sermon more problematic, so that a kind of vacuum was created, one which the preachers were unable to fill immediately. The universal character of the sermon, addressed as it was to the broader public who did not identify clearly with any particular school of thought, made it more difficult for the preachers to find a direction which would satisfy all elements of their audience. Where could the Italian preachers turn in this atmosphere of crisis surrounding scholastic philosophy? The natural solution would have seemed to be for them to make more extensive use of midrashic literature and to attempt to develop

[143] See Galletti, *L'eloquenza*, 128 ff.; T. M. Charland, 'Artes Praedicandi contribution a l'histoire de la rhetorique au Moyen Age', *Publications de l'Institut d'Études Medievales*, 7 (Paris and Ottawa, 1936). This type of sermon originated with those delivered in the University of Paris, which were generally known as 'thematic' sermons—that is, sermons on a 'subject' or 'theme'—or at times were even referred to as 'university sermons', because of their association with that world. On this question see also M. Zink, *La Prédication en langue Romane avant 1300* (Paris, 1976).

[144] See e.g. U. Cassuto, 'Un rabbino fiorentino del sec. XV', *RI* 3 (1906), 116–28, 224–8; ibid. 4 (1907), 33–7, 156–61, 225–9; R. Judah Moscato, *Nefuẓot Yehudah*, Sermons 12, 17. Many bibliographical notes concerning the *exordium* have been gathered recently by D. Ruderman, *The World of a Renaissance Jew; the Life and Thought of Abraham ben Mordecai Farissol* (Cincinnati, 1981), 177 nn. 35–6.

[145] See Cassuto, 'Un Rabbino Fiorentino'.

ways of exploiting this literature for homiletical purposes. But from those few sermons which have survived from the period, it is clear that this did not occur.

In so far as the rabbis did turn to midrashic literature in their sermons, they generally cited aggadic passages from the Talmud rather than the Midrash *per se*.[146] Of course, in the case of this later period it is difficult to state with certainty in each case the source from which a certain rabbi drew the *midrashim* which he used in his sermons; one sometimes gains the impression that *midrashim* taken from other than Talmudic sources were borrowed from secondary sources.[147] In any event, the explanation given of these *midrashim* generally did not stray too far from their simple literal meaning (*peshat*). Even those rabbis whose intellectual approach remained purely rationalistic refrained from developing allegorical interpretations for those few *midrashim* which they quoted in their sermons. One hardly need add that the same was true for a figure such as R. Moses Provenzali, who instilled in his disciples a belief in the literal meaning of rabbinic *aggadot*, even when these seemed opposed to empirical knowledge and common sense. Provenzali was a dogmatic believer, who imposed his belief in the scholastic philosophy to which he adhered.[148] But the same was true of R. Obadiah Sforno, whose philosophical approach was certainly not dogmatic.[149] Even more surprising, prior to the publication of the *Zohar* even rabbis of a Kabbalistic orientation did the same. For example, the one extant sermon of R. Isaac Joshua da Lattes,[150] one of the noted scholars and teachers of Kabbalah, does not draw upon the rich and colourful store of Kabbalistic literature apart from one passing allusion, and even that by chance and with a play on words.

What does this surprising phenomenon mean? It seems to me that we would not be far wrong in concluding that this was

[146] See e.g. the sermon by R. Abraham ha-Kohen of Bologna, cited in Document 63, pp. 289–91 of the Hebrew version of this book, and the three extant sermons of R. Obadiah Sforno. See Bonfil, 'R. Obadiah Sforno', Appendices.

[147] At times, it is even clear that the homiletical arguments and *midrashim* cited there were borrowed from other sources—see e.g. the sermon of R. Azriel Trabot given in Document 64 in the Hebrew edition of this book, pp. 291–3.

[148] See Bonfil, 'R. Moses Provenzali's Commentary'. To the best of my knowledge, only one sermon of his is extant, in MS Moscow—Günzberg 334 (Yad Ben-Zvi Microfilm 38; IMHM 27967), fos. 47–8. However, reading this microfilm was so difficult that I was forced to forgo my intention to attempt an edition of the sermon.

[149] See the afore-mentioned sermon of R. Obadiah Sforno.

[150] See the sermon of R. Isaac de Lattes, MS Günzberg 160, fo. 6.

largely due to the fact that the texts of even the major midrashic works were simply not widely available until their massive printing at the end of the 1540s. In any event, the involvement of the public in Midrash was limited, which is why its use by preachers was also extremely limited, even if they themselves had access to rare copies of midrashic texts. Indeed, in all the lists of books which I have examined, in only one case were midrashic works listed.[151] When publishers began to publish midrashic works after 1540, they testified that these books were scarcely extant. For example, in the colophon of the 1546 Venice edition of the *Sifra* and *Sifre*, it is stressed that:

> Here is completed the holy labour, that of the *Sifra* and *Sifre*, which until now were rare finds, and whose memory had nearly disappeared from the earth, had not the sage . . . R. Jacob Mantino the Spaniard, may he live long, been moved to publish hidden things from these two books, which are found in his library . . .[152]

Why did not the Jews of Italy engage in the study of such works throughout the fifteenth century and in the first half of the sixteenth century? It is difficult to give an unequivocal answer to this question, since the methods of studying Midrash during the generations immediately preceding this period—in Germany and France, on the one hand, and in Spain, Provence, and Italy, on the other—have not yet been adequately studied. Despite all that has been written concerning the great controversy over the proper way to understand *midrashim*, a controversy which produced much excitement in R. Solomon ben Adret's time, there are still profound gaps in our knowledge of this issue.[153] In any event, it seems to me that one can state, at least with regard to Germany and France, that the attitude towards the study of Midrash, at least from the fourteenth century onwards, was connected with the extremely limited involvement in the study of the Bible and its commentators, which was one of the typical features of Franco-German Jewry. Scholars from these circles

[151] i.e. List 33, and see my previous comments on the uniqueness of this list. In the inventory published by Trasselli, and among the 581 items in the inventory from Sicily published by Bresc, there is only one copy of the *Midrash Tanḥuma*. See Bresc, *Livre et Société en Sicile*, 65. On the latter, see n. 18.

[152] Sonne has already alluded to the absence of midrashic literature in the cultural milieu of 15th century Italian Jewry in his excellent article, 'Book Lists'. Cf. Bonfil, 'R. Obadiah Sforno', 218 n. 80.

[153] See the studies noted in Sect. 3 above.

gave a wide gamut of explanations for this limited involvement, ranging from apologetics concerning the progressive decline of the generations to an idealization of the study of Talmud, which was supposed to include everything in it.[154] Thus, the study of the Bible was restricted, generally speaking, to study of the commentary of Rashi (R. Solomon ben Isaac, 1040–1105) to the Pentateuch and to dialectical super-commentaries on Rashi.[155] During the fifteenth century, Ashkenazic Jews brought with them to Italy this method of studying the Bible, characteristic examples of which are the commentaries on Rashi by Rabbi Israel Isserlin (1390–1460), on the one hand, and of R. Joseph Colon and his disciples, on the other. This remained the case until the German and French immigrants began to be influenced by the Italian method of study, which placed great stress upon knowledge of the language and grammar of the Bible, in which people of those generations took great pride.[156] Thus, the limited study of the Bible and its commentators, combined with the restricted involvement in the study of philosophy characteristic of the Jews of France and Germany during this period appears to have brought about a superficial involvement in *midrashim*, based upon an exclusively literal or nearly literal reading. This was aptly summarized by R. Don Isaac Abrabanel when he said that, 'the first way [*of understanding the midrashim*] is the literal way, which is in my view inadequate and incorrect, but this is the way of the Ashkenazim'.[157] This method was certainly far from satisfying for those trained in the philosophic school. On the other hand, the great controversy which exploded during R. Solomon ben Adret's time seems to have left a deep impression, discouraging many from studying *midrashim* of which the literal meaning seemed unconvincing, if not impossible, and whose allegorical interpretation aroused the fear of accusations of heresy.[158] This

[154] See M. Breuer, 'The Ashkenazic Yeshivah', Doctoral Dissertation, Jerusalem, 1967, pp. 59–63.

[155] See S. Assaf, *Mekorot*, i. 44.

[156] See e.g. the sources cited by S. Simonsohn, 'The World of a Jewish Youth During the Renaissance' (Heb.), *Hagut 'Ivrit be-Europa* (Tel Aviv, 1969), 334–5. The youth himself was the son of an Ashkenazic family and educated among Ashkenazim (ibid. p. 338) in the atmosphere of the Italian Renaissance.

[157] *Yeshu'ot Meshiḥo*, Part 2, Ch. 2 (in the 1862 Königsburg edition: fo. 39b).

[158] Moreover, throughout the entire period there is a growing criticism of Maimonides' approach. Maimonides himself, despite his insistence upon the argument that the *aggadot* are not to be understood literally, offered very few interpretations of the difficult or

situation continued until the acceptance of the Kabbalistic approach, which considered its own interpretations as correct tradition, as opposed to the allegorical interpretations of the philosophically inclined. We may add to this the decline in the prestige of philosophy from the middle of the fifteenth century onwards, which also contributed to the distancing of Italian Jewry from the study of books of philosophical sermons, such as *Malmad ha-Talmidim*. On the other hand, in Provence and Spain, where Kabbalah blossomed, the process of the incorporation of the commentaries of Kabbalists into the study of Midrash was a rapid one and, at least in Spain, these commentaries were published together with the rationalistic commentaries, as we learn from such authors as Nahmanides, R. Isaac Arama, R. Abraham Saba, R. Joseph Javeẓ, R. Isaac Abrabanel, and their like.

So long as the Provençal, and particularly the Spanish, elements were not a significant factor in the shaping of the cultural atmosphere in Italy, the works of *midrash* and *aggadah* were not of interest to the general public. Thus, during the transitional period between the increasing challenge to scholastic philosophy which, as we said, reached its peak in the first half of the sixteenth century, until the printing of the classical works of *midrash* and *aggadah* as well as the Zoharic literature, around the 1550s and 1560s, the preachers could not easily resort to Midrashic literature to quench the spiritual thirst of their generation. Even following the publication of the various Midrashic works, a certain transitional period was necessary until these books entered people's homes, permitting a deeper absorption of their contents. During this period, sermons were extremely simple, concentrating upon the exegetical elements of the theme and its ethical-religious lessons, which the preachers reflected upon in an extremely linear manner. Even those few departures from the literal manner of explaining the *midrashim* were, it seems to me, based upon the popular classical literature, such as R. Joseph Albo's *Sefer ha-ʿIkkarim*, in which the philosophical element had long been

problematic *aggadot*. On criticism of Maimonides, see Ben-Sasson, *Trial and Achievement*, 230–42. On Maimonides' attitude towards the *aggadot*, see W. G. Braude, 'Maimonides' Attitude to Midrash', in *Studies in Jewish Bibliography, History and Literature in Honor of I. Edward Kiev* (New York, 1971), 75–82. On the attacks of the Kabbalists against Maimonides and his system *re* the understanding of *aggadot*, see G. Scholem, *Reshit ha-Kabbalah (1150–1250)* (Jerusalem, 1948), 133–5, and the parallels in his *Ursprung und Afgänge der Kabbala* (Berlin, 1962) and *Les origines de la Kabbale* (Paris, 1966).

combined in an organic way with ethical-religious elements.[159] Once the immigrants from Spain became a factor in shaping the cultural atmosphere in Italy, and after the publication of the aggadic and midrashic works,[160] followed shortly thereafter by the *Zohar*, the interest in *aggadah* and *midrash* experienced a great outburst, while at the same time the old disputes were revived—all against the background of the challenge to scholastic rationalism and the overwhelming success of Kabbalistic studies.[161]

Scholars of the Ashkenazic school saw the great interest aroused by the literature of the *aggadah* and *midrash* as a clear sign of spiritual decline. For example, R. Samuel Judah Katzenellenbogen stated that 'once the generations had declined . . . in almost all the communities they fled from hearing laws and *halakhot* and instead expounded *midrash* and *aggadah*'.[162] This literature rapidly won over the hearts and preachers made great use of it, especially in eclectic works,[163] such as in R. Isaac Arama's '*Akedat Yiẓḥak*, which was universally read.[164] Katzenellenbogen no longer saw any way of accepting this new tendency, and therefore advised that:

> The wise preacher will have his eyes in his head, and behave with them as the expert physician does with his patient. When a physician sees that he requires some potion and is afraid that he [the patient] will resist him and refuse to receive it, he places a bit of sugar on it to make it tasty to his mouth,[165] although his main intent is to [introduce] the medicine needed for the disease. In the same way the preacher shall hold fast: first his mouth shall speak *aggadot* and *midrashim* which draw the heart, but the main [part of] his sermon shall consist of those laws and *halakhot* required at the time.[166]

R. Samuel Judah said this in his eulogy for R. Judah Moscato who, as is well known, was not among those who made use of

[159] See e.g. the sermon of R. Azriel Trabot, in Document 64, pp. 291–3 and n. 24, in the Hebrew edition of this book. It is worth noting that he was also a French rabbi.

[160] Cf. the remarks of the printers of the *Sifra* and *Sifre* (Venice, 1546), that prior to this printing, midrashic works were totally unavailable save in the library of Jacob Mantino, the Spaniard!

[161] See e.g. *Minḥat Kena'ot*, 14–18.

[162] Katzenellenbogen, *Derashot Maharshi"k*, Sermon 3, fo. 19a.

[163] e.g. in R. Judah Moscato's *Nefuẓot Yehudah*, about half of the sermons are developed around Rabbinic sayings taken from the midrashic literature.

[164] Cf. Bettan, *Studies in Jewish Preaching*, 133.

[165] Cf. on this motif the remarks by Torquato Tasso, *La Gerusalemme Liberata*, i. 3.

[166] *Derashot Maharshi"k*, Sermon 3, fo. 19a.

midrashim and *aggadot* in his sermons only in order to make palatable their legal contents! Nevertheless, even though *midrashim* were used by Moscato and others in an eclectic fashion, in the context of the breakdown of scholastic rationalism, yet some criticism developed against this usage within the camp of the conservative scholars, especially among the Kabbalists, who were intensely opposed to the 'figures' by which such preachers as R. Judah Moscato 'depicted' the *aggadah*.[167]

In his sharp criticism of the Ferrara ordinances of 1554, R. Moses Basola complained that 'they did not turn their hearts towards the books which were already printed by Shlomo Attia, and the commentary on the *aggadot* which was recently printed and other vanities which deserve to be burned and which it is forbidden to read'.[168] Note that this criticism was specifically directed against the commentary on the *aggadot*, and not against the printing of the aggadic texts themselves, as the latter served the Kabbalists well, who saw in them a stratum of hidden meaning in addition to the literal meaning.[169]

The afore-mentioned eclectic trend, adopted by some of the more talented preachers among the Italian rabbinate, each in his own manner and style,[170] certainly obscured the intellectual foundations of any given system. This was doubtless motivated as well by a deliberate wish to deepen the religious consciousness of the listening public, and to prevent doubts in the realm of philosophical thought from impinging upon the very foundations of faith. However, one should certainly not regard these scholars as representatives of a moderate anti-rationalism, depending upon the degree to which they addressed themselves to non-Jewish literary and philosophic works.[171] For example, R. Samuel Judah Katzenellenbogen—who in nearly every one of his twelve published sermons relates to the subject of the human soul, the unique characteristics of the soul of the Jewish person, and its

[167] On the term 'figures' (*ẓurot*), see the note of D. Kaufmann, *Bet Talmud* ii (1882), 117 n. 4. On the debates in Italy at the end of this period, see D. Kaufmann, 'The Dispute About the Sermons of David del Bene of Mantua', *JQR* 8 (1896), 413–524.

[168] See the discussion by M. Benayahu, *Haskamah u-reshut be-Defusei Veneẓiah* (Jerusalem, 1971), 86–9.

[169] See Scholem, 'New Information Concerning R. Joseph Ashkenazi', 81.

[170] e.g. in Katzenellenbogen's sermons, the Kabbalistic element began to outweigh the philosophic one, while in those of R. Judah Moscato the opposite was the case.

[171] As is done systematically by Barzilay in his book; see e.g. the chapter devoted to R. Judah Moscato (in *Between Reason and Faith*, 167–91).

survival after death[172]—stresses in one passage that 'among the essential points and roots of the primary elements of our holy Torah is to believe . . . [that] the intellective soul within man is a separate being, which stands by itself and possessed a spiritual existence before it was implanted within the body'. This reality is obviously that mentioned by Nahmanides:[173] 'For it is the spirit of the great Lord, from whose mouth is knowledge and understanding, for one who blows into the nostrils of another gives of his own soul, and that is what is meant by, "and the soul of the Almighty understand in them" [Job 32: 8]—for it comes from *binah* [*understanding, also one of the Sefiroth*], in truth and faith.'[174] On the other hand, one reads elsewhere, 'for the soul of the one who studies will be substantiated by the intelligible reached by the study, when it will be unified with the object of cognition'.[175] We thus find here, in a discourse regarding the soul, an expression characteristic of the Maimonidean doctrine—which, as is known, would certainly not recognize the separate existence of the human soul except at the conclusion of the process of cognition within the framework of the unity of the intellect, the subject of intelligence, and the object of intellection—combined with the doctrine of the emanation of souls—'separate bodies standing by themselves'—like the Sefirah of *Binah* in the Kabbalistic schema! The substantiation of the soul as understood by Katzenellenbogen is certainly quite different from the substantiation of the soul in Maimonidean thought; indeed, he denies the latter's entire philosophical position on this point.[176] Nevertheless, the use of semantics characteristic of the Maimonidean system is more than accidental. Concepts from the Maimonidean world are used in a manner which certainly did not fit Maimonides elsewhere in his work. For example, what he wrote concerning human perfection,[177] allegedly following Maimonides,[178] relied in his case upon the statement that:

172 See *Derashot Maharshi"k*, Sermons 1, 2, 4–8, and cf. G. Nigal, 'The Sermons of R. Samuel David Katzenellenbogen' (Heb.), *Sinai*, 70 (1972), 80–1.

173 See Nahmanides' *Commentary* to Gen. 2: 7.

174 See *Derashot Maharshi"k*, Sermon 2, fos. 7b–10a.

175 Ibid., Sermon 4, fo. 22b.

176 Ibid. Sermon 7, fos. 35b–36a, and cf. Nigal, 'The Sermons of R. Samuel David Katzenellenbogen'.

177 *Derashot Maharshi"k*, Sermon 6, fos. 32b–33a.

178 But note that of Maimonides' writings on this subject, he refers especially to the *Shemonah Perakim* and not to the final chapter of the *Guide*!

True blessing does not reside in these three perfections [i.e. *perfection of ethical virtues, bodily health, and wealth*] . . . but in that which is hidden from the eye, [namely], true human perfection whose final purpose is none other than the reward which is destined for him in the world to come.[179]

In a different style, arising from a different mental constitution, R. Judah Moscato begins one of his sermons[180] with the words of the *Zohar*. He writes there in praise of the seven human wisdoms in a manner very similar to that of R. Levi, who was the cause of the great controversy in the time of R. Solomon ben Adret.[181] However, the entire sermon is designed to prove that these seven wisdoms 'will not reach perfection in the realm of morals and physics, and *a fortiori* in metaphysics . . . for without doubt their hands are inadequate to attain the truth'.[182] We thus find, formulated positively, certain ideas which are very similar in content to what was stated negatively by R. Vitale da Pisa.

If, from the 1570s onwards, Kabbalistic literature and its interpretations of the *aggadot* were increasingly used by those preachers who adopted an eclectic approach, they were used constantly in the sermons of the enthusiastic Kabbalists. The latter drew freely upon the colourful motifs found in the broad spectrum of the Kabbalah, to which they added various arguments based upon *notarikon* and *gematria* (interpretations based upon the numerical values of the letters in a given word, re-combination of its letters, etc.), thereby restoring to the sermon its freshness and vitality. The element of surprise upon which the structure of the sermon relied,[183] in one way or another was now provided with a new source, allowing the preachers to enchant their audience even if their literary talents were not particularly well developed. In a world filled with mythology, as was the case both of contemporary *belles lettres* and of the widespread Platonic philosophical thought, the mythological dimension of these mystical images offered the preacher's audience a refreshing experience. This latter fact seems to have been one of the leading factors contributing to the further transformation which took place during that same period in the realm of the sermon. The

179 But note Maimonides' own remarks in *Guide* III: 54.

180 *Nefuẓot Yehudah*, Sermon 14.

181 See C. Touati, 'La Pensée Philosophique de Gersonide', Paris, 1972, i. 12.

182 Cf. also *Nefuẓot Yehudah*, Sermon 13.

limited number of basic concepts in Kabbalah, which was out of proportion to the complexity of the ideational and homiletical combinations, which these concepts permitted to the Kabbalists, did not require a complex or convoluted technical vocabulary as did the philosophical sermon of the previous generations. Kabbalistic sermons might thus be written in languages other than Hebrew. Take, for example, the Italian-language sermons of R. Mordecai Dato, notable both for their conceptual simplicity and their lively freshness. In these sermons—which are, incidentally, important sources for the study of the Judaeo-Italian dialect of those days—Dato presented his theories in which 'nature, senses and philosophy'[184] combine together into homiletics. This rabbi absorbed Kabbalistic teaching in Safed, and returned to Italy full of enthusiasm. His sermons, written in a heavy Italian style, lacking in confidence as well as in mannerism, are nevertheless impressive in their freshness, drawing upon colourful Kabbalistic motifs, which come one after the other and are woven together into a unified literary creation.[185] These sermons combine, with great simplicity yet impressive power, all those ideas and motifs most characteristic of the period, namely: the uniqueness of the Israelite nation; the essential distinction between the Jewish soul and that of the Gentile; the decisive importance of practical commandments within the cosmic framework; etc.[186]

Others followed in R. Mordecai Dato's footsteps, such as R. Menaḥem Azariah da Fano, who said of himself that wherever he went he spoke in the synagogues and houses of study on Kabbalistic matters,[187] or R. Menahem Rava (sixteenth century), who gathered his Hebrew sermons into a book, entitled *Bet Mo'ed*, after showing them to R. Menaḥem Azariah da Fano.[188] Those who preached on Kabbalistic matters saw themselves as thoroughly exempt from any necessity to justify their esoteric interpretations of the *aggadah*. The tradition tracing the transmission of the Kabbalah from one person to another, going back to the time of R. Simeon bar Yoḥai, seemed to them sufficient evidence of the

[183] See Dan, 'Hebrew Homiletical Literature', 564–6.

[184] See at the end of Sect. 3, and cf. I. Tishby, 'The Image of R. Moses Cordovero in the work of R. Mordecai Dato' (Heb.), *Sefunot*, 7 (1963), 135 n. 89.

[185] For an example, see Bonfil, 'One of Dato's Sermons'.

[186] Cf. in Sect. 3 above.

[187] See his introductory remarks to *Sefer Pelaḥ ha-Rimmon* (Venice, 1605), 2a.

[188] See Menaḥem Rava, *Bet Mo'ed* (Venice, 1605), 2b.

truth of these interpretations and of their constituting a layer of additional meaning beyond the literal meaning of the texts.[189] This approach added a dimension of continuity with the Jewish cultural-religious tradition in general, and thus provided one of the main elements of Jewish pride in Italy during this period.[190] We should add that, to this feeling of cultural continuity, which strengthened fideism *vis-à-vis* scholastic-rationalistic thought and which held fast against the cultural split that occurred in the Renaissance world in general, there emerged in a natural way a renewed interest in the historical-philosophical œuvre of R. Judah ha-Levi, which was based upon these very same elements. R. Obadiah Sforno scoffed at the certainty of those who believed without rational arguments, and took to task those rabbis who cultivated this type of faith.[191] However, the renewed interest in Judah ha-Levi's teaching during this period in Italy is sufficient indication of the deep roots struck by the outlook described above among Italian Jewry during this time.[192]

This development was also reflected in the area of the Jewish-Christian polemic. In my opinion, this confirms an awareness on the part of both Jews and Christians that the two cultural phenomena were in contrast. Thus, during the very period in which Christian scholars routinely turned to the Jews in order to learn the *Hebraica Veritas*, the apostate Gerardus Veltwick

[189] See at the end of Ch. 5.

[190] See Bonfil, 'The Uniqueness of the Jewish People', 40. R. Elijah del Medigo, one of the opponents of the Kabbalah, felt the power of the argument of the continuity of the tradition invoked by the supporters of the Kabbalah against those who relied upon philosophical reasoning. He attempted to refute this by arguments disproving the antiquity of the Kabbalah. See *Sefer Beḥinat ha-Dat* (Basel, 1629), 5b–6b, and cf. Modena, *Ari Nohem*, ed. Leibovitz, 33–4.

[191] See his Introduction to *'Or Amim*, and cf. Bonfil, 'The Interpretation of R. Moses Provenzali', 153.

[192] See above, Sect. 3. It is perhaps not superfluous to note that R. Judah Moscato composed his extensive commentary on the *Kuzari* during this period. See, in its introduction, the four reasons given for calling it *Kol Yehudah* (the Voice of Judah): 'for in its name are included its four causes: the material, the formal, the active, and the final. For the material is the voice of R. Judah ha-Levi, in the narration of things as they came out; the formal is the voice of the Jew (*yehudi*; a reference to the *Ḥaver*, the protagonist in the theological dialogue which constitutes the heart of the book), who propounds his arguments with strength and glory . . .; the active is to spark the voice of Judah, each person in his own work . . .; and the final cause is that the voice be the voice of Judah and Israel in general, to thank God for the perfection of His Torah, which brings perfection to the soul of the people upon it and spirit to those who walk in it.'

wrote his book, *Shevilei Tohu*,[193] in which he said about the claims of the Jews:

And if you say, do not the Christians themselves say that we are their scribes and God gave them to be a scattered nation carrying books in order to prove the truth . . . The answer is . . . that at the beginning the Bible was written in the Holy Tongue, and from it all other books were translated. However, although it is your language, it was not known, and your rabbis [*namely, the sages of the Talmud*] were not educated . . . therefore they erred [in it].

That is, while the Bible was indeed written in Hebrew, its earliest translators and commentators did not know this language clearly, and thus introduced mistakes and distortions into their interpretations. This continued until the Tiberian grammarians appeared 'and set their heart and laboured with all their souls to make a lost language readable', followed by the Spanish grammarians, 'who lent a hand, for they are wealthy and tranquil and know our wisdoms, and they are learned in philosophy, and they opened their eyes [to realize] that their teachers and forefathers were foolish'.[194] Thus, in his opinion, Hebrew underwent in the Middle Ages what Greek and Latin underwent during the Renaissance. It was forgotten and rediscovered, undergoing a kind of linguistic-literary renascence in which Christian culture also participated. In this manner, the author sought to refute the continuity of the Jewish tradition and to deny the special status which this feeling of continuity granted to Jewish culture during this period, in contrast with earlier periods, within the framework of the Jewish–Christian confrontation.

Unlike the Kabbalistic preachers, who felt no obligation to justify their non-literal interpretations of the *aggadot*, the eclectic preachers, particularly those for whom the rationalistic element was predominant, felt the need to justify their turning to allegory. To this end, they used the arguments of the Kabbalists: namely, that the allegorical interpretation is essentially an additional layer of meaning beyond the literal, and that one is not to reject the literal meaning of Scripture. Thus, R. Judah Moscato declared that 'I will also accept [the words of] whoever wishes to understand this saying in its literal meaning, for I do not wish

[193] The book was published in Venice in 1539. See Y. Mehlmann, 'Daniel Bomberg's Printing House in Venice' (Heb.), *'Areshet*, 3 (1961), 96–8.

[194] G. Veltwick, *Shevilei Tohu* (Venice, 1539), xiv. 4b.

less than they to believe in the law of the divine ability to do thus and more than thus.'[195] Moscato follows here his own approach, in which the four levels of interpretation—*peshat*, *remez*, *derash*, *sod* (literal, allegorical, homiletical, and esoteric)—are intertwined with one another in the multi-tiered exegetical approach which was widespread within the Christian world and which underlay the medieval Christian sermon,[196] where allegory reigned supreme.[197] Nevertheless, preachers of the type of R. Judah Moscato felt that they needed to behave with care when they turned towards allegory; a need which left its mark on their literary creativity, which seemed less vital and alive, its slow development following the polished manneristic style.

To conclude: it seems clear that the publication of the midrashic works in Italy towards the middle of the sixteenth century signified the beginning of the renewed flowering of the interest in *aggadah* and its use in sermons, in the context of the cultural trends just described. Thus, the classical type of sermon, both aesthetically complete and rich in contents, returned to its rightful place after half a century of decay.

5. Theory and Practice

Another change in the cultural area stemmed, to a large extent, from the afore-mentioned tendencies, whose essence was the shift in emphasis from hermeneutics and philosophical thought, which had constituted the main element in the sermons of the earlier period, to praxis and ethics, which characterized the period under discussion here. This change particularly fitted the activity of the

[195] *Nefuzot Yehudah*, Sermon 12. This is certainly an expression of confrontation and competition, a clear sign that the ferment characteristic of the substantive confrontation did not completely bypass the sermon!

[196] Ibid. Sermon 7: 'The four kinds of exegesis, which are called in the vernacular *senso letterale*, *senso allegorico* or *morale*, *senso anagogico* and *senso tropologico* . . . are those known to us as *peshaṭ* (literal meaning), *derekh ha-derash* (homiletics), *derekh ha-sekhel* (philosophical allegory), and *derekh ha-emet* (Kabbalistic symbolic interpretation).'

[197] See e.g. striking examples of this in ibid. Sermons 7 and 8. The author's intention in Sermon 7 is 'to clarify the saying of Rabbi Hoshaiah at the beginning of *Genesis Rabba*, concerning the Torah being on the level of the six causes mentioned by Plato—active, material, formal, final, instrumental and intellectual . . .' In Sermon 8, the author elaborates upon the allegorical interpretation of the rabbinic dictum that, at the Creation, God wrapped Himself in light like a garment and made the whole world shine with His light, 'according to Plato's view, as the first cause'—i.e. by the neo-Platonic system of emanation.

rabbis, who saw themselves and were perceived by the public as the spiritual leaders of the generation. This phenomenon was also shared by the Jewish and Christian milieus for, as is well known, during the Renaissance the main interest was placed in the fields of ethics and politics, as opposed to the preoccupation with logic, metaphysics, etc., which had characterized the previous period.

When R. Joseph ben Shem Tov discussed the question of those topics which a preacher ought to deal with in his sermons, 'if it is fitting that these must be only the true subjects of the Torah, or may they be [taken from] other arts and sciences, or from all of them',[198] he concluded by saying that, as everything depended upon the 'illness' of the soul and what was required in order to correct it,[199] the preacher must deal with all of the topics mentioned without exception. On the other hand, when R. Jacob b. Kalonymos ha-Levi enumerated the subjects which the preachers of his generation attempted to present before their congregations, he wrote:

> While I was going about and doing thus and such, I saw the tears and efforts of those engaged in the labour of sermonizing, which is very burdensome, and their pondering the path by which to find new and profitable, appropriate subjects: whether in the [weekly] Torah lesson or the festivals; whether in praise of a [given] commandment or virtue or in the condemnation of some sin or vice; whether involving the way to repentance or charity or the redemption of captives and the needs of the orphan and the marriage of the virgin; whether for the celebration of a circumcision or marriage or in praise of a certain individual or whether, Heaven forbid, at a eulogy or the like. And at times he may find a good subject, and find himself half naked for the lack of Biblical verses and Rabbinic sayings and homilies and the like, which are of great usefulness . . . For which reason I set my heart to prepare a table before them containing various subjects deserving acceptance by the thirsty soul, to build upon them worthwhile sermons . . .[200]

Conspicuous by their absence here are any mention of 'the other professions and speculative sciences', or even of the 'true sections of the Torah' which do not bear upon the specific subjects mentioned by R. Jacob b. Kalonymos ha-Levi.[201] On the contrary,

[198] See Shem-Tov, 'Sefer 'Ein ha-Kore', 92b. [199] See Sect. 4.

[200] Introduction to Jacob b. Kalonymos Segal, 'Sefer Kol Ya'akov'.

[201] Cf. the remarks by I. Rosenzweig, *Hogeh Yehudi mi-Keẓ ha-Renessans* (Tel Aviv, 1972).

in his opinion, were it not for the difficulty in finding 'appropriate subjects', then:

> The other aspects of [composing] the sermon are easy and ready at hand, as I truly have practised for a long time . . . for often, when the preacher seeks a [certain] verse or saying, there immediately comes into his mind another verse or saying, upon which, in the twinkling of an eye, he invents a charming explanation, as though God had answered him, and this is a remarkable thing. Moreover, he finds an allusion or confirmation in a [Scriptural] verse or [rabbinic] saying for whatever he may think of, provided that it is a true thing . . . And this is an axiom, known to all the practitioners of the art of sermonizing.[202]

Within the context of the cultural phenomenon described above, one must also take account of the renewed flowering of ethical literature during the second half of the sixteenth century, expressed both in the publication of ethical treatises[203] and in the founding of an ever-increasing number of confraternities for Torah study and the practice of good deeds. While it would be somewhat exaggerated to say that, towards the end of the sixteenth century, the study of Torah ceased to be thought of as a matter of intellectual development and became primarily a matter of religious piety,[204] there can be no doubt that, at least within the orbit of the various confraternities for Torah study which sprang up throughout Italy, the practical side of Torah study as the fulfilment of a precept for its own sake was strongly emphasized. The founding of confraternities for study took place alongside the founding of societies for religious worship, whose main concern was with intensive involvement in prayer, and of charitable confraternities—all within the context of the growth of the pietistic phenomenon, as we have noted. Thus, for example, R. Menaḥem Rava saw the perfection of Jewish society in the observance of the Torah and the religious precepts, with the aim of the rabbis being to educate towards this goal—an education whose purpose was fulfilled by the establishment of confraternities of the type mentioned:

[202] Ibid. [203] Cf. Scholem, *Major Trends*, 251.

[204] See Shulvass, 'The Study of Torah', 110, 126–7, and the sources cited by him. Cf. Shulvass, 'Religious Life', 18–19. Shulvass, loyal to the historiographic approach, did not see this phenomenon, which he described in an exaggerated manner, as one which grew in an organic way from the Jewish cultural nexus, and therefore did not pursue the question of its nature or its roots. Nevertheless, his distinction in this subject is deserving of special note.

One must therefore take great care for the education of the young boys, to guide them in Torah and precepts . . . and one likewise ought to educate them to read words of Torah in public . . . and to bring them into the society of those who perform the religious precepts and good deeds. And all the confraternities are included under three rubrics—namely, Torah, Divine worship, and good deeds—upon which the entire world depends:[205] the confraternity of Torah study, as its name implies, is involved with the laws and statutes which are appropriate to a Torah scholar; the confraternities for religious worship, such as the 'Confraternity of Watchers for the Morning' [*those who keep vigil at dawn*], for prayers and songs of praise which are a substitute for the [Temple] service, or the confraternity of those who go about the city to supervise the fulfilment of those precepts which require such and to remind the people of the need for repentance; and the Confraternity for Charity, of those who do good with the living and the dead [i.e. *the Burial Society*] . . . And in order to benefit the public, to educate towards Torah and good deeds, one ought to preach in praise of the founders of the confraternities and of those who inform the public of the way in which they ought to go and the deeds that they must do [Exod. 18: 20], for by these they truly resemble their Creator, who does good to all His creatures.[206] And now, as to be a Talmudic scholar is a cause fulfilling all the commandments, preparation and involvement in the Torah being weighed against and equal to all [other] preparations,[207] we shall therefore close our sermon with praise of the preparation for the involvement in Torah and training to its study in public . . .[208]

When R. Menaḥem Rava spoke about bringing young men into the confraternities for the performance of religious precepts, he meant this in the literal sense. Indeed, one of the most interesting phenomena of the period, which points to the central place held by the confraternities in the field of education, was the introduction of young boys into these confraternities at a younger and younger age. Thus, for example, Elisha Itai, the son of R. Menaḥem Azariah da Fano, who was born in 1583, was listed as a member of the Charity Confraternity of Ferrara from the year 1593 onwards, while Israel b. Ḥezekiah da Fano, who was born at the end of 1572, was listed as a member of the same society from

205 Based upon *Mishnah Avot* 1: 2.

206 On this motif see Bonfil, 'R. Obadiah Sforno'.

207 Cf. N. Lamm, *Torah li-Shemah be-Mishnat R. Ḥayyim mi-Volozhin uve-Maḥshevet ha-Dor* (Jerusalem, 1972), 77–8.

208 Rava, *Bet Mo'ed*, Sermon 43, p. 190b.

1584 onwards. There were even those who were listed among the members of the confraternity from the day of their circumcision.[209]

A concrete expression of the growing importance of faith and praxis appears in the ethical literature created or printed during this period. Although the main tendency of this literature was highly eclectic, so much so that it seemed to one sage that the authors were nothing more than plagiarists,[210] the books of R. Raphael Norzi[211] are entirely based upon the central importance of faith in Jewish thought, philosophical understanding being inadequate to supply a firm basis for the spiritual world of the Jew.[212] The emphasis was therefore transferred from the intellectual-philosophical realm to that of faith in a personal God, who guides the world by individual providence.[213] He goes on from there to discourse upon the importance of prayer[214] and of intention (*kavanah*),[215] on the love and fear of God,[216] upon repentance[217] and upon the cultivation of ethical purity both of the individual and of society,[218] even by means of withdrawal and asceticism.[219] One need hardly add that, according to R. Raphael Norzi, the Torah's understanding of the human soul is rather different from that of philosophical opinions,[220] and that particular importance is attached to the unique qualities of the chosen Jewish people.[221] The same is true of R. Elijah de Vidas's work, *Reshit Ḥokhmah*, in which the entire Torah is made dependent upon faith alone. This book was printed in Venice in the year 1579, and involved individuals from the circle of R. Menaḥem Azariah da Fano, who during this period devoted most of his energy and enthusiasm to the dissemination of Kabbalistic teachings.[222] Within a year of its publication, the

[209] See R. Menaḥem Azariah da Fano's Ledger of Circumcisions and the Ordinances of the *Ḥevrat Gema"ḥ* of Ferrara, published in Bonfil, 'New Information', 116–33.

[210] See N. Brüll, *Jahrbücher für Jüdische Geschichte und Literatur*, 2 (1876), 168–71.

[211] See H. G. Enelow, 'Raphael Norzi: a Rabbi of the Renaissance', *Hebrew Union College Jubilee Volume* (Cincinnati, 1925), 335–78.

[212] Ibid. 338–9, and cf. Katzenellenbogen's remarks to his congregation concerning the importance of faith (*Derashot Maharshi"k*, Sermon 9), and my previous remarks in Sect. 3 concerning R. Vitale da Pisa.

[213] Enelow, 'Raphael Norzi', 351.

[214] Ibid. 353–4, 356–7.

[215] Ibid. 341.

[216] Ibid. 345–50, 365–8.

[217] Ibid. 354–5.

[218] Ibid. 357, 368–71.

[219] Ibid. 360–1.

[220] Ibid. 373–4.

[221] Ibid. 344–5, 350.

[222] The editor of the book was R. Yizhak Gershon, who was close to R. Menaḥem Azariah da Fano, and was also the publisher of most of those books which he edited. I would like to mention here that the book *Reshit Ḥokhmah* based Kabbalistic Mussar upon the foundations of Jewish ethics, and therefore attempts to convey the basic theoretical

book *Reshit Ḥokhmah* enjoyed the distinction of having an abbreviated version published, written by R. Jacob Poggetto,[223] also from Asti, where R. Abraham b. R. Meshullam resided.[224] It is perhaps appropriate to mention here as well the work *Tapuḥei Zahav*, another abridgement of *Reshit Ḥokhmah*, written by R. Jehiel Melli, although this latter work was not published until 1623.[225] The common denominator of all these abridgements, which were extremely popular, was their emphasis upon ethics and praxis as against theory.[226]

What has been said thus far exemplifies the nature of the transformation in the cultural-religious milieu in Italy over a period of approximately one hundred years: the centre of gravity of spiritual interest within the world of the Jew moved from philosophical activity to praxis. This process began with the questioning of the role of scholastic philosophy against the theoretical criticism which was directed against it. It was continued in the challenge posed by Kabbalah as an alternative to philosophical thought, in the light of the feeling of Jewish cultural continuity and the uniqueness of Jewish nationhood—all this in confrontation with the wider world of the Renaissance, which ceaselessly sought connections with the ancient world. This process was expressed in the creation of a vibrant literature, in constant dialectical tension between two extremes, namely, between the advocates of philosophy and its opponents, who gravitated towards the mystical world of the Kabbalists. The tranformation culminated in the cultivation of the practical elements of Judaism rather than its more theoretical aspects. The rabbis played an active role in this complex process, although they were not necessarily an anti-rationalistic element turning

concepts of Kabbalah to the broad public, in a manner which its author considered to be popular, as without these concepts involvement in Kabbalah, and thereby in Ethics, would be impossible. See M. Pechter, 'Elijah de Vidas' book *Reshit Ḥokhmah* and its Abridgements' (Heb.), *KS* 47 (1972), 689–90. R. Menaḥem Azariah da Fano and his circle were engaged with precisely the same concerns during that period in Venice. I will discuss da Fano, who lived in Venice until the end of the 1530s, at greater length in a forthcoming separate article to be devoted to his life. On R. Isaac Gershon and his activity in disseminating the works of the Safed Kabbalists, see M. Pechter, 'R. Moses Alshekh's *Ḥazut Kashah*' (Heb.), *Shalem: Meḥkarim le-toldot Ereẓ Yisra'el ve-yishuvah*, 1 (1974), 158.

[223] See Pechter, 'Elijah de Vidas' book *Reshit Ḥokhmah*', 696–8, and n. 66 concerning the first editions of this abridged version.

[224] See n. 114 above. [225] See Pechter, 'Elijah de Vidas', 704–9.

[226] See Pechter's lengthy discussion, ibid.

inwards, but rather loyal representatives of a variety of streams of thought, only some of which have been presented here. As teachers within Jewish society and as its spiritual shepherds, these rabbis attempted to stabilize the spiritual world of their contemporaries amidst the confusion introduced into it by the confrontation between opposing systems. True, by the end of this process Jewish cultural developments had become cut off from the wider cultural milieu, in which the foundations of modern philosophy flourished on the ruins of Renaissance philosophy without Jewish participation. But this was not necessarily the outcome of the pressures of the Counter Reformation and the forced isolation in ghettos, nor of the resurgence of 'dark' elements drawing upon the benighted spirit of the Middle Ages, which the rabbis, who allegedly hated culture and enlightenment, supposedly held up as their banner. The process was a prolonged one, rich in inner problematics, from which emerged a new sphere of cultural creativity.

To the crystallization of this cultural phenomenon, as it has been briefly summarized here, external factors certainly contributed as well—factors such as the positive humanistic echoes aroused by Jewish historical traditions,[227] the tightening of the pressures of the Counter Reformation upon the Jewish camp, the battle of the Church against the Talmud, and so on. But these factors were not the essential ones. In this context, even the attraction to the world of charms, and magic, and oaths, against which rationalism fought[228] and which the Kabbalists praised,[229] was not a mere remnant of superstition, which aided the wave of Kabbalistic mysticism and pietism which came about in its wake,[230] but a direct consequence of the historical turnabout and an organic expression of the phenomenon in general, which

[227] Although the general understanding of these traditions by such people as Pico della Mirandola or Egidio da Viterbo was radically different from that of the Jews.

[228] See the remarks of Moses da Rieti in his poem in defence of philosophy ('The Loud Cry Against . . . R. Solomon ben Adret'), and the remarks by R. Obadiah Sforno in his commentary to Psalm 15.

[229] See the remarks of R. Vitale da Pisa in *Sefer Minḥat Kena'ot*, 48–51, as well as those of R. Joseph Ashkenazi who, in the context of his severe criticism of Maimonides, defends belief in demons and magic 'whose marvelous acts our eyes witness every day' (Scholem, 'New Information Concerning R. Joseph Ashkenazi', 76–7).

[230] As explained e.g. by Shulvass, 'Religious Life', 8 ff.

bore a clear parallel to the widespead attraction in the Christian world to magic and astrology.[231]

The enhanced sense of Jewish national uniqueness, within the context of the cultural phenomenon described here, isolated Jewish thought from general thought and brought about the end of the period of fruitful co-operation between the Jewish rabbinate in Italy and Christian scholars. There now opened a period in which the relations between the Italian rabbis and their counterparts in other Jewish communities throughout the world were strengthened, particularly with the sages of the Land of Israel (especially those of Safed) and with those of Germany and Poland.[232] During this period, the rabbis of Italy came to play a new and central role in the history of Jewish culture.

[231] See Garin, *Medioevo e Rinascimento*, 150–69, also H. Wirszubski, *Sheloshah Perakim be-toldot ha-Kabbalah ha-Noẓrit* (Jerusalem, 1975), 39 ff.

[232] Cf. Rosenzweig's accurate observation in *Hogeh Yehudi mi-Keẓ ha-Renessans*, 37.

APPENDIX 1. *Doctoral Diplomas and Rabbinic Ordinations*

A. From the doctoral certificate awarded to Angelo di Francesco Bruogi on June 19, 1409, in Siena.[1]

Humana conditio a sui primordio in lucem inerudita
perveniens, si sapientie lumine illustratur, dignis et
altis est laudibus extollenda;
illique gloriosum nomen habere merentur, qui longa
assiduitate laborum et vigiliarum instantia, per arduum
doctrine callem ambulantes, ad perfectionem sui studii
inclitam pervenerunt . . .
Cuius discipline fructus in gloria requiescit, que
benemeritis, ut ad illam indocti ferveant, est illustri
laudum preconio tribuenda.
Cum igitur venerabilis et spectabilis vir Magister
Angelus Francisci Bruogii . . . ab olim insistens in
diversis Studiis et presertim in hoc . . . Studio Senensi,
sic in Philosophia et Artibus profuerit . . .
idemque magister Angelus taliter se habuit in . . .
examini, puncta sibi assignata . . . seriose legendo,
argumenta et replicationes . . . doctorum sibi successive
arguentium, reassumendo seu recitando et eisdem
sufficienter respondendo, quod . . . idem magister
Angelus . . . sufficiens . . . extitit approbatus,
Idcirco Nos Antonius, episcopus et cancellarius . . . de
concordi consilio et consensu . . . doctorum . . . Collegii . . .
nominamus, denuntiamus et publice declaramus fore
doctorem et magistrum . . .
ipsique Magistro Angelo presenti et humiliter
acceptanti, ut digno et benemerito, et hac promotione
dignissimo,
legendi, doctorandi,[2] cathedram magistralem ascendendi
illamque regendi . . . publice exercendi Senis et ubique
locorum . . . plenam et liberam licentiam tribuimus et
concessimus . . .

[1] Cited in Lodovico Zdekauer, *Lo studio di Siena nel Rinascimento* (Milan, 1894), 151–3.

[2] Note that this prerogative is missing in R. Sforno's doctorate.

B. From the doctoral diploma awarded to R. Obadiah Sforno in Ferrara on 27 April 1501.[3]

Humane conditionis fragilitas a sui primordio in lucem ineruditam[4] perveniens, si sapientie lumine illustretur dignis et altis est laudibus extollenda; illique gloriosi nominis famam adipisci promerentur, qui indefessis laboribus et vigiliarum instantiam,[5] per arduum doctrine callem ambulantes, ad perfectum studiorum suorum apicem laudabiliter pervenerunt; et in duro certamine sue facultatis victoriam consequentes inter mortales se claros et spectabiles reddiderunt.

Cum igitur doctus vir Magister Servideus Jaboci Sfurni hebreus hactenus in artium et medicine facultatibus studens Rome et alibi, ubi studia vigent generalia, sic in eisdem facultatibus profecerit . . . suppositusque hodie rigoroso ac pertremendo
examini . . . taliter se habuit idem magister Servideus in dicto examine puncta sibi assignata doctoreo modo legendo, argumenta doctorum reassumendo, ipsis respondendo, et ea solvendo, ut ipsum magistrum Servideum . . . ab ipsis . . . doctoribs . . . approbatum et suficientem reputatum . . .
dominus vicarius, auctoritate et licentia sibi . . . concessa . . . pronuntiavit, constituit, decrevit et declaravit verum et legitimum . . . doctorem.
eidem presenti et humiliter recipienti, tamquam sufficienti et idoneo . . .
legendi, disputandi, docendi, terminandi, interpretandi, glosandi, cathedram magistralem ascendendi illamque regendi . . . ubique locorum uti earumdem facultatum doctori, et insignia doctoratus recipiendi . . . plenam et omnimodam licentiam dedit et concessit . . .

[3] From Vittore Colorni, 'Spigolature su Obadiah Sforno', *Volume . . . in memoria di Federico Luzzatto* [*RMI* 28/3–4 (1962)], 86–8.

[4] Should read: inerudita.

[5] Should read: instantia.

C. Text of the Ordination granted by R. Isaac ben Emmanuel de Lattes to R. Samuel Kazani.[6]

I have seen you as a venerable old student, who has imbibed of the breasts of Mother Wisdom, and been weaned on the milk of Torah,[7] and you have arrived at [the level of] instruction, and if you prevent yourself from doing so, Heaven forfend, you enter into the category of those of whom it is said 'for it has felled many corpses'.[8] And a good thing was done in its time by the *Ga'on* and Exalted Rabbi, who sits on the throne of teaching, Rabbi Samuel, son of the *Ga'on* Meir Katzenellenbogen, who came to enjoy the mitzvah of adorning you with the crown of the rabbinate, and I will come after his honour to join him and be joined with him[9] in this matter. And from the day that you came to Venice and brought forth pearls from your mouth, I have judged you to be a sharp person, who pursues justice and seeks truth, and you have found favour in my eyes, to be the judge upon the earth within the congregation of God. And if you have set your heart to know the science of healing, and for this reason you have lifted up your hand, the weak hand, the left of every person,[10] in external wisdoms, you have not withheld yourself from studying much Torah, and the right hand of God, the Torah of God which is perfect with you, does mightily—the right hand of God is uplifted, and a golden bowl[11]—for you have given to the crown of Torah an added quality, that it is the ruling mistress, and you have made the other wisdoms as handmaidens which serve it,[12] as they have been

6 From *Teshuvot R. Yiẓḥak mi-Lattes* ii, fo. 128; published in the Hebrew edition of this book, Document No. 8, p. 222. On the Cazani family of Candia, see M. Steinschneider, *ZfHB*, 17, 91; idem, *Mose*, 2 (1879), 415-6; ibid. 3 (1880), 284; idem, CB, 2591; U. Cassuto, *Codices Vaticani Hebraica* (Rome, 1950), 36; Z. Ankori, 'Hebrew Inscriptions in Crete', *PAAJR* 28-9 (1972), 43. At the end of 'Tikkun 'Ezra', MS Warsaw 243 (IMHM 10117), written at the request of one of the members of the Cazani family in 1636, there is a list of members of the family on behalf of whom one was to recite the memorial prayer, from which various details pertaining to the family's geneaological tree may be inferred. Concerning Samuel Kazani, see A. Ankori, op. cit., 43; S. Simonsohn, introduction to *Teshuvot Ziknei Yehudah*, 58; M. Steinschneider, *Catalogus librarum Hebraeorum in bibliotheca Bodleiana*, 2nd edn. (Berlin, 1931), 22565; idem, *ZfHB* 17 (1914), 86; I. Barzilay, *Yosef Shlomo Delmedigo, Yashar of Candia: His Life, Works and Times* (Leiden, 1974), 30. R. Samuel Cazani wrote in praise of *Sefer Or ha-Sekhel* (Venice, 1567) and, according to R. Jacob Soresina, settled a dispute among the rabbis of Candia—see the ruling of R. Jacob at the end of *Teshuvot ha-Rosh*, (Venice, 1607). In the book the name of the family is printed as *Cazano*, a mistake perpetuated by Steinschneider, *ZfHB* 17 (1914), 92.

7 Based on Isa. 28: 9, and see below, n. 5.

8 Prov. 7: 26, and see what is expounded on this verse in Sotah 22a.

9 The reading here should clearly be *senif* (to be joined to) and not *ẓenif* (a diadem), as in the manuscript.

10 Cf. Menaḥot 37a.

11 A crown of gold—a synonym for ordination. See Bava Mezia 85a.

placed under your hand. And the diligence which was in your hand for the beautification of Torah, shall uplift you, and you shall sit upon the throne of kings[13]—'and who are the kings? The rabbis'. You shall stand in the place of the great [ones], for behold I come to you, your honour, Rabbi Samuel Kazani, son of our rabbi, the wise man, Shabbetai, may he long live, of Candia. And lay on my hand, and add light to your light, to be called 'Rabbi' in all matters pertaining to holiness, and there shall be placed in your hands the garments of the rabbis:[14] a stick and a whip with which to beat those deserving of it by the needs of the hour; a shofar with which to excommunicate every man who rebels against you, by your ordinances and limitations to add further limitations to the sanctions of the Torah to those that the Torah has given us in matters of forbidden and permitted; a shoe to perform *ḥaliẓah*; and a quill with which to correct divorces and to issue judgement and to rule in marital issues, for you are expert in their nature. And who shall teach knowledge or explicit traditions[15] when the heads of the people are gathered together in the holy congregation with them, your honour shall be with them and amongst them you shall be counted, for such is befitting to you. For the above-mentioned Rabbi Samuel is fit to be a righteous teacher and to do justice and righteousness in the land, and with mercy shall his seat be established forever, and he shall live long on his kingdom. Amen.

Isaac Joshua b. R. Emmanuel de Lattes

Ferrara, 12 Nissan 5329 [*1569*]

12 A common motif among people of that generation, in the wake of the words of Maimonides. See e.g. Blau (ed.), *Teshuvot ha-Rambam* (Jerusalem, 1961), iii. 57.

13 See *Tosafot* to Eruvin 65a, s.v. *ba-zar*, and to Bava Kama 92b, s.v. *meshulash*.

14 See Document 6, p. 220 n. 123 in the Hebrew edition of this book.

15 Isa. 28: 9, which was the verse with which he began—see above, n. 7.

APPENDIX 2. *Appointments of Communal Rabbis During the Sixteenth Century*

The Hebrew year 5300 was the equivalent of 1539/40 CE; other dates may be calculated from that basis.

Date	*Source*
Verona	
24 Ellul 5299	'Pinkas Verona' i. fo. 190a (see Sonne, 'Basic Premisses', 152–4).
7 Tammuz 5302	'Pinkas Verona' i. fo. 48a (cited as Document 17 in the Hebrew edition of this book; partly cited by Sonne, 'Basic Premisses', 155–6).
18 Tammuz 5305	'Pinkas Verona' i. fo. 57a (see Sonne, 'Basic Premisses', 158–9).
10 Adar II 5309	'Pinkas Verona' ii. fo. 14a (cited as Document 18 in the Hebrew edition).
19 Ellul 5317	'Pinkas Verona' ii. fo. 42b (see Sonne, 'Basic Premisses', 168).
24 Ellul 5319	'Pinkas Verona' ii. fo. 49b (renewal of the appointment and conditions from 5317).
26 Tammuz 5322	'Pinkas Verona' ii. fo. 56a (renewal of the appointment from 5317).
21 Tevet 5325	'Pinkas Verona' ii. fo. 65a (cited as Document 19 in the Hebrew edition).
17 Tevet 5327	'Pinkas Verona' ii. fo. 69b (renewal of the previous appointment for a two-year period).
4 Tishri 5329	'Pinkas Verona' ii. fo. 77a (cited as Document 20 in the Hebrew edition).
2 Tevet 5331	'Pinkas Verona' ii. fo. 83a (renewal of the previous appointment in all particulars).
19 Tevet 5333	'Pinkas Verona' ii. fo. 91a (renewal of the appointment of 4 Tishri 5329).
13 Tevet 5335	'Pinkas Verona' ii. fo. 96b (ditto).
6 Shevet 5337	'Pinkas Verona' ii, fo. 107a (ditto).
27 Tevet 5339	'Pinkas Verona' ii. fo. 114a (ditto).
11 Kislev 5340	'Pinkas Verona' ii. fo. 119a (cited as Document 21 in the Hebrew edition).

1 Tevet 5343	'Pinkas Verona' ii. fo. 134b (renewal of the previous appointment with the addition of the clause: 'but when some people from the Holy Congregation shall come to learn their [daily] lesson, R. Yo'eẓ shall be required to teach them, but if they do not come he is not required to teach, and will in any event receive his salary from their portion').
12 Ellul 5344	'Pinkas Verona' ii. fos. 142b–3a (see Sonne, 'Basic Premisses', 169–71).
27 Adar 5346	'Pinkas Verona' ii. fo. 151a (see Sonne, 'Basic Premisses', 172).
26 December 5349	'Pinkas Verona' ii. fos. 161a–2a (see Sonne, 'Basic Premisses', 171).
26 April 5352	'Pinkas Verona' ii, fo. 173a (see Sonne, 'Basic Premisses', 176–7).
20 December 5353	'Pinkas Verona' ii. fo. 174b (see Sonne, 'Basic Premisses', 178).
25 December 5356	'Pinkas Verona' ii. fo. 184a (renewal of the previous appointment in all particulars).
25 December 5359	'Pinkas Verona' ii. fo. 191a (cited as Document 22 in the Hebrew edition).

Padua

7 Iyyar 5339	*Pinkas Padua*, sects. 41, 87.
22 Av 5341	*Pinkas Padua*, sects. 63, 118.
17 Heshvan 5345	*Pinkas Padua*, sects. 176, 172.
[Tishri 5349 ?]	*Pinkas Padua*, sects. 345, 251–2; see also sects. 328, 241–2.
24 Nissan 5353	*Pinkas Padua*, sects. 504, 311.
2 Shevet 5356	*Pinkas Padua*, sects. 576, 336–7.

Casale

5349–5356	'Pinkas Casale', fo. 15 (cited as Document 23 in Hebrew edition).
28 August 5358	'Pinkas Casale', fo. 20 (cited as Document 24 in Hebrew edition).
22 Ellul 5359	'Pinkas Casale', fo. 25 (cited as Document 25 in Hebrew edition).
2 September 5362	'Pinkas Casale', fo. 32 (renewal of the previous appointment for a two-year period).
17 Adar II 5366	'Pinkas Casale', fo. 37—with an additional

	clause dated 22 Ellul 5356, fo. 38 (cited as Document 26 in Hebrew edition).

Cremona

Second half of 16th century	S. Simonsohn, 'Cremona', 271–2.

APPENDIX 3. *Selected Rabbinic Appointments*

A. Rabbinic Appointment from Verona, 7 Tammuz 5302[1]

[On Wednesday, the 7th day of Tammuz, 5302.] As acts are greater than the one who performs them, and the reward of those who support the students of Torah is very great, we, the two lay leaders of the city at present, R. Abram of Conegliano and R. Seligman Ḥefetz, agreed to propose the following: First of all, we accept and take upon ourselves as leader, prince, judge and teacher the distinguished rabbi, R. Joḥanan son of Saadyah, to be the head of the Academy here in the Holy Congregation of Verona, to teach Torah among us, as follows: the distinguished rabbi shall be required every day, early in the morning, following the conclusion of the prayer in the synagogue, to teach the Talmudic text to those who wish to hear it; he shall also be required to do so every day, for one hour or more, prior to the Afternoon Prayer, to come to the synagogue to teach the *Tosafot* in the special place set aside for study in the synagogue. And he shall likewise be required to teach in the synagogue, as well as between terms,[2] for an hour or more before Afternoon Prayer, one of the books of the codifiers, as the majority of his students shall decide. And he will not be allowed to teach[3] more than seven hours a day at most, and the rest of the time left to him, he shall peruse and involve himself with matters which are to the benefit of the holy community, to chastise, to set aright, and to punish those who behave wrongly, to direct them in the way of ethics, and to strengthen those who study [Torah] and to require them to learn, by any means at his disposal. And he shall be required, upon the request of the Holy Congregation of Verona or of the majority of the leaders at the time, to enact or to ban or to agree to whatever matter or edict [they may ask], provided that it is correct and proper and for the general good. And in payment for his trouble and his loss of time, he shall receive every six months seven and a half ducats, each ducat worth 4 lire 13

[1] 'Pinkas Verona' i. 48a. Printed in the Hebrew edition of this book, Document 17, p. 238.

[2] The two periods of time during which there is no activity at the yeshivah were generally the Hebrew month of Nissan (i.e. around Passover), and between the end of Ellul and Rosh Hodesh Heshvan (the season of the High Holy Days). See N. Porges, 'Elie Capsali et sa chronique de Venice', *REJ* 77 (1923), 33; M. Breuer, 'The Ashkenazic Yeshivah', Doctoral Dissertation, Jerusalem, 1967, pp. 56–7.

[3] i.e. his students; see Ch. 3, Sect. 7 and n. 283.

scudi.[4] And if the distinguished rabbi does not—heaven forfend—fulfil these conditions, then the members of the congregation shall likewise not be required to confirm and to fulfil these conditions with him. And these conditions shall continue for three years running, from New Year 5303 [i.e. *Autumn 1542*] until New Year 5306, may it come upon us for good. And these moneys will be paid to the honourable rabbi R. Joḥanan from the charity strongbox here in Verona periodically, as stipulated above. And the incumbent treasurers shall pay the distinguished rabbi his salary from that fund, without any delay, postponement, or excuse whatsoever.

The decision was approved, 16 for, 3 against, 1 abstaining.

B. Rabbinic Appointment from Verona, 4 Tishre 5329 [1568][5]

There was further proposed on Sunday, 4 Tishri 5329, on the part of the three lay leaders, Mr. Shemariah and Mr. Moshe Melamed and Mr. Joseph son of Mr. Leib Shwabbe, to confirm the appointment of R. Yo'eẓ, that he be our Head of Court in the same manner and condition as he was previously, as stated in the previous decision. Furthermore, R. Yo'eẓ shall teach in the synagogue after the evening prayer, as he has done until now, and shall receive as salary fourteen ducats per year, each ducat valued at 4 lire 13 *scudi*,[6] and this procedure shall continue for two years from the above-mentioned date. And he shall receive his salary in the following manner: ten ducats from the fund of the provisions, to be disbursed by the treasurers, and four ducats from the moneys of the holy community, disbursed by the lay leaders. And the treasurers and lay leaders shall pay R. Yo'eẓ half of his salary at the beginning of the year—that is, at this time[7] the treasurers are now required to pay him 5 ducats and the lay leaders 2 ducats in payment for the next six months, that is, from New Year's Day 5329, which is just past, until the end of the coming month of Adar 5329, and on the coming *Rosh Ḥodesh* [New Moon] of Nissan he shall receive [a total of] seven ducats from the treasurers and lay leaders, as stipulated, and so on every six months according to that arrangement, until the conclusion of the period of his employment. And it is [further] understood that R. Yo'eẓ shall receive the ten ducats annual salary for acting as Head of the Court, and the four ducats annually for teaching in the evening after the

4 See above, Ch. 3, n. 263.

5 'Pinkas Verona' ii. 77a; published in the Hebrew edition of this book, Document 20, p. 240.

6 See above, Ch. 3, n. 263.

7 i.e. 4 Tishri, which was immediately after the New Year's festival.

synagogue [i.e. *after Evening Prayers*]. Furthermore, the four ducats to be paid by the leaders from the congregational funds each year are understood as being included within the ten ducats which he is to receive for serving as judge, it being understood that if the funds in the treasury for provisions shall not suffice for the ten ducats mentioned above, he shall receive the balance from the charity funds, and four ducats will be paid by the lay leaders.

The decision was approved, 16 for, 5 against, 1 abstaining.

C. Appointment of Rabbi Abraham Provenzali in Casale, 5394 [1594][8]

Let it hereby be known that I, Abraham Provenzali, was accepted here in Casale to be the rabbi of the Holy Community, for an initial period of three years, that is, during the years 5349, 5350 and 5351 [*1588–91*], with the stipend given me, by voluntary contributions of each individual, as attested by their signatures upon a list which is in my possession. Afterwards I was continued[9] further in that manner for two additional years, that is, 5352, 5353 [*1591–3*]. After that, at the beginning of the term of office of the leader (*parnas*), the noble rabbi and *kohen* R. Moshe Katz Rapa and the honourable M. Manasseh Yonah, who began their term on this New Year, which is the year 5354 [*1593/94*], as stated above on page 13 [i.e. *of the communal ledger*], they and other outstanding people in the community began to speak about me and to say that it would be better that they provide my salary through an assessment on the Holy Community, like the other needs of the community which are imposed upon couples[10] by assessment[11] of the community, and that it no longer be raised by voluntary contributions, as it has been during the first five years, and that they make me a new contract[12] for another three consecutive years, namely, 5354, 5355, 5356 [*1593–6*]. And after they discussed this matter for many days, the people of the community met in the meeting place in my absence, on Sunday, 17 Tevet, 5354 [i.e. *January 1594*], and there they chose three people to arrive at an agreement with me concerning my salary from the community, which was to total one hundred *scudi* of seven florins each[13] per year, to always be paid in advance for each six months. They likewise agreed with me upon the sum of one hundred *scudi* for the next three years.

8 'Pinkas Casale', fo. 15; published in the Hebrew edition of this book, Document 23, pp. 241–2.

9 i.e. my appointment was confirmed.

10 See Document 22, note 7, in the Hebrew edition of this book.

11 Assessments laid upon property.

12 A contract of obligation. For the precise meaning of this term in medieval halakhic literature, see J. J. Rabinowitz, *Jewish Law; Its Influence on the Development of Legal Institutions* (New York, 1956), 208.

13 See Ch. 3, n. 275.

Furthermore, at the order of those leaders during whose term of office this agreement was made, and at the order of those lay leaders who are to be in the future, I copy here that agreement, as it was given to me in the hand of the honourable *Ḥaver* Jacob Segre, and those two lay leaders also came and signed with their own hand. And I also copy here the agreement of the three chosen ones who reappointed me for those three years with the provision mentioned, and they also signed with their own hand.

Today, Sunday, 17 Tevet, 5354, there gathered together the members of the community mentioned here by name opposite,[14] and a decision was taken for the benefit of the public that those three mentioned by name below be given the authority to hire a rabbi for the community for the next three years, beginning on New Year 5354; and the three chosen, or two of them who will agree to one opinion, will come to an agreement with Rabbi Abraham Provenzali son of R. David to be rabbi and teacher of the congregation, and upon him [is imposed] the office and the burden of this people, as has been until now the law for any rabbi and sage in Israel. And the salary to be allocated by those chosen to said Rabbi Provenzali will be paid promptly every six months in advance for the three years, beginning on New Year 5354, under the condition that they are not allowed to hire him for more than one hundred *scudi* for the year, of nine florins each. And the leaders shall collect this sum every six months from the assessment of the congregation, like any other regular expense and payment divided among the congregation.

Passed by a vote of eighteen positive ballots.

D. Renewal of Rabbi Provenzali's Appointment, 5360 [1600][15]

It was decided on the above date [*22 Ellul 5359*, i.e. *September 1599*], further agreeing that for the next two years the Distinguished Rabbi, the Head of the Court, Rabbi Provenzali, should be the rabbi of the Holy Community as he has been until now, with an annual salary of one hundred *scudi* of nine florins each,[16] per annum, as he has been until now, and upon the assessment of the holy community,[17] with the condition that he may not decide concerning financial questions regarding members of the community without the agreement of the

[14] The names of those present at the gathering were recorded on the margins of the page, opposite this passage.

[15] 'Pinkas Casale', fo. 25; published in the Hebrew edition of this book, Document 25, p. 243.

[16] See Ch. 3, n. 275.

[17] i.e. his wage shall be paid from the collection of taxes to be imposed on the basis of wealth. Cf. the previous appointment document.

two lay leaders who shall be at that time, or of one of them, should the other be an interested party or relative, or the like. And it is understood that all this is conditional upon the necessary agreement of His Majesty the Prince. And that rabbi will also be required each morning, as has been his practice until now, to read and to repeat a lesson in Talmud every day, whether much or little, for the benefit of the public, or he may place another in his stead if he so wishes. And on Sabbaths and festivals he shall also preach in public following the Morning Meal, as this is a time when most of the members of the community are available.

Passed, 21 in favour, 4 against, and R. Dan did not put in a ballot.

APPENDIX 4. *Christian and Jewish Arbitration Agreements* (Compromesso)

A Christian Text of *Compromissum*[1]

In nomine Domini Amen etc. Iacobus etc. ex una parte et Franciscus etc. ex alia sponte etc. ex certa scientia et non aliquo errore iuris uel facti ducti compromiserunt sese et compromissum et commissionem fecerunt et faciunt per rationem transactionem et amicabilem compositionem et per omnem alium modum uiam et formam[2]: per quem et quam infrascripta omnia et singula et quaecunque dicenda et facienda per infrascriptum dominum arbitratorem[3] melius ualeant et teneant et pleniorem fortiantur effectum in nobilem uirum dominum Simonem etc. licet absentem tanquam praesentem tanquam in arbitrum et arbitratorem et amicabilem compositorem et amicum communem communiter et concorditer electum nominatim de lite causa et questione inter ipsas partes uersa et uertente[4] coram domino uicario magnifici domini potestatis Placentiae ex causa et occasione cuiusdam petiae terrae positae etc. et prout ex actis ipsius domini uicarii apparet et de connexis et dependentibus ac emergentibus ab ea: itaque ipse dominus arbiter et arbitrator possit et ualeat inter dictas partes procedere dicere pronunciare sententiare declarare condemnare absoluere adiudicare appropriare cedere arbitrari et arbitramentari et amicabiliter componere: et dicere et facere quicquid et prout sibi uidebitu[5] de iure et de facto: et de amicabili compositione: et de iure tantum et de facto tantum: et de amicabili compositione tantum iuris

[1] From *Formularius instrumentorum* ... *Petri Dominici de Mussis* ... (Venice, 1530), 35b.

[2] Take note that all of these phrases appeared as well, if in abbreviated form, in the early Hebrew arbitration agreements, and disappeared over the course of time, as stated in Ch. 5, Sect. 3.

[3] As we noted in Ch. 5, Sect. 3, 'arbitrator' is used interchangeably with 'arbiter'. Cf. below, where the appointment is designated by the terms 'arbitrum et arbitratorem et amicabilem compositorem'. Further on, the mediator is referred to as 'arbiter et arbitrator', and finally only as 'arbitrator'.

[4] In the Hebrew *compromissum* cited below, many of these terms are used in accordance with the details of Jewish law ('disputes, differences, quarrels, and matters leading to [obligations of] money ... or benefit or any matter involving valuation of judges ...').

[5] Parallel to: 'by law or close to law, without compromise or by compromise, as their eyes see fit.'

ordine seruato et non seruato stando sedendo et ambulando[6] partibus praesentibus et absentibus: una parte praesente et altera absente[7]: citatis partibus et non citatis monitis nec requisitis: una parte citata et alia non citata monita nec requisita: diebus feriatis et non feriatis[8]: quibus feriis et diebus feriatis et omnibus aliis et singulis praemissis et cuiuscunque ex eis beneficio et auxilio dictae partes pacto renunciauerunt et renunciant expresso et per pactum expressum[9]: et quicquid ipse dominus arbiter et arbitrator dixerit pronunciauerit sententiauerit declarauerit condemnauerit taxauerit absoluerit appropriauerit cesserit arbitratus et arbitramentatus fuerit: et amicabiliter composuerit et dixerit et fecerit inter dictas partes ipsae partes uel aliqua ex eis non dicent uel dicet nullum iniquum uel iniustum in totum uel pro parte nec ab eo uel eius parte uel occasione appellabunt querelabunt uel aliqualiter supplicabunt: nec reducent nec reduci petent ad arbitrium boni uiri cui reductioni et eius petitioni et cuicunque reclamationi: et aliis premissis dictae partes renunciauerunt et renuciant expresso et per pactum expressum.[10] quae omnia et singula suprascripta et quaecunque declaranda per ipsum dominum arbitratorem uigore praesentis compromissi et cuiuscunque prorogrationis fiendae dictae partes per solemnem stipulationem promiserunt et conuenerunt sibi uicissim perpetuo firma rata et grata habere tenere attendere et obseruare et efficaciter adimplere: et non contrauenire uel contrafacere de iure uel de facto per sese uel alium aliqua ratione uel causa modo casu uel iure: siue ullo legum uel decretorum seu rescriptorum auxilio: sub omnium damnorum interesse et expensarum litis et extra restitutione et refectione: de quibus et earum quantitate stari et credi debeat et ita consenserunt et consentiunt soli et simplici dicto et assertioni partis attendentis et petentis sine sacramento et onere cuiuscunque probationis et taxationis iudicis inde prestando et fiendae.[11] et ulterius in poena et sub poena ducatorum decem toties committenda et exigenda cum effectu quoties in praedictis uel aliquo praedictorum fuerit contrafactum seu etiam contrauentum. qua commissa soluta uel non firma et rata maneant omnia et singula

[6] In the Hebrew document: 'and even while walking.'

[7] In the following Hebrew Document: 'whether in the presence of his fellow or not in the presence of his fellow.' Note there are many details missing here, incorporated in the general phrase, 'iuris ordine seruato et non seruato'.

[8] Ibid. 'whether by day or by night'.

[9] Ibid. 'And they disqualified any testimony or evidence or cause that might weaken the power of their ruling.'

[10] Ibid. 'as they rule and ordain, so shall it be forever, without any *appellazione* or *revisione* (appeal or revision) before any Jewish or Gentile court in the world . . . everything shall be approved and ratified by us as if performed by the Great Court in Jerusalem'.

[11] Ibid. 'and they shall not refuse . . . for each one has sworn before us by the force of fine and a severe oath . . .'

suprascripta cum eadem stipulatione poenae. pro quibus omnibus et singulis suprascriptis attendendis et firmiter obseruandis dicte partes obligauerunt sibi uicissim pignori omnia sua bona presentia et futura[12]: et uoluerunt et uolunt dictae partes praesens compromissum et terminum ipsius ualere et durare debere usque ad unum mensem proxime futurum.[13] et de praedictis dictae partes rogauerunt me notarium ut inde publicum conficiam instrumentum.[14]

A Hebrew Arbitration Document (*Compromissum*)[15]

It truly being so, that in all matters of disputes, differences, quarrels and matters leading to [obligations of] money, "and even in matters for which there is a fine," or benefit, or any matter involving valuation of judges or financial damage that may exist between *X* and *Y*, from the day they were born until now, they have chosen for themselves as arbiters and as judges to issue a ruling *A* and *B*, *A* being chosen by *X* and *B* being chosen by *Y*. And they have been given all the powers which we shall mention, by means of legal transfer,[16] . . . that they may receive and hear the claims and responses of each one of the litigants—whether once or many times, whether in the presence of his fellow or not in the presence of his fellow, whether verbally or in writing, whether from their own mouths or that of their attorneys, whether by day or by night, [and even while walking][17]—and they may likewise receive the testimony of witnesses or disqualify their testimony, and they may receive witnesses not in the presence of [his fellow] litigant, even without duress, and even to receive witnesses who are [formally] disqualified or are interested parties, until they know things as clearly as they wish. And they may receive testimony at night, and they may disqualify witnesses as they see fit, as if we had disqualified them ourselves, and they may excommunicate

[12] This section is absent in Hebrew *compromissa*. It may be that, because the Hebrew documents were issued as a *kinyan* and not as *asmakhta*—i.e. as itself an instrument of legal transfer, and not as a supporting document—so that the property of the litigating parties was automatically mortgaged to it. In any event, they appealed to the Gentile courts for execution—cf. Ch. 5, Sect. 7.

[13] This clause only appears in some of the Hebrew documents; cf. Document 38, p. 249 ff., in the Hebrew edition of this book.

[14] This section corresponds to the signature of the witnesses, which makes the Hebrew *shetar* valid in terms of Jewish law—see above, Ch. 5, Sect. 3.

[15] A sample Hebrew *compromissum*, from MS British Musueum Add. 27011, fos. 150a–155a. In the manuscript, the text of the sample is followed by an extensive commentary by R. Abraham del Vecchio. The full Hebrew text appears in the Hebrew version of this book as Document 50, pp. 263–4; the commentary and notes follow on pp. 264–74.

[16] Hebrew: *kinyan sudar* or *kinyan 'agav karka'*.

[17] The additions given in angle brackets, here and below, are based upon the text quoted in del Vecchio's commentary.

and administer oaths and interrupt the synagogue service,[18] as if they are acting in our stead, and they have been authorized to act as if they had the authority of [the Great] Court of Seventy One [i.e. *the Sanhedrin in Jerusalem*]. And after they have heard their claims and responses sufficiently, so that matters are clarified, they are allowed to issue ruling—by law or close to law, "without compromise or by compromise," as their eyes see fit . . . at any time they wish, whether by day or by night, whether in the presence of the litigants or not in their presence, whether in writing or orally—and as they rule and ordain so shall it be, forever, without any *appellazione* or *revisione* before any Jewish or Gentile court in the world, and without them [i.e. *the litigants*] being permitted to ask, 'show us by what reason you have ruled thus'. And all this is included in the act of accepting them upon themselves as judges—whether by law or by error, whether they err in the law itself, in a matter of knowledge, or in their judgment, whether they take money away from this one and give it to that one—everything shall be approved and ratified by us as if performed by the Great Court in Jerusalem, and they [the litigating parties] may not refuse or repudiate their ruling. And they may extend[19] time as they wish to the litigants, that they may bring all the evidence they have within the period that seems proper to them, and after this time it will be like broken pottery [i.e. *utterly worthless*]; and from this moment each one of them has assumed his rights with regard to the above court, which is considered as the Court of Seventy-one, that by the force of that legal transfer these rights shall be nullified if they do not bring it within the period of time set for them by the court, and they [the Court] shall disqualify any testimony or evidence or reason or claim that may weaken the force of their ruling, and their [the litigants] silence immediately upon the announcement of the ruling shall be viewed as the admission of a litigant, and as one who has completely accepted upon himself the ruling. And neither one of them may argue any claim that may weaken their ruling, for each one of them has obligated themselves in our presence, by means of the transfer and under a severe oath, and it shall be within the right of the arbitrators to order that they sign their decision before it is read, and to carry it out in any way that is effective, whether by Jewish court or by Gentile court; in such a manner that there shall not remain any possible dispute whatsoever following their ruling. And they may also reserve them the authority and right to clarify any doubt that may come about in their understanding of their words from now on and for ever. And in

18 See Ch. 5, Sect. 7.

19 In the text of the commentary: 'to record' or 'register'. This is evidently the correct reading.

accordance with their words, so shall it be upheld, without them being required to give any explanation of their words "and even if their decision may seem contrary to some precedent ruling issued by them"; and if the distinguished arbitrators do not agree upon one view, they shall choose a third party, and follow the majority [among themselves], and the third one which they shall select shall henceforth be given all of the powers enumerated in the above-mentioned transfer, and they [the litigants] took a verbal oath and stated, by our opinion and that of the above-mentioned arbiters, without any deceit or cunning, to confirm and ratify everything written above, without any objection or hesitation whatsoever.

Bibliographical Abbreviations

CAHJP	Central Archive for the History of the Jewish People, Israel Historical Society, Jerusalem.
IMHM	Institute for Microfilms of Hebrew Manuscripts, Hebrew University and Jewish National Library, Jerusalem.
AHR	*American Historical Review*
BHR	*Bibliothèque d'Humanisme et Renaissance*
CI	*Corriere Israelitico*
DS	*Dikdukei Sofrim*
HJ	*Historia Judaica*
HUCA	*Hebrew Union College Annual*
JHI	*Journal of the History of Ideas*
JJLG	*Jahrbuch der jüdisch-literarischen Gesellschaft*
JMH	*Journal of Modern History*
JQR	*Jewish Quarterly Review*
JSS	*Jewish Social Studies*
JWH	*Journal of World History*
KS	*Kiryat Sefer*
MGWJ	*Monatsschrift für Geschichte und Wissenschaft des Judenthums*
PAAJR	*Proceedings of the American Academy of Jewish Research*
RI	*Rivista Israelitica*
RMI	*Rassegna mensile di Israel*
RQ	*Renaissance Quarterly*
REJ	*Revue des études juives*
RSI	*Rivista storica italiana*
ZfHB	*Zeitschrift für hebräische Bibliographie*

Selected Bibliography

Abraham ha-Kohen of Bologna, R., 'Derashah' [a single sermon], in MS Parma Pereau 42: 3540 (IMHM 14047) and MS Oxford Bod. 2192 (IMHM 20475), 127–8. Published as Document 63 in the Hebrew version of this book, pp. 289–91.

Aloni, Nehemiah, 'Two Book Lists from Italy' (Heb.), *Sefer Assaf* (Jerusalem, 1953), 33–9.

—— 'Book Lists: 15th Century Manuscripts from Tivoli in Italy' (Heb.), *Areshet*, 1 (1959), 44–60.

—— 'Ancient Book Lists in the Vatican' (Heb.), *Areshet*, 4 (1966), 213–33.

Ari Nohem. See Modena.

Assaf, Simḥah, *Mekorot le-Toldot ha-Ḥinukh be-Yisra'el* [*Sources for the History of Jewish Education*], 4 vols. (Tel Aviv, 1928–43). Short title: *Mekorot*.

—— 'Book Lists from the Beginning of the 16th Century' (Heb.), *KS* 24 (1947–8), 248–9.

—— 'Towards a History of the Rabbinate' (Heb.), in *Be-'ohalei Ya'akov; Perakim mi-ḥayyei ha-Tarbut shel ha-Yehudim be-yemei ha-Beinayim* (Jerusalem, 1973), 27–61. Originally published in *Reshumot*, 2 (1927), 259–300.

Bachur, R. Elijah, *Sefer Tishby* (Isny, 1541).

Baer, Yiẓḥak, 'The Origins and Foundations of Jewish Communal Organization in the Middle Ages' (Heb.), *Ẓion*, 15 (1950), 1–51.

—— *A History of the Jews in Christian Spain* (Philadelphia, 1971).

Balletti, Andrea, *Gli ebrei e gli estensi* (Reggio-Emilia, 1930; repr. Bologna, 1969).

Baron, Salo W., 'The Controversy of the Communities of Verona according to the Responsa of R. Mordecai Bassan' (Heb.), *Sefer ha-Yovel le-Professor Shmuel Krauss* (Jerusalem, 1937), 217–54.

—— *The Jewish Community*, 3 vols. (Philadelphia, 1942).

—— *A Social and Religious History of the Jews*, 16 vols. (Philadelphia, 1952–76).

Barzilay, Isaac E., 'The Italian and Berlin Haskalah: Parallels and Differences', *PAAJR* 31 (1960–1), 17–54.

—— *Between Reason and Faith: Anti-rationalism in Italian Jewish Thought, 1250–1650* (The Hague, 1967).

—— *Yosef Shlomo Delmedigo, Yashar of Candia: His Life, Works and Times* (Leiden, 1974).

BEINART, ḤAYYIM, 'Jewish Settlement in the Duchy of Savoy in the Wake of the *Privilegio* of 1572' (Heb.), *Sefer Zikaron le-Aryeh Leone Carpi* (Milan and Jerusalem, 1967), Hebrew section, 72–118.

BENAYAHU, MEIR, *Marbiẓ Torah* (Jerusalem, 1953).

—— *ha-Defus ha-'Ivri be-Kremona* [*Hebrew Publishing in Cremona*] (Jerusalem, 1971).

—— *Haskamah u-reshut be-Defusei Veneẓia; ha-Sefer ha-'Ivri me-'et hava'ato li-defus ve-'ad ẓeto la-'or* [*Approbation and Approval in the Hebrew Press in Venice*] (Jerusalem, 1971). Short title: *Haskamah u-reshut*.

—— and LARAS, JOSEPH, 'The Appointment of Health Officials in Cremona in 1575 and the Dispute between R. Eliezer Ashkenazi and R. Abraham Menahem Porto ha-Kohen' (Heb.), *Mikhael*, 1 (Tel Aviv, 1973), 78–143. Short title: 'Health Officials'.

BEN-SASSON, ḤAYYIM HILLEL, *Hagut ve-Hanhagah; Hashkafotehem ha-Ḥevrati'ot shel Yehudei Polin be-shilhei Yemei ha-Beinayim* [*Leadership and Ideology; The Political Thought of Polish Jewry in the Late Middle Ages*] (Jerusalem, 1960).

—— ed., *A History of the Jewish People*, translated from the Hebrew (Cambridge, Mass., 1976).

BERLINER, ADOLF, *Geschichte der Juden in Rom von den ältesten Zeiten bis zum Gegenwart*, 2 vols. (Frankfurt-on-Main, 1893).

—— *Sarid me-'Ir; kolel ma'amarim shonim ha-nog'im be-korot ha-Yehudim ba-'ir . . . Roma* (*articles pertaining to the history of the Jews in Rome*) *Kobeẓ 'al Yad*, 5 (1893).

—— 'Aus Handschriften', in *Festschrift zum siebigsten Geburtstage David Hoffmans* (Berlin, 1914), 281–92.

BERNHEIMER, CARLO, 'Una collezione privata di duecento manoscritti ebraici del XV secolo', *La Bibliofilia*, 26 (1925), 300–25.

BERNSTEIN, H. Y., 'The Law of Ordination and its History' (Heb.), *ha-Tekufah*, 4 (1913), 394–426.

BERNSTEIN, SHIMON, 'New Poems of R. Samuel de Archivolti' (Heb.), *Tarbiẓ*, 8 (1937), 55–68, 237.

Bet Mo'ed. See RAVA.

BETTAN, ISRAEL, *Studies in Jewish Preaching* (Cincinnati, 1939).

Bi'ur zeh yaẓa Rishonah. See PROVENZALI.

BOKSENBOIM, JACOB, ed., *She'elot u-Teshuvot Matanot ba-Adam* (Tel Aviv, 1983).

—— ed., *'Iggerot Melammedim; Italia 5315–5351* [*Letters of Jewish Teachers in Renaissance Italy, 1555–1591*] (Tel Aviv, 1985).

BONFIL, ROBERT, 'Expressions in Italy of the Uniqueness of the Jewish People during the Renaissance' (Heb.), *Sinai*, 76 (1975), 36–46. Short title: 'Uniqueness of the Jewish People'.

—— 'R. Moses Provenzali's Commentary to Maimonides' 25 Axioms' (Heb.), *KS*, 50 (1975), 157–76.
—— 'Aspects of the Social and Spiritual Life of the Jews in the Venetian Territories at the Beginning of the 16th Century' (Heb.), *Ẓion*, 41 (1976), 69–96. Short title: 'Jews in the Venetian Territories'.
—— 'One of the Italian Sermons of R. Mordecai Dato' (Heb.), *Iṭalyah; ketav-ʿet le-ḥeker tarbutam ve-sifrutam shel Yehudei Iṭalyah*, 1 (1976), 1–32.
—— 'The Doctrine of the Human Soul and its Holiness in the Thought of R. Obadiah Sforno' (Heb.), *'Eshel Be'er Shevaʿ*, 1 (1976), 200–57. Short title: 'R. Obadiah Sforno'.
—— 'A List of Hebrew Books from Imola from the end of the 14th Century' (Heb.), *Sefer Zikaron li-Shelomo Umberto Naḥon* (Jerusalem, 1979), 47–62.
—— 'New Information Concerning Rabbi Menahem Azariah da Fano and his Age' (Heb.), in *Perakim be-toldot ha-Ḥevrah ha-Yehudit bi-yemei ha-Beinayim uva-ʿet ha-Ḥadashah* [*Jacob Katz Festschrift*] (Jerusalem, 1980), 98–135.
—— 'Introduction' (Heb.), to the facsimile edition of R. Judah Messer Leon's *Sefer Nofet Ẓufim* (Jerusalem, 1981), 7–53. Short title: 'Introduction to *Nofet Ẓufim*'.
—— 'The Historian's Perception of the Jews in the Italian Renaissance; Towards a Reappraisal', *REJ* 143 (1984), 59–82.
—— 'Change in Cultural Patterns of Jewish Society in Crisis: The Case of Italian Jewry at the Close of the 16th Century', Proceedings of the Conference on Jewish Societies in Transformation in the 16th and 17th Centuries, Jerusalem, 1986 (forthcoming).
—— 'Cultura e mistica a Venezia nel Cinquecento', in *Gli ebrei a Venezia, secoli XIV–XVIII, a cura di Gaetano Cozzi* (Milan, 1987), 469–506.
—— 'Halakhah, Kabbalah and Society: Some Insights into Menahem Azariah da Fano's Inner World', in *Jewish Thought in the 17th Century*, eds. I. Twersky and B. Septimus (Cambridge, Mass., 1987), 39–61.
Bresc, Henri, *Livre et Société en Sicile, 1299–1499* (Palermo, 1971).
Breuer, Mordecai, 'ha-Yeshivah ha-Ashkenazit be-Shilhey yemei ha-Beinayim' [The Ashkenazic Yeshivah at the Close of the Middle Ages (Heb.)], Doctoral Dissertation, Hebrew University, Jerusalem, 1967. Short title: 'The Ashkenazic Yeshivah'.
—— 'Ashkenazic Ordination' (Heb.), *Ẓion*, 33 (1968), 15–46.
—— 'The Growth of *Pilpul* and *Ḥiluk* in the Ashkenazic Yeshivot' (Heb.), *Sefer Zikaron le-Morenu . . . Y. Y. Weinberg* (Jerusalem, 1970), 241–55.

—— *Rabbanut Ashkenaz be-yemei ha-Beinayim* [*The Medieval German Rabbinate*] (Jerusalem, 1976).

—— 'The Position of the Rabbinate in the Leadership of Ashkenazic Communities in the 15th Century' (Heb.), *Ẓion*, 41 (1976), 47–67. Originally published in *Divrei ha-Kongress ha-'Olami ha-Shishi le-Mad'ei ha-Yahadut*, 2 (Jerusalem, 1976), 141–7.

BRÜLL, N., 'Das Geschlecht der Treves', *Jahrbücher für jüdische Geschichte und Literatur*, 1 (1874), 87–122.

BURCKHARDT, JACOB, *The Civilisation of the Renaissance in Italy*, 2 vols. (New York, 1958).

CARPI, DANIEL, 'ha-Yehudim be-Padua be-tekufat ha-Renessans' [Jews in Padua During the Renaissance (Heb.)], Doctoral Dissertation, Jerusalem, Hebrew University, 1967.

—— 'The Expulsion of the Jews from the Papal States During the Reign of Pope Pius V and the Inquisition Against the Jews of Bologna, 1566–1569' (Heb.), *Sefer Zikaron le-Ḥayyim Enzo Sereni* (Jerusalem, 1971), 145–65.

—— 'R. Judah Messer Leon and his Activity as Physician' (Heb.), *Mikhael; Me'asef le-Toldot ha-Yehudim ba-Tefuẓot* (Tel Aviv, 1973), 277–301. In English: 'Notes on the Life of Rabbi Judah Messer Leon', *Studi sull'ebraismo italiano in memoria di Cecil Roth* (Rome, 1974), 37–62.

—— ed., *Pinkas Va'ad Kehillah Kedoshah Padua, 5338–5363* [*Padua Communal Minute Book, 1578–1603*] (Jerusalem, 1974). Short title: *Pinkas Padua*.

CASSUTO, UMBERTO, 'Un rabbino fiorentino del sec. XV', *RI* 3 (1906), 116–28, 224–8; 4 (1907), 33–7, 156–61, 225–9.

—— 'I piu antichi capitoli del ghetto di Firenze', *RI* 9 (1912), 203–11; 10 (1913) 32–40, 71–80.

—— *Gli ebrei a Firenze nell'età del Rinascimento* (Florence, 1918). Short title: *Firenze*.

—— 'Ein hebräischer Dichter des 15. Jahrhunderts', *MGWJ* 77 (1933), 365–84.

—— *I Manoscritti Palatini della Biblioteca Apostolica Vaticana e la loro storia* (Vatican City, 1935).

—— ed. *Codices Vaticani Hebraici*, codices 1–115 (Rome, 1956).

COHEN, GERSON, 'On the History of the Controversy Concerning the Matter of Gentile Wine in Italy and its Sources' (Heb.), *Sinai*, 77 (1975), 62–90.

COLON, JOSEPH, *She'elot u-Teshuvot . . . Yosef Kolon* (Venice, 1519). Short title: *Teshuvot Mahari''k*.

—— *She'elot u-Teshuvot u-Piskei Mahari''k ha-Ḥadashim*, ed. S. Pines (Jerusalem, 1970).

COLORNI, VITTORE, 'Note per la biografia di alcuni dotti ebrei vissuti a Mantova nel secolo XV', *Annuario di studi ebraica*, 1 (1934), 169–82.

—— *Legge ebraica e leggi locali* (Milan, 1945).

—— 'Sull'ammissibilità degli ebrei alla laurea anteriormente al secolo XIX', *Scritti in onore di Riccardo Bachi*, *RMI* 16 (1950), 202–16.

—— 'Spigolature su Obadia Sforno', *Volume . . . in memoria di Federico Luzzatto* [*RMI* 28/3–4 (1962)], 78–88.

CONNELL, S. 'Books and their Owners in Venice, 1345–1480', *Journal of the Warburg and Courtald Institutes*, 35 (1972), 163–86.

DA FANO, MENAḤEM AZARIAH, *Pinkas Milot* (list of circumcisions performed), published in BONFIL, R., 'New Information . . .', 116–33.

—— *Teshuvot RM"A mi-Fano*, (Jerusalem, 1963).

DA PISA, VITALE [JEḤIEL NISSIM], *Sefer Minḥat Kina'ot*, ed. D. Kaufmann (Berlin, 1898). Critical text based upon Pozen, *ZfHB* 4, 92–5.

—— *Ma'amar Ḥayyei 'Olam 'al 'Inyan Ribit* [*Banking and Finance among Jews in Renaissance Italy; A Critical Edition of The Eternal Life* (*Haye Olam*)], ed. and trans., G. S. Rosenthal (New York, 1962).

DAN, JOSEPH, 'Hebrew Homiletical Literature (*Derush*) and its Literary Values' (Heb.), *ha-Sifrut*, 3 (1971–2), 558–67.

—— *Sifrut ha-Mussar veha-Derush* [*Hebrew Ethical and Homiletical Literature*] (Jerusalem, 1975).

DATO, MORDECAI, 'Derashot' [Sermons] in MSS British Museum, Add. 27050 (IMHM 5726; Margoliouth Catalogue No. 380) and Add. 27007 (IMHM 5686; Margoliouth Catalogue No. 381). Short title: *Derashot Dato*.

DAVID HA-KOHEN OF CORFU, R., *Zeh Sefer Teshuvot* (Constantinople, 1537–8). Short title: *Teshuvot Maharda"kh*.

DE' POMIS, DAVID, *Ẓemaḥ David*, Hebrew, Latin and Italian dictionary (Venice, 1587).

DELLA TORRE, LELLIO, 'In qual lingua si predicò in Italia nei tempi passati', *CI* 1 (1862–3), 94–8.

DELMEDIGO, ELIJAH, *Sefer Beḥinat ha-Dat* (Basle, 1629); see also the new edn. of J. Ross (Tel Aviv, 1985).

Derashot R. Azriel Trabot. See TRABOT.

Derashot Dato. See DATO.

Derashot Maharshi"k. See KATZENELLENBOGEN.

Derashot R. Nathan Finzi. See FINZI.

DE ROSSI, G. B., *MSS Codices Hebraici Bibliothecae I. B. De Rossi . . .* (Parma, 1803).

DIENA, AZRIEL, *Teshuvot R. Azriel Diena*, ed. J. Boksenboim, 2 vols. (Tel Aviv, 1979).

DIMITROVSKY, ḤAYYIM Z., 'History of the Jews in Milan Before the Expulsion of 1597' (Heb.), *Talpiyot*, 6 (1955), 336–45, 701–22.

—— 'On the Method of *Pilpul*' (Heb.), *Salo Wittmeyer Baron Jubilee Volume, Hebrew Section*, iii [*Sefer ha-Yovel li-khavod Shalom Baron*] (Jerusalem, 1975), 111–81.

DINARI, YEDIDYA A., *Ḥakhmei Ashkenaz be-Shilhei yemei ha-Benayim; Darkeihem ve-khitveihem ba-Halakhah* [*Ashkenazic Sages of the Late Middle Ages: Their Halakhic Method and Writings*] (Jerusalem, 1984). Short title: *Ḥakhmei Ashkenaz*.

DISEGNI, DARIO, 'Due contratti di rabbini Medici di Ancona del 1692 e 1752', *Annuario di studi ebraici* (1969–72), 97–104.

Divrei Rivot . . . le-ge'onei Iṭalyah be-reshit ha-me'ah ha-shelishit la-elef ha-shishi [*Controversies . . . of Italian Rabbis of the 15th Century*] (Hussiatyn, 1902).

Eleh ha-Devarim (Mantua, 1566); record of the controversy between R. Samuel of Perugia and his fiancée.

ELBOGEN, ISMAR, 'Una nota di spese sel secolo XVI', *RI* 3 (1906), 155–62.

'Ein ha-Kore. See SHEM-TOV.

ELON, MENAḤEM, 'On the Nature of Communal Ordinances in Jewish Law' (Heb.), *Meḥkerei Mishpaṭ le-zekher Avraham Rosenthal* (Jerusalem, 1964), 1–54.

—— *ha-Mishpaṭ ha-'Ivri*, 2 vols. (Jerusalem, 1973).

EMANUEL b. JEKUTIEL OF BENEVENTO, *Sefer Livyat Ḥen* (Mantua, 1557).

ENELOW, H. G., 'Raphael Norzi: a Rabbi of the Renaissance', *Hebrew Union College Jubilee Volume* (Cincinnati, 1925), 333–78.

FERGUSON, W. K., *The Renaissance in Historical Thought; Five Centuries of Interpretation* (Cambridge, 1948).

FINKELSTEIN, LOUIS, *Jewish Self-government in the Middle Ages* (New York, 1924; 2nd edn., 1964).

FINZI, AHARON BEN ISRAEL, 'Teshuvot R. Aharon b. Yisra'el Finzi [of Reggio]', MS Jerusalem—Ben-Zvi Makhon 4040.

FINZI, JACOB ISRAEL, 'Makkabi: Perush ha-Tefillot ve-Ṭa'amei ha-Dinim' [Commentary on the Liturgy and the Reasoning behind the Laws], MS Cambridge Add. 512 (IMHM 16805).

—— 'Teshuvot R. Ya'akov Yisra'el b. Rafael Finzi' [Responsa], MS Montefiore 113 (IMHM 4627); some responsa were copied from this MS in MS Jerusalem Heb. 8to 1992.

FINZI, NATHAN b. BINYAMIN, 'Derashot' [Sermons], MS London 932 (IMHM 5726).

FOA, SALVATORE, *Gli ebrei nel Monferrato nei secoli XVI e XVII* (Alessandria, 1914; repr. Bologna, 1965).

FRANKEL, D., 'Three Letters Concerning the Biography of R. Isaac Joshua de Lattes' (Heb.), *'Alim le-Bibliographiyah ve-korot Yisra'el*, 3/2 (1937–8), 23–6.

FREIMANN, AARON H., 'Jewish Scribes in Medieval Italy', in *Alexander Marx Jubilee Volume* (New York, 1950), English Section, 231–342.

—— *Seder Kiddushin ve-Nisu'in me-aḥarei Ḥatimat ha-Talmud ve-'ad yameinu* [*Jewish Marriage Laws from the Post-Talmudic Age to the Present*] (Jerusalem, 1965).

GALLETTI, ALFREDO, *L'eloquenza dalle origini al XVI secolo* (Milan, 1938).

GARIN, EUGENIO, *La cultura filosofica del Rinascimento; motivi della cultura filosofica Ferrarese nel Rinascimento* (Florence, 1961).

—— *L'educazione in Europa, 1400–1600* (Bari, 1966).

—— *Medioevo e rinascimento* (Bari, 1966).

—— *La cultura del rinascimento* (Bari, 1971).

GOITEIN, SHLOMO D., *Sidrei Ḥinukh be-yemei ha-Ge'onim u-Vet ha-Rambam: Mekorot Ḥadashim u-min ha-Genizah* [*Jewish Education in Muslim Countries*] (Jerusalem, 1962). Short title: *Sidrei Hinukh*.

—— 'New Information on the *Negiddim* of Kairouan and Rabbenu Nissim' (Heb.), *Ẓion*, 27 (1962), 11–23.

GRAZIANO, ABRAHAM, 'Teshuvot Ma'arvei Naḥal' [Responsa], MS New York JTS 61455 (R 1356). Most of these responsa duplicate those found in BOKSENBOIM, ed., *Teshuvot Matanot ba-Adam*; cf. BENAYAHU, *Haskamah u-Reshut*, 92.

GREEN, JOSEPH, 'The Trabot Family' (Heb.), *Sinai*, 79 (1976), 147–63.

GÜDEMANN, MORITZ, 'Dei Neugestaltung des Rabbinerwesens und deren Einfluss auf die talmudische Wissenschaft im Mittelalter', *MGWJ* 13 (1864), 68–70, 97–110, 384–95, 421–44.

—— *Sefer ha-Torah veha-Ḥayyim be-arẓot ha-Ma'arav be-yemei ha-Beinayim* [*Torah and Life in Western Countries in the Middle Ages*], ed. A. S. Friedberg, 3 vols. (Warsaw, 1897–9; photo edn., Jerusalem, 1972). Short title: *ha-Torah veha-Ḥayyim*.

GULAK, A., *Yesodei ha-Mishpaṭ ha-'Ivri*, 4 vols. (Jerusalem and Berlin, 1923).

—— *Oẓar ha-Sheṭarot ha-nehugot be-Yisra'el* (Jerusalem, 1926).

GUTTMANN, JULIUS, *Philosophies of Judaism* (Philadelphia, 1964).

HABERMANN, ABRAHAM M., *Toldot ha-Sefer ha-'Ivri* [*The History of the Hebrew Book*] (Jerusalem, 1945).

HALBERSTAMM, S. Z. H., 'The Ordinances of 1554' (Heb.), *'Ivri Anokhi*, 31 (1879), 266–7.

HARRIS, A. C., 'La Demografia del Ghetto in Italia, 1516–1797 circa', *RMI* 33 (1937), Suppl.

HARTOM, ELIJAH S., and CASSUTO, UMBERTO, *Takkanot Kandia ve-Zikhronoteha* [*The Ordinances of Candia*] (Jerusalem, 1943).

Ḥayyei 'Olam. See DA PISA.

Haẓa'ah 'al 'odot ha-Geṭ (Venice, 1566). A proposal concerning the writ of divorce issued by Samuel Venturozzo.

HEKSHER, SHIMON, 'Leader, Judge and Teacher' (Heb.), in *'Ish 'al ha-'Edah*, ed. Y. Eisner (Jerusalem, 1973), 161–93.

HOROVITZ, MARCUS, *Rabbanei Frankfurt* (Jerusalem, 1972). [German: *Frankfurter Rabbinen*, ed. J. Unna (Kfar ha-Roeh, 1969)].

IBN YAḤYA, GEDALYAH, *Sefer Shalshelet ha-Kabbalah* (Amsterdam, 1697).

ISSERLES, R. MOSES, *Teshuvot ha-RaMA*, ed. A. Siev (Jerusalem, 1971).

JOEL, ISSACHAR, 'Italian Marriage Contracts in the Library' (Heb.), *KS* 22 (1945–6), 266–304.

JUDAH AL-BARGELONI, *Sefer ha-Sheṭarot*, ed. S. J. Halberstamm (Berlin, 1898).

KATZ, JACOB, 'On the History of the Rabbinate at the Close of the Middle Ages' (Heb.), *Sefer Zikaron le-Binyamin de Preis* (Jerusalem, 1969), 281–94.

—— *Tradition and Crisis; Jewish Society at the End of the Middle Ages* (New York, 1971).

KATZENELLENBOGEN, SAMUEL JUDAH, *Shneim 'Asar Derashot* [*Twelve Sermons*] (Venice, 1594). Short title: *Derashot Maharshi"k*.

KAUFMANN, DAVID, 'Liste de rabbins dressée par Azriel Trabotto', *REJ* 4 (1882), 208–25.

—— 'The Ordinances of *Ḥevrat Yeshivat Shalom* of 1589' (Heb.), *ha-Assif*, 3 (1886), 209–20.

Kevod Ḥakhamim. See MESSER LEON.

KIBRE, PEARL, *Scholarly Privileges in the Middle Ages: The Rights, Privileges and Immunities of Scholars and Universities at Bologna, Padua, Paris and Oxford* (London, 1961).

KIESZKOWSKI, BODHAN, 'Les Rapports entre Elie del Medigo et Pice la Mirandole', *Rinascimento*, series 2, 4 (1964), 41–91.

KOREN, NATHAN, *Jewish Physicians; a Biographical Index* (Jerusalem, 1973).

KRISTELLER, P. O., 'Changing Views of the Intellectual History of the Renaissance since Jacob Burckhardt', in *The Renaissance: A Reconsideration of the Theories and Interpretations of the Age*, ed. T. Helton (Madison, Wis., 1961), 27–52.

KUPFER, EPHRAIM, 'The Disqualification and Reinstatement of Joseph of Arles as *Ḥaver* and Rabbi' (Heb.), *KS* 41 (1966), 117–32.

—— 'R. Abraham b. Menahem of Rovigo and his Removal from the Rabbinate', *Sinai*, 61 (1967), 142–62.

—— 'The Removal of the Crown of Torah from R. Moses Provenzali' (Heb.), *Sinai*, 63 (1968), 137–60.

—— ed., 'Visions of R. Asher b. Meir, known as Emlain Roitlingen' (Heb.), *Koveẓ 'al Yad*, 8 [18] (1976), 385–423.

LATTES, ISAAC DE, 'Teshuvot R. Yiẓḥak mi-Lattes', MS Vienna National Library 80 (IMHM 1303).

—— *Teshuvot R. Yiẓḥak mi-Lattes*, ed. M. Z. Friedlander (Vienna, 1860; photo edn., Jerusalem, 1970).

LEVITA, ELIJAH [BAḤUR], *Sefer Tishby* (Isny, 1541).

LIONTI, F., 'I ministri della religione presso gli ebrei di Sicilia', *Archivio storico Siciliano* NS 10 (1885).

MARGOLIOUTH, GEORGE, *Catalogue of the Hebrew and Samaritan Manuscripts*, i (London, 1899).

MARMORSTEIN, ARTHUR, 'R. David Kohen und das Rabbinerwesen in der ersten Haelfte des XVI Jahrhunderts', *Jeshurun*, 14 (1927), 174–89.

MARX, ALEXANDER, 'Glimpses of the Life of an Italian Rabbi of the First Half of the Sixteenth Century', *HUCA* 1 (1924), 605–24. Short title: 'Life of an Italian Rabbi'.

—— 'A Jewish Cause Célèbre in Sixteenth Century Italy', in his *Studies in Bibliography and Booklore* (New York, 1944), 107–54. First published in *Abhandlungen zur Erinnerung an H. P. Chajes* (Vienna, 1933), 149–93.

—— 'The Removal of R. Joseph d'Arles from the Rabbinate and his Reinstatement' *Tarbiẓ*, 8 (1937), 171–84.

—— 'R. Joseph d'Arles and R. Johanan Treves' (Heb.), *Koveẓ Mada'i le-zekher Moshe Shur* (New York, 1945), 189–219.

—— 'R. Joseph D'Arles as Teacher and Head of an Academy in Siena' (Heb.), in *Louis Ginzberg Jubilee Volume. Hebrew Section* [*Sefer ha-Yovel li-khevod Levi Ginzberg*] (New York, 1946), 271–304.

Matanot ba-Adam. See BOKSENBOIM (ed.), *She'elot u-Teshuvot Matanot ba-Adam*.

Medabber Tahapukhot. See YIẒḤAK MIN HA-LEVI'IM.

MELLI, R. ELI'EZER, *Sefer le-kol Ḥefeẓ* (Venice, 1552).

MESSER LEON, DAVID b. JUDAH, *Kevod Ḥakhamim . . . pesak she-katav . . . 'al ha-maḥloket she-haytah be-Yom ha-Kippurim be-Kahal Evilona* [*The Honour of Sages—halakhic responsum concerning the controversy in the community of Valona*], ed. S. Bernfeld (Berlin, 1899; photo edn. Jerusalem, 1970). Short title: *Kevod Ḥakhamim*.

Mikveh Yisrael. See SALTARO.

MILANO, ATTILIO, 'I "Capitoli" di Daniel da Pisa e la comunità di Roma', *RMI* 10 (1935–6), 324–38, 409–26.

—— *Storia degli ebrei in Italia* (Turin, 1963).

—— *Il Ghetto di Roma* (Rome, 1964).

Minḥat Kina'ot. See DA PISA, *Sefer Minḥat Kina'ot*.

MINZ, JUDAH, *Teshuvot* [Responsa] (Venice, 1553).

—— *Pesak ha-Ḥerem*. See *Pesak ha-Ḥerem*.

MODENA, LEONE, *Historia di gli riti hebraica* (Paris, 1637). Hebrew translation: *Shulḥan 'Arukh le . . . Yehudah Aryeh mi-Modena*, ed. S. Rabin and A. Jellinek (Vienna, 1937).

—— *Kitvei R. Yehudah Aryeh mi-Modena*, ed. J. Blau (Budapest, 1906).

—— *Diwan le-Rabbi Yehudah Aryeh Modena*, ed. S. Bernstein (Philadelphia, 1932).

—— *She'elot u-Teshuvot Ziknei Yehudah* [*Responsa of the Elders of Judah*], ed. S. Simonsohn (Jerusalem, 1955).

—— *'Iggerot Rabbi Yehudah Aryeh mi-Modena* [Letters], ed. J. Boksenboim (Tel Aviv, 1984). Cited in this volume from MODENA (Blau, ed.), *Kitvei* . . ..

—— *Ḥayyei Yehudah*, ed. D. Carpi (Tel Aviv, 1985).

MORTARA, MARCO, 'Notizie di alcune collezioni di consulti MSS di rabbini italiani possedute e pubblicate da Marco Mortara', *Mose*, 5 (1882), 125–6, 155–6, 191–3, 231–2, 265–6, 306–7, 377–9; 6 (1883), 52–3, 133–4, 191–3, 263–5, 337–8.

—— *Indice alfabetico dei rabbini e scrittori israeliti* (Padua, 1886). Short title: *Indice alfabetico*.

MOSCATO, JUDAH, *Sefer Nefuẓot Yehudah. Derushim* . . . (Venice, 1589).

MOSES b. SAMUEL IBN BASSA OF BLANES, 'Tena'ei ha-Darshan', in MSS NY Columbia 15Q X893T (IMHM 23348) and MS Livorno T"T 34 (IMHM 12463).

MÜNSTER, LADISLAO, 'Una luminosa figura di medico ebreo del Quattrocento—aestro Elia di Sabbato da Fermo, Archiatra Pontificio', in *Saggi sull'ebraismo italiano; scritti in memoria di Sally Mayer* (Jerusalem, 1956), 224–58.

Nefuẓot Yehudah. See MOSCATO, *Sefer Nefuẓot Yehudah*.

GHIRONDI, MORDECAI SAMUEL, and NEPI, GRAZIADO, *Toldot Gedolei Yisra'el u-Ge'onei Iṭalyah* (Trieste, 1853).

NIIGAL, GEDALYAH, 'The Sermons of R. Samuel David Katzenellenbogen' (Heb.), *Sinai*, 70 (1972), 79–85.

Pesak ha-Ḥerem. See WIENER.

Pesakim (Venice 1519). Rulings of the Venetian Rabbis. Republished in *Parshiyot me-ḥayyei Yehudei Iṭalyah be-me'ah ha-ṭ"z*, ed. J. Boksenboim (Tel Aviv, 1986), 4–29 (introduction), 55–233 (text).

'Pinkas ha-Medinah shel Azor Padua'. Minute Book of Padua Region, including Padua, Monselice, Montagnana, and Cividale. MS in Padua Communal Archives. Short title: 'Pinkas ha-Medinah be-Padua'.

'Pinkas Kehillah Kedoshah be-Casale', MS in local communal archives. Short title: 'Pinkas Casale'.

'Pinkas ha-Kehillah be-Verona'. Verona Communal Minute Book, 2 vols., MS Jerusalem National Library Heb. 4to 555 (vol. i); and 552 (vol. ii). Short title: 'Pinkas Verona'. See also S. Simonsohn, 'The Communal Ledger in Verona'.

Pinkas Va'ad Kehillah Kedoshah Padua, 5338–5363 [*Padua Communal Minute Book, 1578–1603*], ed. D. Carpi, (Jerusalem, 1974). Short title: 'Pinkas Padua'.

PORGES, N., 'Elie Capsali et sa chronique de Venise', *REJ* 77 (1923), 20–40; 78 (1924), 15–34; 79 (1925), 28–60.

PORTO HA-KOHEN, R. ABRAHAM MENAḤEM, 'Teshuvot', in MSS Jerusalem Heb. 8to 3904, Montefiore 480 and Mantua 38. I primarily used the Jerusalem MS, supplemented by MS Montefiore.

PROVENZALI, R. MOSES, 'Teshuvot', MS Jerusalem Heb. 8to 1999. Cf. R. Bonfil, *KS* 50 (1975), 164–5.

—— Miscellaneous Responsa, in MS Los Angeles 12 (IMHM 28085).

—— *Bi'ur zeh yaẓa Rishonah* (Mantua, 1567).

RABINOWICZ, HARRY, 'Rabbi Joseph Colon and the Jewish Ban', *HJ* 22 (1960), 61–70.

RABINOWITZ, RAPHAEL N., *Ma'amar 'al Hadpasat ha-Talmud; Toldot Hadpasat ha-Talmud* [*History of the Printing of the Talmud*], ed. A. M. Habermann (Jerusalem, 1965).

RABINOWITZ, ISAAC, 'A Rectification of the Date of Judah Messer Leon's Death', *Studies in Jewish Bibliography, History and Literature in Honor of I. Edward Kiev* (New York, 1971), 399–406.

RAVA, R. MENAḤEM, *Bet Mo'ed* (Venice, 1605). Contains fifty of his sermons.

ROSENBERG, H., 'Alcuni cenni biografici di rabbini e letterati della communità israelitica di Ancona', Introduction to *Kitvei R. David Avraham Ḥai ve-Rabbi Yiẓḥak Refa'el Ashkenazi* (Ancona, 1932).

ROTH, CECIL, *Venice* (Jewish Community Series; Philadelphia, 1930).

—— *The History of the Jews of Italy* (Philadelphia, 1946).

—— 'The Rabbis of Ancona', *Sinai*, 21 (1947), 323–6.

—— 'The Qualification of Jewish Physicians in the Middle Ages', *Speculum*, 28 (1953), 834–43.

—— *The Jews in the Renaissance*, (Philadelphia, 1959).

RUDERMAN, DAVID, *The World of a Renaissance Jew; the Life and Thought of Abraham ben Mordecai Farissol* (Cincinnati, 1981).

SALTARO, R. JUDAH b. MOSES, *Mikveh Yisra'el* (Venice, 1607). Response to the work *Mashbit Milḥamot* pertaining to the ritual bath controversy in Rovigo.

—— *Palgei Mayim* (Venice, 1608).

SCHECHTER, SOLOMON, 'Notes sur Messer David Leon tirées de manuscrits', *REJ* 24 (1892), 118–38.

SCHOLEM, GERSHOM, *Major Trends in Jewish Mysticism* (New York, 1961).

SCHWARZ, ARTHUR ZACHARIAS, *Die hebräischen Handschriften der Nationalbibliothek in Wien* (Leipzig, 1925).

SCHWARZFUCHS, S., *Études sur l'origine et le developpement du rabbinat au Moyen-Age* (Paris, 1957).

—— 'I responsi di Rabbi Meir da Padova come fonte storica', in *Scritti in memoria di Leone Carpi* (Milan and Jerusalem, 1967), 112–32.

Sefer ha-Sheṭarot. See ISAAC OF BARCELONA.

Sefer le-kol Ḥefeẓ. see MELLI.

Sefer Yefeh Nof (Venice, 1552). Formularum.

SEGAL, JACOB b. KALONYMUS, 'Sefer Kol Ya'akov' (alphabetical listing of subjects for sermons), MS Columbia X893 J151Q (IMHM 23318).

SEGRE, RENATA, *Gli ebrei Lombardi nell'età Spagnola* (Turin, 1973).

SHEM-TOV, JOSEPH, 'Sefer 'Ein ha-Kore'. Preserved in the following manuscripts: Paris BN 325 (IMHM 20237); MS Oxford Bodl. 2052 (IMHM 19337); MS Montefiore 61 (IMHM 4580); etc., of which I used the Paris MS. The introduction to this work is published in A. Jellinek, *Kuntres ha-Mafteaḥ* (Vienna, 1881), 30–2.

SHILO, S., *Dina de-Malkhuta Dina* [*The Law of the Land is Law*] (Jerusalem, 1975).

SHULVASS, MOSES AVIGDOR, 'The Religious Life of Italian Jewry During the Period of the Renaissance' (Heb.), *PAAJR* 17 (1947–8), 1–22. Short title: 'Reliigious Life'.

—— 'The Jews of Italy in the Framework of Renaissance Culture' (Heb.), *Sinai*, 22 (1948), 44–8.

—— 'The Study of Torah Among Italian Jews During the Renaissance' (Heb.), *Ḥoreb*, 10 (1948), 105–28. Short title: 'The Study of Torah'.

—— 'Books and Libraries Among Italian Jews During the Renaissance' (Heb.), *Talpiyot*, 4 (1950), 591–605.

—— *The Jews in the World of the Renaissance* (Leiden and Chicago, 1973). Short title: *Renaissance*.

SIMONSOHN, SHLOMO, 'The Organization of Jewish Autonomous Rule in Mantua, 1511–1630' (Heb.), *Ẓion*, 21 (1956), 143–82. Short title: 'Organization of Jewish Rule'.

—— 'The Scandal of the Tamari-Venturozzo Divorce' (Heb.), *Tarbiẓ*, 28 (1959), 375–92.

—— 'The Communal Ledger in Verona' (Heb.), *KS* 35 (1960), 127–36, 250–68.

—— 'The Ghetto in Italy and its Government' (Heb.), *Sefer ha-Yovel le-Yiẓḥak Baer* (Jerusalem, 1961), 270–90.

—— 'Books and Libraries of the Jews of Mantua, 1595' (Heb.), *KS* 37 (1962), 103–22.

—— 'The Jews of Syracuse and their Cemetery' (Heb.), *Sefunot*, 8 (1964), 273–82.

—— 'The Jewish Community in Italy and the Christian Corporation' (Heb.), in *Dat ve-Ḥevrah be-Toldot Yisra'el uve-Toldot ha-'Amim* (Jerusalem, 1968), 81–102.

—— 'The World of a Jewish Youth during the Renaissance' (Heb.), *Hagut 'Ivrit be-Europa* (Tel Aviv, 1969), 334–49.
—— *History of the Jews in the Duchy of Mantua* (Jerusalem, 1972). Short title: *Mantua*.
—— 'I banchieri da Rieti in Toscana', *RMI* 38 (1972), 406–23, 487–99.
—— 'Remnants of the Communal Minute Book in Cremona' (Heb.), *Mikhael*, 1 (Tel Aviv, 1973), 254–76. Short title: 'Cremona'.
—— (ed.), *Teshuvot Ziknei Yehudah*. See MODENA, *She'elot u-Teshuvot Ziknei Yehudah*.
SIRAT, COLETTE, and BET-ARYEH, MALAKHI, *Oẓar Kitvei-Yad 'Ivri'im mi-yemei ha-Beinayim, be-Ẓiyunei Ta'arikh 'ad Shenat 'HSh"* [Medieval Hebrew Manuscript Collections, Dated to 1560; Part I: Manuscripts in Libraries in Israel and France in Large Formats] (Jerusalem and Paris, 1972).
SONNE, ISAIAH, 'Basic Premisses for the History of the Jews in Verona' (Heb.), *Koveẓ 'al Yad*, 3 [13] (Jerusalem, 1939–40), 145–90. Short title: 'Basic Premisses'.
—— 'On the History of the Community of Bologna at the Beginning of the 16th Century' (Heb.), *HUCA* 16 (1942), 35–100.
—— 'The General Synod in Italy, Father of the *Va'ad Arba Araẓot* in Poland' (Heb.)', *ha-Tekufah*, 32–3 (1948), 617–89.
—— 'Excursions into History and Bibliography' (Heb.), *Alexander Marx Jubilee Volume* (New York, 1950), Hebrew Section, 209–35. Short title: 'Excursions'.
—— 'Documents Concerning Rabbinic Messengers in Italy at the Beginning of the 17th Century' (Heb.), *Koveẓ 'al Yad*, 5 [15] (1951), 186–97.
—— ed., *mi-Pavlo ha-Revi'i 'ad Pius ha-Ḥamishi; Chronika 'Ivrit meha-me'ah ha-Shesh 'Esreh* [*A Sixteenth Century Hebrew Chronicle*] (Jerusalem, 1954).
—— 'Book Lists through Three Centuries; A: First Half of the Fifteenth Century, Italy', *Studies in Bibliography and Booklore*, 2 (1955), 3–19.
STEINSCHNEIDER, MORITZ, 'Jüdische Aerzte', *ZfHB* 17 (1914), 63–96, 121–67; 18 (1915), 25–57.
STERN, MORITZ, *Urkundliche Beiträge über die Stellung der Päpste zu den Juden* (Kiel, 1891–3), 2 vols.
STOW, KENNETH R., 'The Burning of the Talmud in 1553, in the Light of Sixteenth-century Catholic Attitudes toward the Talmud', *Bibliothèque d'Humanisme et Renaissance*, 34 (1972), 435–45.
'Takkanot Ancona', MS Los Angeles 44 (IMHM 28088).
'Takkanot Ḥevrat Gemillut Ḥessed be-Ferrara, 5275–5303' [Ordinances of the Mutual Aid Society in Ferrara, 1515–63], MS Haifa, Municipal Scientific Library (AHJP HM 5231).

'Takkanot Ḥevrat Nizharim be-Bologna', MS New York Public Library, Jewish Items 34 (IMHM 31161).

'Takkanot Ḥevrat Yeshivat Shalom be-Ancona'. See KAUFMANN, 'Ordinances.'

TAMAR, DAVID, 'On R. David Messer Leon's *Kevod Ḥakhamim*' (Heb.), *KS* 26 (1950), 96–100. Repr. in *Meḥkarim be-Toldot ha-Yehudim be-Ereẓ Yisra'el uve-Iṭalyah* (Jerusalem, 1970), 48–52.

'Teshuvot Bat Rabim', MS Moscow-Günzburg 129 (IMHM 6809).

Teshuvot ha-RaMA. See ISSERLES.

Teshuvot Ma'arvei Naḥal. See GRAZIANO.

Teshuvot Maharda"kh. See DAVID HA-KOHEN OF CORFU.

Teshuvot Mahari"k. See COLON.

Teshuvot Matanot ba-Adam. See BOKSENBOIM.

'Teshuvot mi-Rabbanei Iṭalyah' [Responsa of Italian Rabbis], MS Kaufmann 150. Cf. Mortara, *Teshuvot be-Kitvei Yad*, 5, 265–6, 306–7; 6, 52–3, 133–4.

'Teshuvot u-Pesakim mi-Rabbanei Iṭalyah', MS Copenhagen, Royal Library 115; MS Strasbourg 154, 155; MS Mantua 88.

Teshuvot Ziknei Yehudah. See MODENA.

TISHBY, ISAIAH, 'The Figure of R. Moses Cordovero in the Work of R. Mordecai Dato' (Heb.), *Sefunot*, 7 (1963), 119–66.

—— 'The Controversy Concerning *Sefer ha-Zohar* in 16th Century Italy' (Heb.), in his *Ḥikrei Kabbalah u-Sheluḥoteha*, i (Jerusalem, 1982), 79–130. Originally published in *Perakim*, 1 (1967–8), 131–82.

TRABOT, AZRIEL, 'Derashot' (Sermons), in MS Oxford Bod. 2266 (IMHM 20547), fos. 21a–28a. Cf. Document 64, pp. 291–3 in the Hebrew edition of this book.

—— 'Teshuvot', MS Jerusalem, National Library Heb. 8to 101.

URBACH, EPHRAIM E., 'Lists of Hebrew Books from the Beginning of Printing' (Heb.), *KS* 15 (1938–9), 237–9.

—— *Ba'alei ha-Tosafot* [*The Tosaphists*] (Jerusalem, 1980), 2 vols.

VAJDA, GEORGES, 'Un Inventaire de Bibliotheque Juive d'Italie', *REJ* 126 (1967), 473–83.

VOGELSTEIN, H., and RIEGER, P., *Geschichte der Juden in Rom*, 2 vols. (Berlin, 1895–6). Short title: *Geschichte*.

WADISLOWSKI, JUDAH ARYEH LEIB, *Sefer Toldot Rabbenu Menaḥem 'Azaryah mi-Fano* (Pietrkow, 1902).

WALK, JOSEPH, 'R. Obadiah Sforno, Exegete and Humanist' (Heb.), *Sefer Zikaron le-Zekher David Neiger* (Jerusalem, 1959), 277–302.

WEIL, GERARD E., *Elie Levita* (Leiden, 1963).

WIENER, SAMUEL, ed., *Pesak ha-Ḥerem shel ha-Rav Ya'akov Polak neged . . . RABa"H Minz* (St. Petersburg, 1897). Documents concerning the excommunication issued by R. Jacob Polak against R. Judah Minz in the Norzi controversy. Short title: *Pesak ha-Ḥerem.*

—— *Mazkeret Rabbanei Iṭalyah 1520–1818*, in his *Pesak ha-Ḥerem.*

WILENSKY, MORDECAI, 'On the Rabbis of Ancona', *Sinai*, 25 (1949), 64–82.

YIẒḤAK MIN HA-LEVI'IM, R., *Medabber Tahapukhot*, ed. D. Carpi, *ha-Ẓofeh le-Ḥokhmat Yisra'el* (1912), 168–86; (1913), 45–54; (1914), 69–96.

ZIMMER, ERIC, 'Biographical Details Concerning Italian Jewry from Abraham Graziano's Handwritten Notes' (Heb.) *KS* 49 (1974), 400–44.

ZINBERG, ISRAEL, *A History of Jewish Literature; iv: Italian Jewry in the Renaissance Era* (Cincinnati and New York, 1974).

ZOTENBERG, HERMAM, *Catalogues des Manuscrits Hébreux et Samaritains de la Bibliothèque Impériale* (Paris, 1866).

Index

kohanim (sing. *kohen*) *see* priesthood, Jewish
Kohen, Simeon, scribe in Padua 125
Kohen-Zedek, Avigdor 178 n.
Kol Ya'akov 301, 317
Kol Yehudah see Moscato, Judah
Kuzari see Judah ha-Levi

Lampronti, Isaac 112, 113 n.
Lattes, Bonet de 179–82, 189
Lattes, Isaac Emmanuel de 24, 84 n., 103, 104, 108 n., 121, 162–3, 165, 189–90, 200, 227, 229 n., 230, 305, 326
Lattes, Isaac Joshua de *see* Lattes, Isaac Emmanuel de
'law of the land is law' *see dina de malkhuta dina*
law, church 264
law, Jewish *see halakhah*
law, Roman 207, 221, 264
lay leaders *see* communal heads (lay leaders)
Leo X, pope 166
letters, writing of *see* scribe, scribes
Levantines 109, 113, 172 n., 226, 243
Levi (author of *Liviat Ḥen*) 312
levirate separation *see ḥaliẓah*
Levita, Elijah 18, 36
Livorno 211 n.
Loans, Meir 47 n.
Lumen Gentium 293
Luria, Solomon (Maharshal) 258
Luria, Isaac 295
Luria, Israel 128 n.

Ma'amar Ḥayyei 'Olam see Pisa, Yeḥiel Nissim (Vitale)
Macerata 69 n.
magic 78 n., 322
Maimonides 46, 48, 146, 148, 255, 257, 260, 262, 263, 265, 272 n., 278, 288 n., 290, 294, 307, 311
Malmad ha-Talmidim 276 n., 308
Manetti 198
Manoscrivi, Ahavah Kohen 185
Mantino, Jacob 277 n., 306, 309 n.
Mantua 3, 62, 64–5, 69 n., 70 n., 76, 81, 98, 108, 171, 172, 175, 176, 182 n., 189, 197 n., 211 n., 213–14, 229 n., 234 n., 242, 250 n., 273
mara de-atra see titles
marbiẓ Torah 110, 143–50, 153, 155, 165, 176, 177, 187
Marcaria, Jacob 190, 192 n.
Marches (region) 69 n., 153, 210 n.
Margalit, Jacob 188
marriages 65, 66–7, 76, 85, 89, 92, 150, 151, 170–1, 177–81, 192
Martin V (pope) 208 n., 209 n.
matchmaking 192
mathematics 287
Maximilian I, Duke of Bavaria 279
Mazzara 144 n.
meat, ritual supervision of 182
Medici, Ferdinando de 211 n.
Meir ha-Levi of Vienna 32
Meir of Padua (Maharam) *see* Katzenellenbogen, Meir
Meiri, Menahem 90–1, 94 n.
Melamed, Moshe 332
Melli, Jehiel 321
Melli, Phineas Elia 229 n., 243
memorization 264 n.
menstruation and purification 259–61, 262 n.
Meshulam, Abraham b. Asher 191
Meshulam Kaufmann b. Shemaiah 113, 191 n.
Messer, Leon *see* Judah, Messer Leon
metaphysics 287, 312
midrash 298–316
Milan (duchy of) 134, 212
Mingeit, wife of rabbi in Padua 77
Minḥat Kena'ot see Pisa, Yeḥiel Nissim (Vitale)
Minz, Abraham b. Judah 54 n., 57, 60, 63, 108 n., 110, 113 n., 121, 132, 188
Minz, Judah 26–7, 51 n., 61 n., 77, 104 n., 105–7, 109, 110, 111, 132, 152 n., 154, 179, 187, 188, 256
Mirandola, Pico della 293, 322 n.